PRAISE FOR *AID ON THE EDGE OF CHAOS*

'Thought-provoking . . . Has much to offer the world of aid . . . Aid agencies ignore complexity to their own detriment. They must listen, learn from their mistakes and then adapt their solutions.'

The Economist

'An exhaustive tour of phenomena as diverse as climate change, food price rises, ethnic segregation and the Arab spring . . . Ramalingam's ideas are important and relevant for the aid world, especially as pressures on aid budgets, and demands to show better results, mount.'

The Financial Times

'Compelling and comprehensive . . . Practitioners and scholars concerned with development must read this book. It will be the standard reference on the topic for years to come.'

Global Governance Journal

'*Aid on the Edge of Chaos* sets a new milestone in the aid debate . . . Ramalingam takes readers on an impressive interdisciplinary tour and provides an important compass for navigating the edge of chaos, where aid can realise its greatest innovative potential.'

The Guardian

'This is a most unusual book, not only for its potential importance but also because its coverage is much wider than its title suggests. Many books promise more than they deliver; this one delivers more than it promises. It has changed the way I see the world and I am glad to have read it.'

The International Union for Conservation of Nature Newsletter

'Ramalingam's book is rich in good values and respect for the challenges of development. Aid agencies would do well to move robustly in the directions he proposes. It is not surprising that these challenged organisations seek fairly simple approaches. But they can certainly do better. Ramalingam's book illuminates how much of that learning needs to happen.'

The Lancet

'Fosters a new aid paradigm, of an open innovation network, catalysing and leveraging change in countries around the world.'

Nature

'This book explains an importa   lerstand, and
important scientific ideas that n

New Scientist

'This masterful book represents an important step towards changing our institutions and organizations: a shift away from outmoded, one-size-fits-all, top-down planning and towards responsive and adaptive innovation. If that were to happen in international development alone, the effects could be profound—but as Ramalingam implies, this needs to be a part of a much broader change in political and economic thinking. Ramalingam skillfully draws upon a diverse body of ideas and research to deliver a vital message for aid and beyond.'

Philip Ball, author of *Critical Mass*, Winner of the Aventis Royal Society Book of the Year

'That the world is complex and difficult to manipulate is a proposition with which few would disagree. This optimistic book argues that modern science— particularly in the fields of systems thinking, network science, agent based modeling and non linear dynamics—has the chance to significantly improve the way that the aid business operates. What is clear is that the scientific approach to complex problems and the appropriate use of evidence advocated by Ramalingam has to be the way forward in development.'

Sir John Beddington, UK Government Chief Scientific Advisor, 2008–2013

'Ben Ramalingam's tour de force of a book provides an unorthodox and fascinating insight into today's global aid sector: its current practices and sometimes faulty theories of action. Beyond the criticism it manages to explore several avenues on how to unlock the most obstructive problems that are facing the sector. Borrowing from scientific fields generally ignored by the aid industry, Ben Ramalingam also opens up new perspectives on possible humanitarian and development futures. This book is a vital source of inspiration for the ICRC and for the aid community as a whole.'

Yves Daccord, Director General, International Committee of the Red Cross (ICRC)

'We are all on this small planet together. Ultimately, our fates cannot be separated. In a broad ranging discussion of our global 'network of mutuality', Ben Ramalingam expertly shows how those in the wealthier countries can best help the severely disadvantaged in this time of massive change and dislocation. Marrying science, policy and practice with a deep moral conscience, this important book points to a future that we should all be working towards.'

Peter Doherty, Nobel Laureate, Medicine

'This is a superb book, boldly facing in this age of globalization the complexity of aid to developing countries. Ben Ramalingam presents lucid exposition and insightful analysis, derived from hundreds of interviews, empirically tested studies, and real-life episodes. His findings make a compelling case to transform aid, from the "external push" of unrealistic panaceas to "internal catalysis" that can help recipient societies evolve their own future. Impressive and inspiring, this work is destined to become a 21st century classic.'

Dudley Herschbach, Nobel Laureate, Chemistry

'*Aid on the Edge of Chaos* is an important and insightful book, a work of original and well documented scholarship that is also highly accessible. Fresh thoughts and new ideas bubble on virtually every page. Ramalingam sets out a challenge to researchers and practitioners in international cooperation to rethink our basic assumptions and act in ways that are more attuned to the real world in all its complexities. This is one to read and reread.'

Sir Richard Jolly, Assistant Secretary General, United Nations

'Foreign aid to poor countries has had a checkered history, in part because well intentioned aid agencies sometimes oversimplify the problems they need to solve. Ben Ramalingam's book makes the good case that the growing field of complex adaptive systems can help prevent such errors from being repeated.'

Eric Maskin, Nobel Laureate, Economics

'This brilliant book will energise the struggle to make big government, big money and big aid sensitive to contexts, humble about what they can achieve, and sophisticated about the connectedness of things. It won't make simple panaceas any less attractive. But it points the way to a common sense far more appropriate to the 21st century world.'

Geoff Mulgan, Chief Executive, NESTA

'*Aid on the Edge of Chaos* is a magnificent piece of work, highly readable notwithstanding the complex topics it deals with, and a major contribution to the debate about how to rethink and improve the way we deliver aid world-wide... I fully endorse Ben Ramalingam's call for more catalytic approaches to aid, that empower and enable local communities to find and develop their own answers, which are in keeping with the richness, interconnectedness and intricacy of their lives.'

Sir Nick Young, Chief Executive Officer, British Red Cross

AID ON THE EDGE OF CHAOS

RETHINKING INTERNATIONAL
COOPERATION IN A COMPLEX WORLD

BEN RAMALINGAM

OXFORD
UNIVERSITY PRESS

OXFORD
UNIVERSITY PRESS

Great Clarendon Street, Oxford, OX2 6DP,
United Kingdom

Oxford University Press is a department of the University of Oxford.
It furthers the University's objective of excellence in research, scholarship,
and education by publishing worldwide. Oxford is a registered trade mark of
Oxford University Press in the UK and in certain other countries

First published 2013
First published in paperback 2015

Several sections of this book first appeared in different
form on the Aid on the Edge of Chaos blog <www.aidontheedge.info>

Impression: 1

Published in the United States of America by Oxford University Press
198 Madison Avenue, New York, NY 10016, United States of America

British Library Cataloguing in Publication Data

Data available

Library of Congress Cataloging in Publication Data

Data available

ISBN 978–0–19–957802–3 (Hbk.)
ISBN 978–0–19–872824–5 (Pbk.)

Printed and bound in Great Britain by
Clays Ltd, St Ives plc

To Mum, for values; to Naomi, for belief and inspiration; and to Koby, for joy.

PREFACE: GLOBALIZATION, DEVELOPMENT, AND COMPLEXITY

The Globalization of Vulnerability

I am sitting on an open terrace overlooking paddy fields, sketching the land-scape in a grubby notebook. The vista is one of rice terraces delicately contoured with the undulating hillsides, gently flowing rivers, diligently maintained tributaries, and myriad shades of green. Here and there, tiered buildings rise elegantly from the tall waving grass. As the sun moves, each paddy shimmers, like individual facets of a jewel slowly turning in the light, giving the landscape a magical, otherworldly feel. It is one of those views that makes you want to 'burst into spontaneous applause'.[1]

I'm here in Bali to better understand how this picture-postcard-beautiful, thousand-year-old farming system has somehow, miraculously, survived the vagaries of human nature and the disruptions of history. My experience so far has been a rather incongruous one. I have spent most of my time with small-holder farmers and agricultural experts. This has involved visiting numerous farms and plots of land, traipsing along hand-hewn irrigation channels on the edge of paddy fields, past water storage facilities and small temples. I have interviewed quite a few people, asking them to describe their lives and liveli-hoods, how they make decisions, and how they cooperate, and why. I close every interview with the same question, about the factors that sustain or threaten the resilience of the Balinese farming system and way of life. The previous day, one of the interviewees had given a particularly memorable answer to the threats. Raising two fingers, he counted one off and said, 'One, globalization.' Then, counting off the other finger, 'Also, two, development.'

Today my time has been time spent accompanying a high-level delegation from the United Nations Educational, Scientific and Cultural Organization (UNESCO), including its new director-general, on a motorcade through the jungles. The delegation is here to review an application for World Heritage Status for the unique social–ecological system that covers much of the central region of Bali, centred on the island's indigenous agricultural methods. The experience is a stark and at times surreal contrast to the previous days' activities: moving around the island in the wake of high praise and garlands.

Behind me, the members of the convoy are shuffling back into mud-splattered cars. As I pause to examine my sketch, I find myself reflecting on the farmers' answer, and my day so far.

Like the members of the delegation, and indeed all visitors to the island, I carry the sinuous fingerprints of globalization with me. Look at my notepad, my pen, my mobile phone, which vibrates occasionally as SMS messages arrive, the bag containing my scratched and battered laptop slung across the back of my chair. The laptop: Korea for the manufactured components, China for the assembly, Japan for the marketing, and India for the case. The phone is American, powered by chips made from metals mined in the Democratic Republic of Congo. My pen is from a German firm but was made in Taiwan. The notepad I picked up at a small shop on my way through Denpasar, Bali's capital—it was made in China.

Examining my immediate vicinity, the marks of globalization prove just as pervasive. Next to me there is a glass of tea with a plastic lid and a bowl of cashew nuts. The nuts come from Java, the neighbouring island. The drink: Vietnam for the tea, Australia for the milk, South Africa for the sugar, and Bangladesh for the glass. The terrace is part of a restaurant whose old-world charm is only slightly marred by prominent cabinets full of American soft drinks.

As I sketch, sip, chew, text, and reflect, I am actively participating in a global network of trade relations and value chains, of purchases and legal obligations, of brand identities and cultural symbols. I am plugged into this network in many ways: economically, socially, physically, technologically, and emotionally. So too, although in rather different ways, are the Balinese rice farmers.

You too are 'online', as you read these words. You might be browsing in a bookshop or a library, surfing on the Internet using Google Books, scrolling through a free first chapter on an electronic reading device; you might have picked the book off a friend's shelf or even have purchased it and opened it up on the train or bus home. You and I are connected across time and space through a distinct and unique pathway consisting of many hundreds of decisions and actions. And there are countless connections like ours taking place around the world, often in astonishing ways. There are garment workers in China sweating in David Beckham T-shirts; Maasai tribespeople in Kenya SMSing on Finnish mobile phones; Irish technology workers buying (now very expensive) rounds of Mexican bottled beers; British sixth formers donning bindhis and sarongs (the boys, naturally); Japanese women learning exuberant flamenco moves in the south of Spain. Such seemingly random connections have increasingly become the norm, in ways reminiscent of the quip: 'Million-to-one chances crop up nine times out of ten.'[2] A global coalition of scientists has even come up with a name for such linkages and feedbacks: 'telecoupling'. These appropriately dispersed systems thinkers have shown that, as with the television and the telephone, 'coupling at distance' is increasingly transforming our lives.

Martin Luther King described something instantly recognizable when he said, 'We are caught in an inescapable network of mutuality... whatever affects one directly, affects all indirectly.'[3] Like so many of Dr King's reflections, this one seems to accrue relevance with time. It describes with unerring precision our world today. Our whole world is increasingly interconnected and interdependent. But in the new millennium, this inescapable network of global mutuality has become ever more unpredictable. It is expansive in its potential, but it also has many hidden fragilities. It propagates both staggering opportunity and terrible vulnerability. Astonishing wealth has been the outcome for a lucky few, and persistent exclusion for the majority.[4] A noted development academic, Dani Rodrik of Harvard University, has argued that globalization 'works best when it is not pushed too far'.[5] But because we are now so connected and interdependent, we seem to be living in a world that not only has been pushed too far, but also may well be teetering on the edge of the precipice if not actually plummeting straight downward. Uncertainty rules the roost. It has politicians doing contortions worthy of prize gymnasts. It routinely confounds policymakers and confuses practitioners. It has experts and academics contradicting themselves several times, often in the same paragraph.

One of the chief ways we can better understand this network of mutuality today—its reach, its connectivity, and its remarkable and troubling dynamics— is through the branch of science known as complex adaptive systems research. My argument in this book builds on a wealth of examples, all of which employ tools and approaches from this new movement in scientific thinking to better understand the dynamic complexity of the real world. For some, like noted science writer Philip Ball, increasing globalization and the growing interest in complex adaptive systems go hand-in-hand: 'It is exactly the growing connectivity that has led our global society to take on the emergent properties of systems that have long been the focus of the complexity scientists.'[6] But it is not just global theorists who have turned to complexity. Here in Bali, researchers have made use of the same approaches when seeking to understand the intricate workings of the island-wide rice farming system. Indeed, my visit was motivated by the desire to better understand how ideas from the cutting edge of science have been used to understand and enhance the unique resilience of the Balinese social–ecological system. Part of the power of these ideas is precisely from the fact they can be used at multiple scales.

Few areas illustrate the dynamics of globalization and the potential of complex systems thinking as well as the global financial system: simultaneously a powerful articulation and a key driver of globalization. Scientists in New England have recently mapped the entire global economy using network modelling techniques: collecting and carefully analysing a huge amount of data. Their preliminary findings are unsurprising, if depressing: a few dominant players control the vast majority of money in the global financial network. Yet even those wielding power in this network are not free from its volatility:

consider the thousands of wealthy financiers who still live in fear of the days when the numbers on their screens start to turn red.

Perhaps appropriately, the metaphor of a precipice has underpinned an unlikely collaboration between a leading banker and an eminent biologist, who wanted to explore how and why the system fell off the edge of a cliff in 2008.[7] By studying the financial system using ecological techniques, Andy Haldane and Robert May were able to show that the network had evolved to a critical state, much like an ecosystem on the verge of a radical tipping point. Then all that had to happen was a shove—which happened with the collapse of Lehman Brothers in 2008.

The notion of a global meltdown is no longer just a metaphor, according to Joseph Stiglitz, former Chief Economist at the World Bank and Nobel Laureate in Economics. Comparing the global economic system with the nuclear industry, and drawing on the work of complex systems scholars Charles Perrow and Joseph Tainter, Stiglitz argues that these crises share some common roots. In both economic and nuclear systems, they are caused by growing interconnectedness between different types of risks, by practitioners having few incentives to think hard about this connectedness, by experts seriously underestimating the collective risks, by policymakers turning a blind eye, and by vested interests actively and repeatedly denying the accumulating systemic problems.[8] The net effect is that we are—as a global society—gambling with both our present and our future. 'Recent events cannot help but lead one to question the social, environmental, and technological world we are constructing for ourselves.'[9]

What is increasingly clear is that not having access to globalization's benefits is no insurance against its downsides.[10] Suicide rates and labour unrest in Chinese factories are spiking as workers feel the pressure of working around the clock to meet Western demand for the latest smartphones. Kenyan market traders sell fuel and wood at escalating prices to an increasingly dissatisfied population, and live in fear of a metaphorical spark of violence. British single mothers are turning to loan sharks to afford the weekly food shop, and end up paying interest rates of several thousand per cent for bread and packets of cornflakes. Here in Bali farmers can list globalization as one the greatest threats to their way of life.

We all seem to be scrambling to make sense of a world in which established norms—of working, living, and even thinking—seem troublingly out of date. And although our understanding is slowly growing, for many this is happening far too slowly. From this perspective, there are probably few who would completely disagree with the first part of my interviewee's response. It is not just opportunities, but also threats and vulnerabilities, that have been globalized.

This extraordinary and unpredictable global network in which I, you, the Balinese farmer, the UNESCO delegation, and approximately seven billion (at time of writing) others are caught up is by turn the stage, the backdrop, and the prompt for the story I want to tell in this book. But my narrative and argument focus on a sub-system that is embedded within, and shaped by, these broader dynamics: the international foreign aid system. This system is directly implicated in the second, perhaps more controversial, part of my respondent's answer: that development poses the second major threat to the Balinese way of work and life. This may seem somewhat contradictory: surely development, as human betterment, is an inherently good thing? Unfortunately, it has become important to separate out development as a legitimate and worthy aspiration from 'development aid' as the ideas and practices promoted, delivered, and supported by the international community to low and middle income countries as the route to development. The recent history of the breathtaking landscape in front of me illustrates this distinction all too well.

Development Disasters Averted … For Once

Perhaps the most fascinating thing about the undulating terrains of Balinese rice farming is how improbable they are. These remarkable terraces and the social structures that are intertwined with them have sustained the local population through the comings and goings of entire dynasties of Balinese kings, the rise of Hinduism, colonial invasion and domination, Japanese occupation, and Indonesian self-determination. The arrangement has survived against all the odds.

That they even exist is testament to an intricate social system: a remarkable system of farmer cooperation. Without sufficient water, pests proliferate, rice plants are decimated, and harvests are ruined. Those landowners closest to the river have the obvious upper hand when it comes to water access, but somehow water gets from the rivers to even those farms and terraces that are the furthest away. This happens through a collective decision-making mechanism unique to Bali, known as the *subaks*. Centred on the hundreds of tiered water temples, each *subak* cooperative performs not just agrarian functions but also legal and spiritual ones. At their best, they are profoundly egalitarian in nature, serving the interests of all the farmers in a given district, and ensuring cooperation between districts. They are also tremendously successful, with the highest yields per hectare on the sub-continental Indonesian archipelago.[11]

Records indicate that rice yields have been consistently high and stable. One exception was during the 1970s when the system was subject to an external aid-supported agricultural reform process, designed and implemented in the name of development aid.

During the 1970s and 1980s, the Asian Development Bank designed and funded an external intervention in an attempt to improve and modernize the agricultural system. The result was a dramatic crash in rice paddy productivity.[12] For all its resilience and beauty, the system was sent into meltdown by foreign aid interventions. Under the auspices of the Green Revolution, Balinese farmers were subjected to large-scale reforms and enforced changes to their thousand-year old practices. New chemical fertilizers were provided. Growth and harvest patterns were re-engineered and enforced. Cooperation was viewed as a relic of the outmoded past: the *subak* systems were effectively disregarded. Evidently without any hint of irony, the programme was named Massive Guidance.

Massive Guidance ignored contexts and seriously underestimated risks. It denied systemic problems, and therefore allowed them to propagate. Vested interests were as rife as the pest populations that explosively grew, infesting the paddies. And the rice yields became highly unpredictable, crashing one harvest, levelling the next, spiking in another, and then crashing again. In the name of development, this thousand-year-old system was uprooted, literally sent into chaos. Brian Atwood, Bill Clinton's Chief of the United States Agency for International Development, argued that 'sustainable development can become an antidote to chaos'.[13] The Balinese experience suggests that the opposite holds true for *un*sustainable development.

Many aspects of this development intervention echo the problems Joseph Stiglitz has observed in globalization. Indeed, a more appropriate name for the 1970s intervention, following Stiglitz, may have been Massive Gamble.

This is not an uncommon story. So well established is the 'development disaster' narrative that it has become the topic of a widely distributed satirical cartoon, which tells the cautionary tale of two development workers arriving in a peaceful and self-sufficient forest-dwelling community. The text accompanying the first few panels depicting the encounter is a poignant echo of the Bali story: 'Our original aim was the same as usual: to bring them sustainable development. However, in this specific case we encountered an unexpected challenge. It turns out that these people, in their own strange kind of way, were already sustainable. So all we could really bring them was…development.'[14]

The foreign aid workers proceed to implement a number of aid's standard approaches—participatory community development, income generation, and empowerment—all of which fail miserably. They then establish an 'integrated multi-stakeholder process' that results in big industry razing the forest to the ground. They implement measures that, in the name of environmental protection, prevent people accessing the now much-depleted forest resources, they create cash-for-work programmes to replace livelihoods decimated by their interventions, and they set up safety nets to help those who have inevitably fallen below the poverty line. The interventions create a spiralling situation of subjugation and squalor. In the penultimate panels, the aid specialists sincerely acknowledge the difficulties of the process, and commit to learning lessons to apply elsewhere. The community members, meanwhile, are left pictured against a grim background of urbanization, industrialization, and pollution. The accompanying text is the sucker punch, and echoes the sentiment expressed by my Balinese interviewee: 'Welcome to the Global Village.'

The 'development disaster' period in Balinese rice agriculture lasted over a decade. It didn't lead to the dire consequences predicted in the cartoon, thanks in part to the work of an inspired anthropologist called Stephen Lansing and colleagues associated with an exceptional scientific institution based in Santa Fe, New Mexico. Using the tools of complex adaptive systems research, they started teasing out what had made the old system work so well for so long. They designed a computer simulation to calculate the effect of the various imposed reforms and changing environmental conditions on rice yields. This showed conclusively that the island-wide system of *subaks*, marginalized by the Massive Guidance programme, was central to the effective functioning and resilience of the rice terraces. Drawing on the same family of approaches employed to analyse the dynamics of the global financial network I mentioned earlier, the researchers showed the *subaks* were self-organizing networks, optimally suited to the problem of allocating water in a subtle and elaborate social–ecological system. According to Lansing, the *subaks* operated on the 'edge of chaos', a delicate balance between the socio-cultural system, economic needs, and the environmental limits of the landscape. Development aid, and the recommendations of development agencies, pushed the system away from this balance. Lansing found that the agricultural system had literally been tipped into chaos by the external intervention.

The *subaks*—so vital to the functioning of the agricultural system—were considered by external actors to be a relic of an outmoded past, pre-modern, backward even—and the focus on religious rites didn't help the case. Such lack of respect for institutions is widespread in aid. In discussion, the late Elinor Ostrom, who won the 2009 Nobel Prize for her work on institutional economics, drew a comparison between colonialism and aid: both, she told me, treated local knowledge as non-existent, and assumed the developing world presented a series of institutional blank slates. '"Fitting" is all important... Agencies today have blue prints for situation A... They are so ingrained they can't deal with B, C, D, and E.'[15] The difference in Bali was that the colonial powers never sought to overwrite the *subaks* because they didn't see that the system would generate enough surpluses to be worth the effort. It took development aid to *really* put the system at risk. The logic of my respondent's answer ('one, globalization; also, two, development') starts to become clearer.

Eventually, after much advocacy and lobbying by Lansing and others, and many presentations of the model, international development agencies recognized the *subaks* for their unique contribution to agricultural productivity. Local cooperative practices were re-instated. Yields returned to their pre-development highs. This was a remarkable fusion of cutting-edge science with traditional knowledge, whereby the former was used to explain, substantiate, and affirm the latter. The result was a remarkable turnaround in development policies relating to Balinese rice farming. Threats are still looming, not just from globalization and development, but also from climate change, water scarcity, and demographic changes. But for now, it would appear, the system has returned to the delicate balance Lansing observed at the 'edge of chaos'.

Nine months after my visit, a UNESCO official announced that the *subaks* had made the grade and would be recognized as a World Heritage Site. Steve Lansing incidentally also played a major role in the UNESCO application process.

I will return to the story of the *subaks* later, but the message it delivers is worth reflecting on here. One obvious message is that, while globalization and development pose threats and challenges, the farmers' response is not the whole story: they also provide new ways of thinking and opportunities. Steve Lansing and complexity thinking came to Bali through a convoluted process of globalization. This 'science of the real world' provided a new set of tools and a new, more precise, form of language to describe and understand the vital importance of the *subaks* in the Balinese rice-growing system. And the development agency in question listened and learned and the systems are more resilient as a result. It took another global development agency, UNESCO, to give the *subaks* official status and provide an assurance of their future preservation. It will be very difficult indeed for other, more hubristically minded, development agencies to ignore the *subak* systems in future agricultural development schemes.

In the wake of the financial crisis, with the benefit of analysis and insights from experts like Haldane and May, and numerous calls for a more adaptive and intelligent form of regulatory system, one cannot help but wonder whether the principles underlying the *subaks* have some relevance, can somehow be adapted and adopted, writ large, to enhance financial resilience. Whether such an egalitarian system for regulating the balance between risks and opportunities could ever play a role in the harshest of global markets is of course an open question. Similarly whether the financial system could also be said to be most effective—the equivalent of highest yield rice fields—at the edge of chaos also needs thorough examination.

Such conjectures aside, a second, more fundamental message also arises from the *subaks*. To my mind, the story of this beautiful landscape is so important because it exemplifies Albert Einstein's adage that we can't solve problems until we change the way of thinking that led to those problems in the first place. Sadly, as the satirical cartoon suggests, such transformations of understanding are all too uncommon in development aid. Instead, the system too often resembles the old joke: we've learned from our mistakes and are pretty sure we can repeat them exactly.

Complexity and Aid at the Crossroads: The Journey Ahead

The restoration of the status of Bali *subaks* is one example of how the growing movement in scientific thinking—known as complex adaptive systems research—is helping change the way we think about, and thereby shed new and important light on, thorny problems faced in many areas of research, policy, and practice. The contrasting examples in this brief introduction—from the global financial system to small-scale farming—illustrate the power and potential of this diverse set of scientific ideas. Although very different in their focus and the level of analysis, these examples provide useful initial pointers to the argument I want to make in this book. They help think about the aid system, both as it is, and how it might be.

As I argue in the first chapter, foreign aid is at something of a crossroads. There are those who seek to protect and increase it, there are those who seek to attack and reduce it, and there are those who seek to re-think and improve it. These are not mutually exclusive pathways, but I should state up front that my feet are firmly planted in this third camp. Let's make aid better, let's increase the good and reduce the bad, both of which we should be able to find in reasonable abundance.

There are many thinkers and practitioners following such an approach: it is a broad church. The school I am most drawn to, and within which this book is positioned, argues that there are no simple, replicable prescriptions for development: that Massive Guidance and similar efforts play little part in positive change. In keeping with the approach of these thinkers and practitioners, I want to focus on a more relevant, appropriate, realistic, and innovative approach to aid, one that puts 'best fit' before best practices. In doing so, I am as interested in the 'how' as the 'what' of successful development efforts.

My aim in this book is to examine the system of international foreign aid: how it works, how it doesn't, and how it might be improved. Many have undertaken such assessments in the past, to good and often controversial effect. My own approach is informed—and I hope distinguished—by my enduring fascination with how the ideas and insights from complex systems research can help us think differently about foreign aid and the challenges it faces.

Although work to apply these ideas is at relatively early stages, I hope to show that it is already yielding promising results in a variety of settings. My argument is informed by over six years of work on this issue, during which time I have published working papers and book chapters, undertaken numerous research projects and evaluations, run workshops and roundtables, spoken at conferences and events, and launched a blog.

I start with a brief account of the aid system. I then reflect on the aid 'business model' and 'institutions': the observable and dominant patterns in how the system works. This covers four areas of development and humanitarian work in turn: how aid agencies learn and 'think', how they develop strategies and policies, how organizations and relationships work, and finally how they ensure accountability and performance.

I then go into an exploration of ideas from the complexity sciences. In the second part, I aim to set out the key ideas of complexity research, providing examples relevant to social, political, and economic contexts. This part looks at complexity through four 'lenses': systems, behaviours, networks, and dynamics. Building on material originally published by the Overseas Development Institute, this work owes a considerable debt to the work of scholars around the world, especially at the Santa Fe Institute, the London School of Economics Complexity Group, and the International Institute for Applied Systems Analysis.

In the third part of the book, I show how growing numbers of development and humanitarian analysts and practitioners have started challenging conventional approaches and using the ideas of complex adaptive systems to discover and delineate what a more relevant, appropriate, realistic, and innovative approach to aid might look like. As well as returning to look at the *subaks* in more detail, Part 3 looks at over 25 examples from across the development and humanitarian spectrum. This part is broadly organized so as to mesh together ideas from Parts 1 and 2 and explore what the existing aid business model might look like through the lens of complexity. My aim in Part 3 is to show how the four lenses of system, behaviours, networks, and dynamics have direct relevance for the challenges in aid—learning and knowledge, strategies and policies, organizations and relationships, performance, and accountability. I conclude with reflections on what the aid system might look like in the future.

A few provisos are worth making upfront. As alluded to earlier, complex systems work is just part, one strand, of a broad movement to try and improve the way aid works. I may get too over-excited or push the implications of complexity research too far. I will of course try to resist this temptation, and want to acknowledge from the outset that what I am documenting is very much a work in progress.

It is also a diverse body of work I present here, both geographically and intellectually. There are many cases I couldn't include for lack of space, and there are no doubt some great examples of which I am not aware. As noted above, some of this work comes from researchers and analysts who have sought to explore ideas of complex adaptive systems in the new and different context of development and humanitarian work. As in the case of the *subaks*, these ideas are sometimes a form of resistance from those working at the margins of the traditional aid system who have worked to diminish the insensitivities and vicissitudes of aid. There are also many practitioners and thinkers within aid agencies who are picking up new ideas and exploring them as a means by which to rethink and improve their work. I have drawn a lot of this work together in this book, in order to illustrate my overall argument. But this not a single coherent movement: the battle to understand and navigate complexity has many fronts.

But perhaps the most important proviso is this: if you are hoping for a definitive step-by-step guide, a gleaming toolkit for how to deal with a complex adaptive world, this may not be the right book for you. Although in some cases people have derived some new and fascinating solutions, the most important lesson of complexity science (echoing the Einstein quote) is that the focus is less on potential solutions and more on the new mindsets we need to employ. This resonates strongly with the view of colleagues at the Santa Fe Institute, who argue that complex systems research is best seen as an engine for intuition.

If I were to distil my overarching message in the pages to come into a few words, it would be hard to better the wonderful phrase of Marcel Proust: 'The true voyage of discovery lies not in seeking new landscapes, but in having new eyes.' Even here among the rice paddies of central Bali, with this breathtaking vista before me, this notion holds true. It sums up perhaps the most important lesson I have learnt in the course of writing this book. I hope in the chapters ahead to do justice to this idea, and the remarkable people who in different ways have conveyed it to me.

ACKNOWLEDGEMENTS

This book has been the result of several years of work, and owes a debt to many people, colleagues, friends, and family alike.

First, to all at Oxford University Press, especially to Aimee Wright for guidance, exceptional patience, and good humour throughout, Adam Swallow for support and feedback and Sarah Caro for getting the whole thing rolling. International Development Research Centre (IDRC) provided invaluable financial support, through Sarah Earl and Fred Carden of the Evaluation Unit, without whose encouragement and mentorship this book would not have been possible. The Knowledge Management For Development (KM4Dev) Innovation Fund provided funding for research into knowledge, learning, and complexity which provided invaluable inputs for chapters 2 and 15.

Roo Griffiths provided superb and invaluable editorial work, support, and advice on all of the chapters and the final manuscript. Deborah Eade provided clear and honest insights and editorial work on early versions of Part 1 and 2. Nina Behrman edited the first version of the manuscript in 2010. Fran Orford drew, and redrew, cartoons with enthusiasm and energy.

Peer reviews and comments on early chapter drafts were gratefully received from Simon Maxwell, Ralph Stacey, Lauchlan Munroe, Owen Barder, Randolph Kent, Carl Jackson, Robert Chambers, Mike Powell, Dave Snowden, Paul Knox-Clarke, Sean Lowrie, Nigel Timmins, Rick Davies, Sarah Earl, and Ricardo Grau-Wilson. I have learnt that nothing is more valuable for a would-be author than thoughtful criticism. The book has been improved immeasurably by my peer reviewers' careful, considered, and extensive feedback.

A number of institutions and colleagues have provided support along the way. The Overseas Development Institute (ODI) provided a crucible for these ideas to ferment in. Special thanks go to Simon Maxwell and Alison Evans for their intellectual leadership; and to John Young for mentoring and supporting me during the Research and Policy in Development (RAPID) years, and for first suggesting the idea that turned into this book, on a pub roof-garden in July 2003. This book would not have been possible without the 2008 Working Paper 'Exploring the Science of Complexity', which I worked on with Harry Jones, Toussaint Reba, and John Young, and the emergent meeting series that followed it, which both helped in germinating and growing many ideas, insights, and reflections. The readers of the 'Aid on the Edge of Chaos' blog (<www.aidontheedge.info>) deserve a special mention: they helped me learn a lot more about how to get these ideas clear in my own mind, and how to write about them (hopefully!) in a more accessible way.

I am grateful to John Mitchell at the Active Learning Network for Accountability and Performance in Humanitarian Action (ALNAP) for his kind support and calm leadership in day-to-day matters away from the book, and considerable support and flexibility while the first draft was being written. Randolph Kent of the Humanitarian Futures Programme has been an enduring source of ideas, vision, and encouragement. Jemilah Mahmood has been and remains a truly inspiring and energizing figure. Owen Barder of the Centre for Global Development (CGD) and Duncan Green of Oxfam have both been fonts of vital ideas, healthy scepticism, and much web traffic. Eve Mittleton-Kelly at the London School of Economics (LSE) Complexity Group provided both a space to think and an office to work in, as well as access to a much-used library. Eve is also one of the best-networked people in the social complexity community, and shared her contacts, resources, and ideas generously. Robert Chambers, Danny Burns, and all at the Participation Team at Institute of Development Studies (IDS) deserve special thanks for support over several years, for my continually-extended Visiting Fellowship, office space, time to think, regular confidence boosters, fun retreats, and access to another marvellous library. Bill Frej opened up a new world of possibilities through his residency at the Santa Fe Institute (SFI)—it is safe to say this book was completely transformed for the better as a result of the opportunity he provided. I am grateful to him and Anne Frej for the hospitality. Jerry and Paula Sabloff and Murray Gell-Mann at SFI were kind and supportive during my time there and afterwards. Steve Lansing, Sukmaa Sushanti, and Alit Artha were indispensable before, during, and after the Bali trip. Elinor Ostrom, who sadly passed away as this book was being finalized, was another tremendous source of inspiration, ideas, and encouragement.

Three specific thinkers and their books have provided a vital roadmap for my own explorations and ideas. Eric Beinhocker, formerly McKinsey and now Institute of New Economic Thinking (INET)@Oxford, is a source of inspiration and ideas: this book follows in the wake of his impressive *Origin of Wealth*, which set out the ideas of complexity and economics with great clarity and insight. Work by Tim Harford in *Adapt* and Philip Ball in *Critical Mass* proved similarly inspiring and they were both generous with their time and support.

I have interviewed hundreds of people, including aid leaders, practitioners, and researchers; complex systems specialists, numerous eminent scientists, and leading policymakers from the world beyond aid. A huge debt of thanks is owed to those who undertook the various case studies included here and so kindly shared their experiences in open and honest fashion. Without them this book would be much shorter—and not worth reading.

They include: Steve Lansing, Sukmaa Sushanti, and Alit Artha; Allan Savory; Rob Ricigliano; Alberto Concha-Eastman; David Waltner-Toews; Monique Sternin; Dudley Herschbach; Lant Pritchett; Mark Abdollahian; Barbara Nunberg;

Ken Arrow; Francois Bousquet; Eva Schiffer; Patrick Moriarty and all at Triple S; Karl Blanchet; Ricardo Hausmann; Cesar Hidalgo; Rick Davies; Sugata Mitra; Nathan Eagle; Matt Ferrari; Melissa Leach, Ian Scoones, Gerry Bloom and all at the STEPS Centre; Luca Alinovi and Alnoor Ebrahim.

Of course, it goes without saying that all mistakes remain my own, and the best bits are largely thanks to these many others.

On a more personal level, I have had continual encouragement, support and teasing from a circle of close friends. In particular, Chris Kiefer, Phil Teare, and Mike Grozsmann share my passion for complex systems thinking and practise it in their own areas of expertise. Our conversations were always a morale boost and a great way to access new insights from very different fields to my own. Vince and Becca Eames, Alex Groszmann, and Chris Waghorn provided unflagging support and encouragement in this as they have done in everything else I do. Special mention goes to Vince for convincing me—with uncompromising firmness—to take the Oxford path.

A wider circle of friends have encouraged and supported my writing ambitions for more years than I, and they, probably care to remember. They include: Michael Arnold, Stuart Caldwell, Nick Edstroem, Jesse Fahnestock, Simon Massey, Giles Parker, Sophie Richards, Mark Sellings, Simon Teesdale, Tony Tregidgo, Justin Wasielewski, and Catherine Williams. Thanks are also due to my in-laws for their support: John and Patricia Alexander and Sue and Ken Guy.

My mother Saraswathy, brother Saravana, and sister Thurka provided both continuous encouragement and the occasional total bafflement during the writing of this book. My mother taught me from an early age about the value of curiosity and the importance of caring. She got me started on the path that has led me to where I am today, and provided so much vital support along the way.

My wonderful son Koby was born just after the first draft of this book was completed, started toddling with the second draft, and was chatting during the final draft. He teaches me about complex adaptive change every single day.

Last, not least, my wife Naomi. Thanks are due not just for her patience and support during the intense last few months of writing, when I was working almost every hour of every day, but for everything else she has given me and continues to give daily. Without her, I would never have had the confidence to start this book, the time and space to continue it, or the drive to finish it.

BR, Brighton, October 2012

CONTENTS

LIST OF FIGURES

LIST OF TABLES

PART 1
The way aid works

CHAPTER I

A System to Change 'The System'?

'How selfish soever man may be supposed, there are evidently some principles in his nature, which interest him in the fortune of others, and render their happiness necessary to him, though he derives nothing from it, except the pleasure of seeing it.'

Adam Smith.[1]

Cirque du irrationel

Ethiopia is one of the most heavily assisted countries in the world. Net official aid to the country is around the US$2 billion mark, putting it among the top ten largest recipients of aid. Ranked 174th out of 187 countries on the Human Development Index,[2] with an average food intake routinely 15–20 per cent below minimum accepted calorific levels, famously Band-Aided by Bob Geldof in the 1980s, it is also notable for the numbers of aid workers who spend thousands of dollars living long term in four-star hotels in the country's capital, Addis Ababa.

Aid to Ethiopia has the dubious honour of being the focus of one of the most fragmented of all international aid efforts. More than 51 per cent of projects are for less than US$100k, making up less than 2 per cent of all aid by volume.[3] Of course, in and of itself, this is not necessarily a bad thing. Small is often beautiful.[4] But this fragmentation is far from being cost-neutral in terms of its burden on such developing countries: the aid machine needs a lot of metaphorical tracks to be laid and infrastructure to be built. Figures from aid effectiveness work illustrate this well: the global aid system supports some 15,000 donor missions in 54 recipient countries per year—and in some countries this amounts to over 20 official visits per week.[5] In some Sub-Saharan African countries, health workers are so busy meeting Western delegates they can only do their proper jobs in the evenings.[6] In some developing countries, civil servants can have up to 2,400 reports on aid projects to produce each year: in some cases, this means spending a quarter of their time on reports.[7] Estimates are that Ethiopian Ministry of Health officials spend more than half their time responding to foreign donor requirements, instead of working on national health policy issues. A more startling example of the impact of such fragmentation is from the Indian Ocean tsunami response, where a doctor in Banda Aceh made the following notes: 'In February, in Riga (close to Calang) we had a case of measles, a little girl. Immediately, all epidemiologists of Banda Aceh came in, because they were afraid of a propagation of measles among displaced people, but the little girl recovered very fast. Then, we realized that this was not a normal case of measles and we discovered that this girl has received the same vaccine three times, from three different [aid] organizations. The measles symptoms were a result of the three vaccines she received.'[8]

How has this situation come about? Although these are all instances of particularly high levels of aid fragmentation, such complaints are not uncommon whenever aid is given. Kevin Rudd, the Australian Foreign Minister and former Prime Minister, made his own viewpoint very clear after the devastating 2011 floods, when his government faced domestic pressures to *accept* foreign aid. He argued publicly that one of the worst things Australia could have done would have been to accept 'a whole lot of uncoordinated delivery of stuff from around the globe plonked on [our] doorstep'.[9] Rudd, incidentally, had previously overseen a promise to double the Australian foreign assistance budget, aid presumably being among those things which one is more blessed to give than to receive.

It turns out that such fragmentation can be found throughout the aid system. Consider the multiple starting points of aid: usually political or social institutions in high-income countries. Think of parliamentary bodies voting on new global or country-specific measures, legislatures passing bills for assistance, civil society organizations campaigning, people tentatively stopping in front of a charmingly attractive 'charity mugger' in the street or reaching for their phone after seeing a heart-rending advert on the television. Every country on earth is part of the aid system, as donor or recipient or, increasingly, both. Aid flows to poor and middle-income countries alike; it is given to countries, like India and China, which themselves give considerable amounts of aid to others. Most working adults in the high-income world and—increasingly—the middle-income world have contributed aid, either directly in the form of personal donations or indirectly through taxes. In total, development aid given just by the countries of the Organization for Economic Cooperation and Development (OECD) in 2011 amounted to some US$134 billion, with an estimated further US$12.5 billion for humanitarian assistance.[10] This of course doesn't include all non-OECD aid: Brazil, China, India, and Russia, and also Iran, Israel, South Africa, and Turkey are getting in on the act. Private individuals gave a further US$4.6 billion in humanitarian aid, while figures for private giving on development are not collated.

This money supports everything from multi-billion dollar reconstruction projects to microfinance loans of less than US$10. It funds health services and the expansion of primary education. It helps administer vaccines and support cutting-edge research on new drugs. It is intimately tied up in the process of macroeconomic reforms and frequently used for small business development. It funds the strengthening of both parliamentary systems and civil society movements. Aid resources are allocated to decades-long climate change adaptation programmes and rapid, immediate, life-saving humanitarian relief.[11] It can be used for knowledge and technical expertise on women's empowerment, or the subsidized purchase of equipment and machinery for dams.

Foreign aid employs many different intermediaries to deliver these physical, financial, and knowledge assets. These include UN bodies, international financial institutions, government departments giving and receiving aid, the Red Cross and Red Crescent Movement, non-governmental organizations both large and small, grant-making foundations, small private trusts, think tanks and universities, and multinational corporations. These organizations bring together passionate and caffeine-fuelled campaigners, media savvy and fashionable fundraisers, hyperactive policy wonks, toe-the-line bureaucrats, hairy engineers, warm-hearted community facilitators, burnt-out programme managers, techie nutritionists, obsessive agricultural scientists, geeky economic modellers, poll-obsessed politicians, billionaire philanthropists, ambitious civil servants, grumpy male rock stars, and millions of well-intentioned charitable givers and people who volunteer their time and energy.

The aid system also includes many actors who are often invisible to the many funders of aid work, but who nonetheless are essential for much of the system to work: local non-governmental organizations, civil society movements, local governments, community-based organizations, small businesses, and the millions of people who work endlessly to help others in their communities and families. It is also made up, nominally speaking at least, of the billion or so poor and vulnerable people who are the 'target' of all of its good works. They might live in rural settings like those in Bali or much of Ethiopia, but they equally—indeed more frequently—might be in precarious teeming slums on the edge of traffic-choked cities, stricken coastal regions hit by flood surges, dusty refugee camps in politically contested borderlands, or oppressively hot cities where unwanted Western military forces face a thousand faceless enemies.

Today, we are dealing with what has been called a 'many-to-many' world of aid. There are more agencies using more money and more frameworks to deliver more projects in more countries with more partners employing more staff specializing in more disciplines. The relationships and interdependencies between existing and new organizations have increased, and so too have the pathways and channels through which aid resources can flow (Figure 1.1).[12]

Some have argued this messy confluence of intentions, actors, and activities does not deserve the label 'system'. Work I was involved in to assess the

Old reality:

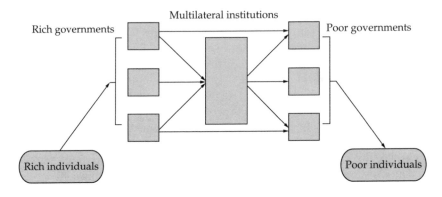

New reality:

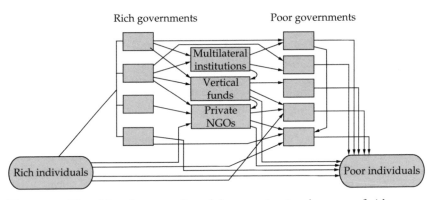

Figure 1.1 The old and new reality of the organizational system of aid

Source: Fengler, W. and Kharas, H. (2010), *Delivering Aid Differently: Lessons from the Field* (Washington, DC: Brookings Institution Press).

performance of the overall global humanitarian aid effort, which we entitled 'The State of the Humanitarian System', was met by one experienced and garrulous colleague with the memorable phrase, 'What ****ing system?' Ethiopians have long referred to the aid system as 'a permanent entourage', 'the circus that never leaves town'. A rather more sober—if abstract— conclusion reached by researchers working in the OECD's Poverty Unit was that development aid was, in a wonderfully Orwellian phrase, a 'non-system'.[13] Former UK Secretary of State, Hillary Benn, argued that the system works in highly irrational ways.

That Special Feeling

The saving grace in all this fragmentation, mission creep, and irrationality should be the ultimate benevolent intentions of aid. The ever-expanding and imperfectly formed agenda that weighs on the shoulders of aid agencies is not an end in itself. Foreign aid supports a multitude of activities with a collective eye fixed on a set of grand ambitions. Broadly speaking, aid agencies seek to ease (if not erase) the ills of poverty, to alleviate suffering. At its *most* idealistic and ambitious, aid aims to transform the entire global network of social, economic, and political relations within which it sits, rebalancing it in favour of the poor and vulnerable.

Aid is intended to be 'a system to change the system'. Aid dreams are of a more even, fair, and just world. As the head of one major European bilateral agency told me, 'it is not just the amount of amount of aid we give, the 0.5 per cent or 0.7 per cent or 1 per cent of gross domestic product. It is how we use that to transform the other 99 per cent of what our government spends that really matters.'[14]

In pursuit of a world that is fair and humane, international agencies are carefully positioned not just as the intermediaries for the delivery of resources to poor and vulnerable communities. They are also the 'middlemen' for the delivery of salves of conscience to Western governments and their citizens. They give their donating stakeholders—some of whom are keenly aware of the need for fairness and justice in the world—a sense that they are doing *something*.

On its good days, its champions argue, foreign aid is one of the most humane expressions of the idea of global mutuality: that what happens on the *other side* of the world is of concern to everyone *in* the world. At its best, the system is the manifestation of another form of globalization to add to the opportunity and vulnerability I described earlier: aid is an expression of global compassion.

In a world marked by competition and scepticism, however, aid intermediaries have to sell their goals hard to funders—be they individual or institutional supporters. Heart-tugging adverts, sophisticated marketing material, detailed policies and proposals all serve to communicate urgent demands in the developing world, and the credentials of aid organizations to meet them.

Witness, for example, this excerpt from the campaign of one development non-governmental organization, which I spotted at a London underground station (I no doubt puzzled my fellow commuters by taking out my notebook and transcribing the text): 'We're hoping to inspire thousands more people to join us and get the special feeling that comes from helping to end poverty, together.'

It turns out that the 'special feeling' is different for different people. There are four adverts running simultaneously for this organization, each focusing on a different type of person, with a different feeling. For example, 'Barbara' in the advert in front of me feels angry about poverty. So she donates funds to the organization to 'transform the lives of the poorest women around the world [and this] gives Barbara the chance to turn that anger into action and make a difference'. And as 'Barbara' herself puts it, 'It's just such a good feeling. You know that at the end of the road there is going to be a change for people and that just produces a real joyfulness.' The tagline urges me and my fellow commuters to donate to the organization and 'Get your feeling!'

Many would argue that the global aid network is triggered, supported, and sustained first and foremost by self-interest—much of it more malign and self-serving than Barbara's. Consider the fall in aid after the end of the Cold War, or the equivalent spike during the Global War on Terror. Consider the 'lost decade of development' in the 1980s, when aid agencies peddled structural adjustment programmes that deepened poverty and vulnerability. Consider the disproportionate support for emergencies across countries: the 2010 Haiti earthquake saw US$1,166 given per person affected, while the Pakistan floods later the same year received US$135 per person.[15] Think about the long roster of development disasters that didn't see a turnaround like the Bali *subaks*. Think about decades of 'high-level' pronouncements and rhetoric about enhancing ownership and autonomy, and the continual chagrin of aid donors when their 'clients' display exactly these qualities. 'Irrational' and 'baffling' start to sound like charitable terms. Aid is uneven and disproportionate, politicized and undemocratic, less a global welfare system and more a global postcode lottery with few handpicked winners and many, many more losers. It seldom adds up even to the sum of its rapidly multiplying parts, let alone coming close to exceeding them. Some conclude it doesn't have enough good days, and has rather too many bad ones.

Experienced aid practitioner and author Roger Riddell suggests that, against the reality of the ambiguous results of aid, there are three options for aid communications: to say that it works sometimes; to say that they are doing their best to improve it to reduce failures; or to admit that aid is a complex endeavour where some degree of failure is inevitable. The overwhelming effort by aid agencies has been in the first two areas—the third has been avoided 'almost entirely'.[16] At the end of the day, though, tales of 'do-gooders gone/done bad, and with *our* cash!' stick more, are more compelling, headline grabbing, memorable, just simply more interesting, than 'do-gooders who did a reasonably okay job in difficult circumstances while navigating a really quite challenging set of compromises with limited resources, and achieved some limited success'.

Pearl Diving in the Bermuda Triangle

There is more to aid than just carefully marketed messages for Western audiences, of course. The simplification of the 'aid sales pitch' is in direct contrast with the ambiguity of the subsequent endeavour. Dig a little, and you quickly find yourself overwhelmed with conflicting information about what needs to be done, by whom, why, and the results that will ensue. Not for nothing have development consultants been labelled 'a plague of seagulls' by frustrated developing country counterparts: 'They fly in, flap around for a while, drop large white wads, and then fly off again.'[17]

Collectively, aid organizations churn out (or dump) enough documents on an annual basis to paper over a small but statistically significant portion of the developing world, adding Dali-esque problems to already troubled lands.

Maybe the volume of material is justified. David Ellerman, former Senior Advisor to Joseph Stiglitz, then World Bank Chief Economist, has noted that aid agencies deal with some of the most complex and ill-defined questions facing all of humanity.[18] Another experienced aid official, Robert Calderisi, has argued that 'helping other nations successfully can be like looking for pearls in a murky sea'.[19] Maybe the documents and policy papers are just an indispensable means of helping aid agencies navigate this murky sea on a daily basis.

And yet research done over ten years by the Overseas Development Institute suggests evidence informs aid policy and practice only when the political context, the networks, and the knowledge are all in alignment. When the political context is not right, research is bypassed, evaluations are forgotten, studies are ignored, and aid itself can be curtailed.[20] Wheels are reinvented that, in many cases, never really worked in the first place.[21]

Even the simplest of questions about aid are hard to deal with. What is it and why is it given? Does it work? Who benefits and how much? One study concludes that any answers generated today 'would be inappropriate by tomorrow'.[22] One of the most credible and wide-ranging assessments of aid undertaken to date—and a success by any measure—is Roger Riddell's *Does Foreign Aid Really Work?*,[23] which found no conclusive evidence either way in response to the question posed in the title.

The great American international relations scholar and policymaker, Hans Morgenthau, dryly summed up the ambiguities and contradictions that shape aid to this day. In 1962, he wrote, 'Foreign aid is among the few real innovations which the modern age has introduced into the practice of foreign policy [but] none has proven more baffling to both understanding and action.'[24]

Morgenthau, it seems, was not far wrong. For those posing these beguilingly simple questions, foreign aid may seem rather like the public policy equivalent of the fabled Bermuda Triangle. Numerous policy evaluations and research studies start out with grand ambitions to address such critical questions, but end up wrecked, abandoned, or disappearing altogether.

I noted in the preface the propensity of aid agencies to repeat mistakes ad infinitum. A frequent critique of aid evaluations is that they tell us nothing new or different to previous assessments. Perhaps this is grounded in beliefs and practices—unspoken, but pervasive—that it is better for reputational purposes to fail conventionally than to succeed unconventionally. Repetition of mistakes and conventional failures is not unique to the aid system, of course: market crashes, corporate corruption, political co-option, and military abuses all attest to this. But many believe, perhaps because of the way that development and humanitarian agencies have become vendors of compassion, they should be better: being on a higher plane of morality seems to demand a higher level of effectiveness.

The lack of change and improvement despite growing investment in trying to understand development and disasters has led to growing criticism from all quarters. Much of this is strident, and quite a lot is misplaced. Aid is only as good as—can only ever be as good as—the politics surrounding it allows it to be.

When the stated aims are so lofty, though, ineffectiveness and failure perhaps inevitably become a scandal. And sometimes, of course, they are. The narratives woven by aid agencies themselves do not help matters. The higher the expectations are ramped up, the simpler the messages that are sold, the more out of touch with reality aid agencies risk becoming.

Aid at the Crossroads

For many critics, there is no better example of high altitude aid than the Millennium Development Goals (MDGs), set out by the UN and ratified in 2000 by world governments and the majority of aid actors. Addressing areas such as hunger, education, and health, these set out a series of targets attempting to change the world in favour of poor people.

Let's take the area of education to illustrate this briefly—I will return to this in more detail in a subsequent chapter. On education, the UN set the goal that, by 2015, every child on the planet between the ages of three and eleven would go to school. Education stands out from the other goals not just because it was the only one that predated the MDG process, but also because it was the only universal goal: poverty would be halved, water access would be doubled, and so on. The universality and absolute nature of the education target reinforced the importance of the goal both in its own terms but also as a requirement for the achievement of the other seven goals.

There is something about the education goal—and the idea behind it—which is clearly very compelling. It seems to say something important about humanity, and our advancement as a species. Journalists, academics, and activists often seek to put less inspiring data—from US consumer spending on second bathroom refurbishments to the amount spent on erectile dysfunction drugs globally—into perspective by comparing them with the anticipated bill for achieving universal education. In the exhibition on war at the UN headquarters, the total defence budgets of the world are presented as a multiple of this same number (the multiple is, of course, depressingly high). Our ability and willingness to pay for the world's children to be educated seems somehow to put our less humane and more ignoble activities into a sharp, shared, moral context.

But what does the Goal amount to? As a whole, the MDGs suggest better and more spending will lead to better goods and services, which will in turn lead to achievement of the targets. Therefore, by spending in the right areas, the world would be able to achieve universal primary education by 2015.

From spending cash to building schools and providing textbooks, to increased enrolment and engagement, to positive societal effects, the model of developmental change is presented as a linear, step-by-step progression. Similarly, better access to, use of, and satisfaction with educational services will have a range of positive effects on key dimensions of wellbeing. It is nothing if not enchanting, this vision of social change.

But problems clearly remain. The Millennium Campaign website suggests that, despite some progress, the education goal is very unlikely to be met by 2015. The World Bank's Global Monitoring Report states that, while primary school enrolment rates are up, completion rates, especially for girls, remain a major concern.[25] UNESCO reports that, in one-third of countries with available data, less than two-thirds of children enrolling in primary education are reaching the final class, let alone graduating.[26] Other sources go further and argue that the global education target will not be reached until the year 2030. The most extreme example was the 2007 work of Social Watch, a think tank, which calculated that at present rates of progress universal primary education would be achieved by 2036 in the Middle East and North Africa and by 2079 in Sub-Saharan Africa.[27] Just to spell it out, a girl in Africa coming of primary school age in 2015 may, if she is lucky, get to see her great-grandchildren benefit from the target that should have been reached when she herself was a child.

Overseas Development Institute analysis notes that the span of the MDGs was barely long enough for five to six new cohorts of children to both enter and finish primary school by 2015.[28] This is insufficient time to conclusively reform a *single aspect* of education policy in a Western country, let alone scale up the entire global system to universal coverage for a rapidly growing population. This sobering tale gives us a good indication of how realistic the MDGs were from the outset. It is also worth noting that the education target was originally set in 1990 to be met by 2000, and then 're-booted' in 2000 to be met by 2015. With 2015 approaching, there is much talk of what will replace the MDGs, or whether another re-boot is necessary.

The MDGs have been referred to by academics at Manchester University as 'the world's biggest promise'.[29] On the above reckoning, and in relation to education at least, one needs to add in 'unrealistic', or 'empty', in the appropriate place.

The endless revising of targets has something of the feel of the burden of Sisyphus, the mythical villain cursed by the Greek gods to spend eternity pushing a rock to the top of a hill. Every time he nears the top, the rock slips loose and rolls back down the hill, and Sisyphus has to start over again from the bottom. The analogy only goes so far, however: with aid, it seems as though the burden is getting bigger and harder to get a handle on with each successive attempt. But the task is not one that can be put aside, as the UN itself has noted: 'The myriad difficulties and uneven progress notwithstanding, continued pursuit of these ideals is essential; even if Sisyphus is unhappy, he must fulfil his duty.'[30] (In his farewell address as Secretary-General in 2006, Kofi Annan made the following pertinent remarks: 'Together we have pushed some big rocks to the top of the mountain, even if others have slipped from our grasp and rolled back...It's been difficult and challenging, but at times also thrillingly rewarding. And while I look forward to resting my shoulder from those stubborn rocks...I know I shall miss the mountain.')[31]

What should be done in the face of such an apparently fundamental mismatch between moral ambitions, goals, and realities? One answer is to call for an increase in aid spending, on the assumption that more inputs will lead to more and better outcomes. There have been recent calls to double aid, to meet decades-old targets for spending as a proportion of donor GDP, to increase and protect financial commitments. Prominent in the mid-noughties, and still favoured by some influential academics and leaders, for the most part, this has a rather Pollyanna-ish air to it. The likelihood of such increases appears increasingly remote in the current economic climate—except in those cases where spending on aid has become part of a domestic political calculation. Even in these situations, such as in the UK, the lack of economic growth as a result of the global financial crisis means that targets of meeting 0.7 per cent of GDP can be actually met by cutting projected aid volumes. This is before one considers the diversion of aid—for example toward the military.

A second set of answers is that the aid system itself is to blame for its ills, and should be put out of its—and everyone else's—misery. After all, what on earth could aid be doing well if one of its most important goals is going to be missed by the order of several generations? Through wilfulness and moral decrepitude, shameless co-option and political obsequiousness, or just plain old incompetence and inadequacy, the aid agencies deserve to get it squarely in the neck. There is a thriving coalition of those now willing to challenge what is widely perceived as the moral superiority and innate smugness of aid workers. The solution, from the perspective of these 'aid hawks', is unambiguous: wage a global war on aid. For many, this means discarding aid with all its imperfections, and attempting to achieve development through other means.

Suggestions abound. Give the job of development to trade interests or corporate power. Let the financial markets sort things out. Hand the whole thing over to the military. But such transformations are likely to permanently affect the developmental and humanitarian objectives of aid. Which member of the public would have given money to the tsunami effort if TNT were doing the fundraising and would have made profits from the endeavour? Which company can legitimately say to its shareholders that it is investing in Africa in the interests of poor and vulnerable people? Which community would readily accept aid from the military forces that are—rightly or wrongly—seen as creating the problems in the first place?

Although in some cases the anger is understandable, the argument for ridding the world of aid agencies may be as kneejerk and simplistic as the call for doubling their budgets. As Amartya Sen has argued, in the context of aid agency effectiveness, there is a difference between curing an affliction and eliminating the afflicted.[32] There is little evidence to suggest that any other kind of actor will be much more successful because of the systemic nature of the problems.

A third answer is to accept that longstanding failures and new intractable challenges require us to radically rethink what aid agencies do and how. This school also has its long-term and passionate adherents.

The argument that aid agencies need to undergo fundamental reforms and changes in mindsets now occupies a predictable place in the rhetoric of aid agencies. 'This calls for a step-change in our work!' is the frenzied claim of many a policy analyst. And yet there is a lack of clarity and precision about what this means. There is a pronounced tendency to point to technical issues: 'we need better evidence/results/information technology/communication' (delete as appropriate); developing country governments: 'we need developmental states'; or even poor people themselves: 'why won't they adopt what we know they need?' However, a reasonable amount of the problem can be attributed to ideas and incentives within the aid system.

As Richard Manning, one of the leading aid thinkers and practitioners working today, with an distinguished career in UK's Department for International Development and the Development Assistance Committee of the OECD, has argued, 'any assessment of aid has to start from a realistic appreciation of how societies and institutions develop, and an understanding that injections of external finance and expertise can only complement local resources, systems and processes'.[33] He goes on,

> aid [is] intrinsically a second-best solution as compared to 'home-grown' development, but still a necessary one given the impossibility of local resources financing basic government services in many poor countries (and the potential of relatively modest amounts of aid in transferring skills to lower middle income countries and helping them deal more appropriately with their own marginalized communities)...the challenge for those involved in aid...is how to manage this 'secondbest' solution...by recognizing areas of weakness and by putting in place approaches which mitigate them...[34]

Rosalind Eyben, former Chief Social Scientist at the UK Department for International Development, has argued that, 'Even if we are unconscious of it, we all use theory for explaining the world to ourselves and to each other. Our usual way of thinking about the world and its problems shapes our practice. *New ways of thinking offer the potential to make choices about practice*' (emphasis added).[35]

New ways of thinking can arise from the process of asking forthright questions about the relevance and appropriateness of aid. Some of this, laudably, has been done by aid actors themselves. The Tsunami Evaluation Coalition—a group of 43 international aid agencies including donors, non-governmental organizations, UN agencies, the Red Cross, and researchers—analysed the unprecedented flow of funding after the catastrophe: the largest-ever assessment of humanitarian aid. Their report,[36] prefaced by former US President and Special Envoy for Tsunami Relief Bill Clinton, was a sobering catalogue of failures of international assistance. It argued that international agencies needed to devote as much time to *how they do things* as to *what they actually do*.

An equivalent single review of development aid—the largest to date, which sought to assess progress against high-profile OECD donor commitments made to improving aid in Paris in 2005—found that what started off as a political commitment to change behaviour and enhance development soon became interpreted and used as mainly a 'technical' and 'process-oriented' agreement that failed to 'enlist the political and societal engagement needed to push through some of the most important changes'.[37]

The challenge, as those involved in such assessments would no doubt concur, is how to get such findings front and centre of the effort to improve aid. The rather damning reality is that new ways of thinking and hard-learned lessons are seldom prominent among the multitude of propositions bouncing around the shiny recycling depot of aid reforms. Among the visions that are regularly set out by the highest echelons of foreign aid, there is not nearly enough reflection on *the way we think and act*. The focus has been on technical fixes instead of behavioural changes, on bolt-ons instead of changed business models, on spin instead of substance. According to Riddell, despite reinventing itself throughout history, the aid industry retains many of its old problems—by not facing up to these systemic problems, those who would seek to transform aid are in fact busily streamlining and improving a system that is known to be flawed.[38]

This general phenomenon is not unique to aid agencies, of course. The late great Russell Ackoff, a systems thinking pioneer, used to argue that much public policy is built on the assumption that we can do 'the wrong thing righter'.[39]

> The righter we do the wrong thing, the wronger we become. When we make a mistake doing the wrong thing and correct it, we become wronger. When we make a mistake doing the right thing and correct it, we become righter. Therefore, it is better to do the right thing wrong than the wrong thing right.

The pronounced tendency to 'do the wrong things right' reinforces the 'second best' nature of aid solutions. In fact, in many cases, aid attaining 'second best' status would be a tremendous step up from its typical ranking.

How Aid Works

In the next four chapters, I want to examine the inner workings of foreign aid. I want to take a look inside the 'black box' of aid, to show *how* aid goes about doing what it does. I have taken inspiration from a range of thinkers—Elinor Ostrom, Douglass North, Oliver Williamson, Amartya Sen, Bill Easterly, Lant

Pritchett, Owen Barder, David Booth, and others—who have helped further our understanding of the institutions and mental models of aid.

My starting point is that aid works within a set of constraints: the 'rules of the game' that shape what can and can't be done in aid, that shape behaviours and actions, that determine rewards and punishments. These lie at the heart of the aid system—and indeed any socio-economic system—but are often unwritten and unspoken. My approach has been to investigate these rules of the game by examining how they have become embedded in four key aspects of aid: learning, strategies, organization, and performance.

Aid actors are characterized by the 'mental models' that reflect their understanding of the world and which they use to **learn** about the world, frame decisions, share knowledge, and guide objectives and actions. These mental models change over time and can provide impetus for institutional changes; equally, rigid mental models may reinforce particular forms of skills and knowledge, and be underpinned by certain kinds of institutions. With this in mind, I first look at how the mental models of aid manifest themselves in a number of different settings, and try to draw some generalizations about the way that aid learns, what it learns, and with what effects.

Aid agencies act in ways they believe will help them achieve their objectives: they set out and follow strategies, and they may even occasionally correct and revise them. I look at **strategy and policy** as key mechanisms by which formal aid decisions are made, programmes designed, and new interventions launched. I try to take a discriminating approach to strategy—to understand what the key strategic approaches are in aid, how they work, when they work, and what happens when they do not.

The institutions and rules that shape aid present opportunities for individuals to work together in groups, bound by what one would hope is their common purpose. If institutions are the rules of the game, then aid organizations and their multiple stakeholders are the players. In my third lens on the workings of aid, I look at the nature of the **organizations and relationships** found in foreign aid, the way they are structured and managed, cultures and 'thought worlds'. I examine whether and how internal relationships influence development outcomes, as well as how aid organizations interact with and relate to those they seek to help.

Finally, aid agencies also increasingly have some form of feedback from their environment, some means by which they can assess performance and enforce it. I look at **performance and accountability** approaches and examine how aid agencies deal with issues of trust and legitimacy inherent to the aid chain. How do aid agencies show they are accountable, and how do they prove their worth? What are the challenges, and how have these been dealt with? I end Part 1 by reflecting on the lessons from across these four areas, to draw general conclusions about the way aid thinks and works.

CHAPTER 2

Thinking Inside the Box

'Learning is not compulsory... neither is survival.'

W. Edwards Deming.

In 1949, in Point 4 of his inaugural speech, US President Harry Truman talked about 'our inexhaustible stores of technical knowledge', which would be made available to 'underdeveloped countries'.[1] *Since then, the burgeoning international development sector has treated knowledge as a central part of aid efforts. Both by itself and alongside other transfers, especially technology, knowledge was produced in 'developed' donor countries, then captured, translated, and transferred, with the ultimate aim of being absorbed by recipient countries.*

As well as articulating the process of knowledge transfer, from the early days of development the sector has also prescribed the kinds of knowledge that are best for developing countries. Walt Rostow identified developed countries as those that had firmly subscribed to a Newtonian view of the world:[2] *a developed society was one anchored in linear cause-and-effect processes that could be distilled into a set of underlying laws. Developing countries therefore needed to absorb and act on those cause and effect laws that developed countries had found to govern the world. The implications are revealing: 'X causes Y in Western Europe, then let's make sure we do X in Asia to ensure we get Y.'*

But, as sociologists well understand, knowledge is not a commodity; it is dynamic, social, and unpredictable; it is less given, more earned. Equally, not all social processes are amenable to the principles of Newtonian mechanics. The commodification and reductionism has had a distorting effect on what is considered useful knowledge for development, how it is thought about, how it is managed, and how it is applied.

Over time, these tendencies have become more deeply embedded in foreign aid efforts, more intricately woven into the political economy of development. They have a fundamental effect on who learns about development, what they learn, how, and why. For many working on 'knowledge for development' issues, myself

included, observing the limitations of such efforts has been a vital starting point for
understanding the relevance of complex systems thinking to aid efforts.

Text for Survival

A 2007 article in *The Economist*, drawing on a press release from the World
Food Programme (WFP), recounted a dramatic call for help from an aid
recipient struggling to survive in a refugee camp. The message was as follows:
'My name is Mohammed Sokor, writing to you from Dagahaley refugee camp
in Dadaab. Dear Sir, there is an alarming issue here. People are given too few
kilograms of food. You must help.'[3]
   The article went on:

> A crumpled note, delivered to a passing rock star-turned-philanthropist? No,
> Mr Sokor is a much sharper communicator than that. He texted this appeal
> from his own mobile phone to the mobiles of two UN officials, in London and
> Nairobi. He got the numbers by surfing at an internet café at the north Kenyan
> camp. As Mr Sokor's bemused London recipient points out, two worlds were
> colliding. The age-old scourge of famine in the Horn of Africa had found a
> 21st-century response.

As the piece concluded, this was an unusual event: there are few examples of
messages from unhappy aid recipients making it through the organizational
information network and out into the mainstream media: 'A familiar flow of
power and authority, from rich donor to grateful recipient, had been reversed.'
The sense of surprise expressed in the piece was echoed within the aid sector
and more widely.
   Within a couple of years, research by the UN Foundation would show aid
agencies as especially insensitive to new mobile technologies such as Twitter and
SMS and unable to tap into their 'user-driven' potential.[4] Agencies were far
more comfortable with predictable vertical information flows up and down the
hierarchies of the organization, than with the emergent, wayward swirl generated by social media. Many in the aid sector recognized this picture, although it
clearly made them uncomfortable. The report begged the question: how did the
supposed 'reversal' between Mr Sokor and WFP actually happen, and in
particular how did it happen through that agencies' own press release? This
apparent paradox has some salient lessons on how aid agencies learn.

The Limits of Organizational Enlightenment

Imagine putting on a pair of goggles that gives you a different perspective on
this story and the organization from which it emerged.[5] They are like infrared

goggles, but instead of showing up heat patterns, they reveal the information flows, communications, and interactions happening across the organization.

Let's say that, from our privileged vantage point, we are able to examine the flows within aid agencies at different points in history. Pick one whose history extends way back, such as the anti-slavery movement which was formed in the late eighteenth century. In the 1830s, we might see a letter posted in England, crawling for six months to Africa or India, with a reply coming back in anything up to two years. In 1870, the newly formed Red Cross mobilized its response to the Franco-Prussian War, it included for the first time a mechanism for captured but unwounded soldiers to write to their families. These desperately awaited letters would take several weeks to get home. In the 1920s, King George V sent a telegram from the British Empire Exhibition that traversed the world and returned in 80 seconds.[6] This mode of communication helped fledgling aid agencies: when Eglantyne Jebb was arrested for distributing pictures of starving Austrian children at the end of World War I, the emerging membership of the Save the Children Fund received the information by telegram. Radio, television, email, the Internet, mobile phones: with each new invention, the x-ray of an organization transforms, becoming brighter, more connected, and faster.

Let's use our goggles to look at a modern aid agency: the WFP in the story above. Something like an airline brochure flight map might appear: a globally distributed, interconnected networks of lines, with intensely bright hubs in Rome, many lines shooting off from other capital cities such as Bangkok or Nairobi or Delhi, lots of exchange and interchange, but slowing as the lines get further away from capitals and closer to the end points of projects and programmes. New events may cause a wave of energy across the network—a new humanitarian crisis here, or a change in donor priorities there. Very occasionally, we might see the whole map pulse with energy because a new idea or piece of information spreads out across the network. In 2007, a text from Mohammed Sokor in a north Kenyan refugee camp crosses the world and causes a burst of new lines and networks around the globe. The whole network shimmies with energy afterwards.

Such moments of organizational enlightenment[7] have become the Holy Grail for a whole generation of business thinkers. Whatever the sector or industry, thinkers and practitioners argue that knowledge and learning are the primary basis of its effectiveness. Knowledge is increasingly seen to be at the heart of competitive advantage, performance, accountability, efficiency, and adaptiveness.[8] Knowledge is increasingly referred to as the central economic input, of greater importance than land, labour, or capital, likened to the central nervous system of modern organizations. The Renaissance idea that knowledge itself is power seems to have withstood the tests of both geography and time.[9]

But such idealized images of information and knowledge hide more than they reveal. The speed of information flow hasn't necessarily enhanced the speed of insight or the pace of enlightenment. Even in 1934—before television, Internet, mobile phones, email, and social media—the poet T.S. Eliot was worried about this: 'Where is the wisdom we have lost in knowledge? Where is the knowledge we have lost in information?'[10]

The reversal of the direction of information flow between Mr Sokor and the WFP was presented in *The Economist* as a signal that power dynamics had also been reversed. The implication is that new signals can emanate from anywhere in the world, even from recipients, and reshape the organization's actions. But did the WFP, the largest humanitarian agency in the world, really voluntarily relinquish its power and authority because of the sheer audacity and uniqueness of Mr Sokor's communication? Was this truly a moment of organizational enlightenment?

I would argue that the story of Mohammed Sokor's text message represents a moment of organizational enlightenment more because of *where* it came from than because of *what* it actually said. The text to the officials, and the press release that followed, is in fact a good—albeit dramatic—example of what organizational learning specialists call single-loop learning, following a model developed by Chris Argyris and Donald Schön, two of the pioneers of organizational learning.[11] Henry Ford reportedly understood single-loop learning well: 'If I asked people what they wanted, they would have said a faster horse.'

For most of its history, food aid has been based on knowing exactly what is needed and how much. Famine and starvation are about a lack of food, ergo give more food. As one commentator puts it, 'children are starving...They need food...an X–Y relationship'.[12] This is not a startlingly new insight, of course. Noted systems thinker, Peter Senge, observed this in the 1990s: that food aid is underpinned by short-term, linear, and 'non-systemic' thinking. This was based on the assumption that if there is hunger, the solution must be more food.[13] This Newtonian logic—of which Walt Rostow would presumably have been proud—is reinforced in the minds of critics by the role food aid has played and continues to play in channelling Western grain surpluses. At its worst, food aid is a means for high-income countries to dump agricultural surplus on markets in developing countries. Simple and linear equations of human need and morally driven supply may well prove helpful in this regard.

I may give the impression with the story above that I am singling out the WFP for criticism; this is certainly not my intention, as the agency has in recent years proved among the most progressive deliverers of food aid, with serious attempts underway to make a strategic shift from food aid towards 'food assistance'. Although the evidence suggests this transformation—which I will return to later in this chapter—is still a work in progress, the organization deserves credit for its efforts to acknowledge and address longstanding problems.[14]

Taken on its own terms, however, it is hard to avoid the conclusion that Mr Sokor's communication, and the way it was broadcast more widely, was consistent with a dominant simple narrative about hunger and the lack of food. His text message communicated a shortfall in food, which needed to be addressed urgently. The agency, its stakeholders, and donors had the power and institutional mandate to address it. Rather than reversing the status quo then, as *The Economist* suggested, Mr Sokor's communication was used to reinforce it in a number of crucial ways. Although the medium was new, the message was little different from the kinds of public fundraising generated by the organization itself. As the agency's press release itself notes, 'Mohammed's *direct appeal* has to be a first'[15] (emphasis added).

Aid agencies—much like all other organizations—want their stakeholders to experience the world as a collection of codified, abstract representations that drive certain behaviours. Gatekeepers at different levels of the organization would have checked the story before it ended up in the mainstream media. On this basis, Mr Sokor's story caused little problem for the political, economic, or administrative survival strategies of the agency, and in fact arguably supported them. Mr Sokor's own survival strategy, in this instance, aligned well with the organizational survival strategy. Paul Currion, a refreshingly critical aid commentator, concurs that the Sokor story does not illustrate any kind of dramatic change—far from it: 'the "familiar flow of authority" is still intact, except now it comes with a customised ringtone'.[16]

Official Views and Simple Narratives

In the work of Argyris and Schön, a truly radical story would have been one that demonstrated 'double-loop learning', that questioned the existing practices and policies informing how things were done in food aid efforts. To truly reverse the power dynamic, Mr Sokor's communication would have needed to question the underlying causes of problems, and challenged the basis of and justification for standard operating procedures and policies. Such challenges are often inhibited by individual and organizational 'defensive routines', firmly entrenched in minds, setting cognitive and social limits on learning. This makes double-loop learning relatively rare; when it does occur, it can pose serious threats and risks of embarrassment to managers and employers.

Along these lines, it would arguably have been more remarkable if Mr Sokor's text had said, 'we are starving, but please do not send more food, it is not the answer, we need cash'. Cash distributions have now gained the status of a mainstream strategy for aid agencies. Yet as recently as the 1980s, researchers who had the temerity to even *study* the potential of cash ran the risk of being blackballed by leading international food aid agencies. Knowledge was necessary, but clearly not sufficient in the face of entrenched institutional defensiveness. As noted above, although institutional attitudes towards cash in the WFP have shifted in recent years, such a message would undoubtedly have had a more challenging path through the organization, conflicting as it does with dominant narratives, political pressures, bureaucratic inertia, and existing incentive structures.[17]

David Ellerman, formerly Senior Advisor to the Chief Economist at the World Bank, has written eloquently about the dominant visions of development and the role they play in aid organizations. He sees development agencies as modelled on the idea of a 'development church', 'giving definitive ex cathedra "official views" on the substantive and controversial questions of development'.[18] As with the dogmas of a church, 'the brand name of the organization is invested with its views'. The Institute of Development Studies makes the case strongly for an equivalent concept of development narratives that shape aid policy and practices. These 'define the world in certain ways [and] provide both a diagnosis and a set of measures and interventions. They define a problem, explain how it comes about, and show what needs to be done to avert disaster or bring about a happy ending'.[19] Another account, this time by the Overseas Development Institute, suggests such simplified narratives are an attempt to 'bring order to the complex multitude of interactions and processes which characterise development situations'. There is a clear attempt to tease 'some order out of chaos, to weed out some threads of causation from very complex situations'.[20]

This may not seem too much of a problem. After all, this process basically involves asking 'What is wrong?' and 'What is needed to make it right?' Almost every profession is based on such assessments. In foreign aid, however, such 'official views' are problematic because lack of feedback from the end-user means high-level narratives can easily turn to imposed dogma: 'They often gain validity despite (or even because of) the fact that they frequently simplify complex issues and processes. This simplification is seductive in that it sidesteps fuzziness and suggests a programme of action.'

Development scholar Emery Roe highlights several such narratives, including one that neatly captures the above text story—the ubiquitous 'aid crisis narrative', whereby situations are framed as being in urgent need of action, with dire consequences if action is not taken.[21] Of course, this narrative underpins pretty much all humanitarian aid: 'every single catastrophe goes through a similar trope'.[22] Many examples illustrate how certain simple mentalities have been transferred from one set of challenges to another, with dire consequences: 'AIDS is messier than smallpox; dealing with water pollution is more puzzling than building sewage systems; automobile congestion isn't solved by simply building more freeways; macro-economic policies are a whole lot messier in a global economy.'[23]

Scholars looking at the phenomenon of development narratives have found they develop a kind of 'cultural paradigm' as they become influential. In information technology parlance, we might say such narratives provide a kind of operating system, or platform, upon which aid efforts are launched: 'Certain types of development programmes, methods of data collection and analysis become associated with particular narratives.'[24] At their worst, these narratives underpin 'blueprint development'—'a prescribed set of solutions to an issue used at times and in places where it may not be applicable'.[25] (We see numerous cases of this in the next chapter on aid strategies.)

In a few instances, however, such simple, official narratives have been countered with different, more appropriate, and more relevant perspectives on the challenges faced. The body of research cited above implies, however, that successful counter-narratives are the exception and not the norm. Ellerman argues that, given the existence of official views, adverse opinions and critical reasoning tend to give way to authority, rules, and bureaucratic reasoning shaped by hierarchies within the organization: 'Once an "Official View" has been adopted, then to question it is to attack the agency itself and the value of its franchise. As a result, new learning at the expense of established Official Views is not encouraged.'[26] In India, the anthropologist David Mosse found that that 'Actors [in international aid] devote their energies to maintaining coherent representations regardless of events.'[27] And, 'Even when they embrace debate, such debates often reduce the world to two dimensions in a simplified and ultimately unhelpful way.'[28]

A startling example is urbanization. World Bank estimates are that more than 750 million of those living on less than US$2 a day live in urban areas.[29] And yet, according to 2006 research by Lund University in Sweden, international organizations that focus on poverty have tended to give very low priority to urban issues. This has been related to a number of 'official myths', such as the perception that 'Urban poverty is not as bad as rural poverty',[30] and a variety of institutional and historical factors. As the Chief Executive of Care International, Helen Gayle, argues, neither donors nor non-governmental organizations have 'co-evolved in the direction of facing urban poverty as rapidly as urban poverty has occurred'.[31]

However, this isn't just about big 'Development Narratives' with capital letters, but might equally relate to pragmatic concerns about how to do aid work in different contexts. To take just one example, in one research project I led, we interviewed senior agency managers about sources of innovation. They shared the view that it was very rare for developing country partners to say they had their own ideas and ever have these accepted by Northern counterparts—regardless of their local knowledge and experience.[32]

Received wisdoms gain their power because they are embedded in particular institutional structures, are sustained by particular networks, have strong cultural and historical roots, and are often underpinned by existing scientific theories. They are also repeated wisdoms. As Nobel Laureate Daniel Kahneman puts it, 'A reliable way to make people believe in falsehoods is frequent repetition, because familiarity is not easily distinguished from truth. Authoritarian institutions and marketers have always known this fact.'[33] Familiarity provides an 'oasis of certainty' that organizations seldom leave voluntarily, and leads to aid blindspots that are seldom overcome.

The concept of an institutional 'thought-world' is useful to draw on here.[34] Mary Douglas, who developed the term, suggested that 'institutions think' by generating a world of images, symbols, ideas, and past experiences. Those working in an institution have to accept the given 'thought-world' in order to function, as it shapes decisions, orders experience and memory, exercises a degree of control over institutional responses, and facilitates 'social cognition'. Séverine Autesserre, whose work on the Democratic Republic of the Congo I examine later on in this chapter, gives a useful account of how the thought-world of aid is dominated by simple narratives that lead to unquestioned best practices:

> Simple narratives help shape the way we perceive the social and material worlds, and thus orient how we act upon our environment. They make action possible: they authorize, enable, and justify specific practices and policies while precluding others. These actions in turn reproduce and reinforce both the dominant practices and the meanings, embodied in frames and narratives, upon which they are predicated. *Over time, the narratives and the practices they authorize come to be taken as natural, granted, and the only conceivable ones*[35] (emphasis added).

The 'Best-practicitis' Epidemic

Such simple narratives dominate the way aid thinks and, by extension, how it works. Evidence of this can be found throughout the system. Consider Joseph Stiglitz's 2002 assessment of the workings of the international financial institutions as involving 'outmoded, inappropriate, if "standard" solutions. Rarely did I see thoughtful discussions and analyses of the consequences of alternative policies. There was a single prescription.'[36] This prescription inhibits open debate and advice based on facts and evidence. Stiglitz observed that, instead, 'Academics involved in making policy recommendations become politicized and start to bend the evidence to fit the ideas of those in charge.' On the humanitarian side of the aid system—arguably as far removed from macroeconomic policymaking as it is possible to be while still being in the aid world—there is evidence that agencies consistently apply a 'cookie-cutter' approach to solving problems,[37] with food aid being the most prominent example.

Having come through the heady global aid optimism of the noughties into an era of greater cynicism and criticism, one of the ideas we do seem to be left with is that of a 'worldwide standardisation of development strategies'.[38] This, rather ironically, has happened alongside increasing efforts to make aid agencies better 'learning organizations'. One might expect the two pushes to be contradictory, but in fact there are numerous examples of a kind of symbiosis emerging, whereby standardization—based on Northern models—is seen as a main route to improving aid, and learning as the means by which it can be achieved.[39] This, however, is not learning that helps us challenge and innovate (double-loop learning—think cash or the Model T), but learning to reinforce and improve existing practices (single-loop learning—think food or faster horses).

In the 1990s, there was a movement towards 'knowledge for development', led in particular by the World Bank. The fundamental idea was that aid agencies could, and should, be employing their existing knowledge to transform development. Consider the vision the Bank set out in 1998: 'Knowledge is like light. Weightless and intangible, it can easily travel the world, enlightening the lives of people everywhere. Yet billions of people still live in the darkness of poverty— unnecessarily.'[40] Steve Denning, former Chief Knowledge Officer at the World Bank, reiterated the specific role of aid agencies in such knowledge transfers.

> A health worker in Kamana, Zambia, was struggling to find a solution for treating malaria. In this tiny and remote rural town, the health worker logged on to the Web site of the U.S.'s Centers for Disease Control and Prevention and got an answer: 'The most striking aspect of the picture is this: [The World Bank] doesn't have its know-how and expertise organized so that someone like the health worker in Zambia can have access to it. But just imagine if it did!'[41]

James Wolfensohn, then President of the World Bank, even suggested his institution rebrand itself as the 'Knowledge Bank'. In his inaugural speech to the assembled finance ministers of the world, he argued that the Bank should be just as focused on collecting and disbursing knowledge that poor and developing countries need as it was on providing loans and finance.

This Truman-esque optimism has become mired in the old adage that context counts: poor nations include an incredible variety of institutions, cultures, and histories. To paraphrase Easterly, the idea of aggregating all this diversity into a developing world that will readily absorb existing foreign aid knowledge is a 'heroic simplification'.[42]

Over time, the knowledge for development vision has been found to be at odds with, and too disconnected from, the core business of the aid system. Instead of serving to meet clients' needs better—arguably the saving grace of the Knowledge Bank idea—knowledge and learning have become more focused on existing operations—in effect, a knowledge-based support function for what organizations already do, to help them do it faster and better. This can be seen clearly in the evaluation of the World Bank's efforts, still undoubtedly the most high-profile and well-supported knowledge and learning strategy of any aid agency.[43] The Operations Evaluations Department recommended as the most important change the linking of knowledge practices with existing lending operations. Knowledge and learning, in other words, needed to be subordinated to the *existing* culture and way of doing things. Single-loop learning was to be placed front and centre of the knowledge for development agenda.

It is interesting to contrast all of this with the ideas contained in *Learning to Fly*, a text by two former BP knowledge specialists that is almost certainly the most widely read text on knowledge and learning in the aid sector. In the first few pages of this book, the authors argue that 'rarely can something that has worked well in one location and in one situation be applied directly to another. The solution often disappoints...we've always struggled with the question, who can define good practice? We believe it is the person who uses the practice next, who determines whether it makes a difference to what they are doing.'[44] Sadly, this principle has seen relatively little take-up in the knowledge for development movement, let alone in foreign aid more generally.

As a result of the dominance of single-loop learning, which has only been reinforced by the formal movement, I would argue that an epidemic of 'best-practicitis' is afflicting aid agencies. This may seem like a facetious framing, but my intention is a serious one: aid is suffering from a non-trivial ailment. The symptoms include the following: organizations spend all their time looking for the single right answer rather than diverse solutions; people spend more time trying to do things right than doing the right things; there is much more focus on knowledge transfer than on knowledge creation; the whole enterprise is underpinned by a search for efficiency and cost-based value-for-money measures that assume that what is known is needed (and should be cheap, although that is another issue). Limits are placed on the kind of learning that is acknowledged and rewarded, and the creation of new technological systems, handbooks, and guidelines simultaneously take precedence over and undermine any attempts to change existing culture or incentives in favour of interaction and dialogue. Assumptions are implicitly made that the existing paradigm is in fact the right one, and that single-loop learning is sufficient. But as Riddell laments, 'sustainable development is unlikely to be achieved by slavishly following the "how-to" guidelines of off-the-shelf manuals'.[45]

Another obvious symptom of best-practicitis is the dominance of spurious judgements and questionable evidence that 'fit our existing models'. Despite recent pushes for greater scientific accuracy, development and humanitarian work is still not strictly speaking evidence-based. Instead, the framing of the problem permits certain kinds of information and inhibits others (think back to the remarkable journey of Mohammed Sokor's text message). As one informant put it, 'certainty' in a development context is first and foremost a matter of bureaucratic convenience rather than scientific accuracy.[46] In 12 years of studying the role of evidence in development policy processes, the Research and Policy in Development programme at the Overseas Development Institute found that the most important determinant by far was not the quality of evidence, nor linkages between researchers and policymakers, but the political context. Examining a number of large-scale changes in aid policy and practice, including the emergence of poverty reduction strategy papers, The Sphere Project, and livelihood approaches,[47] the programme found that evidence is seldom, if ever, the sole or even major driving force for change in aid policy and practice. To sum-up the core message: there is far more policy-based evidence than evidence-based policy.

The same holds true at operational levels. The UN High Commissioner for Refugees' Policy Director found that, between Iraq in 1991 and Kosovo in 1999, there were some 'easy lessons' that could be incorporated through technical adaptations, but also other more challenging lessons, which were recognized in principle but where behaviours remained constrained by cognitive and political factors playing out in the agency.[48]

As Robert Chambers of the Institute of Development Studies wrote in the 1990s, power determines whose knowledge counts, what knowledge counts, and how it counts.[49] Mr Sokor's text from the camps constituted acceptable knowledge for WFP. But in many other cases, knowledge—of local contexts, the multiple problems being faced, and the minimal results being achieved—is distorted, blocked, or simply ignored. Let's move away from food aid and consider the closely related issue of dealing with drought in one of the most vulnerable and aid-heavy regions of the world: the African Sahel. A review published in 2007, extracts from which are shared in Box 2.1, illustrates the numerous ways in which over-simplistic narratives shape policy and practice to the detriment of understanding the real dynamics of drought.

Box 2.1 Beyond any drought[50]

'There is a nominal understanding of the nature and causes of vulnerability among the people in different international development and donor agencies. However, the analyses are often simplistic and contain many generalizations that would not hold for many specific circumstances... In five or six years there could be a complete change of staff in all the major development agencies, leading to institutional forgetfulness and a lack of profound understanding of the issues.'

'... the development paradigm is still largely based upon an assumption that the development agencies can "bring a solution to a problem" and deliver change in very short periods of time. The rapid replacement of one approach with another implies an inexhaustible optimism that solutions can be found. There remains insufficient participation of local people and little use made of traditional knowledge (notwithstanding the lip service paid to "participation"). Farmers and pastoralists are acutely aware of the problems they face but are rarely included in formulating solutions

(*continued*)

Box 2.1 Continued

because of the uncertainty that this represents for donors and development agencies in the short term.'

'Programme and project support is often . . . designed and managed in ways that are not sufficiently flexible to cope with the uncertainty of the Sahelian situation. There is a tendency to apply simplistic attempts to increase productivity that are not appropriate to the high-risk environment of the Sahel.'

'Many analyses of the situation of vulnerable populations in the Sahel do not examine the root causes and tend to divide causes into immediate and structural issues, allowing the structural issues to be largely ignored The situations of vulnerable people in the Sahel are complex and nuanced . . . Vulnerability can be influenced by gender, ethnic group and generation issues, and by contemporary and historical social processes that are often not analysed and not explained. The short-term nature of many contracts in international development makes it difficult for staff members to develop profound and detailed understanding of the situation, and the management systems in development agencies do not demand such understanding.'

'Many aid initiatives are based on the shallow analyses mentioned above and are almost always driven by externally imposed ideas of development. Notwithstanding the lip service paid to "participation", the majority of aid organizations develop their programmes on the basis of their own priorities and their own visions. In most cases there is an external analysis of what local people lack, and plans are designed to address this lack.'

Source: Trench, P., Rowley, J., Diarra, M., Sano, F., and Keita, B. (2007), 'Beyond Any Drought: Root Causes of Chronic Vulnerability in the Sahel', The Sahel Working Group (London: IIED).

As the Sahel example suggests, the real victims of this kind of mentality are individuals, communities, and countries that are the unwitting focus of such narratives and the actions that follow. In some of the worst cases, best-practicitis undermines, diminishes, and hurts those aid seeks to help.

If we accept the premise that real change in any sector is grounded in new ways of thinking and perceiving,[51] then clearly aid is in some trouble. A lack of focus on supporting learning, and the emphasis on transferring knowledge, has meant that the mental models of aid work have become less diverse and less creative, even as the scope and ambition of aid has expanded.[52] This has reinforced conservative mindsets, outdated aid approaches, entrenched attitudes, and sclerotic processes.[53]

In the rest of this chapter, I am going to look at three specific examples of aid best-practicitis: malaria responses, aid amid conflict, and natural resource management. I selected these three because they span the aid portfolio, because they illustrate clearly the challenges of repeatedly pushing simple solutions to complex problems, and because they reveal the flawed mentalities that have proved so resilient.

How Do You Solve a Problem Like Malaria?[54]

One in every five childhood deaths in Sub-Saharan Africa is due to the effects of malaria. Around the world, every 30 seconds a child dies of malaria. According to the WHO, in a single year, the disease killed almost 800,000 people and afflicted 225 *million* others.[55] Yet numerous accounts suggest current global attempts to eradicate the disease may be doing more harm than good.[56] In particular, approaches tend to be focused narrowly on the delivery of, or search for, a limited number of technical solutions:

No other disease has so many guises – so many radically permuted facets of epidemiology, entomology, or genetics – that enable it to defeat the monolithic 'silver bullet' approach attempted during the eradication era. Yet donors understand and are attracted to the drama of silver bullets, which far and away appeal more than the Byzantine complexity of a sustained malaria control program.[57]

For modern examples of silver bullets, think of the infamous insecticide-treated bednets. A more recent example is a blue laser, proposed by a former Microsoft employee as a state-of-the art technology to 'zap' mosquitoes out of the air. The prototype received considerable publicity in 2010, but has the key problem that it has been trialled only in laboratory settings, and, more fundamentally, that many malaria-affected areas also lack adequate and reliable electricity supplies to support such a system at scale.

The tendency to think in terms of silver bullets to attack malaria has been a constant feature over the past 40 years. In 1969, the Pearson Commission confidently pronounced the disease 'virtually eliminated'.[58] How, then, did the situation reported in 2010 come about? '[The 1960s eradication campaign] was far too monodimensional, relied too much on DDT [insecticide] spraying, and neglected the palpable problem that the delivery infrastructure was not in place in too many parts of the malarious world. The emergence of widespread mosquito resistance to DDT, and parasite resistance to the cheap mainstay of therapy compounded the difficulties.'[59] As Don Henderson, architect of the successful smallpox eradication effort of the 1960s and 1970s, later put it:

> . . . all malaria programmes were obliged to adhere rigidly to a highly detailed, standard manual of operations. It mandated, for example, *identical job descriptions in every country and even prescribed specific charts to be displayed on each office wall at each administrative level. The programme was conceived and executed as a military operation to be conducted in an identical manner whatever the battlefield* . . . the premise of the programme was that the needed technology was available and that success depended solely on meticulous attention to administrative detail in implementing the effort. Accordingly, research was considered unnecessary and was effectively suspended from the launch of the programme . . . (emphasis added).

In short, the narrowness of the response allowed the mosquito to become resistant. The silver bullet problem has, unfortunately, also proved resilient. As clinical microbiologists Richard Carter and Kamini Mendis see it, for the most part, the *types* of tools available and used for malaria control today are the same as those during the 'virtual elimination' era.[60]

This point does need some nuancing. There was one approved insecticide during the first eradication effort; there are now a dozen. And the use of treated nets—which weren't around in the 1960s—has been responsible for a large decline in malaria incidence in some countries. However, even in these countries, there is growing acknowledgement of the need for a better combination of responses if progress is to be made.

Resistance to responses—whether among mosquitoes or the parasite itself—has been identified as an evolutionary phenomenon. Ecology 101 tells us that all populations of organisms display genetic variation across members, which enable some to handle particular environmental stresses and opportunities better than others. Natural selection favours the evolution of pathogen populations that can resist the drugs and insecticides in their environments. In the face of an evolving enemy, 'cheap mainstays' will not do the trick.

While there has been some basic research to bring an understanding of such complexity to the design of better drugs, pesticides, and even vaccines, there are still questions as to whether this knowledge is ready to be applied in aid programmes and at the necessary scale. For example, the Global Malaria Action Plan of the Roll-back Malaria initiative sought to spray 172 million houses annually and distribute 730 million insecticide-impregnated bednets in 2009. If this were implemented with existing insecticides, with no acknowledgement of the scope for evolutionary responses, the programme would create unprecedented opportunities for the development of resistance among mosquitoes, and may also create new variants.[61]

Some of these fears may be becoming reality. It has been suggested that the mosquito strain responsible for most disease transmission is in the process of evolving rapidly into two genetically distinct species, in reaction to differences in environment and the challenges they face. Researchers at Imperial College, London, have confirmed that this development is likely to undermine efforts to control and treat malaria: conventional strategies are unlikely to be effective against both strains.[62]

Global efforts to prevent malaria through bednets and sprays reduced cases from 233 million in 2000 to 225 million in 2009, and from 985,000 deaths to 781,000 in 2009. However, tellingly, several African countries saw a resurgence of the disease—attributed to evolving resistance and changing contextual factors.[63]

Eradication and control strategies that do not take account of these complex evolutionary dynamics may well make things worse, and could 'substantially exacerbate the significance of malaria in coming decades'.[64] Forty years ago, malaria eradication failed at least in part because of a lack of diversity in the mechanisms employed, and the related evolution of resistance. Although global responses are broader than before, there are still questions about whether they are sufficiently diverse, and whether the full breadth of approaches and knowledge are being applied at scale. And yet, narrowness in responses continues and, in the worst case scenarios, is making human populations more vulnerable to malaria. For a variety of global diseases, we are discovering that best practices in control achieve the exact opposite of what is intended. And yet, as I will show in the next chapter by revisiting the work of Don Henderson and his colleagues, the most remarkable successes in disease control have come about through more open and exploratory approaches.

The Simple Heart of Darkness

The Democratic Republic of Congo is one of the grimmest places on earth to live in poverty. It is ranked lowest on the UN Development Programme Human Development Index 2011,[65] at 187 out of 187 countries. It is also one of the most corrupt countries in the world, ranking 168th in 2011 according to Transparency International.[66] It has a population of 60 million in a territory the size of Western Europe, but paved road coverage of only 1,226 km,[67] just over a tenth of that of its former colonial occupier, Belgium.[68] The war that raged during the 1990s killed millions; over 2 million are internally displaced. There are hundreds of armed groups and militias, and it hosts the largest UN peacekeeping force in the world, numbering over 20,000 at an annual cost of US$1.4 billion.[69] The country is now a prime example of the Orwellian 'not war, but not peace either' classification developed by the Bolsheviks. Margot Wall-ström, UN Special Representative on Sexual Violence in Conflict, has described the Eastern region as the 'rape capital of the world' and the 'most dangerous place on earth to be a woman', because of continued and egregious abuses by armed groups.[70]

Bad as all of this is, according to Severine Autesserre, a political scientist at Columbia University, the situation has been made even worse by the simple narratives created by the international community. Based on ten years of ethnographic research and over 500 interviews, he provides an account of the heuristics and biases shaping foreign aid interventions. Between 2005 and 2010, three narratives dominated assumptions about the country and had a profound influence on aid strategies, focusing on 'a primary cause of violence, the illegal exploitation of natural resources; a main consequence, sexual abuse against women and girls; and a central solution, reconstructing state authority'.[71]

While not questioning the significance or importance of any of these three issues, Autesserre found that they represent serious simplifications of the context, in ways that are counterproductive and demonstrably damaging—and in certain cases making the situation worse. I want to take a look at Autesserre's findings for two of these narratives: minerals as a source of violence, and sexual abuse.

Although the UN estimates that only 8 per cent of all the conflicts in the Democratic Republic of Congo relate to natural resources, the conflict mineral narrative 'often eclipses all the others'.[72] As a result, the dominant solution to the problem of violence in the country is to end the illegal trafficking of resources. As with the malaria case, 'By focusing exclusively on one cause...and one solution...the proponents of this narrative have inadvertently exacerbated the very problems they were combating.'[73] The dominance of the 'conflict mineral narrative' means less attention has been paid to policy actions to address other critical issues such as conflict resolution, tackling corruption, and adminis-trative reform.

Much political and media attention has also been paid to the problem of sexual abuse in the Eastern region. Rape commands attention in the UN Security Council, in the US Department of State, and among foreign ministers. While acknowledging the horrors of such abuses, Autesserre suggests this has diverted attention away from other forms of violence being perpetrated. For example, UN support to the reconstruction of the justice system focuses on enabling officials to respond to sexual abuses rather than all crimes. Similarly, the European Union police deployment focuses exclusively on the fight against sexual abuse. The provision of health services has become so focused on sexual violence that sometimes the best and only way to obtain care is to claim to have been raped:

> ...according to donors and aid workers, sexual violence is such a buzzword that many foreign and Congolese organizations insert references to it in all kinds of project proposals to increase their chances of obtaining funding...Congolese and foreign aid workers regularly complained that they cannot draw the attention of the media or donors to horrific events that have no sexual dimension.[74]

Most worryingly, aware of the media, political, and international attention that will ensue, certain armed groups have been given orders to systematically rape, so as to draw attention and facilitate invitations to the negotiating table.

These are startling consequences of the best-practicitis phenomenon, and they lead to questions as to how this sorry state of affairs might have transpired. Autesserre refers to Daniel Kahneman and Amos Tversky's work in behavioural psychology, and in particular the notion of 'frames', which helps explain how certain narratives can become dominant and what happens as a consequence (see Box 2.2).

This is not to say that such simple narratives go uncontested, nor that there are no benefits from their application in aid settings. But when they are used at the expense of all other kinds of narratives, they contribute to bureaucratic conservatism and a reliance on those predictable actions and routines that are justified by the narratives, regardless of the reality on the ground. Variations in the narratives do, over time, lead to a gradual evolution in how things are understood: 'change in frames and narratives—and in the practices and policies they enable—usually takes place slowly and incrementally.'[75] But as noted by David Ellerman, more radical change usually threatens entrenched organizational cultures and interests.

As with malaria, the exclusive focus on straightforward, silver bullet solutions for overly simplified problems means international efforts can often exacerbate the problems they aim to address. In the Congo in particular, they 'obscure most interveners' understanding of the multi-layered problems [and] orient the intervention toward a series of technical responses and hinder the search for a comprehensive solution'.[76] This is precisely why such simple models can survive for a long time in aid, reinforced by notions of best practice and technical expertise.

Box 2.2. Follow the simplicity—the Congo case

'Certain stories resonate more, and thus are more effective at influencing action, when they assign clear causes of the problems and a short and clear causal chain assigning responsibility; when they suggest a simple solution; and when they can latch on to pre-existing narratives...the aspect of "simplicity"—notably an uncomplicated story line, which builds on elements already familiar, and a straightforward solution—is particularly important in enabling a narrative to achieve and maintain prominence.'[77]

This then plays out across a network of actors who need simple, dominant narratives as 'a way out of their predicament. Such narratives emphasize a few themes to focus on; interveners can then believe that they have a grasp of the most important features of the situation, instead of feeling lost and deprived of the knowledge necessary to properly accomplish their work.'[78]

The actors and their motivations include:

- 'Media outlets need to find a story that fits in a few pages, or can be told in a few minutes, and that their audience can easily understand and remember.'[79]

- 'Policymakers based in headquarters, such as desk officers and advisors to foreign and defence ministers, face a similar challenge, for internal bureaucratic reasons. They are granted only a few minutes or a short memo to brief their superiors, who decide on the main policy directions but usually have only a superficial knowledge of various development problems. They thus have to find a brief and straightforward presentation of the situation, with clear policy recommendations that their superiors can readily grasp and approve.'[80]

- 'Aid organizations need to raise funds for their programmes, and advocacy agencies need to mobilize followers.'[81] 'Apart from rare exceptions, international agencies involved in the country recruit their staff on the basis of their technical expertise...and not on their knowledge of the country...Most interveners therefore lack contextual knowledge...time to read the extensive literature on the conflict [and] reliable information on current events.'[82]

- 'To make matters worse, meetings and reports usually provide factual information on security events, but rarely put these facts into a broader context, and almost never infer their meaning for the overall political, social, and economic situation. The rapid turnover of most international staff, who usually stay in the country for a period ranging between a few months and three years, compounds the lack of in-depth understanding of the conflict.'[83]

Having already looked at health and conflict, I want to turn to how similar processes of simplification have been employed with disastrous consequences in the field of natural resource management.

Down on the Ranch

Rangelands are one of the most common ecological landscapes on earth, collectively covering around a fifth of the land surface in diverse forms: grasslands, shrublands, open woodlands, wetlands, semi-deserts, and savannas. They are also an intrinsic part of our species' story: current paleo-anthropological thinking is that our species took a dramatic turn towards our current evolutionary state whilst in the rangelands of Africa some 7 million years ago. We have been living on and using rangelands since before we were fully human.

International development projects focusing on rangeland management in Africa began around the 1960s, and followed in the wake of numerous colonial efforts to manage these vast open spaces. The early focus of these projects was technology transfer and heightened productivity. The idea was that through capital- and labour-intensive ranching methods—combined with investments in range restoration, water, and fodder—rangelands could start to generate produce for both urban and international markets.[84] These projects singularly failed to achieve these ambitions: production did not increase, and some projects were very destructive for local livelihoods and poverty levels.[85]

An immediately obvious shortcoming was that the international agencies involved typically aimed to work *for* rangeland users, but not *with* them. But there were even more fundamental flaws in the approach. During most of the development era, and the preceding colonial period, the management of dry rangelands in Africa drew on the assumptions of the classic ranching model that had been employed in the temperate climate of North America. Ideas such as rotational grazing, fenced paddocks, and fixed carrying capacity were considered to be 'context independent'. But the success of the US system—also used in Canada and Australia—was dependent on a number of factors and assumptions that simply did not hold true in many parts of Africa.

The late 1970s and early 1980s saw the rise of integrated rural development projects, which were more service-oriented and had at least some degree of appreciation for local perspectives. In many cases, however, the blueprint mentality persisted[86] and the assumptions of the North American model were not seriously challenged, despite the continual finding that local 'spatial and temporal dynamics made such [imported] solutions unworkable'.[87] Research undertaken by the Overseas Development Institute in the 1970s and 1980s on integrated rangeland management projects in Lesotho, Somalia, and Tanzania[88] found that each of the projects was based on similar designs and was broadly in line with other pastoral development projects. All of the projects sought to

- demarcate a controlled grazing area;
- create a grazing association to manage the area;
- establish a rotational grazing system to improve the range;
- upgrade veterinary services;
- train government staff in range management;
- use the market to improve breeds;
- increase commercial meat or fibre production.

As the researchers found:

> The similarity [of] these projects illustrates the assumed universality of Western range management. It is as though a standard list of range-livestock development objectives existed that could be inserted into any development project design. There was very little modification of this standard list to fit local context. Most of the expatriates involved in the design of these projects lacked an understanding of local livestock and range resource management strategies and showed little awareness of previous work in the area.[89]

The designs reflected the imported paradigm whereby a high level of definition and control over the grazing resource was deemed necessary and proposed through exclusive rights and defined boundaries, clear group membership, enforced seasonal movements, centralized decision making, and a variety of other ingredients corresponding to the left hand side of Table 2.1.

The reality, however, was more aligned with the right hand side, and the diverse, dynamic livelihoods of African pastoralist groups. More recent research done at the STEPS (Social, Technological and Environmental Pathways to Sustainability) Centre at the University of Sussex in the UK has shown that, in stark contrast to the imported model, local livestock keepers have their own 'non-equilibrium' approach to rangeland management, involving flexible movements, decentralized decision-making, and the adaptive use of changing resources.

Table 2.1 The North American and Sub-Saharan range management models compared

North American model	Sub-Saharan African model
Agricultural systems geared to the commercial production of meat and fibre.	Pastoral systems generally have multiple goals, emphasizing human survival, milk production, capital accumulation in livestock, and risk aversion. Commercial meat and fibre production tend to be low priorities.
Focused on cattle and sheep as livestock.	In many pastoral systems, species other than cattle and sheep are important.
Livestock are generally controlled by fencing rather than herding.	In most pastoral systems, livestock are herded.
In most cases, producer households have exclusive grazing rights to their range resources, whether these are on private or public land.	Land use is communal or open access.
Operate in industrial countries with well-developed infrastructure for transportation, communication, marketing, research, and education.	In many non-industrial nations, infrastructure is poorly developed, isolating rural populations and constraining government services.
Producers are generally integrated into the political process so government is both accountable to producers and aware of producer needs.	Pastoral populations are frequently politically weak, with little influence on official policy.
Producers tend to share a common Northern European cultural heritage.	Pastoral people come from a wide variety of cultural, religious, and historical backgrounds, creating a diversity of cultural mindsets.

Source: Based on Perrier, G.K. (1990), 'The Contextual Nature of Range Management', Paper 30C (London: ODI).

This lack of fit between the proposed solutions and the local context created numerous conflicts, which agency staff struggled to deal with. Modifications were made to deal with lack of cooperation and compliance among target populations. But, interestingly, the most common response of the range managers was to suggest changes to the local context to make it better suited to the imposed solutions. For example, there were attempts to create bounded and controlled areas to which households were to restrict grazing, as well as to create centralized decision-making bodies. But these changes were resisted because the pastoralists' existing systems were—unsurprisingly—better suited to the ecological and social context: 'The local contexts proved to be too complex and resilient for a context modification strategy to work.'[90] The alternative approach of adapting range management to the contexts doesn't appear to have been seriously considered: the whole endeavour was a classic example of 'doing the wrong thing righter'. 'By the end of the projects, few of the grazing management objectives had been achieved...the contextual nature of Western range management contributed to these results.'[91]

To paraphrase Gregory Bateson, the major problems in this area are the result of the difference between how nature works and how people think.[92] There is some cause for hope: while imposed solutions have repeatedly failed, local versions are gradually, slowly, being taken up as a more effective basis for development.[93]

Power Itself is Knowledge

> Much of the history of development – from colonial times to the present – can be read as a history of the export of inappropriate, doctrinal models... Whether in economic policy or the management of forests, soils, agriculture or water resources we see time and time again the confident assumption that a particular model applied in Europe or North America will work when transplanted into Africa or Asia. And, whether in neo-liberal prescriptions for economic reform and adjustment or sustained yield management of forests, we see such models too often failing the intended beneficiaries.[94]

The examples that I covered here are all symptoms of foreign aid best-practicitis at its most worrying: as Oscar Wilde might have put it, the immovable in pursuit of the impractical. As the STEPS Centre quote above implies, many more examples could have made the list. A comprehensive compilation could easily fill several (rather depressing) books.

Gareth Morgan writes, 'organizational horror stories always seem blatantly stupid and shortsighted [but] they are inevitable in any situation where people are encouraged to *edit their understanding of reality to suit narrow purposes*'[95] (emphasis added). The power and weakness of such editing of reality is evident in many of the cases I have highlighted in this chapter. Such editing of reality, I would argue, typifies the way the aid industry learns and works. Its power is precisely why Mr Sokor's story is even known outside the refugee camp where he lived. Its weakness is it leads directly to a series of 'travelling orthodoxies...[that] are remarkably resilient and sustain over-optimism about the possible applications of the [imposed] model'.[96] We might conclude that power shapes knowledge far more than knowledge confers power.

Aid tends to try and solve simple problems through narrow, prescribed interventions. Aid professionals are not encouraged to learn about the complexities of development, at least not formally. Simple theories that pay implicit homage to Newton and Rostow, and clear-cut directive policy prescriptions, are the order of the day. In holding such ideas and principles sacred, in giving them official status, agencies have not brought about positive change in developing countries: they have instead illustrated how entrenched and conservative they are, often making things worse for the poor and vulnerable.

We might, as a result of this chapter, identify a constant in aid: it has continually been represented as the missing piece in a puzzle—its very existence hinges on the politicized notion that exported solutions and knowledge can fix or improve things. The underlying assumption is that the development and humanitarian challenges of a given developing country are simple, closed, predictable problems that are amenable to such exported solutions.

The old joke is that for every complex problem there is a solution that is simple, neat, and wrong. The account so far suggests the following addition: 'and peddled by foreign aid agencies'. Aid agencies persist in treating the world in a certain way, so their *available* solution becomes *the solution*. When an institutionally embedded set of simple solutions fails, yet again, the underlying belief that the right solution is just around the corner—just a case of 'doing things righter'—keeps the system going. Little wonder that seasoned aid professionals like Roger Riddell can raise the following concerns:

> The longer I have worked in the field of aid and development, the more concerned, and at times alarmed I have become about the limited knowledge and appreciation of so many full-time aid professionals of the complexities of development, and the gaps in our knowledge about the role that aid can play in assisting the process of sustainable development.[97]

Of course, it may be that focusing on these examples may well lead to accusations of exaggeration and generalization. It is always easier to identify others' mistakes than our own.[98] My critique should not be taken to mean aid agencies do not engage with complexity—they do, in some cases, and in some ways—or that they have learned nothing from their experiences—they have. But the reality is that the many examples of good practice are occasional, 'below the radar' rather than built into the formal mechanisms and processes of aid.[99] People learn despite the system, rather than because of it. Because power is knowledge, and power above all else seeks to sustain itself, we can see that the rhetoric around development knowledge—'like light'—is not just optimistic but also clearly wildly inaccurate.

So what about instances where the system has demonstrably learned? Information may be like light but knowledge and learning is slow and heavy. There is evidence for this in all instances where the system has demonstrably 'learned'. The move from small-scale cash experiments to wider acceptance of cash in aid was not simply a case of using knowledge in rational ways to change existing practices. A whole host of other factors mattered: relationships, networks, and policy context. A cynical perspective would be that perspectives on the benefits of cash transfers in the aid system changed (1) just as the era of cheap food ended, and (2) in the context of an emergency response—to the Indian Ocean tsunami—that was awash with cash. Even when change does take place in aid work, as this example illustrates, it is hard to say conclusively that it is because knowledge has finally been accepted. It could be argued that change happens when a readily appropriated form of knowledge is in the right place at the right time to enable maintenance of some form of the status quo. As two noted Swedish development scholars put it:

> In development oriented organisations, with their multitude of objectives and activities, it is not an easy task to state with some confidence that the organisational knowledge structure has changed, i.e. the agency has learned something. We can observe changes in the practice of development aid. We will, however, have a hard time to establish whether these changes were driven by increased knowledge and accumulated experience, or whether agencies were simply reacting to external changes to the best of their ability.[100]

There are of course some people and some aid agencies who have driven change against the odds and in the face of fierce opposition. After all, we know so much about the learning failures of aid highlighted in this chapter largely because of the work of aid agencies themselves, and the openness of staff working in difficult conditions and questioning the rationale of what they are doing, often at considerable personal cost. The experiences of these iconoclasts—literally, those who burn the over-simplistic icons of aid—can be held up as evidence of the failure of narrow, simplified approaches, as well as to the fact that there *is* some valuable learning happening in the aid system after all. One might apply a simple rule of thumb to all this: such learning is slow and often painful, and any aid agency who says otherwise is usually selling something.

I started this chapter with an example of what I described as very effective, if unconventional, single-loop learning in the World Food Programme. As noted earlier, WFP has proved itself to be one of the most progressive aid agencies under the leadership of Josette Sheeran, a former tech CEO, senior US diplomat, and trade negotiator who many view as the most visionary leader in the UN system for a generation. A 2010 book on rethinking food aid showcased just how far the agency had come in reverting the usual power balances in aid[101]—the argument was made strongly that the 'modern WFP not only delivers food—it delivers hunger solutions. It is not instrument-based, but problem-based'.

In Sheeran's words: 'WFP is in the process of...chang[ing] from a food aid agency to what I call a "food assistance" agency, embedding local purchase and more nuanced, market sensitive interventions alongside life-saving emergency commodity contribution...'.

She described the transformation in a language which resonates strongly with the ideas of double- and triple-loop learning introduced earlier, calling for 'a revolution in food aid, where *the way we intervene becomes part of the solution*'[102] (emphasis added).

Sadly, such transformations are more the exception than the norm. Those aid agencies that continue to emphasize simple, exported solutions to development problems risk losing sight of a fundamental adage. This is one that should underpin the social, political, and economic changes they are supposed to be working towards: that nothing is more important than the freedom to question what is important.

Promoting such freedoms in aid efforts would mean placing less emphasis on knowledge as product and as power, and more emphasis on learning as means of mutual transformation.[103] It would mean aid agencies having the courage and vision to follow the paths walked by their own most creative thinkers and practitioners, and—even more importantly—by those practical and resourceful innovators on the margins of the system who they seek to help. It would mean responding to longstanding problems and repeated mistakes with a concerted attempt to challenge existing understanding and assumptions; to learn not just at a tactical level of *doing things right*, but also at a strategic level of *doing the right things*.

CHAPTER 3

Strategic Mismanagement

'None can see the strategy out of which victory is evolved. Strategy without tactics is the slowest route to victory. Tactics without strategy is the noise before defeat.'

Sun Tzu, *Art of War.*

Today, strategies and policies are employed—in name at least—at just about every level of the aid system, and for almost every kind of initiative. They are usually formalized in documents containing goals, frameworks, and indicators of progress. In principle, strategies at different levels should talk to each other, in a cascade of intentions. Most aid organizations are, at any given point, engaged in dozens of simultaneous strategy development and implementation processes, focusing on a breathtaking variety of issues and problems.

Research on strategic approaches in the public sector found senior leaders faced increasing pressure to be strategically innovative, adaptable, and reliable, all in the face of economic and technological changes and growing political and social complexities.[1] Growing expectations amid changing contexts 'require new ways of thinking about organizations and their strategic management'.[2] However, it is also widely acknowledged that the theoretical frameworks that have historically dominated strategic management have not been able to deal with these demands. They have been dominated by certain fixed mental models, assumptions, and ideas and as a result do not match—in theory or in practice—the world faced today. Many public sector strategies are, put simply, not fit for purpose.

Identical critiques have been made of aid agencies and the ways they plan and strategize, most recently and vociferously by Bill Easterly in the White Man's Burden.[3] *In this chapter I want to explore how strategy works at different levels of the aid system and within different types of organization. I take a look at the assumptions and frameworks used in aid strategies, and draw conclusions on their relevance and appropriateness. I try to show that a more reasoned and realistic approach to strategy is required if we are going to understand and improve strategic processes in foreign aid. I close by pointing to what this might look like in practice.*

Smallpox and the 'Strategy Safari'

The World Health Organization (WHO) global strategy for dealing with smallpox, launched in 1967 and declared successful in 1980, is a unique story in foreign aid, because of *what* was achieved: smallpox was one of the biggest killers in human history, estimated to be responsible for at least 300 million deaths in the twentieth century, some 2 million of which occurred in the same year the global strategy was launched. Twelve years later, and at a cost of US$300 million, roughly the same as one modern Hollywood blockbuster in digital 3D, there were no naturally occurring cases anywhere in the world. It was the first—and still the only—time a human disease has been eradicated.

When the last case of smallpox was announced in 1980, WHO Director-General H. Mahler described the achievement as 'a triumph of management, not of medicine'.[4] It may seem odd that he chose to mark this great achievement—arguably one of the greatest medical achievements in human history—with such a statement. After all, his organization was and is a health agency par excellence: the principles of medical achievement and excellence underpin the entire institution, its goals, incentives, values, and career paths. Mahler's emphasis on the importance of management in smallpox eradication indicates that *how* this staggering achievement came about may be just as interesting as *what* was achieved. And yet much of the official history makes only passing reference to this, focusing instead on the medical approach—mass vaccination—that rid the world of smallpox. Not only that, but mass vaccination is typically described in very straightforward ways, involving the roll-out of simple standardized processes. It leaves one wondering what the managerial triumph described by Mahler amounted to.

This seeming contradiction is an appropriate starting point for this chapter, in which I look into the widespread but often convoluted practice of strategy, focusing on how it has been taken up and applied in foreign aid. The smallpox case illustrates powerfully some of the ambiguities in aid strategies that I want to examine. Why is the triumph of management so often remembered today as a triumph of medicine? Why have we in the aid system, and the international community as a whole, learned what seems to be the wrong lesson from this remarkable achievement? And what are the implications for the plethora of aid strategies underway today?

There are of course a great diversity of approaches to strategy, planning, and policy. Thanks to the work of Henry Mintzberg, a leading business academic and author, and colleagues,[5] who researched several thousand books and articles on strategy, we can classify this diversity into one of three traditions.

- *The prescriptive philosophy focuses on how strategy should be formulated.* This is a broad church and includes some who see strategy as a process of design to match internal capabilities with external possibilities; some who extol the virtues of formal planning processes; and some who stress the importance of positioning organizations optimally in their sector or market.

- *The descriptive philosophy looks at how strategy does, in fact, get made.* Here, thinkers emphasize the importance of visionary leaders, of cognitive processes, of learning, of power struggles and negotiations, of collective social action, and of external events shaping actions. Less interested in prescribing idealized behaviours, this approach focuses on strategy's messy, inconsistent, reality.

- *The integrative philosophy seeks to combine other mindsets and approaches according to context and the needs of the strategy and organization in question.* Here, strategy is transformative and evolving, moving between different approaches depending on the circumstances.

Using these three approaches, we can start to take a more detailed look at how researchers and academics have understood strategy. The smallpox case study helps illustrate key points, but I also look at how these three approaches can be used to understand aid strategies more generally.

Prescriptive Approaches: Assembly Lines

The prescriptive approach to strategy carries a number of assumptions: about strategists, the world they live in, and the implementers they charge to carry forth their plans. As Mintzberg and his colleagues put it, 'underlying the whole... exercise [i]s the machine assumption: produce each of the component parts as specified, assemble them according to the blueprint, and the end product (strategy) will result'.[6] Not for nothing have close parallels been drawn between the prescriptive school and factory work of the early twentieth century.

So, prescriptive strategies are 'guided by a cadre of highly educated planners, part of a specialized strategic planning department'.[7] They are expected to think on *behalf of* an organization or entity and do so in some specific ways. First, they establish clear and unambiguous goals and objectives, so one strategy can be seen as preferable to all others. They then analyse all alternative solutions (or policies), weighing up each one carefully in relation to the objectives. They understand perfectly the implications of different alternatives and their consequences, now and in the future. They then select the optimal programmes—those that get closest to the stated objectives and deliver maximum benefits. These are then implemented by numerous operational units, staffed by rational, reasonable, and non-political people, who take on board the strategy and implement actions in perfect accordance with strategic vision and directions. Strategists monitor progress via a system of appraisal and control. A core assumption is of predictable, stable cause-and-effect relations, so the separation of formulation and implementation of strategy does not lead to irrelevance and inappropriateness down the line.

Top-down, blueprint approaches to planning were seen as integral to government and business in the first half of the twentieth century—whether in the growth of big firms in the USA, the rapid industrialization of the Soviet Union in the 1920s, the 1930s' strategy for dealing with worldwide depression, or the post-war economic boom of the 1950s. The mentality reached a peak of acceptance in the 1960s, thanks to a group of influential US businessmen and policymakers, foremost among whom was Robert McNamara, former Ford Chairman and US Defense Secretary, who would become the fifth President of the World Bank. McNamara's story (Box 3.1) is both illuminating and tragic.

Box 3.1. Robert McNamara and the failures of prescriptive planning in Vietnam

Robert McNamara was the brightest of a group of ten military analysts who worked together in Air Force Statistical Control during World War II and who were hired *en masse* by Henry Ford II in 1946. They became a strategic planning unit within Ford, initially dubbed the Quiz Kids because of their seemingly endless questions and youth, but eventually renamed the Whiz Kids, thanks in no small part to the efforts of McNamara.

There were 'four McNamara steps to changing the thinking of any organisation':[8] state an objective, work out how to get there, apply costings, and systematically monitor progress against the plan. In the 1960s, appointed by J.F. Kennedy as Secretary of Defense after just a week as Chair of Ford, McNamara created another Strategic Planning Unit in the Department of Defense, also called the Whiz Kids, with a similar ethos of formal analysis. McNamara spelled out his approach to defence strategy: 'We first determine what our foreign policy is to be, formulate a military strategy to carry out that policy, then build the military forces to conduct that strategy.'[9]

Obsessed with the 'formal and the analytical' to select and order data, McNamara and his team famously developed a statistical strategy for winning the Vietnam War. 'In essence, McNamara had taken the management concepts from his experiences at the Ford Motor Company, where he worked in a variety of positions for 15 years, eventually

(continued)

Box 3.1 Continued

becoming president in 1960, and applied them to his management of the Department of Defense.'[10]

But the gap between the ideal and the reality was stark. Colin Powell describes his experience on the ground in Vietnam in his biography:

> Secretary McNamara...made a visit to South Vietnam. Every quantitative measurement, he concluded, after forty-eight hours there, shows that we are winning the war. Measure it and it has meaning. Measure it and it is real. Yet, nothing I had witnessed...indicated we were beating the Viet Cong. Beating them? Most of the time we could not even find them.[11]

Powell goes on, in language that echoes later critiques of prescriptive strategies as dogma and ritual:

> McNamara's slide-rule commandos had devised *precise indices to measure the immeasurable*. This *conspiracy of illusion* would reach full flower in the years ahead, as we added to the secure-hamlet nonsense, the search-and-sweep nonsense, the body-count nonsense, all of which we knew was nonsense, even as we did it (emphasis added).[12]

McNamara then used the same principles to transform the World Bank's systems and operations. Sonja Amadae, a historian of rational choice theory, suggests that, 'over time...the objective, cost-benefit strategy of policy formation would become the universal status quo in development economics—a position it still holds today.'[13]

Towards the end of his life, McNamara himself started to acknowledge that, 'Amid all the objective-setting and evaluating, the careful counting and the cost-benefit analysis, stood ordinary human beings [who] behaved unpredictably.'[14] 'Rationality', he concluded poignantly, 'would not save us'.[15]

The experience of the US military in Vietnam has been replicated in many other contexts, and has met with much the same level of success. Mintzberg wrote the following in *The Financial Times* in 2008: 'We hear a great deal about micro managing these days—managers who meddle in the work of those who report to them...it can be a problem...but more serious now is macro managing—managers who sit on "top", pronouncing their great visions, grand strategies, and abstract performance standards while everyone else is supposed to scurry around implementing...I call this "management by deeming."'[16]

Of course, 'management by deeming' can work well for certain, static, straightforward problems, including notably for a certain class of development problem. Charles Kenny, in his 2011 book, *Getting Better: Why Global Development is Succeeding* sets out a number of development problems that are today less pronounced because of the effective diffusion of cheap technologies.[17] But as his colleague at the Centre for Global Development, Lant Pritchett points out, 'in many country contexts ... many simple problems—those susceptible to logistical solutions (e.g. vaccinations, expanding enrollments)—have been solved'.[18]

For many of the more complex and thorny problems faced in public and social life, prescriptive blueprint approaches to strategy have proved woefully inadequate, and have indeed been the focus of much ire. In the extreme, the prescriptive approach puts such faith in *ex-ante* rationality—in the power of *deeming*—that it leads to the belief that there is no need for learning as strategies progress. But as Winston Churchill famously put it, 'however beautiful the strategy, you should occasionally look at the results'.

Other prominent failures of the approach illustrate exactly this lack of interest in learning and, by contrast, a dogmatic faith in predefined strategic intentions. This may be, in large part, why such 'rational' intentions have repeatedly been described as ritualistic and superstitious. Business strategy scholars Richard Foster and Sarah Kaplan, had dismissive—if perhaps culturally insensitive—views of the prescriptive approach to strategy: '[It's] like a primitive tribal ritual: there is a lot of noise, dancing, waving of feathers, beating of drums, and still no one is exactly sure why we do it, but still there is an almost mystical hope that something good will eventually come of it.'[19]

Others have argued that the prescriptive approach has widespread acceptance 'not only because choosing means to achieve defined ends is attractive to planners, but it also appeals to modern publics as a common sense way to *anticipate the future*' (emphasis added).[20] More scathing is the assessment by two editors of *The Economist*, who use a quote from David Hume, the eighteenth-century Scottish philosopher known for his work on empiricism and scepticism, simultaneously to explain and condemn the efforts of what they call the 'witch doctors' of strategy: 'Managers are constantly embracing techniques that promise to control the uncertainty at the heart of their jobs ... we are reminded of David Hume's insight: "in proportion as any man's course of life, we always find that he increases in superstition."'[21] Such ritual strategies offer, in Colin Powell's words, a 'conspiracy of illusion' in the face of uncertainty.[22] They also enable, and facilitate, the expression of control by the powerful. It may also, of course, be that *ex post* imposition of linearity and predictability of outcomes and rationality of intent is simply part of the way that humans make sense of things.

Some aspects of the smallpox strategy fit well with the prescriptive approach. The original call for a new global eradication effort was made at the 1958 World Health Assembly by the deputy health minister of the Soviet Union, and was formally approved in 1959, but saw little progress until 1966 when a dedicated team was established, under the leadership of a US physician and epidemiologist called Don Henderson. The goal of the programme was initially defined as the complete eradication of smallpox, and mass vaccination was prescribed as the means by which to achieve it. Based on what was already 'known' to work in developed countries, the vaccination approach was seen as the best way forward: 'With the epidemiological experience available in 1966, the choice of mass vaccination as a strategy *appeared rational*'[23] (emphasis added). It was firmly linked to a package of standardized responses. The official records present a clear mechanical image '[of] the many different cogs of a complex administrative wheel ... work[ing] in almost perfect unison, causing orders from the top of the organisational pyramid to be implemented in localities across the globe'.[24]

The original 1960s strategy initially took a prescriptive approach: puzzle solving; blueprinted, designed, and specified at the top; and implemented by rote at the bottom. Issues such as the diversity of country contexts, how populations would respond, and the capacities of implementers were seen largely as straightforward matters for implementers to overcome. 'Such an interpretation would have us believe that the calculations and actions of a few senior managers controlled the actions of a huge number of public health and medical personnel of different educational backgrounds, nationalities, political affiliations and gender, over the course of more than a decade.'[25] This is as clear a description of management by deeming as one could hope for. Echoing this, Charles Kenny's account in *Getting Better* focuses on the fact that vaccines were 'cheap, stable, long lasting and easy to administer', and an example of a general rule 'the most effective health technologies are very cheap and very simple'.[26] But this again begs the question: if this cheap simple technology was all that was needed, why did the WHO director describe the eradication as a triumph of management, not medicine? If mass vaccination worked just as designed, was that really a triumph of management? What exactly did Mahler mean by his statement?

Descriptive Approaches: Muddling Through

During the 1950s and 1960s—the heyday of the prescriptive approach to strategy and policy—a Harvard political scientist called Charles Lindblom was arguing that policy and strategy were rather different to how McNamara and his contemporaries presented them. He was not alone: Herbert Simon, whose Nobel-winning work we will come to in Part 2, was arguing for new theories of decision making, based on the fact that human problems are far more complex than our limited capacities and resources can handle. Simon's colleagues, Richard Cyert and James March, were writing on the importance of learning in policy and strategy. These authors all called for an alternative to the prescriptive strategy. Aware of the 'conspiracy of illusion', they suggested that what was needed was a more realistic, empirically sound view of how strategies actually get formulated and implemented.

In reality, Lindblom argued, strategies do not start in the mind of strategists, and they are certainly not a clean movement toward predetermined goals. They are better described as a series of small, incremental steps in a 'science of muddling through'. 'Muddling through' emerges from the interaction between organizations and their environment, and also the accretion of many hundreds of ad hoc decisions. Strategists may partly capture this, and reflect it back to the organization, which then leads to more ad hoc behaviours and actions. Strategy is not rigid and predefined, but dynamic, iterative, and emergent: it is 'a never-ending process of successive steps in which continual nibbling is a substitute for a good bite'.[27] The dynamic interplay between intent and outcome is at the heart of the descriptive approach.

However, although muddling is a prominent feature of policy and strategy in almost all contexts, Lindblom observed that this is *not* how scholars and practitioners of policy and strategy describe what they do, or what they tell others to do. This leaves those 'who handle complex decisions in the position of practicing what few preach'.[28]

This 'science of muddling through' is underpinned by a set of assumptions that contrast with those of the prescriptive approach. Lindblom and others argued that

- Defining objectives clearly and unambiguously is very difficult, given the multiple, interacting trade-offs faced in any given context.

- It is impossible and inefficient to identify and analyse every policy solution and implication upfront; for all but the most narrow policy choices, it takes too much time and too many resources, and so only a few means are considered.

- Choices among these different means are determined more by agreement among interested parties based on past experience and group dynamics than on perfect information, and are often highly politicized.

- It is impossible to aggregate the values and objectives of the various constituencies to determine exactly which preferences are most important: one person's efficiency criterion is another's professional anathema.

- The separation of ends and means—strategic objectives from recommended actions—is also impossible: solutions are always bound up with objectives. We often know what the ends might be only by thinking through the implications of different means, and so the means shape the objectives and vice versa.

- Finally, unpredictability and instability mean adjustments need to be made in an ongoing process. Strategy is never complete; it is an endless repetition of imperfect decisions in the face of changing aspirations and conditions.

'Lindblom's notions... violated virtually every premise of "rational" management, but they struck a chord by describing behavior with which everyone was familiar, and in business no less than government.'[29] Because of this, those working on the descriptive approach are often seen as providing a more empirically sound basis on which to understand strategy, despite 'the absence of sufficient human skill in both calculation and control to permit [even] a single complex policy decision'.[30]

As one might imagine, Lindblom's attack on the dominant approach to strategy did not go undefended. Counter-criticisms[31] of the science of muddling through included the claim that such an approach was purposeless—insufficiently goal oriented and ambitious, inviting 'complacent acceptance of our imperfections'[32] and justifying 'a policy of "no effort"',[33] and proceeding 'without knowing where we are going'.[34] Rightly or wrongly, the possibility of a lack of strategic direction and discipline is a key worry for those not convinced by the 'muddling through' approach.

The notion of muddling through enables us to make sense of those accounts of the smallpox story—personal histories of those involved, research in the *British Medical Journal*, and of course, Mahler's enigmatic statement—that paint a very different picture to the one given in the official history. First, 'the initial definition of the problem as mass vaccination was a classic symptom of a confusion between ends and means';[35] relatively early on in the process, the original epidemiologically sound analysis in fact proved to be wrong. The prescriptive strategy contained in the official account is not just challenged by this evidence, but completely contradicted. This leaves us at something of a loss in seeking to understand the success of the strategy—either they got it right up front and it worked, or they didn't and it didn't work. How could they have got it wrong and still been successful in the eradication effort? This is precisely the kind of confusion that Lindblom argued occurs when the assumptions of the prescriptive strategy school—about the perfect knowledge of strategists, about the predictability of cause and effect, and about the simplicity of implementation—do not hold true.

A variety of contextual factors blew the smallpox eradication plans off course. As Don Henderson wrote, 'The program had to surmount numerous problems, including lack of organization and discipline in national health services, epidemic smallpox among refugees fleeing areas stricken by civil war and famine, shortages of funds and vaccine, and a host of other problems posed by difficult terrain, climate, and cultural beliefs.'[36] The reality of agreeing different implementation processes, and the related aid packages, was far more complex and elaborate than the official story suggests. The sucker punch to the top-down strategy was the discovery that its core assumptions did not (to paraphrase the old military saying) survive its encounter with reality: 'It was soon learned that even when 80 per cent of the population was vaccinated, smallpox often persisted.'[37]

The enterprise was much more complicated than the official account suggests. The reality was that the eventual strategy and policy that led to the eradication of smallpox was not deliberately and rationally planned for or even envisaged by senior managers: 'WHO and its staff *were not in control of the unfolding strategy.*' The process of implementation was far from being a series of cleanly meshed and efficiently whirring cogs, put into motion by senior managers.

As described in the previous chapter, Don Henderson subsequently compared the smallpox strategy to the doomed malaria eradication strategy of the 1950s and 1960s. I share his views that the failure of malaria was largely because of the heavily prescriptive approach. For smallpox, however, a different approach was needed. Remarkably, it was put in place despite considerable resistance:

> The smallpox eradication campaign had to function differently... *This occurred despite the opposition of senior WHO leadership who insisted that the tools were in hand and the epidemiology was sufficiently well understood*[38] (emphasis added).

This is not, however, to detract in any way from the smallpox achievement. Rather, these glossed-over complexities 'highligh[t] the enormity of the achievement, which many officials and politicians considered impossible during the 1960s and 1970s'.[39]

The smallpox case study suggests critiques of the 'muddling' approach are not *wholly* true. Taking a more incremental approach to implementation enabled the revision of the original faulty assumptions, a focus on innovation and adaptation, and a move away from the initial conservative, epidemiological approach. However, some of the mud that the prescriptive school would no doubt sling does in fact stick. The unavoidable question is as follows: had the WHO *begun* in 1967 with an incremental approach, would smallpox have been eradicated? Clearly not: some combination of the two approaches was necessary. A goal and initial strategy was clearly needed to mobilize attention and set the level of ambition, but it also needed to be quickly shelved in favour of a different, more adaptive approach that emerged during the implementation process. This insight takes us to the third strategic approach: the integrative approach.

Integrated Approaches: Strategic Adaptation

In his 2011 book,[40] Tim Harford, journalist for *The Financial Times*, tells a story about 'the surge' in Iraq, widely attributed to the troop surge put in place by David Petraeus in 2007 (long before his career ended in scandal and disgrace). In fact, the changes that contributed to success in the campaign had already been brought about, thanks to the work of a visionary colonel who had realized the key to counter-insurgency wasn't more troops or more sorties, but rather ensuring the protection of local civilians. David Kilkullen, an Australian counter-insurgency specialist, composed a set of tips entitled '28 Articles: Fundamentals of Company Level Insurgency' over a bottle of whisky, which was circulated widely in the field. He later said that a key principle of this work was simply to emphasize that 'Foreigners can't fix all these issues' and that instead they needed to accept their role as one of a number of actors in a complex, dynamic 'conflict ecosystem'.[41] When Petraeus got to command, he requested that the existing counter-insurgency manual be replaced with the field-based lessons. Much of the organizational change necessary for success against the insurgents had already happened by the time the new strategy became official. In an echo of the WHO smallpox effort, however, it was the top-down surge strategy of more troops that got the credit. As Harford writes,

> We associate Gen Petraeus with the successful 'surge' in Iraq because he was the man in charge at the time – the equivalent of the chief executive of the US Army in Iraq. But much of the process of organisational change had already happened when he took over. Gen Petraeus had recognised the army was,

piece by piece, adapting its strategy. And he had catalysed the bottom-up process before taking the leadership role for which he is recognised today.[42]

What Petraeus did was more intelligent than top-down planning or muddling through alone; like Don Henderson, albeit with very different purposes, he combined both to good effect.

The integration approach to strategy is based on the idea that different strategic approaches are needed for different issues or at different stages. This is supported by both empirical research and observational studies, which show that, instead of sticking rigidly to one approach or framework, effective organizations and groups often make use of different approaches as the context suits. This points to the 'possibility of reconciliation' between the two opposing schools—a marriage between McNamara and Lindblom, or strategic opportunism. The classic work on this philosophy was undertaken by a doctoral student on one of the most dramatic episodes in UN history, the Cuban missile crisis. Graham Allison argued that the key players 'th[ought] about problems of foreign and military policy in terms of largely implicit conceptual models that [had] significant consequences for the content of their thought'.[43] He described three distinct approaches—rational actor, organizational process, and government politics—which map onto our prescriptive and descriptive schools. The key, from his perspective, was that each model was useful but needed to be supplemented with—and on occasion supplanted by—the others. He did, however, reserve special criticism for the dangers of the 'rational actor' approach, which he saw as unscientific and 'unfalsifiable': smart analysts will be able to find rational choice underpinning virtually any decision.

How to know when a particular approach is relevant or not? One common way is to draw an analogy with ecological adaptation. One strategic practitioner, David Hurst, argues that different types of strategies need to match where an organization is in an imagined 'ecocycle'. The hypothesis is that just as complex systems such as forests and rangelands transition from phases of growth and exploitation to conservation followed by destruction, so too do organizations. Different kinds of strategic action are most appropriate at different stages of the cycle. Drawing on the ideas of Buzz Holling, which have become widely applied in recent years, Hurst argued that human beings are not able to be perfectly rational like a machine, but are able to pick up cues from the environment, to adapt to context, and to shift their perspectives and ideas—what he describes as being 'ecologically rational'.[44]

If we relate these ideas to the strategy that *eventually* helped advance the fight against smallpox, we can now say it involved a *strategic adaptation* in *how* the WHO approached the problem, moving *between* the prescriptive and the descriptive approaches, using both or either when necessary, depending on the context and the stakeholders concerned. First, the rational action stage ran into problems, which led to a point of crisis, which required strategic leadership to steer the process. This takes us to the emergent action phase, where a creative global network of actors swung into action. A broad array of measures emerged over time from the local practices of field teams that worked to invent effective procedures that blended with local customs and conditions. What eventually eliminated smallpox was the *combined approach* of top-down problem solving—what are rightly called 'vertical programmes' for mass vaccination to reduce disease incidence—and bottom-up emergent experimental innovations in early detection, isolation, and control.[45] This is a clear evolution from the prescriptive model towards a learning, evolutionary, politically savvy approach, in which the context shaped the approach and conscious effort was put into adapting the project as it progressed. It was an 'emergent' success. Notably, Henderson argued that the success of the programme was attributable to this process of strategic adaptation and learning, 'more than any other single factor'.[46] The true 'triumph of management' Dr Mahler referred to was a system for *evolving* appropriate strategies in the face of context, change, and complexity.

I want to use these ideas to delve deeper into the detail, patterns, and trends of strategy development and implementation in aid. I will look at a range of strategies underway at three different levels of the system: global strategic frameworks that are supposed to shape aid as a whole, country-specific strategies, and organizational strategies. The Millennium Development Goals (MDGs) take up the first part, followed by country-specific strategies—covering the once-popular poverty reduction strategy papers and also country strategies of particular agencies. I then look at organizational strategies—both organization wide and issue specific. I draw on research studies, evaluations and perspectives of those involved, a mix of sources across which I attempt to 'join the dots' to provide an overall picture of strategies and policies within foreign aid.

A Polarizing Consensus: the Millennium Development Goals

The Millennium Development Goals are the commitments made by the 189 UN member states in 2000 to reduce extreme poverty and its many manifestations. Setting out quantitative objectives to be achieved by 2015, they represent the international community's most broadly agreed commitment to improving the lives of the poor. The intention was 'to create an environment—at the national and global levels alike—which is conducive to development and the elimination of poverty'.[47] Little wonder they have been described as 'the world's biggest promise'.[48]

The Millennium Development Goals are broad, aiming to eradicate poverty and hunger, achieve universal primary education and gender equality, reduce child mortality, improve maternal health, combat disease, ensure environmental sustainability, and create a global partnership for development. The 8 goals are underpinned by 18 targets, which themselves have 48 indicators below them. They have become central to the development aid strategies and policies being pursued by large numbers of countries and organizations. All member states of the United Nations endorsed the goals in 2000. Today a number of major agencies—including many donors, all UN agencies, and most NGOs—judge the overall value of their activities on the basis of their contribution to the Goals. And yet, despite this remarkable level of take-up, the MDGs still manage to polarize opinions within the aid community.

On the positive side, it is argued that the Goals amount to a grand strategic vision for international development. They have the strength of good intentions and of creating solidarity and purpose: 'They fare best when viewed as a minimum set of objectives that all or most in the international community would subscribe to.'[49] They also command a sense of legitimacy and consensus rarely seen in international politics.[50] One early and notable critic told me he had underestimated the political value of the MDGs in this regard. Jeffrey Sachs talks about 'a slow gravitation towards the goals' that he has observed among politicians, government bodies, and civil society. The MDGs are also eminently suited to the existing bureaucracy of aid, with a system of targets that can—in theory at least—be tracked and measured. This has led to their widespread use as a framework to organize policy, planning, and action. So far, so prescriptive, but not necessarily bad: remember that similar prescriptive approaches were a necessary but not sufficient element of smallpox eradication.

However, a number of more critical views also need to be taken into account. The MDGs are seen as utopian—part of 'a long and controversial tradition of setting demanding—and sometimes frankly unrealistic—goals at the inter-national level'.[51] Relatedly, they are based on an almost inevitable simplification of the world: 'from the outset, there have been concerns that the MDGs present too simplistic a picture of a complex reality... This is perhaps less a criticism of the MDG framework than of the way in which it has been interpreted and used.'[52]

The way the goals have been 'interpreted and used'—that is the strategic approach for achieving them—is the subject of numerous critiques. Most common is the accusation that they are insensitive to diverse and dynamic contexts. This is unsurprising, given the ambition of setting common goals for every single developing country in the world to be achieved in a decade and a half. Also unsurprisingly, the MDGs are not especially future-ready: 'the exercise...does not deign to touch the important, if difficult, issue of the anticipation of emerging and future needs'.[53] Questions also arise about the comprehensiveness of the MDGs. A number of critical, but harder to measure and quantify, dimensions such as governance, voice, participation, and vulnerability are missing: 'the MDGs' process...avoided the messy, uncertain, and contested aspects of development in favour of a more singular approach'.[54] This may be unsurprising given the imperatives that shaped the MDGs. Here is Sachs again, describing the approach of Claire Short, the then UK Secretary of State for International Development: 'her view was "just focus on this, don't deviate", and once when I said "well maybe we should do something else also", she said, "no! we have one set of goals. This is what we are focusing on, we will not talk about or do anything else." I learned to see the wisdom of that.'[55]

Such prescription would be fine if the Goals were developed through some systematic and scientific process. However, the rather more arbitrary way in which the Goals were developed was illuminated by one of the principal authors, Lord Mark Malloch-Brown, in an interview in 2013. Shortly after the MDG document had gone to press, as he tells the story, 'I was walking along the corridor, relieved at job done, when I ran into the beaming head of the UN environment programme and a terrible swearword crossed my mind when I realised we'd forgotten an environmental goal . . . we raced back to put in the sustainable development goal.'[56] Reflections from the STEPS Centre are pertinent here: 'Without acknowledgment of power relations and the political dynamics fostered within the process, the ability to achieve sustainable goals which prioritise the needs of the poor and marginalised as effectively as possible is diminished.'[57]

The MDGs also 'ghettoize' the problem of development.[58] Despite the commitments developed countries made to mobilize behind the MDGs, all the targets focus on changes in the developing world, with few goals pertaining to the changes in behaviour among rich countries: the goals fail to recognize the fact that international development begins at home, and focus 'entirely on "development" as a process or activities to be exported or supported in other countries'.[59] As well as neglecting the importance of global interdependence, this separation of goal setting from results has a very McNamara-ish feel to it. It is hard to dismiss the feeling—and the considerable evidence—that rich countries acted as the strategists, with developing countries viewed as the implementers of this new 'global' commitment. This is reinforced by the findings of a mid-term review for the European Union, which found 'a sense of lack of ownership of the MDGs in developing countries . . . [which] are often seen as instruments for the developed countries'.[60]

There are also concerns that the goals and targets that are in place are not in fact well matched to the problems they seek to address. Many of the MDGs are compelling, but the related targets often fail to capture or even allude to important dimensions of the issue they cover. For example, there are now major questions arising about what meeting targets such as primary enrolment—a key education target—really says about the quality and relevance of formal schooling. We will see more instances of such mismatches between comprehensive goals and narrowly-defined targets in a subsequent chapter on performance approaches.

Along similar lines, critics have also been quick to point out the potential distortions that arise from the technocratic scaffolding that supports the whole enterprise. One critique refers to the MDGs as human development plus results-based management.[61] I explore the challenge of results-based management in a later chapter; for now, all that needs noting is that this approach has a track record of creating numerous distortions in policy and practice, whatever the context: 'power is wished away in managerial goals'.

At their best, then, the MDGs are a courageous call for multidimensional poverty reduction and a set of indicators for holding international agencies and governments accountable to citizens. At their worst, they are a donor-led, top-down, reductionist agenda—'minimum development goals'—that pays little attention to locally defined and owned definitions of progress and development and the responsibilities of rich countries in bringing about change. Perhaps the best summary is that of Richard Manning, former Chair of the Development Assistance Committee of the Organisation for Economic Co-operation and Development, who argues that 'the MDGs...are good servants but bad masters'.[62] At the time of writing, although the champions and critics are holding firm to their positions, the objective jury is still out.

What is clear is that, without radical progress, many of the MDGs will not even be nearly met for the poorest people in the world by 2015. This is true across and within countries: 'Women, rural inhabitants, ethnic minorities and other poor people are typically progressing slower than national averages—or showing no progress—even where countries as a whole are moving towards the Goals.'[63] In entire groups of countries, moreover—notably those described as fragile states and parts of Sub-Saharan Africa—very few if any MDGs will be achieved in the timeframe specified. If this situation doesn't change, and fast, then surely the MDGs deserve to go down as another major failure of the prescriptive approach to strategy.

Let's take another look at education, which I examined briefly in Chapter 1. Most actors in the aid system have looked to increases in spending as a key strategy to meet the MDGs, and the education goal is no different—there has been a spate of studies examining the spending required to achieve each goal, the relationship between spending and outcomes, and the rate of progress needed to meet the goal. While this is fine if coverage is the *goal*, the reality is that we should be as interested in the *quality* of educational outcomes. As noted earlier: access doesn't mean completion, or quality education, or enhanced capabilities.

Take the example of India, where a 1996 Public Report on Basic Education identified that absentee rates among teachers in rural states was 48 per cent. This led to a nationwide programme to support improvements in the quality of education, which saw an increased budget for schools, infrastructure, hiring, training, and other investments. This led to an increase in enrolment rates and other indicators. It has been claimed that the MDGs made a contribution to this effort. However, a revisited version of the Public Report in 2008 found that teacher absentee rates remained at 48 per cent. And although the key target indicator of enrolment had improved, there was almost no improvement in basic literacy or mathematics.[64]

As a World Bank evaluation found, 'The MDGs primarily address the issue of access to primary education and do not include an explicit goal with respect to either the quality of instruction or to learning outcomes, such as literacy or numeracy'.[65] It continues,

> The MDG push for universal primary enrolment and completion, although a valuable intermediate goal, *will not suffice to ensure that children achieve the basic literacy and numeracy that are essential to poverty reduction*. To reduce poverty, countries in partnership with the Bank need to make *improved learning outcomes a core objective in their primary education plans and focus on the factors—shown by country-level analysis—most likely to influence such outcomes in the local context*, recognizing that improving learning outcomes for all will require higher unit costs than universal completion[66] (emphasis added).

Separately, a major multi-donor evaluation of progress against basic education found that attachment to 'prescribed solutions' has consistently undermined durable and lasting progress.[67] Specifically,

> There has been a strong tendency for external agencies to place increasing emphasis on the use of external support for accelerating progress in basic education, especially in relation to the education goals of the Millennium Development Goals (MDGs)...This tendency has been accompanied...by a reliance on blueprints, templates and prescribed solutions that has been detrimental to a commitment to partnership, has been inconsistent with the capacities of partners and has sometimes limited the relevance of programmes and projects.[68]

It concluded that while there is a commitment to partnership among donor agencies for improving outcomes, 'What is most lacking, however, is a willingness and determination to improve basic education through locally developed solutions, which are most relevant to the contexts of partner countries and which are built from the "ground up" rather than through the application of blueprints and templates developed at a global level.'[69]

When the record on the rest of the MDGs is examined, similar messages seem to come up time and time again. If one consider these issues across the whole set of MDGs, it becomes clear there are genuine risks and an inherent danger that 'even if the targets are achieved, the inequalities within a nation across people and places would still persist'.[70] Given all of this, it is entirely possible for the development system to 'hit the target and miss the point'.[71]

Incidentally, the arguments above were not made by tub-thumping civil society organizations or irascible East Coast academics. They are admissions and acknowledgements of those organizations that have heavily bought into—and in some cases were principle architects of—the strategic approach and process taken to meet the Goals. If the world's biggest promise is *not* to be an empty one, clearly there needs to be serious attention paid to *how* education, and indeed all the other goals, is approached.

Critics like Bill Easterly say that bottom-up innovation—'searching'—should replace planning mechanisms like the MDGs altogether, allowing for localized responses. This was one of the core arguments in his popular book, *The White Man's Burden*, which attributed the failure of 60 years of aid to the dominance of 'planner' mentalities. Because of the complex and unknowable nature of development, Easterly argues, it would be better to replace such planners with searchers, who experiment, adapt, and muddle through. But this is going too far in the opposite direction for the prescriptive school. While Easterly sees the top-down approach as failed and unnecessary, others suggest simply that it is not sufficient. As the World Bank evaluation of education says:

> The optimal strategy to improve learning outcomes for the disadvantaged in any given country will depend on local conditions and institutions. Those countries where Bank support has led to improved learning for the disadvantaged have taken quite different routes, consistent with their conditions and constraints. What has had the largest impact in Ghana may not have the same impact in Uganda; what is effective in Honduras may not be so in Peru...Adopting international good practice norms without sufficient experimentation can lead to unanticipated results that can undermine program effectiveness.[72]

Similarly, UNESCO has grappled with the alternative strategic approaches in relation to its work on education. In a paper published five years before the MDGs were agreed, UNESCO strategists painted a picture that clearly illustrated a nuanced understanding of the task ahead of them:

> Education planning cannot be purely technical or linear. It deals with an educational enterprise that is not characterized by unambiguous issues, clearly defined objectives, undisputed causal relationships, predictable rationalities and rational decision-makers...Education policy planning, as such, is by necessity a series of untidy and overlapping episodes in which a variety of people and organizations with diversified perspectives are actively involved in the processes through which issues are analyzed and policies are generated, implemented, assessed and adjusted or redesigned. Education planners thus need *a methodological approach [which] capture[s] the intricacies of both policies and processes, to give deliberate attention to every element of the policy-planning process, and to gauge the evolving dynamics of the system*[73] (emphasis added).

The Malloch-Brown story about the environmental goal highlights one of the many ironies of the MDGs: that a framework that is so based on the notions of formal rationality, in fact resulted from a messy, muddled negotiation. Let's backtrack momentarily to examine how the MDGs came about: a clear case of strategic adaptation at play. Diane Stone, one of the leading global policy analysts working anywhere in the world today, developed the concept of a global policy agora, drawing on the Ancient Greek concept of a public space where social, economic, and political life came together: a kind of platform for 'muddling through' to take place. She describes international policy vividly, as characterized by, '…fluid, dynamic and intermeshed relations of politics, markets, culture and society. This public [social and political] space is shaped by the interactions of its actors. [It is] a domain of relative disorder and uncertainty where institutions are under-developed and political authority unclear, and dispersed through multiple institutions and networks…policy activity is opaque and as likely to take place inside private associations as in inter-governmental conferences.'[74] Researchers at Manchester University's Brooks World Poverty Institute picked up Stone's idea, arguing that 'The global agora provides a valuable image of the inherently complex, messy and unpredictable processes that incrementally, sometimes by design and sometimes by accident, gave birth to the MDGs.'[75] This description brings to mind the old American adage that cheap sausages and laws are two things you never want to see being made. International aid policy is just as problematic in the making, but there may be even fewer opportunities to witness the process. It should go without saying that the process of *implementing* the MDGs is no less complex, messy, and unpredictable than the one that led to their creation: the MDGs didn't pass from an agora into a perfectly rational world. Instead they were introduced into 189 diverse, fluid, and opaque national policy agoras.

The irony is that the messy MDG formulation process would lead to such a triumph of the rational, technocratic school of strategy. The way the MDGS were packaged and communicated perhaps made this inevitable. Malloch-Brown described in his autobiography the rich countries' desire to make the MDGs cost as little as possible, which led to an emphasis on identifying simple, low-cost solutions that would achieve development progress on all fronts. This was nothing if not 'wishing power away'.

The challenge is whether a more complex understanding can somehow be brought to bear on the post-MDG agenda, despite the countervailing system that continues to push the formal MDG approach. There seem to be some genuine attempts to do just this, but whether the new post-2015 agenda is really able to draw the appropriate lessons from the pre-2015 effort remains to be seen.

Technocratic Experiments with Documents: The Poverty Reduction Strategy Paper

In a 2003 review of the resurgence of planning approaches in aid,[76] the ODI Director at the time, Simon Maxwell, argued that one of the benefits of the then new wave was the multiple levels at which new poverty-planning thinking was being applied. Alongside the MDGs at the macro level were a number of country-led processes, including new mechanisms for delivering aid associated with budget support to developing countries, a commitment to results-based management, and a mechanism for operationalizing strategies at a national level, in the form of the Poverty Reduction Strategy Paper (PRSP).

The idea of long-term visions for development had become a central element of aid thinking for some time before PRSPs came onto the scene. The World Bank's Comprehensive Development Framework emphasized a multisector, multidisciplinary, long-term development vision and approach, based on country leadership and country-level donor cooperation. This philosophy was applied more widely following the 2001 World Bank/International Monetary Fund (IMF) Board decision to adopt the PRSP approach, which built on similar principles.

PRSPs are—nominally—national plans of action for tackling poverty. As the name implies, they are formal documents that set out an analysis of poverty in a country and define a national strategy for dealing with it. Designed to replace the heavily criticized structural adjustment programmes, each PRSP was intended to have a number of common elements:

- Country-driven and consultative—involving broad-based participation by civil society and the private sector in all operational steps.

- Results-oriented—focusing on outcomes that benefit the poor—and comprehensive—recognizing the multidimensional nature of poverty (economic and social dimensions).

- Partnership-oriented—involving coordinated participation of development partners (bilateral, multilateral, and non-governmental).

- Long-term—based on a long-term perspective for poverty reduction.

Over the course of the 2000s, PRSPs became a key tool for all low-income countries seeking access to expanded debt relief and funding from the IMF and World Bank. A number of major donors, including the European Commission and the UK, have provided strong support for the approach and made their own grants conditional on effective PRSP processes.

The PRSP process involved a cycle of steps, with poverty analysis followed by objective setting, policy decisions, implementation, and monitoring, which then subsequently fed back to inform future analysis and formulation. As with the MDGs, the PRSP is underpinned by the prescriptive planning model. And, just like the MDGs, PRSPs have had their supporters and detractors. The champions of the approach—the international financial institutions—were responsible for some of the most detailed critiques, adding one more to a list of paradoxes that surround the PRSPs. The criticisms were, as with the MDGs, wide-ranging, and, like the MDGs, many focused on the assumptions and ideas held about the strategy process and its effects. From the outset, although the PRSPs were supposed to be led by national governments and stakeholders, the process was designed and developed almost entirely in the context of the Bank and the IMF. Tellingly, there was 'no mechanism or guidance to adapt the [PRSP] Initiative's processes and requirements to differing country conditions'.[77]

Given that the PRSP was, for the duration of the 2000s, 'the primary means through which multilateral assistance was granted, and managed',[78] producing the strategy in a way that would lead to successful sign-off was critical.

The PRSPs also involved conditions on the part of the IMF and the Bank, and needed both institutions to sign-off on releasing funds, which was 'perceived as undermining the principle of country ownership—as "Washington signing off" on a supposedly country-owned strategy'.[79] As one commentator told me, 'ownership in PRSPs relates to ownership of the need to jump through a hoop in order to get a credit line'.[80]

This led to a preoccupation with responding to PRSP requirements with formulaic statements and standardized strategies, at the expense of any adaptation to country circumstances. There was also evidence of self-censorship among governments for fear of not qualifying for funding, to the point that 'Country governments have little control over the structure, content, and policy prescriptions in their PRSPs.'[81] Analytically, many PRSPs took a shallow reading of poverty, focusing mainly on income-based measures and not making use of the advances in multidimensional measures that had come about as a result of the Human Development Report process.

Another demonstration of the prescriptive school in action was the separation of analysis, formulation, and implementation. In many cases, as a Bank evaluation found, there was 'too much emphasis on producing documents, rather than improving underlying policy processes'.[82] Indeed, the PRSPs took this to new levels, whereby major 'nationally owned' strategies were being drafted in Western capitals, by foreign consultants.

The implementation of PRSPs was also found to be problematic. The Bank evaluation found that, in general, the process did not generate meaningful discussions about policy options and implementation issues outside a narrow, senior official circle.[83] It also noted that 'monitoring of implementation does not ... inform policy design'.[84] A related issue was that, because of the weakness of in-country monitoring systems, there was a tendency towards donor-focused monitoring, leading to further issues with ownership and accountability.

In many cases, moreover, 'The process has not proved able to adapt to unanticipated developments—such as changes in macroeconomic conditions.'[85] David Booth argued in 2005 that the PRSP process, while useful in some ways, contained a naïve set of assumptions about the nature of political change in developing countries: PRSP designers saw the process of developing and implementing strategies as essentially apolitical and technocratic, but the reality was fundamentally political.[86]

The impacts of the PRSP experiment have been questionable. The World Bank evaluation of PRSPs in 2004 found that: 'the PRS Initiative has *not yet* fulfilled its full potential to enhance poverty reduction efforts in low-income countries'[87] (emphasis added). A rare statistical review of the impact of PRSPs, which used non-PRSP countries as a counterfactual, found that the net difference in poverty reduction or growth between the two groups was negligible,[88] leading some to wonder what the fuss was all about.

The same thing may be true of the MDGs; as explained at the start of Chapter 4, China has done more than any other country towards achieving them, despite not subscribing to the MDGs or the accompanying tenets and principles of foreign aid. Perhaps it is little wonder that in recent years a number of countries have abandoned the PRSP process entirely, or allowed the strategies to fall into disuse.

Overall, many of the findings about these strategies highlight the internal contradictions of a process that had moved only imperfectly and partially away from the ideas of high-level, top-down control inherent to prescriptive strategies.

'We Are Currently Experiencing Policy Turbulence': Donor Country Strategies

While MDGs and PRSPs are (or should that be 'were'?) important strategic processes in the aid system, they are just one specific form of strategy to be found in the aid sector. Every aid agency also has a veritable library of strategy papers and policy documents, which are variously supposed to help them deal with new issues, contexts, and problems; focus organizational efforts at different levels or over different time-spans; improve organizational effectiveness; or respond to specific political or institutional demands. Among the most prominent of these are country programme strategies. Typically three to five years in length, these are used to bring many of the 'big picture' efforts to bear on specific contexts. They have been growing in symbolic importance over the past few decades despite longstanding issues with their performance and concerns about blueprint approaches. As a review of US country strategies by the Overseas Development Institute in 1974 recommended, 'Country programming should serve as a multidimensional framework for making...aid more relevant to the complexities of the development process, and not as a guide and stimulus to detailed economic and social engineering.'[89]

How far has this vision from the 1970s been enacted today? Evaluations of the country strategies of two major donors—the UK and Sweden—provide some useful insights. For the UK, country strategies are periodic exercises that 'aim to set out a series of objectives and describe how they will be met',[90] with a starting point of 'very sound analyses'. The Department for International Development (DFID) either itself does, or brings in external consultants to do, the analytical work that shapes the country strategy. Some of this analytical work is used in strategic objective setting, but in some cases strategies were found to contradict the key findings of this analysis.

In some cases, there are assumptions made about the value and efficacy of 'higher-level' strategies that are proven incorrect, having a knock-on effect on how well country strategies work. So in one country, DFID aligned itself very strongly with the PRSP, assuming the government was genuinely intending to implement it. However, the document was poorly formulated, with little national ownership or realism in its objectives. A blind faith in the higher-level strategy led to these flaws being mirrored in the country strategy. More generally, there is an assumption of a 'linear cascade of policy objectives'[91] from high-level policy pronouncements to global agreements, regional plans, country strategies, and individual investments and influencing initiatives.

Another key factor across all country strategies reviewed was that of context: 'Major programming decisions are often driven by processes either not envisaged in the development of the CAPs [Country Assistance Plans], or that are external to the DFID country office...significant elements of country programmes were found to be driven by such processes.'[92] The ideal is for strategies to have sufficient scope to be able to cope with changes in country and organizational contexts, and 'not become out-dated soon after being written'.[93] The risk is that many strategies—based no doubt on a keen awareness of how context changes—would head in the opposite direction, and become 'so permissive as to accommodate any course of action'.[94]

In the UK system, another challenge was the continual evolution of policy and its effects on country strategies. This was important to ensure effective high-level objectives; for instance, the MDG commitment made by DFID institutionally was reflected strongly in all country strategies. But there was a downside, relating to what one country office referred to as 'policy turbulence' emanating from the centre: 'The volume of policy work emanating from headquarters can become overwhelming, or may be interpreted in such a way that it distorts country programmes.'[95]

This is consistent with findings from the 2006 peer review of DFID, which identified 'a very wide range of policies, practice papers and other directive materials, some of which are not necessarily linked to field needs or realities'.[96]

One interesting issue is the potential scope for country strategies to signal meaningful objectives for programming. Legacy matters a great deal, given the normal project cycle of five to eight years and a typical country strategy cycle of three years. This strategic incongruence, not anticipated in the linear cascade of policy objectives, leads to a 'super tanker effect': one has to steer like crazy to see any change in direction. For example, in one DFID office, it was found that many current achievements and innovations were owed to 'choices taken and activities commenced under much earlier strategies, rather than the implementation of the present hierarchy of objectives'.[97] The reviews suggested that more honesty about the legacy effects and the 'inherently incremental' nature of the strategy would improve the strategy process.

In Swedish aid, country strategies serve a similar purpose: to frame specific organizational and country objectives in ways that are relevant to the changing context. Again, this meant asking what changes were necessary, both in Swedish development work and in the country context. This resulted in country strategy documents that were clear in terms of overall objectives and specific in terms of what would be done or not done, but the links between overall objectives and particular alternative policies and practices were, at best, ambiguous. The options were not chosen in a transparent or clear way: 'The country strategy document does not provide the argumentation to link overall and intermediate objectives, to explain why a particular area of activity rather than an alternative is the best way to achieve an objective. Rather the linkage is assumed to be self-evident.'[98]

There was a 'middle step missing between the analysis and the naming of activities: the explicit identification of assumptions and immediate objectives'.[99] Much of the concern here related to the lack of strategic alternatives: in too many cases, 'the only alternatives taken into consideration are "business as usual", mere "incrementalis[m]" or some readily available "default alternatives"'.[100]

> ... it could be argued, for example, that opening up roads does not assure access to the market for producers ... who produce maize for an often glutted market and whose transport costs are high even with better roads. In this case a market for peasant produce is assumed to exist. If it does not, then roads will not have the expected benefit for rural incomes. At most, they may merely speed up out-migration from the area, or become ... 'roads to nowhere'. Another, or complementary alternative such as experimentation with non-traditional exports could be more relevant than building more roads.[101]

As in the UK aid programme, there were issues about the scope for country strategies to have a meaningful impact, given the cycle of ongoing projects and programmes. The country strategy in reality is a process of 'managing the margin', namely, examining the space that actually becomes available and determining what to do with it in light of strategic objectives.

Another similarity was the issue of strategic flexibility in adapting to changing circumstances: 'Some of the ongoing activities within the strategy period may only come to completion towards the end of the horizon, when circumstances may have changed.'[102] In Sweden, this led to debates about the value of the country strategy, because of the 'rigidity it imposes on aid action and of its perceived failure to respond to changing circumstances'.[103] The counter-argument was that, absent strategy, decision making becomes random: 'the sum total of discrete choices made at successive points in time'.[104] In the extreme, this leads to projects that 'go on forever', because renewal is often the easiest default option. But 'reassessing tactics in the light of changing circumstances ... *should be* part and parcel of strategic thinking and implementation ... Operationalisation is not just a question of simple coherence with a blueprint [but] requires the construction of relevance in the light of a guiding strategy' (emphasis added).[105]

A fundamental issue was the degree of external and internal flux facing the Swedish International Development Cooperation Agency (Sida) in given country contexts. While external flux was reasonably well observed, internal flux received less attention. This is the equivalent of DFID's 'policy turbulence', but was seen as broader, including organizational restructuring processes, changing relationships between the agency and the Swedish embassy, and more day-to-day flux of staff rotations and turnover.

A curious paradox underpinning Sida's strategies is that the *same* set of strategies have alternatively been perceived as 'a straightjacket, rather than as a flexible tool, capable to deal with changing conditions over the strategy horizon'[106] *and* as 'vague and void of steering power'.[107] Perhaps the reality is that strategies are simply subjective processes, determined by social context and political imperatives and less by technocratic concerns than is usually understood to be the case.

Strategic Myopia: Organizational Strategies

Like every other type of organization, aid agencies develop strategic plans, which are supposed to set the high-level priorities and outline the key approaches and assumptions of their work. These strategies can be organization-wide, or focus on specific issues (say, HIV and AIDS, or gender), or geographies (South Asia, Sub-Saharan Africa), or both (gender in Latin America). We have already looked at country strategies, so here I focus on organization-wide strategies and those relating to particular themes or ideas.

The Inter-American Development Bank (IADB), the regional development bank for Latin America, evaluated its organization-wide strategies, taking care to look at these in relation to broader development trends and ideas. Strategies are a central part of the Bank's organizational approach to development, yet the evaluation found organizational strategies 'tend to be based on prevailing opinion within the international development community, rather than on deep understanding of country or sector level detail...the empirical basis for stating that strategy X will work well in context y is weak'.[108] Box 3.2 pulls out some of the key findings from a separate assessment report.[109]

The IADB evaluation also notes a strategic reality outlined in the evaluation which did not play much of a role in formal strategies: '[There is] inherent uncertainty surrounding any given piece of strategic guidance [and] a widespread recognition that circumstances matter and that country-focus, innovation, and experimentation are appropriate responses...People expect strategic thinking to evolve through experience, and there is thus an instinctive reluctance to cede too much authority to formal documents approved some years earlier.'[110] This has an influence on incentive structures in aid agencies, as we will see in the next chapter.

The evaluators of the International Organization for Migration (IOM) reached very similar conclusions. The humanitarian strategy was developed over three years and includes a twelve-point framework, which was approved in 2007. According to the Swedish-funded evaluation, there was a general view in the organization that 'It was the process of developing the strategy, with full involvement of member states, rather than the result that was the most important.'[111] It is unclear whether this was intended from the outset, however. A year

Box 3.2. Inter-American Development Bank strategies[112]

Strategies are seen as too conservative: 'Strategies rarely break new ground, or push beyond the boundaries of the prevailing conventional wisdom. By design, strategies are intended to articulate an existing consensus with regard to best practice in an area.'

They also tend to be overly standardized: 'The "best practice" approach biases strategies in favor of a "one-size fits all" strategic guidance . . . There is a strong tendency for strategies to propose "best practice" approaches to an area based on currently popular theories or models.'

They also tend to be based on an assumption of certainty and predictability: 'There is a tone of certainty ("do this and the problem will improve") rather than a recognition that much is unknown about how to address a problem in the current context . . . Strategy documents tend to presume that learning on a subject has already taken place, rather than that operations are themselves an opportunity for learning.'

The basis of strategies in prevailing development theories and ideas is not especially sound: 'Thinking about most areas of development is very much an ongoing process. The prevailing wisdom in an area is subject to constant change and sometimes has seen complete reversal over the course of a few years.'

Strategies are not well disseminated and in some cases are simply not known, let alone understood: 'Strategies are not well-disseminated internally, nor are they widely shared with executing agencies in . . . member countries. Awareness of the simple existence of strategies is low, and awareness of their explicit content is even lower.'

Implementation is consistently weak: 'Operations in an area covered by a strategy often do not contain key elements established in the strategy, and sometimes are developed along lines explicitly mentioned as risky or inappropriate in the strategy documents.'

Finally, there are weak processes for monitoring or evaluating strategies: 'There is virtually no process for monitoring strategy execution. Strategies are not evaluated systematically, either by the organizational units creating them or by the regional departments implementing them.

> In design terms, strategies have low evaluability, and it is generally
> impossible to determine whether predicted results are flowing from the
> recommended actions...Compliance is often difficult to determine (given
> the generality of the strategies) and rarely enforced.'

after the strategy was finalized, the evaluation found the mandate and strategy
to be 'very broad', that it did 'not provide any clear focus' and had 'not yet really
affected or restricted the operations of IOM'.[113] Nonetheless, the evaluation
found the organization 'confident that a large-scale internal information campaign with an ambition to incorporate the strategy into the IOM culture has
reached its objectives'—but that this confidence was misplaced: few if any of the
individuals met were fully aware of the twelve-point strategy. Damningly, 'no
one claims that the new strategy has given IOM a new and different focus...As
the strategy does not really tell the organisation what it shall not do, it matters
little if the new strategy has had any impact on country level.'[114] There are clear
and obvious contradictions between the stated intent, process, and outcome: the
executive management had chosen '*not* to primarily steer the organisation's
direction and operation through traditional measures such as policy/strategies,
operational plans, objectives, allocation of resources to operations and analyses
of performance and results'.[115] Instead, as in the IADB, the agency's direction
and operations are steered mainly through a 'market-oriented approach' with a
large degree of decentralization.

At the other end of the strategic spectrum to both the IADB and the IOM is
the Global Fund to Fight AIDS, Tuberculosis and Malaria. Strategy for this
relatively new entity in the aid landscape seems to be an example of incrementalism run riot, leaving it open to much the same criticisms made of 'muddling
through' strategies. For the first five years of its existence, strategic decisions
were made largely in the form of 'add-ons and piecemeal adjustments'.[116]
A strategy *was* formally approved in 2007, but this did little to advance the
situation: 'The process being followed is mostly incremental.'[117] There is a lack
of clear organizational vision, which has a knock-on effect on operations, and
especially partners, which are 'left to "wait and see" where the Fund is going,
unable to anticipate its approach to new issues and realign their efforts accordingly. Given the size of its portfolio, uncertainty in [its] strategic intentions
affects the certainty with which other organizations can articulate their strategic
intentions.'[118] The first five-year evaluation found the Board 'left largely
unaddressed the critical issue of strategy development. Absent a shared organizational vision, the ad hoc growth and reactive evolution of the Global
Fund architecture has brought with it increased procedural complexities and
a spate of policy changes that have led to confusion, and in some cases,
contradictions.'[119]

The same kinds of issues are apparent in thematically focused strategies. A recent review of the Swiss Development Cooperation's gender strategy highlights interesting points about strategic culture in that organization:

> New issues ... are meant to be implemented without anything being removed from the plate. Some of this is driven by opportunities, some by increased capacity ... As one informant told us, 'If you are in headquarters working on patent rights, the natural outcome is a policy paper and guidelines.' Without a rigorous and disciplined effort by senior management to maintain strategic coherence, issues proliferate ... As one senior informant noted, 'When you have 50 priorities you have none.'[120]

Against this continual stream of strategic requirements and guidelines, the gender strategy was perceived as just one more document within an incoherent mass. As such, and along with all other strategic priorities, it became devalued. As one senior staff member joked with me at the time, 'here, there are more important things than priorities'. In fact, at that point in the organization's evolution, the continual dissemination of documents seemed to take the place of any meaningful implementation effort to follow the publication of these documents. This was similar to the strategic evaporation identified in the IADB and the IOM: strategies that simply disappear after formulation. The key tool in the strategy, a gender toolkit, was not used extensively if at all.

Echoing this, an earlier Overseas Development Institute review of human rights strategy in the same agency found the strategy documents were not sufficiently operational: their effectiveness in terms of human rights awareness, policy coherence, and increased programming was limited: 'It is not sufficient to just send a policy document to staff and partners and expect change to occur.'[121] The strategy also highlighted the challenges of implementation in globally dispersed organizations, especially the tension between institute-wide policies and localized strategies. The agency was described as having a range of strategic principles, a portfolio of country-focused projects, and a 'missing middle' between the two. On-the-ground contextual sensitivity and flexibility are valued and widely championed, and most staff members see the idea of global strategic coherence as being in conflict with decentralized autonomy. There seemed to be no organizational imperative to balance and optimize both.

The second thematic strategy of interest is from the UN Development Programme (UNDP), whose HIV and AIDS strategy for Africa was evaluated in 2006. Again, there is strong evidence of 'a disconnect' between corporate-level strategies and implementation by regional and country offices, and a similar disconnect between country strategies and actual activities: 'Broad frameworks were not consistent nor did they adequately capture what UNDP actually planned and executed at the country level.'[122] These disconnects seem to be the subject of some uncertainty, depending on the assumptions made about the strategy process. On the one hand, the disparity could indicate 'adaptation, evolution, and flexibility in the UNDP response'.[123] On the other, they might be the result of fractures between the various strategies and paradigms at different levels of the organization. During the period under review, there was a major increase in political attention to HIV and AIDS, alongside expanded funding. However, it was not evident whether the agency had been successful in 'strategically adapting its HIV/AIDS responses to the dramatically changing global and country-level environment'.[124] Overall, the review identifies a 'large delivery gap' between strategies as governance tools and on-the-ground actions that hopefully mitigate and reduce the incidence and impacts of HIV/AIDS: 'Leveraging policy and strategic change has been easier in words than in action.'[125]

A third set of strategies are the strategies designed and implemented by Oxfam International for poverty reduction across their country portfolio. Echoing the other strategies looked at above, these strategies are seen as presenting very good context analysis, but not always being clear as to how strategic choices emanate from such analysis: 'They are rarely explicit about how the choices they make are rooted in lessons and achievements from the past.'[126] When looking at how the strategies dealt with notions and concepts of change, it was found that, largely, 'assumptions underpinning change hypotheses usually remain invisible'.

I want to emphasize that I am not singling out these agencies for criticism; if anything, they should be lauded for their transparency and remarkable frankness. Most aid agencies' strategies closely fit the findings in this section, but the organizations in question either fail to recognize it or conceal and/or deny it.

Straightjackets or Vague Voids?

Having served time as a corporate strategy consultant, I was initially rather taken-aback by the ways in which strategies were devised in aid organizations. Each process I became involved in or observed seemed to exist primarily to move from ritual obligations, through symbolic consultation processes, to argumentative write-ups, which were massaged into ambiguous recommendations, all leading to unopened dust-covered boxes of final reports beneath random unoccupied desks. It wasn't until I came to examine these strategies in more detail that I learned that this was an endemic problem.

The main finding of the review above is how all the strategies covered reveal similar stories about the challenges of formulating strategies and then making them work in reality. There is a clear tendency to try and get the content right—with several years and millions of dollars sometimes spent in the attempt—but often using the flawed and irrelevant conceptual models explored in the previous chapter. Such an approach, taken to extremes, does not lend itself to relevance in the face of shifting contexts or emerging problems.

These conceptual models are then grafted onto processes that borrow heavily—and directly, given his tenure at the World Bank—from the McNamara school of strategic thinking. The theory of change in these frameworks is broadly linear and sequential, assuming a move from outputs to outcomes to impacts. This created— or responded to—an expectation of predictability and stability, leaving subsequent implementation unable to adapt to the challenges that inevitably arose.

This inability to adapt then leaves those overseeing strategies with two options if they are going to stay the course with their stated approach. First, strategies can evaporate in the face of incoherent thinking, be made irrelevant by a changing policy context, or be neutralized by apathetic or actively resistant country-level staff. As well as resistance, there are countless examples of incomprehension leading to hollow compliance. In those few cases where no explicit strategy existed, or where the strategy was deliberately left open, there was no coherent story about what the aid effort was doing and why, and the effort was seen as highly disjointed. This echoes critiques of the incremental, muddling through approach.

Second, they can stick to their guns, keep calm and carry on, but the results are not much better. Those strategies most clearly wedded to the idea of formulating goals, policies, programmes, and actions upfront—to the conspiracy of illusion—have perhaps predictably struggled the most with the reality of the complex problems faced in the real world. In each generation of development thinkers, recognized experts have pointed out the inadequacies of top-down planning approaches. If this is a straw man, as no doubt some readers will conclude, then clearly it is one that many have felt to be worth airing in public and burning to the ground on a regular basis.[127]

The underlying assumptions of this school of strategy have proved resilient in aid practice, and this is despite the fact that many of its exponents understand— and in private often accept—that they do not match reality. The approach casts a heavy shadow over what is done in aid agencies and too often can lead to overoptimism in the strategy process. Even where the limitations of the approach are understood and acknowledged, there is little evidence of attempts to change or adapt the assumptions underlying strategic processes. As a result, strategies are clumsily undertaken, supply-oriented, and riddled with naïve assumptions about people, political processes, and the nature of change. At their worst, such ill-conceived aid strategies can drive out exactly the kind of behaviours that they are supposed to promote.

Overall, it is hard to disagree with Amartya Sen when he critiques Easterly,[128] and calls for more nuance and balance when exploring the issue of planners versus searchers in aid agencies. What is interesting is that few, if any, of these strategies seem to be aiming for or occupying the middle ground of integrated strategic thinking. As the smallpox case illustrates, there is a strong case to be made for intelligently combining the prescriptive with the descriptive approaches. Perhaps the key message to take away from the strategies looked at here is that, while there *is* a dominance of the prescriptive approach, as well as evident discomfort with and distrust of the descriptive approach, success does not come about from abandoning one or the other. Instead, it is vital to allow them to come together in different ways, depending on the nature and the context of the strategy in question.

However, many strategies, in the aid sector and elsewhere, do not go through such an adaptation as a matter of course, nor is such an adaptive effort routinely seen as integral to the success of strategies. Strategists stick with the top-down approach, despite the known failures and growing irrelevance, and claim the process was what mattered most. Or the strategies are abandoned, and there is a free-for-all, which may or may not be successful.

Ensuring such adaptations happen as a matter of course is the major recommendation for how aid strategies might be improved and increase their relevance and impact. Why hasn't this very simple idea had more take-up? The reality is that this may simply not fit with the organizational imperatives and mechanisms through which aid is delivered. This is what I turn to in the next chapter.

CHAPTER 4

The Goats in the Machine

'Organizations can never be a substitute for initiative and for judgement.'
Louis D. Brandeis.

Think of aid, of any type. For many readers, it will be very difficult to do so without picturing an organization of some form. A logo might be prominent, a senior and high-profile leader, newspaper reports or TV interviews, urgent appeals, fleeting images of projects or programmes, notable campaigns, changes the agency has helped bring about, particular countries or contexts in which it has been involved. For some, an organizational creation story or myth may come to mind—how the agency was formed after a war, as the result of a particular campaign, or motivated by some need. Those with more intimate knowledge may think of particular areas of expertise, where the organization in question has provided intellectual and operational leadership—innovative ways of conceiving of or doing aid work, perhaps influential reports or publications.

What is remarkable is that, despite their diversity, aid agencies face remarkably similar organizational challenges: I have led studies where the lessons from the tiniest of non-governmental organizations were echoed directly in the experience of the largest multilaterals. In this chapter I draw on ideas from organizational scholars and practitioners to take a look at aid organizations and their workings: their structure, culture, and ways of relating internally and externally. For a number of reasons I will explain, the evidence on aid organizations is patchy, but thankfully it is also slowly improving. If we want a rounded picture of the successes and failures of aid delivery, the organizational lens—enabling us to understand cultures, relationships, power dynamics, and management philosophies—may need to become much more prominent than it is at present.

Dogs That Don't Bark

If foreign aid is defined as 'the transfer of money, goods, and knowledge from developed to developing countries',[1] then it is a relatively straightforward matter to think about the variety of roles that organizations might play. Many raise funds for these transfers, through taxes for government bodies, member contributions for international organizations like the UN, and directly from the general public or member and constituency groups. Some run their own commercial activities—from High Street charity shops to greetings cards, calendars, and 'poverty gifts' to consultancy services. Some can lobby for and initiate official transfers and negotiate related terms and conditions. Many are directly involved in transfers through the design, implementation, and assessment of aid projects and programmes. Others work with developing country governments and civil society organizations to help implement these projects or programmes, or provide support through appropriate technical expertise. Some advocate for more and better transfers, or for specific conditions to be placed on—or removed from—such transfers.

The literature on foreign aid contains applications of almost every social scientific lens available, from economic theory and foreign relations to sociology and history, from social psychology to anthropology, and interdisciplinary approaches such as political science and development studies. And yet, despite the fundamental role of agencies in the delivery of aid, there are very few examples of empirical work on organizational issues. In 1986, Samuel Paul wrote that management had always been a neglected factor in development aid activities; some 25 years on, it is hard to argue that this has changed significantly—knowledge of organizational issues 'has not been adequately utilised or indeed tested in development studies research'.[2] There are frequent mentions of the 'aid machinery' in official documents and policy statements—but precious few accounts of its actual workings.

This highlights a curious contrast between the apparent central importance of organizations in aid delivery efforts on the one hand, and the relatively few applications of the organizational lens in aid research on the other. In the world outside of aid, there is extensive research exploring 'the impact of . . . practices on the achievement of organizational objectives'.[3] And yet Rosalind Eyben says that 'no official aid agency has been prepared to undertake a study that aims to learn about their staff's everyday practices—what they are doing, as distinct from what they report they are doing—and their effects'.[4] An earlier account argues, more pointedly, that the literature has been 'ominously silent' on the matter of what actually goes on in aid organizations: 'Like one's personal sex life, it is not a topic deemed worthy of public discourse.'[5] Worthiness may in fact be a key consideration: organizational lines of enquiry have long been seen as rather superficial and irrelevant, and less important than the plethora of other factors—technical expertise, policies, politics, funding, needs, and so on—that supposedly determine development effectiveness. This argument was made by Simon Maxwell, a former director of the Overseas Development Institute, in his review of the relevance of organizational issues for food security.[6]

In many cases, it seems that aid organizational issues may be as apparent as much from the situations when they are *not* mentioned as from those when they are. As Sherlock Holmes noted in the story the 'Silver Blaze', when he was able to solve the mystery because of a curiously quiet canine on the night of the crime, 'the dog that doesn't bark may be just as important as the one that does'.[7] For example, numerous studies do draw conclusions about the importance of understanding organizations for furthering poverty reduction, but these have almost entirely focused on agencies in developing countries.[8] These studies almost always fail to consider the effectiveness of *international* aid organizations—which are, after all, the main deliverers (and, some might argue, primary recipients) of foreign aid. As one senior manager in a leading international non-governmental organization told me, 'In our work with our counterparts in the South, we want to make them more like us. But we don't really pay enough attention to what we, or they, are really like.'[9]

It is not that organizational issues do not feature at all in aid debates—far from it. Get a group of aid workers together and they will often discuss little else: there is 'a rich, somewhat clandestine, oral tradition'.[10] Operationally, there has been a rapid growth in organizational change efforts, often driven and propagated by senior leaders. Driven alternately by fashion ('everyone else is changing, we should too'), events ('the new chief executive had a clear plan of change for her first hundred days'), and the desire for growth ('we should double our turnover in the next ten years'), such efforts have become all too common in aid. But although there is a wealth of work in the corporate sector on such issues, there is no equivalent body of work in development—aid leaders tend to draw on the experiences and insights of top-end business consultants.

This lack of attention belies the potential importance of organizations in achieving development and humanitarian goals. Researchers at Manchester make the point firmly: 'to ignore their internal management processes, capacity and interface within the wider policy framework is to negate the well-established fact that the *effectiveness of organisations is central to [...] social and economic development*'[11] (emphasis added).

My aim in this chapter is to identify key trends and patterns in the way aid organizations in the narrow sense, and aid delivery mechanisms in a broader sense, are thought about and managed. I refer to a number of specific themes derived from the wider literature on organizations, including the diversity of 'theories, nostrums and semi-sacrosanct beliefs'[12] about how different organizational and relationship characteristics contribute to success or failure in different settings. These include organizational models, managerial approaches, culture and relationship dynamics, and last but not least, structural aspects.

I draw on my research of a range of agencies, as well as the slowly growing body of reports, evaluations, and studies. However, the lack of coverage discussed above means some detective work and reading between the lines is also necessary to fulfil my aims. Let's listen for the silent dogs.

The Aid Conveyor Belt

Over the past 50 years or so, there has been a noticeable change in the working approach of aid organizations. The fledgling sector, like many niche areas, was highly informal and ad hoc in nature. Stories abound of how, even as recently as the late 1980s, a recent graduate would phone the offices of an international non-governmental organization to enquire about possible vacancies, to find herself on the next flight out to run an entire country-wide operation. As the aid sector has grown, and taken on growing importance in global public policy, it has been formalized and consolidated, with the introduction of 'professional-ization' and 'modern management' approaches.

The expectations are also higher, with many seeing aid agencies as account-able to the same extent as national government and civil society in developed countries. Kenneth King and Simon McGrath, of Edinburgh and Nottingham Universities respectively, in their 2003 book on how development agencies use and share knowledge,[13] find that the central challenge of changing aid agencies is all too often sidestepped in aid reforms and replaced by a language of 'working smarter'. This 'stealth approach' carries with it the implication that a change in practices will inevitably lead to changes in organizational culture. But it may also be because the culture of change is one of cautious incrementalism.

> Aid tends to be 'tweaked', i.e. changed in appearance from time to time, without addressing fundamental and well-understood problems, because of a set of mutually reinforcing factors which taken together prevent reform from taking place. These include a lack of clarity and rigour; the unfitness-for-purpose of the aid institutions; a mutually reinforcing web of vested interests; and the genuine difficulty of getting agreement among diverse stakeholders with different interests.[14]

Interestingly, some of the most noteworthy changes relate to growth. As one aid observer puts it, agencies have put in place elaborate machinery for raising and spending money.[15] (The wry Sir Humphrey's Law from *Yes Minister* seems tailor-made for aid: 'By definition a big department is more successful than a small one...this simple proposition is the basis of our whole system.'[16]) Any-thing that helps them do this bigger, better, faster will get prioritized. On the other hand, things that grow slowly—participation, ownership, contextual understanding—will be sidelined.

I noted earlier the relative lack of attention to organizational issues within the aid research community. One notable exception to this stems from the work of a British consultant and researcher, Paul Clarke, who is a perfect example of what might be termed 'an organization watcher'. He has spent years observing the ebb and flow of aid organizations as they reposition their work and campaign on new issues, market their efforts and fundraise, and deliver on the ground in ever more countries. His fascination stems from personal experience at both policy and operational levels within high-profile agencies. Until recently director of a successful consultancy operation on change issues, he could count every kind of aid organization among his clients and every kind of change process in his portfolio—from organizational restructuring to corporate downsizing, building strategic partnerships, and process re-engineering.

Perhaps the most striking thing for Clarke in all of this work is the similarities between organizational charts and engineering diagrams such as those representing electrical circuits. As Clarke told me when we first worked together, the organizational chart is a visual metaphor for organizations, and it makes a powerful statement about the nature of the organization it describes and how it should be understood and managed; indeed its origin in US rail companies in the 1850s tells us a good deal. In work that Clarke and I did together in 2007, we found that one of the most prevalent metaphors for aid organizations was the machine—one need only look at the language of aid to see its manifestations. 'It leads to technical recommendations, "levers" for change, and re-engineering organizations for maximum efficiency.'[17] Relationships are formal and can be readily 'reconfigured and restructured'. Aid is also packed to the brim with 'mechanisms'—for everything from learning, accountability, strategy, and change to ownership and participation. Many of these are described as needing to be 'bolted on to existing operations'.[18]

Clarke's observations echo a landmark study by Tom Burns and G.M. Stalker, two Scottish social scientists.[19] Burns and Stalker identified two managerial paradigms, which had different levels of suitability depending on the industrial context. The first was 'mechanistic firms', which were most successful in static or stable environments. This was the prevalent paradigm of organizations at that time, and arguably still is today. This 'classical model' draws on corporate models of the early twentieth century and European notions of bureaucratic government, which in turn are based on 'a nineteenth-century physics deeply committed to a mechanical philosophy'.[20] In the model, the formality of the organizational chart and a predictable hierarchy negates any need for messy, social relations. The dehumanizing implications were famously parodied by Charlie Chaplin in *Modern Times* in 1932, still the machine approach to organizational design has proved surprisingly resilient. Its adherents argue that it is so widespread and prevalent precisely because of its potential value. But this value also has limitations: 'Mechanical approaches to organizations work well in situations where machines work well—where there is a straightforward task to perform, a stable operating environment, and compliant, predictable and reliable parts, including the human "components."'[21]

The second type of firms, 'organic firms', thrive in changing or dynamic environments. For example, software development organizations need to promote creativity to be successful. This means placing a high premium on regular informal interpersonal communications. The group dynamic is a vital part of problem solving. As a result of Burns and Stalker's work, a number of the underlying assumptions about organizations started to surface and be discussed, along with their contribution (or indeed otherwise) to management success.

This led to suggestions that *appropriate* organizational 'paradigms' are the key to success.[22] The organizational paradigm approach suggests every organizational model is a collection of assumptions about what organizations are, what they mean, what they do, how they bring people together to achieve coherence, and why. At the heart of each model are firmly held, although often implicit, beliefs about the world, change, human nature, and human relationships. In his 1980s work, Gareth Morgan, a British-Canadian organizational theorist, consultant, and academic,[23] argued that using the wrong organizational model can lead to inappropriate strategies and poorly conceived actions, both inside and outside the organization. Although he identified a range of possible models, like Burns and Stalker, Morgan found the machine metaphor to be a dominant 'image of organisation'.

What exactly does this mean for organization realities? In engineering design, the task is to define a system of parts arranged in a specific sequence, anchored by precisely defined flows of fuel, energy, or information. Similarly, organizations committed to mechanical paradigms are expected to operate as rationally as possible. The overall 'chain of command' (itself a machine metaphor) is maintained through the hierarchical structuring of authority and decision making, which in turn governs the flows of resources and information. From this perspective, organizations are as machines that receive inputs, work to transform them in routine and standardized ways, and produce predictable outputs and outcomes.

There are now several institutionalized mechanisms for bringing about improvements and change within aid agencies: policies, learning initiatives, evaluations, and training programmes. Echoing the range of strategic tools being applied in the aid system (see Chapter 3), Clarke and I found that these are all built on a mechanical perspective: that somehow the organization will automatically be able to absorb the lessons and ideas generated from these efforts. The overarching emphasis is on standardization and corrective alignment.

> The machine metaphor leads to belief on how the 'system' can be improved: If the system is not working as planned, then identify the broken part and replace it. If the system is too costly, then work towards economies of scale. If the system is not working in a coordinated fashion, then tighten the interconnections between parts of the system.[24]

If the mechanical mentality were simply restricted to how aid agencies view themselves that would be problematic enough. But there is also evidence that this mechanical bias extends to how aid agencies view the world and contexts in which they work. David Mosse has argued that there is an overt mechanical rationality to aid discussions.[25] These models work to achieve cognitive control and social regulation, to enhance agency capacity and expand bureaucratic relations control, particularly over marginal areas and people, to reproduce hierarchies of knowledge (scientific over indigenous) and society (developer over 'to be developed'), and to fragment, subjugate, silence, or erase the local. It has also been argued that aid agencies, despite good intentions, are boxed into a self-reinforcing 'collective illusion' centred on an engineering philosophy, which is reinforced and supported by the way the aid organizations are themselves viewed:

> We do not follow the implications of what we have come to understand, but act as if development were something else...these organizational imperatives not only make it easy for us to act as if development were something other than the complex and often opaque set of interactions that we know it to be, but also box us into a collective illusion...because of our urgency to end poverty, we act as if development is a construction, a matter of planning and engineering. While we rarely use the term engineering, we do regularly use engineering lexicon.[26]

Mechanistic management models can isolate interventions from the history and social and political realities of the 'third world', or bend these realities into 'the discipline-bound logics of diagnosis and prescription'.[27] This leaves agencies unable to deal with uncertainty and change, in contrast with the idea of organic firms identified by Burns and Stalker:

> Venturing into the unknown normally means that the organisation's standard operating procedures can no longer deal with the types of information it is receiving, and are no longer suitable. Such departures occur when the organisation is on the brink of collapse or is being forced – by means no longer in its control – to change its procedures fundamentally. It often takes a long time for an [aid] organization to realise that it has hit the point where there is no alternative to change; often, that point comes too late.[28]

This failure to adapt to changing contexts is one form of what has been termed a 'systemic leadership failure' in aid agencies. When the world outside proves to be organic and not mechanical, the machine inside all too quickly breaks down. The organizational and relational problems that arise in aid agencies are exactly those anticipated by Burns, Stalker, and Morgan when mechanical models are applied in dynamic settings.[29]

The engineering, mass production, conveyor belt mentality is deeply embedded in aid agencies' managerial approaches—as well as in their strategies, processes, and structures—all of which work to reinforce each other. This inhibits the space for change and leads agencies to 'whisk...political effects out of sight through technical discourses that naturalize poverty and objectify the poor and simplify development'.[30]

It is perhaps unsurprising that leading analysts have compared aid 'clients' to Ford's Model T customers. As Henry Ford famously quipped about the Model T car—that most famous product of scientific management—customers could 'have a car painted any color...so long as it is black'.[31] Richard Ellerman echoes Ford's joke: 'The clients who wish to receive assistance are free to...do so in conformity with Official Views.'[32] Robert Chambers, one of the world's best-known development scholars, whose vision and ideas have exerted a powerful influence on the sector for the past three decades (and who led the vanguard of applying complex systems approaches in development), wrote a rhyme about the philosophy underpinning aid efforts in his book *Whose Reality Counts?* (1997), which concludes:

> The poor are look-alikes and weak
> We know their needs. They need not speak.
> Our mass production's sure to please.
> Let's make our programmes Model-Ts.[33]

Chambers' wit should not hide his serious point: the mechanical philosophy is most effective in a 'product push' environment where external stakeholders have little say about what is done. Aid is produced by those at the top of the pipeline: donors, the rich, the developed. It is delivered by means of 'experts' and other 'knowledgeable persons' of the 'pipeline' down to 'beneficiaries' such as local development agents, policymakers, advisors, farmers, and researchers at the receiving end.

However, the Ford Model T is useful because it highlights another important point: there are organizations that enjoy significant and even spectacular success using the mechanistic model, because the various mechanical assumptions are fulfilled. The logistical underpinning of most of the simple solutions outlined in Charles Kenny's *Getting Better* provide a good example of this.

However, as I argued previously, these conditions do not always, or even mostly, hold true in development. There is a growing view that the machine metaphor fails to represent the reality of twenty-first-century organizational life. To paraphrase Duncan Watt's quip about Newtonian science, the mechanical approach is staggering about the aid stage like a mortally wounded Shakespearean actor, forever being on the verge of collapsing entirely but never quite doing so.[34]

Mind the Leadership Gap

In many aid agencies, the machine mindset is reinforced by institutionally approved approaches to management. There is a widespread assumption of the manager as the 'controlling head', which does the thinking, with subordinates as the unthinking body that follows. The reductionist model found in strategic planning applies equally to day-to-day interactions. Echoing Chapter 3 on Strategic Mismanagement, there is an assumption of cascading intentions—that somehow, once a course of action is determined, initiative flows from managers to subordinates. Instructions are 'communicated and rolled out' through the ranks, sometimes with a 'veneer of participation to engender buy-in'.[35]

In the UN Development Programme, for example, work on HIV and AIDS cited in the previous chapter shows the effort has been limited by 'an "individualistic" paradigm [that] underpins the notion of leadership, management and its development in many UNDP country office strategies'.[36] Of course, this may be appropriate in some settings. But the profound challenges posed by the pandemic were seen as requiring a more culturally appropriate model of leadership, more collective, emergent approaches that go beyond the individual to focus on common values and knowledge that bind people together. Interestingly, in those country offices where notions of leadership and management moved towards a more collective, networked approach, there were also some shifts toward a more robust and systematic approach to responses to the disease.

While there have been remarkable examples of successful management and leadership in the aid sector, this is often despite, rather than because of, organizationally mandated approaches. Many of those interviewed for a study on humanitarian leadership suggested that the reality of aid leadership means gaming the system[37]—working out how things work, and then how to do the things that matter despite, and occasionally in active conflict with, the formal system. For many of the leaders interviewed, this meant focusing on the stated goals and values of the organization—the moral drive—to the detriment of career paths, reputation, and political standing. Although this may be a sensible way to work in a context that constrains judgement and initiative, a sorry consequence is a weakened management *culture* within aid agencies. It also places a high personal cost on more 'organic' approaches to leadership.

Tellingly, the same focus on hierarchy and individual leaders applies to how development and humanitarian agencies engage with developing country counterparts. A review of World Bank efforts in civil service reform over an 18-year period is telling, and resonant of the findings vis-à-vis strategies such as poverty reduction strategy papers: 'Rather than engaging civil services and dynamic systems that are influenced by multiple stakeholders, Bank operations relied on small groups of interlocuters... to design and implement one-size-fits all civil service reform blueprints in diverse country settings.'[38]

The case study in Box 4.1 is a more in-depth example, drawn from evaluative material focusing on the international aid response to Cyclone Nargis. It illustrates powerfully the mismatch between the kinds of organic management that *should* be used to address aid problems and the kinds of mechanical management practices that are in fact in place. It illustrates how, in the extreme, this mismatch leads to profound conflicts and dysfunctions—sometimes at the expense of lives and livelihoods.

Box 4.1. Case study—Cyclone Nargis

On 2 May 2008, Cyclone Nargis struck the coast of Myanmar, resulting in vast human loss and suffering: nearly 140,000 dead or missing and 2.4 million severely affected. UN estimates suggest the number of people displaced may have been as high as 800,000 with some 260,000 seeking refuge in temporary settlements in the immediate aftermath.

Considerable international attention was paid to the nature and scale of the disaster, and the aid effort that followed. On 6 May, the Myanmar Government formally appealed to the UN for help, but stated a firm preference for bilateral assistance. Entry visas were issued slowly, and many flights and aid agency staff were held at the airport or in Thailand. There were also the considerable logistical difficulties of working in the affected areas, as most were accessible only by air or by boat.

In terms of the response itself, it is useful to distinguish between the preparation, or pre-emergency, phase in the build-up to Nargis, an emergency phase related to the period of the immediate response—which lasted approximately a month—and a third phase, when things started to get more systematized and strategic.

Preparation was poor, at national and perhaps also international level. There is evidence that the Myanmar Government had information about the impending cyclone, but did not announce it nationally. At international level, there was also awareness of the vulnerability of the region

(*continued*)

Box 4.1. Continued

to multiple hazards related to climate change. The operating environment for international agencies was also fraught, with some, such as the World Health Organization, working well with corresponding ministries and others, such as Oxfam GB, repeatedly being refused permits to set up a dedicated in-country office. These issues were not fully resolved when the cyclone hit, increasing the challenges facing the response.

Arguably, there was insufficient strategic leadership, nationally or internationally, to enable sufficient preparedness for the crisis. This may have been the crucial factor preventing awareness of the potential for crisis from translating into greater *institutional* sensitivity to the impending disaster. One hypothesis would be that organizations want to stay in their comfort zones until they have no choice but to move out of them.

In the emergency phase, barriers to international aid agencies meant the initial response amounted to what could be delivered through presence already on the ground and through national actors. Much of the immediate relief work lacked clear strategy, and was characterized by small-scale and ineffectual activities. Numerous evaluations concluded that there was a 'pattern of systemic leadership gaps':[39] circumstances, structure, and organizational culture combined to deliver sub-optimal leadership *despite* the presence of good leaders. Specifically, 'bad leadership' was generated by institutional interactions between a number of agencies' organizational cultures and structures.

Following the emergency phase, there were noticeable changes in attitude and understanding of participation in the response. 'By the end of November, [the agency] was perceived as adaptive and flexible by donors and was described as being on top of changing needs.'[40]

How did this transformation come about, given the challenges faced in the emergency phase? The evaluation of the effort is quite clear:

> The need for speed, flexibility, adaptability, risk-taking and rapid decision-making declined. What became more important was the ability to administer regular, quality focused, large-scale, well monitored and reported activities . . . within a programming context that became increasingly long-term with the shift towards transition . . . Over the following months the machinery gradually started working. And it started working well. Food was delivered in the right quantities, to the right people, at the right times. The initial mess was cleaned up, the process involving a great deal of work which could have been avoided had proper systems and structures been in place early on.[41]

Although a success in the terms of the evaluation, this stage of the Nargis response saw a reversion to the 'comfort zone' of standard operating procedures. As a result, it seems reasonable to suppose that future crises in Myanmar, and possibly elsewhere, will be dealt with in similar ways to the Nargis cyclone. Indeed, the evaluation concluded that this pattern of systemic leadership gaps would persist in future crisis situations unless the agency in question managed to address an 'organizational leadership culture that respects turf at the expense of performance'.[42]

Note the telling phrase used in the case study: 'The machinery started working. And it started working well.' Although in the case in Box 4.1 the reversion to standard operating procedures and predictability is framed as a good thing, the overwhelming sense from aid managers is that the 'space for leadership' is being eroded by the focus on targets and clearly pre-specified deliverables. This was reinforced by findings from Active Learning Network for Accountability and Performance (ALNAP) research, which found that many examples of humanitarian leadership happened despite, rather than because of, the existing organizational context and incentives.[43]

This has some obvious implications for ongoing aid efforts. Many new initiatives are over-defined, over-specified, and over-controlled, with little latitude or scope for flexibility. Successful project proposals are those that define upfront the specific protocols, targets, and modes of operation that will guide the work. The irony is that over-control of this kind negates the innovative potential of the proposed work because the attention is focused on internal legitimacy and control rather than shifting external challenges. This works to fold the aid management process neatly into the architecture and mentality of results-based management—a Fordist dream if there ever was one. But few individuals and jobs are the cogs in the organizational machine that this kind of approach assumes. In reality, this results-oriented approach has led to an overt bureaucratization and little or no strategy. Specifically, aid management is becoming characterized by

- Cumbersome reporting obligations that pull staff away from focusing on delivery realities, but give the illusion of control.
- Painfully bureaucratic and formalized procedures both within and between aid agencies and donors.
- The assumption that change can be rolled out and positive results achieved in predictable ways.
- Evaluation procedures that tend to penalize rather than reward flexibility and adaptation.

- The widespread acknowledgement that calculated risk taking and innovation can damage rather than enhance an individual career or an organization's reputation.

It is little wonder that successful leaders feel unsupported by organizational systems and processes, if they lead to such a mismatch between behaviours that are proscribed and those that are best suited to developmental and humanitarian realities. Aid managers and analysts are exhausting themselves trying to give the impression of oversight and control to many unpredictable and indeed unmanageable aspects of complex organizational systems. Structural or systemic issues are ignored or set aside for a later date. Where such issues are embraced, this is often 'under the wire' and away from the organizational mainstream.

DFID's former Chief Social Scientist, Rosalind Eyben,[44] argues that there is a profound irony in such 'gaming of the system':

> ... An aid agency staff member, for example, told me he was hiding from his line manager what he considered to be the most effective initiatives that he had supported in a conflict-ridden country, because these involved supporting cross-community relations at the local level and ran counter to management's high-level strategy. Another told me she believed many of her agency's most effective country-level interventions in support of gender equality had not been reported because these concerned investing in relationships, rather than achieving the kind of outcomes that had been incorporated in formal plans ...

Eyben's findings are damning: effective aid needs to build on precisely those relational and dynamic issues that the formal, machine, side of aid agencies works to deny and suppress.

Culture and Relationships

> Hierarchical, centralized, and control-oriented organizations are inclined [towards] top-down flows [which] are inimical to teamwork within and across units ... mastery of the operating system is of greater consequence than appreciating the context and probing the quality of a policy or operation. Conformity – not local accountability, flexibility, innovation, or critical reflection – is rewarded ... Field staff members find themselves at the bottom of the hierarchy, their views and interpretations overlooked or overruled.[45]

The quote above is revealing about the nature of relationships within aid agencies. Growing numbers of researchers are focusing on the role of relations, values, beliefs, social norms, and ideals in the workplace. Instead of the value-free results-orientation of the mechanical approach to organizations, many are now arguing that work is fundamentally shaped by an organization's cultural and social dynamics. By implication, organizations should try, whenever possible, to adjust relationships to the external demands and constraints they face.

The challenge for many organizations is that culture, values, and relationships are slippery and frequently uncomfortable topics to tackle head-on, and this is especially so for organizations that have social and moral ambitions.

Most aid agencies do not have a single culture, because of variations in geography, language, and, of course, cultures in the sense of value systems, ethos, and ways of relating to peers and hierarchies. This may be due to different locations (head office or field). Age, gender, country of origin, or founders' personalities can all shape the dominant belief system. And the function different organizational sub-units perform influences their 'micro-cultures'.

What we do have are some common patterns and themes. Of course, culture is manifest in everything aid agencies do, but here I want to look at values, partnerships, and participation as three areas where the fingerprints of aid agency relationship culture can be seen most visibly.

Aid agencies usually place their goals within a broader normative framework, emphasizing, for example, poverty reduction, human rights, political reform, or economic trade and growth. Morals and values play a major role: agencies often retain a set of moral statements to govern their effort. Secular organizations might use a rights-based discourse; others might mention the 'modalities' of their aid work, such as capacity building or partnership; faith-based organizations refer to their religious values as key guiding principles. Morals and values act as a signpost for the organization and the wider world, and can also play an important role in an organization's marketing and fundraising strategies.

However, moral values are not sufficient to push organizations towards new ways of doing things, even though they should be the strongest motivating factor.[46] In particular, while aid agencies want to do good, they also want to do well, and so the fundraising imperative can start to dominate the moral one. And so morals are usually articulated only in narrow, institutionally determined ways, and supported by a culture of 'institutional bystanders', such that, when things go in directions that might conflict with these high-level values and morals, they are not brought back into the fold.

> Agencies want to help others while advancing their organizational interests, and are likely to pursue actions that they believe will resonate with those interests...From this perspective, the objectives of aid agencies can be paraphrased as: to assist targeted beneficiaries in such a way that our good works are seen and valued by donor communities and the profile of our agency is enhanced, so we can do more good works in the future.[47]

While this is not necessarily a bad thing, in the extreme it can become very damaging. It can lead to those who fund aid overtly shaping its agendas, and it can leave aid efforts without any clear strategic purpose or direction beyond dancing to the tune of these stakeholders. This then has implications for the ideas and approaches delivered by aid agencies: making them subject more to the whim of donors than to what is actually understood about development progress.

Nowhere is the narrow take on morality more apparent than in the relationships between aid agencies and their counterparts in developing countries. The moral case for better engagement, ownership, and so on, is clear and well established. Calls have been made for a greater focus on developing country actors since the very start of the aid effort. And yet, if you ask anyone in any part of the aid sector today 'Who calls the shots?', you are likely to be directed to an actor higher up the 'aid chain'. Southern non-governmental organizations are controlled by Northern ones, non-governmental organizations by UN agencies, both of these latter by donors, donors by political powers, political powers by immediate electoral demands and more shadowy 'strategic interests'. (Incidentally, the strong domestic interests in aid—citizenship, commercial, and political—run counter to the popular press idea that somehow aid exists for the benefit of 'big men' in developing countries. To paraphrase the old joke, 'Foreign aid is the transfer of money from poor people in rich countries to rich people in poor countries'—and for the benefit of rich people in rich countries.)

The power relations within aid have a self-similarity throughout the sector. Southern NGOs make *identical* complaints about Northern NGOs as Northern NGOs make about donor agencies. Donors make similar complaints about treasury departments, parliaments, and political influence, albeit rather more quietly. The pattern is one where everyone looks upwards and mutters, 'They aren't willing to hear the realities of our situation.' What this means is that the ultimate recipients of aid are consistently found to be the least powerful stakeholders in the system, because they neither purchase, pay for, nor specify the delivered service.[48]

This clearly conflicts with the stated moral position of aid agencies of existing to help others. One of the ways this is maintained is through an almost legitimized lack of sensitivity to context, which allows a narrow, self-interested morality to prevail. External relationships suffer as a result. The damning point made by Richard Dowden, Director of the Africa Institute—that aid agencies pay less attention to context than did their colonial forerunners[49]—is sadly hard to deny: 'Oxfam GB was run by former colonial "hands" when I started, all of them motivated in fact by managing the independence process. Many spoke local languages, had engaged with local power structures at the lowest to the highest levels, were expected to develop knowledge to inform the UK government.'[50] Contrast this with an account from the same practitioner, whereby a credible aid doctor argued that, as Salvadoran refugees stayed put while humanitarian expatriates only did six-month tours, the refugees should try to learn the language of the aid agency. Consider the global impact of a system which propagates such attitudes, and which comes with handfuls of money and 'best practices': it is little wonder that a World Bank Vice President saw fit to remark that donors were 'undermining capacity faster than they are building it'.[51] As the tsunami evaluation bemoaned, agencies were driven by 'frenzied self-interest', with a predictable effect on quality, performance, and local actors. In the pithy words of one Sri Lankan government official: 'I don't know which was worse, the first wave of water or the second wave of aid.'[52]

Of course, there have been attempts to enhance participation and local ownership in aid programmes, many of them well meaning, and some of them very effective. The participation research team at the Institute of Development Studies has been one of the most influential in shaping development practice over the years. But as the experts there are all too well aware, participatory development can simply end up reinforcing the status quo by defining upfront the *kind* of participation the aid agency wants, rather than thinking about the kind of participation that might be needed and appropriate to the context. Box 4.2 illustrates this with a case study on participatory approaches to enhancing goat farming in Brazil.

Box 4.2. Case study—the World Bank, participation, and goats

In the wake of the structural adjustment plans of the 1980s, the Bank and others started to support more participatory approaches, to ensure minimal levels of investment in public services and infrastructure and in social programmes to protect the most vulnerable. However, massive spending has 'proceeded with rather little effort to understand the challenges entailed in inducing participation or to understand why

(continued)

Box 4.2. Continued

earlier programs failed. The process has been driven more by belief or ideology and optimism than by systematic analysis, either theoretical or empirical.'[53]

This is not unique to the Bank. As Cornwall argues in a review of participation in Swedish support, 'Who participates, how they participate and what happens as a result is not something that conforms to any linear set of procedures or prescriptions. Making sense of these complexities requires not generic definitions but context-specific social analysis.'[54]

A good example is given by Joabe Cavalcanti, a Brazilian social development specialist.[55] In 1999, the World Bank signed off on a project in the town of Gravata in northeast Brazil. Run by the Brazilian development agency, it sought to engage community members and farmers in improving the living conditions of rural producers.

The community, which consisted of subsistence farmers, each family working on its own, was encouraged to start breeding goats. The Bank grant included a lot of stipulations, including that this should be a collective project, using common land and collective management of shelters for the goats. Each recipient was to get three goats and two kids, and people could sell the kids and the milk as long as they retained at least five goats. Three years after the project started, it was disbanded, 'after a series of discussions within the community which made clear that members had been pushed to act in a way that was not in accordance with their own way of life'.[56]

The project had induced participation and the formation of new networks, but the participants went along with this in order to benefit from the cash and other material pay-offs provided. Even in successful projects, such networks and forms of participation 'melt away when the incentives are withdrawn'. In this case, the benefits never started to accrue in the manner anticipated, so the participants pulled out. This was not a rejection of development, but of the Bank's version of it.

As Cavalcanti soberly concludes,

Development today has become a kind of missionary vocation in which the bearers of knowledge and techniques are understood to be superior, and then embrace the cause of changing the way of life of populations who think and live in a different fashion. When I questioned other development technicians about the cultural violence committed against communities in the name of development, two of them agreed that they themselves were indeed guilty of this, but argued that it was an unintended consequence of their job. With regard to this case study, what happened was a conflict between different views of life, of the world, of culture, and of the very concept of what development should mean. It can be argued that these small farmers were not interested in improving their lives, if 'improving' meant disruption and destabilisation of their way of life. For them, development should not mean more work, more headaches, even if it meant also more consumer goods and money. They were not interested in making more money and having no time to enjoy it. The crux of the matter is that the changes required as a means to get more money would mean an even greater loss of the opportunity to enjoy their lives.[57]

The conclusions of the recent study on the World Bank and participation, still draft at time of writing, highlight the importance of organizational cultural change to be able to cope with the kinds of responses found in Brazil:

Project structures need to change to allow for flexible, long-term engagement. Projects need to be informed more seriously by carefully done political and social analyses, in addition to the usual economic analysis, so that both project design and expected outcomes can be adapted to deal with the specific challenges posed by country or regional context . . . Most importantly, there needs to be a tolerance for honest feedback to facilitate learning, instead of a tendency to rush to judgment coupled with a pervasive fear of failure. The complexity of development requires, if anything, a higher tolerance for failure. This requires a change in the mindset of management and clear incentives for project team leaders to investigate what does and does not work in their projects and to report on it.[58]

The sad reality is that, all too often, participation ends up reinforcing the dominant culture of aid, which asks the puzzled question, 'Why don't they want what we know they need?'[59] Or, to put it another way, the so-called 'soft stuff' of relationships is actually the hard stuff for aid agencies.[60]

This is not just a moral issue, of course. The lack of feedback between beneficiary and donor, and the insensitivity of aid agencies to the needs of local and national actors, is seen by many as being at the heart of the problems facing the relevance and effectiveness of aid activities. As one recent review of international aid put it, 'Improving the welfare of beneficiaries is the ultimate goal of aid agencies [but] links between beneficiaries and a donor are weak to non-existent [. . .] activities do not focus on beneficiaries as much as on policy goals.'[61] As well as facing numerous accountability tests themselves (about which more in the next chapter), aid agencies can have a damaging effect on accountability structures within developing countries. By receiving basic services from external aid agencies, populations can become disenfranchised and less able to hold their own leaders accountable.

Meghnad Desai argues that 'We are not paying enough attention to how poor people get themselves out of poverty. We always assume we have to *do it for them*'[62] (emphasis added). He has also posed a radical suggestion that the Make Aid History contingent would no doubt have relished:

> We are giving fifty billion dollars of overseas aid. There are a billion poor people in the world. Why don't we just find the poor and give them one dollar a week and do nothing else . . . no questions asked. What they do with the money is not our concern. That would probably do more to alleviate poverty than anything else.[63]

At the moment, the system is far from this democratic ideal, not least because of all the aid agencies that are busy spending the billions of dollars given in aid. The sorry account given in *Why Nations Fail*, one of the most lauded books on development in recent years, tells all too common a story:

> Villagers in a remote district in the central valley of Afghanistan heard a radio announcement about a new multi-million dollar program to restore shelter to their area. After a long while, a few wooden beams . . . were delivered. But they were too big to be used for anything in the district, so the villagers put them to the only possible use: firewood. So what had happened to the millions of dollars promised? Of the promised money, 20 percent of it was taken as UN head office costs in Geneva. The remainder was contracted to an NGO which took another 20 percent for its own head office costs in Brussels, and so on, for another three layers . . . the little money that reached Afghanistan was used to buy wood from Western Iran, and much of it was paid to [the] trucking cartel . . . What happened in the central valley of Afghanistan is not an isolated incident . . . most of the waste resulting from foreign aid is not fraud . . . simply business as usual for aid organizations.[64]

Lost in the Matrix

Changes to organizational structures are among the most visible 'results' of efforts to reform aid, suggesting an implicit recognition of the need to reorganize aid agencies' internal relationships in order to maximize aid effectiveness. This assumption is not uncommon: organizational structure is widely seen as having a profound influence on organizational life. It provides a foundation on which standard operating procedures and routines are played out, and sets out the parameters for decision-making processes by specifying lines of authority, responsibility, and control. A sound structure provides a shared framework for identifying and meeting stakeholder and customer needs as well as achieving effectiveness and efficiency. It indicates the kinds of internal relationships of coordination and collaboration that are expected in an organization and gives employees a shared picture of the overall organization and how their department and specific role 'fit' in the whole.[65]

As in the wider world, aid organizational structure is seen as having an influence on roles, responsibilities, reporting, accountability lines, and decision-making power.[66] Three specific relational features get a lot of attention in aid agencies' own internal management processes: centralization, differentiation, and design.

A focus on *centralization* highlights the question of who makes the decisions in an organization. Different aid agencies position their functions at different points on a spectrum between decentralization and centralization, with most clustered somewhere in the middle. An ongoing challenge is striking a balance between the degree of centralization needed for control and the decentralization needed to gain commitment, participation, and context-specific learning. According to research by the Overseas Development Institute, those agencies with greater decentralization of staff, resources, and responsibilities to the field are able to harmonize better with others and respond to local circumstances: decentralization allows more effective collaboration with other agencies at country level.[67]

Many of the donor agencies included in the ODI research were in the process of decentralizing. However, separate research I have done suggests the effectiveness of such processes depends on recognizing that headquarters still has an important, if different, role to play in the new decentralized structure.[68] The ideal is that some elements are decentralized but others are retained at the centre, the latter including the provision of strategic coherence, clear guidelines, and ongoing technical support; monitoring and evaluation; dissemination of good practices; research; and professionalization efforts. However, this recognition appears to be lacking in many aid agencies, with field offices complaining about a lack of clear guidance from headquarters about what to do, when, and where. By contrast, headquarters are often totally unaware of the full scale of activities at country level, and seek to address this with continual competing demands for information, all requiring instant responses.

Differentiation, by contrast, looks at how tasks and functions, expertise, and geographical locations are managed and thought about within an organization. This has a direct bearing on organizational structure: choices about the priority of particular forms of differentiation superimpose themselves onto the organizational structure. Aid work is increasingly specialized in line with different geographies, functions, and themes, with overarching structures that are supposed to show how these different kinds of specializations fit together.

Paolo De Renzio, then at ODI, identifies the need for a *balanced and reciprocal relationship*[69] between geographic lines and thematic/sectoral lines, although this has proved hard to establish in practice. Different agencies use different arguments about the kind of differentiation that should take priority. For example, two bilateral agencies, the Swedish International Development Cooperation Agency and the Japan International Cooperation Agency, have restructured in opposing directions: '[Sweden's] most visible reform has been an organizational restructuring of the entire agency...Country teams are now grouped by the type of challenge faced in the partner country and the modalities that Sweden is likely to use, rather than by geographical location. This means that countries from different continents will be in the same departments.'[70] Separately, '[Japan] is considering an organizational structure that is not based on the nature of aid but on geographical regions...This is seen as a welcome direction, as it would enable the workflow to be organized...to properly manage aid operations on the basis of program units that bundle together various projects.'[71]

If these structural changes are successful, the incentives within each agency would of course end up looking rather different. In general terms, country staff give more attention to external actors, and are more aware of the imperatives and politics of local contexts. By contrast, thematic or sector specialists focus on technical soundness and formulation of coherent programme packages, following global standards for such work.

These different categorizations of the work of aid agencies help order information and facilitate mental models. They can often give the impression of a state of structural equilibrium. The reality is rather different. Because of high degrees of structured specialization and low levels of coordination and interaction, aid agencies now demonstrate a startling compartmentalization. As Riddell argues, 'The compartmentalisation of different sub-groups within the field of development, often lead[s] to isolation from, ignorance about, and sometimes even indifference to other dimensions of development.'[72] Another leading business thinker described the problem as follows: 'Organisations...are very prone to the practice of "boxing the problem". That is, having identified a continuing issue, they create a box somewhere on the organization chart, give it the name of the problem, and put some people in it in the hope that they will deal with it. Unfortunately, this only adds to the bureaucratic tangle.'[73]

One common response to these multiple simultaneous challenges posed by spans of control has been the rise of *matrix approaches* to management. These typically work by superimposing a set of goals or geographies across different forms of internal expertise and functions. Functions might include core processes such as fundraising or programme management, and support services such as human resources or finance. This tool originated in NASA in the 1960s, where there was a need to move away from the 'traditional hierarchical structure', 'which tends to diminish the visibility of authority and to emphasize consensus as an operative mode'.[74] The reality in aid, however, is that it seems to emphasize confusion as an operative mode.

So how does matrix management work in practice? There is surprisingly little evidence on its application in aid agencies—whether in terms of rationale or results. Journalistic research on its application in international businesses suggests a key theme of 'utter frustration of operating in [such] complex and shifting matrix management systems'.[75] The frustration stems from

- multiple and complex reporting lines;
- confusion over accountability;
- competing geographical and functional targets;
- unclear roles;
- too many people involved in decisions;
- lack of support from senior managers;
- politics and conflicts arising from continual organizational restructuring.

Many of those working in aid organizations will recognize these issues: the reality of matrix organizations is far from the mechanical perfection suggested in the theory of the matrix approach. Listen to this description of the experience of one middle manager:

> [He had] direct, indirect and 'dual solid' lines of reporting across multiple functions, product lines, and geographic regions . . . In addition to running his own virtual team that spanned three time zones, he had responsibility for several head office projects, with the added problem of dealing with a line manager on one project who was his peer on another . . . As he went through each layer of complexity and challenge, he began to laugh – amusedly at first, but then with increasing despair. He confessed he was exhausted by the sheer complexity of the situation and was unable to answer my question: 'At what point does all this become unworkable?'[76]

What research there has been on aid matrix structures indicates that they are not flexible and dynamic enough to enable new institutional approaches, often resulting in work on new issues being marginalized. Even longstanding issues, such as gender, HIV and AIDS, or disaster risk reduction, can 'fall between the cracks' of the grander conceptual frameworks of development cooperation and emergency relief.[77] There are numerous informal examples of matrix structures in non-governmental organizations causing misunderstanding or confusion about relationships and obligations. One Canadian NGO leader has stated:

> We have not grown in a neat, linear fashion; we have not evolved predictably or coherently; and we have not been able to apply machine precision to the coordination of work among us. Growth and change have usually caused stress, frustration, dissension and anxiety. Internal confusion

and ambiguity have nearly torn the organization apart at points when we were facing some of our most exciting opportunities. The lack of coherence during these periods of change has made even the mavericks in the organization's leadership uncomfortable; some, at times, were nearly ready to jump ship.[78]

More often than not, mechanisms for management and collaboration in the 'new' matrix structures are poorly defined and inadequately promoted. The various structural elements of aid agencies end up relating to each other largely as they always have done. For the new structures to really achieve their design objectives—a refocusing of agency resources and approaches—would require a shift in power and influence away from existing managers and department heads. As Olivier Serrat of the Asian Development Bank argues, hierarchical, centralized, or control-oriented structures present formidable roadblocks to change in most aid agencies.[79] In keeping with this, the implementation of matrix structures has been largely ineffectual. The most common result of restructuring seems to be the superimposing of a new symbolic framework—or a revised matrix—on an otherwise unchanged hierarchical organization.

The reduction of aid agencies to sets of structurally defined components also presents the organization as less than the sum of its parts. Organizations managed in this way can lose out on potentially valuable relationships between different parts that lead to new and emergent approaches and ideas. Cross-matrix sharing of ideas, often a key goal of senior management meetings, seldom 'trickles down' into closer sharing between operational units. Instead, practice is driven by bureaucratic obligations and financial reporting requirements, from both head office and donors. Agencies find it difficult to adopt new ideas that do not fit easily into matrices, limiting both cross-organizational analysis and operational innovation. For example, how might two 'parallel' themes in a matrix—say gender and climate change—interact to create a new understanding of specific problems in a particular setting—say Darfur—which might require new kinds of programming approaches? Or how about urbanization and food security? Development research has raced ahead of agencies' ability to integrate these issues. The problem isn't simply one of insufficient resources, but instead is related to how those resources are prioritized and allocated, and the institutional context in which these decisions take place.

The result of all of this is that organizations swing between entrenched turf interests and profound confusion about responsibilities and authorities. This is what one informant referred to as 'structural conundrums'.[80] Although this is far from being a passive process—think of the amount of effort needed to stay still when swimming against a current—the image from the outside is of organizational obfuscation and tardiness.

Despite the high drama of organizational restructuring, the distribution of power and influence within aid organizations—and between aid organizations and their stakeholders—has remained largely unchanged. For example: the structural problems of international financial institutions continue to reflect 'their origins as essentially technical agencies dealing with issues of international coordination'.[81] Despite changing global conditions and challenges, US foreign aid programmes, their organizational structures and statutory underpinnings, have been described as still reflecting the Cold War environment in which they originated.[82] A recent review of the Canadian International Development Agency highlighted severe restrictions on its mission and effectiveness which, according to its staff members, did not owe to problems in the concept or mission or the work it supports, but rather issues *in the organizational structure*.[83] There are no doubt many more examples.

There remains an abiding sense that the structures of most aid agencies are still inappropriate, and certainly do not reflect the needs and priorities of poor and vulnerable people. The introduction of matrices may have led to only symbolic rearranging of the proverbial organizational 'deckchairs on the *Titanic*'. The changes have been limited because they have not been accompanied by a shift in power dynamics. In effect, despite new structures, the same people and positions remain in charge. This is not surprising, because the very people who are the architects of structural change also tend to be those with most to lose by its being too dramatic or wholesale in nature.[84]

This finding is not unique to the aid sector. As a former IBM chief executive wrote, 'Nothing would have changed (except polite platitudes and timely head nodding) if we didn't redirect the levers of power. This meant making changes in who controlled the budgets, who signed off on employee's salary increases and bonuses, and who made the final decisions.'[85]

Organizations Start to Think For You[86]

In his best-known work, Aldous Huxley imagined a 'brave new world' built on the principles of Henry Ford's production line. Henry Ford is himself revered as a deity—with common utterances being 'By Ford!' or 'Our Ford'. The calendar counts up from Year 1, which is 1908 AD, the date of the first Model T. The ubiquitous religious symbol is a cross with the top cut off to make a 'T'.

Were Henry Ford alive today, what he would see would clearly not stand up to Huxley's exaggerated satirical vision. After perhaps some initial disappointment, though, he would do well to take a look inside a public sector or civil society organization. He would be able to take solace in the fact that at least some of his legacy was still alive and well in certain quarters.

The ideals and images of mass production and scientific management, which were themselves grounded in Newtonian mechanics and nineteenth-century science, had considerable influence on subsequent business and public management thinking. In the business world, the era of mass production gave way to new strategic approaches and new kinds of organizations, but the public sector and civil society seem to have moved ever more forcefully and intentionally towards the model that business slowly discarded. The Fordist paradigm is thriving, although, ironically, this is under the rubric of 'modern management techniques'. Despite longstanding and widely accepted critiques, this way of thinking and working has proved remarkably hard to change. The implications are far from trivial.

Sir Ken Robinson, a leading British educationalist, argues that modern educational systems are akin to nineteenth-century factories—where children go in one end depending on their 'date of manufacture', are subjected to a whole range of mechanical learning processes, and then are packaged and put out into the world of work.[87] Robinson sees this neo-Newtonian mindset as underpinning the major flaws in the educational system today. Health care systems and hospitals are also built on a reductionist, mechanical, factory model. Children are not being freed by education, they are being bound by it.

Aid, too, is an early industrial dream, and its agencies package and deliver development like so many Model Ts. This is to the detriment of more organic approaches. As noted in the previous chapter in relation to strategies, a blend of approaches is needed if a given organization is to effectively balance internal pressures with external interests, environmental context, and dynamics. But such nuance and balance in the management of aid agencies is noticeable predominately by its absence. Aid agencies are expected to act as mechanical entities, be equal to if not more than the sum of their parts, and use information in a logical and systematic fashion. Aid organizations work to fit Newton's *Principa Mathematica* precisely onto societal, political, and economic problems.

All of this points us towards an answer to the often-asked question: why has there not been a rise in innovative and dynamic new aid agencies to fill the niches in development and humanitarian work?[88] The reality is that few existing aid agencies are structured, managed, staffed, resourced, or generally thought about in ways that would enable innovative practices to emerge and flourish. And the system as a whole reflects nothing so much as an entrenched oligopoly: 'Taken as a whole, the institutions of the aid sector are in some ways redolent of the old "military-industrial complex" of the Cold War, with vested interests resisting changes in the analysis which might lead to their exclusion from opportunities.'[89]

This reinforces the notion of aid's 'travelling orthodoxies' mentioned in Chapter 2: mental models co-evolve with institutions; they are reinforced and supported by them. When institutions don't die but merely expand in size and number, perhaps it is inevitable that mental models are adjusted and adapted but never radically rethought.

Aid organizations, worryingly, continue to try to do a lot of the thinking for their staff. They seek to replace judgement and initiative with prescribed decision formulae and trigger points; inspiration with bureaucracy; trust with contracts; human relationships with matrices; moral values with value for money. What is more troubling is that because of the sheer weight of conformity that is overwhelming the system, all too often they succeed.

CHAPTER 5

Watching the Watchmen

'The government are very keen on amassing statistics. They collect them, add them, raise them to the n-th power, take the cube root and prepare wonderful diagrams. But you must never forget that every one of these figures comes in the first instance from the village watchman, who just puts down what he damn well pleases.'

Sir Josiah Stamp.

Think about any of the decisions you make in a day, month, year, or a decade: buying an item of food, choosing a utility provider, getting on a bus or train, moving house or changing jobs, sharing a difficult experience with a friend, proposing or accepting an offer of marriage. After just a few moments' reflection, most people would probably agree that 'trust is one of the most pervasive, but also least noticed, features of social life ... We all exercise it unthinkingly every day.'[1]

But trust isn't what it used to be. The sociologist, Anthony Giddens, describes a transformation that has happened as a result of modernity, away from traditional models of trust based on social relations and, in particular, deference to received authority and status—think family, faith, and monarchy.[2] However, these forms of trust and confidence can no longer be taken for granted.[3] Instead, modern institutions are characterized by systems designed to earn—rather than simply expect—trust. A review of accountability in medical practices makes the case clearly: 'Trust is conditional and is earned *through a variety of strategies that demonstrate honesty, reliability, competence, accessibility'*[4] (emphasis added). As a result, we are surrounded by a dizzying variety of shapes and forms of accountability and performance mechanisms. There is growing investment in, and acceleration of, 'aspirations and attempts to make business and professionals, public servants and politicians more accountable in more ways to more stakeholders'. There is no part of our lives that is not subject to this cultural turn: health, education, work, purchases, sales, civic life—the list goes on. 'Management by objectives', 'results-based management', 'performance measurement', 'target indicators', 'league tables', and 'total quality management' are all being applied—often simultaneously—with a variety of aims, in corporations, public sector bodies, and civil society organizations.

This chapter focuses on how similar accountability and performance approaches have been brought into foreign aid, and on what the effort amounts to. It looks at the range of methods employed and philosophies underpinning them, as well as assumptions about how they will contribute to enhanced trust and confidences. I want to examine what is being gained and lost in current trends in aid account-ability and performance. Is trust, in fact, increasing? Or are we headed in the opposite direction?

The Poverty of Numbers

In the space of one week in early 2012, both the World Bank and the UN announced major successes in development. The Bank told the world that the first Millennium Development Goal (MDG) on poverty had been met in 2010, two years previously.[5] A week later, the UN announced that the goal on access to safe water had also been met, also in 2010.[6] While meeting such goals should be heartening, it is also very easy to be seduced by good news. What did this flurry of claims to have met these goals two years ago actually mean?

More specifically, the World Bank stated that the percentage of people living on less than US$1.25 a day—the absolute poverty measure for the poorest developing countries—had declined in every region of the developing world between 2005 and 2008 for the first time since it started measurements in 1981. However, there were qualifications. While the proportion of abjectly poor people globally did fall—from 43 per cent in 1990 to 22 per cent in 2008—much of the reduction—around half—was attributable to China. Take China out of the equation, and the figures look markedly different. Outside China, the absolute number of people living on less than US$1.25 per day hardly moved between 1981 and 2008, staying fixed at approximately 1.1 billion people. As one might expect, various critiques sprang up about the veracity of the China data, which were robustly defended by the Bank. However, this back-and-forth missed an underlying issue: as Joseph Stiglitz argued in 2003, China had succeeded despite aid agency advice, not because of it.[7] To what extent could foreign aid, and the MDGs, take credit for this 'achievement'? In the wake of the Bank's announcement nine years later, Dani Rodrik of Harvard made the same point:

> The goal of halving extreme poverty [measured by the number of people living on less than $1.25 a day] is likely to be achieved ahead of time, largely thanks to China's phenomenal growth. At the same time, there is little evidence to suggest those successes were the result of the MDGs themselves. China implemented the policies [for] history's greatest poverty eradication pro-gramme prior to, and independently from, the millennium declaration and the MDGs.[8]

It is also important to take into account how such targets are dealt with in other contexts. According to the Bank figures, there will still be a 'bottom billion' of poor people worldwide in 2015, by the 'low' US$1.25 poverty line. However, the number of people living between US$1.25 and US$2 a day doubled to 1.18 billion people between 1981 and 2008. This 'bunching-up' effect, acknowledged by the Bank, can mean one of two things. First, the move out of poverty is not nearly as profound as 'meeting the MDG on poverty' would imply. Second, it takes a special kind of optimism to ignore the fact that such 'bunching-up' frequently occurs when targets are set. To pick just one from potentially thousands of examples, when the UK ambulance service set a target of 13 minutes for emergency response, 70 per cent of subsequent cases were found to have been responded to in 12 minutes.

The announcement itself also deftly spun the 'good news'. It stated emphatic-ally in several places that the goal of halving poverty had been reached. In fact, the goal is made up of three targets and nine separate indicators. The Bank provided data to show that one of these nine subsidiary indicators had been met—the one on income poverty. This was *not* the goal set in 2000. This may seem pedantic, but the conflation of goals and indicators is far from a trivial issue. Set aside the other eight indicators and what they look like for a second, and look only at the target that had been 'reached'. There is a long history of research showing that income poverty is only one aspect of deprivation; it is important to acknowledge other factors, such as under-nutrition, access to services, and minimum basic needs. The MDGs are underpinned by the human development approach, which takes the limitation of income poverty measures as one of its founding principles. In the worst case, as some human development experts argue, the income number is a meaningless and arbitrary line drawn across the complexity of poor peoples' lives. How much progress was made on the other indicators for the MDG? The Bank report fails to mention any of them. Nor does the press release or the report mention the other targets set for the goal.[9]

On the water goal, MDG 7, the lauded achievement also looks shaky under even light scrutiny. The World Health Organization and the UN Children's Fund[10] announced that the MDG to halve the number of people without access to safe drinking water had been met, five years before the deadline. Between 1990 and 2010, more than 2 billion people gained access to improved drinking water sources—meaning piped supplies and protected wells. According to household surveys and censuses, 89 per cent of the world population used improved drinking water sources. However, the detail suggests this was an optimistic assessment.

The report qualified its statement with the message that the target to meet basic sanitation—access to toilets and waste collection—was some way from being met, with 2.5 billion people still lacking basic sanitation. Given that sanitation and water cannot always easily be separated, how exactly can these figures hold water, if the pun can be forgiven? It turns out that they don't: in the opening pages of the 2012 report that announced the MDG had been met, the qualification was made that some of these improved sources may not be maintained and therefore may not, in fact, provide 'safe' water.[11] As Jamie Skinner of the International Institute for Environment and Development asked, 'The question few people ask is whether the target is even the right one. Does it measure what really matters? ...[The] news sparked a predictable media fanfare, but it also obscured some important facts.'[12]

As with poverty, there was a massive China uplift, the country accounting for almost a quarter of the 2 billion people who had gained access to drinking water since 1990. Another quarter lived in India. The report also identified massive regional disparities: many countries in Africa were not on track to meet the target by 2015, and a number were falling back to pre-1990 levels. There were also massive disparities within countries—between urban and rural, between the poorest and richest. Reviewing 35 African countries, the monitoring system found the richest 20 per cent enjoying close to full access and the poorest with no access to piped water and still largely practising open defecation.

Again, there was also a confusion of indicators and goals—MDG 7 is not to provide access to safe drinking water but to achieve environmental sustainability, and has four targets and ten indicators. One of the targets is access to safe and sustainable drinking water and basic sanitation, which has two indicators: the proportion of people with access to improved drinking water and the proportion of people with access to basic sanitation. 'There is a fierce debate over the accuracy of the data set that is frankly somewhat exhausting. The core issue that is real is that there is a big difference between simplistic views of access and substantive views of functionality.'[13]

By measuring only *access* to improved water sources, and focusing on the types of facilities used, there is nothing said about water quality, available quantities, reliability, time spent on accessing and using water facilities, functionality of the water source, and the cost or sustainability of the sources. One sobering finding is that much of Africa's water supply infrastructure is failing owing to a lack of maintenance: estimates are that some 50,000 water infrastructures across the continent are in a state of disrepair. In effect, the achievement of the indicator of access tells us very little about the target of *sustainable*, safe water, and even less about the overall goal of environmental sustainability. The report itself warns that 'It is likely that the number of people using safe water supplies has been overestimated', making one wonder whether this should have been reflected upfront in the report about the MDG having been met. At the risk of sounding cynical, 'water improvement indicator has been met, if we ignore the very likely possibility of overestimations, and the places where it hasn't been met' makes rather less of a headline.

Ban Ki Moon referred to the water report as 'a great achievement for the people of the world'.[14] He went on, 'The successful efforts to provide greater access to drinking water are a testament to all who see the MDGs not as a dream, but as a vital tool for improving the lives of millions of the poorest people.'[15] Leave the confusion between goals, targets, and indicators aside for a moment, and we still need to ask whether the targets were actually 'achieved'— or were both just cases of *post hoc ergo propter hoc* logical fallacies at play? What exactly was the contribution of this 'vital tool'?[16] Both the reports were noticeably silent on the details of the contribution of the MDGs or aid to either of these targets being 'met'. They measure whether the MDG indicators are being reached, albeit with the qualifications made above. But we are none the wiser as to what international efforts have contributed to these outcomes.

Echoing the words of a senior UK Department for International Development (DFID) official, cited in Chapter 3, it would seem that these are both instances of the aid system hitting the target, but missing the point.

Take the two stories together, and it is hard to escape the sense that these announcements of progress tell us more about the measurers than the measured. The quote from Josiah Stamp, a former director of the Bank of England, that opens this chapter is especially pertinent. We might justifiably employ another Latin tag, and ask '*Quis custodiet ipsos custodes?* Who watches the watchmen?'

Why Getting out of Bed is so Hard

Arguably, it is not accountability itself, but what accountability *generates* that plays so central a role in our social, economic, and political lives. Accountability confers trust, and trust matters a great deal. Niklas Luhmann, the renowned German sociologist, may not have been overstating the case when he argued that 'A complete absence of trust would prevent [one] even getting up in the morning.'[17]

An absence of trust and confidence underpins phenomena as disparate as credit crunches, troubled health care bills, and climate change negotiations. 'Every day we read of untrustworthy action by politicians and officials, by hospitals and exam boards, by companies and schools.'[18] Although, we may need more trust the act of trusting 'often seems hard and risky'.[19] The world, it seems, faces 'a deepening crisis of trust'.[20]

From all sides—politicians, campaigning groups, academics, and journalists— there is pressure for all kinds of organizations to make effective decisions, work to objective standards, take responsibility for their impact on the wider world, be open and transparent to their wider stakeholders, and be attentive and responsive to stakeholders' feedback. These pressures have played a crucial role in redefining the modern public sector.

> . . . work on the 'new accountability agenda' suggest[s] that to understand accountability one needs to ask a series of questions: who is demanding

accountability; from whom is accountability being sought; where – in what forum – are they being held to account; how is accountability being delivered; and, for what are people/institutions being held accountable? In recent years, the range of answers to these questions has expanded.[21]

Research on a range of different approaches suggests some common assumptions underpinning many of these accountability frameworks:

- *Clear responsibilities* for achieving goals, undertaking tasks, making decisions, adhering to sets of codes or standards, fulfilling certain values and principles, or being responsive to certain stakeholders.

- *Honest reporting* of information about actions and behaviours, in which an organization renders public an account of how it fulfilled its responsibilities.

- Some form of *evaluation or appraisal process* for those to whom the organization is accountable to judge the results of actions against the predetermined standard and measures.

- Some *concrete mechanisms* for holding an organization to task, in terms of *sanctions and rewards* in response to certain kinds of performance or behaviours, to eliminate unwanted differences between standards and practice.

These systems work to create a 'self-correcting, dynamic feedback loop'.[22] Behaviour (of individuals, groups, systems) can be specified, comparisons made between expectations and reality, which then feedback to inform another round of specifications. This is underpinned by principal–agent theory, from human relations research, whereby a 'principal' delegates authority to an 'agent' and the principal has formal authority to hold agents to account by means of economic and legal incentives and sanctions.[23] A good analogy for such accountability systems is a thermostat: we set the desired temperature in a room, wait to see the result, and adjust it as necessary. Much like this, principal–agent approaches tend to assume a direct one-to-one relationship between principal and agent, a single coherent set of goals, and an immediate and unambiguous feedback loop. In the absence of trust, it seems, we should have greater control.

The push for greater control as a means of ensuring trust has been sadly counterproductive in many settings. In Western contexts, where these ideas originated, there is growing cynicism about results. Beryl Radin, responsible for the design and delivery of major systems of public accountability in the USA in the 1990s, suggests a curious paradox in all of this work. Even as public institutions are subjected to ever more weighty and detailed judgements, the complexity of their tasks is increasing, and the scope to objectively assess performance is diminishing.[24]

Related studies and assessments have identified a number of common problems with the accountability agenda (see Box 5.1).

> **Box 5.1. Accountable problems**
>
> 1. Displacement: targets displace goals and become the focus of effort, such that efforts hit the target but miss the point.
>
> 2. Excessive focus on what can be counted as opposed to what counts.
>
> 3. Focus on those closest to the target, leading to bunching-up effects.
>
> 4. Neglecting harder areas, focusing on easier things.
>
> 5. Manipulating numbers and data.
>
> 6. Inability to perceive or account for the unexpected, except as misbehaviour: 'If my theory about reality doesn't yield the right results, it is reality that needs to wake up.'

Despite its best intentions, the accountability revolution has left us 'overwhelmed by the proliferation of laws, standards, auditing and targets that aspire, *at least on paper*, to hold [others] to account'[25] (emphasis added). For many, trust seems further away than ever. The temptation to simply stay in bed must surely be growing.

Aid Accountability: Highways or Pileups?

In the past few decades, the international aid sector has seen its own version of Giddens' cultural transformation. The motivation for this is hard to argue against: 'It is not enough to simply do good, it must be done well.'[26] Like other public and private organizations, aid agencies too need to become more accountable in more ways to more people. Although, as Riddell notes, aid has been subject to scrutiny ever since it was first given,[27] many argue there has been a 'quiet revolution in aid accountability'[28] in the past two decades. Once considered angelic deliverers of urgently needed sustenance or high-minded advocates for the redistribution of wealth, all aspects of aid agencies are now increasingly questioned and criticized, from their motivations through to their results.

Click through the online archives of almost any newspaper and you will find academics, journalists, former agency staffers, politicians, and international commissions routinely expressing opinions about aid and its role. Even celebrities have had their say. Some of these are vehement and widely publicized critiques, questioning its entire rationale. Others are more tempered and point to the lack of speed, quality, effectiveness, or results. The typical retort from those working in foreign aid tends to be that such critiques oversimplify, veer into ideology, and overgeneralize and sensationalize the bad while ignoring the good. 'Damned if we do, and damned if we don't', comes the surly response from many quarters. They might also point to systems that have been set up to address exactly these issues within aid: mechanisms to further trust and confidence have become commonplace. Abstract notions of accountability have been made concrete in a number of distinct ways. These were described by one leading expert, John Mitchell, as a 'three-lane highway for aid accountability'. The three lanes are: monitoring and evaluation approaches; results-based management approaches; and standards and codes for aid effectiveness.[29]

These three approaches have been applied in different kinds of aid work, each of which present particular challenges to the assumptions and ideas of the accountability movement. Humanitarian activities address urgent survival needs, such as food and temporary shelter, as well as disaster, crisis, and conflict mitigation and risk reduction. Service delivery addresses basic needs, such as education, health care, longer-term shelter, community development, employment, and income generation, at both small, local and large, regional, or national scales. And policy and rights advocacy addresses structural issues of rights, public policy and regulation, and societal norms.[30]

All of these applications grapple, to differing extents and in different ways, with the burning questions of aid accountability and effectiveness, how to analyse the successes and failures of aid, and what to do about them. The basic assumption across all three lanes of the aid accountability highway is exactly of a closed, controllable, thermostatic system in which the principal–agent relations I described above can be clearly and unambiguously articulated. In much of this effort, donors are positioned as the ultimate controllers or *principals* of aid, who seek to influence the behaviours of aid agencies or recipient governments by attaching conditions to aid delivery that act as a form of feedback. 'Such a contract—for example the "performance assessment framework"— consists of agreeing in advance on the intended results (e.g. more girls in school, reduced numbers of women dying in childbirth), the quantity of resources required to achieve these results, and the means by which the parties to the contract will know whether these results have been achieved.'[31]

Implementing such thermostatic approaches obviously requires the establishment of control systems, 'formal, information-based routines and procedures which aid managers use to maintain or alter patterns in organisational activities'.[32] These are useful in theory because they can create incentives for effective performance and delivery. But how well do they work in practice? Before looking at three specific examples of the accountability movement in aid, I want to look at the more general critiques that have been made of this way of thinking. Can such abstracted notions of trust actually be employed in aid efforts?

The first, and best-rehearsed, critique relates to structural flaws in the system. If you benefit from, say, health policies in a developed country, you are usually able to make some judgement about the service, provide feedback, and have some recourse to some form of accountability. If your problem is with the policymakers, you usually have the option of voting against them. If it is with the practitioners, you have some form of ombudsman, standards, and even legal procedures. For poor people in developed countries receiving health via international agencies, such forms of feedback are weak or non-existent. There is a structural gap—which leads to a vacuum alluded to in the previous chapter—between those who pay for aid and those who are supposed to benefit from it. This gap can of course be filled—by researchers, the media, and sometimes aid agencies themselves. But as the Tsunami Evaluation Coalition put it: 'The flow of information back to [donors] is rather haphazard. The principle route is the agency's own information, which is normally intended to promote the agency's brand rather than provide an unbiased and balanced account of their performance.'[33]

The second issue that most raise relates to the composition of the system. Most accountability approaches are firmly bound up with an idealized principal–agent model, described earlier. The problem is that the thermostat model doesn't come close to matching the 'many-many' reality of the aid sector outlined in Chapter 1. Bill Easterly argues that,

> Trying to do everything with aid creates many principals and many agents... multiple principals (many rich-country governments and issue lobbies) weaken the incentives for the agent (the international agency)...Each principal (say, each issue lobby) influences the agent to pursue its objectives; together this weakens incentives for the agent to achieve any one objective...Aid is also complicated by having many agents – many different aid agencies who answer to different bosses. None of the agencies is responsible for a particular outcome, and the effects of their individual efforts are unobservable. However, they jointly have an effect, for example on economic development. When something goes wrong, after years of effort by these agencies, which one is to blame? We don't know, so no one agency is accountable. This weakens the incentives of agencies to behave, and principals don't know who to hold accountable. The problem gets more severe as the objective becomes more general, with more agents that could have contributed to the outcome.[34]

The third issue is that there are many mechanisms to generate trust in the system, and they often crowd each other out. As in the wider world, aid has seen a proliferation of accountability and performance mechanisms, established at different levels, for different purposes, at different times, and by different actors. New systems often overlay rather than replace old ones, adding administrative burdens to the already considerable political ones. The picture is less of a nice neat parallel three-lane highway and more of an institutional traffic jam or, even worse, a motorway pileup. There is a general lack of attention to 'how organizations deal with multiple and ... competing accountability demands'.[35] Of course, one could argue if one was being cynical, that letting a thousand accountability flowers bloom is one way of ensuring the revolution remains relatively quiet, encumbered by internal debates and inevitable disagreements.

Finally, issues arise around what are termed 'theories of change'. Aid is assumed to work in a certain way—as already explored in the first three chapters of Part 1. In general, accountability mechanisms have been a key contributing factor to these assumptions, and have served to reinforce them at critical points in the decision-making process. At best, approaches to performance and accountability have sat on top of these assumptions instead of challenging them. Many have failed to shed light on the actual processes of change involved in development or disaster recovery. To take one obvious example, every framework for assessing performance comes with associated indicators, which call for agencies to specify not just what will be achieved but also exactly how, with clear articulation of achievements all along the aid chain, and upfront. However, many of the questions purse-holders would like answered upfront simply cannot be answered given the complexity and 'noise' along links in the chain.[36] Aid effectiveness approaches as a whole were reviewed by the World Bank's Development Effectiveness Team, which found that 'the complex causality chain linking external aid to final outcomes' has largely been ignored, with the relationship between aid and development being treated as a black box.[37] 'Making further progress on aid effectiveness requires opening that box.'[38]

There is a need for accountability mechanisms that can help open up the black box of development success and failure. Questions of how well specific mechanisms deal with these challenges shape the rest of this chapter.

Logics and Trials: Aid Evaluation

For almost as long as aid has been given, there have been efforts to assess its effectiveness. This has been for (at least) three reasons: *learning* in the sense of understanding what causes what effects, which is useful to everyone interested in improving development projects, and *accountability* in the sense of giving account to parliaments, taxpayers, and donor publics. Both of these are underpinned by a deeper goal of trust, because an emphasis on transparent assessments should boost credibility and *legitimacy*. In theory, evaluation should be a straightforward matter of objectively assessing what an intervention achieves and whether it met its stated goals, and explaining differences between hoped-for and actual effects. In practice, as always, things are a little more tricky that that.

To date, evaluations have not been seen as especially important for development spending decisions: 'An evaluation continues to be a concern for a very limited proportion of all those who have an interest in a project and are affected by its outcome.'[39] A review of evaluations in a major agency highlighted that staff members did not find evaluations useful in general.[40] Supporters of evaluation point out that donors do use evaluations to make decisions about continuing or stopping funding but there are counterarguments as well—in one agency internal assessment, almost half the staff considered the evaluation irrelevant to the assessment of the success of a project. Evaluation is often seen as predominately a tool for external accountability, and therefore faces a great deal of defensiveness and resistance: for many, evaluations may as well be called inquisitions.

More problematic is the finding that those at the receiving end in developing countries think assessments and reports are in fact the *main purpose* of aid: 'Foreign assistance concentrates on reports. If they are well prepared, the reality is not considered.'[41]

It's logical, Captain

The most prominent tool used in aid planning and evaluation, borrowed from NASA in the 1960s, is the *logical framework analysis*, or the *logframe* for short. This enables agencies to systematically set out programme or project objectives, spell out the causal relationships between these objectives and certain activities, provide indicators for success, and describe the assumptions and risks that underpin the design process—and to plot all of these on a matrix. At the point of evaluation, the logframe is used as a basis for investigating whether objectives have been achieved and how well. Done right, the logframe makes users think carefully and systematically about their plans, and how activities will contribute to goals. Donors often suggest its real value is that it confers clarity on an otherwise messy and opaque process. It can also help air issues and forge consensus about a shared, albeit linear, way forward on a given issue.

The problem is that it is not always done well. A number of researchers have explored the use and abuse of the logframe in recent years, providing insights into how the ideal image of evaluation works in practice. Alnoor Ebrahim of Harvard University sees a number of issues with the approach, chief among which is its highly technocratic nature, which 'organizes and reduces complex social and political realities into simple and discrete components'.[42]

The logical sequencing of activities, outputs, and outcomes that is seen as the advantage of the logframe is also its downfall: a frequent issue is the highly linear logic, which suggests the world is much simpler and more predictable than in fact it is:

> ... there are so many factors involved which lie beyond the scope of the planned initiative that will change the way things work. Although the LFA [logical framework approach] makes some attempt to capture these through the consideration of the risks and assumptions, these are limited by the imagination and experience of those involved. As a result the LFA tends to be one-dimensional and fails to reflect the messy realities facing development actors.[43]

This 'tendency towards simplification and quantification make[s] the logical framework, in its current form, inadequate for monitoring complex development interventions'.[44]

Consider the following comment from a representative of a major donor, speaking at a meeting to discuss problems with logframes: 'We don't pretend that it matches reality, but we still find it useful.'[45] Why might a tool that, in the extreme, enables its users to maintain a firm grip on fantasy prove useful? One key use, it would seem, is that it enables the establishment of an idealized principal–agent relationship between donor and aid agency. Little wonder that, perhaps even more than aid strategic processes, such efforts have been seen as embodying the prescriptive thinking processes so beloved of Robert McNamara. However, 'Despite heavy criticisms from a wide range of field practitioners, it and its cousins have survived and remain the dominant frameworks in the development sector for planning, monitoring and evaluation.'[46]

Assessing impact

Even with tools such as the logframe, there are limits to how far aid projects can go in terms of assessing their achievements. A continual problem has been assessing and understanding impacts—the difference an intervention has made. Despite high expectations, evaluations have historically been dismal at providing such information. A review of humanitarian evaluations published over an eight-year period concludes that 'A standard sentence could almost be inserted into all [evaluation] reports along the lines of: "It was not possible to assess the impact of the intervention because of the lack of adequate indicators, clear objectives, baseline data and monitoring."'[47] Similarly, on the development side, 'The finding that donors are unable to ascertain their effectiveness beyond intermediate outcomes is repeated in virtually all the evaluations surveyed.'[48]

Until quite recently, there was a diversity of opinions as to whether such assessment was feasible. Some suggest that, 'In most cases changes in development outcomes in a specific country cannot be attributed to aid in general, let alone to an individual donor.'[49] Others suggest it is possible to do this, but 'The evidence on development impacts is patchy, and generally lacks sufficient information on the links between outcomes and [an agency's] actions.'[50]

This divide has flared up strongly in recent years, with considerable implications for how aid evaluation is thought about and practised, and for aid as a whole. The past ten years has seen a gradual shift towards statistical approaches to impact evaluation, described by its champions variously as 'rigorous evaluation' and the 'gold standard'. Borrowing from medical practices, this form of evaluation seeks to prove causality between intervention and effect by using randomized control trials (RCTs). This means that, as in drug trials, the recipients of an aid programme are determined randomly at the outset, and the assumption is made that the recipients and non-recipients are broadly similar *except* for the presence of the intervention. Data are gathered against key indicators, and comparisons are made between 'treatment' and 'non-treatment' sites. 'If the groups are randomly selected and the samples are large enough, the average differences in the groups' development can be traced back to the causes. For assessments to be precise, it is important to prevent interaction between the groups as best one can.'[51]

The proponents of experimental designs argue that multilateral development banks and UN agencies already spend considerable sums on operational assessments of projects (monitoring and evaluation) but not nearly enough on impact evaluations. They also argue for greater methodological rigour in order to understand what works in development. They have had considerable success in influencing donors. This presents a considerable shift in the aid evaluation world, with donors seeing RCTs as promising evidence of impacts and outcomes hitherto not available, enabling them to solidify the principal–agent relationship.

There has been a loud chorus of complaints about the limitations of such approaches. The counterargument school argues that this kind of methodology is based on such serious and flawed assumptions that, were they to be made transparent, they would invalidate the entire rationale for their use in social settings. They argue that the methodology is best known for its use in clinical field trials of new medications precisely because it is fairly straightforward in separating those who receive treatment from those who do not, and because the interventions are discrete and homogenous and impacts are easy to track along key indicators. At a more technical level, there are those who argue that the dependence of RCTs on the statistics of averages and on supposedly 'isolated' populations makes them less suited to more complex, dynamic, and interactive phenomena.

A major danger is that if, as some of the 'randomistas' suggest, anyone not doing an RCT is equivalent to a mediaeval leech doctor, the kinds of programmes that will be delivered will be limited to those that can be randomized, potentially putting severe limits on the scope of aid programming:

> It is noteworthy, however, that randomised experiments are pertinent only for certain types of interventions. This tool is not of any use for assessing the results of budget support, advice to governments and policy dialogue at the national level. It only serves to evaluate the results of reform implementation at the municipal or household levels, but not to assess a reform process and its origins as such.[52]

Experimental approaches, just as with logframes, have seen challenges from development practitioners and scholars who urge greater methodological pluralism. They contend that rigour in impact evaluation requires multiple types of comparisons and triangulation, supported by explicit linkages to theories of change and action. RCT may be well suited to the provision of vaccines, conditional cash transfers to the poor, or the distribution of new seed varieties to farmers. However, they are less appropriate for activities where a comparison group or counterfactual is hard to isolate, such as in policy advocacy, macroeconomic policy changes, reforms in labour markets, or even some investments in infrastructure. Nor are they suited to examining complicated development pathways involving multiple, interacting, and non-linear causal factors. One leading evaluator has argued that less that 10 per cent of aid interventions are amenable to such assessments.[53] Finally, even on their own terms, RCTs provide insights that are hard to generalize: 'If you find that using flipcharts in classrooms raises test scores in one experiment, does that mean that aid agencies should buy flipcharts for every school in the world? Context matters—the effect of flipcharts depends on the existing educational level of students and teachers, availability of other educational methods, and about a thousand other things.'[54]

The move towards a more pluralistic approach seems to have been at least partly successful, with some arguing that RCTs have been 'oversold' as the gold standard for issues of aid accountability and performance. Even its champions are suggesting that the *accumulated* knowledge from RCTs, and what this says about *systemic* issues, is one of the most valuable contributions[55] of the movement. But if the aim is to get a broad systemic picture of a particular problem, it is worth asking if stacking up a whole lot of RCTs is the best way of doing this.

The Aid Counter-bureaucracy: What Results From Results?

'Modern management techniques'—the darling of public sector reform efforts—are increasingly at the heart of aid reform processes. In the vast majority of cases, this means results-based management (RBM), an element of the New Public Management Movement that spread across Western governments in the 1990s. The World Bank *Sourcebook on Managing for Development Results* provides the following, eminently sensible, rationale for RBM:

> Development stakeholders now recognise that the process of improving conditions in the world, a country, or an organization is a process of change management. Defining clear results provides a better target for change. Periodically measuring results provides guideposts or markers that allow for correction to keep programs or projects on track toward their stated outcomes. Ultimately, better managing for results helps demonstrate more clearly whether development outcomes have been achieved.[56]

The reality is somewhat different. A review of RBM among donor agencies identifies a persistent emphasis on activities and outputs—those things within the control of a particular organization—despite the fundamental problem this raises with the actual rationale for RBM approaches.[57] Managing for results is seen as 'a relatively new and unfamiliar challenge' and 'a very difficult one to master in many fields'. This is amply evidenced by the struggles some donor agencies, and their own governments, report when they admit that the clarity of certain indicators and conceptual understandings are still internally debated. In some areas, such as general budget support, it is extremely difficult to measure and attribute results. In more traditional approaches, 'A lack of clarity about the *level at which results* are to be defined leads to confusion about assessing how externally supported interventions should contribute to the development objectives.'[58]

In 2003, UK DFID established a Multilateral Effectiveness Framework for assessing the effectiveness of agencies to which it provided core funding. The initial focus was to be a synthesis of the results gathered by the 23 agencies in question. But, given a severe lack of information on the results achieved by these agencies, the Department shifted the focus to organizational effectiveness, defined as 'the enabling system that needs to be in place to produce these results'.[59] This was based on the assumption that 'An effective organisation is one that incorporates a results focus into all its business processes and uses the results to continually improve performance.'[60] The final report suggests 'We have become aware of the limitations of the RBM approach, particularly that establishing results-based organisational systems is only one part of the effectiveness story.'[61]

A more recent and demanding evaluation of RBM among UN agencies sheds more light on why such a framework faces problems, indicating a range of conceptual and practical concerns. First, the original design of RBM is frequently inadequate, statements of results are often vague, and the determination of success does not lend itself to impartial, transparent, and precise measurement. Performance measures that exist frequently lack baselines and targets, and many are not regularly tracked. Many of the planned-for results are expressed in a self-serving manner, lack credible methods for verification, and involve reporting based on subjective judgement. RBM takes no account of the fact that multiple actors and external risk factors influence outcomes. Although aspirational results are used to justify approval of budgets, actual attainment or non-attainment of results is found to be of no discernible consequence to subsequent resource allocation or other decision making. What accountability does exist is not based on a review of outcomes but instead only on ascertaining that there is no negligence, misconduct, or breach of rules and regulations. In addition, the formalistic approach to codifying how to achieve outcomes, inherent to RBM, can in fact stifle the very innovation and flexibility required to achieve those outcomes. In fact, the review of RBM in the UN found the extensive effort had made virtually no contribution to strategic decisions.[62]

Although organizational approaches to RBM are important, it is the Millennium Development Goals that are the real 'poster child' for RBM in the sector. Described as human development plus results-based management,[63] this formal hierarchical system of goals, objectives, and performance targets is the basis of resource, mobilization, and corporate motivation in many aid agencies. At the time the MDGs were being developed, RBM was in the ascendancy in the North: 'Its common sense nature and linearity added to its attraction—set targets, monitor achievement and reward on the basis of performance.'[64] This attractiveness carried over to aid donors and multilaterals: 'The widely reported underperformance of aid in earlier years would not occur in the future as RBM methods would ensure high levels of performance.'[65]

RBM manifested itself in a number of ways in the MDGs, each of which smacks of the prescriptive model of strategy. First, the MDGs are structured as a nested hierarchy of over 40 targets and 150 indicators based on time-bound outcomes. Second, targets and indicators were screened for how well they fit with the RBM philosophy and assumptions, and the judgements made on this basis affected specific goals and targets. Third, the focus on quantifiable results and measurements means MDGs that were hard to analyse and measure didn't make the grade. Finally, the reliance on RBM amounts to a weakness in theory: there is no deeper theory of causation linking policy to outcomes. All of this illustrates how, as with logframes and RCTs in evaluation, the pressures of accountability can loom large over the design of aid efforts. Ambition can be held back by the need to 'formulate realistic and measurable goals'.[66] This is tricky territory, as it creates the incentive of only doing those things that can be measured, and thereby locking in existing attitudes and prejudices. Echoing a previous chapter title, this really is thinking inside the box.

Perhaps unsurprisingly, the same critiques made of results-based approaches in developed countries have been made of the MDGs. With targets and indicators come considerable potential for misuse, manipulation, and misrepresentation: perverse incentives and gaming behaviours can run rife. Ashwani Saith of the Institute of Social Studies (ISS) in The Hague notes, for example, the likely targeting of *those nearest the poverty lines* rather than *the poorest* to maximize the apparent impact of interventions on target indicators such as headcount poverty, and the switching from *non-target groups* (e.g. the disabled) to those groups more related to the targets (e.g. children).[67] 'It is also possible that such indicators might post satisfactory progress while there might well be significant concurrent deteriorations on a wide number of more relevant but patchily reported and largely un-monitored dimensions.'[68] Indeed, the two examples of water and poverty with which I opened this chapter arguably display all of these issues.

There are, of course, numerous contexts where the MDGs are being used in an effective and intelligent way, to serve development (as defined by the top-down strategists, at least). But nowhere do they seem to be fulfilling the eminently sensible vision set out by one analyst: keep the goals clear and simple, allow national and local definition and measurement, and use action research with poor people to explore the multidimensionality of poverty and to report on progress.[69]

I want to give the final word on RBM to Andrew Natsios, former Head of the US Agency for International Development. It has been long established that, in aid, there are often no adequate baselines or suitable indicators against which to measure progress, and results cannot always be captured in 'hard' data: 'There is a danger of a fixation on available data at the cost of dialogue and monitoring on genuine policy priorities.'[70] Natsios, who oversaw a major RBM process in the world's largest bilateral aid agency, took this further in a searing critique. He argued that the mentality of results was gutting the sector, replacing development imagination with bureaucratic requirements—what he called the 'aid counter-bureaucracy'. His final assessment was damning, for both the results approach and the randomista school of evaluation: 'Measurability should not be confused with development significance.'[71]

Standard Bearers

The third and final form of aid accountability I want to look at in this chapter concerns standards and codes of practice. Long established as part of corporate quality management, such practices are an important—if contested and often questioned—feature of the development and humanitarian landscape. This is one area where, to the best of my knowledge, the humanitarian aid side of the system may have been a step or two ahead of the development side.

In the wake of the 1994 genocide in Rwanda and the tragic failures of aid in that crisis, international agencies combined to create a variety of mechanisms to strengthen accountability, performance, and learning. One of these was a network to strengthen evaluations as a key tool of accountability and learning. Another was a set of standards, known as the Sphere Project, which set out minimum requirements of delivery of assistance, down to the level of the amount of water and calories that should be delivered. A third was the Humanitarian Ombudsman, now the Humanitarian Accountability Partnership International, which applies quality assurance approaches to make aid providers more responsive and accountable to aid recipients. The positives and negatives of these approaches aside, what is interesting is that they were set up in response to particular recommendations, but where the spirit of the recommendations was resisted. Indeed, prior to Rwanda, the best such mechanism for humanitarian aid was the Red Cross–NGO Code of Practice, developed in 1994 and now with over 400 signatories. What one critique made of this mechanism has proved more generally true: 'The code does not provide...clear proactive regulation with respect to the provision of humanitarian aid. The code is not regulatory because of its cautious language, with phrases like "we shall endeavour to", instead of "we shall". By using this language, room for manoeuvre is also created for international NGOs with different approaches.'[72]

So, in the wake of the Rwanda crisis, one recommendation was to establish an independent, international accreditation mechanism to ensure the performance and accountability of aid organizations. However, these suggestions were actively resisted by aid agencies. Instead, Sphere and others formed a series of voluntary standards and codes intended to address different aspects of perform-ance and accountability. Instead of external regulation, the key had become self-regulation (the same, of course, applies in business sectors—better to pre-empt harsh external measures by adopting soft internal ones).[73] A similar set of recommendations for an NGO policing mechanism following the 2004 Asian tsunami was simply ignored by most agencies.

Despite the ineffectual nature of the mechanisms, they also met with some resistance in certain quarters for fear of the unintended consequences. Franco-phone agencies, led by Médecins Sans Frontières, strongly opposed the assur-ance initiatives on the grounds that they risked creating a set of rigid, lowest common-denominator standards; inhibited innovation and independence; were open to manipulation by donor governments; and solidified the dominance of the core group of major NGOs.

The development system, as noted, was a little slower to pick up on such approaches, but did so with aplomb in the 2000s with the Paris Declaration on Aid Effectiveness (which, incidentally, was preceded by the Rome Declaration, and followed by Accra and Busan). Several high-profile conferences held after 2000 established that the MDGs (Chapter 3) were to be tracked regularly at country, regional, and global levels. This agreement included recognition of the need to identify the programmes, mechanisms, and strategies that can best achieve the MDGs. Collectively labelled the aid effectiveness agenda, this effort culminated in the 2005 Paris Declaration, which included the following state-ment: 'We the ministers of developed and developing countries responsible for promoting development and Heads of multilateral and bilateral development institutions, meeting in Paris on 2 March 2005, resolve to take far-reaching and monitorable actions to reform the ways we deliver and manage aid.'[74]

The Paris Declaration has itself been evaluated, in a first-phase report published in 2008 and a final report published in 2011. This is in fact the largest aid evaluation ever conducted, with more than 200 people in 40 countries working on 35 subsidiary reports.[75] The results are depressingly similar to those achieved by the assurance mechanisms found in humanitarian aid. The principles and commitments have been applied, if gradually and unevenly, among partner countries, and much more unevenly among donors and agencies. Other comments include that 'progress is slow' and 'disappointing in relation to the original hopes'.[76]

Mechanisms for holding agencies to account are the most controversial and politically sensitive of all aspects of accountability and performance. There is a distinct lack of willingness among organizations to be held to account in tangible ways to the demands of external stakeholders—shareholders, political masters, clients, the tax-paying and donating public. This area of aid account-ability has seen least progress in the past 15 years, although not for the lack of recommendations or suggestions by leading aid analysts. Interestingly, among the few mechanisms that explicitly try to hold some part of the aid system to account, are two focusing on recipient governments—the Millennium Challenge Account and the movement towards cash-based incentives for development results.

It seems that significant conceptual and practical problems characterize every aspect of aid accountability mechanisms, and that the various mechanisms and tools lack political 'teeth' in terms of holding aid agencies to account for their actions and performance. Growing numbers of frameworks and commitments indicate that the sector sets itself high rhetorical standards. Yet 'There are no rewards for agencies that meet them or penalty for agencies that don't. It is for each agency to decide whether they are meeting the standards themselves.'[77]

Distorted Reflections

Although the tools covered here are just a few among many, they exemplify the issues faced generally with aid performance and accountability approaches. The mentality is clearly evident in the performance and accountability demands of donors—standardized reports, emphasis on measurable inputs and outputs, centralization of information, and many other aspects that seek to reinforce the principal–agent model of working: 'The type of appraisal, monitoring and evaluation procedures insisted upon by donors...distort accountability by emphasising short-term quantitative targets and favouring hierarchical management structure—a tendency to "accountancy" rather than "accountability."'[78]

While aid reporting mechanisms are very well established, there is a distinct sense that the process dominates the purpose. Most organizations delivering aid programmes have a huge number of separate reporting lines to their donors, each based on specific formats and templates, each of which usually includes some statement of how monies were spent, where, and with what results. For a programme manager, the burden of reporting can be so heavy that this is widely seen as the one of the most time-consuming and stressful aspects of running an aid programme. And this is just the basic reporting task, focused on meeting contractual obligations, which doesn't involve assessment or judgement. Inter-national agencies complain about donors but pass on exactly the same restric-tions and rigidities to their national counterparts.

For many organizations, the information gathered as part of such processes is of little use for programming. Meeting donor needs means not meeting your own needs. This leads to compensating systems, and parallel systems—one for funders, one for managers. Despite many in the aid sector complaining of an onerous reporting burden, those requesting the information do not seem to be satisfied. Many government and institutional donors complain about the lack of data and evidence about aid performance, but they are also clear about the lack of political engagement with the complexities of performance: 'We say we want evaluation, but we don't, we want results, results we can put in our glossy reports, we can put on our websites, that we can give to ministers to present in Parliament.'[79]

This has led to some peculiar contradictions in the accountability landscape. Ian Smillie, development researcher and author, and Henny Helmich of the OECD development centre, had this to say in 1996:

> ...having promised too much to the donor and the public, however, [aid agencies are] trapped in a vicious circle. If funding is to be maintained or is to increase in the face of growing demands, success is essential. Often it is exaggerated, while failures are downplayed or concealed. Important lessons are not learned, and only the successes – often highly situational – are disseminated, usually in a public relations format.[80]

This situation has evidently not improved in the past decade and a half, despite the growth and acceleration of aid accountability. Much the same trap has continued to be identified in assessments of a report published ten years after Smillie and Helmich:

> Transparency about programmes and operations, as opposed to basic financial accounts, is not easy when there is pressure ... to demonstrate results in short timeframes, and in quantitative form ... organisations are locked in a dilemma of knowing that a lack of transparency is both damaging the sector, and contradictory to its values. At the same time they fear that a greater openness about performance by the sector will lead to a negative reaction by the media, donors, and the general public.[81]

One major cross-sector survey of managers found that organizations rated themselves most highly on 'donor care' but lowest on transparency and accountability, begging the question as to exactly what kind of donor care they are extending.[82]

Participation, ownership, and rights-based approaches are supposed to cut across these three areas. There are participatory evaluations, codes for recipient and partner accountability and ownership, and a focus on results. But, despite technically sophisticated efforts to develop tools, techniques, and frameworks, the majority of accountability solutions and practices retain an upward focus to donors. As Doug Reeler of the Community Development Research Association, Cape Town, notes, 'In an age where the "speak" is becoming more participatory, bottom-up or horizontal there is, paradoxically, a strengthening of pressure for upward, vertical accountability to the North.'[83] This finding is not consistent with the current rhetoric of aid accountability, which emphasizes ownership as a keystone for effectiveness. Even rights-based approaches, in many ways a reaction against the growth of the service delivery orientation in aid delivery, have been implemented in largely instrumental and mechanical ways, and are facing challenges from donors who pay lip service to the idea while pursuing a more technocratic approach.[84] This focuses on information flowing 'up' the system, leaving little space for downward accountability to partners or recipients. In fact, there is little genuine downward accountability anywhere in the aid system, and attempts to set up such mechanisms are usually greeted with obfuscation and disagreement.

These problems are embedded in a set of wider institutional and political issues: the coexistence of multiple objectives for aid, which makes it unclear what should be measured; high rates of aid staff turnover, which means staff focus on tasks that are more likely to be rewarded in the short term; institutional pressure to raise and spend aid funds; and the problem of the presence of many actors—donors, agencies, and recipients—which means the whole enterprise is riven with collective action problems and spiralling transaction costs.

While aid agencies have not conformed fully to these pressures, nor have they resisted explicitly. Instead, the shift has been evolutionary, involving 'push-me-pull-you interactions',[85] and a strange middle ground between co-option and standing up for values. Eyben has described how this works in practice, suggesting that aid agencies are characterized by two cultures: a dominant formal culture, which matches the accountability needs and fulfils information demands with largely ritualized accounts based on the 'silver bullets' of log-frames, RBM, RCT, and so on; and an invisible, informal culture, which gets on with managing the messy realties, uncertainties, and relationships central to effective aid work. As the staff in one major multilateral body have argued, concepts such as efficiency are tied to an agenda which 'is not a noble one . . . it is almost the duty of staff to resist such change'.[86] Perhaps more reasonable and practical is the point made by Deborah Eade, development author and editor, of the vital need to draw a line between 'transparent compromise and blind co-option'.[87]

Overall, the success of accountability and effectiveness mechanisms has been partial at best.

Despite the understanding that no system can be all things to all people, aid accountability mechanisms are increasingly being used to serve multiple purposes for multiple stakeholders—for example both control and learning, both innovation and improvement, both furthering national ownership and international reforms. These various intentions may not be compatible and mean that, in trying to do too much, nothing is achieved.

The 'quiet revolution in accountability' has failed to increase trust in the aid sector. As a result of the lack of clarity and understanding that surrounds this area of work, and the often vehement disagreements, there is a growing sense of distrust in the very mechanisms established to further trust and build confidence. On the contrary, agencies are often accused of being a 'cosy club'. Despite the growth in accountability frameworks, tools, and approaches, a 2007 opinion poll by AccountAbility and Edelman on the state of accountability in relation to 'global public goods' issues, such as poverty, disease, and climate change, found many respondents 'very unsure about who should be held to account—let alone how—for the things that matter most to them'.[88]

Perhaps the most challenging issue, and one consistent with the findings of earlier chapters, is the fact that accountability systems have reinforced certain framings of the world that are simply not consistent with reality. There is a widespread assumption that 'Accountability is a one-to-one relationship between agents with fixed specific roles and identities, brokered by formal mechanisms.'[89] However, while 'this simple static model . . . is a useful starting point, it is unlikely to provide the tools needed to understand the real-world complexities of accountability'.[90]

However, this relative failure does not appear to have been a major cause for concern for those promoting such approaches. Public management scholars Geert Bouckaert and John Halligan dryly note that RBM and accompanying top-down control processes have not themselves needed results to be championed and implemented with ever-greater enthusiasm.[91] Similarly, another highly critical review of performance approaches in UN agencies has glumly acknowledged that the RBM agenda is here to stay. Politics clearly plays a part in the resilience of these approaches.

So too, perhaps, does the lack of other options for generating the hoped-for levels of trust: 'We are resolute in our commitment to measures of performance; we are trained in them, we feel comfortable with them, and in some cases, we are legally obligated to them. But our commitment is mostly the result of knowing no alternative.'[92]

CHAPTER 6

Part 1 Epilogue—The Trouble with Physics Envy

Santarem, a popular tourist destination in the western Amazon region, is known as the Brazilian Caribbean for its stunning freshwater beaches. A quirky stop on the circuit is about a hundred kilometres away: a deserted town of fabricated buildings, overgrown roads, and road signs in English.

This is Fordlandia, created in the 1920s in an effort to bring American-style industrial development to the Brazilian rainforest. Using the approaches he had perfected on the factory floor, Henry Ford spent millions attempting to create the world's largest rubber production facility. This was not just a business venture, but an attempt at agricultural development. As Ford put it at the time: 'We are not going to South America to make money but to help develop that wonderful and fertile land . . . We'll train the Brazilians and they'll work as well as any others.'[1]

The main reason most readers won't have heard about Fordlandia is simple: it was an abject failure. A British journalist who accompanied Ford on a visit in the 1930s concluded that 'In a long history of tropical agriculture, never has such a vast scheme been entered in such a lavish manner, and with so little to show for the money.'[2]

What is most interesting about Fordlandia are the assumptions that shaped the effort. Local knowledge was ignored—whether of culture, of soil, or even of rubber plants. Astonishingly, no botanists were employed on the project—the wealth of knowledge about rubber trees and how they could be cultivated was simply brushed aside. Ford attempted to bring in US culture, requiring workers to live in American-style houses, not drink alcohol, attend weekly line dancing, eat hamburgers, and, of course, drive Model T cars on newly laid and tarmacked roads. In effect, the project was an attempt to import 50 square miles of American life into the Amazonian rainforest. As well as numerous violent reprisals, Fordlandia lost the company US$240 million in today's prices over 17 years.

The remnants of Fordlandia today stand as a monument to exported hubris: squatted by locals and a surreal stop on tours. But it could well be argued that the philosophy behind it is still alive and well—thriving, even—in development and humanitarian agencies. It is apparent in the way aid agencies learn, strategize, organize, and analyse their work.

Of course, borrowing philosophies from other settings is not problematic in and of itself: it is just when these approaches are applied without due—or indeed, any—consideration of the context in which they are being used that they become dangerous. To the extent that aid agencies do this, they can be seen as implementing Fordlandia on a global scale.

This is no mere coincidence. One can trace the intellectual history of the modern aid mentality, as Andrew Natsios, former chief of USAID, did in his justly famous paper:[3] Henry Ford passed the torch of scientific management to Robert McNamara, who oversaw the ultimate failure of such approaches in the jungles of Vietnam, and then brought the approaches firmly into development mainstream during his ten years at the World Bank. They have remained there ever since. As Andrew Natsios put it, with some understatement, 'McNamara's rigid, measurement-based approach has not translated well to the complex and dynamic field of development.'[4]

Whether for political expediency or administrative convenience, or because of conceptual small-mindedness, there is a pervasive and longstanding bias towards treating the world as a simple, predictable place in which aid can be delivered, as if on a global conveyor belt, to bring about positive changes. To reiterate Dichter's critique, 'We act as if development is a construction, a matter of planning and engineering.'[5]

One of the too-few reviews of aid from a historical perspective rather depressingly concludes, 'There has been...one constant in the history of aid, namely that the development objectives of aid programmes have been distorted by the use of aid for donor...advantage.'[6] Slavery is conveniently combated through colonial expansion. Food is delivered because of lobbying by subsidized domestic farmers, and to open up markets. Technology is provided to ease the way to lucrative service contracts. Knowledge is imported through expensive consultants. The tsunami provides a fantastic opportunity to show the world we care. Non-governmental organizations become force multipliers. Aid donors are net *recipients* of resources from developing countries. And so on.

Drawing on the four chapters that comprise Part 1 of this book, we could surmise there is another candidate for a constant feature in the history of aid: that aid agencies have carried forward a series of scripts, of cognitive templates often unthinkingly enacted, thereby reproducing similar patterns of behaviour across different domains of their work.[7] This has resulted in powerful tendencies towards simplification and standardization, which are apparent across four integral elements of the aid business model I have looked at here. Although this is not the intention of aid agencies, what this adds up to is a system where simplicity is repeatedly, consistently, and damagingly chosen over relevance and appropriateness.

This 'conventional model' summarizes the chapters in Part 1, and illustrates how modern aid work is underpinned by a set of implicit and explicit assumptions and biases about the systems and problems they work on, about human agency, about the structure of social relations, and about the nature of change (see Figure 6.1).

I am not arguing that these assumptions underpin all of aid, or that these are the only ideas that specific aid agency staff have in their minds as they go about their work, or indeed that any given individual believes firmly in this model. What I am arguing is more subtle than that: that the aid system, through a variety of means, uses these as its underlying theories-in-action, as an implicit framework of beliefs. These assumptions about systems and problems, about human agency, social structures, and the nature of change—rather than any stated ambition or approach—are embedded in the DNA of the system.

They quietly but pervasively shape how the system learns, makes decisions, develops strategies, organizes internally, relates to actors externally, and assesses itself. This is of course not always a bad thing: there may be lots of situations where *exactly* these assumptions are *exactly* what are needed. The trouble is that much of development and humanitarian work simply doesn't match these assumptions.

A fascinating example of how this mentality gets reinforced comes from the autobiography of one of the genuine development leaders of the past few decades, Mark Malloch-Brown, former head of the UN Development Programme and subsequently Chief of Staff to Kofi Annan. He described the

	Conventional aid thinking
Systems and problems	Systems and problems are closed, static, linear systems; reductionist—parts would reveal the whole
Human agency	Individuals use rational deduction; behaviour and action can be specified from top-down; perfect knowledge of future outcomes is possible
Social structures	Formal relations between actors are most important; relationships are ahistorical and can be designed; actors can be treated as independent and atomized
The nature of change	Change is direct result of actions; proportional, additive and predictable; can hold things constant; simple cause and effect

Figure 6.1 Conventional approaches in aid

Source: Adapted by the author from Beinhocker, E.D. (2006), *Origin of Wealth: Evolution, Complexity, and the Radical Remaking of Economics* (Cambridge, MA: Harvard Business School).

mood around the time of the Millennium Development Goals (MDGs) as one of incremental ambition that stressed the affordability of change. When he commissioned Jeffrey Sachs to lead a team to calculate the cost of meeting the MDGs, the answer was broken up into 'the ten dollar malaria bed net... or the increasingly low cost of AIDS treatment. Many of these interventions... would cost each of us less than we spend at Starbucks in a week.'[8] Given the need to provide simple, low cost, incremental solutions, the problems faced by aid are presented as closed, controllable, 'tame', to be solved in isolation from others. This quote could have been tailor-made for the MDG cost accounting process: 'We solve tame problems through analytical methods—breaking things down into parts, fixing components, assessing the probabilit[ies].'[9]

The problems that arise as a result of such biases are largely predictable and observable in settings outside of the aid world. Leading British economist Paul Ormerod argues that this is a feature of many public policy systems: 'The world is seen as a machine, admittedly a complicated one, but one which can be controlled with the right pressure on this button, just the right amount of pull on that lever... everything can be quantified and targets can be not only set but also achieved, thanks to the cleverness of experts.'[10]

As Andy Lo of the Massachusetts Institute of Technology puts it, 'Physical systems are inherently simpler and more stable than economic systems... hence deduction based on a few fundamental postulates is likely to be more successful in the former case than in the latter.'[11] Or, in a rather less understated way, 'Physics envy can be bad for your wealth.'[12] In a blog post on the MIT work, Bill Easterly argued that aid agencies were even more wedded to physics than financiers.[13] On the basis of Part 1, there are numerous strong cases for concurring with this. As Erik Reinert suggests, 'the abstract standard theory as it is used today toward the poor countries of the world assumes a world without variation or diversity, without friction, conflicts or trade-offs'[14] and that these assumptions exist 'because... proponents [of development] chose to model society based on the physics of the 1880s'.[15]

Eighteenth- and nineteenth-century intellectual traditions in physical sciences—with their focus on predictability, linearity, and equilibrium—have been extended far beyond their original remit, and are today deeply embedded within a variety of professions and sectors across the world. 'These, in turn, became interlocked with institutions, policy frameworks and professional practices—in natural resources policy, public health and economic planning— persisting even as the science moved on.'[16]

These conventions are not aberrations or one-offs but part of the rules of the game of foreign aid. They amount to a widespread bias towards seeing interconnected, dynamic, open problems as simple, closed problems that can be planned for, controlled, and measured. This leads to a whole host of ill-advised actions and mistakes: 'While it may seem appealing in the short run, attempting to tame a wicked problem will always fail in the long run. The problem will simply reassert itself, perhaps in a different guise, as if nothing had been done; or worse, the tame solution will exacerbate the problem.'[17] This leads to systemic failures of understanding, of design, and of function.[18] As one senior donor manager put it (as much out of frustration as anything else, I suspect), 'I want a simple problem with a simple solution so I can measure value for money.'[19]

As a result, the underlying problems addressed by aid don't go away. In many cases, they are simply sustained over time, or even get worse. In following this model, aid agencies are simply creating more problems for themselves in the future. Instead of working themselves out of a job—the stated aim of many social entities once upon a time—they are doing the exact opposite.

Development failures lead to humanitarian crises, and back again. Malaria interventions lead to the evolution of resistance. Agricultural development leads to the crashing of local systems and the collapse of hoped-for productivity. And still the best practices get rolled out, in an unstoppable global conveyor belt.

In the face of widespread institutional inertia, the resilient cookie cutters and travelling orthodoxies of foreign aid, the strategy most commonly found is to simply give up on trying to find a good solution. Just follow orders, do your job, and try not to get in trouble. Let the system do what it will. If these ideas are so powerful and pervasive, what alternative do we have but to blindly follow them? Of course, as Reinert has darkly suggested, 'The system made me do it' may no longer be an acceptable excuse.[20]

This is precisely what Natsios bemoans in his assessment of the US Agency for International Development, by some way the largest bilateral donor operating today: 'The command and control system for foreign aid programs is out of control ... and has become a major impediment to aligning good development practice with the best research on good development theory.'[21]

To take an example described by David Waltner-Toews, if we want to deal with Avian flu in developing countries, we could import a North American model as best practice. This would involve industrialization of livestock and caging chickens (to say nothing of swans, pigeons, ducks, geese, and other semi-domesticated fowl) en masse. But such imported solutions also deny history: 'The particular approach worked where it did because of a whole range of factors, urbanisation, transportation, technology, the availability of fossil fuels, the prevailing political and social context. You can't just drop this into sub-Saharan Africa and then get annoyed when it doesn't work or have impact.'[22]

The sad reality is that exactly this kind of thing happens every day in the aid system—what Alex Evans has called 'institutional mono-cropping'.[23] Lant Pritchett and Michael Woolcock have termed the practice of transferring principles of bureaucratic rationality from place to place 'skipping straight to Weber', following the famous principles of an 'ideal bureaucracy' developed by German sociologist Max Weber in the 1920s.[24]

Such efforts are based on mythologies that conceal the fact that, in reality, institutional solutions 'emerge from an internal historical process of trial and error and a political struggle'.[25] Pritchett and Woolcock go as far as to argue that a fundamental part of 'the aid solution' is to hide this enduring and widespread truth. This 'hiding' takes place in all aid, from the smallest to the largest of interventions.

That this pattern should be a consistent one, from the innovations in vaccine delivery to attempts to stabilize entire regions, is remarkable. There is a 'resolute optimism' about the favoured approaches and solutions for development and humanitarian work, enabling aid agencies to 'overplay impact', 'blur the normative and the actual', and enact a 'denial of history'.[26]

Despite the grander claims of some recent movements, development and humanitarian work is not a knowledge industry—except in the most idealistic interpretation. It is an export industry, and an exceptionally blunt, supply-oriented one at that. It gathers up poverty, vulnerability, and suffering from the South, packages them for sale in the West, and exports off-the-peg solutions back in relentless waves of best-practicitis. In contrast with the classic evolutionary formulation of 'variation, selection, amplification', numerous aid efforts are scaled up despite repeated failures, while many potential successes are killed off before they have a chance to flourish. While such behaviours may be appropriate in highly stable sectors, the world has changed and with it the context for aid has become transformed almost beyond recognition. To put it simply: aid agencies are dealing with a world for which their learning, strategic, organizational, and performance frameworks were not designed.

As is now being witnessed on a daily basis, complexity and unpredictability pose serious challenges to researchers, practitioners, and policymakers in virtually every area of human endeavour. The global financial crisis, the food price crisis, climate change, urbanization, the increasing scarcity of the fuels on which industrialization has been built, population growth: these are all challenges that mean rethinking our way of analysing and acting in the world[27].

The influential Millennium Project[28] has developed and regularly updates a comprehensive list of 'global challenges'. Their most recent results—drawing on a participatory process involving over 2,500 experts in 40 countries—are reproduced in Box 6.1.

Box 6.1. 15 global challenges facing humanity[29]

1. How can sustainable development be achieved for all while addressing global climate change?

2. How can everyone have sufficient clean water without conflict?

3. How can population growth and resources be brought into balance?

4. How can genuine democracy emerge from authoritarian regimes?

5. How can policymaking be made more sensitive to global long-term perspectives?

6. How can the global convergence of information and communications technologies work for everyone?

7. How can ethical market economies be encouraged to help reduce the gap between rich and poor?

8. How can the threat of new and re-emerging diseases and immune micro-organisms be reduced?

9. How can the capacity to decide be improved as the nature of work and institutions change?

10. How can shared values and new security strategies reduce ethnic conflicts, terrorism, and the use of weapons of mass destruction?

11. How can the changing status of women help improve the human condition?

12. How can transnational organized crime networks be stopped from becoming more powerful and sophisticated global enterprises?

13. How can growing energy demands be met safely and efficiently?

14. How can scientific and technological breakthroughs be accelerated to improve the human condition?

15. How can ethical considerations become more routinely incorporated into global decisions?

The Millennium Project Report's reflections on these challenges are instructive: they 'show that the world is increasingly interdependent and intricate, requiring improved abilities for collaborative decision making across institutional, political, and cultural boundaries'. By worrying contrast, 'many of the world's decision making processes are inefficient, slow, and ill informed.'[30]

It is hard not to think of aid when one reads this. But the problem is not unique to aid. Serious mistakes in all walks of public and political life are increasingly being attributed to a bias towards seeing interconnected, messy problems as simple, closed, controllable ones. With the interconnectedness that globalization has wrought, this bias has become ubiquitous, transcending sectors and geographies with ease. Business, government, and charities are all facing a whole host of challenges and their philosophies and ways of working are uniquely 'unfit for purpose'. What can be said with reasonable confidence is that this bias finds its most startling manifestations in those sectors, like aid, that are most firmly wedded to the principles of nineteenth-century physics and the associated 'world as machine' mentality.

This reiterates the point made throughout Part 1: aid agencies are increasingly dealing with a world for which their learning, strategic, performance, and organizational frameworks were not designed.

So how can we better understand the complex problems so commonly found in development and humanitarian efforts? And how can we navigate such problems better in the context of aid? These questions shape Parts 2 and 3 of the book.

PART 2
The way the world works

CHAPTER 7

Introducing Complexity

'I think the next century will be the century of complexity.'

Stephen Hawking (2000).

The World's Future Depends On It

In 1948, *Scientific American* published a paper called 'Science and Complexity' by Warren Weaver,[1] Chief Scientist of the Rockefeller Foundation. Frequently referred to as the 'founding text of complexity theory',[2] at six pages it may also be the shortest piece to have inspired a new movement in scientific thinking.

That Weaver himself is not better known today is one of the peculiar anomalies of history. A brilliant mathematician, he helped kick-start the field of molecular biology and financed the first mass-production of penicillin in the UK, spearheaded new approaches to cancer research, and oversaw ground-breaking agricultural research programmes. He was decorated by the USA, Canada, the UK, and France for his wartime efforts in bringing a scientific understanding to bear on aircraft detection, military organization, and communication. He wrote a text that contributed to the formation of the RAND Corporation and co-authored the first book on information theory, which many see as having ushered in the digital age. He was a pioneer of machine translation, now being used in everything from Internet search engines to global weather reports. He personally mentored and supported almost 20 future Nobel Laureates.[3]

Weaver's aim in his paper was straightforward but ambitious: he wanted to examine how science had dealt with different kinds of problems. His credentials for doing so were clearly well established.

Until the nineteenth century, Weaver argued, physical sciences had been concerned largely with problems of two or three variables, with relationships characterized as 'organized simplicity'. This kind of thinking led to some major scientific advances and innovations and also had a major influence on business and government: from it we have the telephone, the radio, the automobile, the airplane, the phonograph, moving pictures, the turbine, the diesel engine, and the modern hydroelectric power plant; it also brought new levels of public health, corporate law, and sanitation, and much more besides.

Recounting this list makes me think of the 'What did the Romans ever do for us?' scene in Monty Python's 'Life of Brian'. Impressive as these achievements were, however, there were clearly many issues nineteenth-century physics and its assumptions couldn't help with—as Henry Ford discovered in the rainforests of Brazil.

According to Weaver, starting in the nineteenth century, and more so in the twentieth, science had 'leapt' to the other extreme, becoming obsessed with the behaviour of systems, with many variables interacting randomly. Problems included the motion of atoms, the thermodynamics of gases, the death rate in a human population, and the growth of the universe. While it was difficult to pinpoint the behaviour and history of a specific element in such systems, scientists could, through the application of statistics, explain average behaviours across systems, thereby generating insights. The tools used to understand and predict the motion of gases were, by and large, the same ones insurance companies used to assess risks across a population and thereby turn a profit. These were not simple problems, but instead were problems of 'disorganized complexity'.

The greatest challenge, Weaver argued, was that a large number of real-world problems could not be put into either category. He gave the following examples from economics: 'On what does the price of wheat depend? ...How can currency be wisely and effectively stabilized? To what extent is it safe to depend on the free interplay of such economic forces as supply and demand? To what extent must systems of economic control be employed to prevent the wide swings from prosperity to depression?'[4]

He went on to explain that these problems involve

> ...dealing simultaneously with a *sizable number of factors which are interrelated into an organic whole*. They are all...problems of *organized complexity* [that] involve analyzing systems...with their parts in close interrelation [and] These problems – and a wide range of similar problems in the biological, medical, psychological, economic, and political sciences – are just too complicated to yield to the old nineteenth-century techniques which were so dramatically successful on two-, three-, or four-variable problems of simplicity (emphasis in the original).[5]

These new problems, moreover, cannot be handled with the statistical techniques so effective in describing average behaviour in problems of disorganized complexity.

Dealing with the ubiquitous problems of *organized complexity* demanded a 'third great advance' in scientific thinking, to follow in the wake of two earlier successes: addressing *organized simplicity* through the application of classical mechanics and thermodynamics and addressing *disorganized complexity* through statistical mechanics and probability theory.

Weaver provided suggestions for the way forward on his third great advance. 'Out of the wickedness of war'[6] came two distinct possibilities. The first was the use of what he (rather touchingly, from the perspective of a modern reader) called 'electronic computing devices', which 'will make it possible to deal with problems which previously were too complicated, and, more importantly, they will justify and inspire the development of new methods of analysis applicable to these new problems of organized complexity'.[7]

The second was what he called a 'mixed team' approach to operations analysis, with teams pooling their resources and focusing all their different insights on common problems to tackle certain problems of organized complexity, in spite of modern tendencies towards intense scientific specialization.

The third advance would need to be greater in scope and ambition than either of these considerable achievements, but Weaver justified it on the basis of an urgent need to progress the organized complexity agenda precisely because *'the future of the world depends on many of them'*[8] (emphasis added).

The Unfinished 'Third Great Advance'

Weaver's work on complexity had an influence across the intellectual, political, and ideological spectrum. The 1948 article and variants thereupon directly inspired some of the most influential thinkers of the second half of the twentieth century. Take three of the most prominent. Frederick Hayek cited Weaver's work and used the idea of organized complexity to provide intellectual support to his notion of 'spontaneous order' of free markets. As he famously put it in his Nobel acceptance speech in 1974,

> [Mankind] will have to learn that in this, as in all other fields where *essential complexity of an organized kind prevails*, he cannot acquire the full knowledge which would make mastery of the events possible. He will therefore have to use what knowledge he can achieve, not to shape the results as the craftsman shapes his handiwork, but rather to cultivate a growth by providing the appropriate environment, in the manner in which the gardener does this for his plants (emphasis added).[9]

Another Nobel Laureate, Herb Simon, made an immeasurable contribution to our current understanding of organized complexity. This included a number of ideas about the limits of rationality and decision making, and the architecture of complex systems, all concepts we look at later in Part 2. Simon's seminal work on complex systems, a 1962 paper on the 'The Architecture of Complexity',[10] was peer reviewed by Weaver. One subsequent account described him as 'the inheritor of the legacy of Warren Weaver'.[11]

Last but not least, Jane Jacobs, one of the great social thinkers of the twentieth century, was also influenced by Weaver's thinking on organized complexity. Jacobs used Weaver's ideas to conclude her influential book, *Death and Life of Great American Cities*, the final chapter of which—entitled 'The Kind of Problem a City Is'—contained the following passage about urban life in New York:

> It is a complex order. Its essence is intricacy of sidewalk use, bringing with it a constant succession of eyes. This order is all composed of movement and change, and although it is life, not art, we may fancifully call it the art form of the city and liken it to the dance – not to a simple-minded precision dance with everyone kicking up at the same time, twirling in unison and bowing off en masse, but to an intricate ballet in which the individual dancers and ensembles all have distinctive parts which miraculously reinforce each other and compose an orderly whole. The ballet of the good city sidewalk never repeats itself from place to place, and in any one place is always replete with new improvisations.[12]

Through the work of these three and others who followed in Weaver's visionary wake, ideas of organized complexity have been brought to bear on many different fields. However, despite inspiring significant intellectuals and shaping a new movement in scientific thinking, it seems fair to say that the third great advance is yet to fully come to fruition. Some have suggested that Weaver was simply too optimistic about the future of complexity research, and that 60 years had been not nearly long enough for the kind of transformation he outlined.[13] As James Crutchfield and Karoline Wiesner of the Santa Fe Institute External Faculty put it in 2010,

> In hindsight, however, we know that Weaver glimpsed only the beginning of a new era of science – what came to be known as the science of complex systems. Perhaps Weaver, who died in 1978, would be disappointed to learn that, at the start of the second decade of the 21st century, the exact nature of organized complexity remains the subject of ongoing debate.[14]

Others argue that he may have actually been too prescient, and that it took the best part of 50 years for the rest of the world to catch up with him on the need for such an advance. Another argument is a pragmatic one: when I asked him why the creation of the Santa Fe Institute occurred almost 40 years after the publication of Weaver's piece, Murray Gell-Mann suggested that only in the 1980s did computing become cheap enough to enable a critical mass of researchers to work on such issues.[15] While all of these explanations are interesting, they don't to my mind get to the heart of the issue. I would argue that the means by which we deal with problems are no longer shaped solely by the concerns of scientific advancement—if indeed they ever were.

At the heart of the scientific method is the need to apply the relevant approach to the relevant problem. And yet this entails numerous challenges in science. We know much more about this thanks to the work of Thomas Kuhn in the 1960s, who famously argued that, 'Under normal conditions the research scientist is not an innovator but a solver of puzzles, and the puzzles upon which he concentrates are just those which he believes can be both stated and solved within the existing scientific tradition.'[16]

As biologist Robert L. Dorit explains in a 2011 *American Scientist* piece, at one stage in his field there was a naïve hope in the biological sciences that complexity was 'a by-product of incomplete understanding, an illusion that would fall away once the parts were fully understood'.[17] In effect, this means problems of organized complexity will eventually reveal themselves to be amenable to simple or random system approaches. But the reality is that, despite successes in organized simplicity and disorganized complexity, many of the problems Weaver identified—in biology and more widely—have not been resolved adequately or even partially.

Just as Weaver warned, much is being missed, especially given the globalized nature of the world today. We focus on the immediate at the expense of the important: 'Scientists know the mathematics which describe individual air and water molecules [but] building up a picture of what billions of them will do when mixed together around the globe is extremely complicated.'[18] Biologists have 'captured the intricacies of photosynthesis, and yet the consequences of rising carbon-dioxide levels for the future of the rain forests remain frustratingly hazy'.[19] Medical researchers have explained the cellular evolution of disease but remain baffled by patterns of epidemics or the onset of cancer. Economists have unpacked microeconomic behaviours and macroeconomic trends, but cannot adequately explain—let alone predict—stock market crashes, financial crises, or economic growth. Anthropologists explain kinship structures in remote Amazonian tribes but are at a loss as to how many modern cultures form and interact. Development economists can evaluate microenterprise development, but not fully explain the dynamics of national innovation and growth. Humanitarians can deal with individual child malnutrition but find understanding overall national- or even community-level food security much harder to achieve.

Dorit's description is especially pertinent: 'We are ... the king's horses and the king's men: We stare at the pieces, knowing what Humpty should look like, but unable to put him together again.'[20]

The limitations of science have their equivalents in public policy. Institutions, government bodies, and social movements have invested time, resources, and reputations in particular approaches to the problems they face. Thousands of careers depend on sustaining certain ways of looking at the world. The third great advance has faced not just an intellectual challenge but also a cognitive, social, and political one.

The worlds of business and policy are still wedded to a mentality that sees their diverse systems as a series of wind-up clocks that can be predicted and managed with precision and accuracy.[21] Many failures in public policy, business, and civil society can be attributed to the application of inappropriate assumptions and principles to problems. 'Some of the greatest mistakes are made when dealing with a complex mess, by not seeing its dimensions in their entirety, carving off a part, and dealing with this part as if it were a complicated problem, and then solving it as if it were a simple puzzle, all the while ignoring the linkages and connections to other dimensions of the mess.'[22]

This gives us a useful way of framing the arguments and evidence in the first part of this book. As I argued in the epilogue of Part 1, there is in foreign aid a widespread bias towards seeing interconnected, dynamic, open problems as simple, closed problems that can be planned for, controlled, and measured.

One could argue that resistance to Weaver's third great advance is apparent in some startling ways within foreign aid agencies. In the way aid agencies learn, strategize, organize, and perform, there is a clear manifestation of an obsession with organized simplicity, with the ideas and principles of nineteenth-century physical sciences. Aid organizations frequently—perhaps consistently—misunderstand and misrepresent the systems they seek to change and the problems with which they deal. In Weaver's terms, effectively, aid agencies have spent the best part of 60 years treating problems of organized complexity as if they were problems of organized simplicity or disorganized complexity.[23]

Ironically, Weaver even anticipated the foreign aid movement. He closed his exploration of the possibilities of organized complexity with the following words: 'What sacrifices of present self-interest will most effectively contribute to a stable, decent and peaceful world?'[24] One wonders whether, if Truman or one of his aides had read—and understood—Weaver's article and the implications for knowledge transfer, the Point 4 speech given the following year would have sounded any different. I would suggest that it would and—further—that this would have had serious implications for the aid system that emerged and grew.

Despite being a work in progress, many today agree with Weaver that these ideas are of vital importance for 'the future of the world'. Eminent British scientist Alan Wilson has argued that *all* of the grand challenges we face today are in fact problems of organized complexity.[25] He remarked when I shared the list on grand challenges in Chapter 6 with him: 'It's a no-brainer that these are all problems of organized complexity—this is precisely because of the interconnected nature of our globalized world.'[26]

It is not just scientists who have come to this conclusion. Jocelyn Bourgon, former Head of the Canadian International Development Agency and Chief of the Canadian civil service, directs a project called New Synthesis, which brings together senior decision makers at the highest level of four major governments.

As she said to me, 'There have always been complex issues to deal with in public policy. But the argument I would make is that there are increasing numbers of them today... Today, the lot of a public policy actor is to deal with increasing numbers of these complex, interconnected, dynamic issues.'[27]

This gives us a simple choice: do we continue to struggle to answer questions with an intellectual toolkit not designed with such problems in mind, and a policy and operational toolkit that lags even further behind? Or do we keep calm and carry on, applying a 'divide and conquer' approach that is unhelpful, in many cases increasingly meaningless, and in the extreme downright damaging? Nobel Laureate Ilya Prirogine put it well, describing the sciences of complexity: 'We are witnessing the emergence of a science that is no longer limited to simplified, idealised situations but rather one which confronts the complexity of the world and allows human creativity to flourish.'[28]

I believe that dealing with our current realities in ways that allow human creativity to flourish means facing up to some of the fundamental questions Weaver posed. This means identifying what is known about problems of organized complexity, what alternatives they provide to current ways of thinking, and the ways in which these alternatives have informed thinking and action. This is what I want to do in the rest of Part 2.

Unguarded Borders, Diverse Inhabitants

One exponent of complex systems, an archaeologist, recently made a lovely analogy, likening complexity science to a new scientific continent, whose 'borders are unguarded and... inhabitants diverse'.[29] In the Complexity Territories— for which Warren Weaver is surely a Columbus-like character—we can today spot representatives of every discipline and background, from archaeologists to zoologists. Biologists and ecologists wander around with a strange sense of déjà vu, while physicists ponder the firmament. Mathematicians and computer scientists occupy the high ground, and occasionally suffer from altitude sickness. Sociologists roam about, some aimlessly, almost at random, others taking small steps with great care. A few anthropologists are having a great time. Economists are slowly growing in number, many with a rather guilty, furtive air to them.

The inhabitants of and visitors to the Complexity Territories are not limited to scientists and researchers. There is a small, growing band of senior civil servants, civil society activists, and community development specialists. Journalists are semi-regular visitors—alternatively 'breezily hyped and unjustly derogatory'[30] about the work they observe. Opportunistic consultants have set up stalls selling dubious maps for the unwary traveller: 'Here be complexity'. Politicians are noticeable by their absence, at least during terms in office.

The Complexity Territories aren't full of wandering nomads. There are numerous institutional hubs of activity and energy, with new ones forming all the time. Significant organizations include the Michigan University Complexity Group, the New England Complex Systems Institute, the Complexity Group, and the Institute for New Economic Thinking at the London School of Economics, Warwick, Southampton, and Oxford. Programmes are also springing up in middle-income countries: Indonesia, the Philippines, and China. Arguably, all of these institutes have been connected by two remarkable organizations, which have been at the forefront of the third great advance over the past few decades.

The International Institute for Applied Analysis (IIASA) in Austria is perhaps the most important research institute that readers will have never have heard of. Formed by US President Lyndon Johnson and Soviet Premier Alexei Kosygin, IIASA represents one of the world's most remarkable examples of scientific cooperation, formed against the backdrop of the Cold War. Since 1972, it has brought together scientists from around the world to work on problems of common concern, to establish a focus for 'international cooperation in solving problems arising from social, economic, technological, and environmental change' and to 'develop and formalize systems analysis and the sciences contributing to it, and promote the use of analytical techniques needed to evaluate and address complex problems'.[31] Weaver's thinking seems to have been important—as an early handbook put it, 'Tackling problems using a systems approach implies not being reductionist and examining [different] problem situations using the ideas of "organized complexity."'[32] In just one example of its work, IIASA was responsible for the formal model of greenhouse gases that underpinned the 1989 Montreal Accord. This is still the only scientific assessment accepted by all parties to an international treaty—in itself a considerable achievement of navigating organized complexity. It is also the focus of ongoing study at the institute.

Around 9,000 miles away from IIASA as a very tired crow flies is the Santa Fe Institute (SFI) in New Mexico. Since 1984, SFI has been the best-known centre in the world for the study of complex adaptive systems, for the past 25 years posing significant challenges to the simple, predictable model of the world. In its mission and its execution, SFI is perhaps the most direct and prominent flag-bearer of Weaver's third great advance. In correspondence, George Cowan, whose brainchild SFI was, told me he was well aware of Weaver's ideas, and that it was safe to assume they influenced his thinking in setting up the institute.

So, if we were to marshal the knowledge and ideas of all these inhabitants, tourists, and drifters in the Complexity Territories, what would we learn? There is much debate about exactly what the value of complexity is—and much of this starts within the Territories, among its dispersed communities. But many long-term inhabitants and regular visitors have at least three shared beliefs.

First is the notion that reductionist approaches to problems—what might be termed the 'divide and conquer' approach—are no longer sufficient to tackle a number of real-world problems, described as problems of organized complexity or, in more recent parlance, complex adaptive systems. These are 'systems with a large number of mutually interacting parts, often open to their environment, [which] self-organize their internal structure and their dynamics with novel and sometimes surprising macroscopic ("emergent") properties'.[33]

Such problems are interconnected and interdependent, characterized by processes of feedback that shape how the system in question behaves. Influential approaches such as 'effective complexity', developed by Murray Gell-Mann and Seth Lloyd, suggesting that complexity is highest between total order and total randomness, owe an intellectual debt to Weaver.[34] Numerous other frameworks, developed by social scientists and organizational development consultants, also borrow—consciously or unconsciously—from Weaver's thinking.

Second is the idea that there are alternative ways of understanding complex problems by using a diverse set of tools, techniques, and approaches. The properties of complex adaptive systems are the focus of intensive study: a global network of researchers and practitioners is obsessed with better understanding how to approach, analyse, explain, and navigate problems of organized complexity. Through this, a dizzying set of concepts, principles, propositions, and ideas have emerged from different disciplines and have slowly coalesced. As Wikipedia—itself often described as a complex adaptive system—suggests: 'Complexity science is not a single theory—it encompasses more than one theoretical framework and is highly interdisciplinary, seeking the answers to some fundamental questions about living, adaptable, changeable systems.'[35] Thanks to complex systems researchers, we now know more about the interactions that underlie organized complexity, and the *systemic* phenomena that emerge from them. We know more about how *adaptive* agents—from humans to amoebae, and anything in between—behave in systems of organized complexity, and about the structure of such systems—the *relational* patterns and effects. And we know more about how such systems change over time—their *dynamics and trajectories*.[36]

Figure 7.1 extends the summary table in the previous chapter, and compares the traditional assumptions of aid to those emerging from complex systems research. It builds on work I did with Harry Jones, John Young, and Toussaint Reba while at the Overseas Development Institute. The overall approach owes a debt to Eric Beinhocker's similar framing of the difference between conventional and new approaches to economics. It is an initial attempt to outline the kind of alternative intellectual framework that might be needed in aid if we are to move away from the entrenched and often implicit theories that guide it.

The ideas set out in the right-hand column represent a set of alternatives to the conventional, mainstream approach that can be observed in foreign aid. These alternative assumptions and ways of thinking, which underpin Parts 2

	Conventional aid thinking	New Perspectives
Systems and problems	Systems and problems are closed, static, linear systems; reductionist—parts would reveal the whole	Systems are open, dynamic, non-linear systems far from equilibrium. Macro patterns emerge from micro behaviours and interactions
Human agency	Individuals use rational deduction; behaviour and action can be specified from top-down; perfect knowledge of future outcomes is possible	Heterogeneous agents that mix deductive/inductive decisions, are subject to errors and biases, and which learn, adapt, self-organize and co-evolve over time
Social structures	Formal relations between actors are most important; relationships are ahistorical and can be designed; actors can be treated as independent and atomized	Interpersonal relationships and interactions matter in form of culture, ties, values, beliefs, peers. Informal matters, relationships are path dependent and historical
The nature of change	Change is direct result of actions; proportional, additive and predictable; can hold things constant; simple cause and effect	Change is non-linear, unpredictable, with phase transitions

Figure 7.1 Conventional and alternative approaches

Source: Adapted by the author from Beinhocker, E.D. (2006), *Origin of Wealth: Evolution, Complexity, and the Radical Remaking of Economics* (Cambridge, MA: Harvard Business School).

and 3 of the book, draw heavily on the ideas of complex adaptive systems researchers. As Beinhocker argues in the context of economics as a whole, this kind of framing can help set out broad parameters for an aid system that 'has much greater fidelity to the real world'.[37]

Many leading thinkers believe that modern complex systems research has a lot to say about the world we live in, characterized as it is by interconnectedness, networks, emergence, non-linear change, phase transitions and tipping points, intelligent actors adapting to their circumstances and each other, and systems that evolve together over time. The sheer breadth of coverage of the ideas means that few fields of scientific endeavour have not been examined, in one way or another. The potential significance of these ideas is also noteworthy: 'There is a growing recognition that progress in most of these disciplines, in many of the pressing issues for our future welfare as well as for the management of our everyday life, will need such a systemic complex system and multidisciplinary approach.'[38]

This is not to imply these ideas are in and of themselves the sole answer to the ailments of aid: far from it. What they do provide, as I hope to show, is a more realistic and relevant set of assumptions for aid than nineteenth-century physics: assumptions and ideas that could usefully inform the way aid thinks and works. They provide empirically sound alternatives, and these are vital for effecting change. The Nobel Laureate Herb Simon argued that science and politics shared some common ground in this regard. In politics, it wasn't possible to defeat a new piece of legislation, a new measure, or a candidate simply by pointing to flaws and problems—usually an alternative must be offered. Similarly, in science, 'once a theory is well entrenched, it will survive many assaults of empirical evidence that purports to refute it unless an alternative theory, consistent with the evidence, stands ready to replace it'.[39]

Third, and an important qualification of the previous points, is the idea that complexity research—and, as argued earlier, Weaver's third great advance—is a work-in-progress.[40] Murray Gell-Mann suggests the biggest drawback to complexity science advancing is that people think it already exists.[41] Alan Wilson concurs, suggesting that, in complexity terms, we are akin to biology *before* the discovery of DNA.[42] Eric Beinhocker has described complexity as a 'revolution still very much in progress'.[43] However, hopes are high—perhaps to the point of being counterproductive. Melanie Mitchell, one of the most eloquent writers on complex systems today, argues that 'complex systems scientists have at times made promises and set up expectations that are hard for any young science to fulfill'.[44]

In the following chapters, I show how ideas of complex adaptive systems have been used to understand and navigate problems of organized complexity, such as climate change, food price spikes, conflicts, the financial crisis, the Arab Spring, power grids, forest fires, terrorist networks, urbanization, and ethnic segregation. I have deliberately chosen applications that lie outside the conventional understanding of development and humanitarian work, although all of these issues profoundly, and increasingly, shape the context within which the aid industry operates.

I must reiterate the qualification made above: for many of these areas, the insights are still emerging even if the findings are promising and the implications tantalizing. But, as science writer Philip Ball argued in a speech entitled '2011 and All That',[45] the nature of the problems we face today, and the blatantly inadequate nature of existing models, means we would be crazy not to even try to see what relevance there is. The next chapters are a compendium of lessons from those scientists, policymakers, and practitioners who have done just this. Part 3 will look at how these same ideas have been applied in aid contexts, to rethink and re-envision learning, strategies, relationships, and performance.

CHAPTER 8

More Than, and Different To, The Parts

'By a complex system I mean one made up of a number of parts that interact in a non-simple way. In such systems, the whole is more than the sum of the parts . . . given the properties of the parts and the laws of their interaction, it is not a trivial matter to infer the properties of the whole.'

Herbert Simon.[1]

Boiling Down Complexity

In Brighton, England, where I live, there is a now sadly infrequent display of natural beauty. At dusk, hundreds of starlings gradually flock together from every direction, engaging in an intricate, and often breath-taking, dance as the sun sets. Shapes emerge—a heart, a whale, a face. The birds coalesce into tight groups, flowing into an invisible, swaying centre of gravity, and then seem to burst free, shooting away in random directions until some unseen forces start to pull them back together. The rusty, skeletal remains of the once-magnificent West Pier provide an anchor point for the ever-expanding flock's performance, as a surreal, Dali-esque stage.

Although few watchers would think of it in this way, this avian performance is an important manifestation of a complex system. The birds are an example of how complex systems are characterized by *emergent properties* not present in their component parts. The natural world is replete with other examples of emergence—from the formations of crystals, clouds, and hurricanes to the social behaviour of insects and mammals. All of these are, as Weaver put it, systems of organized complexity.

Certain experts in complexity research argue that their object of study, like pornography, is something 'you know when you see it'. In the absence of the more obvious responses that might be associated with the latter phenomenon, a key question is whether complex systems have any distinguishing features and characteristics by means of which they might be recognized. The current work-in-progress answer is: yes, we think so. Researchers are trying to figure out the various fingerprints, signatures, and trails of complexity.[2] This may make them sound like forensic detectives, which in some cases is not too far from the truth.

Although emergence is one of these signatures, it is not limited to such systems. Think about the examples Weaver gave of disorganized complexity—the behaviour of gases, the mortality of humans as analysed by insurance companies, the evolution of galaxies. These are also emergent properties. However, there is a difference between this and the behaviour of the birds, which provides us with one of the fundamental tenets of complexity research.

In systems of organized simplicity or disorganized complexity, the emergent properties of the overall system can be reduced to averages that give a pretty good indication of the overall behaviour of the system. The classic example is rolling a six-sided dice. The average expected value of a roll, given that any number is as likely as any other, is 1 + 2 + 3 + 4 + 5 + 6 divided by 6: 3.5. With enough rolls, the average value will slowly tend towards this number—this average is an emergent property of the system. The variations around this average—all the actual numbers that might occur—will eventually cancel each other out.

By the same token, in other systems the conditions for random sampling—many independent events—will tend towards a normal distribution. So, if we look at, say, the heights of toddlers in a particular playgroup, we can anticipate that they will cluster around a central average. This is because the events are independent of each other; and large diversions from the norm—whether towards the right or the left—cancel each other out. It might be argued that 'average thinking' dominates social and economic policy, and—at the risk of seeming mischievous—this may well be in both senses of the word 'average'.

However, in complex systems, like the Brighton starlings, markets, or societies, the average tells us little about the overall properties of the system. As British software innovator Phil Teare puts it, 'When we try to boil down complex systems, the key finding is that they *cannot* be boiled down.'[3] Instead of averages, we see 'unexpected statistical regularities'.[4] A good example of this is the skewed nature of wealth distribution, as famously demonstrated by Wilfred Pareto in nineteenth-century Italy, which arises from the fact that 'Interactions reinforce one another... result[ing] in behaviour that is very different from the norm.'[5]

To better explain these emergent features, scientists have been exploring the interactions that characterize complex systems. The feedback processes between the different components—be they ants, birds, car drivers, or market traders—can be modelled using computers to better understand the principles that guide behaviours, which make more explicit the interactions that occur in complex systems, namely, the gathering, processing, and enacting of information by adaptive agents based on their interactions with each other and with their environment. By developing models of populations of agents operating under different 'rule sets', complexity scientists have been able to simulate emergence 'as it happens'.

One of the most famous examples of such emergence is the application developed by Craig Reynolds.[6] Reynolds programmed a series of computerized birds—or 'boids'—to move across a screen following three simple rules: separation of flight path from that of local boids, alignment of steering with average direction of the local flock, and cohesion to move towards the average position of the local flock. Using these rules, the boids display a dance that is recognizably that of a flock of birds. Similarly, the Australian cathedral termite is famous for creating mounds that reach to well over ten feet simply by following simple rules of behaviour.

The boids take us rather neatly to the notion of the 'edge of chaos'. Some have described this as a good candidate for a general law of complexity, but it is currently better described as a widely used hypothesis about such systems. In keeping with the work-in-progress nature of the whole complex systems field, there are numerous interpretations of the concept, many of which I will touch on in this part of the book.

The first interpretation is what some have called the 'grand incarnation' of the idea: the edge of chaos is seen as descriptive of, and helps define, the fundamental behaviour of complex systems. According to this thinking, some systems are ordered, some are chaotic, and complex phenomena are at the interface of the two, 'at the edge of chaos'. A common comparison is with water, which exists in three phases: solid, gas, and a liquid state in between. The liquid state of water is at the 'edge of chaos'. According to Kauffman, 'All complex adaptive systems in the biosphere—from single cells to economies... evolve to a natural state between order and chaos, a grand compromise between structure and surprise.'[7]

Chris Langton, a computer scientist at the Santa Fe Institute, did the work that provided the intellectual ballast for this widely cited idea.[8] He showed that, for a given computational system—such as the boids—there is an 'edge' where the overall ability of the system to learn and adapt is highest, that is, where it is maximally effective. Stuart Kauffman has described the nature of emergence at this stage: 'Here, at this poised state, small and large avalanches of coevolutionary change propagate through the system as a consequence of the small, best choices of the actors themselves, competing and cooperating to survive.'[9]

Both qualitatively and instinctively, many have found this a compelling argument. There is some evidence of this notion in biology and physics but, despite this, the 'grand' form is not without its detractors—as one well-known complexity researcher at SFI said to me: 'Edge of chaos? God, Ben, I can feel my spleen start to rupture.'[10] Less dramatically, there are those who argue that, while the edge of chaos idea *is* a useful one, there is no evidence that any given complex system will naturally move toward such an edge. Furthermore, prevailing conditions will determine whether being at the edge is actually a good, desirable thing.

Think back to the water analogy: it would be hard to say that the liquid state is inherently any better or worse than any other state that water takes. However, even critics of the idea agree that there is emerging support for more subtle interpretations of the edge of chaos idea. I will explore these in subsequent chapters.

Because of our ability to process and communicate information in highly sophisticated ways, some of the most interesting forms of emergence are those that arise in systems and structures created by humans. A great example of emergence in human systems is a traffic jam.[11] Each driver is trying to get somewhere, and is doing so in accordance with, or in defiance of, a range of rules. These rules can be legal (e.g. the speed limit, driving on a particular side of the road), behavioural (e.g. slowing down to let someone come into your lane), and social (as evidenced by 'Baby on board' stickers or 'Kill your speed, not a child' road signs). A traffic jam is a distinct phenomenon that emerges from all of these individual behaviours in the face of rules, and can sometimes work in very different ways to the individual behaviours from which it arises: 'Gridlock on a highway...can travel backward for no apparent reason, even as the cars are moving forward.'[12] Human emergence can also be the hardest model to analyse, precisely because the rules that govern our behaviour are so dynamic, diverse, and dense.

But such emergent phenomena are not just 'academic curiosities' or interesting analogies; they also 'lie beneath the surface of many mysteries in the business world'. Consider these three: 'How prices are set in a free market...Why...do employee bonuses and other incentives sometimes lead to reduced productivity? Why do some products—like collapsible scooters—generate tremendous buzz, seemingly out of nowhere, while others languish, despite their multimillion-dollar marketing campaigns?'[13] Ideas of emergence have helped improve our understanding of a whole range of social processes and phenomena, from collective action to diffusion of cultural norms to sharing of information. Standing ovations and crowd surges are also emergent phenomena. Emergence has been found to play a major role in how social structures arise and evolve, in the development of markets, how personalities form, the rise of cities.[14] Social movements too are characterized as emergent phenomena: one of the most remarkable examples of recent times is the 2008 US presidential campaign led by Barack Obama. The victory resulted from not just the charismatic and remarkable candidate, but also the efforts of a distributed and emergent movement that owed much to Obama's roots as a community organizer, and to the civil rights movements of an earlier generation. In a Massachusetts Institute of Technology lecture, Marshall Ganz, veteran of the 1960s civil rights movement and key activist in the Obama election campaign, described 'emergent leadership' as 'taking responsibility to enable others to achieve purpose in the face of uncertainty'.[15] Leaders 'recruit, motivate and develop others, constructing a community around common interests, and building capacity from within the community'.[16] Importantly, this massive movement couldn't rely on rigid hierarchies or command-and-control structures but was instead focused on enabling many thousands of volunteers to become 'adaptive in the face of uncertainty'.[17] The 'distributed leadership' of the Obama 2008 campaign resonates with a number of ideas of emergence I described above, from standing ovation surges to flocking birds.

Once your senses have become aware of the connections between these diverse phenomena, it becomes hard to let them go. Whenever I see images of social insects like ants or bees I cannot help but think of our own messy urban equivalents: not for nothing do we so often talk about the 'buzz' of the city. Apart from humans and our tiny—and similarly successful—companions, it is hard to think of a species where so many individuals and groups work cooperatively in such close confines.

One of the fundamental challenges of emergent phenomena—and arguably the reason they remain poorly recognized and acknowledged—is that they are 'devilishly difficult to analyze, let alone predict'.[18] Emergence, as Herb Simon pointed out, arises from the interactions of individual units in an unpredictable and often inexplicable manner. Conventional analytical tools are unable to pick up emergence precisely because 'Such approaches work from the top down... whereas [emergence] is formed from the bottom up, starting with the local interactions of the different independent agents.'[19] This raises an abiding issue: how can we engage with complexity and emergence without paralyzing analysis and decision making with the unpredictable and inexplicable?

One area where this is already starting to happen through the use of complex systems tools is urban planning and management. It could easily be argued that the most remarkable form of emergence happening in the world today is that of urbanization: unplanned, unpredictable, but transforming the surface of the planet and leading to what some have described as the most profound change in human–environment interactions since the rise of agriculture.

Until quite recently, individual cities had not been studied as emergent phenomena. There have been a number of very suggestive works—including those of Jacobs and Geddes. Jacobs famously closed her bestselling book with a chapter on 'What Kind of Problem a City Is', and cited extensively from Weaver: 'Cities happen to be problems in organised complexity, like the life sciences.'[20] Jacobs used these ideas to argue that the mechanistic way cities were being conceived and planned was counter to this organized complexity, with the result that post-war urban planning was killing the diversity and energy of cities. More recent assessments of planned capital cities have come to the same conclusion: 'The development they are supposed to promote never comes, the images they are intended to project soon lose relevance, and, centuries later, they retain an artificial air which continues to hamper their growth.'[21]

Four decades after Jacobs, John Holland of SFI made the following rather poetic observation: 'Buyers, sellers, administrations, streets... are always changing, so that a city's coherence is somehow imposed on a perpetual flux of people and structures. Like the standing wave in front of a rock in a fast-moving stream, a city is a pattern in time. No constituent remains in place but the city persists.'[22]

Modern complex systems researchers have focused increasing attention on how cities grow and evolve, 'to how the patterns that we observe with respect to urban form and structure emerge from a myriad of decisions from the bottom-up'.[23] According to Michael Batty of University College London, this underpins everything from how cities form to how people interact in urban settings.[24]

Batty has developed and tested various models of urban change, both at the macro level of urban formation and shorter-term processes like large-scale urban gatherings. Both are of particular interest to scholars of complexity. He has found five key factors that shape the formation of cities:

- Randomness—that certain decisions about cities are just down to random noise.

- Historical accident—that cities grow from the decisions of founders whose decisions are a result of historical expedience.

- Physical determinism—that cities emerge in certain places where it is possible to build streets and buildings, given existing technologies.

- Natural advantage—that natural resources exist in a form that can be exploited for economic gain.

- Comparative advantage—that certain sites may be relatively advantageous to each other.

Urban development, as Batty sees it, is a combination of these drivers, interacting in different and highly localized ways. The generator of urban development and growth is the feedback playing out between them. We might see positive feedback between factors—for example where natural and comparative advantage has played off historical accidents to generate thriving urban centres and vast perilous slums. We can see negative feedback, where change is dampened over time, in areas of urban decline. Batty's modelling of the growth of cities successfully demonstrates what we understand from boids and ants: that this most exemplary of human achievements—the city—is the result of 'local rules based on limited interaction with immediate neighbours [that] can effectively generate global order of a kind that cannot be anticipated'.[25] Batty sees the notion of the edge of chaos as being important for cities as they can be shown to exist 'at the edge of chaos—illustrating a resilience whose signature is the ability to respond to changes'.[26]

Another example of emergent urban phenomena relates to large group events in cities. The annual Notting Hill Carnival in the UK attracts well over 2 million people into a small district of the city. The challenges of crowd management and safety provision are considerable. I vividly remember one year when the crowd surge down one street was so sudden and spontaneous that I was lifted about ten centimetres off the ground and carried a metre or two in a single human body mass before my feet touched the ground again.

Batty's model examines the 40 entry points into the area and simulates attendees' decisions about which stations to use and routes to employ into and through the carnival. He shows that small, localized decisions can have profound effects on levels of crowding and the dynamics of movement. The crowd surge I experienced was an example of flocking—positive feedback that arises between carnival goers taking paths shaped by the noises they hear and the feedback from other walkers leading to aggregate movements. The mass movement could easily have turned into a tragedy, but there were enough points for dispersal—where negative feedback processes could dampen the build-up of the crowd.

This approach enabled Helbing and Mukerji to counteract some commonly held assumptions of the crowd crush disaster that took place at the Love Parade festival in Duisberg, Germany, in 2010.[27] Accepted wisdom is that mass panic causes such tragedies. By looking at available data—especially videos published by eyewitnesses—and ordering chronologically, they were able to see that most attendees were far from being wild with mass panic. Instead, what happened was that, as the crowd built up, they slowly got closer and closer until they were all touching each other. At this point of connectivity, all intentional and unintentional movements are transmitted through the crowd. For example, if someone stumbles, this can lead to a domino effect. The surge I experienced in the Notting Hill crowd was clearly this kind of 'crowd quake'. According to Helbing and Mukerji, the cause of crowd disasters is less to do with psychology and more to do with physics: 'The problem with the concept of "mass panic" is that it blames the crowd for the tragedy. This makes it difficult to draw the right conclusions...i.e. to learn the lessons [on] how to make future mass events safer.'[28] For example, fear of triggering panic is often used as a justification for not informing crowds about the threat of crushing. However, this is not the way to go: the lack of communication heightened the disaster.

This example of swarming is just as tangible as that of the Brighton starlings: 'These switches of collective motion...emerge spontaneously even as individual predispositions are altered only incrementally.'[29] The key to understanding this, according to Batty, is understanding the interactions and feedbacks that make up the crowd movement, to think about crowd dynamics as an emergent phenomena, and to plan safety and crowd management with this in mind.

The way forward, if the lessons from urban contexts are more widely applicable, is to engage with the diverse and emergent reality of such complex systems: to understand better the way cities are structured and how they evolve. Accepting this has meant rethinking the very nature of policy and practice: 'Planning, rather than being imposed from the top, becomes interwoven with its outcome in an iterative and interactive manner.'[30] Urban planners have even developed a whole school of thinking to address this, with growing attention to 'wicked problems', which builds on Jacobs' work on cities as problems of organized complexity.

Through the idea of emergence, which is so intrinsic to how complex systems behave and change over time, and given the work of growing numbers of researchers examining and modelling such systems, we are increasingly able to 'know complexity when we see it'.

However, the way feedback plays out is highly dependent on context, and incredibly hard to prepare for and capitalize on in advance. Getting better clarity on the nature of feedback itself is therefore essential. Some very useful lessons are emerging from a network of scientists in an ongoing effort to understand complex and emergent global interactions and their implications for how we live and work. Rather ironically, the story starts on a day that for many still typifies the unpredictability of globalization.

The Science of Global Feedback

On 11 September 2001, Jack Liu, then a visiting scholar at Stanford University, was in Washington, DC attending a conference. He found himself stranded in the chaos of the events of that fateful day. One of his conference participants was a fellow Stanford academic called Paul Ehrlich. Having found one of the last rental cars available in the city, the two academics set off for a road trip. During the two-day journey, they identified a mutual fascination in the interactions and feedbacks that occur between humans and their environment. In particular, they were interested in coupled human and natural systems where 'people and nature interact reciprocally and form complex feedback loops'.[31] Ehrlich had made his name in this area: his infamous 1968 book *The Population Bomb*[32] argued that the rapidly growing human population could not be fed effectively and was placing tremendous strain on all aspects of the environment.

Liu had just completed a study on the use of forests for firewood by local residents in Sichuan province of China, and the impact of government policies on these behaviours. Communities were using bamboo, the staple food and habitat of the panda bear, as fuel, which had led to massive negative impacts for the animals. Recognizing this, the government offered households subsidies to prevent excessive use of forest resources. However, these became an incentive for household fragmentation: there was a growth in the number of households and a consequent *increase* in resource use, even though fuel use per household did decrease. Liu subsequently worked with Ehrlich and others on a broader study building on this work, the first ever to examine at a global level the feedback between household numbers and resource use,[33] although of course many had focused on population size and resource use.

The study showed that household splintering and growth was a global trend, and a more important determinant of resource use and environmental impact than total population size. Worryingly, this growth was found to be fastest in 'biodiversity hotspots'—areas rich in species and threatened by human activities. This and subsequent work led Liu to develop the idea of 'telecoupling', a concept that originated in atmospheric science work on tele-connections (with 'tele' meaning 'at a distance'), used to describe linkages between different and geographically separate weather systems. By close ana-logy, telecoupling has been defined as 'the correlation between specific planet-ary processes in one region of the world to distant and seemingly unconnected regions elsewhere'.[34] This is the cutting edge of the study of feedback and its role in global emergence.

Today, Liu runs an international network to strengthen links between scientists working on problems encountered in 'coupled human and natural systems'.[35] A key ambition of the network is to build on the findings of individual projects to generate insights that are more broadly significant. In an interview, he rationalized the project as follows:

> At the global level right now, because everything is connected, there are feedbacks. The feedbacks are very important. Usually people don't pay attention to them because they take time to emerge and people usually don't see them easily. Because of the time lags, people usually see things in short term. Sometimes the impacts might not be seen until years or even decades later. It's not just a linear relationship. It's a very complex system we are looking at.[36]

In a *Science* synthesis study,[37] senior advisors to the network together with the coordinators examined six separate case studies of interdisciplinary programmes that aimed to further understand coupled human and natural systems. These were spread across five continents, in developed and developing countries, and in rural, peri-urban, and urban areas, and covered a variety of problems. They included the China example as well as deforestation in Kenya, agriculture in Altamira in Spain, and tourism in Wisconsin in the USA. All the case studies 'explicitly address[ed] complex interactions and feedback between human and natural systems'.[38]

All of the projects were context specific and longitudinal, enabling an understanding of how dynamics feedbacks were established and changed over time. The teams concerned found that many factors influenced such processes, including government policies, markets, and context. For example, rural and urban feedback processes were very different, shaped by 'urban forms, infrastructure, location and consumption preferences of diverse households'.[39] A key finding is that *surprise* was a routine affair and should be expected.

The review teams' conclusions are significant for this chapter: that the studies 'offered unique interdisciplinary insights into complexit[y]'[40] specifically by providing greater understanding of the scope and dynamics of feedback. All the study teams were interdisciplinary, employing both ecological and social science tools, following the 'mixed teams' approaches to organized complexity that Warren Weaver had called for 60 years earlier. They also made the most of latest technologies, including mobile phone monitoring and satellite imagery.

Liu has no shortage of ambition for this new area of work: 'This is a beginning of exploring the new frontier. Telecoupling is about connecting both human and natural systems across boundaries. There are new and faster ways of connecting the whole planet—from big events like earthquakes and floods to tourism, trade, migration, pollution, climate change, flows of information and financial capital, and invasion of animal and plant species.'[41] He sees telecoupling as a way to 'express one of the often-overwhelming consequences of globalization—the way an event or phenomenon in one corner of the world can have an impact far away'.[42]

Telecoupling can be seen as an attempt to use the concept of feedback to better understand the million-to-one chance global connections described in the opening chapter of this book. It is especially evident in the area of human health. Although there are subsets of all populations that are more vulnerable to emerging diseases, telecoupling often works to connect these populations in surprising ways. The emergence in 2003 of Severe Acute Respiratory Syndrome in Southeast Asia demonstrates the mechanism for telecoupling of vulnerabilities, leading to sudden and dynamic changes in vulnerability.

Ecologist Ruth DeFries has worked on the role of telecoupling in deforestation patterns. She shows that, while once it would have been shaped predominately by local factors, today it is the demands of urbanization and globalization that drive deforestation:

> In the case of the Brazilian Amazon, much of that demand is for soy that goes to feed farm animals, which then goes to meet the growing demand for meat around the world. The price of soy and the rate of deforestation in the Amazon were linked – and since growing affluence in developing Asia is pushing up demand for food, that was bad news for the rainforest. It's a bit like the old butterfly effect – only instead of a butterfly flapping its wings in Peking and creating a storm in America, it's an urban laborer in Beijing buying a bowl of pork noodles and causing a tree to be cut down in Brazil.[43]

But the same telecoupling that can lead to ecological destruction can also have a beneficial effect. DeFries noted that, when the link between soy and deforestation became clear, consumers and activists in developed nations put pressure on the soy industry to stop planting on clear-cut land. In 2006, the soy industry imposed a moratorium on recently deforested land, which has been extremely successful in reducing the rate of forest loss. Instead, soy growers used degraded land—and still were able to produce enough to meet demand.[44] So, while the telecoupling caused the problem, it also led directly to its solution. And therein lies perhaps the biggest challenge: 'There are good sides and bad sides to telecoupling. We have challenges and we have opportunities.'[45]

Much the same point is made repeatedly about urbanization, population growth, and numerous other global challenges. The undoubted poster child of telecoupling, however, is climate change. Because of the growing scientific consensus around this and its potential effects, understanding our interactions with the earth's atmosphere may well be the single most important area for understanding feedback and its implications in complex systems.

Emergent Monsters

With a few notable exceptions, people living in developed countries tend to view climate change as a far-off possibility, even though it is already having a drastic impact on millions of lives and livelihoods around the world. Thanks to the emergent phenomenon of temperature rises resulting from the carbon dependence of modern industrial societies, our earth system is pushing back in a variety of ways. Dunes are encroaching on villages, rivers are bulging and bursting their beds, typhoons and cyclones are battering coastlines, and rainfall patterns are being disrupted. And, of course, ice is disappearing.

Uusaqqak Qujaukitsoq, from northern Greenland, is a man of many parts. He is a political activist who cut his teeth campaigning against US military base policies on his Cold War-contested homeland. He is a firm advocate of local approaches to natural resource and conservation issues and a former Greenland parliamentary member. But first and foremost, like generations of Inuit leaders who preceded him, he is a hunter, and this gives him a unique perspective on the world around him. In 2007, when he was asked to give evidence to the Arctic Climate Impact Assessment on how climate change was affecting indigenous populations, he spoke primarily as a hunter. Here's an extract from what he shared with the assessment team:

> Change has been so dramatic that during the coldest month of the year...our outermost hunting grounds were not covered by sea ice because of shifting wind conditions and sea currents...We used to go hunting to these areas... only four or five years ago...The ice is generally thinner and is slower to form off the smaller forelands...Glaciers are very notably receding...our place names are no longer consistent with the appearance of the land.[46]

While the changing weather patterns of Greenland are clearly unique, Qujaukitsoq's message echoes among all those communities facing the advance party of global climate change. His sobering summary is much more widely relevant: 'It is hard to tell what impact such conditions will have...it is hard to say what can be done about these conditions.'[47]

Although global warming sceptics' favourite argument is that climate scientists are scaremongering alarmists, the rather more worrying reality is that the latter group often seems to err on the side of caution. Some argue, for example, that there is an inherent conservatism in the way the Intergovernmental Panel on Climate Change (IPCC) develops its reports, which lead to it consistently underestimating the rates and impacts of climate change.[48] For example, in 2001, the IPCC stated that hurricanes could well grow in frequency and intensity by the twenty-second century. By 2007, the report stated that this was already happening.

But it is also becoming clear that the different ways *we think about and analyse the phenomena of climate change* also play a significant role in such underestimations. Paleoclimatologist and climate risk specialist Stephan Harrison has suggested that many of the uncertainties and ambiguities 'come down to the tension between reductionist and emergent responses to highly complex, coupled and dynamic systems'.[49] The climate is 'an extremely complex coupled system involving significant physical processes for the atmosphere, ocean, and land over a wide range of spatial scales from millimeters to thousands of kilometers and time scales from minutes to decades or centuries'.[50] There are many variables interacting, albeit not in a random fashion. Because of the numbers and interactions of the feedbacks involved, unpredictability and uncertainty are inherent features of climate change. Cause and effect are not related in simple fashion. There are no obvious controls for the overall system; indeed, there is often no 'outside' position in which would-be controllers can place themselves. Little wonder that Neil Johnson describes global warming as an emergent monster[51]—the climate is an emblematic version of the class of 'organized complexity' problems described by Warren Weaver.

Policymakers are picking up this reality more slowly than scientists. In a recent interview, Leon Fuerth—former National Security Advisor to Al Gore—elaborated on this point from a complex systems perspective. He described climate change as an 'interaction between human beings as a highly organised industrial civilisation, and the world's physics and chemistry'.[52] He argued that complex systems thinking has 'developed a path that runs towards human events...especially the interaction between physical and human events, which makes it very interesting for the purpose of dealing with...climate change'.[53] These ideas are slowly being picked up in policy circles.

One key idea from complex systems thinking is the idea of feedback. In its simplest form, feedback is a way of describing a process by which a 'change in an element or relationship...alters others, which in turn affect the original one'.[54]

The IPCC describes climate feedback as 'an interaction mechanism between processes in the climate system ... when the result of an initial process triggers changes in a second process that in turn influences the initial one. A positive feedback intensifies the original process, and a negative feedback reduces it.'[55] There are also many different climate feedbacks. Positive feedback processes include emissions from degraded soils and permafrost, dying forests, melting ice, ocean evaporation, and desertification.[56] Scientists have also identified some dampening negative feedback processes. The last IPCC report found that 'Complex feedbacks and interactions occur on all scales from local to global'.[57]

One of the leading worldwide authorities on climate change is James Hansen, Chief Climate Scientist at NASA. His famous testimony to the US Congress in 1988 is credited as the first serious wake-up call on global warming. In a 2008 article, co-authored by several other leading climate scientists, Hansen concluded that feedback effects were the *predominate* reason the earth's climate displayed such high levels of sensitivity to global 'forcing' factors such as the rise in CO_2 concentrations.[58] The implications drawn by the Center for Strategic and International Studies Age of Consequences study were clear:

> The models used to project future warming either omit or do not account for uncertainty in potentially important positive feedbacks that could amplify warming [and] recent observations of climate system responses to warming (e.g., changes in global ice cover, sea level rise, tropical storm activity) suggest that IPCC models underestimate the responsiveness of some aspects of the climate system to a given amount of warming.[59]

In other words, feedbacks are one of the 'main sources of uncertainty in our attempts to predict the effects of global environmental change'.[60]

In general, regardless of the system, feedbacks can be amplifying or dampening, slow or fast, predictable or unpredictable. Markets rely on emergent feedback processes, as Adam Smith noted with his famous 'invisible hand' hypothesis. When Alan Greenspan moved markets, he was participating in, and shaped by, a staggeringly complex system of feedback processes and dynamics. Social systems rely on feedback: the Arab Spring would not have happened without it. It underpins widely used analogies to describe patterns in our social lives: think of vicious and virtuous circles, 'coming full circle', 'cycles of violence' or 'snowballing', 'cascading' events.

As Jack Liu and his colleagues in CHANS-Net have found, the intricate patterns of feedback observable in our climate are echoed in many other complex human systems.

Work by the Organisation for Economic Co-operation and Development on global shocks and their increasing prevalence provides some useful analytical tools for thinking through these patterns of feedback. Tools such as dependency analysis and conceptual mapping—described in Box 8.1—are a useful starting point for engaging with complex systems.

Box 8.1 Systems thinking for water and energy distribution systems[61]

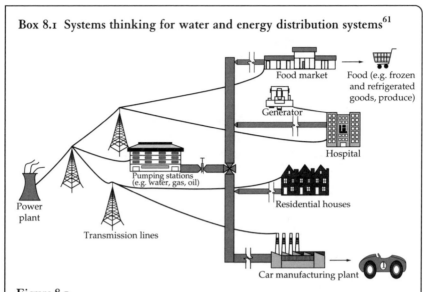

Figure 8.1

Source: Pederson, P., Dudenhoeffer, D., Hartley, S., and Permann, M. (2006), 'Critical Infrastructure Interdependency Modeling: A Survey of U.S. and International Research' (Boise, ID: Idaho National Laboratory).

A key characteristic of complex systems is for effects to propagate in ways that produce wide-ranging and long-lasting secondary consequences that may have little to do with the initial trigger.

Figure 8.1 above provides a highly simplified diagram of an electricity and water distribution system. The power plant provides electricity to a network of transmission lines. Electricity is then distributed to various customers, including businesses, residences, and public utilities—such as the water-pumping station that then supplies water to the same customers as the power plant. All these components together make up a system, as they are all linked to each other in some way—spatially or otherwise.

Now imagine the power plant has been taken offline, for any of a variety of reasons. The effects of the loss of power propagate through the system, with some components affected and others not. In many cases, the severity of the impact depends on the longevity of the event (the power outage) and the criticality of the specific components adversely affected. For example, at the food market, a loss of power might shut down cash registers, making it difficult to conduct business, and might even mean a loss of perishable goods. The hospital is equipped with a generator to provide a back-up supply of electricity, which ensures short-term disruptions do not jeopardize the lives of patients on life support for example. A sustained loss of electricity could create far more severe consequences for the system's elements. For instance, sanitation problems in houses could ensue if water-pumping stations lack sufficient back-up power. The hospital's generator requires only fuel, but a long-term electricity disruption might impede delivery systems. This could require the prioritization of medical services, resulting in backlogs.

Even in this very simple system, there are numerous variables—and interactions between them—to consider. The initial loss of electricity results in a variety of knock-on effects that follow from, but may only be loosely linked to, the initial event. In relatively simple systems—where there are only a few elements and their relationships and interconnections are well understood—it is quite easy to determine how an event will propagate. This is not the case in complex systems, because they are 'composed of many parts that interact with and adapt to each other and, in so doing, affect their own individual environments and, hence, their own futures. The combined system-level behaviour arises from the interactions of parts that are, in turn, influenced by the overall state of the system. Global patterns emerge from the autonomous but interdependent mutual adjustments of the components.'[62]

In the electricity example above, the geographic location of the various components in the system does not reveal much about their interdependencies; a conceptual map describing the linkages within the system would be useful for asking the right questions and can lead to actionable information. For example, what are the energy sources for electricity generation within the system's scope? What structures and activities rely on the electricity being provided? Where are the back-up facilities and how/where could they be set up quickly in the event of a prolonged blackout?

Figure 8.2 below is a dependency matrix for critical infrastructures that begins to answer some of these questions. It identifies the degree of dependencies between critical infrastructure sectors by ranking them as high, medium, or low. It depicts, for example, water purification as highly dependent on electrical power, whereas the oil and gas industries, although often thought of as closely linked, are not strongly dependent on one another.

(*continued*)

Box 8.1 Continued

Sector		Energy and utilities					Services		
Element		Electrical power	Water purification	Sewage treatment	Natural gas	Oil industry	Customs and immigration	Hospitals and health care	Food industry
Energy and utilities	Electrical power	–	L	N/A	N/A	M	N/A	N/A	N/A
	Water purification	H	–	N/A	N/A	M	N/A	N/A	N/A
	Sewage treatment	L	H	–		H	N/A	N/A	N/A
	Natural gas	M	N/A	N/A	–	L	N/A	N/A	N/A
	Oil industry	H	L	N/A	N/A	–	N/A	N/A	N/A
Oil industry	Customs and immigration	H	L	L	L	L	–	L	N/A
	Hospital and health care	H	H	L	H	H	M	–	H
	Food industry	H	H	H	L	M	M	L	–

Key: H = High; M = Medium; L = Low

Figure 8.2

Source: Pederson, P., Dudenhoeffer, D., Hartley, S., and Permann, M. (2006), 'Critical Infrastructure Interdependency Modeling: A Survey of U.S. and International Research' (Boise, ID: Idaho National Laboratory).

Mapping a complex system might require a combined approach which cuts across disciplines. Critical infrastructures, for example, have both important geographical and conceptual components. The geographical component provides essential information about the location of various assets as well as their spatial relationships. As some elements of critical infrastructures are physically and geospatially interdependent, this provides information about the time required to accomplish certain tasks, such as providing raw materials to manufacturing plants, delivering fuel for electricity production, or protecting the assets at risk from a natural disaster. The interdependencies in modern critical infrastructure, however, go deeper than simple physical and geospatial links. There are also informational and policy interdependencies that represent key components of the system.

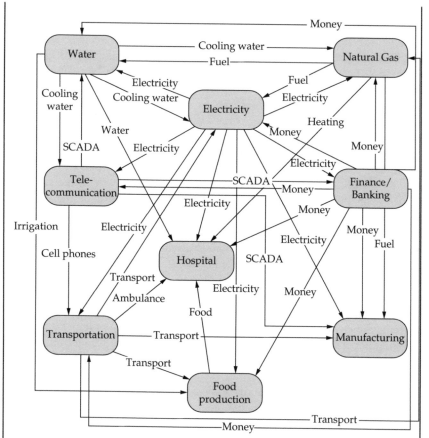

Figure 8.3

Source: Based on Zhang, W.J., Liu, X., Chai, C.L., Deters, R., Liu, D., Dyachuk, D., Tu, Y.L., and Baber, Z. (2008), 'Social Network Analysis of the Vulnerabilities of Interdependent Critical Infrastructures'. *International Journal of Critical Infrastructure* 4(3): 256–73.

Understanding these aspects of the system requires a conceptual map, such as in Figure 8.3 above. Physical interdependencies are included, such as the provision of cooling water to the production of electricity and natural gas, and the distribution of electricity to the different infrastructure sectors. The figure also shows linkages that would have been impossible to present adequately on a geographical map. For example, the finance and banking system provides cash for continuous operation in the other sectors.

The Age of Systemic Consequences

Of all the climate feedbacks currently being investigated, many would agree that the most critical are those playing out in the Arctic region. Two pieces of data illustrate this dramatically. According to the Arctic Climate Impact Assessment,[63] while global average surface temperatures rose 0.8°C between the end of the nineteenth century and the start of the twenty-first, the Arctic region warmed over twice as fast, by 1.9°C. This 'feedback within a feedback' is affecting wind patterns, disrupting Arctic flora and fauna, turning fragile ecosystems upside-down, and leaving indigenous lifestyles and economies in disarray. Separately, Arctic climate feedback processes have been shown to have a disproportionate influence on the entire global climate system. For example, the latest Arctic Monitoring and Assessment Programme[64] estimates that, driven by the sea ice temperature and other feedbacks, Arctic sea levels will rise by between 0.9 and 1.6 metres by the end of the century. This is significantly more than the IPCC's 2007 projections and will prove disastrous for low-lying areas and small island states[65]— with millions of climate refugees a very likely prospect.[66] Arctic feedbacks, and the devastating effect they might have on the rest of the world, are why the region has become known as a 'canary in a cage' for global warming: it is an early warning messenger of change processes that are underway in the whole climate system.

While not accounting for feedback can lead to significant underestimates of the severity of long-term future climate change, accounting for it effectively is still very hard to do. John Harte, an external faculty member of SFI, and his students at the Rocky Mountain Biological Laboratory in Colorado have developed an innovative experimental method for analysing likely climate feedbacks. Starting in 1988, Harte and his team chose five experimental plots of meadowland, 30 metres squared, on the western slope of the Rockies. Each plot was matched to five control plots. They then suspended overhead electric heaters over the experimental sites, and warmed the plots by an amount anticipated by global warming models. In 1990, the data gathering started. The team has been monitoring the impact of the artificial warming on soil microclimate, carbon and nitrogen fluxes, CO_2 and methane exchanges with the atmosphere, plant growth, flowering success, and species diversity. Their findings indicate a profound impact of warming on soils and vegetation, and these ecosystem effects will have a profound feedback to the climate.[67]

Separately, Harte and Torn have studied the impact of feedback processes at a global level, by examining the glacial data record. They conclude that 'there is a higher risk that we will experience more severe, not less severe, climate change than is currently forecast'.[68]

While debates continue about the relative contribution of these feedback processes to global warming, there is some emerging consensus that positive feedbacks are outweighing negative ones. Meanwhile, John Holdren, Barack

Obama's Chief Scientific Advisor, was far from alone when he suggested that 'The feedbacks in climate change can be positive or negative, but what we are seeing is more positive feedbacks than negative ones.'[69] This was supported by a group of scientists examining the potential for climate tipping points: 'Since there are countless feedbacks and thresholds, rapid amplification of potentially exploding variables becomes highly probable, and sharp, abrupt climate change should then be the norm, as appears to be suggested by the past records of climate change.'[70] This suggests, if nothing else, that the world is going to be much hotter than we imagined.

The faltering promise of timely mitigation has given way to a desperate need for immediate adaptation measures. Inuit fishers who can no longer hunt are culling dogs by the hundreds. International and local organizations are suggesting adaptation strategies, one especially ironic example being the redeployment of hunting dogs and sledges for travellers engaging in 'climate tourism'— motivated by a desire to 'see it before it goes'. This is a last-ditch attempt to locally tame what must surely be the exemplary wicked problem of our time.

Little wonder some aid agencies have started using an old humanitarian refrain in the context of climate change. Like those desperate situations where human rights are being abused, a key role of external agencies is to 'bear witness'.

Part of the reason special interests can contest climate change so easily is because it is taking place in the context of an interactive and dynamic system that crosses intellectual and policy boundaries.[71] Such change occurs at the interface between socio-economic, biological, geophysical, and atmospheric systems. The impacts of change are as multifaceted and hard to predict as the climate itself. The field of earth systems science emerged in the 1980s in response to this kind of segmentation. In 1988, the Earth System Science Committee of the NASA Advisory Council, led by Francis Bretherton, published its landmark report *Earth System Science: A Closer View.*[72] This argued that studying earth as a single complex system is essential to understanding the causes and consequences of climate change and other global environmental issues. This meant new ways of conducting science—NASA called for new technologies, research methods, and conceptual models to better express growing understandings of the complex feedback processes that play out in the dynamic earth system.

Bretherton's model, shown in Figure 8.4, divides the earth system into the physical climate system and biogeochemical cycles. These broad areas are made up of many sub-systems—the atmosphere, the hydrosphere, the biosphere, society, space, and so on. Because of feedback—because the output from one system is the input into another—none of these categories can be evaluated in isolation. With its roots in systems dynamics, the Bretherton model is supposed to equally emphasize all the various sub-systems and their interconnections, couplings, and dynamics (although in practice different disciplines have focused

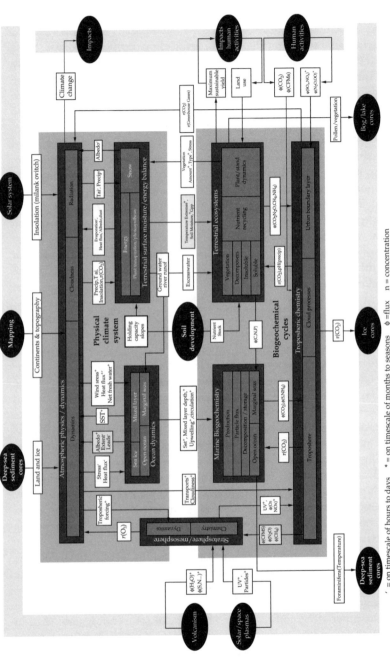

Figure 8.4 Bretherton complex model of the earth system and related processes

Source: Bretherton, F. et al. (1988), *Earth System Science: A Closer View* (Washington, DC: NASA).

on their sphere of interest).[73] This can be seen as a more elaborate and multifaceted version of the systems map I shared in Box 8.1. The dependency framework could be developed for that rather simpler system. For the earth system, such a map of dependencies and feedbacks will quickly get beyond the ability of any human being to hold in their heads, and the sheer number of dimensions would make tabular representation very difficult. Again, we can see the prophetic nature of Weaver's vision: without computers, it would be almost impossible to develop and explore realistic climate scenarios that take account of all of the possible dependencies and interrelationships.

Earth systems science today calls for a focus on the earth as a unified system shaped by interactions, feedbacks, and dynamics between different physical and biological systems. As the Bretherton model clearly indicates, a trans-disciplinary perspective is essential. What is also important is changing the way analysis is undertaken. Four international global change research programmes joined forces in the 1990s to further earth systems science, and identified certain fundamental principles, all of which echo complex systems research.

The overarching message is a sobering one: human activities—which are having an increasing and fundamental influence on earth systems in ways that go beyond any natural variability—have the potential to switch the earth system to alternative modes of operation that may prove far less hospitable to humans and other forms of life, and irreversible to boot. Some policymakers are waking up to this rather harsh reality, but still much too slowly.

Part of the challenge is that this also means acknowledging that, in systems of organized complexity, feedbacks emerge and interact in dynamic and unpredictable ways, so there are clear limits to what can be known and understood in advance.[74] Perhaps the most commonly used example of a feedback loop that occurs in systems of organized simplicity is the daily ritual many of us perform to balance the hot and cold shower taps. Theoretically, this kind of simple system is characterized by feedback that is linear, predictable, and controllable. However—as anyone who has leapt like a startled colt in the shower cubicle will know—even in such simple systems feedback isn't always all that straightforward. But within certain parameters, and given cooperative housemates, we can still probably exert some modicum of control over the feedbacks.

This is seldom the case in systems of *organized complexity*. Here, feedback processes are much harder to analyse and understand. Just as in the simple system, feedback can be positive, such that a change in a particular direction or of a particular kind leads to spontaneous reinforcing pressures that lead to escalating change in the system.[75] Feedback can also be damping, such that the change triggers forces that counteract the initial change, thereby tending to decrease change in the system. The feedback isn't generated solely by actors or forces outside the system—some forms will emerge endogenously from the dynamics of the system. In such systems, the shower taps stop being a meaningful analogy. There is no place one can stand, no tools one can employ, no perspective one can take to exert meaningful and volitional control over the whole system. Somewhere, unbeknown to the would-be controller, some hidden or unexpected feedback process will be quietly slipping a lead into the boxing glove. 'It is when the forcing grows to a point in which the positive feedback takes over that its explosive amplification produces the nonlinear effects that we see in the data. Thus, a critical threshold may in fact be the point at which the two competing feedback effects are just balanced.'[76]

Even for a relatively simple system, anticipating change and interdependencies can be challenging. For dynamic feedbacks and interactions in complex phenomena like climate change and the economy, analysis will always be, and cannot help but be, incomplete and partial. Like other emergent effects in complex systems, climate change faces 'inherent epistemological challenges';[77] because it is caused by and impacts a dizzying number of processes at so many different scales and in so many different places, there are many feedback effects that need to be understood,[78] some already at work, and others yet to kick in or even be discovered.[79] The limits of our understanding exacerbate the complexity of the system. When it comes to the climate, and a whole host of other complex systems, we are clearly talking about more than just balancing taps, of turning one effect 'up' and another 'down'.

It is interesting to note, given this, how many of the solutions to climate change seem to assume that we can 'adjust the taps' to make things better. A major challenge in understanding real-world feedback processes is precisely this tendency to look at problems not as they actually are but in line with existing intellectual and conceptual frameworks—at least until it is too late. Bill Clinton, after the 2011 Nobel Laureates Global Symposium on Sustainability, made a passionate call for 'synthesis thinking', especially on challenges like climate change. But he also soberly suggested that, during his time as president, a hostile Congress largely inhibited such thinking. Of course, one of the challenges is that many leaders are restrained by their own constituencies. As I have argued elsewhere, although many talk about the challenge of speaking truth to power, there may be just as much of a challenge getting power to speak truths.[80]

It is hard to avoid ending on this rather depressing note, at least in the context of climate change. There may well be limits to how much we can understand, and there is no dial, no tap, no dashboard that can really help us. But, more than that, so much of the climate change problem is about dealing with 'the consequences of things we already have done, and set in motion, before we were smart enough to recognise the patterns'.[81] The planetary bill is already in the post, and we are busy trying to extend our overdraft limit. This is a grim echo of Gabriel García Márquez's definition of wisdom—itself arguably a form of slow feedback—that it is precisely knowledge which comes too late to be of any use.[82]

CHAPTER 9

The Madness of Men

'I can calculate the movements of heavenly bodies, but not the madness of men.'
Isaac Newton, speaking after the crash
of the South Sea Bubble.[1]

The Great Plausibility of Intelligent Leaves

October 1962 was a month that was emblematic of the whole tumultuous decade
in which it fell. Over the course of 31 days, Uganda gained independence from
the UK and became the 110th member of the UN. There were race riots over
the admission of an African American student to Mississippi State University.
The Beatles released their first single, 'Love Me Do'. And for 13 of those 31
days, the world stared down 'the gun barrel of nuclear war'.[2]

The Cuban Missile Crisis has been described as the single most-studied
international incident of the twentieth century.[3] It started on 16 October when
the Central Intelligence Agency reported to the Oval Office that there were
ballistic weapons in Cuba trained on the USA. This was a Soviet response to the
famously botched Bay of Pigs invasion a year earlier. Six tense days later,
Kennedy publicly denounced the Soviets' actions, announced a naval blockade
of Cuba, and threatened the Soviets with a nuclear counter-attack were any
missiles to be launched. The tension was heightened by the fact that some
hawkish players on both sides were demanding military action regardless of
the consequences. After six days of public posturing and frantic behind-the-
scenes manoeuvres by both sides, Nikita Krushchev announced that the missiles
would be dismantled and brought home.

The official history usually refers to John F. Kennedy's decision-making
prowess as a key factor in the result: a master class in inspired international
crisis management, with widespread praise for his diplomatic skills. But this

view was far from the only one. Curtis LeMay, Chief of the US Air Force and notoriously disdainful of the Kennedy administration, called the peaceful resolution of the crisis 'the greatest defeat in [US] history'.[4] Defense Secretary Robert McNamara—whose work at the World Bank has proved so influential in development efforts—gave another rather different version of events: 'At the end we lucked out. It was luck that prevented nuclear war...Kennedy was rational; Khrushchev was rational; Castro was rational. Rational individuals came that close to total destruction of their societies.'[5]

That everyone involved was rational but pushed towards conflict by the 'fog of war'[6] is an intriguing interpretation. Kennedy himself observed with reference to the crisis that 'The essence of ultimate decision remains impenetrable to the observer—often, indeed, to the decider himself. There will always be the dark and tangled stretches in the decision-making process—mysterious even to those who may be most intimately involved.'[7]

Several of the most influential studies of the crisis, most notably that by Graham Allison, *The Essence of Decision*,[8] made the same point. Allison explored the nature of decision making in international relations, specifically the use of rational choice theories to describe how the Cuban Missile Crisis played out. He saw rational choice models as having saturated the political sciences, thanks to the work of policymakers such as Henry Kissinger and McNamara and economists such as Milton Friedman. Such principles suggested that states made decisions by considering all possible options and then acted rationally to maximize their utility. Allison's argument was that, in situations such as the Cuban Missile Crisis—and Pearl Harbour before it—the use of such theories was not just misguided but also downright dangerous.

A number of principles—which, along with efficient markets hypothesis, are often pointed to as the paradigmatic core of economics—underpin the 'perfectly rational' model of decision making. According to these principles, rational individuals—referred to as *Homo economicus*—are able to perfectly define a given problem; have perfect knowledge of all alternative approaches to it; can identify all relevant criteria for making a decision, including being able to accurately calibrate the future value of any present decisions and compare them systematically and consistently with all other available choices; and can finally choose the option that yields the highest value.[9] Rational choice assumes all individuals are self-interested utility maximizers with stable, well-defined preferences and perfect knowledge of the present and the future, which can be unambiguously linked to preferred outcomes. When economists and political scientists speak of rational behaviour, it usually means behaviour consistent with the above. As even its proponents admit, these assumptions are not an accurate description of real-world decision making. They do not accurately describe how most of us go about buying food in a supermarket,[10] let alone how global leaders make decisions in major crises.

Karl Weick makes an interesting analogy in a description of formal strategic approaches:

The young lieutenant of a small Hungarian detachment in the Alps sent a reconnaissance unit out into the icy wilderness. It began to snow immediately, snowed for two days, and the unit did not return. The lieutenant suffered, fearing that he had dispatched his own people to death. But the third day the unit came back. Where had they been? How had they made their way? Yes, they said, we considered ourselves lost and waited for the end. And then one of us found a map in his pocket. That calmed us down. We pitched camp, lasted out the snowstorm, and then with the map we discovered our bearings. And here we are. The lieutenant borrowed this remarkable map and had a good look at it. He discovered to his astonishment that it was not a map of the Alps but of the Pyrenees.[11]

One of the major proponents of rational choice theories, Nobel Laureate Milton Friedman, would probably have enjoyed this story. He famously dismissed the need for realism in assumptions. The key for him was whether a given theory makes 'good enough' predictions. He gave an example of his rationale with reference to how leaves grow on a tree:

> I suggest the hypothesis that the leaves are positioned as if each leaf deliber-ately sought to maximize the amount of sunlight it receives, given the position of its neighbors, as if it knew the physical laws determining the amount of sunlight that would be received in various positions and could move rapidly or instantaneously from any one position to any other desired and unoccupied position ... Despite the apparent falsity of the 'assumptions' of the hypothesis, it has *great plausibility* because of the conformity of its implications with observation (emphasis added).[12]

It is worth reflecting on the implications of this statement: it suggests that the reality of decision-making processes in the Oval Office, the Kremlin, or Havana Presidential Palace in October 1962 didn't actually matter, that it doesn't matter if assumptions are incorrect as long as theory is consistent with observations. By extension, for Friedman the key lessons from the Hungarian detachment would have been (1) that they had a map and (2) that they used it to navigate the situation. The assumption that the map gave clear and precise instructions and helped guide them out of their conundrum would have had, for Friedman, great plausibility because it was consistent with the outcome.

At the risk of dipping into hyperbole, to take this line of thinking to its natural conclusion, if Friedman were to assume (1) that his cat was a table and (2) all tables have four legs, he would be able to rationally deduce that his cat will have four legs. This Monty Pythonesque train of thought leads to a prediction that conforms to observations, and therefore, by Friedman's reckoning, the overall hypothesis carries 'great plausibility'. The fact that that this could conceivably have led him to serve a three-course meal on the back of his cat is immaterial.

It is hard not to have a strong sense of irony in learning that Friedman—who was, after all, the champion of free markets and individual freedoms—promoted a model of decision making that essentially assumed that the actual way individuals made decisions was immaterial. Allison's critique hinged on the fact that this was far from trivial: flawed assumptions could have disastrous consequences, whether we are talking about leaders, lieutenants, or leaves.

Fumbling with Galileo's Telescope

The assumptions of rational choice theory have been critiqued for almost as long as they have been around. In 1955, Herb Simon set out the ideas that would form the basis of bounded rationality and win him a Nobel Prize in 1978—one of the earliest challenges to the rational choice way of thinking. Allison used Simon's work to explore more realistic alternatives to rational choice theory, and numerous behavioural economists and experimental psychologists have since shown that judgement, decision making, and behaviours are not exclusively— or in some cases even partly—based on logical reasoning, discounting, and comparative analysis.

Instead, decisions are distorted by cognitive biases: they are anchored in first impressions, they fit within existing value and belief systems, they filter out information that doesn't match prior experience, they employ rules of thumb, they are shaped by learning and failing, and they involve experimentation. Decision makers don't always know—and in some cases can never know— the outcomes of their actions with any degree of certainty. The Bay of Pigs Invasion in 1961 led to the identification of 'groupthink' phenomena, whereby dissenting voices are shut out because of the social dynamics that reinforce a particular world view.

That rational choice assumptions do not hold in complex crises may not be entirely surprising. Such interactions might very quickly become too complex to gather all relevant information. Decision makers may misinterpret information owing to biases and errors. These and other factors amount to 'systematic violations' of the assumptions so central to rational choice theory.

Herb Simon pointed out that 'the assumptions of perfect rationality... do *not even remotely describe* the process that human beings use for making decisions in complex situations'[13] (emphasis added) and are 'so wildly at odds with known scientific understanding of human behavior and decision making that the model is of little use in describing or predicting actual behavior outside a narrow set of parameter values'.[14] Graham Allison argued in the *Essence of Decision* that 'An imaginative analyst can construct an account of value-maximizing choice for any action or set of actions performed by a government',[15] but only provided he or she is willing to ignore a lot of the available facts. (As one can imagine, his position led to a bit of academic cut and thrust with Milton Freidman.) Robert McNamara's eventual conclusions echoed Allison, suggesting towards the end of his life that 'Rationality will not save us.'[16]

This lesson does not appear to have been learnt, however, as Cramer's witty article, '*Homo Economicus* Goes to War',[17] indicates. Forty years after the missile crisis and 30 years after Allison's work, ideas from rational choice theory were still playing a major but misguided role in how academics, governments, and non-governmental organizations thought about and worked in conflict contexts:

> Rational choice theories of conflict based on neoclassical economics are unconvincing theoretically and where they have empirical content this is largely arbitrary... faced with the complexity of conflicts, and indeed of the social in general, [we] insist on the myth of rational choice individualism, even in the midst of evidence of a range of structural constraints on individualism and of compulsions other than utility maximization that constrain choice.[18]

If critiques have been made consistently for several decades, and this unrealistic and flawed model was shown to be flawed in one of the defining texts on one of the major international incidents of the twentieth century—and has even been denounced by its leading exponents—then why does it still hold such sway?

The problem, as Ken Arrow has suggested, is that relaxing assumptions of rational choice leads to a breakdown of mainstream policy thinking.[19] Amartya Sen has also suggested that the approach is hard to replace, because of its simplicity and usability: 'There is little hope of finding an alternative assumption structure that will be *as simple and usable*' (emphasis added).[20] For these reasons, rational principles have continued to wield a disproportionate influence on economic and other forms of policymaking. However, recent events have put paid to the idea that assumptions don't have to match reality as long as the predictions are accurate: the biggest financial crisis since the 1920s has taken place in a system dominated by rational choice theories and its variants.

Tools of the Trade

I am staring at two computer screens on the trading floor of one of the medium-sized investment banks. It is by far the biggest room I have ever worked in. Imagine half a football pitch, housing hundreds of people, sitting in parallel rows of screens and flashing numbers. The year is 2000, late July. The week, and the month, has been an odd one. Dotcoms are crashing daily and concerns about economic prospects are widespread. Traders are holding their positions. The feeling across the City of London has been one of listlessness. But today there is a sense of tension almost hovering in the air. Throats are dry. Fingers tap nervously at keyboards. As I look around, a lot of people are, like me, staring at screens or up at the televisions dotted around the floor. Everyone, it seems, is waiting. For what, I don't know.

And then, just like that, while I am distracted by an incoming email, the floor comes to life with a Mexican wave, pulsing energy. Phones start ringing like crazy. People are shouting at each other, seemingly at random. The director of the trading floor, accustomed to wandering the aisles with a small red bat to whack underperforming staffers, is standing on a desk and swinging his bat above his head like a delirious fan at a sports stadium. Imagine a gigantic call centre dominated by pink shirts, pinstripes, and super-charged egos and you will have a reasonable sense of what it feels like around me. The screens are now flashing green, not red. In another thousand rooms just like this, information is being digested and responded to instantly. All those decisions are being aggregated, minute by minute, on the screen in front of me. It was as though someone had just flicked a switch on the raw power of markets.

The feeling wouldn't last. Within a day, many corporations reported their earnings and the shares dropped again. Reality bit back. The listless feeling returned. The director's red bat returned to its previous, more violent, trajectories.

Two of the Santa Fe Institute's external faculty members, based at Columbia University, conducted an in-depth ethnographic study of trade-floor activities. They likened a trading room to a gigantic laboratory in which traders are engaged in a process of search and experimentation.[21]

In theory, the game was a simple one: it was the economists' textbook game of rational choice, albeit enhanced by high-speed connectivity. The key was to gather timely information and use mathematical tools to process it to make buy or sell decisions and maximize value, based on precise calculations of future gains.

But the reality is that, at the level of professional trading, while the tools and theories were necessary to play the game, everyone else had them too. And little was actually certain in terms of future outcomes and the value attached to them. Nobody knew where value would be the moment before Alan Greenspan made his statements, or before a particular share offering. There was no straightforward value 'out there' to be captured and delivered to corporate paymasters. Instead, the Columbia researchers found that the act of trading was one of adaptation and innovation: 'searching for something that is not yet named and categorized'.[22]

The real-world strategies employed by my trade-floor colleagues had much more in common with this than the textbook approach. Their approaches focused on recognizing patterns in the external environment, navigating the range of potential opportunities and risks, understanding the multiple pathways through which actions could yield value for different stakeholders, leveraging a dynamic network of internal and external actors, selecting from a range of suitable evaluative tools, and then designing and executing transactions that would hopefully generate unique 'value propositions' in the face of all of this.

This stood in contrast to the textbook assumptions of rational choice that traders gather timely information and use mathematical tools to process that information to make buy or sell decisions and maximize value, based on precise calculations of future gains. A trader who used only rational choice theory would have struggled in this world of adaptive innovators.

As recent history has shown, some forms of adaptive innovation in financial markets can result in rather dire consequences. One explanation is that regulatory structures were built around the formal assumptions of rational choice theory. Regulators have all the tools and theories but never really come close to understanding these strategies-in-action.

Andy Lo of the Massachusetts Institute of Technology makes a grim assessment of the financial system, which we will hear more about in the next chapter. He argues that the regulatory framework was developed for 'a very boring system'[23]—one populated by rational maximizers—and was simply not suitable; instead what was needed was *adaptive regulation*. As he puts it, 'interesting systems' needed dynamic forms of regulation that change in response to innovations and, based on thresholds, to changing market conditions. But this required a paradigm shift in how regulators think about financial markets, away from efficient market hypothesis and its limited assumptions and, perhaps more importantly, in how they thought about individuals and the rationality of their choices.

One would imagine that only the most bullish of rational choice economists would argue that the axioms of perfect rationality retain 'great plausibility' in understanding the current global economic crisis. As one senior figure in the actuarial world has put it, 'Our models of behavior and, more important, our recommendations for new policies and practices should be based on what people actually do rather than what they are supposed to be doing under the assumption that they are completely rational.'[24]

John Kay, the noted economic journalist, goes further, arguing that the maintenance of rational expectations in the face of sustained critiques and recent crises is equivalent to the Church Inquisition refusing to look through Galileo's telescope when he protested they did so to get evidence that the earth moved. They didn't have to look because they *knew* that whatever Galileo saw wasn't there.

But what alternatives are there? Are we destined to fumble with Galileo's telescope, finding flaws with our view of the world but refusing to seek alternatives? Are we, like Robert McNamara, going to continue steadfastly affirming the rationality of all actors in the face of the evidence, until it is too late? Is our learning in this area destined to be of the 'catastrophe-first' school? Or can we find some different lens to use to understand these issues of decisions and behaviours?

Agents of Change

In the 1960s, political scientist Tom Schelling, who had been involved in the heyday of the Marshall Plan, was travelling on a plane from Chicago to Boston and started to think about racial segregation. He wanted to work out why racial segregation was persisting despite increasing levels of tolerance in American neighbourhoods. Using a pencil and paper, and later his son's chessboard and a collection of copper and zinc coins, he mapped out an imagined community, placing black and white people randomly in a grid.[25] Then he let them move about the grid to reach a location where they were best satisfied with the racial distribution around them, developing simple rules for why people moved and where they moved to, and then let his imaginary community work out their prejudices.[26]

In the first few rounds, Schelling set the affinity levels low. No black person would want to stay next to a white person and vice versa. Unsurprisingly, the board quickly evolved into a highly segregated landscape. However, curiously, segregation also occurred when the prejudices were far weaker. Even with relatively tolerant preferences—where each person wanted at least one person of the same colour in their neighbourhood but was happy with all other racial configurations—the experimental community would still end up being highly segregated. Individual behavioural choices could aggregate into system-wide social phenomenon that were unintended, unexpected, and, in this case, undesirable.

Schelling wrote up his work in 1978 in *Micromotives and Macrobehaviour*, in which he examined the emergence of such behaviours among other 'binary groups'—men and women, officers and personnel, and so on.[27] His exploration of how complex phenomena arose from relatively simple rules proved influential. This work has been used to explore a number of longstanding social issues—including the resilience of racial segregation despite progressive legislation, policies, and attitudes—and also other forms of aggregate processes—for example the formation of urban enclaves of particular kinds of businesses or restaurants, and religious or ethnic segregation in Ireland. For example, the Chinese business community in a given city will be made up of diverse actors with a range of preferences about how close they are to others. But interactions between them may change these preferences. There will be feedback loops, whereby emergent patterns of aggregation in a particular neighbourhood have an effect on the attitudes and actions of newcomers. Several non-linear cascades of behaviour and tipping points later and you have a Chinatown in every major city in the world. Linking such models to empirical data has meant making them more realistic and bringing in more elements of human behaviours.[28]

Schelling was one of the inspirations for a step-change in a new field of research, known today as agent-based modelling (ABM). Since he used his son's chessboard, things have advanced considerably in terms of computational power, as have applications of the basic principles. One of the most significant subsequent breakthroughs was made by John Holland of the Santa Fe Institute (SFI), who developed a model of an adaptive agent able to display a range of possible decision rules, together forming an evolving population of such rules. It is fair to say that Holland's work put the 'adaptive' into complex adaptive systems. Adaptive agent approaches brought perception, reflection, conscious action, and diversity into the complexity research perspective.

Modern agent-based modelling attempts to build social systems '*in silico*' and from the bottom up. One of the foremost authorities is Joshua Epstein, formerly Director at the Brookings Institution and now Professor of Emergency Medicine at Johns Hopkins. Epstein has developed what must surely be one of most extensive models to date—an attempt to simulate the entire US population of 300 million people for the purpose of running disease transmission scenarios. Although this may seem a million miles away from Schelling's chessboard, the basic principles are very similar:

> We basically build artificial societies where people ... can be connected in networks, but they're very diverse. They can have partial or even bad information – what we call bounded rationality; they use ... rules in deciding how to behave. They move and interact with neighbors ... the basic idea is that if we're interested in some social phenomenon – like an epidemic or distribution of wealth or a settlement pattern – we try to grow it in an artificial society composed of individual agents.[29]

ABM permits researchers to move beyond the limitations of the aggregate approach underlying system dynamics models, encouraging them to identify and experiment with the micro-processes involved in the production of emergent macro-scale social patterns or distributions.[30] Researchers attempt to understand the complex relationships of critical actors involved in socio-political instability—that is, civilians, government (at various organizational levels), rebels, and government forces (military or police). Epstein and Axtell's Sugarscape model was one of the first ABM simulations to demonstrate the significance of this 'emergence' method.[31] With a few simple rules, Sugarscape was able to reproduce macro-social patterns in the abstract, permitting experimental investigation of micro-dynamics capable of driving conflict, as well as of other economic and social dynamics (e.g. wealth distributions).

So how does ABM actually work? According to the latest research from cognitive and evolutionary psychology, all living creatures can be seen as adaptive agents. So too can the groups they form—the aggregations of agents into institutions creates 'meta agents' of differing sizes and scales. Simulated adaptive agents are the 'people' of artificial societies—the equivalent of Schelling's coins. Each agent has a range of internal states and follows certain behavioural rules. Some of these might be fixed for the agent's life (e.g. genetic makeup, ethnicity, language); others change through interaction with other agents or with the external environment (e.g. religious or economic preferences, sexuality, wealth, cultural identity). Regardless of their diversity, agents all share certain characteristics in terms of their relationship to other agents and their environment.[32] These include the following aspects:

- Agents perceive their own state, that of other agents, and that of the environment. This includes physical, social, and cultural factors. This perception is a filtering process: some information may be discarded, some distorted, and some partially assimilated.

- They gather information about themselves, other agents, their environment, and their own and others' interaction with the environment. They identify regularities and patterns in the information they gather.

- They condense these patterns into a model of 'rules of thumb'—'world views'—and select the best ones to guide their actions. Different agents can adopt different schema, which may relate to desired local states, goals, rewards, needs, or negative outcomes that need to be avoided or minimized. They may work with multiple schema at any given time.

- They act in the world on the basis of their selected schema, using anticipation of certain future states, with external environments and/or other agents. Interactions with other agents can include observation, communication, physical interaction, spread of knowledge or disease, imitation of perceived successful behaviour, cooperation to achieve common goals, competition for resources, and so on.

- They use information generated by their actions to reinforce, adapt, or challenge their selected models. They can learn from experience, switching strategies according to what others are doing and changing opportunities.

- As a result of all of these factors, agents will generally be diverse in their properties and behaviours. This is not only because they have divergent properties, but also because their experienced history of the environment and other agents is diverse. Even in a system where the agents begin with the same properties, differences arise over time. Importantly, rules and behaviours can be determined and changed through direct interactions with other agents.[33]

These ideas are the starting point for complexity scientists' explorations of decision making and behaviours. This work provides an explanation of human behaviour that includes perfect rationality as one of a number of ways in which decisions are made. Humans are adaptive actors guided by different 'schema' that can be seen as guiding behaviours and can gradually become more refined, based on trial and error and goal-directed learning. Human behaviour can therefore be modelled more realistically: as changing and adaptable, not merely as an outcome reasoned from general propositions. The introspective qualities of agents and cultural factors directly create and change the social processes. The agent is allowed to re-examine his/her own behaviour step by step and thus learns by trial and error.

I have already written about Herb Simon as the successor to Warren Weaver's vision, and one of the few true geniuses of complexity. We will be drawing on his thinking in each of the chapters in the current part of the book, and one would think that his contribution in the present chapter on the importance of bounded rationality would have been sufficient. However, he also anticipated the agent-based approach in a follow-up work. Some four decades before the development of what is now the most famous agent-based model, Sugarscape, Simon described with unerring precision what the actual system developed by Epstein and Axtell might look like and how it would work.[34]

Unlike rational choice theory, however, ABM isn't a specific theory of decision making. Importantly, adaptive agents do not maximize utility based on perfect information and foresight. Rather than rational choice, agents in such models display an approximation of 'naturalistic decision-making'. Cognitive scientists identify this as the means by which most decisions are made, especially under pressure. It relies heavily on intuition, past experience, and pattern recognition in order to inform appropriate courses of action. Gary Klein compares it to the way a rock climber scales a cliff face he or she has never attempted before.

> Expert rock climbers learn...to identify leverage points during their climb. These points have no single common characteristic...What is more, there are no 'absolute' leverage points: The environment (visibility, wet or dry, hot or cold) and condition of the climber (fresh or tired, relative strength, size, and weight) all play a part in determining what may be used...The same holds

> will not work for everyone, even on the same climb. Rock climbers must learn
> to make rapid and effective real-life decisions... to improvise and to exercise
> adaptability.[35]

Perfect rationality is just one of the set of rules *potentially* available to agents, and in many cases it may be unattainable. It allows agents a diversity of preferences and mental models, and seeks to explore the social outcomes that result from the interactions of these agents with each other and their environment.

The hopes for agent-based approaches at the time of writing are pitched high, specifically as an alternative to rational choice theories. The applications go well beyond economics. Joshua Epstein, one of the developers of Sugarscape, is responsible for the Models of Infectious Disease Agent Study (MIDAS) of the US National Institutes of Health (NIH). As the name implies, the programme focuses on agent-based models of the interactions between infectious agents and their hosts, how diseases spread, and how response strategies might influence this. MIDAS members have developed models of the whole USA—300 million people; and of global pandemics involving 155 of the largest cities in the world. Not only has the programme won awards, but also it is being taken seriously: at the time of writing, US guidance for slowing a pandemic flu attack without pharmaceutical interventions is based on MIDAS modelling results.[36]

Economists are also paying attention. That stalwart of the discipline, *The Economist*, acknowledged in the wake of the financial crisis that 'Many of the assumptions, including efficient financial markets and rational expectations... were clearly too simplistic.'[37] It also identified ABM as 'one of the most promising alternatives'[38] (see Box 9.1).

This potential had already been realized to some extent in the work of two of Rob Axtell and Joshua Epstein's students, Vincent Darley and Alexander Outkin, both of whom also worked with Stuart Kauffman at his BiosGroup outfit. The idea was that 'agent-based models... would emulate well the complex "ecology" of traders, market makers, and investors buying, selling, and competing for orders, while simultaneously adapting their behavior and strategies in a continual struggle for survival'.[39]

> Think of this particular agent-based simulation as a kind of laboratory for investigating the market's dynamics as a function of the trading regulations in place, the types of strategies used by investors and market makers, and certain exogenous factors such as tick size (the smallest possible increment of change in a stock's price), and the arrival of new information. What is most exciting about this faster-than-real-time laboratory is that it means regulators can study what might happen with the introduction of new rules without making risky early concept tests in the real-life marketplace where real money is made and lost by real people.[40]

Chairman of the Nasdaq, Michael Brown, later argued that the model had proved itself: 'overwhelming evidence points to its uncanny prescience'.[41] This

---

Box 9.1. The value of agent-based models, according to *The Economist*

ABM does not assume the economy can achieve a settled equilibrium. No order or design is imposed on the economy from the top down. Unlike many models, agent-based models are not populated with 'representative agents'—identical traders, firms, or households whose individual behaviour mirrors the economy as a whole. Rather, ABM uses a bottom-up approach that assigns particular behavioural rules to each agent. For example, some may believe prices reflect fundamentals; others may rely on empirical observations of past price trends.

Crucially, agents' behaviour may be determined (and altered) by direct interactions between them, whereas in conventional models interaction happens only indirectly through pricing. This feature of ABM enables, for example, the copycat behaviour that leads to 'herding' among investors. Agents may learn from experience or switch their strategies according to majority opinion. They can aggregate into institutional structures such as banks and firms. These things are very hard, sometimes impossible, to build into conventional models. But in an agent-based model you simply run a computer simulation to see what emerges, free from any top-down assumptions.

ABM makes no assumptions about the existence of efficient markets. The markets it generates are more like a turbulent river or the weather system, subject to constant storms and seizures of all sizes. Big fluctuations and even crashes are an inherent feature. This is because models contain feedback mechanisms that can amplify small effects, such as the herding and panic that generate bubbles and crashes. In mathematical terms, they are 'non-linear', meaning that effects need not be proportional to their causes.

---

highlights some of the real-world value of ABM: these approaches allow for more realistic assumptions about human behaviours that conventional models miss out. The findings of various modellers are that humans are adaptively rational rather than omnisciently rational. That is, how a human approaches or deals with a given problem depends on their background, memory, knowledge, and skills. They face limited information, continually adjusting to each other and their environment, and make use of patterns, analogies, narratives, and rules of thumb. As such, and as Schelling showed, ABM is more a mindset than a technology.[42]

The Adaptive Search for Excellence

Herb Simon described his 'bounded rationality' approach as a Darwinian model, arguing that human problem solving was one example of the adaptive systems found more widely in nature.[43] Drawing on work by evolutionary economists, cognitive psychologists, and behavioural theorists, the notion of adaptation and evolution has become widely used as a means to understand social and political phenomena, from conflict dynamics to political institutions, technological change, and economic growth.

Echoing Klein's analogy of decision makers as rock climbers, one of the most widespread metaphors used in such work is that of the fitness landscape, which draws on the work of influential biologist Sewell Wright in the 1930s.[44] The determinant of such landscapes in biology is genetic and behavioural. Thanks to work by—among others—Stuart Kauffman and Simon Levin, this model has found its way into social, economic, and political contexts as a new metaphor for thinking about adaptability and evolution. In these more social settings, fitness can be determined by simple criteria—as in Schelling's segregation model. Or they might be broader and more comprehensive, including factors such as behavioural characteristics, relationships with others, personalities, and so on. Take the example of a firm in a given industry. The firm can be seen as populated by actors competing with others for survival and resources. It is a complex system, made up of many agents—generally people—in a network of relationships following certain kinds of behaviours. The system moves between different possible combinations of relationships, networks, and behaviours (also known as its 'design space') to find the particular combination that will best enable it to survive and thrive.[45] This adaptive search, shaped by a given industries' 'fitness function', underpins whether a given firm survives and thrives, does the opposite, or slopes around just being mediocre.

Any given fitness landscape will be a dynamic combination of peaks and troughs of different heights and depths. In his book *Adapt*, Tim Harford gives a marvellous description:

> ...imagine a vast, flat landscape, divided into a grid of billions of squares. On each square is a document, a recipe describing a particular strategy...if the fitness landscape is biological, each strategy is a different genetic recipe: some squares describe fish, some describe birds, some describe humans...the fitness landscape might equally represent recipes for dinner....[or] business strategies: different ways to run an airline or a fast-food chain...each recipe is very similar to its neighbours...two neighbouring business strategies might advocate doing everything the same, except that one prescribes slightly higher

prices and a bit more marketing....Now let's change the picture and say that on our fitness landscape, the better the solution, the higher the altitude of the square that contains it. Now the fitness landscape is a jumble of cliffs and chasms, plateaus and jagged summits. Valleys represent bad solutions, mountaintops are good...in a biological ecosystem or an economy, the peaks keep moving, sometimes slowly, sometimes quickly...[46]

He goes on to describe how some firms went out of business because the peak they were on suddenly disappeared (sewing machines), how others have been around for some time and are slowly moving, others are fast-moving, like a rolling wave.

According to modern evolutionary thinking, adaptation is a search across the fitness landscape. This search is based on three simple principles: through **variation**, different strategies can be developed, and then **selection** pressures mean that certain of these are shown to be more or less fit than others, allowing for **amplification** of successes and reduction of failures.

So we can imagine a group of adaptive agents (such as firms) located on a landscape. Each agent seeks to increase its fitness simultaneously, moving across the landscape to attain greater fitness. This search is often described as an algorithm—literally, a set of instructions, or a programme—built around the processes of experimentation and random mutation. These activities have an influence on the landscape and the potential of others. This leads to an ongoing series of actions, interactions, adaptations, and landscape movements.

Experimentation depends on trial and error attempts to try out different combinations of qualities, and on cognitive processes such as memory and intuition. Random mutation can be seen as wild jumps that can result in much higher—or lower—fitness levels. Following either experimentation or mutation, new positions may be selected and replicated. Different qualities or traits will be amplified and spread across populations if they do not decrease the 'fitness' of individuals. The overall movement of the tribe across its fitness landscape is likely to be a combination of adaptive walks and random jumps. Harford suggests that there are 'many ways to search for peaks in this changeable and mysterious landscape', ranging from 'small steps with occasional wild leaps' through 'clinging to a familiar summit as it shifts around', through 'darting off to find a new peak rising'.

Although this is a simplified model for thinking about the diversity and multifaceted nature of human decision making, socio-biologists have found that this kind of adaptive learning algorithm does indeed underpin human social learning, and can be seen to be at the heart of group decision making, problem solving, and cultural diffusion. The variation, selection, amplification formulation has proved popular among economists, notably being used by Eric Beinhocker in *The Origin of Wealth* and Tim Harford in *Adapt* to describe processes of successful adaptation—and maladaptation—in complex settings.

Elinor Ostrom also used this as an analogy for policy in the face of complexity: 'different solutions need to find their niche in an evolving landscape'.[47] The model can also be used more generally to describe how groups of actors make decisions in complex systems.

The nature of the landscape, usually referred to as its 'ruggedness', is also an important consideration. A smooth fitness landscape relates to just a few high fitness solutions; a more rugged one will have a more jagged topography. The landscape itself can also change, sometimes slowly, sometimes quickly, because of either actors' strategies or exogenous events. 'And the fitness landscape of one species changes because the other species that form its niche themselves adapt on their own fitness landscapes.'[48]

This approach can help us understand the nature of adaptation in more detail. Some adaptations that take place for one reason can prove useful in other contexts; the formal term for this is 'exaptation'. There may be high peaks that are unattainable because they involve too big a leap or too much of a drop to start the climb. The often-used example of this is the reason animals don't have wheels. It may be possible to imagine the biological constructions that would be needed for blood, bone, and sinew to form an axle and a wheel arrangement. But what would the path across the fitness landscape look like? Almost impossible, according to Richard Dawkins, who refers to the peak of wheeled animals as 'Mount Improbable'.[49]

What this highlights is that evolution is a recipe not for optimization but for trial and error experimentation. Just as it has not yielded a cast of optimally adapted organisms, other forms of evolution tend not to result in 'single best solutions'. What Stephen Jay Gould famously said about the evolution of humanity not being inevitable—'replay the tape a million times . . . and I doubt that anything like Homo sapiens would ever evolve again'—applies to life forms,[50] and equally to all social, political, and economic institutions, all behaviours, and so on. As Kauffman describes it, 'Evolution is a story of . . . populations [wandering] under the drives of mutation, selection, and random drift across the landscape seeking peaks, but perhaps never achieving them.'[51] And, 'Each coevolving partner chases peaks that move away from it faster than it can climb, each clambering forever uphill on deforming landscapes. Tracking peaks on deforming landscapes is central to survival. Landscapes, in short, are part of the search for excellence—the best compromises we can make.'[52]

Co-evolution can also lead to sub-optimal solutions: where groups and individuals are competing for resources, fitness is relative. An agent might get to a local peak that is better than its neighbour's and stay there, with the overall system drifting into sub-optimal solutions as a result.

Evolutionary biologists have identified two forms of co-evolution: that between agents and that between agents and the system. To take one widely cited example of system co-evolution, elephants thrive on acacia trees but, after a while, they destroy the trees, drastically changing the wildlife the area can sustain and even affecting the physical shape of the land. In the process, they render the area uncongenial to themselves, and either die or move on. The land is adapting to the elephants just as they are to it. As one Maasai proverb has it, 'Cows grow trees, elephants grow grasslands.'[53]

As with ABM, computers have been essential to exploring these principles. One of the most powerful applications is in the design of new drugs. Effective drug activity requires the binding of a molecule to a relevant part of another, known as the 'lock and key' principle. Evolutionary computing practices have been employed to synthesize trial drugs and then test their compatibility with the target molecule, by generating billions of random drug molecules, which are tested by letting them search across a fitness landscape, with compatibility with the target molecule defining the peaks. The most successful molecules are selected and variants created and tested using the same fitness test. The same process is repeated until the best drug is obtained. As one expert has put it, 'Evolutionary breeding of drugs is the future of biotechnology.'[54]

A tool called Rosetta@Home, developed in the early noughties, uses volunteers' desktop machines to undertake the computational processing necessary to evolve new and more accurate structures of proteins in HIV and AIDS, vital to developing effective treatments. At the heart of the approach is the idea of an 'energy landscape' that maps all the possible arrangements of molecules in a protein against the associated energy contained in each structure. While the landscapes will be very rugged, one common finding is that the lowest points—troughs corresponding to lowest energy structures—indicate a stable structure for a given protein. The application develops different trajectories along the energy landscape and thereby approximates different solutions to the problem of developing protein structures. A screensaver shows the progress of the evolutionary process: different protein shapes are continually adapted in one corner of the screen, while in the centre the energy levels associated with each new attempt are indicated.[55] The process is networked, so volunteers can also see the structure of the most recently accepted protein from across the user community. Watch it run for a few minutes, and one is reminded of nothing so much as a massive, 3D game of Tetris.

The same notion clearly occurred to the Rosetta volunteers, who in 2008 asked for an interactive version of the system where they could do the computational work themselves.[56] The Foldit game involved working out appropriate ways for each human user to evolve solutions to the protein puzzle, and the similarities to 3D Tetris are reinforced when you see this process in action. Users are given a series of starting structures and use controls to tweak, wiggle, shake, and freeze the different components of the molecule. Users compete with each other to share solutions and discuss strategies and approaches. In 2011, research by the Foldit developers showed that the human computer version was actually better than the pure computational approach at solving these problems: users could deduce the protein structure of a simian version of the HIV virus in under three weeks.[57] As the lead researcher noted afterwards: 'This is the first instance that we are aware of in which online gamers solved a longstanding scientific problem.'[58]

The co-evolutionary approach has generated some valuable insights for social and political scientists, and has been used to understand a variety of different problems, from how institutions arise, to how industries change when new technologies are introduced, to organizational knowledge processes, to political analysis, and even violent conflict and war.

Starting with the work of economists Nelson and Winter in the 1980s,[59] there has been steady growth in such evolutionary applications in the social and political sciences. These studies examine not only how a particular agent adapts to and is shaped by other agents in a system, but also how the same dynamic plays out between agents and wider institutions and environmental conditions.

Arie Lewin of Duke University sets out a co-evolutionary theory of organizational change, seeing organizations, their populations (i.e. industries), and their environments as interdependent outcomes of deliberate choices, institutional influences, and environmental changes. By focusing on the firm, Lewin and his colleagues emphasized institutional factors such as regulation, rules and norms, educational systems, governance structures, employment relations, and capital markets; and environmental factors such as technologies, social movements, new entrants, global interdependence, and management approaches.[60] Together, these aspects all form the fitness landscape for firms in a given context.

In political science too there has been a growing interest in using such thinking to examine interactions and change. Building on notions of competition to examine multiparty competition in democracies, Michael Laver of New York University together with Ernest Sengeti of the World Bank showed that many mainstream models of party competition are static—with fixed rules and parameters. However, party competition is in continual flux: what political agents do at one point in time has a profound influence on future behaviours, and is about carving out niches in a transforming electoral landscape. In short, political competition can be seen as a co-evolving complex system.[61] Ken Kollman, working with Scott Page and John Miller of SFI, developed the notion of electoral landscapes more fully, to explore how changing voter preferences influence party political positions.[62] One of the assumptions of democratic theory is that electoral processes encourage candidates and parties to adapt to, or at the very least appeal to, voter preferences, meaning parties can use information to take positions as close to voter preferences as possible, thereby ensuring success.[63]

However, political theorists have not succeeded in fully describing how changing voter preferences influence party positions. When changes in preferences lead to changes in party positions, it bodes well for democracy. But parties may not be able to adapt to, or have other interests that dominate, voter preferences. This can be modelled using electoral landscapes.[64] Like fitness landscapes, these have peaks and troughs, with the height equivalent to expected vote count. Each political agent starts at a particular position—which represents their political platform—and seeks to climb higher. Such 'start from where you are' adaptations may be the only way to ensure electoral success, for a number of reasons. Limited information and foresight mean local adaptation is the only way of winning. Ideology may make parties unlikely to move far from their start point. Opposing party positions may limit scope for movement, because parties want to avoid platforms that resemble those of their opponents. Finally, sudden or radical moves across the electoral landscape may lose core voters. There may be imagined high ground for votes, but a given party would lose too much to get there—equivalent to the wheeled animal discussed earlier.

Another area where evolutionary approaches have been applied is in the conduct of war. ABM has been used to simulate opposing armies in battle, examine the possible behaviours of terrorist groups, and understand outbreaks of violence. Peter Coleman has developed a detailed model of conflicts taking place across a fitness landscape shaped by peaks (peace) and troughs (conflict), which may exert weak and strong pulls on warring parties and may be explicit or latent. The search of the different parties for peace takes place across a landscape, with each point relating to a particular combination of qualities, more precisely a solution to the problem of optimizing the mix of different kinds of benefits to the warring parties. Some points of peace may be of low fitness, and lead to war being reinitiated. Some conflicts are intractable: the landscape is extremely jagged, with numerous forces pulling the parties down into conflict, and options and responses may be very limited. It is much easier to simply go headlong down the slope. Other landscapes may evolve to the point that peace succeeds against the odds.[65]

Here again, the concept of the 'edge of chaos' has been employed by a number of analysts, including Peter Coleman. From the perspective of adaptive agents, the edge of chaos is hypothesized as the optimal position for learning: being at the edge of chaos means populations are capable of learning from their fitness landscapes, facing terrains low enough that peaks can be found but rugged enough that aimless behaviour can be avoided: 'Adapting populations that are too methodical and timid in their explorations are likely to get stuck in the foothills ... but a search that is too wide-ranging is also likely to fail.'[66] The edge of chaos also applies to co-evolution: 'Each partner clambers up its fitness landscape toward fitness peaks, even as that landscape is constantly deformed by the adaptive moves of its co-evolutionary partners.'[67] The ideal is to be sufficiently coordinated to permit mutually beneficial interaction, but sufficiently loose to avoid immobilization from conflicting constraints. True learning happens when organizations are coupled at the edge, where new ideas come into an environment that is flexible and adaptable.[68]

John Miller and Scott Page take this idea further, suggesting the edge of chaos is a phenomenon that occurs in the *rules* that shape agents' behaviour. So the boids may follow three rules, and this will lead to complex behaviour. What if we change one of the rules slightly? Or if the rules are replaced wholesale? For Page and Miller, the empirical search for the edge of chaos has become a search for how small changes in a rule impacts on the emergent behaviour of a system. Miller and Page use the stock market as an example of a system where agents actively adapt and alter the fundamental behaviour of the system, thereby forcing it into new 'realms of activity': 'If stockmarkets are too predictable ... adaptation [will] create agents that can exploit this [their] emergence should wipe out the predictability and push the system toward a more chaotic regime.'[69]

Along similar lines, Elinor Ostrom argued that policy in the face of complexity needed to be less about applying pre-set solutions and more about creating systems that embody the search for such solutions. The search for new and better rules is itself something that needs to be conducted 'on a rugged landscape with many peaks and valleys' and effort made to seek out 'appropriate types of solutions for specific niches'.[70] The key here, according to Ostrom, is to move away from 'best practices' towards 'best fit' for the rule system in question.

Anti-war Games

One of the most poignant images of World War I is that of the football match that took place between the warring armies on Christmas Day in 1914. The unofficial, unauthorized Christmas truce took hold in various locations along the Western Front. It started in the week before Christmas, when a group of German soldiers decorated their trenches with candles and Christmas trees and starting singing carols. This was greeted by carols from the British side. They started shouting Christmas greetings across No Man's Land. There were many small instances of parties of German and British soldiers walking out to meet their counterparts to exchange small gifts. On Christmas Eve and Christmas Day, this culminated in soldiers from both sides venturing out and socializing, resulting in joint carol singing and the now-infamous games of football. Almost 100,000 soldiers were involved in this remarkable, spontaneous cessation of hostilities.

In fact, there were many incidents of truces occurring at trench level throughout the war, usually against the direct orders of high-ranking leaders. In some cases, trucing soldiers showed more concern for their opposing counterparts than for their own commanding officers. Measures had to be introduced to prevent them happening, including ordering artillery bombardments on Christmas Eve to prevent any lulls in combat and the rotation of troops to prevent over-familiarity with the enemy.

Robert Axelrod studied the truce phenomenon in his work on the evolution of cooperation, and describes it as a 'live-and-let-live system'.[71] He attributed these outbreaks of peace to a series of spontaneous, self-organized movements. Self-organized systems are those that spontaneously produce a new organizational form in response to exogenous or endogenous changes. Axelrod found that, after the first bloody period of the war ending in August 1914, there was a stabilization of the lines and truces emerged spontaneously in numerous locations. The earliest examples resulted from meals being served at the same time on both sides or from bad weather inhibiting aggression, and the truce extended beyond the period of mealtime or after good weather had returned. Following the Christmas truce and the stern reaction of senior officials, small truces would be arranged through shouts and signals between the opposing sides. Arrangements such as 'quiet hours' and 'sniper out-of-bounds areas' emerged. But court martialling was commonplace for those fraternizing with the enemy, which meant other means needed to be established. This often focused on mutually shared points of basic needs. For example, when rations were delivered, it would have been possible for either side to shell the vans, but not doing so indicated a willingness to establish a small-scale truce.

Using a variant of ABM, Axelrod showed that the live-and-let-live system had *evolved* on a fitness landscape of pay-offs for cooperation. Truce behaviours gained a foothold through local exploratory actions, emerging spontaneously through a variety of opportunities and evolving into patterns of 'mutually understood behaviour'. These were sustained over time because of the extensive contact that built up between soldiers facing each other for long periods of time. The evolution of cooperation did not rely on either random mutation or survival of the fittest, but rather was a case of deliberate adaptation and a self-organized, reciprocal form of ethics and rituals. 'Friendship is hardly necessary for cooperation based upon reciprocity to get started. Under suitable circumstances, cooperation can develop even between antagonists.'[72]

Self-organization is a common feature in many complex systems. Nobel Laureate Ilya Prigogine described the economy as 'a self-organising system, in which market structures are spontaneously organised by such things as the demand for labour and demand for goods and services'.[73] In setting key design principles for the emergence of self-government, Ostrom saw Axelrod's work as a key starting point for understanding how users of common pool resources achieve self-organization.[74] Another Nobel Laureate, Paul Krugman, wrote about the self-organizing economy from the perspective of space (the way cities gradually form specialized districts and the distribution of city sizes) and time (business cycles).[75] Perhaps the most remarkable aspect of self-organization is that it runs counter to the idea of entropy, which is that all systems tend toward greater disorder (what Warren Weaver called disorganized complexity). By contrast, a self-organizing system uses energy from its environment to increase the level of internal organization. This is what some have described as 'order for free'. Adam Smith's invisible hand is perhaps the classic example of this in the social sciences.

However, it is important to note that both public goods and public bads can arise in self-organized fashion. A stark example is provided by the Rwandan genocide: levels of mass participation can be explained partly by the self-organized emergence of a norm for extreme violence among the Hutu community. Bhavnani concludes that the frequently attributed causes of the genocide—including the death of the Rwandan president in a plane crash, ethnic tensions, and the post-war culture in Rwanda at the time—are at best partial explanations, which need to be related to the bottom-up collective processes of violence through which the genocide unfolded. This self-organization, which Bhavnani demonstrated using ABM, was driven by complex patterns of interactions among individuals forming Rwandan society, such that killing Tutsis became the norm. The existence of such a norm is proven by the fact that, even in Hutu-only areas, 10 per cent of the population was killed, family members killing each other in acts of astonishing brutality. This suggests that in some parts of the population this self-organized norm turned in on itself.[76]

We started this chapter with the Cuban Missile Crisis, and we have touched on a number of applications of complexity in political contexts over its course. It seems fitting to close on this same theme. Politics is not the rational optimizing discipline it is imagined to be. Political positions—whether democratic, military, or anything in between—do not come from careful consideration and optimization. Instead, we are plagued by biases. Daniel Kahneman and Jonathan Renshon examined biases uncovered in 40 years of psychological research and implications for war. They found that *all* the biases favoured hawkish impulses. 'In short, these biases have the effect of making wars more likely to begin and more difficult to end.'[77]

But our irrationality and adaptiveness is also our saving grace. Kennedy may not have been perfectly rational, but he was certainly adaptive. War and peace do not just co-exist: they co-evolve.

A perhaps surprising analogy can be made with musical forms. Barrett suggests seven features of jazz improvisation that also hold true for improvisation within organizational contexts:[78]

1. Provocative competence: deliberate efforts to interrupt habit patterns.
2. Embracing errors as a source of learning.
3. Shared orientation toward minimal structures that allow maximum flexibility.
4. Distributed task: continual negotiation and dialogue towards dynamic synchronization.
5. Reliance on retrospective sense making.
6. 'Hanging out': membership in a community of practice.
7. Taking turns soloing and supporting.

The similarity between musical improvisation and complexity goes beyond metaphor. For example, work by British researcher Chris Kiefer provides insights into improvised electronic music as an emergent phenomenon occurring as a result of the interactive dialogue between musicians and their instruments. Especially interesting is that this improvisation can in some cases go beyond the music itself to the creation of new *instruments*, with composers working real-time, during performance, to redesign the software tools through which different sonic outputs are generated. This corresponds closely to the notion of the co-evolution of behaviours and rules described earlier.[79]

Along similar lines, Neil Johnson of Oxford University sees modern jazz as the musical equivalent of complexity.

> [It] involves a spontaneous interaction of a collection of objects (i.e. musicians). It exhibits surprising emergent phenomena in that it is improvised and hence what emerges in a given solo is product of the actual feedback which that soloist receives at that moment in time. It is also an open system in that its best performances arise in an environment with audience feedback ... there is a crowd effect in which the whole group begins to synchronise ... it has no ... orchestral conductor or an existing piece of melody that all the players are simply repeating.[80]

The connection between this way of thinking and the conduct of war and peace was made clear to me at the Nobel Laureates Global Symposium in May 2011. Former US President Bill Clinton told the story of a particularly intractable peace negotiation he was involved in. It was his reflection on the kind of shift needed for policymakers to adapt to the demands of sustainability. The story spoke clearly to an issue that all the symposium participants were struggling with. How do we learn to set our knowledge, training and expertise aside and learn to be more adaptive?

One side was headed up by a classically trained pianist turned national politician who was treating the process like a virtuoso performance: he knew the metaphorical score and he clearly believed he would achieve his goals through continual repetition. Time and again, when a deal seemed to be in sight, he restated his goals and ambitions, using the same exact words and phrases each time. Clinton described how he turned to his obstreperous counterpart in frustration and blurted out:

> Why did you have to be a classical pianist? Why couldn't you have been a mediocre jazz player? Because then you would have known how to stay in the same key and riff![81]

CHAPTER 10

Falling Off Cliffs

'Having stripped the study of complexity down to its bare essentials...we discover that it is all built on networks, interconnections between the simple parts that make up a complex system'.

John Gribbins.[1]

Homogeneity Breeds Fragility

Most of us would find it hard to think of a job title more inherently contradictory than director of financial stability. But this is precisely the role held by Andy Haldane, whose work placed him at the forefront of attempts to understand the financial crisis that rocked the world economy in 2008 and that is, at time of writing, showing no signs of subsiding. In 2009, he gave a speech in Amsterdam in which he argued that the crisis presented policy-makers and analysts with a large body of evidence and strong incentives to change the way financial markets are understood.[2] For Haldane, the shift needed was clear: explaining the global crisis required application of complex adaptive systems thinking. Financial stability was, in other words, a problem of organized complexity. He used a branch of complex systems called network science to show how the international financial network had evolved over a 20-year period to become more fragile, highlighting two key aspects. First, in 2005 there were more countries that were holding large external financial stocks, and second, the flows between countries were dramatically larger relative to those countries' GDP. By extension, he argued, ideas from the complex systems field could potentially help protect the financial system from future shocks.

Haldane followed up his speech with what may seem like a rather unlikely collaboration—with one of the world's most eminent biologists. Robert May, former Chief Scientific Advisor to the UK government and life peer in the House of Lords, had already spent some time thinking about the oxymoronic nature of financial stability. A couple of years earlier, May, along with two other noted biologists, Simon Levin and George Sugihara, had published a piece called 'Ecology for Bankers',[3] in which they argued that there was potential value in extending techniques for analysing ecosystems to financial systems. At the time, the world was teetering on the edge of the credit crunch. No scalps had yet been claimed but something was certainly up. May's previous work had shown that, outside the world of financial modellers, such crises were routine occurrences in a wide range of contexts: 'from infectious diseases to power grids, from forest fires to the world wide web'.[4] All these systems are underpinned by the idea of ecological networks.

Perhaps the most common application of the ideas of network to ecological systems is in the form of food webs. These take the idea of simple linear food chains (say, from sun to grass to grazing mammals to carnivores) and introduce the multiple interactions between the species in question. These have been used widely to explore the complexity and fragility of ecosystems, especially in the context of human exploitation of natural resources.

Perhaps the most well-known cases relate to ocean ecosystems and the impact of over-fishing. Hake is by far South Africa's most valuable fish resource. The country's coastline is also home to numerous seal colonies, which the fishing industry has long blamed for the reduction in hake stocks. However, as Peter Yodzis of the University of Guelph has shown, the hake and the seal are part of an immensely complex network. There are potentially 225 *million* different pathways of cause and effect between the two species, some direct but many more through intermediary species such as anchovy and sardines.[5] The actual effect of a seal cull on hake populations is impossible to predict; what is unambiguous is that the over-fishing practices of the industry, which catches some 134,000 tonnes of hake each year, *is* having a dramatic impact. Yodzis's influential food web analysis brings to mind that famous passage from *The Origin of Species*:

> It is interesting to contemplate an entangled bank, clothed with many plants of many kinds, with birds singing on the bushes, with various insects flitting about, and with worms crawling through the damp earth, and to reflect that these elaborately constructed forms, so different from each other, and dependent on each other in so complex a manner, have all been produced by laws acting around us.[6]

As noted several times already, there is no generally accepted theory of complex systems. But there are some elements we could take an educated guess play a major role, and among these network science is one of the most significant. Scientists in diverse fields are starting to appreciate that at the heart of many—if not most—problems of organized complexity are network problems. Building on growing knowledge of these and other food webs, May, Levin, and Sugihara—biologists working on the financial sector— concluded that 'The ephemeral networks that define financial reality and global markets are a key to understanding the ecology of market robustness and its potential vulnerability to collapse.'[7] Economists at one of the US Federal Reserve Banks put the resulting challenge to finance in a rather prophetic manner: '[Conventional finance] models...no longer fully capture the possible channels of propagation and feedback arising from major disturbances.'[8] In conversation, Simon Levin suggested to me that the missing part of this story had traditionally been the lack of links to the social sciences and policy, and that what was needed were 'deep partnerships' between economists, ecologists, and other social scientists. However, one of the challenges he noted was that interdisciplinary ideas often 'extend beyond what a scientific approach would permit'.

The clarity and analytical deftness of Haldane and May's collaboration matched up to Levin's challenge. It was well after the global financial crisis had got into full swing that Haldane and May started working together. The view that traditional methods of analysis were not up to the job was commonplace at the time, even among doyennes of conventional thinking such as Chairman of the US Federal Reserve, Alan Greenspan. Greenspan made the point while giving evidence to Congress in 2008: 'The whole entire intellectual edifice crumbled.'[9] Ezra Klein at *The Washington Post* wrote afterwards 'Ultimately, that's what makes the financial crisis so scary. The complexity of the system far exceeded the capacity of the participants, experts and watchdogs. Even after the crisis happened, it was devilishly hard to understand what was going on.'[10] He continues: 'It is clear that our key systems are going to continue growing more complex, and we're not getting any smarter, or any less able to ignore risks that we know we should be preparing for.'[11]

Haldane and May's collaboration was built on the shared idea that the vulnerability and risks inherent to the banking system urgently needed to be understood better and that the dynamics of ecological systems would help make sense of the contagious consequences of sub-prime mortgage mis-selling, poor risk management, and the failure of Lehman Brothers in late 2008.[12] In an interview, Haldane used a dramatic analogy: 'In October 2008, the financial system, and world economy, fell off a cliff [and] conventional economic models have struggled to make sense of this.'[13] May in turn is scathing about the fact that the mathematics underpinning financial instruments such as derivatives and credit default swaps—Warren Buffett's financial weapons of mass destruction— rested on a series of implicit, idealized assumptions and vague concepts.[14]

In a 2011 cover article in *Nature*, Haldane and May described the scope of applying the tools used by ecologists to understand food webs and by epidemiologists to understand disease transmission.[15] They found, unsurprisingly, that the nodes of the financial network were rather more elaborate than the species in food webs or the individuals in disease networks. However, as May et al had noted three years previously, the banking system had the kind of data ecologists could only dream about. Haldane and May developed ways to model the interconnections and interdependencies between different banks and made further refinements so it was possible to explore the knock-on effects of a single bank failing on the rest of the system. They found that, at certain levels of connectivity, a bank failing could lead to not just one but numerous waves of subsequent failures. They also found that excessive homogeneity—as exhibited by 'herding behaviour' among banks—can in the short term minimize the risk for each individual bank, but in the medium to long term the probability of the entire system collapsing increases. There are clear equivalents in ecology: hives of bees that are genetically similar experience much greater temperature fluctuations than diverse ones.[16] As in ecosystems, economic homogeneity breeds fragility.[17]

This provides several powerful insights that derive from the authors' use of complex systems research. First, on regulation: the traditional view is that setting higher requirements for bank assets helps reduce risks to individual balance sheets, while the ecological perspective is that they also strengthen the system as a whole by reducing the possibility of crises propagating through the network. Second, the financial ecology perspective also suggests that the failure of different institutions carries different implications for the system, given their size or connectivity. The banking system has been characterized by the rise of institutions that are not just too large to fail but also too *connected* to fail. This has a direct equivalent in disease epidemiology and the idea of preventing 'super-spreaders' benefiting the overall system. Another equivalent is the idea of the keystone species, the diminishing of which leads to entire ecosystems crumbling. Third, just as in ecological networks, modularity—what some have called firebreaks—in the banking system limits the potential for cascades and creates systemic resilience. Such buffering is commonplace in complex social-ecological systems.

Haldane and May close their rare collaboration on a serious note. There is still not enough emphasis on understanding the systemic issues underlying the financial crisis, the importance of diversity or flexibility is not being sufficiently emphasized, and not enough is being done to enhance the resilience of the network. Just as ecologists took decades to improve their approach to biological systems, it will take a generation to adapt the mental models in banking and finance. One of the critical issues, for Haldane, is that approaches to regulation need to understand and navigate the complexity of the system without mirroring it. As he put it in a 2012 paper on the topic, 'As you do not fight fire with fire, you do not fight complexity with complexity.'[18]

According to Andy Lo of the Massachusetts Institute of Technology, lack of progress on such regulatory changes means we are missing the window of opportunity the crisis has provided. Lo, whose work has long drawn on complex systems research, reaches a disturbing conclusion: 'No one has learnt anything, nothing has been put in place that will stop it happening again. Five years after the greatest financial crisis of our lifetime, the right people aren't asking the right questions. We are left with a machine for perpetual crisis.'[19]

The Killer App of Organized Complexity

Although it is now the focus of a massive body of work and no small ambition, network science had humble beginnings.

Sociometry was a field of study initiated in April 1933, when psychologist Jacob Moreno presented to a medical conference what must have been the world's first social network diagram. Based on analyses of a spate of runaway girls from the Hudson School for Girls in upstate New York, Moreno hypothesized that the runaways were motivated less by their individual attitudes and conditions and more by their position in an underlying social structure, or what he called a 'sociogram'.[20]

Applying the principles of sociometry, Moreno argued that these links provided a channel for a flow of social influence and ideas among the runaway girls. He suggested that this approach would enable researchers to understand precisely what the interpersonal structure of a group looked like. Moreno's work focused on two aspects of networks: 'agents' and interactions between agents that influence each other's behaviour. Moreno believed that large-scale social phenomena, such as the economy and state, were sustained and reproduced over time by the small-scale configurations formed by people's patterns of friendship, dislike, and other relations. Network analysis has become much more elaborate and sophisticated, but has retained a focus on these basic ingredients and insights.

Moreno's research received a lot of attention, with one of his sociometric network visuals finding its way into *The New York Times*. He set up a journal, called *Sociometry*, which systematically investigated the relationship between psychological wellbeing and 'social configurations'. He would go on to become a leading light in group therapy and counselling. When he died, his epitaph read 'The man who brought laughter to psychiatry.'[21] It could be justifiably added 'and social networks to the world'. Herb Simon alluded to this work in his 1962 paper on the architecture of complexity:

> Almost all societies have elementary units called families, which may be grouped into villages or tribes, and these into larger groupings, and so on. If we make a chart of social interactions, of who talks to whom, the clusters of dense interaction in the chart will identify a rather well-defined ... structure [which] may be defined operationally by some measure of frequency of interaction in this *sociometric matrix*[22] (emphasis added).

Today, the notion of the network is one of the most used—and overused—terms in any context: the popular press, government policies, corporate strategies, blogs, tweets, and everyday conversation. Many social phenomena can be usefully thought of in terms of a network—from families to social communities to the Internet—with the latter at least partly responsible for the dramatic growth in interest in networks. 'Network' seems to play the same role in the social, economic, and political discourse of the twenty-first century that the concept of 'machine' did in the twentieth: it is a fundamental organizational metaphor for our times.

Science too is clearly much enamoured with networks: tools and concepts are being applied across the board, from cellular development to the evolution of galaxies. When in 2010 the International Network for Social Network Analysis held its biannual conference, the proceedings listing the various sessions came to a back-breaking 800 pages.

What all these very different systems share is the fact that they are made up of elements that are connected in a variety of ways. Network scientists focus their attention and considerable toolkit on understanding the pattern of relationships between the elements of a system, and seeing how these patterns affect system behaviour.[23] Through such analyses, common ground has been found between very different kinds of systems—for example, the supply networks feeding car manufacturing plants with machine parts have been found to have very similar characteristics to the neural networks that synchronize the brain and heartbeat of an earthworm. Traffic flow has been likened to the growth of slime mould, as I will show shortly. And we have already seen how the financial network can be likened to an ecological network. Such comparisons are alluring, but they have their critics. Some argue that they are simply a series of meaningless coincidences, an attempt to import insights from biological and physical sciences into social settings. However, as innovation specialist Karl von Hippel has argued, there is considerable scope to transfer ideas and principles from 'parallel ecosystems'—for example car brake manufacturers learning from airplane braking systems, to take an obvious example. The same principle has informed the work of 'biomimicry' specialists, who look for patterns and relationships in ecosystems and then replicate them in engineering approaches.

Moreover, network science does more than simply draw comparisons between social and physical or biological phenomena. It can be used to identify patterns in phenomena that occur at the interface of such systems—in fields such as health: 'an infection, for example, is transmitted more rapidly by people who have many contacts than by people who have few'.[24] Networks can reveal some fundamental insights about the social phenomena in question. As leading network specialist Mark Newman puts it, regardless of the kind of systems we are talking about, without understanding something about the structure of underlying networks we cannot hope to understand how the corresponding systems actually work.[25] And they can be applied in a number of very practical ways—today, network principles are being applied in everything from counterterrorism efforts, to web search engines, to tackling obesity. Little wonder that network analysis is being seen as the 'killer app' of complexity sciences.

At the heart of all of this work are a number of relatively simple questions:[26]

- What measures can be used to characterize properties of networks?
- What properties do different kinds of real-world networks share, and why? How did these properties come about?
- How do these properties affect the dynamics of information (or disease, or other communications) spreading on such networks, and the resilience of such networks to noise, component failures, or targeted attacks?

As Melanie Mitchell of the Santa Fe Institute says, 'Answering these questions could have a large impact not only on our understanding of many natural and social systems, but also on our ability to engineer and effectively use complex networks, ranging from better Web search and Internet routing to controlling the spread of diseases, the effectiveness of organized crime, and the ecological damage resulting from human actions.'[27]

Without doubt one of the major drivers of the rise in network applications has been the effort to understand terrorism networks. There are many network diagrams of Al Qaeda available online, most of them with the late Osama Bin

Laden occupying a central position in a large, dispersed system. The Office of Naval Research at the US Military Academy collected social network data on Al Qaeda, with records starting in 1988. By applying social network analysis (SNA) techniques to this data, they have been able to identify the most important and influential individuals in the network. But the data are inevitably incomplete: terrorists tend not to be too good at filling out the detailed surveys necessary for the relevant authorities to get a full and comprehensive understanding of their networks. Job descriptions for Central Intelligence Agency and Military Intelligence analysts increasingly include SNA skills. Such techniques have been used in counter-insurgency efforts in Afghanistan and Iraq.

Every network—from Al Qaeda to Facebook—is hypothesized as made up of nodes and links. Every actor is a node, an agent in the network, and every line is a link. Typically, nodes represent the agents in a network and links represent agents in some way interacting with each other. Links are often simplified as single lines, but they can be more detailed: multiple lines, indicating different kinds of connectivity. The addition of arrowheads can help indicate relationships that are one way—where one agent influences, provides resource to, or supports another but the relationship is not reciprocated. Or they can be two-way—where there is mutual influence or flow. Links may also be weighted, using relative ranking, or thickness, to indicate the strength of the interaction. Links can be of different kinds—for example information sharing links might be different colours to resource transfer links. Through the application of mathematical techniques to such models, different properties of the underlying network can be established.

In dense, or highly connected, networks, each node has a very large number of connections, and tends to be linked to most of the other nodes in the network. By contrast, in sparse, or low-density, networks, some nodes may have many connections but overall most of them are not directly tied to one another. For example, visualizations of Al Qaeda available online often show greater density around Bin Laden but more sparseness at the edges, with some small neighbourhood clusters.

The degree of a node is the simplest measure of a network, and represents the number of links a given node has. A node's *centrality* hinges on how well integrated and connected it is. There are three main forms: degree centrality, or the number of links each actor has; between-ness centrality, or how much an actor is a bridge between two cliques in a network; and closeness centrality, or the average distance between an actor and all other actors in a network.

Another key network measure is the level of clustering. In general terms, this means the likelihood that any two links from a given node are themselves linked together. Formally, this can be analysed by counting the triangles around a given node. The average *distance* in a network is the average number of steps it takes to 'travel' along the ties from one node to another, with each tie counting as one step. This tells us about the rate of information or resource transfer across the network.

While all of these metrics can be measured for specific nodes, they can also be usefully analysed for the network as a whole. So, for example, one of the most important global properties of a network is the distribution of links—a histogram showing the number of links against the nodes.

This has been found to be a fundamental feature of networks. Some histograms may show a normal distribution, suggesting the networks are more or less random, with a clustering around a central median. Others will exhibit a power law: a few nodes have a large number of links and many have a small number. Power law networks behave very differently to random networks. For example, a scale-free network is likely to retain its overall structure when nodes are randomly removed, whereas random ones will quickly disintegrate into component parts. However, if power law networks are broken up in a targeted manner by removing the hubs, they break up more quickly than random networks. This makes power law networks simultaneously robust and fragile.[28]

SNA uses these and a rapidly growing number of other formulations to look at how patterns of interactions between individuals lead to overall network properties. It is used to analyse a whole range of aspects of a network, from how much the network is held together by intermediaries, to the ability of members to access information, to the density of interactions within the network and the cohesion of relationships into cliques.

In the Christmas movie, 'It's a Wonderful Life', Jimmy Stewart's character George Bailey gets a chance to see what the world would have been like without him. Despite his clear and present troubles, he sees that the alternative world would have been far worse. As his otherworldly guide comments: 'Each life touches so many others…when [one person] isn't around, it leaves an awful hole.' The seemingly minute choices Bailey had made in a changing world affected by war, technology, and capitalism—which he previously deemed so unimportant—had a ripple effect beyond anything he had imagined.

Of course, the town of Bedford Falls was the archetypal small world—and network scientists have been able to show that the whole world displays surprising small world properties. The different possible network 'architectures' can be seen as the larger relationship structures, manifested in the overall pattern of links in a network. Perhaps the most influential network scientists working today are Duncan Watts, Stephen Strogatz, Albert Barabási, and Reka Albert. Their accumulated work suggests two particular structures underlying networks are especially relevant for understanding real-world problems of organized complexity.

Small Worlds, Scale Free

The first model I want to describe is based on the notion of 'six degrees of separation'. Watts and Strogatz started out with a network of 5,000 individuals and linked people up to their ten closest neighbours. This led to some local clustering: for any given ten nodes, around two-thirds were connected in a clique. To get from one part of the network to another, the average number of steps was around 50. The researchers then added some randomness into the mix. For each network of 5,000 people, they added another 50 at random. While this had little effect on the clustering of the network, it had a dramatic effect on the degrees of separation, which suddenly dropped to around seven. They checked their numbers and found them to be solid: a small amount of randomness was enough to turn a large world network into a small world network. This revealed how it was possible for social worlds—like 1960s America—to have only six degrees of separation. It also explained the surprise we feel when confronted with this small world reality: 'The long-distance social shortcuts that make the world small are mostly invisible in our ordinary social lives.'[29]

It turns out that a large number of real-world social networks are made up of many small, tightly knit groups with sparse connections to other groups that would otherwise be remote or isolated. Watts and Strogatz checked their findings against the Internet movie database, and found that the global actor network was indeed a small world network. Unlike the 'six degrees of Kevin Bacon' game so loved by drunken undergraduates, however, the degree of separation was closer to three—and it applied to every actor, not just Mr Bacon. They also showed that the US electrical power grid was a small world network—work that has since inspired the government to study 'complex adaptive systems engineering' to better understand and deal with the network effects in critical infrastructure.[30]

Forest fires have also been shown to exhibit small world properties. By modelling the fuel path in a forest as if it was a small world network, researchers showed that a small world model generated results that were identical to real forest fire patterns in Europe and South Africa, in terms of the rate of spread, the area, and the shape of the burn. Using satellite imagery, they also found that the 'topology' of the fires was accurately predicted by the small world model.

While their findings kick-started a revolution in network thinking that has spread across disciplines over the past decade or so, a couple of questions remained about Watts and Strogatz's assumptions and how closely they matched the reality of how networks form and grow over time. The assumption that you start with a 5,000-node network and then add in random networks works fine as an abstract description of small world networks. But it isn't how our social lives are created, nor—intuitively—does it explain how other real-world networks might have come to be. Second, and just as important, Watts and Strogatz didn't take into account the feature of what is called 'preferential attachment'. Specifically, in their approach to forming networks, the likelihood of highly connected nodes fell away as the number of nodes increased: 'Vertices with large connectivity are practically absent',[31] and the overall distribution of nodes was Gaussian in form, with a scale for cut-offs (akin to human heights).

Barabási and Albert started their work on the basis that Watts and Strogatz had failed to take account of two real-world features of networks. The first was the notion of growth: instead of thinking of nodes as in place already and then the links being added in, Barabási and Albert tried to show that the number of nodes rises and falls over time. Think of your friendship networks as an example. Second, the reality of network connections is that most real networks are 'preferentially connected':

> A new actor is cast most likely in a supporting role, with more established, well known actors. Consequently, the probability that a new actor is cast with an established one is much higher than casting with other less known actors. Similarly, a newly created webpage will more likely include links to well known, popular documents with already high connectivity, or a new manuscript is more likely to cite a well known and thus much cited paper than its less cited and consequently less known peer.[32]

This has been referred to as the 'Matthew effect' from the Bible: 'He that has, shall gain in abundance.'[33] Or, to put it another way, the rich get richer. If the number of links for each actor is mapped in a frequency table, instead of a Gaussian distribution you get a power law distribution with a fat tail that trails off with no cut-off: all scales are present—'scale free'. Such preferential connection seems to be present in the six degrees phenomenon. It turns out that, once again, Herb Simon's work was an important precursor: in a 1955 theoretical paper he showed that social connections in real-world networks were likely to be characterized by power laws—or what he called 'skewed distributions'.[34]

These two elements were shown to generate the small world networks of the kind that Watts and Strogatz identified, with the advantage that they provided a realistic picture of how networks grow and how linkages are distributed across different nodes.[35]

In various studies of real-world networks, including the Internet, electrical power networks, networks of airline city connections, scientific collaboration networks, and metabolic networks in biological organisms, Barabási, Albert, and others, found that the empirical degree distribution was explained well by a power law. They concluded that their 'growth with preferential attachment' mechanism is what drives the evolution of real-world networks: 'Small differences in ability or even purely random fluctuations can get locked in and lead to very large inequalities over time.'[36]

While network scientists will argue about the relative merits of these approaches, the reality is that both are important for understanding real-world networks. Experiments I have run (of which more in the next part of the book) suggest that Barabási's work doesn't generate the kind of community clustering seen in real-world networks, whereas the Watts model doesn't have a decent model of change or distribution. An intelligent combination of the two models is actually the most useful way forward.

In keeping with this line of argument, it has been shown that the financial system is simultaneously a small world, scale-free network. Andy Haldane showed that the past 20 years had seen the financial system being characterized by rising levels of interconnection, a growing tendency towards small world properties, and a long tail degree distribution—what he calls 'an unholy trinity'. And, 'From a stability perspective, it translates into a robust-yet-fragile system, susceptible to a loss of confidence in the key financial hubs and with rapid international transmission of disturbances.'[37]

This begs the question, just how connected is *too* connected? With many of these examples, it becomes evident only after the fact that a system is dangerously interconnected. But interconnectedness is not always a bad thing. Stuart Kauffman of the Santa Fe Institute developed a formal network model to try to explain and perhaps anticipate the interactions that characterize complex systems, be they positive or negative.[38] He uses the analogy of 10,000 buttons on a rug being joined up one at a time. To begin with, you get isolated pairs, then small clusters. To start off with, the system is a simple one. But the way the connections are made slowly results in a remarkable transformation: it is nothing less than the rise of complexity. As the number of connections reaches and exceeds half the number of buttons (i.e. around the 5,000th link,) the system switches rapidly from a lot of buttons with a few connections to another start where there is a lot more structure. This transition point is a phase transition: complexity emerges just through the addition of more connections. But at a certain point, dense interconnections lead to what Kauffman calls complexity catastrophes. Here, too many connections lead the system to be rigid in the face of shocks, despite being robust.[39] Again, balance is key: it turns out network scientists also have a variant of the 'edge of chaos' idea. Kauffmann illustrates this by asking us to imagine the buttons are Christmas tree lights. Each bulb is either on or off, and is wired to k other bulbs. The bulbs are governed by simple rules whereby they turn themselves on or off depending on the state of the neighbouring bulbs. An example of a rule is 'majority wins', that is, if a bulb is connected to three others, and two are on, it turns itself on. It turns out that there are three possible patterns of behaviour for the system.[40]

- Chaotic: where k is large and the bulbs turn on and off chaotically as they switch each other off and on.

- Ordered: where k is small and some lights turn on and off a few times, but quickly the whole set of lights stops twinkling.

- Complex: where k is around 2, where complex patterns will emerge of twinkling islands of lights, slowly changing shape but never freezing into a fixed pattern or becoming chaotic.

This point of complexity is fundamentally dependent on the ability of the system to transmit information. The ordered and chaotic extremes are unable to transform information or adapt. But a complex network—one at the edge of chaos—is able to do both. This point of interconnectedness being 'just right' is where the networks have a balance between stability and change and have the potential to evolve. The message is that, when you have a highly connected network in a dynamic and shifting context, you may be in trouble unless you can quickly mobilize the means to ensure robustness and resilience. This same basic process is at the heart of the contagion in the financial system, in the American forest landscape, and in the growth of Facebook.

One of the most fascinating proofs of this similarity across systems comes from the work of biologists working with slime moulds.[41] Slime moulds are deeply unusual life forms that are somewhere between plant, animal, and fungus. The basic slime mould 'unit' closely resembles an amoeba, and they are found in woodlands and forests in dark, damp, northern, temperate zones. When foraging, a slime mould will put out feelers, create nodes and branches, and grow outwards as an interconnected network of tubes, growing up to a quarter of a metre wide. As they explore forest floors, each mould has to constantly trade off the cost, efficiency, and resilience of this expanding network. Biologists believe they do so by following simple rules to travel, solve problems, and adapt to environmental conditions.

Because the purpose of slime mould networks is to link food sources together and to transport nutrients around as efficiently as possible, there is an obvious analogy with human transportation networks. A Japanese–UK research team set out to find out exactly how similar these processes were, with startling results.

The scientists examined slime network development processes by putting oat flakes (a particularly favoured food of slime moulds) in a pattern that represented the positions of cities around Tokyo. Initially, the mould moved so it was arranged evenly around the flakes. But within hours it began strengthening some nutrient tunnels and connections, while others disappeared. After one day, the slime mould had built a network of nutrient-carrying tubes, with an overall pattern that bore a striking resemblance to the Tokyo rail system.

The process was then repeated by another team at the University of the West of England, who used slime mould to accurately simulate the UK motorway system. Not only had the mould created the shortest possible network that could connect all the 'cities', but it had also included redundant connections that allowed the mould (and, by implication, the real rail and road networks) to be resilient to breakdowns in any part of the network. The tiny slime mould network had adapted to mimic the costs, efficiencies, and resiliencies of the much larger-scale versions.

> The mould's abilities are a wonder of self-optimisation. It has no sense of forward-planning, no overhead maps or intelligence to guide its moves. It creates an efficient network by laying down plasmodia indiscriminately, strengthening whatever works and cutting back on whatever doesn't.[42]

However, this doesn't mean we all need to go foraging for slime moulds in dank northern forests in the hope they will help us with complex project designs. As an article in *The Economist* argued,

> Of course, [the researchers are not] suggesting that rail and road networks should be designed by slime moulds. What they are proposing is that good and complex solutions can emerge from simple rules, and that this principle might be applied elsewhere. The next thing is to discover and use these rules to enable other networks to self-organise in an 'intelligent' fashion.[43]

As an aside, having become enamoured of the field of biomimicry, which uses ideas inspired by nature in engineering and organizational design, I spent some time puzzling as to what organisms, if any, behave like the aid system today. In June 2011, I attended a conference at the International Institute for Applied Systems Analysis chaired by Simon Levin, the eminent ecologist whose work on the banking system I described earlier in this chapter. After my presentation on aid and complexity, I asked him about this specific issue. I described to him carefully the nature of the aid system, the way it absorbs resources and moves and forms in distinctive ways in different parts of the world, putting itself in a central position in new settings while resources are available, then moving on to another location. I asked—with a sense of having talked for too long—if there was any ecological equivalent. He grinned, and replied, 'Slime moulds. That's the organism that best fits your description of the aid system.'

From Broadway Stars to Bug Fixers and Begotten Slums

I want to close this chapter with three stories that all highlight how network analysis, for a long time the province of serious scientists and academics, is becoming more and more practical and usable.

One recent example of the use of SNA has been in understanding the success of Broadway musicals. Brian Uzzi, a sociologist at Northwestern University in Chicago, decided he would combine his academic and personal interests and apply network science to see if he could explain what made one musical successful and another a failure. He gathered data on 321 musicals launched on Broadway over 44 years, focusing on team membership. His findings were intriguing: teams that had never worked together before fared poorly. Teams made up exclusively of people who had worked together previously also tended to produce flops. In between, groups with a balanced mix of new and old participants reliably produced hits. Variation in the density of the ties between individuals allowed for better communication and greater creativity, with fresh ideas combining well with insiders. Ultimately, 'Success came down to the structure of the network binding its team together.'[44]

SNA is growing in popularity, not least because it reveals the truth hidden in organizational charts and matrix diagrams. Hidalgo argues that organizations should be seen not just as collections of individuals but also as networks of individuals who 'interact sometimes through hierarchies, but mostly, despite them'.[45] Echoing Uzzi, he suggests success or failure depends not just on talent but on how employees interact. 'The networks that define an organization [are those] that emerge from the informal interactions that occur between an organization's members. Two firms, with the exact same organizational chart, can have diverging fates. Can we say the same about two organizations characterized by similar informal network structures?'[46]

Kidane and Gloor looked at the relationship between creativity, performance, and network structure in open-source software development.[47] The core finding was that more centralized groups could fix more bugs than less centralized groups, but the latter came up with more new features in a given time period. Again, the balance between performance and creativity was reflected in the social networks.

Another powerful example presents what is, as far as I know, the first use of network analysis as admissible evidence in a court of law. In the television series

'The Wire', the detectives used an ingenious wiretapping process to create a network map of the dealers, carriers, and shadowy bosses of a drug network in Baltimore. Researchers in a social justice organization went through much the same process in trying to uncover a network of 'slumlords' in Los Angeles, whose violations included sewage leaks, high lead levels, and illegal evictions. The organization started to notice some patterns in the buildings housing the tenants and, as the data grew, tried to find different ways of representing this. They eventually turned to social network analysis 'to make sense of the complex interconnectivity'.[48]

The key problem was that the slumlord network was adapting to the situation. The organization passed data on to city officials, who then delivered it to the building owners. When the deadline for fixing things approached, the owners would say the property had changed hands and they were no longer responsible, thereby passing away responsibility for the violations. By analysing the structure of ownership, the organization found that the building owners were members of a large extended family network. The extent of the conspiracy became clear. As well as an obvious network structure, the analysis revealed a shadow network of masterminds, a couple of steps removed from the building owners themselves. These key individuals had numerous business interests across the city, including sitting on the board of a mortgage company, which just happened to have financed the transactions for the property owners. The city attorney used the network analysis along with the findings of a separate investigation to convict the family members. The tenants of one building subsequently used the same evidence to file a civil suit and obtain compensation.[49]

All three of these examples, along with those I shared earlier, illustrate well how the x-ray that is network science is helping researchers, policymakers and practitioners in many diverse fields 'become more self-aware'.[50]

CHAPTER II

The Devil is in the Dynamics

'Consider change: the management of it, the forecasting of it, the predictability of it, the expectation of it, the reliability of it, the surprise of it ... the structure of it. Change is what makes life interesting. It's what makes thinking necessary; change in our world provides the substance of life ... Still, with change all around us, we insist on ... focusing on snapshot pictures of our world. We are like two-dimensional flatliners in a three-dimensional world. We ... disregard the transitions ... We capture measures ... as singular quantities, and record them with precision, believing that greater accuracy will somehow provide greater truth. We don't seem to mind that those measures don't reveal the dynamics of the continually changing [world] they represent ... No-one seems to be concerned about the patterns and structures of change ... This is not a world of constants that can be captured with measures ... it is a world of dynamics.'

Richard Priesmeyer.[1]

Watch What You Heat

Having looked at the systemic, behavioural, and structural aspects of complex adaptive systems, there is one last part of the complexity landscape I want to examine. The focus of this chapter is on *the dynamics of complex systems*. This aspect presents some of the greatest challenges to existing sensibilities in scientific thinking and, by extension, to public policy realms, including foreign aid.

A compelling example of such complexity, precisely because it illuminates the inadequacy of prescribed approaches to dynamic phenomena, is the management of wildfires in national forests in the USA. Fully a third of the country's landmass is covered by forest, almost a quarter of that in official parks and wilderness areas.[2] These forests are diverse; they are also highly dynamic, changing—either fast or slowly—in response to a range of factors that might be internal or external. So, for example, there will be shifts in forest ecosystems in response to climate variations—both longer term and over the course of a single season. There will be responses to disturbances from natural sources—weather events, disease, predatory behaviour of animals. And there are fires—both those caused by natural factors like lightning strikes and those created by the greatest enemy to forests: human beings. Reflecting on all this, one becomes aware that the philosopher's conundrum of whether a tree falling in a forest in fact makes a noise is based on a fundamental oversight: it may in fact be impossible to hear anything over the ongoing din.

So well known is the issue of forest fires that their destructive power forms the basis of numerous theories and models of change in complex systems.[3] And they are not just a metaphor: Buzz Holling, an influential ecologist and one-time Director of the International Institute for Applied Systems Analysis (IIASA), cited forests as exemplars of resilient ecological systems, with fires providing vital forces of 'creative destruction' that enable them to adapt and change.[4]

The national park movement, initiated in the nineteenth century by John Muir, led to the preservation of these vast swathes of natural, dynamic beauty. But the preservation mentality contributed inadvertently to some seriously misjudged policies—especially as relates to the management of these forest dynamics. When the Forest Service was created in the 1890s, there was a strong desire to set what it did as distinct from that of the Native Americans, whose livelihoods often relied on forests. The Indians' 'heathen practices' needed to be eradicated through the application of a 'civilizing mentality' of rationality and control. There was a strong sense that it would not serve the agency to educate people about the appropriate and inappropriate uses of fire. An early forest service chief made the point unambiguously: 'The first measure necessary for the successful practice of forestry is protection from fire.'[5] Fire historian Stephen Pyne wryly observes that propaganda does not thrive on close distinctions.[6] (The same could be said of aid marketing.)

For most of the twentieth century, federal fire policy was geared toward suppressing all fires.[7] While this had some clear and obvious goals on a practical and political level, it simply ignored the benefits fire provided. As well as returning nutrients to soils and encouraging the growth of fire-resistant trees, fires prevented the density of forests from increasing. Periodic fires can support overall forest health through burning lower branches and clearing dead wood from the forest floor, thereby kick-starting regeneration by providing ideal growing conditions. It also improves the habitat for many forest-dwelling species that prefer relatively open spaces. So-called heathen 'light-burning' practices incidentally enabled the regular clearing out of vegetation. In the language of the previous chapter, small fires maintained the modularity and resilience of the forest network. John Muir seems to have realized this rather earlier: 'By forces seemingly antagonistic and destructive Nature accomplishes her beneficent designs—now a flood of fire, now a flood of ice, now a flood of water; and again in the fullness of time an outburst of organic life.'[8]

But massive fires in the early twentieth century and high levels of human fatalities propelled the Forest Service to the forefront of a national movement towards fire protection. Under the Forest Fires Emergency Act of 1908, Congress agreed that *any amount of money* spent by the Forest Service in fire prevention would subsequently be reimbursed.[9]

> Government management of fire suppression on national forests has interfered with ecosystem function and put forests and communities at risk. The Forest Service is staffed by qualified professionals, but they respond to incentives, like anyone else. Bureaucratic incentives do not always encourage responsible stewardship of natural resources. This is exemplified in fire policy decisions that increase[d] the Forest Services budget, but result[ed] in fuel-choked forests of weakened trees.[10]

What this meant was there was no incentive for the Forest Service to determine optimal or efficient levels of fire prevention. Worse than this, the Forest Service is now known to have suppressed evidence of the benefits of light burning for years, swayed by the financial benefits of the 1908 Act. Fire suppression made the forest system become dangerously interconnected—so that a single fire could spread for miles. It has also become vertically interconnected: grasses, shrubs, and saplings form a 'fuel ladder', enabling flames to climb to the forest canopy and leading to the destruction of whole swathes of forest. Overall, there has been a shift from a system where forests burned lightly every 15 to 30 years to one where they burn catastrophically on a more frequent basis. The Act was eventually repealed in 1978, but extreme fires in the late 1980s led to a public outcry and another wave of fire prevention activities, with Congress again supporting a system of fire suppression reimbursement. As of 2001, some 60 million acres of forest was at risk of catastrophic fires. Fire policies have not protected the forests but in fact have placed them at considerably greater risk. In many part of the country, this politically expedient but ecologically vulnerable system remains in place at the time of writing.

The story is a sad but instructive one of poorly conceived human power being clumsily exerted over a dynamic ecological system. The ecological system was interconnected with human decision-making systems in numerous ways, which increased its fragility. Berry concludes that the fire suppression policy backfired precisely because of several generations of management decisions grounded in political concerns instead of local, professional, or scientific knowledge: politicized decision making and fire suppression had major economic and ecological costs. And this is an inherent challenge in the politicized delivery of public goods. Publicly owned forests offer services that are non-rivalrous and non-excludable. This means that individuals cannot be effectively excluded from the use of forests and that use by one individual does not reduce availability to others. However, politicized mismanagement has interfered with ecosystem functions and put forests and communities at risk: 'Bureaucratic incentives do not always encourage responsible stewardship.'[11] Some readers will no doubt already be drawing their own parallels with international aid.

As Muir himself put it, in a prophetic summary of the subsequent century of misguided policy: 'Through all the wonderful, eventful centuries God has cared for these trees, saved them from drought, disease, avalanches, and a thousand straining, leveling tempests and floods; but he cannot save them from fools.'[12]

The Parable of Hora and Tempus

For me, the notion of the world becoming an engine for perpetual crisis echoes the Watchmaker's Parable told by Herb Simon.[13] Two fine watchmakers, Hora and Tempus, were both highly regarded, with a lot of demand for their product. However, while Hora's business went from strength to strength, Tempus ended up poor and lost his shop.

Both craftsmen, Simon tells us, used about a thousand separate pieces in their watches. The difference was in the nature of the assembly process. Tempus assembled each watch part by painstaking part. Whenever he was interrupted, he had to start again. Hora made watches that were no less complex but he put his watches together in a *modular* manner, using small collections of ten parts, which themselves formed larger collections of ten parts, with the larger watch being composed of ten of these larger assemblies. This meant his work was far less susceptible to interruptions, with a dramatic effect on productivity levels. If the probability of interruption is set at 1 per cent (0.01), Hora would complete nine watches in every ten attempts while Tempus would complete only nine watches in around every *two hundred thousand* attempts.

As this example indicates, interconnectedness may occur at various levels of a system. The watch components are interconnected; the ten-part assemblies of Hora are interconnected; the manufacturing system and the sale-order system of both watchmakers is interconnected; the two organizations are interconnected with the wider environment. Different actions are interconnected, ideas and practices are interconnected, intentions and actions are interconnected.[14]

Degrees of connectivity can vary across different parts of a system, over time in a system, and—obviously—across different systems.[15] Understanding this better is central to getting our heads around problems of organized complexity. Herb Simon referred to this as the essential 'architecture of complexity'[16] and showed how other kinds of networks exhibit the same kind of modular structure as Hora's assembly. His wide-ranging analysis—which incidentally was peer reviewed by a certain Warren Weaver—covered biological, physical, and social systems.

In modern parlance, the work of Hora was more resilient to change. Resilient systems are the focus of a growing body of researchers, most notably the global Resilience Alliance founded by Buzz Holling.[17] Resilient systems are widely described as those able to maintain functions in the face of stresses and change. The global financial crisis and its associated uncertainties have led the idea of resilience to take on greater importance in development and humanitarian aid.

Some of the generic characteristics of resilient systems are apparent in the Watchmaker's Parable. As Simon pointed out, Hora's system had an inherent modularity and redundancy, which meant it was better able to cope with pressure, surges, and demands. It was flexible and better able to perform essential tasks under a range of conditions. It distributed the benefits of efforts such that they were not all affected by a given event. Finally, it exhibits safe failure, whereby shocks and challenges can be navigated and absorbed. Safe failure also indicates the 'soft interdependence' of a system, so that failure in one structure or linkage will not lead to cascading effects across the whole system.[18]

Thinking has moved on from the 1960s, when Simon presented his parable, but perhaps not as much as we might imagine. Robert Dorit recently suggested we are just starting to understand that modularity and redundancy are important and inherent features of all living systems, and are characteristic of 'systems that are simultaneously resilient and capable of evolving'.[19]

As Dorit suggests, instead of the chain of command found in mechanical systems with 'simple causes and effects barked down a simple chain of command', complex living systems are characterized by a 'very large web of weak interactions' which leads to interaction among the parts that is less 'a chain of command and more like a complex court intrigue: ambiguous whispers against a noisy and distracting background'.[20] This network form confers certain advantages—networks of weak interactions mean systems can react to a turbulent environment while maintaining a degree of stability.

By implication, what Simon, Dorit, and the work of resilience researchers tells us is that the network underpinning the global financial ecosystem may be more Hora than Tempus. A more resilient financial system would have more modularity, so a degree of stability could be maintained. There would also need to be more flexibility and redundancy in regulatory frameworks, which would be designed for the one-in-ten-million chance events.

The lack of attention to modularity and redundancy in human-designed systems is remarkably consistent. One obvious analogy is with the levees in New Orleans, where lack of investment was compounded by decades of concreting over the mangrove swamps that naturally buffered the coastline from storm surges. This left citizens doubly vulnerable. The forest fire prevention system example above is another good illustration.

What these imagined and real examples show is that the relationships that underpin systems of organized complexity have a profound effect on adaptability and resilience. Highly connected systems—financial markets, Tempus' assembly, electrical grids, forests—are extremely vulnerable if their environment is unstable, because changes in one part will quickly propagate across the system, with potentially devastating effects. The implication seems clear: we have moved from a Hora world to a Tempus world.

The Sandpile Revolutionary

We have a much better understanding of what connects forest fires and a whole range of other complex dynamics, including market crashes, traffic jams, and political landslides, thanks to work of a maverick Danish physicist called Per Bak. For about 20 years after the publication of his 1988 paper on how change happens in complex systems—the so-called sandpile hypothesis—it was the most widely cited scientific paper in the world.

Bak started out by echoing Warren Weaver, describing the tendency of science to reduce problems to one or two body problems or many body problems. The reality was that a great deal of what is seen in the natural world sits between the two extremes: 'for instance, ecological systems are organised such that the different species "support" each other in a way that cannot be understood by studying the individual constituents in isolation'.[21] In a later study, he argued that 'Behavior of systems like these cannot be deduced by examining ever smaller scales to derive microscopic laws; the dynamics and form is "emergent."'[22]

What was the key to all of these phenomena? One answer was to consider an external agent who somehow organized them. For a variety of reasons, this didn't satisfy Bak, who was keen to 'take God out of the equations'.[23] Instead of going through a series of context-specific analyses of different systems and their particular dynamics, he wanted to see if a common self-organizing dynamic could be identified. As he argued,

> Perhaps nature does not need to invent a multitude of mechanisms, one for each system. The view that only a limited number of mechanisms, or principles, lead to complexity in all its manifestations (from the galactic or universal to the molecular) is supported by the observation of regularities that appear in the statistical description of complex systems. These statistical regularities provide hope and encouragement that a science of complexity may eventually emerge.[24]

Bak illustrated his hypothesis with reference to a slowly growing sandpile. Imagine you have just turned an hourglass around and have filmed the sand running through, and then play back the film slowly enough to see each grain drop, one by one. As more grains of sand fall, they naturally form a cone-shaped pile. As the pile continues to build, different grains form clusters, in an intricate network arrangement whereby some grains are loosely connected and others tightly connected. The pile eventually reaches a state of criticality, when a single grain has the potential to simply land and do nothing at all, to slide down the pile, or to 'trigger a domino-like reaction of tumbling grains that can sweep through the entire pile'.[25]

These ideas resonate with thinking on tightly and loosely coupled systems in social science more generally. In tightly coupled systems, relatively trivial changes in one element or dimension can spread rapidly and unpredictably through the system and have dramatic and unpredictable effects. Two of the best-known forays into social complexity science—by Charles Perrow and Joseph Tainter, writing in the 1980s—look specifically at the phenomena of accidents and societal collapse. Both illustrate dramatically the implications of connectedness for change by distinguishing complex and simple systems. Perrow compared accidents in tightly coupled systems such as nuclear power stations to those taking place in loosely coupled systems such as educational systems.[26] Tainter argued that when a society forms there is an increasing return to complexity, but then it reaches a tipping point at which the return on complexity is outweighed by the cost.[27] These ideas also find expression in the network science idea of a 'complexity catastrophe' described in the earlier chapter.

Returning to Bak's model, at the point of criticality a single grain can have an entirely unpredictable effect, whose size cannot be anticipated in advance. The overall system of events does have a pattern to it, however: put simply, small avalanches happen far more frequently than large ones.[28] This 'power law' means the frequency of events of a given size decreases as the size of the event increases. So, for example, when the size of a potential forest fire is doubled, it becomes twice as unlikely to occur. This, incidentally, is the same scale-free phenomenon identified in the connections between nodes of a social network by Barabási and Albert (see Chapter 10). Some readers may be drawing parallels with the edge of chaos notion; in fact, self-organized criticality has been described by Stuart Kauffmann, who also collaborated with Per Bak, as 'a close cousin' of this concept.

Bak also showed how the build-up of undergrowth leads to larger-scale fires, and thus that preventing small fires could indeed lead to large fires. The same lesson is present in traffic jams: trying to eliminate all traffic jams is only likely to create much larger catastrophic standstills. Forest fires have since been shown to exhibit small world properties, with research producing results that are identical to real forest fire patterns in terms of rate of spread, area, and shape of burn. Using satellite imagery, the small world model has been able also to predict the 'topology' of fires accurately.[29]

Bak also showed that the dynamic nature of the feedbacks had led some to evolve to a critical state where power laws dominate and negligible changes can cause catastrophic events. Many other systems—from the workings of the heart to the global economy—have been examined through this lens. In all of these systems, the longer a critical state builds up, the longer the feedback dynamic continues unchecked and the greater the potential for a serious 'avalanche'. In social settings, this can be because of the feedback loops that reinforce potentially damaging and irresponsible behaviours. Andy Lo talks about the self-organized critical state that financial markets reached prior to the crisis, mutually reinforced by the behaviours and actions of financiers, politicians, home owners, and consumers.[30]

Even human psyches might be subject to self-organized criticality. In his book *How Nature Works* Bak explains the implications in the following way:

> The formation of a person's identity is analogous to the formation of the sandpile. A personality reaches the critical state; then the impact of each new experience reverberates throughout the whole person, both directly, and indirectly, by setting the stage for future change. Because these changes are subject to sensitive dependence each person's history and personality is unique.

This insight resonates with some of the latest thinking in systemic therapy, psychology, and psychiatry. However, as with so much in the field of the human mind in sickness and health, things are not that straightforward. According to psychiatrist Mike Groszmann, the social context in which mental illnesses or pathological behaviours emerge has a profound effect, to the extent that one can never be certain until after the event what the 'grain of sand' might have been, or indeed what kinds of resilience enable some individuals to weather storms that bring many others down.[31]

Today, in our globalized world, it is not just individuals or even individual systems that are at facing such risks. The hyper-connectivity of previously distinct systems has contributed to the whole world reaching a critical state, with successive tsunamis of instability cascading around the world. Bertram and Bar-Yam argue that the Arab Spring is a political and social example of just such a critical global cascade. The build-up to the tipping point was the ever-tighter coupling between finance, energy, and food systems:

> The basis for the cascade is an underlying buildup of tensions (like the sandpile) which has to reach a point of crisis at any one location...once something happens in one place, the outbreak cascades. The current unrest can thus be considered as an avalanche in the sandpile of the Middle East. Tensions in the region have built up to a critical state, and the uprising in Tunisia acted as the grain which began the cascade.[32]

Being aware of, and intelligently navigating, these cascades as they emerge is the fundamental challenge. This may bring to mind daredevil snowboarders who get kicks from riding avalanches down mountainsides. This is of course a very optimistic image—and implies that we can learn to apply the science of crises to better weather them.

But the problem remains that, in many contexts, being aware of socio-economic avalanches as they are happening may not always be beneficial, not least because of the social and psychological issues alluded to earlier. We are not always able to collectively act in a clear and calm manner in such situations. Moreover, as the 2008 banking crisis showed so clearly, the way in which different actors weather such storms will be shaped by their existing status and position. To take one obvious example, researchers found that the wealthiest portion of society actually became proportionally richer in the years following the crisis. It seems that resilience—psychological, social, or economic—is seldom evenly distributed.

The Mathematics of 'The New Normal'

Per Bak started his investigation into self-organized criticality to try and explain the common recurrence of power laws in a range of natural phenomena. These statistical regularities, which I touched on previously in the context of networks, are a key signature of complex dynamic systems. Although power laws are now firmly embedded in the toolkit of statistical physics, the first identified power law was in an economic context.

Intrigued as to why so much of the land in his native Italy was concentrated in the hands of so few, nineteenth-century engineer-turned-economist Wilfred Pareto set out to map wealth distribution more generally.[33] Looking at a large variety of datasets, from Swiss tax records to Parisian rental income and personal income from the UK, Prussia, Italy, and Ireland, he found a series of long tails, today known widely as Pareto distributions. Instead of being normally distributed, as he had expected, wealth was concentrated in the hands of a few. This clearly depressed Pareto, who saw it as evidence of a harsh social Darwinism. The notion of democracy was a lie: human nature was base and selfish.

Rather less portentously, Pareto found similar trends in a range of other phenomena, including in the yields of his home-grown broad beans. A lot of research has been done following Pareto's discovery to understand the nature and cause of inequality, and the same long tail has been found in many other countries. But the mathematics of the curve eluded Pareto. The question he and his contemporaries didn't ask, as far as we know, is *why* this pattern occurs.[34]

That said, a few notable thinkers do seem to have grasped its potential, among them Schumpeter, who wrote in the 1940s, 'Nobody seems to have realized that the hunt for, and the interpretation of, *invariants* of this type might lay the foundations for an entirely novel type of theory' (emphasis added).[35]

The 'novel type of theory' that would eventually emerge from Pareto's foundation ended up transcending economics and the social sciences. Researchers working in different fields discovered similar long tails in other contexts. At Harvard in the 1940s, George Zipf found power law distribution when analysing word frequencies in different languages and texts, and also in city sizes.[36] Lewis Fry Richardson found a power law in war casualties.[37] Richter and Gutenberg in the 1950s, in their study of earthquakes, discovered what is perhaps the most famous power law to date, used in the Richter scale.[38] Such diverse examples were drawn together when—surprise, surprise—Herb Simon looked at power laws in a number of contexts in 1955.[39] Simon noted that long tails were so frequent, and so widespread, that they could only signify some common underlying pattern of probability. He explored a number of assumptions against each case and showed that, in all the cases, correlations between events of different kinds played a central role in the creation of the long tail. Simon's analysis is formal and detailed, but is useful because of its focus on assumptions made about the distribution of events in complex systems. Add this to Simon's work on the architecture of complexity, decision making, and network relations, and it is fair to say that his contribution to the various elements of the third great advance is arguably greater than that of any other single individual. It should now become clear why Eric Beinhocker refers to Simon as the 'first true genius of complexity'.[40]

In the normal distribution, events are independent and additive, what has been called the *mild* family of distributions.[41] Independence of events, such as price changes or market movements, means the occurrence of one event is not influenced in any way by the occurrence of another. Normal distribution, which follows in part from this, assumes that, given a large enough number of events, we will see a clustering around some central average. The classic example of independent, normal distribution is the height of a population, which is represented by a bell-curve, with a peak in the centre and a falling-off to zero relatively quickly on either side. This represents 'a baseline theory for what happens when many independent events contribute to some outcome. It is what makes past averages ... useful as guides to the future.'[42]

By contrast, when events are related—when they are interdependent and *multiplicative*—long tails emerge, because 'Positive feedback processes leading to extreme events occur more frequently than "normal", bell-shaped Gaussian-based statistics lead us to expect.'[43] When such events are mapped without forcing them to fit the bell-curve—by eliminating outliers and 'cleaning the data'—one sees a rather different kind of curve. This long tail starts off very high with the smaller events and then drops slowly downward. As Mark Buchanan puts it, 'The Achilles' heel of the bell curve is the word independent. When one event influences another ... when interdependence is important ... the power-law pattern frequently takes the place of the bell curve.'[44] This is the *wild* family of probability distribution. Benoit Mandelbrot, IBM computer scientist-turned-Yale mathematician, famously explored these issues in relation to the stock market in 1963, saying, rather bombastically, this made him the 'first well-trained mathematician to take these tails seriously'.[45]

The problems arise when the wild family is confused with the mild family. In interdependent systems, averages are seldom a useful guide to the future. This has implications for—among other things—risk and how it is understood. Take market fluctuations as one example. Normal distributions suggest crashes are a long way off, and encourage particular forms of risk taking and innovation. The bell-curve predicts a drop of 10 per cent will happen on average around every 500 years. Mandelbrot argued that there were two major flaws in modern finance—that events were viewed as independent and that they were seen as normally distributed. The popular black swan hypothesis put forward by Nassim Nicholas Taleb, about the unexpectedly high frequency of large shocks to complex systems, essentially builds on the idea of power laws and Mandelbrot's thinking on fractals and non-linear dynamics.[46] An earlier study by Paul Krugman argued that power laws are an important indication of a self-organized economy.

A large number of researchers have sought to identify the power law basis of complex systems. As a result, power laws now seem to be everywhere: hurricane intensity, size of firms, number of criminal acts committed by individuals, information and links provided on the worldwide web, and frequency of family names. Gross domestic product growth, that holy grail of development aid efforts, has been shown to follow a power law. So too have casualties following disasters. Each of these phenomena has been created by positive feedbacks, whereby there are far more outliers than would 'normally' be expected.

That said, there is still a need to be careful when looking at events and determining the implications for the dynamics of a system. First of all, just as it is easy to see a mild distribution when there is in fact a wild one, there is also a risk that the opposite can happen. To take one extreme example, researchers have shown that terrorist groups' efforts serve to create the *perception* of fat tail events, which in turn heighten a sense of risk and fear. After the 11 September 2001 terrorist attacks, the perception among the American population of the heightened danger of flying led to a massive shift towards driving, and an increase in road-related incidents, which outweighed the casualties from the attacks.[47] At a more analytical level, the identification of power laws can be complicated by the large fluctuations that occur in the tail of the distribution, and the inability of commonly used methods for analysing power law data to produce accurate assessments.[48]

Another issue is to not read too much into the power law pattern in and of itself. Some see power laws as a statistical signature of complex systems, in that they reflect a typical 'pattern of organization and change'.[49] However, it is becoming clear that a number of different processes can generate power laws, only some of which are directly related to complex dynamics in the underlying phenomena. There are also some phenomena where the big events are even *larger* than one might anticipate given the power law distribution. For example, Didier Sornette has argued that the notion of the black swan is redundant for some phenomena, such as the size of cities, and instead we should talk about 'dragon kings'. London and Paris are good examples of dragon kings—both hugely influential in their respective countries, benefiting from a variety of positive feedback mechanisms, and as a result both cities are orders of magnitude larger than one might expect even with a skewed distribution. The basic message is that the presence of dragon kings in many systems and related datasets means extreme events are even more likely than power laws suggest.[50]

A contrasting view has been presented by Allen and Holling, who suggest the search for power laws has become too ubiquitous among complex systems researchers, and instead scientists need to pay more attention to the precise type of discontinuities that might occur—and thereby expand the different forms of non-linearity that can be recognized.[51]

All of that said, it is still worth appreciating that a power law is a good starting point, but more analysis of a qualitative and quantitative nature is needed to identify whether it has meaning from the perspective of organized complexity. Perhaps the key message is that one shouldn't look for power laws in much the same way as one shouldn't look for a Newtonian model of cause and effect: you might simply end up finding what you were looking for rather than getting a better, more scientific understanding of the problem at hand.

What this wealth of work on power laws and their implications has achieved is to give weight to the argument that we need to be much more careful in analysing the dynamics of systems. For starters, in many systems, power laws suggest that 'Outliers cannot be ignored and that averages are *meaningless*.'[52] Overcoming Gaussian dogma is difficult because it has become so fundamental a part of how we all see and think about the world. Unconsciously, we all employ such assumptions in so many day-to-day decisions. Not only that, but the normal distribution is seen as having greater scientific validity. It is at the heart of all assessments of statistical significance; it is better for career advancement, publication, and so on. But it also places a premium on independent, additive phenomena (i.e. organized simplicity or disorganized complexity) over interdependent, multiplicative phenomena of organized complexity. Perhaps clinging to the mast of normality is the only way to stay sane in a world of extremes and outliers. But it also means we are consigned to treating the irregular and the extreme as continuous shocks.

As Nobel Laureate Phil Anderson put it, 'Much of the real world is controlled as much by the tails of distributions as [by] means or averages . . . by the exceptional not the common place; by the catastrophe, not the steady drip . . . we need to free ourselves from "average" thinking.'[53] Our language itself may need to change—we may need to stop talking about 'normal' events and others, and instead argue for a more precise, scientific explanation of what has been called 'the new normal'.

Lost in Transition

So far in this chapter on the dynamics of complex systems, I have looked at how change happens in complex systems and how power laws are important signatures that can be found when comparing the frequency and size of events in such systems. This begs an obvious question: what are the processes of change in such systems?

Many simple systems are characterized as changing in a gradual, predictable fashion, for example the evolution of species: Darwin argued that natural selection would work to change the average features of a species by preferentially removing less fit individuals from the breeding stock and after a long enough time a given species would transform into a new one. Less formally, this has been described as 'evolution by creeps'. In physics and economics, gradualism has its equivalent in the idea of 'steady state': that after some initial turbulence, systems settle down to a predictable, continuous state of change.

Gradualists put missing links in the species record down to breaks and inconsistencies in the rock record, but Eldridge and Gould argued in 1972 that the fossil record was supportive of a different approach to evolution, one of species undergoing very little evolution for long periods of time and then very rapid changes.[54] Under punctuated equilibrium models, evolutionary change happens under certain conditions, and happens very rapidly—seen as 'evolution by jerks'.

Around the same time, Buzz Holling was developing a similar approach to understanding ecosystem changes.[55] Now popularized in the form of resilience thinking, Holling's work presented different ecosystems as existing in a state of equilibrium but, through various impacts over time, relationships between species get tighter and more interconnected. As the loose peripheral relationships are eradicated, the ones left behind become increasingly vulnerable to change in others. Eventually, at a critical point, the ecosystem tips into a different domain: think for example of the transformation of forest land into prairie after droughts and forest fires.

In the 1990s, David Raup showed that species extinctions followed a power law: small events are common and insignificant, large events are rare and significant.[56] Of course, there may well be 'smoking guns'—like meteorites or giant volcanoes—but it may also be the case that some of the observed pattern of extinctions is just an inherent part of evolutionary dynamics playing out across a complex adaptive system. Per Bak also did work on this issue, building on the sandpile model, and found that some extinctions did indeed have no identifiable cause: evidence, in his mind, that evolution was another example of self-organized criticality in nature. As he argued, 'The trigger may simply be the flap of the butterfly wing—the extinction of a single species—that results in an avalanche that propagates through the entire system.'[57]

More generally, there is a need to distinguish equilibrium models and non-equilibrium systems. A good example of an equilibrium system is a ball that rolls to the bottom of a hill and then settles down into a place of minimum energy. In biology, the viruses being modelled by the FoldIt gamers described previously are complex molecular structures, which, in the right environment, will self-assemble, seeking the state of lowest energy. The most obvious example in social settings is the notion of market equilibrium: the point where supply equals demand and the market is cleared. Once the state of lowest energy is reached, in balls, viruses, or markets, no further energy or inputs are needed to maintain that state.

By contrast, non-equilibrium systems are those that have a constant need for energy to sustain themselves. Also known as 'free-living systems' and 'dissipative structures', these continually exchange energy with their environment in order to maintain their internal order. Because of this process of dissipation, they were named 'dissipative structures' by Ilya Prigogine,[58] who won a Nobel Laureate in Chemistry for his work. Many are now arguing that, like evolution, the economy is a non-equilibrium system, with various implications for its analysis and management.

Gould later expanded the scope of this work, pointing to 'a broader discussion about the nature of change: Is our world ... primarily one of constant change ... or is ... change a "difficult" phenomenon, usually accomplished rapidly when a stable structure is stressed beyond its buffering capacity to resist and absorb.'[59] Given this broadening of the applicability of punctuated equilibrium, these same patterns have since been identified in a variety of other systems, including markets, economies, and the global climate. While the historical climate record, for example, is full of jumps, the challenge is that the scale and timing are inherently unpredictable. The same can be said for a variety of other phenomena, including disease outbreaks, wars, and fashions.

The discontinuous transitions[60] exhibited by all of these systems are an indication of their potential for change. Such transitions have been popularized through the notion of 'tipping points', an idea now so widespread that it runs the risk of losing all scientific meaning. This is the phenomenon that became generic and popularized in *The Tipping Point*.[61] Malcolm Gladwell showed that the kinds of people involved were crucial—those who gather lots of information (mavens), those who can propagate it (salespeople), and those who know lots of very different kinds of people (networkers). This same interactive dynamic underlies many different kinds of 'phase transitions', whereby a complex system moves from one state to another. The most common example—which I used earlier—is how water freezes to form ice at zero degrees. Rather less prosaically, some evolutionary biologists have used the model to describe how a mix of inert molecules in the ancient primordial soup might have reached a degree of diversity and connectivity that enabled the very first life forms to emerge. Such processes may also govern technological innovation—it has been hypothesized that one theory of economic take-off relates to the diversity and interconnectedness of goods and services: 'The origin of life at a threshold of chemical diversity follows the same logic as a theory of economic takeoff at a threshold of diversity of goods and services. Above that critical diversity, new species or molecules, or goods and services, afford niches for yet further new species.'[62]

Work by P.J. Lamberson and Scott Page[63] suggests a need for much more clarity when talking about such tipping point phenomena. For any given 'tipping phenomenon', we should ask two questions. First, is the tipping point direct or contextual? *Direct* tipping points are those that occur when a change in a particular variable leads to a large, discontinuous change in that same variable in the future. A good example is when the sale of a particular stock by traders leads to mass selling of that stock over the course of a trading day, because (as we saw in Chapter 8) these actions have a lot of positive feedbacks, leading to the dramatic reinforcement of change. *Contextual* tipping points are when things change in—surprise, surprise—the context of a system, which then leads to dramatic changes in that system. A good example is how a speech by Alan Greenspan could move markets: he never bought or sold shares himself, but he changed the context in which shares were sold. By being connected to key actors and factors, he influenced behaviours and attitudes. The connection-based approach to contextual tipping points is consistent with accounts of the role of new technologies in uprisings like the Arab Spring: 'Technologies make people more connected and allow for ideas and actions to percolate across the society in ways that were precluded, often purposefully, under some regimes.'[64]

Second, is the tipping point changing the nature of the system in question? If we see systems as simple, complex, and random (broadly following Warren Weaver), tipping points can lead to changes in the overall *state* of a system—for example, moving from one type of simple system to another type of simple system, or from one type of complex regime to another. On the other hand, there may be tipping points that serve to shift a system to a new kind of behavioural regime—from simplicity to complexity, complexity to randomness, and so on.[65]

Whether or not a phase transition actually takes place depends on a range of factors, including boundary conditions, interactions in the system, and, importantly, historical conditions. This last point is closely related to the notion of path dependence. Gould, who developed the punctuated equilibrium model, wrote the following in his 1989 book on evolution: 'We came this close...thousands and thousands of times [to] the veering of history down another sensible channel. Replay the tape a million times...and I doubt that anything like Homo sapiens would ever evolve again. It is, indeed, a wonderful life.'[66]

Like punctuated equilibrium, this idea has proved popular in innovation studies. Technological progress in a number of industries has been observed as consisting of long periods of incremental improvement interrupted by short periods of radical innovation. 'Path dependence' is now commonly used to describe how many alternative technological configurations are possible at an early stage of a system's development but, once one alternative gains an upper hand, it becomes 'locked in' and difficult to shift. For example, standards that are first-to-market can become entrenched 'lock-ins'—the most famous examples being the QWERTY layout in typewriters and the success of VHS over Betamax.[67] Using the tipping point approach, we can see that, for both of these, positive feedbacks leading from small early advantages led to a direct tipping point in the success of that product.

An example of a contextual tipping point here might be how steel and petroleum-based fuel have come to dominate over other fuel alternatives, especially steam and electric, with a considerable effect on the industrial basis of modern society. In urban formation, 'Many cities developed where and how they did not because of the "natural advantages" we are so quick to detect after the fact, but because their establishment set of self-reinforcing expectations and behaviours.'[68]

Clearly, in some contexts the sudden change of a system from one state to another is not a good thing, but in others it is something to be capitalized on. Thomas Homer-Dixon makes the case eloquently: 'To the extent that we are not ready for it, and to the extent that our existing regime of beliefs, values, rules, institutions, and patterns of behaviour are tightly coupled to the former situation, and we don't have any clear plans to adapt to the new situation, then threshold change is basically a bad thing.'[69]

And of course, the converse of all of these points is also true: when we are ready, when existing regimes are loosely coupled, when we have plans to adapt to the new situation, threshold change can be a good thing.

This point between phases brings me to the fourth and final way of thinking about the edge of chaos. The moment of criticality, of transition between phases, when a system is balanced between one point and another, is also known as the edge of chaos. A number of physicists have been able to track how a range of system properties changes as the point of phase transition is reached: variables such as temperature, sound, and so on. Interestingly, at the point when this point is reached, the equations break down, providing an important clue that 'something interesting is happening'.[70]

James Crutchfield, a longstanding member of the Santa Fe Institute (SFI), has made comparisons between the physical state phase transitions and phase transitions in other natural and social systems. In these latter, different states do not depend on changes in parameters such as temperature or pressure. Instead, the key changes that happened as systems flipped from one state to another related to the rate of information processing and memory. He found that the analogy was more than simply a metaphor.

> Just as water changes state in going from ice to liquid with increasing temperature, certain classes of information processing systems show phase transitions between order and chaos. The ordered regime is analogous to a crystalline solid; it literally corresponds to crystalline patterns in time (periodic behaviors). The chaotic regime is analogous to a gas, in which the molecular motion is much more disordered. We demonstrated that at an order-chaos phase transition a new and qualitatively more powerful type of computation appears.[71]

Like Stuart Kauffman, he found that 'complexity arises in the middle ground, at the onset of chaos, the order-disorder border. Natural systems that evolve with and learn from interaction with their immediate environment exhibit both structural order and dynamical chaos.'[72] 'At the very minimum, in a mathematical setting, understanding the interaction of order and chaos and the resulting complexity gives us a powerful set of metaphors for understanding more complicated (possibly complex) systems, such as human culture.'[73] Two other complex systems luminaries, Murray Gell-Mann and Seth Lloyd, have developed a similar framing around the idea of 'effective complexity', which is the length of the shortest description needed to describe a given system. They posit that the effective complexity is highest when the complexity is highest— meaning the relevant description would be large in size. On the other hand, for systems that are ordered, or random, the description will be relatively short. Complex systems are therefore those with high information content, which can be likened to Crutchfield's finding about the computational capacity of simple, complex, and chaotic systems. Through the development of formal definitions, they suggest the effective complexity idea can be used to analyse a variety of systems, including those 'at the so-called edge of chaos'. Bring these two ideas together with the notion of the power law, and one is left with a different and more challenging way of thinking about the edge of chaos. Specifically, the edge of chaos is, like the point of self-organized criticality, the point where novelty is most likely to occur—and, as discussed, this may be in a particular variable, but may also be in an overall context.

But the scale, scope, and desirability of the changes that actually transpire at the point of criticality are highly uncertain. The phase transition in question may be one that was hoped for, one that was *not* hoped for, or something completely different to both. More realistic—and scientifically informed—is not thinking about somehow positioning oneself or one's organization 'at the edge of chaos', but instead having feelers for when particular systems in which one is interested might be approaching such a state, and to anticipate—as far as possible—the full range of possibilities that might transpire. There is a difference, then, between consciously trying to get *to* the edge of chaos, and being aware of the opportunities and risks that occur when one is working on a problem, issue, or system that can be characterized as being *on* the edge of chaos. The state epitomizes the combination of risk and opportunity: it is far from being an unalloyed good.

The Mortally Wounded Paradigm

Ilya Prigogine observed a strong tendency for science to deny 'the complexity and the coming-into-being of the world in the name of a knowable, eternal world that is dictated by a small number of simple, unchanging laws'.[74] Traditional scientific approaches have been strongly influenced by, and have maintained, a firmly Newtonian view of the world, despite the limited applicability of Newton's methods beyond the systems he himself studied: the mechanics of physical motion. This bias in the physical sciences has informed the development of biological, social, economic, and political science, using broad theories of behaviour to generate hypotheses about causal relations between variables of interest[75]—leading to linear equations that describe 'straight lines, discrete phenomena, and an exceedingly small portion of our everyday experience'.[76] This is based on the often entirely unjustifiable idea that relationships can be identified through data gathering and analysis and can be used as the basis of 'laws' of behaviour.

Although linearity is a mathematical formulation, the key principles are easily grasped through description and analogy. In linear systems, it is often assumed that a given system's response is proportional to forces acting on it— that causes are proportional to effects.[77] So, to give a crude example, if a certain amount of social welfare cuts leads to reduced unemployment, then the linear assumption would be that extending the cuts would reduce unemployment even further.

Building on this, such proportionality—and related ideas and propositions— are typically tested by making comparisons between two situations that are identical except for one variable—referred to as the independent variable. This kind of analysis means 'holding all other things constant', so that change in an independent variable produces a related change in a dependent variable. Again, extending the social welfare programme, it could be assumed that welfare payments could be isolated and acted on in such a way that changing them would not have any effects aside from on unemployment.

The third commonly made assumption of linearity is that linear problems can be broken down into pieces, with each piece analysed separately; all the separate answers can be recombined to give the right answer to the original problem. In a linear system, the whole is exactly equivalent to the sum of the parts. So if event A leads to outcome 1, and event B leads to outcome 2, the two events together would automatically lead to both outcomes 1 and 2. Again, if cutting welfare and increasing job-to-work programmes both have an effect on unemployment, then doing both together should have an additive effect.

To summarize, linearity assumes that change is proportional, that key variables of interest can be seen as independent, and that system behaviours are additive. As Thomas Bass has argued, 'For centuries, scientists reduced the world to linear equations because these were what they could solve.'[78] They also helped explain a lot of the world—as Warren Weaver pointed out. And many actions taken by policymakers have sought to treat the world in this way. Work to reduce forest fires, and thereby ensure forest sustainability, is based on a simplistic reading of what a forest is and how it changes over time, for example.

The assumption of linearity is at the heart of traditional science's reductionist approach: split a system into parts and analyse the relationships of each; the computation of the whole then equals the sum of the relationships of the two. Unfortunately, for nearly all complex systems, this approach doesn't work: 'The linear point of view is correct for a simple system near equilibrium...but we do know that large events can happen without external impact.'[79]

In forests, and many other contexts, evidence is growing that many systems operate far from equilibrium and do not work in a linear fashion. As anticipated by Weaver, the number-crunching power of machines revolutionized mathematics and physics by allowing scientists to calculate non-linear equations relating to systems of organized complexity. Key aspects of complex systems—emergence, feedback processes, mutual interdependence, multiple interactions and influences, human behaviours—lead to dynamics that are *non-linear*.

Non-linear dynamics take the three assumptions of linear systems and explode them. Such systems are not proportional: 'The effect is not proportional to the cause. The straw that breaks the camel's back is nonlinear. A small shove can result in a big push. A system evolving in one direction can suddenly veer off in another. Thermometers and bathroom scales are linear. Financial markets yo-yoing between bubbles and crashes are nonlinear.'[80] In complex systems, then, the output is not proportional to the input. Feedback loops and adaptive behaviours and emergent dynamics within the system may mean the relationship between input and output is non-linear. 'Non-linear systems magnify even minor disturbances in unpredictable ways—the so-called butterfly effect—a tree branch touching some power lines in Ohio during a storm can produce a grid collapse.'[81]

Jervis, in his work on the role of non-linear phenomena in international relations, argues that 'Sometimes even a small amount of the variable can do a great deal of work and then the law of diminishing returns sets in [a negative feedback process] . . . in other cases very little impact is felt until a critical mass is assembled.'[82] Non-linear phenomena are also not reducible to simple two or three variable equations, where all other things can be held constant. In such systems, it is impossible to look at just one thing or make only one change.[83]

The notion of additive systems also frequently does not hold, because the consequences of event 1 may depend on the presence or absence of many other factors, which may well be affected by event 2 or what happens as a result of event 2. The sequence in which actions are undertaken also frequently affects the outcome. Take the 2008 financial crisis: this owed to the non-linear 'ratcheting effects' of the combination of low interest rates, rising house prices, and easy access to finance.[84] Although each of these factors alone would have been fine—perhaps positive—together they were the equivalent of taking anti-depressants, sleeping medication, and cold mixture all at the same time.[85]

The implications of non-linearity are far from trivial. Murray Gell-Mann argues that, for any non-linear system, 'It is simply not possible to pick out various aspects in advance, study them separately, and then be able to describe the behavior of the system by putting together the separate pieces'[86]—instead we need to take 'a crude look at the whole'.[87] For others, like Steve Strogatz, it means 'All bets are off'.[88] Jerry Sabloff, President of SFI, talks about SFI's three key contributions as the study of complexity, the trans-disciplinary approach, and the importance of non-linear thinking in the world today. He suggests it is in this third area that the Institute has been *least* successful, and this despite the fact that 'the world and most systems are non-linear'.[89]

An interesting—if disturbing—example of the challenges posed by non-linear phenomena is in the realm of climate change and the policies being formulated to deal with it. We saw in Chapter 8 that climate change itself has been described as a 'manifestation of phenomena that are complex in the technical sense of that word'—meaning it is 'nonlinear and unstable'. Although incremental levels of climate change will have political and economic consequences, a major finding of reviews is that *non-linear climate change will produce non-linear economic and political events*, and moreover that responses will also have non-linear effects. If the environment deteriorates beyond some critical point, natural, social, and economic systems that are adapted to it will break down. 'Beyond a certain level climate change becomes a profound challenge to the foundations of the global industrial civilization that is the mark of our species.'[90] An example of this was provided in the Stern Review of Climate Change:[91] the incorporation of dynamic non-linear feedbacks in response to rising greenhouse gases means that the total average cost of climate change rises from 5 per cent to at least 20 per cent of global per capita consumption.[92]

Policy responses to climate change also have non-linear consequences, although policymakers seldom appreciate this. There is a tendency to rely on a 'linear, direct and one-to-one'[93] relationship between energy efficiency improvements and reductions in energy demand. This serves to 'consistently produce overestimates of the net energy savings and emissions reductions potential of such efficiency measures, with potentially dangerous consequences for climate change mitigation efforts'.[94]

Work on energy efficiency improvements by the Breakthrough Institute shows that the precise macroeconomic consequences of energy improvements are highly uncertain. For this reason, efforts at climate change mitigation need to focus on non-linear effects of different interventions on the carbon load of economic activities—non-linear 'rebound effects' act to reduce the net savings that might result from efficiency improvements. These are typically expressed as a percentage of potential energy savings 'taken back' owing to the potential impact on energy demand. 'A straightforward example of rebound would be a homeowner who installs new insulation to increase ... heating efficiency ... only to take advantage of the resulting decrease in home heating costs to increase the average heating temperature, the amount of time the home is heated, or the number of rooms heated.'[95]

Take one homeowner and their house and the picture is pretty simple. Link a billion households together, add in businesses, governments, and regulatory frameworks, and we get a picture of 'multiple rebound effects operat[ing] at varying scales' and outcomes that are 'the combination of multiple non-linear and reinforcing effects'.[96]

It is precisely this kind of non-linearity that explains why technologies that at one level of analysis—say, an actual product level—appear to save time, energy, or costs incur net costs at a higher, more systemic, level of analysis. The oft-repeated prediction has been that improving the productivity of labour, capital, or materials through new inventions—from vacuum cleaners to emails—would result in a macroeconomic reduction in demand for such inputs. However, the actual result has been just the opposite. 'Through a variety of self-reinforcing and non-linear mechanisms, micro-level improvements in the productivity of labor, capital, or raw materials frequently result in macroeconomic increases in the demand for these factors.'[97]

Despite these rather disheartening examples, it is important to note that non-linearity is not always a bad thing. For example, a counter to the lethal combination of drugs that leads to so many untimely deaths is to be found in combination therapy for HIV/AIDS, which uses a cocktail of three drugs that works precisely because the immune response and viral dynamics are non-linear. The three drugs taken in combination are much more effective than the sum of the three taken separately.

We now understand that vast numbers of naturally occurring systems exhibit non-linearity: 'Every major unresolved problem in science—from consciousness to cancer to the collective craziness of the economy, is nonlinear.'[98] As Stanislaw Ulam dryly suggested in the 1950s, calling a situation non-linear is like going to the zoo and talking about all the interesting non-elephant animals you can see there. The need to develop new ways of thinking cannot be overstated—to paraphrase Duncan Watts, co-developer of the small world hypothesis we explored in the previous chapter, the linear model is staggering about the global stage like a mortally wounded Shakespearean actor.

The 2012 recipient of the UN Champions of the Earth prize, Sander van der Leeuw, argued that, despite the seeming multitude of global crises, there is a fundamental challenge at the heart of them all: 'Our current information processing capacity is insufficient to deal with the dynamics that surround us.'[99] Over the course of this chapter, we have seen a number of approaches that might be put forward as an alternative. Two challenges remain: the first is that alternatives are still a work in progress, and the scope and integration of taking such 'crude looks at the whole' need to be developed, tested, and improved over time. Second, and as numerous Shakespearean characters would no doubt concur, killing and then disposing of a dead monarch is not altogether a straightforward matter.

Part 2 Epilogue—What Lies Between Order and Chaos?

By anyone's measure, Joshua Cooper Ramo is an overachiever. The youngest ever Senior Editor at *Time* magazine, he is also a skilled acrobatic pilot, speaks fluent Chinese, sits on the Board of StarBucks, and won an Emmy in 2008 for his live television coverage of the opening ceremony at the Beijing Olympics. However, all this takes second place to his current day job. Ramo runs the shop at the geostrategic political consultancy set up by former US Secretary of State and Nobel Laureate Henry Kissinger. This means he spends his time at the forefront of some of the most important foreign policy issues facing the world today. It also means that, from time to time, he gets a phone call from his boss with rumbling questions like, 'Joshua, what is Facebook?' and 'Should I tweet?'

In 2009, Ramo distilled his experience and ideas into a book entitled *The Age of the Unthinkable.*[1] His basic message was simple: much of what he saw in the world of serious foreign policy was based on equally serious flawed thinking. Policymakers, politicians, and economists were continuing to use inappropriate tools to explain and predict what may or may not happen in the world, akin to physicists who try to apply Newtonian physics—a science of simplicity and certainty—to understand a complex and uncertain problem. He is convinced that what he calls 'sandpile thinking'—informed by Per Bak's work—needs to routinely inform how we engage with global issues, especially in foreign affairs. His thinking appears to have been influential. In 2011, Mr Y released an article entitled 'A National Strategic Narrative':

> The 21st century is an open system, in which unpredictable external events/ phenomena are constantly disturbing and disrupting the system. In this world control is impossible; the best we can do is to build credible influence – the ability to shape and guide global trends in the direction that serves our values

and interests (prosperity and security) within an interdependent strategic ecosystem. In other words, the U.S. should stop trying to dominate and direct global events. The best we can do is to build our capital so that we can influence events as they arise.[2]

That the special advisors of the most senior military figure in the world would take on these ideas, and use them to place clear limits on the some of the fundamental precepts of the military, is some testament to their perceived value. The challenge they set out is clear: the very nature of power and influence needs to change in a complex world. Perhaps it is unsurprising that Henry Kissinger, describing his protégé's (Ramo's) work, quipped that 'It has one basic theme that is a little difficult for me, which is that my generation is sort of a bunch of dodos, that we stagger through life with just one idea in our minds, which on top of it, is hugely wrong.'[3] However, being a complexity dodo is not unique to that generation. And as Herb Simon argued, in order to replace old and outmoded paradigms we need, first and foremost, alternative approaches that are more accurate and realistic.

We have seen over the course of Part 2 that a number of approaches, models, and experiments have—explicitly or implicitly, consciously or indirectly—built on Warren Weaver's formulation of simplicity and complexity. We have seen that, in a growing number of cases, ideas from complex systems research can yield new and useful insights about how to think about such problems, and, at a minimum, what *not* to do. In broad terms, and in keeping with the chapters in Part 2, we can think about the systems, behaviours, relationships, and dynamics of different phenomena.

In Figure 12.1 I have attempted to provide a visual and conceptual summary of how each of these aspects of systems might be represented using Warren Weaver's influential framing—first through a lens of organized simplicity, next through that of organized complexity, and finally through a lens of disorganized complexity. Below that I present the assumptions of the 'sciences of simplicity'— which underpin foreign aid—and contrast these with the key assumptions underpinning complexity research.

Some reflections on this before we move on. It should be clear that I am *not* arguing that everything is complex. Rather, following Weaver, it is clear that there is a range of social, economic, and political phenomena that are imperfectly or partially described and explained by what might be seen as the 'sciences of simplicity'. The challenge of modern policy and practice is, first, to be able to identify when we're dealing with a complex system or problem and, second, to be able to think and act appropriately: 'We must learn how to discriminate between simple and complex problems which means we must have the intuition to recognize complexity when we encounter it.'[4] But this doesn't mean 'We should jettison all our previous paradigms of management.'[5]

It's also important to note that the insights of complexity research are at different stages of development, in terms of both scientific advancement and

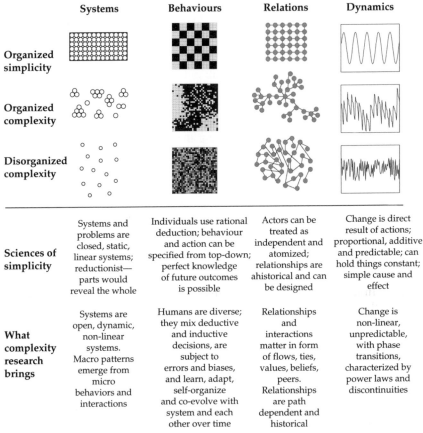

Figure 12.1 Visual signatures and contribution of complexity research

Source: Drawn and adapted from Madhur, A., Gonzalez, A., Guichard, F., Kolasa, J., and Parrott, L. (2010), 'Ecological Systems as Complex Systems: Challenges for an Emerging Science'. *Diversity* 2(3): 395–410; Beinhocker, E.D. (2006), *Origin of Wealth: Evolution, Complexity, and the Radical Remaking of Economics* (Cambridge, MA: Harvard Business School).

real-world applicability. Some of these are scientifically sound; some of them are more tentative. There has been great progress in the use of computers to explain complex phenomena and develop new means of analysis. Some of these have helped transform the way we understand and think about the world and our actions within it. There have also been some notable—if less numerous—instances of mixed team approaches to issues of organized complexity. The ultimate proof of any new intellectual approach, of course is, in the putting into use. Melanie Mitchell suggests that, 'In spite of the hype and the slurs ... some very interesting and worthwhile work has been done in complex systems over the last several years, evidenced ... by real changes in the way people approach science, medicine, economics, business, and ... the study of intelligence in natural and artificial systems.'[6] It is also important to note that the value is different for different kinds of problems. With crowd dynamics, the tools of complexity can already yield insights and be used to help inform decision making in a very direct fashion. At the other end of the spectrum, with climate change, complex systems tools may well yield useful insights, but the key at the moment is seeing whether it helps us ask the right questions. Jocelyn Bourgon is firmly of the view that thinking differently about globalized, interconnected problems is 'precisely where complexity thinking gets it value'.[7] Dorit also argues that complexity research is divulging important insights and ideas in precisely those areas where reductionist science is failing.

The rationale for the use of these ideas is becoming more and more obvious. As some have suggested, 'It is better if we embrace and plan for the inevitable complexity of the problem right from the beginning, rather than be surprised by it along the way.'[8] The late Max Boisot, Professor of Strategic Management at the ESADE business school in Barcelona, summarized the situation in a pithy fashion: 'Insofar as the business environment is getting more complex, [organizations] will need to shift from the complexity-reducing strategies that [previously] secured their success ... and place more emphasis on complexity absorbing ones.'[9] As the leading British health care think tank concluded in an otherwise critical report on the relevance of complex systems research,

> Complex adaptive systems thinking is a way of challenging taken for granted assumptions about how people, organisations and systems interact ... The mere fact that it pushes planners and policy makers to think about their assumptions and challenge their beliefs about knowledge and learning could be seen to have some value. This allows policy makers and researchers to consider deeper underlying causes and interactions than may have been the case with more surface level assumptions.[10]

My final, and perhaps most important, point is that complexity is a work in progress, a revolution in the making. Stephen Jay Gould has argued pointedly that 'The intellectual study dedicated to the study of complex dynamical systems [is] replete, as all fashions must be, with cascades of nonsense, but also imbued with vital, perhaps revolutionary, insights.'[11] As Murray Gell-Mann repeatedly told me, 'Complexity is not yet a science, it is the hope of a science. The biggest problem it faces is all these people saying it is already a science. It is a body of research, sure, and it has done some useful, even powerful, things. But the science of complexity doesn't exist,' adding, with a grin, 'yet'.[12] Separating the wheat from the chaff is therefore an important part of the endeavour.

As I argued in the opening section chapter, complexity research is perhaps best viewed as a means of systematically challenging our way of thinking, of asking the right questions, of working out why problems arose in the first place. As colleagues at the Santa Fe Institute (SFI) describe it, complexity research, at its best, is an 'engine for intuition'.

But it is not an engine that is altogether straightforward. In the popular science fiction film 'The Matrix', the main character is offered two pills, a blue one that returns him to a blissful, fabricated reality and a red one that shows him reality as it really is, taking him 'deeper down the rabbit hole'. Attempts to change our way of thinking seldom have such clear and unambiguous choices. Old paradigms seldom die; they usually just lose their universality. In science, in politics, in our personal lives, we continually find that contradictory mental models need to co-exist. We each have to walk down many roads at the same time. Uncertainty is a fundamental and irresolvable characteristic of our lives, no matter how good our observations and theories.[13]

Therefore we need to develop both the ability to recognize the extent to which our mental models are correct *and* the ability to use different models simultaneously. This is not a case about making value judgements about simplicity or complexity, but instead to see the world as it really is: to have new eyes.

In closing this part of the book, it seems appropriate to return once again to the popular but contested notion of the edge of chaos. From Warren Weaver's explanation of organized complexity, through to notions of emergence, behavioural rules, fitness landscapes and co-evolution, adaptive networks, self-organized criticality and phase transitions, this idea rears up in different ways throughout the Complexity Territories. I have tried to present all sides of this notion, arguments for and against, but it should be clear—not least from the title of this book!—that it is a concept to which I am strongly drawn.

James Crutchfield of SFI has argued that the fundamental challenge of complexity is precisely whether we as individuals can appreciate the dynamic balance of order and chaos.[14] He goes on:

> Will our societies self-organize into a dynamic that moves beyond the least common denominator results characteristic of human groupings, toward an organization that is appreciative of diversity, understands the role of regularity, and that is truly and constructively complex? ... We are beginning to see some glimmers of order amid the chaos, to appreciate the constructive role of randomness, and to understand the dynamic interplay of order and chaos.[15]

Crutchfield closes, 'What lies between order and chaos? The answer now seems remarkably simple: Human innovation.'[16] The beautiful simplicity and evocative power of this answer is an appropriate place to close our tour of the Complexity Territories.

*

I now want to move on to show how these ideas have been, and can and might be, brought to bear on the issues I explored in Part 1. There, I argued that many of the models and assumptions of foreign aid—the 'theories in use'—need a fundamental rethink. Having presented the ideas of complexity, the key next step is to examine the value these ideas have for the approach and ideas of foreign aid agencies.

My aim in Part 3 is to look at how the ideas in Part 2—systems, behaviours, networks, dynamics—have been applied in development efforts and with what results. A running theme throughout will be the issues of learning, strategies, relationships, and performance approaches—but it is not a hard and fast mapping.

I want to show how the innovation of thinkers and practitioners around the world has started to illustrate an alternative, complex systems-informed, approach to development and humanitarian work. It is my thesis that there is considerable value for complexity research to help question, and think of alternatives to, the core assumptions that shape the way that so much of aid works.

One of the key messages Joshua Ramo communicated in his work, echoing Frederick Hayek's Nobel Prize Lecture, was that dealing with complexity, at its heart, means 'changing the role we imagine for ourselves, from architects of a system we can control and manage to gardeners in a living, shifting ecosystem'.[17]

The story of the *subaks* with which I opened this book embodies this message perfectly. I am going to start the next part of our journey through aid and complexity by returning to the rice fields of Bali. We will see how notions of networks, self-organization, and the edge of chaos have helped build a better, more scientific understanding of the nature and role of the *subaks*, and have lent vital support to their bid for future preservation.

PART 3
The way aid could work

CHAPTER 13

From Bali, With Complexity

In the opening chapter of this book, I described the rice paddies of Bali and the cooperative *subak* institutions that enabled them to thrive for centuries against all the odds. Development programmes inspired by the Green Revolution, entitled 'Massive Guidance', ignored these institutions, and as a result severely disrupted the farmer-led system of rice growing common to the island. Eventually, the *subaks* reasserted themselves, and the major development agencies acknowledged them as key to agricultural productivity.

Steve Lansing, an American anthropologist, worked with the Santa Fe Institute (SFI) to employ the tools of complex systems to demonstrate the powerful ecological and social role of the *subaks* and to convince officials in development agencies of the need for a different approach. Part 3 of the book looks at the application of complex systems approaches in development and humanitarian efforts, and therefore it seems appropriate to return to the story of the *subaks*, and Lansing's work, in more depth.

In 1978, the Asian Development Bank approved what seemed to be a fairly straightforward, if ambitious, project in Indonesia. Named Massive Guidance in Indonesian, it focused on the modernization of agricultural practices in Bali to increase productivity. It was part of a considerable economic—and, some argue, political—process to increase and capitalize agriculture across Asia, labelled the Green Revolution by 1960s US Agency for International Development Chief William Gaud. It was development aid as 'solution exporter' in full force.

Things, as I explained earlier, didn't go quite as well as planned. Some years in and rice yields had dropped dramatically. Farmers I spoke to remembered this being a time of desperation and hunger. The approach was encountering considerable resistance in some quarters: the Bank recognized, 12 years later, that the design principles at its heart were 'not what the Subaks wanted'.[1] The rice fields became infested with rats and other pests and the attempt to make yields more constant saw overall outputs plummet. In fact, this was consistent with Green Revolution outcomes elsewhere in Asia, with decentralization and competition often not having the intended effect. Agricultural development has generally had a patchy record: commenting on 15 years of rural development projects in 1990, the Food and Agricultural Organization concluded that a billion dollars had been 'largely wasted'.[2]

Stephen Lansing had lived in Bali as an undergraduate and was well aware of the tensions between the traditional system and the modern approaches. He witnessed first-hand how the scale of the resistance grew even as the pace of modernization intensified. He argued that the problems that were occurring—from pest explosions to chaos in irrigation schedules to sabotage of new machinery by farmers—were arising because development consultants were ignoring the traditional system.[3]

But what actually led him to work on the problem in a new way was his love of surfing, which he shared with a colleague specializing in marine ecology, James Kremer. A chance conversation on a beach in California would make for a valuable contribution to the fortunes of the Bali farmers: 'I told him the story of the water temples, and of my struggles to convince the consultants that they played a vital role in the ecology of the rice terraces. I asked Jim if a simulation model, like the ones he uses to study coastal ecology, might help.[4]

While in Bali, I spent some time learning how the *subak* system worked. Across the island, rice is grown in paddy fields fed by irrigation systems that depend on rainfall. Levels of rainfall vary—obviously—by season and elevation. In combination with groundwater, this determines river flow. Each irrigation system involves a weir in a river, which reroutes the flow into a tunnel. Water then passes through an intricate system of canals and aqueducts to the summit of a terraced hillside. Control of the water flow into terraces enables farmers to dynamically manage key agro-ecological processes relating to soil quality, pest control, and yield levels. Farmers cooperate to create fallow areas that lower pest numbers, but doing so needs to be balanced against subsequent demands for water: 'Water sharing and pest control represent opposing constraints—optimal levels of coordination depend on local conditions.'[5]

It didn't take much to persuade Jim Kremer to join forces with his friend. Once in Bali, he quickly realized it was not a single water temple that needed modelling, but the interacting system of temples. He proposed building a model to examine the dynamics of water-based cooperation for an entire watershed, numbering over 150 interacting *subaks*. At first, this struck Lansing as rather ambitious, but Kremer convinced him this was the way to go if they wanted to understand how the *subaks* contributed to productivity. They focused on the region between the Oos and Petanu Rivers in central Bali, comprising some 172 *subaks*, and gathered a large amount of data, on rainfall, river flows, irrigation schedules, crop use, and pest population dynamics. Kremer then simulated a 12-month schedule of crop planting, which included changes in rainfall, river flow, and pest damage, all based on historical data. The model tracked harvest data and also highlighted where water shortages or pest outbreaks would occur.[6]

In the first test, they ran the model for two seasons, comparing the results with actual data on yields. It was able to predict most of the variation in yields between the *subaks*. After refining the model, they trialled it in several water management scenarios, including a Green Revolution scenario, whereby each *subak* planted rice as often as possible and ignored the water temples; and a water temple scenario, which worked to minimize pests and water shortages. The former produced large crop losses and water shortages and the latter generated the best harvests, just as in the real world.

However, this was no laissez-faire system: the farmers had to decide to cooperate and to display altruism. And altruism had to pay off. In a subsequent study inspired by researchers at SFI and informed by ideas from John Miller[7] (whose work on the edge of chaos I described in Part 2), Lansing found that farmers cooperated on the basis of their particular dominant issues: upstream farmers were more worried about pests and downstream farmers about water shortages. This pattern was common within *subaks*, across groups of *subaks*, and between watersheds. There was an ecological basis for the pattern of cooperation among the rice growers.

Lansing and his colleagues used ecological simulation modelling to illuminate the role of human agency in reshaping the ecosystem and the emergence of cooperative behaviour among Balinese farmers. The behaviour of the network was found to be critically dependent on the structure of the connections between the *subaks*. Drawing on Kauffman's elegant formulation of systems at the edge of chaos, which I described in Chapter 11, they showed that the *subaks* provided 'an unusually clear illustration of this point'.[8] Water temples functioned like nodes in a network, enabling *subaks* to adapt to changing conditions so as to maximize rice harvests.

A process of dynamic self-organization occurred in the simulation model when temples were allowed to react to changing environmental conditions over time. Artificial cooperative networks emerged that bore very close resemblance to actual temple networks. Tellingly, as these cooperative networks formed, average harvest yields rose to a new plateau. Subsequently, the irrigation systems that were organized into networks on the edge of chaos were able to withstand ecological shocks such as pest outbreaks or drought much better than those that lacked connections or were overly connected. Successful *subak* networks had a precise and relevant structure, leading to higher sustained productivity than would be the case if they were randomly or perfectly organized. At this point, at the edge of chaos, the structure of interactions emerged through processes of co-evolution: 'This structure itself is adaptive: perturbations that change local payoffs trigger small cascades of change that allow the entire network to respond effectively to events such as the addition of a new irrigation system or a new rice pest.'[9] The water temple networks were a particular form of social organization, shaped by a process of cooperative agents co-evolving on a changing environment.[10]

Agricultural extension plans—'development-speak' for the application of research and knowledge through farmer education—are based on results from experimental plots at research stations. Farmers are encouraged to imitate these distant models, but this can lead the process of locally relevant adaptation to grind to a halt. With the Green Revolution-inspired approach, which required farmers to plant as often as possible and ignore the local, temple-based process of adaptation, the result was chaos.

Evaluations of the Massive Guidance approach[11] criticized its lack of understanding and appreciation of irrigation systems in mountainous regions, of systems that had been working successfully for centuries, of the local environmental context, and of local cultural practices. The seemingly well-meaning desire to spread development around the island was seen as having disregarded the fundamental principle of equitable water sharing that operated within and between schemes. By intensifying cropping patterns, the project was contributing to environmental issues around pest outbreaks and pollution caused by the subsequent overuse of pesticides. The hoped-for yields did not materialize, and those increases that did occur the *subaks* could have brought about at a fraction of the cost and with none of the environmental damage. The *subaks* on their own could successfully modify the system to suit local conditions and maintain and improve crop production to a level exceeding the projections made during project appraisal.[12] The final audit noted that it was 'difficult to affirm the existence of the project's impact on production'.[13]

The project performance audit report followed the publication of Lansing's study on the *subaks* as a complex adaptive system. It made the point that,

> The numerous subaks are linked in a network of irrigation canals and streams from mountain lanes down to rice plots and terraces...at each higher level, there are water temples of increasing importance where the irrigators periodically meet to reaffirm their interdependence in a ritual form. A complex system...has evolved over time...the increasing involvement of public agencies have weakened the traditional approaches to the management of watershed [and] the Project has in part contributed to this trend.[14]

It also made extensive use of Lansing's work and acknowledged the findings of the model: as a direct result of his work, there would be no further opposition to the management of irrigation by the water temples.

Steve Lansing would become well known in Bali for his work on the *subaks*, and when the government of Bali decided to apply for World Heritage Status for the *subak* landscape, Lansing was asked to take the lead in developing the proposal. My own visit to Bali was timed to coincide with the visit of the Director General of the UN Educational, Scientific, and Cultural Organization and her retinue, giving me the surreal experience of squatting over ditches one day and being driven around in a motorcade in a flurry of garlands and official speeches the next. The story ends well: in June 2012, just as I was putting the finishing touches to this book, the World Heritage application was approved. The *subaks* would be preserved in perpetuity as a vital part of the cultural, economic, and environmental landscape of Bali.

*

So far, I have set out an argument for why foreign aid efforts need to take better account of, rather than ignoring, real-world complexity (Part 1) and illustrated how scientists, policymakers, and practitioners in the world outside of aid are doing just this by drawing on ideas from the cutting edge of science (Part 2). In Part 3, I present a collection of linked stories about how these ideas are being used in development and humanitarian efforts. The *subak* story is just one of the examples I have examined in the course of writing this book. The others include urban change in East Africa, climate change in Southern Africa, epidemic outbreaks in Asia, water sharing in Bhutan, reform efforts in Asia, desertification in Sub-Saharan Africa, subsistence farming in East Africa, disaster responses in Southern Africa, malnutrition programmes in Vietnam, and industrial production globally. This is not a deliberately eclectic selection—these cases are the result of hard work by practitioners and researchers, project managers, and policymakers. All of the people involved in the efforts explored in the following pages share at least three things: a struggle to make sense of the complex realities faced in development and humanitarian efforts, a sense that the ideas of complex systems research carry value for rethinking and improving their efforts, and the space and courage to try something new and to see what might transpire.

This concluding part of the book will look in depth at how the new, more complexity-sensitive, tools and approaches described in Part 2 have helped and are helping those wanting to do development and humanitarian aid differently. Throughout Part 3, I will link these applications back to my reflections on the aid business model in the first part of the book: on learning, on strategies, on organizations, and on performance. I reflect on examples of aid agencies' innovations in these areas, the assumptions and ideas that underpin these efforts, and how the ideas covered in Part 2 have already helped, or might in the future.

Clearly, there are areas of the aid business model for which key complex systems ideas might carry special and particular significance. For example, systems thinking may be especially relevant to learning; evolutionary approaches are very useful to rethinking strategy; networks speak loudly to organizations and relationships; dynamics are especially pertinent for those seeking to rethink accountability and performance approaches.

That said, the reality is that different complexity concepts carry relevance for many aspects of foreign aid simultaneously. In this next part of the book I want to show how the ideas of complex systems research have been used to make aid ideas and aid practices more sensitive to the real-world dynamics of social, economic, and political phenomena.

CHAPTER 14

Systemic Learning

'In an open source development model, we will not always have the control we have grown accustomed to exercising, and we have to get used to that.'

Raj Shah, Administrator, USAID.[1]

The Unconventional Herd Follower

A quarter of the earth's land area is turning into desert and three-quarters of its savannas and grasslands are degrading.[2] Because the main activity on range-lands is grazing livestock, on which 70 per cent of the world's poorest people depend, this is causing widespread poverty.[3] Significant resources have been spent on trying to understand and reverse desertification, but with few successes. There is considerable disagreement and dissent about its causes and possible responses, which obviously doesn't help.

The UN Convention to Combat Desertification (UNCCD)[4] addresses a range of ecological factors that lead to desertification, but all too often practitioners and policymakers are interested in only a sub-set of these and disagree as to which are the most important and therefore most worthy of attention. A thought experiment by a group of researchers working on these issues illustrates the point well. Imagine visiting a large ranch with herds of cattle grazing on open rangeland. You might conclude—as many do—that these patches are the result of overgrazing, but alternative views are possible. For example:[5]

- Some erosion will be the result of natural phenomena affecting the farm at a local (wind and rain) or a global level (climate change).

- Some erosion may have no impact on farm productivity but much greater effects on overall soil salinity or production losses downstream from the farm.

- If overgrazing is the issue, the responsibility may not lie with the farmer. It is also important to consider the land tenure system, broader institutional and political factors, and market dynamics.

We can quickly see that even this seemingly simple issue requires an understanding of the interrelationships between human socio-economic and biophysical factors.[6] The researchers who came up with the experiment above—from Duke, the Commonwealth Scientific and Industrial Research Organisation, and the Université Catholique de Louvain—responded by developing what they call the Dahlem Desertification Paradigm, the key tenets of which are set out in Figure 14.1.

The developers of the Dahlem Paradigm consciously set out to embrace ideas such as non-linear processes, resilience, range ecology, human perceptions, and systems thinking, all seen as essential in developing a new view of an old problem. One of the key problems in this is that:

Assertion 1: Desertification always involves human and environmental drivers	Always expect to include both socio-economic and biophysical variables in any monitoring or intervention scheme
Assertion 2: 'Slow' variables are critical determinants of system dynamics	Identify and manage for the small set of 'slow' variables that drive the 'fast' ecological goods and services that matters at any given scale
Assertion 3: Thresholds are crucial and may change over time	Identify biophysical and socio-economic thresholds, beyond which there is a significant increase in the costs of recovery, and quantify these costs; seek ways to manage the thresholds to increase resilience
Assertion 4: The costs of intervention rise non-linearly with increasing degradation	Intervene early in local degradation where possible; invest to reduce the transaction costs of intervention at increasing scales
Assertion 5: Desertification is a regionally emergent property of local degradation	Take care to define precisely the spatial and temporal extent and process represented in any given measure of local *degradation*. Use the term *desertification* only as a measure of generalized impact at higher scales
Assertion 6: Coupled human–environment systems change over time	Understand and manage the circumstances in which the human and environmental subsystems become 'decoupled'
Assertion 7: The development of appropriate local environmental knowledge (LEK) must be accelerated	Create a better partnership between LEK development and conventional scientific research, involving good experimental design, effective adaptive feedback and monitoring
Assertion 8: Systems are hierarchically nested (manage the hierarchy!)	Recoginze and manage the fact that changes at one level affect others, create flexible but linked institutions across the hierarchical levels, and ensure processes are managed through scale-matched institutions
Assertion 9: A limited suite of processes and variables at any scale makes the problem tractable	Analyze the types of syndromes at different scales, and seek the investment levers that best control their effects – awareness and regulation where the drivers are natural, changed policy and institutions where the drivers are social

Figure 14.1 The Dahlem Desertification Paradigm

Source: Stafford Smith, D.M. and Reynolds, J.F. (2002), 'Desertification: A New Paradigm for an Old Problem', in Reynolds, J.F. and Stafford Smith, D.M. (eds), *Global Desertification: Do Humans Cause Deserts?* (Berlin: Dahlem University Press).

Formal science and policymaking is rarely carried out by the inhabitants of arid and semi-arid lands...rather, the many players involved are usually distant, they view these issues through the lenses of their own disciplines and expertise, and are poorly coordinated and often ill-informed despite good intentions. Hence, notwithstanding much rhetoric to the contrary, the end result is usually simplistic, one-dimensional solutions that disregard the coupled nature of human–environment systems.[7]

There is a fascinating exception to this prevalence of simple, narrow, one-dimensional, solutions to desertification. Operation Hope has seen the transformation of 20,000 acres of parched and degraded grasslands belonging to Wange community in Zimbabwe into healthy pastures. When the project started, the rural community was facing poverty, disease, drying rivers, failing crops, dwindling livestock, an exodus of young people, and, of course, desertification. The wider national context was far from straightforward: a situation of spiralling political, social, and environmental turmoil.[8] In partnership with Allan Savory's African Centre for Holistic Management, community members developed a project to address issues of desertification. The story behind it provides some real insights into how systems concepts can help transform development practices on the ground.

Operation Hope was based on an approach called 'holistic management', derived from five decades of work by Savory, who tried to develop a practical theory of semi-arid grassland ecologies to understand and improve rangeland practices. This work was inspired in part by his firm grasp of the limitations of the international agency approaches I described in Chapter 2 on learning.

Perhaps the most surprising thing about the transformation Operation Hope achieved was that it was done by dramatically *increasing* the number of herd animals on the land. Savory had realized that the existing diagnosis of desertification as caused by overgrazing was based on a weak understanding of what overgrazing in fact was. He set out to understand why the 'unmanaged' grassland of the pre-colonial era had supported enormous herds of wild ungulates and recovered from even severe droughts without a loss of biodiversity, whereas land grazed by domestic stock under human management degraded rapidly. He found that overgrazing was not a function of time and space, nor of animal numbers, but occurs when animals return to graze on a plant before it has had time to regenerate. The idea is intuitive, albeit in hindsight; as Savory told me, it was 'profoundly simple but took many years to find'.[9]

On enormous pre-colonial unfenced ranges, existing land use patterns and pack-hunting predators ensured beneficial animal movements and herd behaviours. By contrast, limited lands and time increased pressure on the plants, and therefore on the soil and the wider ecosystem. But it is how animals are managed on limited lands that was the issue: when they are allowed to roam at will, they return to graze on plants that have not fully recovered.

But the animals weren't just grazers—they also provided concentrated, nutrient-rich fertilizers, and their hooves acted as soil regenerators, churning it and trampling dead plants down to enable faster processes of decay. Savory told me that this was one of the really big 'aha moments' in the development of holistic management, as it enabled him to develop the idea of herding animals not only in such a way that they do not re-graze before plants recover, but also to maximize their other benefits.[10]

Although the idea was straightforward, putting it into practice didn't come easy. But the vision Savory had was a powerful one: of livestock being used as a tool for improving soil quality, seed germination, and, ultimately, species diversity and productivity. His approach, too, was clear: he wanted something that worked consistently and was backed by solid science. Using a holistic lens and monitoring all of the ecosystem processes (water cycle, mineral cycle, energy flow, and biological community dynamics), the approach enables management of the whole. Its impacts are comprehensive: it increases plant growth, improves rural livelihoods through additional livestock, and increases wildlife populations. Despite this remarkable success, Savory is not satisfied. But the key is not to try and see overnight change—the team refers to Operation Hope as a 100-year project—with the necessary transformation already underway.

The second big 'aha moment' for Savory was when he first started to seriously grapple with the complexity of the system he was working with. He spent an evening with an associate from a university whose scientists had proved very resistant—to put it mildly—to the ideas of holistic management. His guest explained that their latest results had been exactly as Savory had predicted, and asked how the holistic management approach worked. Savory explained to me what happened next:

> I tried to get him to see the relationships as being like throwing different size rocks into a pond, with the ripples in a pond merging with the overall result being predictable if one viewed the whole and not each ripple. I drew lines connecting influences (things we were doing) to ecosystem processes like water, mineral cycling, community dynamics, etc. and I think he left as confused as he came. But my wife, who had watched my frustration at being unable to explain well what was in my head, said, 'You need to capture that'. So I kept the piece of paper and used it with constant improvements to get others to understand how to address complexity simply in practice. That was the origin of today's holistic framework. Pure accident.[11]

The guiding principles of holistic management as they have evolved from this serendipitous moment are set out below.

- When actions are guided by complex realities, rather than rational and abstract concepts, goals must change continuously.
- Conversations are more important than plans. In a healthy community, discussion of overarching goals never ends.

- A healthy community does not aspire to create the perfect plan and then implement it, but grows and develops goals over time. Each and every managed system—people, land, money—is unique. Just as one cannot step into the same river twice, holistic management does not allow for easy replication of solutions.

- 'Letting things go where they will' implies accepting unexpected turns and being flexible to this, taking up unforeseen opportunities as they arise and being prepared to abandon unrealistic aspirations along the route.

- Think about the means, not the ends: 'You might even say that the means *are* the ends. Whatever you think your goal is, the true goal is to have a process for making decisions on an ongoing basis. Any so-called goal is merely one step along a path.'[12]

Readers will recognize many of these principles from the chapter in Part 2 on emergent systems, and in the principles of the Dahlem Paradigm set out earlier in this chapter. Yet one of the most significant and widespread obstacles encountered by the holistic approach is precisely the pronounced tendency to make conscious decisions—planning and design—in a linear way:

> We have created complex global organizations that are programmed according to the same linear thinking. We manage these by designing missions, or visions, that give the collective entity something to aim for in its linear journey forwards. The trouble stems from our attempts to control a world that is holistic, and fundamentally non-linear, in its makeup. This rational, control-seeking approach makes it almost impossible to deal with such wicked problems as biodiversity loss, desertification, and climate change.[13]

As Savory argues, 'We have been successful in developments of technology—but have failed over and over again to deal with nature and human society.'[14] Put simply, land 'cannot be managed like a production line in a car factory'.[15]

For most of the 50 years that Savory has battled to make the scientific case for his approach, he has had to contend with intense opposition from mainstream range science researchers. John Hall, a World Bank staffer sent to evaluate his work with more experienced colleagues made the following point: 'The other nine men in the evaluation team...were scandalized by Savory because he attacked everything they had been doing. I was a naïf, and I found him interesting. I stayed in touch.'[16] Another observer, Jonathan Teller-Elsberg, has suggested that the reason for the long resistance to Savory's approach is simple:

> Mainstream natural resource management systems were in essence designed to avoid or bypass complexity. They coined the term 'best management practice'—but this was a misnomer. What may be the right thing to do on a farm this year may not be next year, let alone on a different farm. Although their motive was good, complexity—social, environmental and economic—is the implacable reality for management and thus cannot be bypassed or avoided. It has to be embraced through holistic planning processes.[17]

But, after decades of rejecting the basic idea underlying Operation Hope, a growing number of scientists now accept the results claimed by Savory are supported by rigorous data. There is now a growing awareness of the value of the approach. The Africa Holistic Management institute won the prestigious 2010 Buckminster Fuller Prize for designs most likely to advance the future of humanity, and they are shortlisted for several more similar prizes. At the time of writing Savory is on the shortlist for talking at the prestigious TEDGlobal event in 2013. The Savory Institute has also recently received a US$4.2 million grant from USAID's Office of Foreign Disaster Assistance to replicate the work in several other African countries. The UNCCD also seems to be paying attention: a 2012 briefing entitled 'Zero Net Land Degradation' made reference to Savory's work: 'Livestock are often referred to as the *major cause of overgrazing leading to desertification*; but with appropriate decision-making and management techniques such as Holistic Management (Savory, 1999) livestock *could become an essential part of the solution*'[18] (emphasis added).

Savory's acceptance by the mainstream is part of a considerable shift in scientific thinking, away from denying and toward accepting complexity. He is no longer alone in realizing that transfers of energy and nutrients are innate to the growing understanding of ecosystem ecology, which has emerged from biological studies of plants and animals and terrestrial, aquatic, and marine ecosystems. As a result, the approach has far wider implications than for desertification alone: it may well contain the seeds of a whole new approach to agriculture—and, yes, that may well be the oldest pun in the development library. In criticizing the Green Revolution on the Savory Institute website,[19] he posits the necessity of 'a new "Brown Revolution", based on the regeneration of covered, organically rich, biologically thriving soil, and brought to fruition via millions of human beings returning to the land and the production of food'.

Howard Buffet, son of the famous investor Warren, gave a speech at the 2010 World Food Prize symposium in which he argued that a 'Brown Revolution' in soil cultivation was precisely what was needed for the future of African agriculture. To quote directly from his keynote: 'Food security is complicated, agriculture is complicated. Simply distributing seeds and fertilizer, if that's the plan, will fail long term.'[20]

Savory's work can be located in a wider movement that has been called agro-ecology. The formal side of this is decades old, but it often builds on traditional, local knowledge that is far older. In what is now considered the classic text by Miguel Altieri, the link to systems approaches is made explicit: 'The underlying analytical approach owes much to systems theory and the...attempts to integrate the numerous factors that affect agriculture.'[21] Agro-ecologists 'know that they are interpreting complex systems that have co-evolved with people as part of a unique process'.[22] I have met a number of exponents of this movement while writing this book, and the most successful ones seem to share some of Savory's tenacity, passion, and revolutionary spirit. Practitioners at the US Land

Institute have long been attempting to apply ideas from the resilience of prairie ecosystems to agriculture, to try and design farming methods that—like holistic management—steer a middle ground between controlled rigidity and wildness. Janice Benyus, founder of the Biomimicry Institute and author of the leading text in the field, argues that this work resonates strongly with Stuart Kauffman's notions of self-organizing systems that operate at the edge of chaos,[23] a point that may equally be true of Savory's efforts. Elsewhere, Norman Uphoff, an early champion of complex systems thinking in development, has actively promoted an agro-ecological systems view of rice production. Through a widely disseminated approach called System of Rice Intensification, he has shown that crop yields can be improved considerably, while respecting ecological health. Like Savory, Uphoff's story has been one of intense resistance and some astonishing successes.

The overall message does seem to be getting through to some of the senior figures in food and agriculture policy. Olivier de Schutter, UN Special Rapporteur on the Right to Food, said in 2010 that the identification and scaling-up of such agro-ecology approaches held the best potential to solve the impending food security crises that humanity will face in the decades ahead.[24]

A Map for Peace that Lasts

The Wange community's new approach to rangeland management, compared with the earlier example of the failure of imported best practices in this field, illustrates in a very clear way the challenge and potential of learning in development contexts. At the heart of the challenge is the fact that there is 'a whole realm of social planning problems that cannot be successfully treated with traditional linear, analytical approaches'.[25] These frameworks tend to be based on an intellectual principle of 'divide and conquer'. This is not unique to science, of course. Businesses, public sector bodies, and civil society organizations are also built on principles of divide and conquer. In Chapter 2, I showed that there are many examples of simplistic, silo thinking that do not take into account the complex, systemic nature of the problems aid agencies face. I argued in concluding Part 1 that this bias characterizes the way aid 'thinks'. The question is: how to change this? How can we better anticipate the kinds of problems we face when dealing with complex problems that make a mockery of disciplinary and institutional boundaries?

Allan Savory trained as an ecologist and became a politician, but he was also a ranger and a farmer. He seems to be a one-man version of one of Warren Weaver's 'mixed teams'. His insights were based on an in-depth understanding of the rangeland situation. But what about those situations where such multidisciplinary, long-term understanding is simply not possible? Conflict and humanitarian emergencies are the obvious examples in the aid intervention portfolio. In such settings, complexity is a seen as an indulgence: the key is to act first (on the basis of half-formed and spurious assumptions) and ask questions later.

However, a number of researchers and practitioners in different parts of the world suggest that—even in these challenging environments—this needn't be the case. Dr Alberto Concha-Eastman, a former senior staffer at the Pan-American Health Organization, in a career spanning several decades, worked to promote what is today described as an 'ecological approach' to dealing with violence in Latin American cities. This means taking into account how the risk factors for violence are interconnected across different levels of a social ecosystem—individual, interpersonal, communal, and so on—while emphasizing the multiple causes. As he puts it,

> Because the roots and causes are found at different levels of the human interactions and relationships with the social and physical environment, it is not possible to define one intervention to solve the problem. A common error made by politicians is attempting to address violence with a single model or recipe, most frequently looking to establish consequences for violence rather than tackling the root causes.[26]

The key is to take a more experimental approach, defining and testing approaches that work at different levels of the system, *and* to take account of the dynamic interactions that work to promote or inhibit violence. In Bogotá, a mix of cultural and social approaches were implemented over a ten-year period, informed by Concha-Eastman's thinking on the ecological approach to violence. This included both proximate interventions (e.g. voluntary disarmament efforts among youth gangs) and more systemic interventions (e.g. the creation of a public spaces recovery programme to allow for safe gathering and mobility). Homicides fell by over 70 per cent and crime levels by over 30 per cent between 1993 and 2004, and public perceptions of the effectiveness of the police force doubled in favourability terms. Concha-Eastman led a similar process in his hometown of Cali, but a lack of sustained political leadership meant the gains— which at one point were comparable to those in Bogotá—were not sustained.[27]

It is not just at a city-wide level that such a perspective pays off. A review of UN peacekeeping operations in 2007 found, echoing Concha-Eastman, that human societies—especially those under stress—are not systems where one can intervene with only one effect. There are always numerous responses to any intervention— only some of which can be anticipated. Unintended consequences are a result of the interconnected nature of the social, economic, and political system, and, of course, people's attitudes and beliefs. Paying attention to this complex system is essential. It turns out that, even in protracted, state-wide conflicts, taking a systems perspective can be beneficial. David Kilkullen, author of the counter-insurgency handbook that preceded and underpinned the success of the Iraq surge, says this was exactly the thinking there: that the theatre of irregular warfare is an ecosystem in which many groups and actors interact, and that external actors need to see themselves as part of that ecosystem in order to be able to constructively contribute to peace.[28]

Rob Ricigliano of the University of Milwaukee is one of the leading proponents of applying a systems dynamics lens in such contexts. He argues we should be looking at the overall *system of the conflict* and the dynamics that occur— what might be described as 'the ecology of war', following Concha-Eastman. He knows what he is talking about: Ricigliano was Executive Director of the infamous Conflict Management Group, has worked on peace negotiations in Russia, Georgia, Colombia, and South Africa, and was a member of the first US team ever to teach peace negotiation at the Russian Federation's Foreign Ministry Diplomatic Academy in Moscow.

Drawing on complex systems approaches, Ricigliano sees three fundamental principles for a systems-based view of conflict:[29]

- Interconnectedness: events and social phenomena do not exist in a vacuum but are connected to other events and social phenomena.

- Dynamic causality and feedback: causality does not flow in only one direction but any causal event touches off a chain reaction that will eventually have an impact on the initial causal event itself (feedback).

- Holism: seeing the whole reveals more than merely understanding all the parts that make up the whole does.

As Ricigliano explains it, the key is to be able to draw intelligent limits around analysis of conflicts: what he calls 'the level of zoom'[30] is critical—too far away and the details are obscured, too close and the bigger picture is missed. The value of systems thinking is to provide 'a more reasonable set of criteria to set a helpful field of vision for peacebuilders'.[31] This is what Murray Gell-Mann of the Santa Fe Institute calls taking a crude look at the whole, and, interestingly, he also uses a mapmaking analogy: all maps are by necessity coarse-grained pictures of reality, akin to aerial photographs of landscapes, but this doesn't diminish their value in navigation—as long as they are drawn with accuracy.[32]

Ricigliano suggests that any conflict system comprises *structures, systems, and institutions*—such as rule of law, economy, and others intended to meet human needs; *transactions*—the processes and skills used to manage conflict, solve problems, and move from ideas to action; and *attitudes*—those beliefs, norms, and relationships that affect the level of cooperation between groups. Conflict does not arise from any one of these elements in isolation, but is an emergent property of interactions and feedback processes between them.

This gives us the starting point for mapping the system of a conflict. This approach builds on the formal systems dynamics pioneered by Jay Forrester in the 1960s, and the more accessible form developed by his student Peter Senge in the 1980s. Ricigliano has applied it in a variety of conflict contexts, including Cambodia, Sudan, and Afghanistan. Below is an example of the first such map he developed, of the conflict in the Democratic Republic of Congo (DRC), which started his subsequent work. The story of the map is itself instructive.

One of Ricigliano's colleagues was in DRC in 2003–4 and was asked for support by the combatant groups. The work was what is termed Track 1.5 in peace-building terms.[33] The map they developed of the situation was quite crude, as Ricigliano admits, but it did have a very clear message.

In effect, Figure 14.2 shows the national-level peace process that international actors were working to get on track. However, the more it got on track, the more it threatened profiteers (mineral exporters), who then manipulated armed groups through the provision of arms and logistical support, encouraging fighting, ceasefire violations, and mass rape on the peripheries in the east and north of the country. As Ricigliano told me, 'our effectiveness was undermining our effectiveness'.[34] The map helped them make sense of this frustration and stalemate, and they returned to the programme with a clear sense of needing to change the way they had been intervening. In particular, it raised the importance of focusing on local and regional processes rather than simply the national. They managed to get preliminary negotiations with regional militias, which eventually—along with a whole host of other efforts—contributed to the signing of a formal ceasefire. Ricigliano is careful not to overstate the contribution of his group: rather than a causal link, it was something that helped get the ball rolling in the right direction. Clearly, in DRC there is still a huge amount of work to be done. But the process was the first step toward the application of systems thinking to conflicts, as he explained: 'There was real power in the lesson: stepping back, zooming out and looking at the dynamics rather than the task in front of us, we were busy with the national level, but when we stepped back and looked at what we were doing, it made us more productive.'[35]

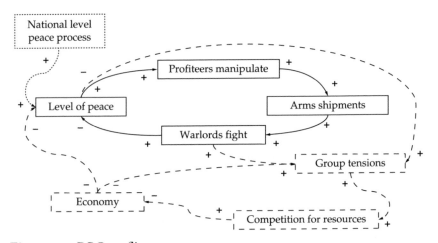

Figure 14.2 DRC conflict map

Source: R. Ricigliano (2012), personal communication.

Ricigliano uses the example of the long-running Israel–Palestine conflict to illustrate the power of the approach. The use of the systemic lens reveals a recurring pattern that moves the actors towards peace and back towards conflict, over and over again. Despite many signs of progress—agreements, accords, reforms—there are continual and significant setbacks—wars, outbreaks of violence, failed negotiations, attacks and reprisals, and expansion of settlements. The key lesson seems to be that progress on one level is not sustainable without progress on others—and shifts in one area have been met with counterbalancing shifts in others—what some analysts have described as 'dynamic stalemate'.[36] Observed over time, the system does not seem to exist to achieve peaceful political settlements, but instead to perpetuate itself.

Ricigliono suggests that, from a systems perspective, the purpose of the peace processes is in fact the *avoidance* of reconciliation:

> The parts of this system deftly interact so as to avoid reaching a political resolution or reconciliation – weaving its way between tangible signs of progress and escalating violence...but never enough violence to cause the system itself to collapse...Neither Israeli nor Palestinian leadership – nor external governments – seem willing to bear the potential costs of a political settlement.[37]

Researchers working with time series data have demonstrated this qualitative understanding of the Israeli–Palestinian conflict.[38] Econometricians from Israel, Switzerland, and the USA worked to analyse in a quantitative fashion how violence on each side occurs in response to aggression by the other side. While previous studies using such techniques indicated that Israeli violence was reactive whereas Palestinian violence was random, the researchers broadened the dataset to look at non-lethal forms of violence and a longer time period. Their findings were clear and echoed Ricigliano's systems analysis: both actors are acting in a pattern of retaliation, but neither side seems to be acknowledging the effects of their actions on the emergent conflict dynamics: 'Well-established cognitive biases may lead participants on each side of the conflict to underappreciate the degree to which the other side's violence is retaliatory, and hence to systematically underestimate their own role in perpetuating the conflict.'[39] We might paraphrase Clausewitz's famous quote here: Middle East peace processes are the continuation of conflict by the same and other means.[40]

This has been described as a fundamental paradox in such protracted conflicts. There is often 'tremendous volatility and change'[41] in these situations. In the above case, for example, there have been major changes in almost every aspect of the situation: 'Leadership, policy, regional circumstances, intensification and de-escalation of violence, intragroup divisions, popular sentiment, and international intervention strategies.'[42] Despite this, overall conflict systems remain remarkably consistent. Peter Coleman of Columbia University, an acknowledged expert in applying complex systems approaches to conflicts, sees this as common to all such conflicts: 'This paradox of stability amidst change is evident in intractable conflicts at all levels, from estranged siblings and neighbors to warring ethno-political factions. They are at once frozen, unyielding, often persisting in hostile states for generations, yet they are also some of the most volatile and dynamic social processes on earth.'[43]

Using this systems lens has strategic implications for the current mentality informing peace interventions, because it highlights its flaws. Let's imagine what actors would do if they employed a solely reductionist approach to the conflict. If conflict is equal to, and no more than, the sum of the parts, then it is about the respective political positions of Israel and Palestine, and therefore external agencies should focus on those key issues that are at the heart of the political disagreement: a settlement over borders, land disputes, security, and status of key assets and locations. Solve each of these, the implicit argument seems to be, and peace will follow, using a mix of brokerage, pressure, and negotiation to try and make deals on each element in ways that are palatable to all parties. Tellingly, this is pretty much exactly what has been done by various configurations of actors over the past half century. These often significant attempts by a whole host of external actors have singularly failed to bring about a change in the system of the conflict—and, in some cases, may have fed that system, worsening the dynamics and the situation.[44]

Ricigliano deals with this with a dose of with measured sarcasm: '"Reductionist" approaches that try to eliminate the confusing aspects of complexity by breaking a messy "whole" into its component parts . . . may be useful when trying to fix a car engine, but it can be very unhelpful when dealing with a social system that produces violence.'[45]

Sadly, there are few indications that any actors in the Israel–Palestine context are seriously considering a systemic approach. However, the system itself may be changing through necessity. A 2012 article in *The Economist* suggested that the requirement that orthodox Jews serve in the military—a duty from which they were traditionally exempt—may lead to a shift in attitudes among this generally hawkish group akin to what has already happened among more moderate communities, and this may be the best chance for the conflict to change in the future.[46] This resonates strongly with the point that 'Systems change best when systems change themselves': the question is whether such assessments can play a role in how international agencies position and develop their interventions.

The Israel–Palestine example highlights one of the challenges of this kind of approach: that all too often it can serve simply to highlight what shouldn't be done, or how not to work, in a complex setting. However, there are ways of using systems dynamics in ways that can benefit the overall process. One notable example is the ceasefire brokered in Aceh after the Indian Ocean tsunami in December 2004. The region had been gripped by three decades of civil war, with a failed peace agreement two years before the tsunami struck and both sides accused of using the ceasefire to strengthen their military position. But only eight months after the Boxing Day tragedy, both sides had signed a memorandum of understanding, brokered by former Finnish President Martti Ahtisaari, which remains in place to the time of writing. As well as the timing—what Ahtisaari called a 'historical juncture' caused by the disaster—the approach taken allowed the peace process to unfold in an emergent fashion.[47] Five rounds of talks were organized, all mediated by Ahtissari, who put one principle first: 'Nothing is agreed until everything is agreed.'[48] This simple principle allowed for the continual reassessment of the overall picture of the resolution, how the different elements contributed, and how changes were affecting the whole. As Ahtisaari subsequently explained, 'Many contested issues are inter-connected, and there will be ebbs and flows in the "give and take" of negotiations. Hence the need to work towards a whole picture and a full agreement before claiming progress.'[49]

The key is not to see the conflict system as a problem to be solved, or to attempt to impose change on it, but instead to map, observe, and listen to the system to identify the spaces where change is already happening and try to encourage and nurture them. Ricigliano explains,

> The key is to focus on learning rather than on solutions. Systems change in unexpected ways, but planners can learn to expect the unexpected. They can learn to embrace the feedback they get based on how their actions affect the behavior of the system. The goal of a development project should not be to meet predetermined benchmarks but to learn which elements of one's initial understanding of the system were right and which were wrong. Which elements of a project nurtured the system in positive ways and which did not? These lessons can bring a sense of humbleness, which will encourage

planners to listen to what the system is telling them instead of assuming they know best.[50]

This also puts paid to some of the concerns that critiques of systems thinking sometimes raise: systems dynamics approaches should not be used as just a new means to control the system but instead be a tool for interactive learning. This, in the terms expressed in Part 2, is where the computational power of the learner is at its highest: at the edge of chaos. But of course it is also where the outcomes may be most unpredictable.

The Ecological Prerequisite for Health

Another area where systems thinking has made a major contribution to the way efforts are designed, developed, and implemented is in health care. Work funded by Canada's International Development Research Centre has led to the development of the 'eco-health' approach, fast becoming a global movement. Instead of bringing an ecological framework to bear on social problems, as in the conflict examples cited above, this is based on understanding the coupled nature of social–ecological systems and how feedback works between the different dimensions of a problem. Although the nature of the problem is very different, here too systems thinking has been employed to good effect: 'Systems thinking helps apply some order to the complex reality of health in the context of social–ecological systems. Systems thinking can lead to a better understanding of the limits of the problem, its scale, and its dynamics. Ultimately, it leads to a richer, more effective research process.'[51]

As in the other examples, systems thinking helps considers the relationships, dynamics, and interactions between and within a number of components in a number of different dimensions—ecological, social–cultural, economic, and governance. There are also issues of scale to consider, both spatial (how villages make up regions, and the implications for disease transmission) and temporal (how different phenomena operate on different timescales, from the daily to the epochal). Like the researchers looking at telecoupling—a community with which there is some overlap—eco-health specialists are also keen to understand the local–global between society and nature, the interactions, and their role in driving health problems. Predictably, this is receiving growing attention from policymakers and the media: as I write this, I have in front of me a *New York Times* article sub-headed 'Destroying Nature Unleashes Infectious Diseases'.[52]

From across these examples, two on malaria interventions serve to illustrate how the insights from systems thinking can lead to changed policies and practices among international agencies. In the Mwea region of Kenya, better control of malarial mosquitoes was achieved by using systems-based approach to analysing and adapting farming practices. In Oaxaca in Mexico, community-based management has meant that DDT—a central plank in malaria interventions in the region for over five decades—is no longer used.[53] Interestingly, in both cases, it was the national government that played a central role in taking a more systems-oriented approach—echoing one of the critical messages from Concha-Eastman's work on urban violence reduction.[54]

Kenya's Mwea region is especially prone to malaria because it is an important rice-growing region, and large paddies provide an ideal breeding ground and habitat for mosquitoes. The application of insecticides and anti-malarial drugs has been widespread, but there has been a marked rise in resistance among both mosquitoes and the parasites themselves. A multidisciplinary team developed and launched an eco-health project, employing and training community members as local researchers, whose first task was to conduct interviews across four villages in the region, to give a first view of the malaria 'system' from the perspective of those most affected by it. The factors involved were almost dizzyingly large in number—from history, to social background, to political conflicts. A subsequent evaluation of the programme referred to this as an admirable feat of analysis.[55]

Using a systems analysis approach that placed malaria in the wider ecological context was a critical part of the programme design. The analogy used to explain this by the programme was coincidentally identical to that used by Rob Ricigliano when analysing conflicts:

> The approach can be compared to using a camera with a zoom lens. The zoom brings the problem into sharp focus – in this case, a mosquito infecting a person with malaria. As the lens pulls back, other elements are brought into the picture: poverty in the villages; farming practices in the rice fields...this 'wide-angle' view helps researchers to determine the reasons behind the malaria statistics and to develop possible interventions.[56]

Particularly noteworthy causative factors were the unforeseen effects of a local resistance movement, whereby farmers had decided to exert local control on irrigation systems, overturning a system of national government control that dated back to the colonial era and was associated with continued impoverishment. However, the change led to 'agricultural chaos in which farmers plant when and where they want'[57] (echoing incidentally the results of *subaks* over-planting in Bali), pushing up both the mosquito population and the number of malaria cases. Mwea also supports a substantial cattle population, which provides an alternative blood source for mosquitoes: the village with the highest number of mosquitoes per household also had the highest cattle population and the lowest malaria prevalence.

A range of solutions were developed and tested, all of which saw a shift away from the ineffective standard medical responses. For example, better coordination of farmers led to a reduction of the paddy flooding time. Rice planting was alternated with soya, a dry crop, which both reduced the mosquito population and improved villagers' diets. Other strategies included the maintenance of cattle populations as bait; the introduction of naturally occurring bacteria to kill mosquito larvae at peak breeding times; planting mosquito-repelling plants around houses; and ensuring vulnerable groups like children and pregnant women always used bednets at night. A subsequent assessment of the 'integrated malaria management approach' found that cases of malaria at the community hospital had declined steadily, from 40 per cent at the start of the project in 2000 to less than 10 per cent in 2004 and zero in 2007, and that the single biggest element of the community-based malaria control strategies consisted of 'environmental management' approaches.[58] Through the System-wide Initiative on Malaria and Agriculture, the Mwea experience is now being disseminated across the country, with the goal of finding ways to reduce malaria while improving people's health and productivity.[59]

The eco-health application in Mexico makes for an interesting contrast. As recently as the 1950s, 2.4 million people contracted malaria annually and up to 10 per cent of these would be fatal cases. In keeping with the espoused global malaria response of the time, the Mexican government made large-scale use of DDT, but, as in Kenya, this was not a silver bullet. The situation came to a head in 2002 when Mexico had to cease use of DDT under the North American Free Trade Agreement. An eco-health initiative convened a multidisciplinary team of specialists to gather data about malaria in 2,000 villages in Oaxaca, and, using geographic information system (GIS) techniques, found mosquito ranges were very limited. They also identified some surprising patterns—for example malaria prevalence was higher in villages next to roads, suggesting humans themselves were vectors of the disease. Enlisting community researchers, the team studied living conditions and found behavioural differences between men and women, which had implications for transmission: women would get bitten in the morning when they fetched water, men in the evenings in the coffee plantations.

The systems view suggested a range of approaches be tried in parallel—from a new, environmentally friendly alternative to DDT, to a more efficient spray-pump and a rapid-testing kit rolled out through volunteers delivering diagnoses in minutes rather than weeks, enabling a more refined first line of response to symptoms of malaria. The number of cases in Oaxaca dropped from 15,000 in 1998 to 400 five years later, with zero usage of DDT.[60]

Given these examples, it is perhaps little wonder that a group of health specialists and ecologists got together in 2011 to make a kind of joint statement on malaria, which argued strongly that ecological understanding was a prerequisite for malaria eradication.[61] But malaria isn't the only disease eco-health approaches have dealt with: *chagas* in Guatemala, avian flu in South East Asia, and HIV/AIDS in West Africa are striking examples of crucial problems that can be addressed using a systems approach that takes into account the link between ecosystems and human health. Both reveal the complex nature of the problem, and the need for multiple parallel solutions that bring together different disciplines and community perspectives. They also identify a kind of 'development sweet-spot': an intervention that in retrospect had all the hallmarks of a systemic response to a systemic problem, but which at the time was just one of a number of approaches launched in parallel with the hope of effecting change. Nor is it applied only in developing country contexts: obesity, diabetes, asthma, and heart disease have all been shown to relate directly to how humans interact with their local ecosystem.

Systems thinking is now being used more widely in health care, and not just for controlling specific diseases. Process issues such as scaling-up new initiatives have been shown to benefit from a systems approach. The World Health Organization has developed a handbook specifically on the use of systems thinking in health system strengthening.[62] Epidemiologists have been using it to look at how diseases emerge and reach contagion point,[63] and are increasingly arguing for utilizing complex systems approaches to avoid health providers becoming 'prisoners of the proximate' (we will see an example of this in a few chapters' time).[64] It has also been employed in an innovative tool called Threshold 21 (T21), a dynamic, quantitative, and planning tool, tailored for use in long-term integrated development planning. This approach uses formal systems dynamics approaches to model the complex dynamic feedbacks and interactions between the three critical 'spheres' of development: economy, society, and the environment. The economy sphere of the model contains the major production sectors (agriculture, industry, and services) and takes into account land, labour, capital, and technology. The social sphere contains detailed population dynamics, health, education, infrastructure, labour, and poverty. The environment sphere tracks land allocation, water and energy demand, energy supply, fossil fuel production, polluting emissions, and the overall 'ecological footprint'. The power of the model is its ability to explore potential trade-offs and synergies between these different elements, something critically absent from much reductionist and siloed development planning tools. T21 has been used to inform national development policies that encourage sustainable development, poverty eradication, and increased wellbeing of vulnerable groups.[65] It has been rolled out in countries as diverse as Malawi and Italy, and for issues as diverse as green growth and malaria management.

There are challenges, of course: systems thinking as a response to panaceas should not be expected to be a panacea itself. A systems approach need not induce paralysis, but equally it doesn't guarantee success. There are challenges of setting boundaries, of determining what is in and what is out, of balancing the need for a comprehensive understanding with the costs of inclusivity. Just as with any analysis, there are trade-offs and hard choices to be made. There needs to be care not simply to replace the simple panacea with a more sophisticated one, which still assumes things can be planned, controlled, and managed with Fordist precision.

One of the most important approaches to breaking down the silos between social and ecological understanding of problems has come from the work of the late Elinor Ostrom, 2009 Nobel Laureate in Economics.

After studying a whole host of coupled social–ecological systems (SES), Ostrom drew some generalizations about these complex systems, posing the question—in what conditions will users of a given resource invest time and energy to avert tragedy scenarios? She worked with political scientists and ecologists to develop this model, testing assumptions and ideas to ensure her work was truly 'transdisciplinary'. The result of this was a framework, a set of design principles she and others subsequently revised to look like the model in Figure 14.3.

Let's pause for a moment to review this model, using examples from this and some previous chapters. First, the framework holds that all human activities are embedded in social, economic, political, and ecological systems. Within these are specific sub-systems common to *all* social–ecological systems: resources and resource units, and users who exploit the resources, who operate under a given governance framework.

So the hardy Greenland fishermen would be users, the resources would be glacial ecosystems, resource units would be fish, and the governance system would include the local practices of fishing at certain times for certain kinds of fish. The delicate balance described by Uusaqqak Qujaukitsoq has been literally upended by climate change, leaving a system in chaos. In the very different context of African rangelands, the resource systems are African savannahs, resource units are grazing animals, users are pastoralists and farmers, and governance systems are the indigenous and imported systems that govern how the rangeland is managed and exploited.

Looking down the list of design factors for emergent self-government, it is also clear that peace can also be viewed as a common pool resource, but just not one that was sustainably managed, if at all. In the World War I trenches, live-and-let-live lacked those principles that related to the wider enabling environment: there was no higher-level support for local self-organization, and the live-and-let-live system was not nested in a wider, supportive incentive structure. In the Palestine–Israel context, the self-organizing forces on either side that might have enabled collective actions for peace were never at the table or in control of the agenda.

There are also different levels nested within these sub-systems—stretching from global to local. So the rangeland management system is embedded in a broader system of governance, which includes but is not limited to community governance, local and municipal governance, national government, and finally international governance frameworks.

In these different contexts, the four sub-systems *interact* to produce *outcomes*. Importantly, these outcomes are more than the sum of their parts. Ostrom provided a useful analogy with organisms, which are made up of organs,

Social, economic, and political settings (S)

Resource system (RS) — Governance system (GS) — Action situation Interactions (I) ↔ Outcomes (O) — Resource units (RU) — Actors (A)

⟶ Direct causal link   Feedback ⟶

Related ecosystems (ECO)

Second-Tier Variables of an SES

Social, Economic, and Political Settings (S)
S1 - Economic development. S2 - Demographic trends. S3 - Political stability.
S4 - Government resources policies. S5 - Market incentives. S6 - Media organization.

Resource Systems (RS)

RS1- Sector (e.g. water, forests, pasture, fish)
RS2- Clarity of system boundaries
RS3- Size of resources system*
RS4- Human-constructed facilities
RS5- Productivity of system*
RS6- Equilibrium properties
RS7- Predictability of system dynamics*
RS8- Storage characteristics
RS9- Location

Governance Systems (GS)

GS1- Government organizations
GS2- Non-government organizations
GS3- Network structure
GS4- Property-rights systems
GS5- Operational rules
GS6- Collective-choice rules*
GS7- Consitutional rules
GS8- Monitoring and sanctioning processes

Resource Units (RU)

RU1- Resource unit mobility*
RU2- Growth or replacement rate
RU3- Interaction among resource units
RU4- Economic value
RU5- Number of units
RU6- Distinctive markings
RU7- Spatial and temporal distribution

Actors (A)

A1- Number of actors*
A2- Socioeconomic attributes of actors
A3- History of use
A4- Location
A5- Leadership/entrepreneurship*
A6- Norms/social capital*
A7- Knowledge of SES mental models*
A8- Importance of resources*
A9- Technology used

ACTION SITUATIONS [Interactions (I) → Outcomes (O)]

I1- Harvesting levels of diverse actors
I2- Information sharing among actors
I3- Deliberation processes
I4- Conflicts among actors
I5- Investment activities
I6- Lobbying activities
I7- Self-organizing activities
I8- Networking activities

O1- Social performance measures
(e.g. efficiency, equity, accountability, sustainability)
O2- Ecological performance measures
(e.g. overharvested, resilience, biodiversity sustainability)
O3- Externalities to other SESs

Related Ecosystems (ECO)
ECO1 - Climate patterns. ECO2 - Pollution patterns. ECO3 - Flows into and out of focal SES.

*Subset of variables found to be associated with self-organization.

Figure 14.3 Analysing coupled social–ecological systems

Source: Adapted from Ostrom, E. (2007), 'A Diagnostic Approach for Going beyond Panaceas'. *Proceedings of the National Academy of Sciences* 104(39): 15181–7.

tissues, cells, proteins, molecules, and atoms; and of different but related anatomical sub-systems: respiratory, digestive, ambulatory, cognitive, and so on. The overall properties of an organism are more than the sum of these parts: think about the social behaviour of swallows, termites, and humans. Similarly, the properties of a social–ecological system are also emergent, as are the processes by which they might be effectively governed. As Ostrom put it, 'Combining variables A, B and C [across the sub-systems] can lead to a system with emergent properties that differ substantially from combining variables A, B and D.'[66]

In discussing the structure of the problems faced in these systems, she cited extensively from work of complex systems researchers:

> These problems tend to be systems problems, where aspects of behaviour are complex and unpredictable and where causes, while at times simple (when finally understood), are always multiple. They are non-linear in nature, cross-scale in time and in space, and have an evolutionary character.[67]

Ostrom argued that building a solid field in sustainability required us to build on the work of complex systems researchers, to stop looking for answers that break problems down to a single cause, and to acknowledge the systems-based nature of reality:

> ...natural and social systems...in fact...are one system, with critical feedbacks across temporal and spatial scales...we need to recognize and understand the complexity to develop diagnostic methods to identify combinations of variables.[68]

Ironically for some policymakers and practitioners, the problem with this framework is precisely the lack of panaceas that it generates. As Ostrom told me, '[It] sets out the key design principles for complex systems which sit on the interface of society and ecology: watersheds, fisheries, increasingly the whole planet. Some of the reaction has been very enthusiastic—some people, the biologists, the ecologists, the complexity scientists, love it. Others hate it, they say it's not science, it's *too* complex.'[69]

However, despite these complaints, this approach presents another complementary approach to systems dynamics, to help guide actions to be effective in the face of complex interconnections, to achieve what Fritjof Capra calls, fittingly, 'ecological literacy'.[70] This has two meanings; one is the sense in which Elinor Ostrom used it, to develop an understanding of the ecological underpinnings of social life. The second is to employ ecological principles to further our understanding of social phenomena. The Ecosystems Services for Poverty Alleviation research programme, established by DFID and two of the UK research councils, has established a series of projects which explore both approaches through a range of complex systems tools and techniques, the results of which are still pending at time of writing, but which promise to further our scientific understanding of social–ecological systems.

As Simon Levin, one of the world's leading ecologists, told me: an ecological perspective is helpful precisely because the banking system, the economy, societies, are all 'kinds of ecological systems, and they should be managed as such'.[71] Levin has done a lot to further such an understanding—through his active role as a Fellow of the Beijer Institute of Ecological Economics, he has been part of an ongoing effort to build bridges between leading thinkers in ecology and economics. The emphasis has been on forging dialogue, building a sense of shared community and partnerships, and informing shared substantive work. Eve Mittleton-Kelly of the London School of Economics Complexity Group, and one of the leading experts on the applications of complexity research to organizations, suggests that complexity's great strength is precisely that it enables us to cross such disciplinary boundaries.[72]

A Resource of the Imagination

These case studies illustrate that, when facing systemic complexity, there is a need to be aware of the risks as much as of the considerable opportunities. The counter to needing to think about multiple interconnections is that one gets a view of how an intervention might address multiple problems at the same time. Because systems are interconnected, the wrong things can go drastically wrong, but the right things can go right just as drastically.

This point is made eloquently by Mike Hulme, climate scientist and founder of the Tyndall Center for Climate Research. In his book *Why We Disagree about Climate Change*, his argument is that the notion of wicked problems 'applies very well to what is conventionally understood as the "problem" of climate change'.[73] He goes on to say that, precisely because the concept of climate change is so *plastic*, it can be put to use in many different contexts and in support of many different undertakings: to 'stimulate new, creative thinking about technology, poverty reduction, demographic management, localised trade and many other such areas'.[74] He suggests, echoing my own conclusions in Part 1 about aid thinking, that climate solutions underestimate the wicked complexity of climate change, and rely too heavily on over-simplistic theories of systems, behaviours, relationships, and change.

Hulme's description of complex problems like climate change as 'a resource of the imagination'[75] is one I find particularly evocative—and have found to be applicable more generally to complex problems and the value of a systems dynamics approach.

A growing and widely cited body of work on 'wicked problems', a term coined by urban planners at the University of California,[76] addresses exactly this issue of ambiguity inherent to complex problems. Wicked problems are difficult to define clearly, deeply interconnected, and driven by many factors; they are problems where any solution is doomed to unforeseen consequences, that are not stable but instead constantly shifting, that generate dissent and disagreement, that cut across many institutional boundaries and responsibilities. These are problems that ultimately require changes in ways of thinking, working, and behaving, which often pose as much of a challenge as the problem being faced. As Michael Batty of University College London, whose work on cities we saw in Chapter 8, notes shrewdly: 'Every solution to a wicked problem is another wicked problem.'[77]

Rittell and Webber contrasted wicked problems with 'tame' problems, which are not necessarily simple—in fact can be technically very complex—but can be tightly defined with a solution fairly readily identified or worked through. Wicked problems cannot be broken down, analysed, and responded to in this manner. 'There is no quick fix for wicked policy problems, no glib formula about "Seven Steps to Crush Social Complexity."'[78]

If readers sense a similarity between this and Weaver's model of simplicity, complexity, and randomness, this is not entirely coincidental. It is not hard to imagine, given their focus on urbanism, that Rittell and Webber had picked up and digested Jane Jacob's famous and influential work. Indeed, in a later essay, one of them used Weaver's concepts, describing how the 'organized complexity of cities' was no longer confined to the specific geography of cities. What was new in their work was their focus on the dissent and disagreement that characterized wicked problems: 'In a pluralistic society there is nothing like the indisputable public good; there is no objective definition of equity; policies that respond to social problems cannot be meaningfully correct or false; and it makes no sense to talk about "optimal solutions" to these problems...Even worse, there are no solutions in the sense of definitive answers.'[79]

This highlights another quality of the stories that open this chapter: none of them has a definitive, single 'answer': different people have wildly different and often irreconcilable views on the best ways to deal with HIV/AIDS, Somali piracy, or overgrazing[80]—and many more problems besides. Nor, obviously, is this limited to developing countries: consider US health care or UK welfare. The notion of the socially constructed nature of knowledge is a central one for the emerging thinking on social complex systems.

Aid agencies seem to be a veritable magnet for wicked problems: they face some of the most complex and ill-defined problems in the world.[81] Most of the *core* work of most aid agencies still takes place in developing countries, and in response to poverty and suffering. These countries are complex social–economic–political systems with specific and particular histories, dynamics, and patterns. They are part of the international aid system, but also part of a whole range of other global systems, including trade, security, media, and so on.

Aid solutions too are wicked: 'Improvements in poverty alleviation, food security and the state of natural resources result from *dynamic, interactive, non-linear, and generally uncertain processes*... It is seldom possible to identify clear, sound cause-and-effect relationships' (emphasis added).[82]

This understanding is slowly percolating into the aid world. A study in Nepal funded by the UK Department for International Development on local views of the impact of climate change in 2009 drew one core conclusion from a whole range of voices and perspectives: that it was vital to engage with the kind of problem climate change was. Nepalese villagers described it as having all of the below characteristics:[83]

- It is a problem that is very difficult to define.

- Attempting to define it exposes many more underlying layers of nested and intractable predicaments.

- There are complex inter-linkages among unforeseen elements.

- There are non-linear relationships that can quickly transform a small perturbation into a catastrophic event.

- Any attempt to tinker and nudge the situation towards a solution requires uncomfortable knowledge or out-of-the-box thinking.

The study concluded that climate change can indeed be called a wicked problem. A separate study on climate change in Nepal came to the same conclusion, but also found that the broad institutional environment needed to be conducive to bold intellectual forays if wickedness was to be navigated. In particular, it found a series of built-in filters among existing knowledge-generating establishments—especially international agencies—and a focus on 'gate-keeping' existing knowledge rather than facilitating new explorations. This was despite the fact that it was widely acknowledged that the uncertainties associated with climate change demand a rethink of development paths and programmes, and that successful efforts would have to be conceived and redesigned several times, and implemented through political compromises in a democratic terrain.

Clearly, some people in development circles were paying attention. Three years later, the Asian Development Bank (ADB) Institute published a paper summarizing Asia's wicked environmental problems and calling for a new approach to dealing with them.[84] Figure 14.4 is a summary of the case studies—which range from hydropower development in the Lower Mekong to deforestation in Indonesia.

Although the research arms of aid may be slowly starting to engage with this way of thinking, the policy and operational sides are lagging. From an institutional perspective, aid agencies are problem tamers that build almost all of their work on the notion of reductionism and simple cause-and-effect relations. This bleeds into politics: taking such an approach enables them to present *their* solution

| Case studies | Problem formulation | Wicked problem characteristics | |
		Interdependency	Solution set
Hydropower development in the Lower Mekong Basin	Development opportunity (power generation, revenues to finance education and growth)? Or development setback (threat to environmental sustainability, food security, political stability)? Dynamic and uncertain outcomes.	Broad and uneven distribution of costs and benefits across stakeholders, countries, economic sectors, and across time. Regional governance structures necessary.	Solution not just yes or no to construction, but damage mitigation measures to employ in planning and operation. Prioritization of solutions depends on weight attributed to environmental sustainability.
Groundwater depletion in India	Many location specific causal factors: contaminated surface water, rural energy subsidies, institutional incapacity, rising agricultural demand, poor urban transmission.	Public good nature of groundwater extraction: many users. Linkages to health, food and water security, climate change adaptation, and, hence, economic development.	Collective management difficult: high transaction costs; broad regulation or market-based solutions require complementary actions. Solutions success location dependent.
Afforestation programmes in the PRC	Man-made sources: logging, corruption, urban sprawl, over-cultivation of agricultural land, 'development first—environment later'. Natural sources: Scarce resources per capita, climate.	Improved regulation 'exporting' deforestation offshore. Solution involves many stakeholders: farmers, forestry workers, local officials, residents of flood-exposed areas.	Stock or 'top-down' solutions counter-productive: tree planting in arid areas furthering desertification. Subjective assessment of success.
Deforestation in Indonesia and THP	Many sources: local incentives, institutional incapacity, decentralization, foreign demand. Is the central problem air pollution (health), sustainable resource use, biodiversity, climate change?	Impacts distributed regionally and globally: health costs from air pollution, atmospheric brown clouds, climate change. External sources: palm oil and timber exports.	Business as usual deforestation hard to calculate. Many potential solutions each requiring another set of supporting solutions.
Regulation of air pollution in Delhi	Sources: population and economic growth, rising incomes, fuel subsidies, poor regulation. Perpetual growth in vehicles.	Public good nature of air quality: many vehicle users, many affected by problem, but individual action ineffective.	Successful solution only 'stop-gap', problem is ever-present 'low-hanging fruit' may already be picked
Indoor air pollution, black carbon, and improved cookstoves	Multiple problem dimensions: poverty, health impacts, gender disparity, regional and global climate change. Disseminating improved cookstoves must overcome many barriers.	Cyclical nature of nexus between poverty, poor health, and biomass fuel use. Non-point source emissions of black carbon and large number of small contributors to ABCs.	No single cookstove design or method of dissemination available. In the PRC, earlier success eroded when problem changed and more coal used in household energy.
Climate change mitigation in the PRC	Many layers to problem, most of which are wicked problems themselves (i.e., carbon pricing, economic reform, energy sector reform). Perpetual growth in energy demand and coal consumption.	Linkage between energy prices and social welfare creates divergence between mitigation and development objectives, making reform difficult.	Broad response required: power pricing reform, energy sector reform, and economic reform. No straightforward solutions or silver bullet'.
Broad problems			
Water management	Combination of multiple demand-side (i.e., usage efficiency, population growth) and supply-side (i.e., pollution, climate change) causal factors.	Competitive uses and users. Two-way linkages to food security, health, welfare, economic growth, and political stability.	Localized manifestation of water issues. Perpetual nature of growing excess water demand renders any solution temporary.
Deforestation and land degradation	Many causal factors, each with own set of origins and many of these sets share factors (i.e., institutional incapacity, poverty).	Circular linkages between poverty and unsustainable exploitation of land-based resources (i.e., arable land, forests).	Growing pressure for over-exploitation as food and timber demand increases, solutions temporary. Success is subjective.
Air pollution	Incessant growth in potential pollution sources. Often non-point source pollution: difficult to control. Many underlying causes.	Linkages across many environmental problems (deforestation, climate change, etc.), affecting many stakeholders.	Many causes (vehicles, industry, energy, growth but also poverty, fire-clearing): many potential solutions for each cause.
Climate change	Hub of complex, cyclical network of causes and effects, encompassing environment, economic, and social factors. Outcomes subject to substantial uncertainty.	Feedback effects render counterfactual analysis redundant. Broad distribution of stakeholder. Intergenerational trade-offs significant, but unclearly defined.	Fundamental and far-reaching changes to development trajectory and social practices required. Solution effectiveness determined ex post.

Figure 14.4 Wicked environmental problems in Asia

Source: Howes, S. and Wyrwoll, P. (2012), 'Asia's Wicked Environmental Problems'. Working Paper 348 (Manila: ADBI).

as *the* solution. As a major donor chief said in interview in 2011, 'In order to really solve problems…you have to break them down to their most transparent and simple pieces.'[85] Another donor senior leader reinforced this: 'I want a simple solution to a simple problem so that I can demonstrate value for money.'[86] One of the newest and perhaps the most prominent of all aid leaders today, Bill Gates, made the following pragmatic—if rather McNamara-esque—points as the centre-piece of a speech entitled 'To Turn Caring into Action' at Harvard University:

> Cutting through complexity to find solutions runs through four predictable stages: determine a goal, find the highest-impact approach, discover the technology ideal for that approach, and in the meantime, use the best applica-tion of the technology that you already have – whether it's something sophisti-cated, like a drug, or something simpler, like a bednet.[87]

As an aside, the 'cutting through complexity' phrasing is reminiscent of the legend of Alexander the Great first attempting to untie the infamous Gordian knot, and then cutting through it with a single sword stroke. While reductionist analytical processes are clearly important for solving certain kinds of problems, as Chapter 2 illustrated, they are contingent on a number of assumptions about the world holding true. Their automatic, knee-jerk use raises issues for aid agencies: about how problems are defined in the first place and whether the definitive solutions that are promoted are possible, desirable, and useful in complex environments. Breaking down a problem into its constituent parts has the advantage of permit-ting a whole range of different solutions to be specified in advance. All well and good. But with wicked problems, 'the world appears so complex and uncertain that not even the possible outcomes are known…in the absence of a specified outcome in the form of a well-defined [solution], it is unclear *how to break up the problem into a set of separable parts*'[88] (emphasis added). Reflecting back on the speech by Gates, this suggests that there are forms of complexity that cannot be 'cut through'—Alexander-style—to 'find solutions'.

On the whole, the aid system's pronounced addiction to seeing the world through a classic reductionist lens is not trivial: such processes lead to problems being defined and solutions chosen prematurely to give a sense of closure and certainty. Little wonder, then, that research and evaluations are replete with examples of aid agencies focusing on one dimension of poverty, crises, or devel-opment—as narrowly defined by their mandates or obligations—and indirectly making the situation worse in a variety of other ways. In the extreme, Rittel and Weber considered it 'morally objectionable for the planner to treat a wicked problem as though it were a tame one, or to tame a wicked problem prematurely, or to refuse to recognize the inherent wickedness of social problems'.[89]

Weaver also argued that most of the real challenges we face—on which the future of humankind depends—were ones of 'organized complexity', the effective management of which is simply not possible through a lens of organized simplicity. This realization is becoming more and more stark: 'Intertwined global-scale challenges spawned by the accelerating scale of human activity…*are outpacing the development of institutions to deal with them and their many interactive effects . . . The difficulty to date is that transnational institutions provide, at best, only partial solutions*[90] (emphasis added).

The challenge is that multidisciplinary and dynamic approaches are for some both questionable and questioned, and are themselves vulnerable to accusations of being partial and unscientific. The concern for many organizations is that, if decisions are not made early, this leads to both the paralysis of indecision and the appearance of being 'flaky'. Reductionism is the 'safe' option, supported by any number of tools and techniques. By contrast, when the situation is complex and demands continual attention and movement without optimal solutions or a sense of closure, there are far fewer resources to draw on: 'The conceptual framework that sees in ambiguity the seeds not of paralysis but of opportunity is not nearly as well developed as the analytical apparatus we routinely use to solve problems.'[91]

So what is to be done? The ADB Institute's work suggests a number of changes are needed—including moving away from the classic development adage of 'one problem, one instrument'.[92] A key element is changing the nature of the science employed: we need a form of systematic thinking that 'facilitates adaptive management as problems evolve and solutions are attempted'.[93] Before any of this, there is a need to establish 'issue linkage': accepting that wicked problems are indeed multifaceted and interrelated.[94]

And it is not just problems external to the development system that can be understood through such an approach. Matt Andrews, Lant Pritchett, and Michael Woolcock, whose work I look at in more detail in the next chapter, suggest an ecosystem model to think about development interventions themselves. They posit that any intervention can be seen as bringing together the ecosystem of aid itself, specific organizations, and individuals. All too often, however, the systemic issues are ignored: individuals are blamed for not making progress or for being corrupt when in fact the system of incentives was the key issue, because 'Agents are themselves often locked into ecosystems and organizational practices beyond their control.'[95] This problem applies as much to the aid chain itself as it does to the interactions between developed and developing country actors.

This chapter has looked at numerous practical examples of systems thinking, at how the practitioners in question used their instincts about a problem, together with the tools of systems dynamics, to bust open the assumptions surrounding conventional approaches in their respective fields. In all of these cases—of natural resource management, conflict, and health—taking a more holistic, systemic approach has led to counterintuitive solutions and some remarkable successes. In some cases, of course, this has merely meant recognition of what *not* to do and how *not* to proceed. But this is also of considerable value at times: as the Lawrence Peter quip goes, 'Some problems are so complex that you have to be highly intelligent and well informed just to be undecided about them.'[96]

Less facetiously, until systemic lessons are learned and absorbed, 'we will be responsible for sustaining a development profession where aid does not make enough difference to the lives of those it is meant to help'.[97]

CHAPTER 15

Adaptive Strategies

'The most difficult challenge at this time is how to modernize our organization, adapting to changes of the 21st century. Technology outpaces our current thinking and people's ideas outpace our way of working. We have to make our organization more nimble, more efficient and effective and transparent and accountable.'

Ban Ki Moon.[1]

From Solution Providers to Solution Evolvers

Where would you go to find the leading experts on dealing with malnutrition? High-profile universities, global think tanks, government bodies, major corporations? The answer—according to one network of researchers—is retrospectively intuitive: the real experts in beating malnutrition are mothers who are living in impoverished conditions but whose children are well nourished.

Thanks to an approach that builds on the aggregated knowledge of exactly these women and their families, malnutrition incidence has been demonstrably reduced in 40 countries around the world. The successes of positive deviance (PD), which builds on principles from the evolutionary branch of complex systems research, don't end there. Other notable achievements include reducing MRSA infection rates in Western hospitals, combating the trafficking of girls in Asia, reintegration of child soldiers in Uganda, reducing female genital mutilation in Egypt, and even enhancing sales force efficiency in Mexico.

Yet the approach had humble beginnings. In December 1991, Jerry and Monique Sternin arrived in Vietnam so Jerry could take up the role of Save the Children US Country Director. The country was still labouring under a US-led economic embargo and had seriously high levels of child malnutrition, affecting 65 per cent of all under fives. Supplementary feeding programmes delivered by international agencies were expensive and the benefits were seldom sustained beyond their lifetime. And the political climate was not welcoming for an American representative of a US non-governmental organization. One high-ranking official told Sternin a week into the visit, 'There are many officials who do not want you in this country. You have six months to demonstrate impact, or I'm afraid my ministry will be unable to extend your visa.'[2]

Just occasionally, just enough pressure is just what is needed to spark new ideas. Sternin remembered a Tufts University colleague, Marian Zeitlin, who was supported by the UN Children's Fund and the (WHO) Organization to examine the phenomenon of positive deviance: the off-the-chart performance— in health, growth, and development—of certain children in a community compared with others, which Zeitlin eventually classified as 'a form of social, behavioural, and physiological adaptability to nutritional stress'.[3] Her 1990 book on the subject expanded on this, and argued that positive deviance was best understood 'in an evolutionary context, as a form of adaptation'.[4] Yet 'operational and behavioural research methods have not...attempted to draw extensively upon the local adaptive wisdom of the mothers and families of the positive-deviant children in low-income communities. Very few studies in nutrition have systematically examined the households whose children are at the top end of the growth performance curve in order to learn from successful adaptations.'[5]

Zeitlin trialled a version of positive deviance in Bangladesh, working with BRAC, to examine diarrhoeal infection and malnutrition in infants. The approach focused on mothers' wisdom and knowledge, especially in relation to positive deviants: Zeitlin and her colleagues used scientific behavioural trials to identify the factors that led to positive deviance, then used this knowledge in the design and roll-out of interventions. The idea was to incorporate the factors that led to positive deviance into 'a consistent pre-tested package of approaches to change based on known methods for improving child survival'.[6] So far, so much business as usual for foreign aid interventions.

However, the Sternins did not have the resources or the time to do this. Instead, they used the principles of positive deviance as the basis for a different approach for dealing with malnutrition. Monique Sternin told me that one of their key goals was to make the positive deviance approach operational, with the community taking the lead, although Zeitlin's work was essential in terms of providing the scientific justification: 'We needed the research, these studies had been done in six to twelve countries, this book gave us the guts to try.'[7] Work the Sternins did in Bangladesh in the 1980s with Grameen and BRAC, both of which were doing considerable experimental work on finance and health, also had a major effect on their thinking.

After numerous negotiations, the Sternins finally obtained a mandate to start working in Quong Xuong district in Than Hoa province, some four hours south of Hanoi. They had just over a dozen weeks to demonstrate impacts before their visas were pulled. In the community, however, the limited amount of money they had was less than pleasing for the local officials involved, who were not happy about promises of 'nothing more than "capacity building" and "self-reliance"'.[8] Eventually, however, the Sternins were allowed to work in four communities with 2,000 under-three year olds, 63 per cent of whom were malnourished.

Driven 'more by faith than by proof',[9] and armed with their belief in the evolutionary principles of positive deviance, the Sternins told the heads of the major village committees that the approach was going to be about finding solutions that were already in the community, which would have to take responsibility for their identification and application. To their considerable surprise, the villagers were very keen on the idea. They had previously experienced only short-term aid projects after which they had watched their children's health gains deteriorate again. This sounded different and more beneficial.

After the children were weighed, they were ranked according to their family's economic status. Volunteer groups then identified the positive deviants. Sternin remembers asking the volunteers, 'Is it possible for a child to be very poor and still well fed?' and the volunteers literally leaping from their benches shouting, 'Co co, co co!' ('It is, it is!').[10] It turned out that much of what was being done differently in the positive deviant families was tacit and unconscious: the individuals in question weren't even consciously aware they were doing anything different or new. Teams of volunteers undertook observations in their homes and found some intriguing things, some of which were common to all the positive deviant families.

The two standout practices related to the content of the diet and the way food was administered. In every positive deviant family, the mother or father was collecting a number of tiny shrimps, crabs, or snails—making for a portion 'the size of one joint of one finger'—from the rice paddies and adding these to the child's diet. 'Although readily available and free for the taking, the conventional wisdom held these foods to be inappropriate, or even dangerous, for young children.'[11] Families also varied the frequency and method of feeding. Other families fed young children only twice a day, before parents headed to the rice fields early in the morning and in the late afternoon after returning from a working day. Because these children had small stomachs, they could only eat a small amount of the available food at each sitting. The positive deviant families, however, instructed the home babysitter (an older sibling, a grandparent, or a neighbour) to feed the child regularly, four or even five times a day. Using exactly the same amount of rice, their children were getting twice the amount of calories as their neighbours who had access to exactly the same resource. Other key factors included atypically high levels of hand hygiene in positive deviant families.

At this point, the Sternins resisted the powerful temptation to 'teach' the community what they had learnt, because 'Our past development work failures...had all occurred exactly at the moment in which we now found ourselves; the moment at which the solution is discovered. The next, almost reflex step, was to go out and spread the word; teach people, tell them, educate them.'[12] This time, they decided, the key would be to give community members the opportunity to share and learn directly from each other, with a focus on fostering and facilitating the exchange of practices. This was uncharted territory: Zeitlin's approach had been very much on the idea of external scientists as knowledge producers. At its core, this meant turning a conventional approach to behavioural change—that of Knowledge–Attitude–Practice (KAP)—on its head. The basic premise of KAP is that, by changing knowledge, you change attitudes and practices. However, the failures in this approach are obvious: millions still smoke, overeat, and so on.

The Sternins reversed the process, to work on Practice–Attitude–Knowledge. 'You start by enabling people to change their practice, which then changes their attitude, and ultimately they internalize new knowledge.'[13] This beguilingly simple idea would become the basis of the positive deviance mantra, and go on to inform thousands of applications around the world over the next two decades: 'It's easier to act your way into a new way of thinking than to think your way into a new way of acting.'[14]

Over a two-week period, the Sternins provided guidance and tools on collecting data on the positive deviant practices. The progress was shared on a board in the town hall, and the charts quickly became a focus of attention and buzz. A few short weeks later, district health staff assessed progress to date. The findings were remarkable: some 40 per cent of the children had already been fully rehabilitated, and a further 20 per cent were well on the way. Granted another six-month visa for their efforts, the Sternins continued their work. By the end of the first year, half the children had participated and 80 per cent were rehabilitated. The model was taken on and applied by the Vietnamese National Institute of Nutrition, and after this by the government, which scaled it nationally. Over time, the positive deviance approach saw a sustained reduction in malnutrition rates of 65–80 per cent, and reached a population of 2.2 million. What's more, it received plaudits from a usually conservative nutrition research community: an external evaluation by researchers at Harvard later found that 'The use of the positive deviance approach had not only solved a complex problem but had achieved behavior and social change.'[15]

Since then, positive deviance has been applied to a whole range of problems. What unifies all its applications is that they focus on 'adaptive problems' that 'are embedded in a complex social system, require behavioral change, and are rife with unintended consequences'.[16] In many cases, its successes have come on the coat-tails of the failure of more technically oriented, externally designed interventions hammered out on the anvil of top-down strategic thinking.[17] As the Sternins found, this creates conditions that are ripe for positive deviance: when the former mentality dominates, it is often met with 'best practice push back'.[18]

'Best practices' evokes the immune system rejection response to a foreign body, and there is also a social immune system rejection response to outsiders coming in and saying: 'Hey, look at the answer here. We have already solved the problem.' With PD, the solution and the host in a sense share the same DNA, so you don't get that push back or rejection.[19]

But the biological relevance doesn't end there. In the definitive text on the approach, the authors argue that 'PD works like nature works...this isn't an analogy; it is the way it is.'[20] At the heart, as identified by Marian Zeitlin, is the evolutionary principle of adaptation. Just as human adaptation happens across generations genetically, some of it occurs between generations behaviourally, and some of it between peers. The positive deviance book published in 2010 put it as follows:

> Nature tinkers with a different shaped bird beak or a slightly larger brain...natural selection does the rest, favouring variations that improve access to food and reproduction...In nature, this all plays out in evolutionary timescales of centuries or millennia. Employing identical principles, the PD process achieves change within months or a few years.[21]

According to Monique Sternin, the original formulation of positive deviance as an evolutionary approach was clear from Zeitlin's work. But underpinning the Sternins' work was an attempt to make this as practical as possible, and some of the original theory was set to one side. 'Over time, however, there was more need to develop the theory and science behind PD, in order to be more systematic about what we were doing, and this is when we got really attached to complexity theory.'[22]

Working with US complexity research institute, Plexus, proved especially useful in efforts to reconnect PD practices to Zeitlin's original evolutionary explanations. Monique Sternin explains,

> We needed to be able to scale it up and tell the story to others, needed to get the tenets and principles that made sense, we needed to be able to label things more clearly scientifically...to do this, we needed to formalize it, and this is why the principles of complexity science were so useful. The resonances were deep: after all, just like positive deviance, complexity thinking is not a magic bullet – it needs to fit a special niche and problem.[23]

It turns out positive deviance relies also on another idea from complex systems: the notion of the power law. Remember that power law curves are characterized by a short 'head' of frequently occurring small events dropping off to a long 'tail' of increasingly rare but much larger ones. For example, if you set 500 sales-people to work independently, their total weekly sales will almost always fall within a narrow range around an average, with large deviations proving very rare.[24] The bell curve reflects an underlying and widely accepted theory of what happens when many independent events or actions contribute to some outcome—and underlies the widespread use of past averages as a guide to the future. The power law can help in formally identifying positive deviants, who might be seen as those individuals who make up the long tail of the curve.

Jerry Sternin held that one of the core tenets of positive deviance was not to be 'blinded by the tyranny of averages because [they] belie the reality'.[25] Nobel Laureate Dudley Herschbach argued that positive deviance has a basis in exactly this aspect of the mathematics of complexity science, and in particular the notion of power laws rather than normal distributions.[26] He explained to me that he had observed this distribution underpinning many different complex social phenomena, from educational attainment to rates of scientific publications. Moreover, he was convinced that the positive deviance approach was one of the best ways available to surface these outliers and enable society at large to learn from them. As he put it to me, 'Change and innovation happen precisely because of these outliers, and so we need a means of being able to learn from them for the benefit of society and the planet, and to preserve our role on it. In this sense, the PD story is a parable of complexity.'[27]

*

Herschbach's insights should serve as a reminder of the point made in Part 2: that the power law curve highlights a key property of complex systems: extremely large outcomes are more likely than they are in 'normal' systems. Power law patterns, with their small, frequent outcomes mixed with rare, hard-to-predict extreme ones, exist in many aspects of economic life. Bill Easterly and his team at New York University identified power laws in international trade, and this approach has been applied to development trade economics. The team looked at manufacturing exports for a sample of 151 countries, and a range of 3,000 products from the UN Comtrade database, to identify a high degree of concentration, or 'big hits', in successful exports.[28] For example:

- 23 per cent of Egypt's manufacturing exports are of one product (ceramic bathroom and kitchen items) to one destination (Italy), capturing 94 per cent of the Italian import market for that product.

- 10 per cent of the Philippines' manufacturing exports are electronic integrated circuits and micro-assemblies to the USA, capturing 80 per cent of US imports of that product.

- Nigeria earns 10 per cent of its manufacturing exports from shipping floating docks and special-function vessels to Norway, making up 84 per cent of Norwegian imports of that product.

Easterly and his fellow researchers conclude that the power law characterization implies that the chance of 'picking a winner' diminishes exponentially with the degree of success. Also, as developing countries are more exposed than rich countries to the vagaries of product demand, this further lowers the benefits of trying to pick single winners. The authors used their analysis to identify what might be called the 'positive deviants' in three African countries and to explore what had contributed to their success. They make some preliminary suggestions about the relative roles and importance of government and the market in picking winners, and the importance of an iterative approach: 'Export success [is] a very uncertain voyage of discovery. This picture of African exports could suggest the advantages of a flexible and decentralized system for continually making these discoveries, while sometimes succeeding also in perpetuating the success of old exports.'[29]

What this illustrates is the importance of the mindset shift needed: the one the Sternins debated on the dusty journey home after they identified the positive deviant practices. This is nothing less than the ability to let go and let the positive deviants self-organize in ways that enable them to find their own solutions. This is especially challenging for actors—be they doctors, teachers, or aid workers—who are imbued with a powerful self-image of being the fixers and the solution providers. These actors need 'to change their role and be willing to trade in their power for a different kind of power...the biggest challenge always is to get those people whose self-image is wrapped up in being the person who knows the answer to become the *ones who know the questions*'[30] (emphasis added).

Given that the first widespread application of positive deviance was in an aid programme, it is still much less well known than it should be in the international development community. I have spoken to senior managers in major agencies who have never heard of it. And yet, outside the development community, it has gone from strength to strength. It is proving particularly effective in dealing with modern superbugs like MRSA. And it is also starting to percolate into the business world: *Harvard Business Review* listed it in 2010 as one of the ten ideas most likely to change the next decade.

Such remarkable successes aside, one of my favourite things about positive deviance is that it originated from the work of the Sternins—remarkable and inspiring examples of 'positive deviants' in their own right.

Iterative Adaptation Writ Large

Matt Andrews and Lant Pritchett of Harvard University together with Michael Woolcock of the World Bank are to be credited for bringing a wonderfully tongue-twisting phrase to development circles: 'isomorphic mimicry'. This is an idea from evolutionary biology, perhaps the most famous of which relates to the famous ant-beetle: a beetle that mimics an ant to the extent that until relatively recently it was thought to be a sub-species. Building on work by Elinor Ostrom and others, they argued that developing country institutions that were built and supported by development agencies were marked by exactly such mimicry.

Again, this is not unique to them: aid agencies do not have a monopoly on systemic problems.

Pritchett told me that one of his favourite examples of isomorphism related to World War II: 'At the beginning of the US engagement in Europe something like half of all line officers got replaced in the first year [because] people who made general in the peacetime army were often not up to the task of actually commanding in a war situation ... when it mattered they got rid of those guys.'[31]

Aid projects create conditions in which developing country organizations— governments, non-governmental organizations, and so on—seek to adopt shapes and frameworks that *look like what the external party wants*, which will therefore gain legitimacy and support from such parties but be ill matched to the specific developing country context in which they are applied.

> Perhaps the most spectacular large-scale contemporary example is that the richest and most powerful nation in the history of humankind has just spent a decade—and enormous amounts of blood (almost 2000 dead) and treasure (over half a *trillion* dollars)—attempting to (re)build state capability in a very small and poor South Asian country. The United States is ... almost certainly leaving behind a state less capable than what Afghanistan had in the 1970s.[32]

These instances of isomorphic mimicry add up to a persistent 'capability trap', whereby 'Governments constantly adopt "reforms" to ensure ongoing flows of external financing and legitimacy yet never actually improve.' This 'suggests the generic "theory of change" on which development initiatives for building state capability are based is deeply flawed'.[33]

Of course, it takes two to pervert incentives. One element is the behavioural response of developing country organizations to the incentives imposed on them; the other is the philosophy and mindset of the external agency, and findings here resonate strongly with my argument in Chapter 3 on Aid Strategies. Capability traps arise when development interventions are based on the reproduction of best practice, which are then delivered through predetermined linear processes, based on close monitoring and compliance and driven from the top down: 'implementation by edict'.

The way out of this is both refreshingly simple and challenging: bringing a different mental model to development policy—'problem-driven iterative adaptation' (PDIA) (see Table 15.1). Importantly, this is not a recipe for success, but rather a set of principles that can be implemented in flexible ways in different settings. Andrews, Pritchett, and Woolcock argue that four principles can be applied at the highest levels of development policy and practice:

- To aim to solve particular problems in particular local contexts.
- To create an environment that encourages experimentation and positive deviance.
- To support active, ongoing learning that feeds back into new solutions.

Table 15.1 Contrasting current approaches and PDIA

Elements of approach	Mainstream development projects/policies/programmes	PDIA
What drives action?	Externally nominated problems or 'solutions' in which deviation from 'best practice' forms is itself defined as the problem	Locally problem driven— looking to solve particular problems
Planning for action?	Lots of advance planning, articulating a plan of action, with implementation regarded as following the planned script	'Muddling through' with the authorization of PD and a purposive crawl of the available design space
Feedback loops	Monitoring (short loops, focused on disbursement and process compliance) and evaluation (long feedback loop on outputs, maybe outcomes)	Tight feedback loops based on the problem and experimentation with information loops integrated with decisions
Plans for scaling-up and diffusion of learning	Top-down: the head learns and leads, the rest listen and follow	Diffusion of feasible practice across organizations and communities of practitioners

Source: Andrews et al (2012), 'Escaping Capability Traps through Problem-driven Iterative Adaptation'. Working Paper 299 (Washington, DC: CGD).

- And to engage broad sets of actors to ensure reforms are legitimate and relevant, that is, politically supportable and practically implementable.

For me, one great example of the problem-driven iterative adaptation approach in practice is—like the story Pritchett tells—a retrospective one. In Chapter 4, we looked at how WHO eradicated smallpox and in particular how it demonstrated the importance, and the limitations, of an endemic form of top-down strategic planning in aid agencies. I argued that what emerged was a more evolutionary approach to strategy, but that this was hard to acknowledge or even talk about for many associated with the programme: the official account barely even mentions the strategic adaptations involved. Looking at them through the problem-driven iterative adaptation lens, they match the principles perfectly in all but one aspect: the intervention wasn't planned that way but evolved into it.

At the heart of the original smallpox strategy was the assumption that the world was predictable and orderly, and that vaccination techniques that had worked in Western countries would work in different developing countries. The systems being created in national contexts reeked of isomorphism, but were not actually getting the job done: smallpox persisted in many countries despite high levels of vaccination.

There then emerged in one particular setting a new kind of strategy, based on local knowledge and a contextualized intervention of surveillance and containment—a combination of the top-down and the emergent. The success of this effort in Nigeria led to an acknowledgement that the 'normal, scientific' puzzle-solving approach to the problem of smallpox was limited. The results spoke for themselves: by 1968, Nigeria was smallpox free. This initial instance of positive deviance in the eradication process provided a niche for the evolution of many more.[34]

Programme managers started to support the development of a new approach to strategy that combined the original rational planning approach with local adaptations around the principles of surveillance and containment. This was used as a kind of learning template, adapted in different ways in different settings. The programme actively encouraged a whole host of local, field-based innovations to facilitate the emerging strategy, strengthen capacity, enable learning, and share knowledge. Examples of other innovations were smallpox recognition cards, watch guards, rewards, rumour registers, and containment books, and all of the most important innovations came from fieldworkers.[35]

As a result of all of this adaptation, the programme was very different in each country, as well as at different times. Each national programme developed its own set of standard operating procedures that were tuned to the local task environment. Throughout the programme, the pursuance of clear and stringent rules and standards concerning vaccination, detection, and containment was matched by an equally fervent spirit of innovation and experimentation in the implementation of those procedures.

WHO recognized early on the critical role of concurrent independent evaluation of the various campaigns to uncover and remedy deficiencies while they were still active. Evaluation procedures evolved constantly in response to new experiences and lessons learnt from the field and were kept flexible so they could be changed to fit each local environment. Initial output-based measures, such as numbers of people vaccinated, were replaced by outcome-based measures, such as trends in incidence. A sensitive feedback and control system was thus established, relying on the extensive, accurate, and rapid collection of data from the field, which were analysed and acted on quickly. Regular review meetings at all levels and special publications and research papers disseminated new techniques or improvements of existing procedures. The programme functioned in a collegial structure of many independent national programmes, each developing its own administrative traditions and adapting to local social and cultural conditions.

The process became ever more politically courageous, with managers who were willing to bend or go outside the rules and operational staff who were empowered to overcome bureaucratic inertia. Managers and supervisors started to encourage the creative solving of problems as they arose, and adopted an attitude of supporting problem-oriented practical experimentation in the field.

Without any formal intention to do so, the smallpox programme developed into a global learning effort, which had a clear focus on 'where to go' but a lot of scope to innovate and adapt around 'how to get there'. Part of the change that took place echoed Bill Clinton's story about adaptation in peace negotiations: the ability to stay in the same key and riff.

This process of strategic adaptation was central to the campaign's success, and was not the strategy WHO originally employed or even envisaged: it emerged from the programme bumping into diverse, dynamic contexts, and was 'a triumph of management, not medicine'.

Armed with these ideas from positive deviance and problem-driven iterative adaptation, we can start to make arguments for such approaches becoming the norm for addressing wicked development problems. Perhaps the greatest need in the world of global health is in malaria response.[36] After all, the problem is evolving, as we saw in Chapter 2, and this is severely limiting the efficacy of existing approaches. For example, within a four-year period in Dielmo in Senegal, the distribution of insecticide-treated bednets had a positive impact in the first two years. After this, however, malarial attacks returned to their pre-bednet levels, almost doubling for adults and children over ten. Separately, researchers found that the resistance-conferring mutation had risen from 8 per cent of the mosquito population to 48 per cent: effectiveness was leading to ineffectiveness.[37]

Professor Karen Day, who has studied the historical evolution of malaria, is clear about the importance of this line of inquiry: 'From Ronald Ross's discovery that malaria is transmitted by mosquitoes came the idea that we could control malaria by impacting the life span of the mosquito. If we can better understand the evolution and diversity of malaria, we may find an Achilles heel in the parasite or new ways to thinking about control.'[38]

Researchers at Maastricht University argue that a fundamental issue is that much malaria modelling does not take into account evolutionary dynamics.[39] By modelling global malaria as a complex adaptive system, they have been able to review the efficacy of strategies. Overall, their conclusion is that continued changes in human behaviour (such as in agricultural methods or urbanization, which presents its own set of challenges), as well as human impacts on the environment, will mean malaria will continue to evolve and confound current interventions in areas of high prevalence.

To 'roll back malaria', it is starting to become clear that there is a need for a more ecologically literate, evolutionarily sound way forward. One option is to apply the ideas of fitness landscapes and agent-based modelling (ABM) to better understand the evolving nature of the problem and how resistance among mosquitoes and malaria parasites is emerging as a result of interactions with various aid-sponsored interventions and treatments. There has been a lot more work in this area in recent years, including—most promisingly—studies that look specifically at how agent-based methods can simulate the potential evolutionary response of mosquitoes to different interventions.[40]

The most important question is not about the research but relates to how to integrate a more adaptive management approach into the strategic decision-making processes of international agencies. This has both policy level implications—can we get problem-driven iterative adaptation approach processes for malaria response?—and more technical ones—how do we adapt bednet programmes to minimize the potential for resistance to evolve?

This general area is what I turn to next, moving away from health to look at how the largest development agency in the world brought evolutionary thinking to bear on some of thorniest challenges it faced in developing countries.

Contours of Influence

The World Bank is the biggest and most influential of all development actors: as my former colleagues at the Overseas Development Institute argued, 'The market structure for aid resembles nothing as much as one Wal-Mart and a whole string of corner shops.'[41] Much of its work relies on reforms in developing countries, which has given rise in the past couple of decades to a much greater focus on governance.[42]

Although understanding the political economy of reforms was widely seen as vital to improving development effectiveness in the Bank—and elsewhere—the available analytical toolkits were limited. Informal political intelligence gleaned by Bank staff and more formal political economy approaches such as macro-level analysis and qualitative stakeholder analysis were found to be subjective, static, and selective. As a whole, the existing tools didn't match up well to the reality of country contexts, where there were typically many diverse stakeholders, interacting dynamically over time and influencing the overall process of change. 'Tracking these dynamics and capturing the knowledge to achieve a desired outcome is a complex process. Such solutions are relatively straightforward in dyadic interactions. In n actor environments they become more unpredictable. This is further complicated in environments where multiple policy or reform issues are present.'[43]

In the face of this organized complexity, the challenge was how to move beyond political economy approaches that were analytically sound but lacked policy relevance or those that were sensible but not rigorous.[44] The practical challenge was clear: to find a robust approach that would fit into the Bank's programmatic work. The team led by Barbara Nunberg, then Head of Governance at the Bank, started to experiment with a tool originally developed within military and security contexts, working with Mark Abdollahian and colleagues from Claremont Graduate University. This built on the principles of traditional stakeholder mapping, combined with a simple agent-based model that allowed the introduction of elements such as interaction, dynamics, and time.

The approach ran along similar lines to the tournaments run by Robert Axelrod in the 'Live and Let Live' work described earlier,[45] which was also one of the inspirations for the work of Steve Lansing in Bali. The starting point was to clarify the driving question for the model, then to draw up an issue map that looked at the range of possible responses and the range of actors involved, their influence, and the salience of the reform issue. Although the actors were diverse in terms of their relative positions and clout on a given issue, they were all subject to 'the same push and pull of the political process'.[46] The process modelled agents making decisions based on their own particular political interests and idiosyncrasies: each agent observed the positions of other actors and acted in ways that furthered their particular calculus of what was a desirable move. The algorithm at the heart of the model specified interactions between each pair of stakeholders over a number of rounds, and allowed actors to get into one of four positions relative to each other: standoffs, compromises, leverage, or imposition.

Multiple simultaneous interactions, iterated over time, led to the emergence of coalitions and fractures of actors that supported, opposed, or remained staunchly ambiguous to reforms. Through repeated interactions, in which different political positions are navigated through *in silico* horse trading, the overall landscape for reform—the space for possibilities—becomes clear. Although it is a model—a dynamic, iterated estimation—it simulates in a powerful way how coalitions, conflicts, and compromises form.[47] The evolving and dynamic nature of the policy process is illuminated, 'opening the black box of political will'. Box 15.1 describes the workings of the model in more detail.

Box 15.1 An agent-based modelling pilot in the World Bank—six key steps

On a practical level, the model was made available through a software application with a variety of visual interfaces and, importantly, the scope to adapt data inputs and issues on the fly. Staff with a political science background were trained to use it as and when they needed it, 'helping to embed political analysis in operational decision making so as to have impact on real-time policy choices'.[48]

Step 1. Framing the question. This involved articulating the overall objective of the political problem and placing the particular issue within the broader political economy landscape.

Step 2. Specifying the issue. This was defined as the continuum of options that stakeholders may support on a particular policy matter, which were given numerical values from 0 to 100. Use of the scale varied: for some cases, 100 meant an actor was in full support and 0 meant full opposition; for others, 0 and 100 represented distinct policy options; and for some, 0 was easy reforms and 100 was challenging reforms. This proved the most difficult part of the exercise, but also one of the most important: 'This step is where substantive expertise and the "art" of analytical creativity are most crucial. Taking time to specify the issue properly is also one of the model's benefits, as it helps the Bank achieve clarity on the reform issue, desired outcomes, and key stakeholders.'[49]

Step 3. Collecting data. A rigorous data collection process involved structured interviews with key internal and external informants with a good understanding of the context, the stakeholders, and the issue itself. The minimum data requirements were a list of all stakeholder groups that might be able to influence the reform: national, international, civil society, private sector, and so on; their current positions on the issue in the given political environment; the influence of each actor on the issue (also rated 0–100); and the importance of the issue to each actor, which then deter-mined the time and effort they would dedicate to the reform process (also rated 0–100). Data were gathered in an iterative fashion.

Step 4. Running the model. After data were entered into the model, it generated a series of pictures of expected stakeholder interactions over time. These included a Base case, where the different actors started out.

(continued)

Box 15.1 Continued

This was examined to explore whether there might be convergence or divergence on a particular issue, and over what kind of timeframe. The model also generated images of the round-by-round simulations, showing how actors moved their own position in response to other actors' repositioning. These visualizations clearly illustrated the different hypothetical coalitions emerging and forming and falling away. The model helped unpick the underlying bargaining dynamics, to see how the overall outcome could evolve from the starting position as a result of the diverse actions of key stakeholder groups. This analysis helped to identify opportunities for the Bank to work with key actors, to build consensus, and to further the reform agenda, as well as to navigate roadblocks on the path to change.

Step 5. Defining and interpreting alternative scenarios. The model was then used to run simulations of strategies the Bank or other actors might employ to improve outcomes in favour of reform. This examined whether, for a given starting condition, different positioning by the Bank would help or hinder the reform process, or how the Bank could work to influence key actors and the possible ramifications. The model also offered sensitivity analysis to determine whether changes in position, salience, or influence scores for certain stakeholders could have a significant impact on the outcome:

'The model can thus provide a detailed illustration of the micro politics surrounding strategies... The model anticipates how these dynamics play out over time and while not a substitute for comprehensive understanding of a country's political economy, [it] can add considerable value to other types of analysis.'[50]

Bank officials, funded by the Dutch government, set up a pilot to roll out the approach across four country offices in the East Asia and Pacific region. The key objective was to integrate the model into the analytical and project cycle and examine its potential benefits for the Bank's core work. The stated aim was no less than to 'elevate the sophistication, accuracy, and operational relevance of political analysis at the Bank'.[51]

From civil service reform in Timor Leste, to accountability and transparency of the public sector and extractive industries in Mongolia and tax administration in the Philippines, the issues to which the approach was applied were all slow moving or in some cases stalled processes of reform. The entry point also varied—from design to refining strategies—as did the stage of the Bank operational cycle at which it was tested (from design to assessment) and the primary purpose of the exercise. The latter included, but was not restricted to, country assistance strategy design; blue sky exploration of new areas of work; identifying potential supporters and opponents and Bank strategies to deal with each; sensitivity testing of existing strategies across a range of actor scenarios; resource and effort allocation; risk mitigation to prevent derailing of reforms; and building consensus for reform. A common driving force across all the country applications was a focus on testing the prevailing strategic assumptions held by Bank staff around a particular reform or political context.

Across the four pilots, hundreds of internal and external interviews were conducted. The positions of different groups were examined, refined, and adapted. Models were built and tested, calibrated, and recalibrated. In Mongolia and Timor Leste, Bank country staff became more circumspect about the path to reform, resulting in more realistic and achievable goals.

In Mongolia, the model revealed the potential for previous unseen splits within the major political parties on mining transparency and the scope for unexpected coalitions. The highly politicized nature of the issue, and the polar-ization of stakeholders around the ongoing national elections, led the Bank to conclude that little could be done to achieve sustained reform. The best option was to maintain an inclusive approach, to keep everyone 'in the ring' on the issue, and to work with actors like civil society organizations that the model revealed to have greater leverage than the Bank over government actors. The model sug-gested this would be a far less divisive approach than trying to push for a specific, timed reform agenda. Within two years, the government itself had drafted guidelines for transparency and was starting to put them into place by publishing the executive budget to the National Assembly.

Similarly, in Timor Leste, the model suggested the Bank should be refocusing its efforts on lower-level and more feasible types of reform. It also highlighted that reforms needed to move through various phases of acceptance, over which external actors had very little positive influence, but which they could unwit-tingly derail through their actions: the model showed the Bank's efforts leading to the fracturing of coalitions or to policy 'regression'. It also highlighted the limits to existing knowledge and the importance of waiting until national actors—notably parliament—took concrete steps towards civil service reform before making a move itself. At the right time, even small changes in the Bank's position were shown to have a positive or negative tipping point effect on the consensus for reform.

In the Philippines, the model was used to highlight a more nuanced picture than Bank staff had previously held. There was considerable desire for tax reform among a wide array of groups, but entrenched opposition from a few powerful stakeholders, notably the Bureau of Internal Revenue, which dominated the issue. The simulation revealed that the actors for change were unable to deal with this powerful group, so the Bank refocused its attention on change management efforts among these groups.

> The analysis of the overall tax reform landscape indicated that revamping the entire system would not be feasible at this time. But the model also identified opportunities to achieve tangible progress through more targeted attention on key micro-level issues, several of which corresponded with [the Bank's work]. These findings validated the program's approach of starting small to build momentum for future reforms.[52]

A common conclusion across the Bank staff trialling the tools was that the process itself had helped guide strategic discussions and supported the development of more realistic and flexible programmes that were more attuned to dynamic, politically intricate contexts. Because of the intensive data gathering that preceded the modelling process, it also highlighted—and in some cases helped address—some critical knowledge gaps.

Country offices found considerable value in the process, in terms of how it helped them think critically about the issues and the dynamic stakeholder landscape. The results helped generate a more detailed understanding of the political economy of the reform process and enabled the testing of new ways to understand and engage in the complexity of reforms, rather than simply ignoring this. When testing the agent-based modelling strategies, staff found them both intuitive and able to yield useful results.

Agent-based modelling has the capacity to support improved understandings of a 'complex, multi-stakeholder reality' in a robust and comprehensive way. Specifically, the model helps capture intricate interactions among a large number of stakeholders in a way that would not be possible using traditional stakeholder tools. Flexibility to change the menu of stakeholders, alter their positions, and test varying scenarios allows the tool to more closely model policymaking conditions in the real world. This dynamic quality, accompanied by accessible and intuitive graphical simulations in the accompanying software, makes the model particularly useful for sifting through intricate political realities to help zero in on more feasible reform strategies. There is a proviso, of course, which relates to the data quality: 'Garbage in, garbage out.'

In summary, and broadly in line with initial high expectations, the model and process were found to be 'a robust way to inject just-in time realism into the design of Bank operations, helping guide the reform support strategy toward achievable goals or, where appropriate, signalling when to jettison programs that are going nowhere politically'.[53] And the pilot 'strongly suggests that mainstreaming [the model] as a regularly applied analytic instrument could significantly improve the operational track record of development institutions such as the World Bank in supporting politically realistic reforms in client countries'.[54]

When I spoke to Barbara Nunberg, the former Bank Head of Governance, who developed, championed, and oversaw the work, she told me that a key driver was to 'move away from armchair analytic to proactively analytic, something that could be tested in the micro-politics'.[55] Having spent 20 years working in very messy, chaotic, or complicated environments, the approach was very intuitive to her. What was especially useful was that it filled a clear and obvious gap: 'You either had these armchair analyses at a macro level by academics or . . . very linear prescriptive approaches to solving a particular problem on the ground.'[56] Neither of these proved especially useful for understanding the complex, dynamic relationships that affected how a reform actually got designed and implemented. I think another important factor was that the tool was less about prediction and more about heuristics: learning and decision making. It was found to be very well suited to strategic assumption busting and brainstorming: 'systematic, just-in-time, and dynamic'. In all of the case studies, what was vital was the integration with the programmes of the Bank; as the synthesis study puts it, this was work at the frontier of practical political economy.

And not just political economy. At the time of writing, I have access to researchers using agent-based approaches to model the growth of cities in Tanzania, to study conflict across Sub-Saharan Africa, to look at food security issues in Asia; the Federal Reserve Bank of India is using an agent-based modelling in its quarterly forecasts; there are many applications in natural resource management, health care—the list goes on and on.

Of course, one of the questions is whether this kind of approach is feasible not just in policy work in air-conditioned offices but also at the coalface of development work. Can the more technically elaborate approach to adaptive strategies be used in the kinds of rural settings the Sternins found themselves in? The answer, perhaps surprisingly, is yes.

Gaming Power

Kenneth Arrow is widely acknowledged as one of the most important economists of the post-war era. He is the youngest ever winner of the Nobel Prize in his field, for his work on the Impossibility theorem, which helped generations of researchers and policymakers make sense of the dynamics of collective decision making.

In 1988, just four years after the Santa Fe Institute (SFI) was established, Arrow took up a role on its science board, giving him a unique insight into the potential of complex systems research for social issues. Indeed, he was a participant in the now infamous meeting of physicists and economists at SFI in 1984. As he explained to me, 'What that meeting did was highlight that we [economists] weren't able to explain a number of phenomena, which the physicists were able to explain with complex systems thinking... so much of what we do that is fundamental to the field, like describing the process by which equilibrium is reached, didn't have well-developed theories.'[57]

When I asked about the value complex systems research brought to the social sciences, he rattled off a list that included dynamics and networks. He also felt there was a lot of potential for agent-based modelling, but suggested that two developments would be important. The first was that it needed to be data driven, based on actors from across a system: 'Let's say we are going to put in a regulation—no mortgage without a down payment. We need to ask the banks, what would you do, and why? Then we need to ask others down the system... We should use theory to guide the questions [and build understanding of the system]... and then we should use computing power... to simulate and stress-test the system.'[58]

This is largely the World Bank process I described in the preceding section. However, Arrow also suggested there was another way in which agent-based modelling could be made relevant to decision making: 'We have to involve real people in developing the models and running them, not just external experts.'[59]

His idea has obvious echoes of the examples in Part 2 of medical researchers combining simulations of viruses with human game players to crack enduring problems. Many other well-known examples of such interactive modelling are also in the 'hard sciences'. On the surface, there may be a reason for this: there may be more of a natural fit with the hard sciences, where there is a longer history of visualizing and manipulating data in computerized form.

Interestingly, the aid sector is starting to address the potential of workshop-based gaming approaches, with an explicit nod to complex systems thinking. Pablo Suarez of the Red Cross is a leading exponent of this approach, designing and running role-playing games specifically intended to help participants navigate complex problems, with a particular focus on disaster response and climate change adaptation. He says the coupled natural–social systems that need to be considered in such efforts have a complex dynamism that is hard to capture through conventional learning approaches: 'Feedbacks, non-linearities, delays, unanticipated "side-effects", and trade-offs between the macro and the micro levels are inherent in risk management decisions and should be part of the learning experience... Games are the medium of complex systems and can help people and organizations improve access, understanding, trust and utilization of information.'[60]

Suarez's work is growing in popularity, but does beg the question as to whether the challenge Ken Arrow posed about a socially driven version of modelling processes, which combines both the participatory and the technological, has any answers that are grounded in development realities. The answer is 'Yes': a community of French development researchers has worked for the past 15 years on exactly this issue. The official name for their approach is 'companion modelling' (ComMod).

Just as in the World Bank case, ComMod emerged from heightened awareness of the limitations of existing analytical and policy research techniques, to respond to the need to understand the dynamics of decision making and to inform ways of resolving conflicts through effective processes of mediation. In particular, in natural resource management, as much attention often needed to be paid to understanding the social dynamics of managing resources as to the ecosystem dynamics, precisely because workable solutions often emerge from interactions among diverse stakeholders.[61] At the heart of the approach is the innovative combination of role-playing games of the kind Suarez facilitated along with an agent-based model very similar to the one the Bank pilot used. ComMod is based on the idea of combining participatory role-playing games associated with agent-based computer models. Francois Bousquet, one of the leading lights in the network, suggested to me that role-playing games *are* in fact a form of agent-based modelling, albeit a largely social one.

ComMod is an interactive process underpinned by evolutionary models 'to support dialogue, shared learning, and collective decision-making'.[62] As well as having an evolutionary principle in the model itself, to match the evolving characteristics of natural resource management, it employs an iterative and evolving process whereby stakeholders are involved in the design of the simulation tools. The idea is that by using this kind of participatory approach, natural resource management practitioners and researchers can be better placed to deal with complex, evolving problems involving dynamic networks of actors.[63] One might describe this as agent-based modelling 2.0.

ComMod has its roots in Bousquet's doctoral research in Mali in the early 1990s, where he came across, and was massively influenced by, Chris Langton's work on the edge of chaos. At the heart of the technique is a way of modelling different stakeholders' preferences and perspectives, and incorporating this into simulation exercises that will enable actors to play out different scenarios. 'Modeling proceeds iteratively by successive approximations usually from simple to more complex representations of system dynamics. This iterative modelling is done in close interaction with stakeholders, who, along with the modelers, use the models for scenario planning.'[64]

It's worth looking at each of the two elements of ComMod quickly before looking at a couple of applications and the implications for strategic thinking. The role-playing game element typically gets participants to invent fictional characters and collaboratively create situations that mirror the actual situation in relation to a particular natural resource: water, land, fisheries, and so on. The characters can observe the situation and make moves based on their assessments. The participants themselves determine behavioural rules based on their characterizations, then play the game under different scenarios. These latter might relate to ecological conditions (e.g. different tide and weather conditions in coastal areas); social conditions (e.g. cooperative scenarios or conflict scenarios); or some combination of the two. The agent-based model is also developed in a participatory way to create and examine scenarios of resource sharing. The agents are programmed with certain characteristics, and make decisions on the basis of a dynamic set of rules. Just as in the role-playing games, scenarios can be created to emulate the real social–ecological conditions. Bousquet suggested to me that the principles of the edge of chaos remained fundamental: 'The concept gives a message that, through the interactions of many entities, the overall behaviour we see is organized complexity, not disordered or ordered, and that within this there will be shifts from one space to another. This completely maps onto our understanding of how humans interact with each other around environmental issues...I still use the [Chris] Langton paper when I teach, and students just get it.'[65]

The role-playing and agent-based elements of ComMod can be brought together in different sequences, or indeed not at all: some applications focus just on the role-playing elements. At its most compelling, the ComMod cycle involves exploiting the synergies between the two approaches in different field-based settings.

The most challenging and intensive element of ComMod is the development of the role-playing game. That said, in some of the most interesting applications, the game preceded the model, with some remarkable results. A group of semi-literate farmers in northern Senegal spent a day or two developing and playing the game, and Bousquet and his fellow researchers spent a night frantically coding a model, the results of which they showed to the farmers the next day. The farmers then started adapting the model, explaining the shortfalls and demanding the inclusion of particular traits. The astonishing thing was that this was the first time any of the participants had seen a computer. When Bousquet and I discussed this subsequently, it became clear that this was another example of the positive deviance principle at work: it's easier to act your way into a new way of thinking than the other way around.

Perhaps the most extensive application of ComMod has been in Bhutan, to look at problems of rural watersheds and water sharing. Water is especially amenable to an evolutionary modelling approach: it is used for many purposes and by many different actors, who have many diverse and often competing goals: 'Inadequate coordination among stakeholders leads to inefficient water use, economic and environmental damage, negative externalities, and social conflicts.'[66] Addressing this challenge was a key motivation for the developers of ComMod in Bhutan: they wanted to strengthen understanding of the dynamics of decision making among water users, and to use this as a means by which to design new rules, or institutions, to enhance decision-making processes.

Bhutan is a landlocked country, and over three-quarters of the population rely on small-scale mountain agriculture and livestock rearing. Access to water in particular is still mainly managed by traditional institutions and norms, based on the caste, location, and history of water users, which the Ministry of Agriculture describes as originating at a time when water was scarce. In general, the more upstream you are, the more established you are, and the higher caste you are, the more likely you are to enjoy water privileges. These customs can lead to conflicts, and violence can break out between villagers over water. In a survey of 60,000 farmers, access to water was seen as the second most significant constraint to production.[67]

The ComMod project focused on the problem of irrigation water sharing between two villages—Limbukha, an upstream village, and Dompola, a downstream village—in a watershed that straddles three *dzongkhags* (district councils) in the mid-western part of the country. Here, two principles from the traditional water sharing system shape water access. The first, 'First come, first served', means existing schemes have an established water right and can prevent newcomers from using it. The second rule is 'More water for upstream communities'. There are also various other, lesser traditional rules, based on caste and status, which determine how water is shared out within a given village.

In the Limbukha–Dompola arrangement, Limbukha has control over the headwater. According to the traditional arrangement, Dompola gets half of the stream flow only from the tenth day of the fifth Bhutanese month every year. Even after this date, the upstream farmers use more than their fair share to irrigate their lands, meaning the Dompola farmers struggle to irrigate their land and transplant their paddy fields. Unsurprisingly, conflicts arise, becoming more pronounced when waters run low.

Against this background, you wouldn't envy the ComMod researchers arriving with a role-playing and agent-based approach to try and examine the situation. But they tackled the problem head on, inviting farmers from both villages to a collective session to build a game of their interaction. The timing also was remarkable: they set it to coincide with the day when the upstream farmers were supposed to share the water with the downstream farmers. The project was billed as a means of fostering dialogue between the villages and enabling the researchers to understand the problem better.

The role-playing game was conceived of using observation of real-life situations, building in factors the participants felt were most critical: plots, crops, rainfall, market, communication systems, and so on. The different types of players were identified, as well as the geographic setting and a range of different events. This provided an immediate test of the researchers' assumptions about individual behaviour, the social–ecological dynamics, and the nature of emergence. The game, which had two rounds separated by a number of months, had a powerful effect on farmers' knowledge about water sharing, and also helped facilitate non-confrontational interactions between the players. It was then transcribed to a computer simulation, and run under a number of different scenarios. A number of the farmers were struck by the realism of the game and the model: as one put it, 'It appeared like playing a game, but recalling in the evening all appeared precisely real and stimulating.'[68]

A number of key findings emerged. First, some assumptions clearly needed to be revised, for example about farmer income levels and cropping patterns. Second, when presented with different scenarios, farmers preferred the cooperative approach: 'It is more fun and interesting to work together in a community, helping each other to pull along.'[69] By the end of the process, almost half were saying that a better approach could be developed. The model also yielded some important results. Specifically, the researchers were able to explore the importance of different issues that had an impact on sharing: natural climate variability, social networks, and exchange rules. Having run a number of different scenarios, it became clear that the most important factor related to the rules of exchange.

The process of gaming and modelling, and the lessons that emerged from it, led to a remarkable breakthrough. At the end of the second round of simulations, the farmers collectively decided to develop a new set of rules for water sharing—to release the water earlier in the calendar—and designed a new institution: a joint committee to oversee overall watershed activities. Clearly informed by their experiences, 'The process went further and faster than the facilitators of the process expected.'[70] However, the success may have been too drastic: the traditional chief subsequently overrode the change in exchange protocols, saying the game should have been accompanied by a legal agreement. Nevertheless, the value of the process is clear: it reveals in stark fashion how simple individual decisions, combined with different interaction protocols, networks, and conditions, can lead to emergent patterns that are meaningful for stakeholders. It has been so influential that a small group of farmers, who had been involved in a very similar mechanism in northern Thailand, presented the model at a major national conference on agricultural development themselves.

The potential implications are considerable. ComMod-style participatory agent-based modelling has been applied to issues outside the natural resource management realm. Work on child poverty in Vietnam showed the traditional researcher-driven approach—collecting facts and subjecting real-world problems to personal biases and mental models—could be complemented by a participatory modelling approach where the diverse stakeholders who were the focus of the model themselves had a say in the process. The value of participatory simulation modelling is that it enables stakeholders to create the strategic conditions and then act in ways that reflect their real-life situation, and to use the emerging patterns as a way of evaluating the potential impact of adjustments to strategies and policies across a range of scenarios.

Clearly, the qualitative principles of a more evolutionary approach to development and humanitarian work are receiving growing amounts of interest from practitioners and policymakers alike. We have seen some examples of the more technically challenging approaches being picked up, adapted, piloted, and proved of tangible value in policy, strategy, and practice. We have also seen that technical sophistication needn't mean 'top down': the ComMod approach shows that poor farmers are more than capable of engaging with the insights and ideas from cutting-edge science, and, moreover, themselves can present the process back to 'higher levels'.

The companion approach might lend itself well to the Bank's approach to stakeholder mapping—and, if the political sensitivities can be navigated, might itself be a tool for participatory reform facilitation. Indeed, the Millennium Institute, whose work I touched upon in the previous chapter, has developed a simulation based on the Threshold 21 model, specifically to help policymakers in Sub-Saharan African nations use games to work together to improve their dynamic decision making and learning capacities when thinking through complex long-term planning processes.[71]

At the other end of the stakeholder spectrum, work led by researchers at the University of Sussex highlights the potential importance of agent-based modelling for understanding the impact of climate change on forced migration.[72] The authors suggest that agent-based approaches could help in developing models that are far more powerful than alternative statistical analysis. This is because of their potential to include real-world cognitive and attitudinal aspects of migrants into the agent attributes and rules of interaction within agent-based modelling: 'Due to the capabilities of ABMs in simulating multifaceted systems where the interactions of agents result in the emergence of complex phenomena, they present a practical and potentially highly effective tool for modelling climate change impacts on migration.'[73] The companion-based approach could be especially powerful if brought to bear on such efforts. The key to all of this, of course, is having the policymakers and practitioners engaged in the process. As Barbara Nunberg suggested in the context of the World Bank pilot work, the key value was that it would enable development practitioners—be they World Bankers or natural resource managers—to start 'thinking about strategy in a more dynamic way, and to start conversations about how we navigate the complexity rather than ignore it'.[74]

Strategic Agnosticism

The idea of a strategic balancing act dates back at least as far as ancient times. *The Art of War* dates to the sixth century BC. The Ancient Greeks assumed both mutual dependence and an irresolvable tension between the two worlds of order—forms and laws—and chaos—multiple, unstable, and unpredictable. Their perception of wisdom was that knowing itself was subjective, interpretive, and unfolding. Wisdom did not mean being able to represent the order of things with objective certainty so that events could be predicted and controlled.

Deliberate strategies, based on rational intentions deriving from formal goals formulated in advance, would literally be 'unwise'. Instead, wisdom (*meteos*, to steer) was seen as the ability to navigate a course between order and chaos, and in particular to move quickly between the two realms and to go in many different directions as needed. Odysseus, the archetypal Greek hero, exemplified this ability.[75]

Balance plays a central role in the latest understanding of strategy, as noted by the editors of the *Oxford Handbook on Strategy*: 'The need for control and integration pulls [organizations] towards stability and eventually ossification. The need for decentralization and innovation pulls them towards instability and eventual disintegration. The left and the right need to remain in balance.'[76]

This leads me to my concluding point in this chapter—the need for balance between the various underlying approaches to strategy. In reality, few strategies are purely deliberate plans, and few are purely the result of searching for solutions and acting in the moment: 'All real world strategies need to mix these in some way: to exercise control while fostering learning.'[77] Effective strategists have to find the balance in ways that reflect the conditions at hand. Some strategies are characterized as 'planned emergence'—such as positive deviance; others might be 'emergent plans'—for example simulation and gaming approaches.

William Easterly sees aid agencies as planners as opposed to searchers, who are the 'real' agents of development. My review indicates that these models relate to two distinct approaches to strategy, one of which clearly appears to prevail in how the aid sector formulates strategy. Although the notion of strategic balance challenges the planner–searcher distinction at the heart of Easterly's argument, the argument retains value as a heuristic device: following Amartya Sen—and the Ancient Greeks—we can appreciate Easterly's general hypothesis even if we do not agree with his specific conclusions. What I think all would agree on is the need for more balance and wisdom in the way aid agencies go about their work.

It's worth reflecting briefly on the influential, lauded, and much-questioned work of the experimental economists—the so-called randomistas. While appreciating their philosophy of a more scientific approach as essential for the future of development, the fact that they are perceived as so strongly wedded to the randomized control trial as *the* gold standard of scientific knowledge is seen by many impartial observers as diminishing their potential contribution.

The work of the randomistas can clearly support evolution of aid in certain contexts. Specifically, where cause and effect are predictable, linear, and sequential; where things can be held constant; where experimental sites are isolated (proponents use the term 'non-contamination' to describe these sites) then we are on firm ground with RCTs. Clearly, the requirements of randomized control trials make it a tool of what Warren Weaver would have called 'organized simplicity'. But even when such 'laboratory conditions' prevail, there is a need for the randomistas to be more humble about the applicability and generalizability of their lessons. Trials tell us less about 'what works in development' than their champions suggest.

Moreover, trials clearly need to be adapted to be of any use in rapidly changing contexts, where the aid intervention *cannot* reasonably be assumed to be the *only* statistically significant difference between the experimental and control communities, where sites *are* connected, where average differences *do not* tell us everything about impacts. I think the overall approach of the experimental economists is laudable, but their reliance on a specific kind of fitness function—based on the randomized control trial—runs the risk of limiting the relevance of their overall arguments. Broadening their work methodologically while maintaining the philosophy of experimentation will be a useful way forward.

Perhaps the most important lesson from all these case studies is what it means for aid strategies and the organizations in which they are executed: how strategies are conceived, developed, and implemented, and within what kind of organizational scaffolding. The principles behind agent-based stakeholder modelling, positive deviance, and problem-driven iterative adaptation can all be likened to an adaptive search on a dynamic fitness landscape. The search might result in a mother feeding her child in a new way, and her neighbours emulating her. It may result in a package of experimental health interventions, used flexibly in response to the particular local manifestation of a global killer disease. It might result in the political space for reforms in developing countries. This principle even applies to development at the grandest scales, as we see in the next chapter in a memorable analogy likening national economic growth to monkeys clambering through trees: this is an alternative—and memorable—way of framing a fitness landscape. Ostrom also argued that *institutions*—the rules of the game—evolve in the face of complexity: different solutions need to find their niche in an evolving landscape:

> The conceptual structure of these problems is a rugged landscape with many peaks and valleys. Finding higher peaks when the number of potential solutions is drastically reduced to a few optimal strategies is grossly inadequate for reaching creative and productive solutions to challenging problems. One can become fixated on a low conceptual hill by trying to optimize specific variables while overlooking better solutions involving ignored variables.[78]

The key lesson seems to be that the development strategic toolkit itself needs to evolve, to develop a more process-based approach more suited to problems that are complex and unstructured, and to find a dynamic balance between no strategy at all and the rigidities of blueprints. For some, this suggests that effective aid strategies are those adaptively positioned between order and chaos. However, as noted in Part 2, this would not be an unalloyed good, but instead brings with it considerable uncertainties and risks as well as opportunities.

The *Oxford Handbook on Strategy* sums up succinctly the key issues facing the strategy field as a whole, which is pertinent for aid strategists: 'a call to drop the baggage, to accept that linearity and traditional planning cannot cope with complexity, to adjourn our repeating of generic strategies, to become analytically softer, to experiment with and take seriously apparently non-traditional approaches... from [our] viewpoint... the view of the future is agnostic.'[79]

BOB WAS FINDING THE NEW STRATEGY TO BE QUITE A MIXED BAG

Any reasoned assessment would conclude that strategic agnosticism is the best way forward for the aid sector. This means that strategic balancing acts need to become more prominent in aid, moving towards evolutionary strategies that seek to balance mindsets, approaches, and philosophies. Of course, this will come with its own set of challenges.

I want to close this chapter with a lovely anecdote from the WHO smallpox eradication effort. Despite its success, many people in WHO believed the programme had bent too many rules. Many also viewed it negatively because it ran outside the regular WHO system. And some remained resolutely sceptical that it would achieve any change. Hopkins recounts how one WHO official commented that, if the India campaign were successful, he would 'eat a tyre off a jeep'. When the last case was reported, the programme director sent the official in question a tyre with a small but encouraging note.[80] If strategic agnosticism means that increasing numbers of the strategic zealots have to eat tyres, or at least their words, this is—to my mind at least—no bad thing.

CHAPTER 16

Networked Organizations

'Woodrow Wilson wished for a League of Nations. We need a League of Networks.'
Robert Zoellick.[1]

Mapping Networks

In 2007, Eva Schiffer was working as a research scientist for the Consultative Group on International Agricultural Research (CGIAR) Challenge Program on Water and Food in Ghana. Her assignment was with the newly established White Volta Basin Board, a sub-committee of the Water Resources Commission of Ghana. Multi-stakeholder groups like this are very common features of the development landscape, not least in water management—where the multi-scale level of issues means thousands are established at supra-national, national, regional, and local levels. There is, however, a fundamental issue with many of these institutions: 'While the belief is strong that these integrated bodies should improve governance, how and to what extent that actually happens is still unclear, not only because of the complexity of the matter but also due to a lack of appropriate research tools for the analysis of complex governance systems.'[2]

Schiffer wanted to find an approach that would help the group understand its own role and work better in a complex policy landscape. The lack of tools led her to experiment with a stakeholder approach she had already used plus a new element—network analysis. Like the researchers involved in developing Com-Mod, described in the previous chapter, she saw untapped potential in bridging the gap between participatory methods and complex systems research. Schiffer's innovation was to take the principles of social network analysis (SNA) and turn it into something that could be applied in a low-tech way, in workshops, using facilitated processes, discussions, and interviews. The Net Map tool gets a group to explore what actors are in a given network, how they are linked, and how influential they are, and by so doing enables groups to better understand complex, real-world relationships. Like so many innovations in development, it was driven by necessity, but it led to a considerable breakthrough for the actors in question.

Board members convened in a workshop to co-create a picture of the relationships between the key actors who influence water usage patterns. The linkages included funding, formal lines of command, support, and advice, and information flows. Having determined the relationships that mattered, board members created maps by drawing the linkages that existed at the present time, through energetic discussions about who was linked to who and why. The next stage was to identify the influential actors and their goal orientations. This process was iterated over time so as to get a picture of the evolving network of interactions.

The benefits were tangible: the process allowed board members to learn more about their individual roles as well as the overall system. It also enabled collective discussion about the board and its role in the policy environment, and helped board members better understand and cope with the complexity of the water governance network. Board members came to the conclusion that they were, collectively, a marginal player in terms of both formal lines of command and funding networks: their centrality was relatively low compared with that of other actors. Their conclusion was that their strongest tool for influencing water governance in the basin was informal, and they needed to focus on providing advice and support. They also drew conclusions about the networks as a whole: despite the multi-stakeholder vision that informed the creation of the commission and others like it, the networks were in fact dominated by single powerful actors who sat in the centre of a hub-and-spoke system. As identified in the networks literature, this also meant the networks were relatively more susceptible to shocks—be they political, social, or environmental.

Schiffer's work helped the actors share their understanding of the policy system of which they were a part, surface and resolve differences of opinion, and think more about a complex phenomenon. Had it been introduced formally as social network analysis, it may have turned a lot of people off at the outset. Purists might argue that this diminishes the science of networks. However, as Schiffer sees it, the value is that it can work as a complement to more technical approaches, and the participatory maps can be used to generate some key network metrics such as centrality, density, and shortest paths and to reflect on the nature of the network. It can also be used to generate hypotheses and research tools for subsequent, more quantitative approaches. At its most effective, this serves to negate the 'science-free analysis' accusation that 'grizzled social scientists' often made of network approaches.

Digitally created, polished products can be intimidating to those who are not accustomed to using them or who are at a different literacy level, which can hold them back from speaking up when they disagree or see something in a different way. The physical aspects of using Net Map allow ownership over the product in a way that computer-generated schematics do not. The data obtained can be put into a social network analysis computer program just the same, but if you just do computer-generated analysis stakeholders will not be nearly as engaged in the process.[3]

In the summer of 2012, I led a team that applied the method to the assessment of a major Gates Foundation-funded rural water programme, Triple S, in Ghana and Uganda and at the global policy level. We used it to understand how the process of reforms that the country teams were kick-starting was influencing the networks that ensure sustainable functionality of water systems. We also examined how the programme was positioning itself in the global landscape of actors involved in delivering rural water programmes. We brought a range of actors together from across the institutional spectrum to look at the nature of the networks between key actors. The feedback was remarkable for its energy, but also the precision with which actors were able to debate and discuss network-related issues at the end of the process: it was literally as though we had provided participants with a new lens to re-examine their existing understanding of the problem.[4]

In 2008, Schiffer was awarded the prestigious Promising Young Scientist of the Year award by CGIAR. Her work has been described as 'a simple way for us to understand and anticipate what can be very confusing and complicated interactions'.[5] Its wider applications include the tracking of avian influenza in Africa and Asia and work on legislative processes in South America, on global advocacy programmes on HIV, and on organizational change processes: remarkably, Merck, a global pharmaceuticals firm, has used it to look at corporate performance issues, in a rare example of a development tool transcending the sector. This range of Net Map applications, and their implications, point to the more general value of network analysis in foreign aid efforts, which I examine in the examples given in the rest of this chapter. First, network analysis can illuminate the *process* of aid and development. In the water management example, it helped generate a better understanding of the inter-organizational structure of relationships and what these meant for aid effectiveness. As we will see, this is a critical feature, and can extend to intra-organizational aspects too. Second, it can also tell us something about the *focus* of aid. In water management contexts, this means illuminating the relationships between actors engaging in water use and the range of stakeholders seeking to improve levels of use. In other contexts, as we shall see, this focus might be communities, innovation processes, national institutions, entire productive economies, or even whole global systems.

When Disaster Strikes

In the first few months of 2000, Mozambique was battered by a devastating sequence of weather events. Torrential rainfall flooded the Limpopo River valley and the capital Maputo, then a cyclone struck land in the coastal region of Beira, and finally flash floods hit the southern part of the country. Individually, the events were not unusual: Mozambique is 'more frequently and severely affected by natural disasters than virtually any other country in Africa'.[6] However, the 'perfect storm' sequence of events made for the most overwhelming floods in the country for over half a century.

Today, after the Asian tsunami, the Haitian earthquake, the Japanese disaster, and the other horrific catastrophes of the decade, the Mozambique 2000 flood death toll of just under 1,000 people may seem tiny. However, this belies the level of devastation across the country. Some 90 per cent of the country's functioning irrigation infrastructure was damaged, and 40,000 hectares of cultivated and grazing land was lost. Almost 250,000 people lost their homes and an estimated 2 million people—some 12 per cent of the total population—were seriously affected, with half that number needing food aid. The impact on the economy was considerable: growth prospects for the year were slashed from 10 per cent to 4 per cent.

A massive fundraising and aid operation was launched, with some US$250 million confirmed at a donor conference in Rome in May 2000. Many countries gave aid, albeit rather less than was promised, and private individuals also reached into their pockets. The media coverage was predictably extensive. Footage of a heavily pregnant woman giving birth in a tree before being airlifted to safety went viral—Sofia Pedro and her new baby Rositha were among the 50,000 to have been rescued in such dramatic fashion.

Scores of international aid organizations and foreign military organizations were involved in the response. Looking through assessments of this a decade on, the messages are rather bland: organizations did well; they made a difference to lives and livelihoods; they didn't elicit enough participation from affected populations; they didn't work enough with local and national organizations. On this basis alone, you might easily come to the conclusion that the success or failure of the response was simply a matter of effective individual agency responses, and that the overall response was largely satisfactory. However, at that time—and even more so today—there was a growing awareness that humanitarian aid effectiveness by necessity went beyond individual agency responses. The Organisation for Economic Co-operation and Development (OECD) had recommended as much just the year before: 'The intervention of a single agency cannot be evaluated in isolation from what others are doing, particularly as what may seem appropriate from the point of view of a single actor may not be appropriate from the point of view of the system as a whole.'[7]

This perspective seems to be largely missing from the publicly available assessments of the Mozambique flood response.

However, interesting insights come from the work of a team of Canadian and American researchers who used social network analysis to understand the overall structure of the flood response.[8] Using data from a Mozambican non-governmental organization that documented the relief and recovery work of 65 international and national NGOs, together with evidence gathered in two stints of field research, the team created a series of network maps based on sector engagement and activities in particular districts. They were particularly interested in exploring the position of different actors in networks, and how this changed over time, by examining the number of ties each actor in the network had to others, the strength of these, and the location of actors as critical brokers between other actors. This in itself was interesting, but the team wanted to go a step further: they wanted to know if there was a relationship between network position and numbers of recipients a particular organization reached. They decided to look at several categories of recipients—individuals and families—in both the emergency and the recovery phases. They also adjusted their findings to take account of factors that might influence beneficiary numbers, including organization size, funding levels, and sectors of operation.

The findings were striking in that they substantiated issues often talked about in humanitarian circles but seldom proved empirically. First, the greatest numbers of beneficiaries were reached by those organizations that were most central to the network: those that had the most and the strongest links and that were key brokers between other organizations. Although intuitive, this is contrary to the 'go it alone' calculus that typically informs agency decisions in the response phase: one major international agency even assesses its effort using the metric of 'speed of response relative to others'.

I examined these issues through a game theoretical lens in a paper written with Michael Barnett, in which we argued that the structural dynamics of the humanitarian system are such that, at the point of crisis, it always *seems* to pay to defect from what would be the overall optimal solution.[9] It may be very well understood that this does not help the overall response, and this was clearly the case in Mozambique, where the network analysis goes some way to demonstrating that a go it alone mentality would not in fact have benefited the individual organizations.

The network analysis revealed other aspects of the structure that were more problematic from a perspective of effectiveness. It was clear that—with the exception of the Mozambican Red Cross, which was the most central actor bar none—international NGOs occupied the most central role in the various district and sectoral response networks. This centrality was especially prominent in the emergency phase, and gave international NGOs considerably more influence and clout than their national counterparts. In some cases, this position may have been abused. One municipal authority described the situation in Chokwe, which had become 'an NGO occupied city... and [they] refused to acknowledge the existence of the municipal authority and municipal assembly'.[10] Research by the Overseas Development Institute the year after the crisis found a system that showed 'determined resistance to cede authority to anyone or any structure... despite the urgency of the task, and the potential impact on human lives of poorly coordinated humanitarian responses'.[11]

Conversely, in the recovery period, as international NGOs started to scale back their efforts, there was evidence of the network deteriorating because national organizations were not in a position to maintain the connectivity. The domestic network was potentially less able to play a role in coordinating recovery and mitigation activities because of its inability to fill the network gaps international actors left.

Although the work was clearly a first step, with numerous areas needing further development and refinement, the researchers concluded that the approach warranted further investigation, for some pretty fundamental reasons: 'Before policies that influence the aid network can be made, policy makers... managers and... practitioners need to know more about the humanitarian aid structure and its effects on aid operations.'[12]

A similar pattern was found for the actors responding in Haiti after the January 2010 earthquake. Researchers at the International Centre for Evidence in Disability worked with the London School of Hygiene and Tropical Medicine to apply a systems and network lens to analyse rehabilitation services provided to disabled people affected by the earthquake. Social network analysis looked at the key actors in the rehabilitation provision system, the relationships between them, and the overall structure that emerged from these relationships. As in Mozambique, they used this evidence to better understand how the system reacted over time and how relationships between actors affected systemic behaviours and the system as a whole. They found that the rehabilitation network had many diverse actors, but they were all oriented around two specific nodes: Christoffel-Blindenmission and Handicap International, which are the two leading international NGOs working on rehabilitation services post-disaster. Worryingly, 'Haitian government ministries and agencies were connected to the centre of the network, but did not have many connections of their own with rehabilitation actors.'[13] A key recommendation was that more effort needed to be put into working out what the rehabilitation sector network should look like after the initial response, and what resources and relationships were needed to bring this improved situation about.

Of course, networks within and between aid agencies are not the only networks that arise at the point of crisis. More important are the networks that exist, and emerge, among affected people themselves. Unfortunately, actors in the international system typically ignore these. The Mozambique response assessment of the Disasters Emergency Committee, a UK NGO network, found that the appropriateness of efforts diminished with time for three reasons, all of which focus on the implicit and explicit assumptions made about disaster-affected communities. First, international agencies consistently underestimated the resilience of the local population. Second, the needs, and capacities, of affected populations grew in their range and complexity over time, 'making the typical "one size fits all" solution ... less appropriate'.[14] Third, over time, the need for greater consultation and engagement with recipients grew more and more important—but the lack of adequate engagement became more and more evident.

Time and time again the evidence shows that local actors and their social networks account for by far the most lifesaving, rehabilitation, and recovery work post-disasters. A study of Italian earthquakes from 1980 found that 97 per cent of those saved were helped by people with shovels and their bare hands, who knew where people might be buried: social networking in desperate circumstances. The 50,000 rescued by international operations in Mozambique, though considerable, are likely to have been far outnumbered by the local, unseen response. In the Asian tsunami, 97 per cent of the lives saved were saved before international agencies even got off the ground. In many ways, none of this should be surprising: during the first period after disaster strikes, the normal working of a social system is suspended, leaving an 'institutional vacuum' often filled by informal social institutions such as networks. Some experts estimate that international aid accounts for no more than 10 per cent in natural disasters.[15]

After the 2008 Sichuan earthquake, the Chinese Academy of Science and Technology for Development conducted the first large-scale example of a post-disaster rapid needs assessment in China.[16] Based on a random sample of 5,000 households in the affected area, a key focus of the assessment was the role of social networks. The researchers used what is known among Chinese social scientists as the 'Spring Festival network indicator' as a baseline. This assessed the extent and composition of post-disaster social networks as compared with the networks respondents had made during the spring festival that preceded the earthquake. They were able to draw numerous conclusions about the role and contribution of these networks.

Around 10 per cent of the sample lost network members, with 4 per cent gaining new networks. In terms of search and rescue, there was a similar pattern of response to the examples I cite above: 95 per cent of those trapped in debris and falling buildings were rescued by relatives, neighbours, and other persons around. Networks were important also for facilitating infor-mation flows (social networks were cited as the third most important source of information, after television and 'local cadres'). They were also vital sources of aid in their own right, with respondents ranking them the second most important source of support, after government aid, with a third placing networks higher than the government. Importantly, social networks were seen as having a significant influence on the amount of support received: a bigger network will bring more social, psychological, and emotional support. The composition of the network also mattered: a dense, horizontal, kin-based network was in fact found to be more supportive than a sparser and more diverse network.

Evidence from numerous other sources suggests that the vertical linkages *within* social networks also have a strong influence on who receives international aid. In Timor Leste, social network analysis funded by the World Bank's Governance Partnership Facility found that individuals with personal relationships with village leaders were *eight times* more likely to hear about a new cash transfer in its first year, giving short shrift to the idea of equality of aid distributions.[17] Work done by researchers at Oxford University found that social networks exerted a powerful influence on food aid allocations, with people with links to officials more likely to receive assistance, with the net effect of a 150 per cent improvement in initial living standards compared with those who didn't have such connections. By examining this relationship over time, the researchers showed that the correlation between aid and networks emerged immediately after a drought, when the formal guidelines for aid allocations were weakest and the resources potentially at their highest.[18] These 'vertical connections' to authority figures also played a role in cash-for-work schemes, with well-connected households receiving substantially higher daily and total payments. Studies done for the National Academy of Sciences in the USA also highlight the potential of network thinking to better understand community-level resilience to disasters.[19]

These examples of network analysis shed light on issues in disaster responses that are typically obscured by the 'fog of humanitarianism'. First, the success of humanitarian operations depends on the ability, capacity, and desire of organizations to work together—not just in bilateral relationships but also in an overarching inter-organizational structure. Position in the overall system really does matter: defecting led to a sub-optimal response in Mozambique, both overall and for individuals. Network analysis findings go some way to providing empirical evidence for this truism.

Network approaches also show that the structure of relationships has a profound effect on the ability of disaster-affected households and communities to self-organize after a crisis and their ability to capitalize on aid efforts. Lack of engagement with affected populations was, and remains, one of the most serious criticisms levelled at international aid agencies. Affected populations should be the primary stakeholders in a response, but instead their views and opinions often seem to be an afterthought: they are over-assessed and under-consulted.

What is especially troubling, from the network perspective, is that the lack of engagement has measurable costs for aid agencies, in terms of the relevance of their work and, ultimately, how effective they are in pursuing their stated goals.

Networks, networks, everywhere

The 'the hub-and-spoke network' is a frequent finding in many applications of network analysis in development. This shows how network analysis can help better understand one of the key challenges in development: namely, whether the benefits of aid will prove sustainable beyond the timeframe of the intervention, in terms of whether a project or programme will have a continued effect on the ground. From a network perspective, the way to understand this is straightforward: apply network analysis over time to examine how the relationships around a particular project or intervention continue to engage with key stakeholders. Looking at the network literature and case studies, it is clear that this has been a major interest of the emerging network analysis movement in aid.

Karl Blanchet of the London School of Hygiene and Tropical Medicine—who led the work in Haiti described earlier—undertook exactly this kind of assessment over a three-year period, looking at health care networks in Ghana. He showed that the eye care system in Brong Ahafo region experienced major changes after an international agency—the Swiss Red Cross—left the country. The study opens in 2006, when the Swiss Red Cross was the central figure in the network: not only was it connected to the highest number of actors, but also over a quarter of all of the shortest paths between any other two actors in the network involved the agency. Together with the regional ophthalmologist, the Swiss Red Cross was involved in almost 50 per cent of the possible paths through the system.

By 2009, the Swiss Red Cross had left the country, and the regional ophthalmologist was the main broker. However, because his networks were not as extensive as those of the Swiss Red Cross, there was no equivalent broker to replace the latter. As a result, 'Several . . . actors at different levels of the network disappeared [and] the positions of nurses and hospital managers changed, creating new relationships and power balances.'[20]

There was a change in the overall structure of the network: 'The system shifted from a centralized and dense hierarchical network towards an enclaved network composed of five sub-networks.'[21] Particularly critical was the fact that the new structure was less able to respond to shocks, circulate information and knowledge across scales, and implement multi-level approaches than the one that it replaced.[22] That said, the departure of the Swiss Red Cross meant some actors were able to take on a more prominent role: for example, the network now catered better for hospital managers' information needs. 'The change of the network over time also showed the influence of the international organization on generating links and creating connections between actors from different levels. The findings of the study reveal the importance of creating international health connections between actors working in different spatial scales of the health system.'[23]

A contrasting application of network analysis was of a US Agency for International Development (USAID)-funded market development programme in Uganda, to look at the transition from subsistence agriculture to commercial farming among smallholder farmers. I am reproducing these maps in full here because they show in a very powerful way how the transition led to changes in network structures. The analysis, developed by Mark Lubell of the University of California, Davis, provided an overview of the interactions between farm producers and the main actors in the agricultural value chain—input suppliers, commodity exporters, and agricultural extension workers—in the district of Kamuli over four years from 2004. In the first year, producers were linked only to middlemen and an NGO in Kamuli. Many actors are simply not connected to the producers—input suppliers, exporters, government extension workers, and credit providers. In the second year, thanks to the USAID-funded programme, a depot committee had taken over the middleman role, giving a better deal to the farmer. In the third year, connections were made to the extension service and a coffee exporter, but there were also new producers coming into the network, bringing with them their connection to another middleman. In the fourth year, this middleman had been pushed out. According to the study, in the final year, 'farmers affiliated with producer organizations in the Kamuli region are now directly linked to buyers of their coffee, rice, and maize and have also formed a relationship with a rural savings and credit cooperative'.[24] With each year that passes, the producers' networks expanded, deepened, and diversified, slowly shifting the 'middlemen' to become peripheral actors. This happens to have been a successful effort—of course network analysis should also be able to show when a programme has *not* been successful. A review of a USAID market development programme, this one in Bolivia, employed participatory approaches to look at information flows around coffee supply chains. The analysis showed clearly that USAID-funded projects were not integrated into the wider coffee network, and were not trusted parties for actors at the centre of the network.[25]

A social network approach has been integrated into the organizational development efforts of the US NGO Pact in its work in a number of countries, including Cambodia, Ecuador, Malawi, the Philippines, and Zambia. As with the examples described earlier, Pact found that international actors played a central role as a hub, distributing resources to and brokering connections between national and local organizations. Links between local organizations are often weak or non-existent. As a World Bank assessment of this work suggested, 'Although hub-and-spoke networks are effective delivery mechanisms for development interventions, they do not necessarily create the links among local actors that would facilitate a sustainable network beyond the life of the funded intervention.'[26]

In Zambia, for example, a network analysis approach was applied halfway through a five-year programme. It showed Pact had established connections to a wide range of actors, but also that it was the central actor bar none, and the network overall had a very high centralization score: were Pact to be removed, the 60-member network would fragment considerably, with the largest component having less than half this number of actors. Pact then worked to incorporate these findings into a major redesign of the programme. In particular, it built on the work of noted network analyst Valdis Krebs to start the process of 'network weaving': 'the creation of new interactions among isolated clusters'.[27] Network analysis findings had helped guide this process in a systematic way, emphasizing creating connections between those actors, other than Pact, that had the highest 'betweenness' scores. In Roger Riddell's mammoth review of the effectiveness of foreign aid, Pact's work on capacity strengthening was singled out for its vision, approach, and sustained benefits to participants.[28]

As these examples and the ones preceding show, networks play as important a role in understanding growth and innovation as in understanding crises and failure. These national and local applications are interesting and valuable, but of course the power of network analysis and complexity research more generally is that it is applicable at multiple scales and levels. I look next at two global applications of network analysis, looking at crisis and growth in turn.

Crouching Networks, Hidden Fragility

In Chapter 10 on Networks, in Part 2, I looked at how a Bank of England executive worked with a former government chief scientist to use network thinking to understand the financial crisis. This approach has also informed the thinking of one of the major financial institutions that form part of the international aid system, the International Monetary Fund (IMF).

As discussed in Part 2, *coupling* is a function of the number of links and the nature of inter-dependencies between organizational sub-systems such as business units, groups, and teams. Russ Marion suggests different degrees of coupling lead to different kinds of organizational systems. This is not a new idea, having been developed by Karl Weick in the 1970s. Broadly, learning is highly dependent on the degree of coupling between actors in a given system, whether within the same organization or across organizational boundaries. Noah Radford of the London School of Economics suggests the ideal organizational system is one that is optimally coupled for the environment in which it operates—which presents an interesting articulation of the 'edge of chaos' principle.

A 2010 study by the IMF Strategy Team[29] notes that rapid financial globalization—indicated in a six-fold increase in the external assets and liabilities of nations as a share of gross domestic product—has also seen a rise in financial interconnectedness. Echoing Haldane's network diagram in Chapter 10, they note that countries have become more interlinked with each other, particularly since the mid 1990s, using language that will by now seem familiar: 'In a highly interconnected world, as agents typically fail to take account of the effects of their actions on others, the *potential* for systemic risk rises . . . pervasive interconnections can result in a rapid transmission of adverse shocks across the global financial system.'[30]

The authors call for *global financial risk maps* to understand interconnectedness, track the build-up of systemic risk concentrations, and improve surveillance. They suggest augmenting macro-financial surveillance with consideration of how a given country's financial system sits in the global financial network.

A follow-up paper in June 2011[31] led by Camelia Minoiu—whose work on poverty I drew on in Part 1—presented empirical data showing how shocks propagate across global financial markets in non-linear ways, with potentially significant real costs to emerging economies. The same team of researchers argues that national defences against such shocks are necessary but not sufficient to eliminate volatility and instability inherent in the inter-connected system. In a direct echo of Haldane and May,[32] they argue that efforts to increase the resilience of the global financial system need to address the trade-off between the benefits and costs of interconnectedness. And they put network approaches at the heart of their approach: 'This trade-off can be understood using insights from network theory, which has been applied to understand the properties of complex financial networks and their implications for financial stability.'[33] They also put forward the notion that such approaches have to inform the IMF's policy advice: 'Pursuing certain policies...cannot be treated in isolation of the broader network to which the system is connected.'[34]

In 2011, researchers at the IMF's Institute for Capacity Development were also inspired by Andy Haldane's work.[35] Camelia Minoiu and Javier Reyes set out to understand the complexity of the financial connections among agents, institutions, and countries, and in particular to take a historical perspective on the evolution of the global banking sector and the implications for periods of instability. The rationale was simple: starting with the 'too interconnected to fail' idea that numerous commentators proposed after the crisis, they wanted to explore the role of interconnectedness in safeguarding the financial stability of member countries. Network analysis was seen as key because of its ability to examine the financial system as 'a set of players connected with one another through financial contracts'.[36]

Reyes and Minoiu mapped banking relationships across countries from the late 1970s using a network lens in order to explore how to assess the level of financial interconnectedness globally, and how this changed over time and around the 2008 financial crisis. Using data from the Bank for International Settlements (BIS)—which collates reports from all licensed banks, securities firms, and offshore banks on a range of financial instruments, including loans, deposits, and debt securities—they constructed 'a worldwide web of financial connections'.[37] Because such data are compiled on the basis of the resident status of the reporting institution, they are amenable to analysing geographical patterns in financial relationships.

The analysis focused on two sets of countries: the core of the network—the 15 developed economies that have reported to BIS consistently since 1978—and the *periphery*—169 countries at various levels of development that either do not report or have started doing so only recently. The two sets of flows captured were those within the core countries and those between the core and the periphery. Their mapping of the relationships between countries where there is a net financial flow in one direction or another showed 'a jumble of intersecting relationships'. By looking at the level of connectivity and clustering, both of which are commonly used to analyse network connectedness, Minoiu and Reyes sought to track the changing density relationships in the global banking network.

- Connectivity measures the density of bilateral relationships, that is, the number of links between countries in the network divided by the total number of possible links.

- Clustering gauges the density of three-way relationships—in which a country's lenders are also lending to each other. It is roughly defined as the number of triangles that appear in the network divided by the total number of possible triangles.

They found that the flows between countries saw a massive increase between 1978 and 2002, to US$230 billion just before the crisis. Core–periphery flows also increased, from US$1.5 to US$6.4 billion before the crisis. Connectedness also rose before the crisis, peaked during it, and fell afterwards. By looking at the core–core patterns over time, the researchers found that both connectivity and clustering reached similar levels before other crises, including the Latin American debt crisis in the 1980s and the East Asian crisis of the 1990s. The core–periphery also saw a pre-crisis increase in connectedness. In the aftermath of the crisis, network density fell to the lowest point of the whole period, and clustering almost disappeared. The crisis appears to have triggered a drop in network density of a magnitude not seen before. While network density in 2007 was comparable to the pre-crisis levels observed earlier, the extent to which it fell in 2008/9 stands out.

Why was this the case? The IMF researchers suggest network analysis helps understand different aspects of the network structure and dynamics that contributed to the crisis. That is, it was not simply that the system was too interconnected to fail: it was *also* too centralized, such that the shock to the hub—or core—destabilized the entire network. Finally, the extent of the flows across the network was the most notable contributor to the crisis, because of the sheer volume of transactions and money moving.

The overall finding was that the simple view of interconnectedness being the main culprit in the severity of the crisis was misplaced. It was also important to get a more detailed understanding of the dynamics and flow across the network, to give a better sense of where in the network the crisis emerged: shocks have differing effects depending on where they materialize. Had network analysis been in the 'policymakers' toolkit', there may have been a better understanding of these nuances. The authors conclude that, 'By looking at agents *and* the links between them, network analysis can add valuable insights about the financial system as a whole, which is a complicated web of interlinked and interdependent players.'[38]

Although the IMF work is clearly very timely, the most extensive work using network analysis to address macro-level development-related issues is less about financial stability and more about growth. I turn to this next.

The Complexity and Wealth of Nations

During the last year of working on this book, I had a series of engagements that took me in succession from Malaysia to Ghana, two countries that development studies books, papers, and lectures have routinely compared. Both were British colonies, and in the early 1950s they were on an economic par: both poor and dependent on raw material exports. Sixty years later, gross domestic product per capita in Ghana is US$333, whereas in Malaysia it is almost US$5,000. While Ghana is still exporting raw materials, Malaysia makes and exports cars, equipment, and oil-based products. Manufacturing in Malaysia accounted for 8 per cent in 1960 and 26.5 per cent in 2009 compared with Ghana's 9.8 per cent in 1965 and 4.3 per cent in 2009. The prevalence of tag lines such as 'Whatever happened to Africa's tigers?' is understandable, if zoologically questionable.

The answer—or part of it, at least—lies in one product: palm oil. Indigenous to West Africa, it became the principle cargo for decommissioned slave trade boats and crew. The British were also instrumental in its transplantation to Asia, where the ecological conditions were rather better for plantations. Ghana exported palm oil throughout the nineteenth century, but had all but ceased by the twentieth century because of the cheap oil that was now coming through from South East Asia. Driven by growing Western demand for chocolate, cocoa took over as West Africa's, including Ghana's, major agricultural export. Although Ghana developed a small palm oil export market in the 1950s, this dissolved after independence, and production is largely for domestic consumption.[39] Exports were limited both by lack of land for plantations and the dominance of vertically integrated global firms that prevented national processors from entering the market and maintained the fragmentation of domestic production.

In Malaysia, by contrast, industrial-level production of palm oil from the early twentieth century went from strength to strength, aided by supportive colonial policies, government decisions, and the dynamics of the world market. Eventually production expanded, and new market opportunities were created by moving from oil exports to secondary processing exports, such as refined palm oil and industrial chemicals. A single product had led in one case to little in the way of domestic development and in the other to a staggering diversity of business opportunities. Ultimately, for one country palm oil was a route to considerable levels of development; for the other it failed to deliver any such gains.

Of course, reducing the economic story to one product and its role is not particularly helpful for examining other countries' growth and development trajectories. If we want to generalize about such aspects of a country's development, we need to find another way of thinking about the nature and dynamics of growth.

This is exactly what has emerged through a collaboration between Ricardo Hausmann, former Chief Economist of the Inter-American Development Bank, and Cesar Hidalgo, a physicist trained under Albert-László Barabási (of preferential networks fame, from Chapter 10) at Notre Dame University. In their very first meeting, Hausmann shared an analogy with Hidalgo of how he understood the idea that would become the basis of their ongoing collaboration:

Think of a product as a tree and the set of all products as a forest. A country is composed of a collection of firms, i.e., of monkeys that live on different trees and exploit those products. The process of growth implies moving from a poorer part of the forest, where trees have little fruit, to better parts of the forest. This implies that monkeys would have to jump distances, that is, redeploy (human, physical, and institutional) capital toward goods that are different from those currently under production.[40]

Hidalgo told me that, at the initial meeting, the forest was seen as a continuous space. However, he decided that this was not a viable assumption:

> Traditional growth theory assumes there is always a tree within reach; hence, the structure of this forest is unimportant. However, if this forest is heterogeneous, with some dense areas and other more-deserted ones, and if monkeys can jump only limited distances, then monkeys may be unable to move through the forest. If this is the case, the structure of this space and a country's orientation within it become of great importance to the development of countries.[41]

One of their starting points, Hidalgo told me, was that much standard development and economic thinking doesn't engage very well with the idea of webs and networks: such ideas run counter to 'standard thinking', which seeks to identify differences between individuals and groups based on their inherent qualities—demographic criteria and suchlike.

> Experts then puzzle over why, for example, communities with the same criteria or countries with very similar starting points end up with very different development pathways and social and wealth outcomes. It turns out that in many cases, their relationships and networks prove to be a key differentiating factor. If the data is available, it is possible to develop very precise and rigorous analysis of these differences.[42]

Having got the data from Hausmann, Hidalgo proceeded to reinterpret the forest as a network, developing network representations of the product forests and using this to obtain a different understanding of a given country's productive structure.

Using the concept of product proximity, meaning goods that might depend on similar institutions, inputs, factors of production, or technologies, he hypothesized that countries would be able to produce and export products that have high levels of proximity to what they are already doing. For example, Peruvian artichoke exporters started to export asparagus. Peru had almost all of the conditions suitable to export asparagus: 'the soil, climate, packing technologies, and frigorific trucks [as well as] skilled agronomists, phytosanitary laws, and trade agreements that could be easily redeployed to the [new] business'.[43] If they had attempted to move into a completely new product—say, toasters—the capabilities developed for exporting vegetables would be of little or no use.

Hidalgo then developed the first visualization of what would become known as the 'product space'. This would eventually look like Figure 16.1 below (albeit in full colour).

Underlying this network map is the notion of product interdependence, which is in turn underpinned by the notion of productive knowledge. As Hausmann notes,

> The wealth of nations is driven by productive knowledge. Individuals are limited in the things they can effectively know and use in production so the only way a society can hold more knowledge is by distributing different chunks of knowledge to different people... to be re-aggregated by connecting people through organizations and markets. The complex web of products and

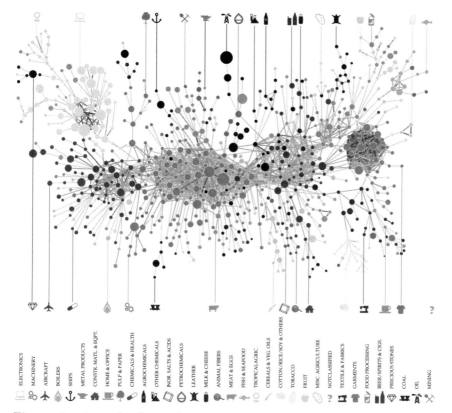

Figure 16.1 Example of a product space map

Source: Hausmann, R., Hidalgo, C.A., Bustos, S., Coscia, M., Chung, S., Jiminez, J., Simoes, A., and Yildrim, M.A. (2011), *The Atlas of Economic Complexity: Mapping Paths to Prosperity* (Boston, MA: Center for Institutional Development, Harvard University, MIT Media Lab).

markets is the other side of the coin of the accumulating productive knowledge. The secret to modernity is that we collectively use large volumes of knowledge, while each one of us holds only a few bits of it. Society functions because its members form webs that allow them to specialize and share their knowledge with others (emphasis added).[44]

Hidalgo and Hausmann's work, the *Atlas of Economic Complexity*, uses a variety of trade and development databases to measure the amount of productive knowledge each economy holds.[45] Through the use of network analysis techniques, they have developed a novel way of understanding the 'complex web of products and markets'.[46] (This, incidentally, is precisely the kind of application Stuart Kauffmann anticipated almost two decades earlier when considering the relevance of biological and evolutionary modelling for economics.)

Hausmann and Hidalgo start by looking at the trade web of countries exporting products. For each country, they examine how many different products it is capable of producing; this is called the country's *diversity*. For each product, they look at how many countries can produce it; this is called the product's *ubiquity*. Based on these two concepts, they introduce two network measures of an economy: the Economic Complexity Index (or ECI, for a country) and the Product Complexity Index (or PCI, for a product).[47]

To put their knowledge into productive use, different countries need to reassemble these distributed products through teams, organizations, and markets. The *Atlas* explores these issues in detail, through the concept of the product space—which in effect is a network map that captures the products made by different countries in terms of their knowledge requirements. These maps provide a visual way of understanding how productive knowledge is accumulated.

Hausmann, Hidalgo, and their team also developed an Index of Economic Complexity to represent their data systematically. This tells us about the richness of the product space of a given country, and, by extension, is one useful indicator of the potential to grow. It can also be used to compare economic complexity across the 128 countries covered in the analysis.

Acknowledging that these ideas are not always easy to grasp, the authors provide a useful thought experiment to help readers get their heads around the implications of the index: if a country can't make a product, in how many other countries can it be made? If the answer is many, the country probably does not have a complex economy. If few other countries can make a product the country can't make, it probably has a complex economy.

For example, Japan and Germany are the two countries with the highest levels of economic complexity: if a good cannot be produced there, the list of other potential countries is likely to be very short. Conversely, if a product can't be made in Mauritania or Sudan, both of which have low economic complexity, the list of other potential countries is likely to be long.

A useful way of understanding the benefits of the product space is to think about what the analysis adds to some of the classic comparisons in growth literature I mentioned earlier. The images (Figures 16.2 and 16.3) below compare Ghana and Malaysia's product space in 2008. Each of the square black nodes indicates a product the country was exporting at that time. Even a cursory glance shows that Malaysia's product space is more complex and diverse than Ghana's. This is because 'Ghana's economic complexity and income stagnated as it remained an exporter of cocoa, aluminium, fish and forest products.' According to the LSE's International Growth Centre, Ghana's economy today resembles that of Malaysia in the 1960s.[48] By contrast, during the preceding 50 years Malaysia underwent a massive increase in economic complexity, and has experienced economic diversification and sustained growth.[49] Although some of the detail is lost with the black and white reproduction, the main difference is clear.

Some of the applications already developed include a regional analysis of growth in East Africa[50] and an intriguing application of the small world idea in the product space, to see where the potential is for future growth and trade patterns.[51] There have also been applications in related areas, such as regional cluster development strategies in Latin America[52] and road network development across the whole of Africa,[53] both of which are fascinating expressions of the same principles.

The Economic Complexity Index has been shown to be a better predictor of economic growth than a number of other existing development indicators.

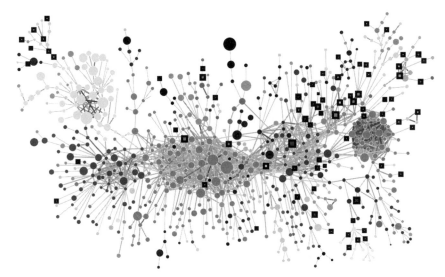

Figure 16.2 Ghana's product space, 2008

Source: Hausmann, R., Hidalgo, C.A., Bustos, S., Coscia, M., Chung, S., Jiminez, J., Simoes, A., and Yildrim, M.A. (2011), *The Atlas of Economic Complexity: Mapping Paths to Prosperity* (Boston, MA: Center for Institutional Development, Harvard University, MIT Media Lab).

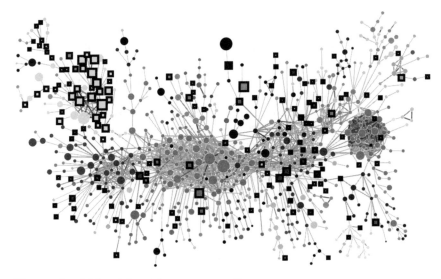

Figure 16.3 Malaysia's product space, 2008

Source: Hausmann, R., Hidalgo, C.A., Bustos, S., Coscia, M., Chung, S., Jiminez, J., Simoes, A., and Yildrim, M.A. (2011), *The Atlas of Economic Complexity: Mapping Paths to Prosperity* (Boston, MA: Center for Institutional Development, Harvard University, MIT Media Lab).

For example, as reported in *The Economist*,[54] it outstrips the World Economic Forum Global Competitiveness Index by a factor of ten in terms of the accuracy of its predictions. It also outperforms the World Governance Indicators and the standard variables used to measure human capital as predictors of growth. The economic complexity approach also gained praise from several economic chiefs among the multilateral development banks, including the World Bank and the Asian Development Bank.

Perhaps the most important contribution of the *Atlas* is the analytical rigour it brings to the complex and dynamic nature of economic growth, and the ability it gives us to ask new and challenging questions more precisely. Hidalgo summed it up for me as follows: 'Our traditional approach to economics has retained measures developed in the 1930s and 1940s to deal with the situations and crises we faced back then. There should be a new breed of measures that bring much more precision and resolution and that mean we don't continue to build our analysis on the over-simplification of a complex system.'[55]

Hausmann and Hidalgo reinforce this, echoing the messages of Bill Easterly's work on international trade that I explored in Chapter 15: 'Ultimately, this Atlas views economic development as a social learning process, but one that is rife with pitfalls and dangers. Countries accumulate productive knowledge by developing the capacity to make a larger variety of products of increasing complexity. This involves trial and error. It is a risky journey in search of the possible.'[56]

Let's hope we see more of this way of thinking in development debates. While there will inevitably be a degree of resistance, it seems to me that no one can disagree with the underlying premise of the report. As I argued in the previous chapter, a more evolutionary approach may be the key to bringing about change in a complex adaptive system, and if this is the case in economic growth, the *Atlas* may well provide us with the maps we need.

Social X-rays

The final example of the application of network thinking to development relates to its use in international organizations. In Chapter 4, I showed there were some perennial issues around the way in which aid agencies saw themselves and their environment. So far in this chapter I have looked at the aid system itself and the world in which agencies operate, and how a network perspective was helping to understand both in a more intelligent and realistic fashion. In this section I want to explore how organizational networks provide a new way of thinking about an aid agency's 'thought world'. The cognitive space created by the thought world determines what an organization does, what information is circulated, what knowledge is valued, what learning is permitted, and what innovations are diffused. The organizational identity is manifest in how all these things happen—they are shaped by motivations, values, and principles.

The thought world influences the meaning of external events, specific project activities, and actions taken. It focuses attention on different issues and shapes resource allocation. It has a crucial role to play in helping an organization's members make sense of the world. It is perhaps the primary enabling and constraining element in the adaptive learning capacity of an organization.

The underlying notion of this analysis resonates with the Hausmann–Hidalgo work on the complexity of the economy, in that both are based on the idea of entities—be they organizations or economies—that are dependent on knowledge. As Hausmann and Hidalgo note,

> For a complex society to exist, and to sustain itself, people who know about design, marketing, finance, technology, human resource management, oper-ations, and trade law must be able to interact and combine their knowledge to make products...Economic complexity, therefore, is expressed in the com-position of a country's productive output and reflects the structures that emerge to hold and combine knowledge...Increased economic complexity is necessary for a society to be able to hold and use a larger amount of productive knowledge.[57]

Replace the words 'society' and 'country' with 'organization' in the above quote and you get a good sense of what organizational network analysts have tried to do. Rob Cross of the University of Virginia argues that all actors in organizations are affected dramatically by information flow and webs of relationships within social networks.[58] Although these networks are not depicted on organizational charts, they have a powerful influence on performance.

Any aid organization (and indeed the entire aid system) is composed of an intricate web of interrelationships, and changes in one area will have effects—often unexpected—elsewhere. At the same time, because each part has multiple relationships within the system, changes to any single part will generally also require changes to the related parts. In complex organizations, transformational change ultimately involves the creation of new organizational realities that can break the hold of dominant patterns in favour of new ones, which are not fully within the control of any one group or individual.[59]

These new patterns cannot be divined precisely in advance—it is possible only to nurture elements of the new reality and create conditions under which the new reality can arise. Especially important here is the idea that, when existing patterns of action are particularly powerful, significant change may not be possible because the organization ends up trying to do new things in old ways.

Figure 16.4 relates to the network of executives in the exploration and production division of a large petroleum organization. Rob Cross conducted social network analysis to help design an appropriate knowledge management strategy for the organization. This revealed a startling contrast between formal and informal parts of the organization. Instead of the hierarchy counting, it was relatively unknown actors who played a central role in the network. However, in this instance, popularity had led to problems for the unseen central actors, who became over-stressed owing to excessive demands for inputs, while simultaneously slowing down the whole schedule. However, this influence is hard to assess and track: individuals tend to have only small parts of the picture. This, incidentally, was part of the rationale Eva Schiffer gave when developing Net Map. If these issues can be overcome, network analysis can be especially powerful for understanding the reality of organizational interactions.[60]

Rob Cross went on to apply his approach in the International Finance Corporation (IFC), a member of the World Bank Group. Created in 1956, the IFC represents the first step by the global community to foster private sector investment in developing nations. It provides loans, equity, structured finance, and risk management products as well as advisory services. It has over 3,100 staff, of whom 51 per cent work in field offices and 49 per cent at the headquarters in Washington, DC. Sustainability is at the core of the strategy and environmental and social expertise is a key differentiator. The agency is currently undergoing a process of decentralization, which will see a progressive delegation of responsibilities to regional hubs.

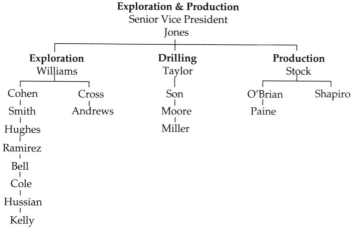

Informal structure as revealed by social network analysis

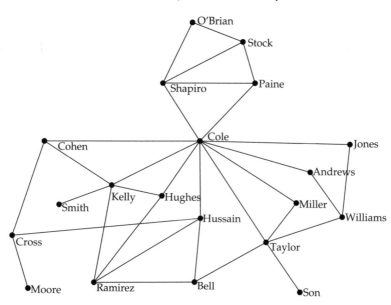

Figure 16.4 Formal hierarchies and real-world networks compared

Source: Cross, R. and Parker, A. (2004), *The Hidden Power of Social Networks: Understanding How Work Really Gets Done in Organizations* (Cambridge, MA: Harvard Business School).

Social network analysis worked to provide baseline data against which to monitor the impact of the decentralization process. It also helped map network flows/communities that would need to be maintained regardless of geographical location of staff and identify key experts and connectors that need special support be able to maintain their influencing role. The manager of the process, Giulio Quaggiotto, says one of the key issues was to analyse knowledge flows, focusing in particular on the issue of new staff integration—the time it takes for new staff to integrate in informal networks within the department.

The assessment revealed some unusual features of the IFC relative to other organizations Cross had examined, notably in the business sector. First of all, it had more linkages between key actors—it was one of the most densely connected networks Cross had come across.[61]

Second, the linkages that were important for work focused more on external relationships; some of these were with staff in the World Bank, but many were classified as 'other', meaning professional associates, friends, and family contacts. Interestingly, networks with clients were seen as very low, which Cross suggested might owe to the nature of the work. On the issue of integration, it typically took three years for staff to become well established in the organization's informal networks, and these tended to have an upward focus: people were less likely to go to a more junior person for advice or support. In addition, the role informal networks played changed as careers progressed: for more junior staff, the primary driver of networking was the need for information, with some support to problem solving; as people progressed, they used networks more for problem-solving support.

> Through this network analysis project, we were able to hone in on a number of strategic areas, such as awareness of expertise, the on-boarding of staff, and cross-unit collaboration, and define priorities for action accordingly. Network analysis was most helpful in translating the sometimes abstract concepts of collaboration and knowledge management into concrete, measurable dimensions. The results of this process will inform the department's strategy moving forward.[62]

A key set of recommendations focused on the strengthening of personal networks: the need to support the building of newcomers' personal networks in a systematic way through structured introductions, making a newcomer's expertise available to others, short rotations, and smart mentoring. The key outcome was a shift in both the way the decentralization process went forward and how new staff were inducted into the programme. I subsequently spoke with some of the staff who explained to me that the network analysis approach had been rolled out more widely, within specific departments and across the organization as a whole, to better understand how to deal with structural change and knowledge flows. In both cases, the approach led to some 'exciting insights into the organization and its workings'.[63] However, a clear proviso was that—as with any analytical technique—the buy-in of management is essential if changes are going to be made. There was also a suggestion that network analysis may be constrained because the managerial dynamics in the organization were not set up to think about such things, but instead operated on a more traditional, mechanistic set of assumptions.

Pact, whose work I explored earlier, has also applied network analysis system-atically to its own organizational management efforts. Pact was particularly keen to work out how to bridge the gaps in the organizational matrix: to get connec-tions happening between clusters of individuals working in different sectors, locations, and cultures. Guided by the idea of 'weak ties' from network theory, Pact undertook a series of assessments of the connections between country offices.

The first assessment showed a baseline picture of collaboration among members of a global network of democracy and governance experts. Along with its associ-ated performance metrics, it shows that much of the interaction occurs within individual country offices. Participants from the Democratic Republic of Congo, Ethiopia, Kenya, and, in particular, Tanzania are all closely clustered by country office and engage in relatively minimal interaction that spans the boundaries among clusters. Headquarters staff play a vital role as brokers, relaying knowledge and resources to the group's diverse regions. In the most extreme case, the headquarters (HQ5) node in Washington, DC, brokers interactions between democracy and governance experts in neighbouring Kenya and Tanzania.

By connecting country-level experts through learning labs and a community of practice, Pact could 'weave' new connections into the network. These span geographic boundaries and facilitate idea and resource exchange in new and powerful ways, with an explicit strategy of 'tapping into the power of weak ties'. 'This example highlights the power of organizational network analysis as a tool for understanding interactions within networks, as well as the power of deliberate network-weaving strategies for developing sustainable networks that support flows of information, ideas, and resources among diverse stakeholders.'[64]

Another pertinent example is a study commissioned by the International Federation of Red Cross and Red Crescent Societies to look at how its National Societies can overcome limitations posed by particular national contexts.[65] The methodology looked to understand organizational development capacities within a select group of National Societies, then ranked these according to the Human Development Index (HDI) of the country in question and with refer-ence to the findings of social network analysis undertaken of the National Societies in question.

A key finding was that associations with actors central to the overall global network could significantly reduce the limitations of low HDI status for National Societies. That said, where National Societies were not strongly connected to central actors, they could still play an active networking role within particular geographic 'cliques' in-country. The most vulnerable were those that were peripheral both globally and locally. One interesting finding, given the recent emphasis in the Red Cross on the decentralization of core features like capacity development, was that Societies with strong ties to regional structures did not do much better than those that did not. Moreover, the nature of the ties within and outside the network matters: Societies with *novel* or *exclusive* ties tended to do better in organizational development terms.

Overall, the network displayed a strong tendency towards a 'rigid core–periphery dynamic'.[66] Developing country National Societies are linked to the overall network almost exclusively through their Northern counterparts and non-Red Cross actors, who play the role of 'global sponsors'. Strong bilateral relationships predominate within a supposedly multilateral system, and these relationships matter a great deal for issues such as organizational development, which had often been viewed in purely technical capacity-building terms.

The Network is the Development

An Australian independent researcher based in Cambridge, Rick Davies has long been arguing for network approaches to be incorporated into development efforts for over a decade now, with some clear arguments for doing so. He suggests a number of points that need to be taken on board more generally by the development sector, echoing the findings from the Red Cross and the other case studies in this chapter.

- Social network analysis power comes from how it can reveal the actors and relationships which are at the heart of development and humanitarian efforts.
- There are a wide range of methods for measuring and visualizing network structures in real-world contexts. There are a similarly wide range of methods of describing expected outcomes of interventions in network terms.
- There are also a wide range of theories about social and other networks that can stimulate thinking about the likely effects of development interventions.
- Network approaches can be used at multiple scales, from very local developments to the global, and can include both formal and informal structures. They are also relevant for understanding recent developments in the delivery of development aid.
- Network models of change can incorporate mutual and circular processes of influence, as well as simple linear processes of change. This enables them to represent systems of relationships exhibiting varying degrees of order, complexity, and chaos.[67]

While such principles are of course useful, putting them into action is the key. Joshua Ramo of Kissinger Associates cites a number of examples of network organizations that are particularly adept at dealing with complex environments: Google, Nintendo, and, somewhat controversially, Hezbollah. These actors are successful because they pay serious attention to context and patterns, and do not try to exert control, but rather foster and facilitate. They are, in other words, network weavers.

It's not just corporations and terrorists that can demonstrate such capabilities. One of my favourite examples of network weaving is in the work of the six non-governmental organizations who founded the International Campaign to Ban Landmines in 1992. The campaign was deliberately maintained as a 'loose coalition of independent groups, without a central office or hierarchy.'[68] What they did build was a powerful network of communications—based on telephones, faxes, and in the final year of the campaign, email. The work of the coalition was built around detailed field research that was quickly shared around the network. As the coordinator of the network, Jody Williams, later wrote: '[the ICBL] galvanized world opinion against antipersonnel land mines to such a degree that within five years a clear and simple ban treaty had been negotiated. Signed by 122 nations in December 1997, the treaty became binding international law more quickly than any such agreement in history. The treaty has, for the first time, comprehensively prohibited a widely used conventional weapon.' In 1997, Williams and the Campaign shared the Nobel Peace Prize. If there is a better example of harnessing network power, I am yet to find it.

All of this carries significant implications for aid agencies. Broadly speaking, a very rigid organization would soon become obsolete, whereas a highly malleable one would be hyperactive, pushing image over substance. Instead, agencies should aim to be a *poised network*, with some clear areas of focus and stability and some scope for flexibility and adaptation.

In such organizations, the role of managers and leaders is not to come up with quick fixes for thorny issues such as structure or culture, but rather to accept the

HEAD OFFICE SAY IT'S A PRIORITY
TO IMPROVE OUR POISE...

inevitable lack of control inherent in these aspects of organizational life. Managers should facilitate, navigate, and make sense of these issues and their impact on organizational performance on an ongoing basis. If networks cannot be designed but instead emerge over time, those who seek to exert control over organizations may need to spend more time using tools like social network analysis to make sense of how this is happening, and then explore how they might adapt their day-to-day practices to 'nudge' the evolving organizational system in preferred directions.

Building on all of this wealth of networks, we might reframe the famous dictum of Sun Microsystems—'The Network *is* the Computer'. For our purposes, we might say 'The Network *is* the Development'. Beyond organizations, network approaches can help us understand development and humanitarian challenges in terms of intricate webs of social, economic, technological, political, and ecological relationships that alternately drive or inhibit change. The changes aid agencies seek to bring about can usefully be framed in terms of bringing about transformative changes in the patterns of these relationships. In fact, it might be argued that no aid can be considered to have a sustainable impact unless it is accompanied by such changes.

CHAPTER 17

Dynamic Change

'There is a need for greater use of more appropriate models... that can take into account undertakings involving multiple partners, multiple causal chains, and outcomes that are emergent and non-linear e.g. with unpredictable or disproportionate outcomes that can only come about in conjunction with the actions of others.'

UK Independent Aid Commission on Development Impact.

Just Another Hole in the Wall

Sugata Mitra is one of those people who can safely be described as a polymath. After getting his PhD in physics in the late 1970s, he designed and produced a revolutionary type of lithium battery, published numerous medical research papers on the human sensory system and the onset of Alzheimer's, then set up India's first local area computer network for newspaper publishing. In 1990 he joined NIIT, a US$2 billion educational and training software company, where he has been credited with dozens of innovations in the field of learning and computer science. All of these remarkable achievements aside, he still doesn't *look* like the kind of person to have inspired a multi-Oscar-winning multi-million dollar blockbuster. But appearances can be deceiving.

Mitra's claim to global fame stemmed from a very simple and familiar idea: that children can quickly learn to do things with computers and other machines that adults cannot. My son Koby, aged less than two, regularly does things to my laptop that have me scratching my head: flipping the screen around 180 degrees, changing the Windows script into Chinese, making his favourite YouTube clip a permanent fixture on my desktop. I wasn't alone, as Mitra discovered.

What is behind this widespread social observation? The adults Mitra talked to were all of limited technological skills? The children were all extraordinary?

Or is this simply just part of the way children learn about new technologies? Whichever way you looked at it, Mitra felt it warranted trying a different approach to computer-based education.

On 26 January 1999, members of Mitra's team at NIIT knocked a hole through the external wall separating the organization's New Delhi headquarters from the adjoining slum, then installed a PC with a high-speed web connection in the hole. Any passer-by could use it, and the terminal was monitored using a remote access machine and a video camera.

The results are—thanks to media coverage and a widely watched TED Talk—well known. The machine proved an instant hit among the slum dwellers, especially the children. With free and public access, the children developed levels of computer literacy with minimum intervention, and were able by the end of the experiment to perform most of the tasks undertaken by the average PC user. They taught themselves enough English to be able to use email, chat, and search engines. Within a few months, they could search the Internet for answers to questions and had improved their English pronunciation. The experiment was well publicized, leading the government of New Delhi to invest in thirty 'holes in the wall' (HiW) in 2000. This was followed by further installations in Madhya Pradesh and Uttar Pradesh. The lessons from the first trial were confirmed, and additional ones were identified, thanks to the use of the machines in areas with some existing educational infrastructure. Users were shown to improve their performance in key subjects at school, especially maths and science. At this point, Mitra coined the name 'minimally invasive education' to describe the approach.

What is less well known is how the process actually works. Mitra's own analysis of the reasons for the learning that occurs is grounded in his physics training, and explicitly builds on ideas of the dynamics inherent in complex systems. In his own words:

> When you allow a system to self-organise, the structure appears without explicit intervention from the outside. The other thing which happens in self-organising systems is emergence. The appearance of a property that's previously not observed as a functional characteristic of the system. Which is why we find a lot of things very surprising...An example of a physical emergent system is [when] there's a breeze and all of that and suddenly like a magic, like a miracle, a little dust devil arrives, and it moves around as though it knows where it's going.[1]

The principle behind HiW is simply that 'The learning environment generate[s] an adequate level of motivation to induce emergent learning in groups of children, with minimal, or no, intervention by a teacher.'[2] If education is a self-organizing system, then learning is its emergent phenomenon—which you can't make happen: 'You can set the stage and allow it to come, when it will...and that to me is the future of learning.'[3]

Five years on from his TED Talk, Sugata Mitra told me more about his findings, and in particular about the complex systems approach that he saw as underpinning the process. He explained that he was even more convinced that the process was indeed self-organizing—first because of the sheer non-linearity of the learning process that would unfold: it would always be surprising and unpredictable. Second, because of the highly emergent nature of the learning that occurs—as he explained, children were able to collectively do things in mathematics or English that were two or three grades higher than their individual levels of attainment—and that this had even happened when they were working in foreign languages that none of the children individually knew. Third, because of the reliance of the hole in the wall learning process on some simple rules, or system boundaries, which would see optimal levels of self-organized learning. After much testing, he told me, he had found that there were certain numbers of children per station, and a certain amount of time that needed to be spent at each station at the start, all of which had key optimal levels. Perhaps most important, he suggested, were the fluid network dynamics that occurred when the process was established. After some time, he observed that the children would swarm or flock between the machines, connecting knowledge, sharing ideas: 'just like birds or insects flocking, although I am not sure which species they most resembled!'[4]

Mitra also told me that there were some obvious implications of this approach for how foreign aid agencies work on educational programmes. For a start, the cost implications are startling: Mitra's project cost on average Rs 1 per child a day, or Rs 365 a year, compared with Rs 15,000 a year for a normal school and Rs 34,000 rupees a year for formal information technology-based schooling. The computer literacy results, five and eight months into the programme, were comparable across all three modes of learning.[5]

As Mitra explains, 'The results have been uniform every time we've done this experiment. You get base level computer literacy almost instantly... with no formal instruction. Therefore any formal instruction for that kind of education is a waste of time and money. You can use that time and money to have a teacher teach something else that children cannot learn on their own.'[6]

Mitra managed to establish a partnership between NIIT and the International Finance Corporation (IFC) to set up a small venture, named Hole in the Wall Education Ltd, to finesse the approach, broaden its scope and applications of the experiments, and conduct more research on the results. IFC's stake was US$1.7 million for a 10 per cent stake, and the plan was to implement the approach in 80 locations across India, both rural and urban. At the time of writing, this had benefited more than 300,000 children. Mitra's paper on the results[7] won a prize for best research article from the prestigious American Educational Research Association in its year of publication.

The project has expanded to Cambodia, eight countries in Africa, and the UK. It now includes online 'learning assistant volunteers', positions that have been filled by numerous retired teachers in the UK, leading to the coining of the wonderful term 'grannycloud'.

But there was also a downside to this: the HiW approach was not something that could easily fit into the standard international or national educational targets and monitoring systems; it was about collective, not individual, attainment and it didn't say anything about how children could memorize and regurgitate, and it didn't treat them as though they were atomized learners. The realization of this was what led Mitra to develop a formal classroom-based approach—the Self-Organized Learning Environment (SOLE)—the results of which, so far, from the perspectives of teachers and pupils, are very promising.

Minimally invasive education has tremendous cultural potential in a country like India, which has long been seen as dominated by 'the teacher pouring forth "words of wisdom" and the students listening passively'.[8] But more than that, the focus on learning outcomes rather than aid inputs—although seemingly obvious—is one that has only slowly come into aid thinking. So pronounced is the gap that Lant Pritchett and colleagues saw fit to call for a new approach— Millennium Learning Goals—to measure educational outcomes rather than the numbers of children schooled.[9] Analysts increasingly agree that achieving universal primary literacy will require innovative solutions, perhaps drawing from outside the traditional schools-based approach, which can complement the more formal approaches of the MDGs.

It is important to note that it was an international agency that supported Mitra: the IFC provided the resources to scale up operations and turn it into a going concern. Could the IFC have done this itself, or one of the agencies working towards the MDGs? Almost certainly not. In most approaches to education, international agencies are not so hands-off, and neither are their interventions: external benefactors design, develop, and finance the apparatus for change. The simple principle that children need to be educated, but also at times need to be left to educate themselves, is hard to bring into the structures of aid. But the IFC could take a risk on supporting Mitra and NIIT, as a way of facilitating a more dynamic and innovative approach to development assistance.

Mitra's 2007 TED Talk became one of the most watched of all time. It also made him one of the most in-demand speakers in global education: requests fly in so frequently that he has hired a leading agent to deal with them all. HiW also inspired an Indian diplomat, Vikas Swarup, to write Q&A, the book that would become 'Slumdog Millionaire'.[10] This film is notable for giving many Western audiences their most visceral vision of poverty in developing countries. That a hole in a wall could achieve such unexpected outcomes is in itself a fascinating example of social complexity.

But, though remarkable and entertaining, the film didn't quite capture one crucial aspect of the lessons from Mitra's work. The idea that one child somehow gained—through his individual and randomly accreted experiences—the precise knowledge needed to win a million dollars in a quiz show seemed to me the exact opposite of the message of the HiW project. The success of Mitra's experiment was all about the networks of children that arose around the computers, and the unpredictable social learning that emerged dynamically from their interactions with each other and the technology. His message was ultimately not about slumdog millionaires, but about the untapped, dynamic learning potential of millions of slumdogs: as he writes in his 2005 paper, '[It] draws upon the expertise of peers, siblings and friends. Each learner is both a learner and a trainer.'[11]

When I put this to him, he laughed and said the following: 'That's a nice way of putting it. You know, I had the same reaction. I wrote to Vikas Swarup, and I asked him, what was it that made him draw this story from my work. It turned out that he saw just the simplest narrative: that a poor slum child could achieve self-betterment. So while my work might have inspired the film, it didn't—strictly speaking—inform it.'[12]

These self-organizing and non-linear dynamics are not just a property of groups of children in slums. As we see in this chapter, they are a common feature of communities, societies, economies; of movements of people and prices; of natural phenomena and the social responses to them.

Mobile Developments

Sugata Mitra is not the only person to have tapped into the human potential of poor people by bringing together the ideas of complex systems with techno-logical innovation. Nathan Eagle is—like Mitra—an extraordinary achiever: a 30-something technology entrepreneur named one of the leading mobile phone innovators in the world by Vodafone, adjunct Professor of Health at Harvard and Technology at the Massachusetts Institute of Technology (MIT), and the youngest-ever winner of the Global Economy Prize (most of the previous winners have been Nobel Laureates). Photogenic to boot, Eagle is the kind of person that the British, in that peculiar national trait, would describe as 'annoyingly successful'.

Eagle's road to success began during a two-year research posting in East Africa starting in 2006. He was working on a mobile text-based system called SMS Bloodbank in a district hospital in Kilifi, on the Kenyan coast. The lack of communications between Kilifi and the central bloodbanks meant emergency support teams working with crash victims would routinely run out of blood for transfusions, at which point hospital staff would become last-minute donors. Clearly, this situation was neither desirable nor sustainable. Working with Eric Magutu, a researcher at the University of Nairobi, Eagle developed an applica-tion to enable Kilifi nurses to text information about blood storage levels to the central banks in Mombasa. The approach was a dismal failure—because nurses were reluctant to use their own airtime to send texts. Eagle hit on the idea of compensating the users with small amounts of airtime when they sent a text. The turnaround was remarkable.[13] A few years later, the system was considered for nationwide deployment.

Eagle then decided to use airtime as a way of compensating mobile phone owners for other types of work that could be performed on low-tech phones, such as filling out surveys or cleaning up data. Other applications of txteagle—today rebranded as Jana—include checking street signs in rural parts of Africa and providing translation services. Three years after its launch, Eagle's firm had access to 2 billion subscribers in 80 countries, and the largest contract labour force in Kenya.[14] Crowdsourcing technologies have become more prominent in the aid delivery chain: tools like Ushahidi and others are being used to generate and share information. However, none of these has the reach Jana has to tap into communities and populations in developing countries. Although Eagle acknowledges that some might find the idea of this large workforce performing tasks for Western corporations challenging, the bottom line is that it delivers an often much-needed source of income in impoverished settings. And, as with HiW, at the heart of the approach is engagement with the distributed intelligence of users.

Another remarkable innovation, launched the same year as txteagle, reinforces the idea that considerable successes can be achieved by understanding the self-organizing dynamics within communities and developing interventions that harness these for developmental goals. In the spring of 2007, at the behest of its owner Vodafone, and with a grant from the UK Department for International Development (DFID), Kenya's largest mobile phone firm, Safaricom, launched a new system called M-Pesa (*pesa* is the Swahili word for cash). Within three years, M-Pesa had almost 12 million users—over half the adult Kenyan population—and transferred an amount equivalent to 11 per cent of the country's gross domestic product. Today, its reach is a staggering 70 per cent of the population. It completes more transactions in Kenya each year than Western Union does across its entire global network.[15] The rocketing of Nathan Eagle's service alongside M-Pesa is a wonderful instance of technological synergy: texteagle paid its suppliers with either airtime or using M-Pesa.[16]

M-Pesa has become a model for mobile money applications around the world, and has brought financial services to a vast population that would not otherwise have had access to a bank account: M-Pesa agents in Kenya outnumber ATMs by a factor of ten.[17] And, 'Almost all [customers] surveyed [responded] that the service was quicker, faster, safer, and more convenient than any alternative money transfer method; 84 per cent of respondents claimed that losing access to M-Pesa would have a significant negative impact on their life.'[18]

However, the model has not been uniformly successful in other countries, such as South Africa. One research study attempted to understand M-Pesa's success by examining the history of its development and acceptance and placing it in context with other money transfer services and methods in Kenya.[19] It turns out that its success was attributable to its fit with existing behaviours and relationships. There was mobile money in Kenya long before the mobile phone, through networks called *halawa*, which enabled agents to communicate with each other across long distances and provide cash brokerage services. Over time, this system evolved to meet the needs of a highly dynamic, urban–rural population. By 2000, people were using airtime as a proxy for cash transfer; when Nathan Eagle set up his text messaging business, M-Pesa and airtime were the two means of payment possible.

As one major review of the M-Pesa approach found, the system doesn't offer a structure in its own right, but instead a flexible tool that can be used in a whole range of different informal transactions across individual social networks, revealing the vast range of interpersonal transactions Kenyans undertake that are endemic to their financial lives:

> These transactions can be understood as embedded in social relationships... Within these social networks, systems of give and take operate in which favours or assistance of various forms are given and received – encompassing a range of resources of which cash is one... Assistance is given with no particular expectation of return and is not necessarily related to need... However, when needs arise, requests for assistance can also be made and resources borrowed or received as a gift. When funds are borrowed, whether or not they are to be returned will be clear but there is rarely a set timetable or interest.[20]

The original intention was for M-Pesa to be a platform for customers to receive and send money and for micro-finance organizations to improve their process and repayment efficiency. Subsequently, it was seen as having potential as a peer-to-peer payment service provider.[21] Today, it is used in a dizzying variety of ways: to pay school fees, send pocket money, pay for drinks in bars, make informal loan repayments, send money for weddings and other social funding drives, pay for public transport, and on and on.[22] This is in itself a testament to the capacity of the tool to tap into the self-organized, networked, and dynamic transactions that characterize Kenya's informal economy. But M-Pesa has also brought things the informal economy didn't have: security, connectivity, volume. Just like Mitra's HiW, M-Pesa used funds from an international agency to get started,[23] but once the process had started it was self-sustaining. Could DFID have anticipated this upfront? It seems unlikely.

Raj Shah, along these lines, tells the following story about a US Agency for International Development (USAID) investment in Egypt:

> A young woman named Gigi Ibrahim... wielded her Blackberry as a weapon of revolution in the rise against President Mubarak of Egypt. She tweeted locations of protests, security alerts, and notes to human rights organizations about the latest arrests or violations. Several months later, Jon Stewart had her on the Daily Show [and] she explained to the rather surprised audience that

she had taken a class at the American University in Cairo called 'Social Mobilization under Authoritarian Regimes' and concentrated on the role of social media as an enabler. I doubt that was an expected outcome when USAID funded the university for over 20 years . . . when we start enabling networks of activity, we simply cannot know what they will end up achieving.[24]

The similarities between HiW, Jana, and M-Pesa are worth reflecting on. Although they work on very different scales, using different technological interfaces, they have a shared reliance on the self-organizing capacity of users. By finding the right set of tools and processes, they have all tapped into the distributed intelligence that lies dormant between groups of people. Their remarkable successes, like the self-organized dynamics on which they rely, carry the hallmarks of non-linearity.

On the Move

Not one to rest on his laurels, in 2010, together with Eric Horvitz, Nathan Eagle set up an initiative called Artificial Intelligence for Development. Their key goal was to use quantitative approaches and 'big data' sources to understand more about the dynamics inherent to development—be they food price fluctuations in Uganda, traffic accidents in Ethiopia, crop failures in Egypt, or urban slum dynamics in Kenya. The initiative published a whole series of working papers, incidentally including one by Hausmann and Hidalgo on product space.

In one of these studies, Eagle worked with Amy Wesolowski, a researcher at Carnegie Mellon, to see how mobile data could reveal more about the movements of people in and around Kibera, the largest slum in Kenya. It was very difficult to track and analyse such a mobile, dynamic population, but, using a year of mobile phone data from June 2008 to June 2009, they set up an exploratory project to develop dynamic models of the slum population.[25]

The dataset was extraordinary: it was a year's worth of information about every call made in Kenya, including the caller, the person called, the location of the cell tower that processed the call, and the date and duration. The data, which were anonymized, were of a larger scale than in any other study by a magnitude of 100: the researchers were able to analyse data from 18,000 residents of Kibera, and at a greater level of detail, thanks to the sheer volume and frequency of the information.

The researchers looked at three specific elements of slum dynamics—migration trends, work trends, and tribal affiliations—chosen because of their relevance to human development issues in the context. Do people move to better neighbourhoods when they leave Kibera? Which parts of Kibera provide possibilities for work over a continued period? Are there any strong ties between slum dwellers and particular tribal groups?

The most striking result, as far as Wesolowski and Eagle were concerned, was the high turnover rate in Kibera, despite overall growth. They found that the average amount of time a Kibera resident spent in central Kibera was just under two months. Close to 50 per cent of individuals were moving every single month. Most of these migrants simply moved to another part of Kibera: there was little evidence of movements to better-off areas. 'The transient nature of this population was evident in our analysis and made harnessing any fundamental properties of Kibera's residents difficult.'[26]

Of course, there are limitations to this work, notably the assumption that one phone relates to one individual continuously. Wesolowski and Eagle did a follow-up study on the heterogeneous nature of mobile phone ownership—that is, one phone is often shared between multiple users—and this was also revealing. Their findings suggested that the sharing is more prevalent in rural settings, and also that, while multiple ownership is likely to skew analyses, the rates of shared ownership can be estimated in ways that allow such factors to be mitigated.

The development community is starting to appreciate these dynamics of urban populations. The *State of African Cities Report* by the UN Human Settlements Programme (UN-HABITAT), published just after the Eagle–Wesolowski study, focuses on the challenges mobility poses to urban development efforts.[27] In particular, it highlights the limitations of censuses as a tool for enumerating slum populations. However, aid agencies as a whole do not appear to have yet (at the time of writing) picked up on the potential of new technologies to address these issues.

The work of Wesolowksi and Eagle was used as one of the starting points for a major study in Haiti after the 2010 earthquake, which used the same approach to look at movements after disasters. Researchers at the Stockholm University found there were no methods to allow timely and accurate assessments of population movements after disasters. Large-scale surveys can give a decent historical perspective, but cannot be deployed in the immediate aftermath of a disaster, while eyewitness accounts are fraught with biases.

By tracking data on SIM card movements through the network of mobile masts, the research team was able to estimate the number of people leaving Port-au-Prince in the first three weeks after the earthquake. The figure of 630,000 correlated closely with a large UN Population Fund survey done afterwards. The team was also able to get a more localized analysis of movements around the cholera outbreak that occurred after the crisis, which was available within hours of the data coming online. The results led the team to conclude that, in areas of high mobile coverage, dynamic analysis could revolutionize the speed and accuracy of population movement assessments. Again, there were limitations: by tracking mobile users, the study missed out groups with low mobile ownership, and there was potential for distortion through the mix of likely ownership arrangements. However, even taking these factors into account, the researchers estimated that the SIMs tracked a minimum of 31 per cent of the

Port-au-Prince population in close to real time—no mean feat, and certainly beyond the scope of any other method. The tremendous potential applicability was clear: the method could be used to estimate size, distribution, and trends in population sizes, and 'could lead to important improvements in the allocation of relief supplies and the quality of needs assessment surveys'.[28] A key recommendation was for analysts to establish relations with mobile operators before disasters to enable effective utilization of the method in the future.

This work has implications in a whole range of areas, including health. Nathan Eagle also happens to hold an adjunct professorship in epidemiology at the Harvard School of Public Health, where he has been a mover in the burgeoning field of 'mHealth' (are the British readers getting annoyed yet?). His first attempt at bringing together big data, mobiles, and health was to track movements of people in Rwanda and use this as a proxy indicator of the likelihood of a cholera outbreak. His hypothesis was that, by tracking people's movements and locations, it might be possible to find correlations with outbreaks. 'For instance, if the movements of 100 people within a 10-mile radius suddenly slow, the cause might be illness—and a looming epidemic.'[29] In fact, people moved around less more because of floods than because of sickness. However, because cholera outbreaks occurred around two weeks after a flood, the model did actually work for cholera.

Meanwhile, one of Eagle's colleagues, Caroline Buckee, used call data in Kenya to track movements of 15 million people and link this to data about malaria, to examine in more detail how human movements influence the spread of the disease. The implications for disease tracking are considerable. As she puts it, 'Never before have we been able to look at individual people on this scale, moving in real time.'[30]

Of course, the proof of the data is in the uptake into decision making. Buckee's plans are to use these models to support a range of interventions: for example sending texts to travellers moving into high-risk areas to remind them to take precautionary measures. Organizations like the UN Children's Fund have already started trialling mHealth interventions, but, perhaps predictably, many of these have been shaped less by the dynamics of community interactions and more by the hierarchies and information flows within the aid system. As the lead author of a UN Foundation review of the potential of these new technologies told the BBC,

> The top-down and centralised nature of aid agencies fails to take advantage of the potential offered by the technologies. It's really quite a different approach from what they've done traditionally...the frame of mind of aid agencies is that it's their job to help...but it may be that actually the best help you can give is letting other people do it. For the first time the people in affected populations could do more to help themselves, but they can't do that if the structures of the people trying to help them don't change.[31]

In Part 2, we saw that forest fires, which can suddenly emerge and tip into massive blazes, generated the classic model of dynamic change in complex systems. This analogy has been used to explain the dynamics of change in a very different system: disease outbreaks in West Africa. Work done at the behest of Médecins Sans Frontières (MSF) and Niger's Ministry of Health on the epidemiology of measles suggests taking a more scientific view of dynamic phenomena has real potential to inform aid programming in practical ways that can enhance relevance and effectiveness.[32]

Although vaccination has brought measles largely under control in many parts of the world, the disease remains a major killer in much of Sub-Saharan Africa and South East Asia. In particular, in Niger, measles epidemics are a big killer of children under five. The problem is that these epidemics are hard to predict: one year there will be no deaths and the next a sudden spike. By analysing the data generated by the government and MSF over a 17-year period, researchers working at the Centre for Infectious Disease Dynamics at Penn State were able to explain the dynamics of measles in Niamey and unpack the challenges faced in terms of effective response.

Their first finding was not unsurprising: the size of outbreaks and transmission rates fluctuated wildly from one season to another.

Second, the timing of outbreaks always coincided with the end of the annual rainy season in November, dropping off in March. The researchers were able to trace this to changes in population density in the capital between Niger's dry and rainy seasons. Cities in Niger tend to swell in population during the dry season because of a lack of agricultural opportunities. When the rains start, agriculture once more becomes a key livelihood strategy. Other factors also play a potential role: dry air promotes aerosol transmission, and there is generally reduced immunity in the dry season. The key message, however, is that aggregate annual measures of measles cases hid the dynamic complexity of the disease.

Third, seasonal dynamics change from year to year, and sometimes you get a year that randomly skips for measles. This is because of an aid-related dynamic that plays out in the population: after an epidemic, measles tends to go locally extinct, and vaccination programmes are cut back. Niger also has the highest birth rate in the world, at 51 births per 1,000, which means there is an increasing 'case load'. This leads to large numbers of children being born without exposure to measles. As the lead researcher explains, 'It is like building up fuel for a fire, in terms of unvaccinated kids. The following year you have added that much more fuel to the fire and that is what creates this erratic fluctuation in the size of outbreaks.'[33] They referred to this behaviour as being 'on the edge of stability'.

A major part of the problem is that Niger's dynamics are not like the epidemic dynamics on which responses are based. 'Just because we understand how measles was tackled in England and Wales with a specific immunization plan does not mean the problem is going to be solved the same way in Niger.'[34]

Despite the erratic nature of epidemics in Niger, researchers say the fact that they are strongly seasonal could help in predicting annual outbreaks, which might help protect susceptible kids from previous years. However, there is a need for greater surveillance to detect potential epidemics and a more strategic and timely vaccination response to control the disease. The existing programme is unlikely to work because it consistently fails to take into account the dynamics of the measles in Niger.

Two doses of the measles vaccine are sufficient to vaccinate at least 95 per cent of children. But a single dose provides only 80 per cent protection from infection. The gap in protection levels is amplified by the social, economic, and environmental dynamics in Niger. 'The key really is that you need to get that second opportunity for vaccination. It stops the fire from burning the fuel.'[35]

These findings offer a cautionary lesson against making assumptions that diseases always follow a predictable pattern. In a *Nature* magazine article published in 2008,[36] the authors called Sahel measles 'The poster-child for non-linear epidemiology'.[37] Matt Ferrari, the lead researcher, told me that at the heart of the problem was the limit that non-linearity places on the ability of public health interventions to project into the future: one runs the risk of either overestimating failure or underestimating success. The goal is to 'come up with strategies and interventions that are robust in the face of underlying uncertainties—but only up to a point. For example, smallpox showed that robust solutions stopped being effective and then you do have to look at a more adaptive, locally focused response.'[38] The challenge, as he saw it, was fundamentally one of a change in culture 'to think about the aid system as one which is *designed, intended* to adapt to change'.[39] In terms of his own work with MSF, he was clear that a vital aspect wasn't just his scientific knowledge and skills, but the 'candid, trustful relationship, which facilitated the acceptance of the new... All too often scientists don't think about the relationship *also* needing to be iterative.'[40]

Taking STEPS Forward

Interestingly, however, the solution to the complexity applied by MSF and the Niger Ministry of Health was not an especially sophisticated one—although it did require a sophisticated understanding of the disease dynamics. This reminds me of a phrase Bridget Rosewell, Chief Economist of the Mayor of London, uses: 'a little bit of complexity can go a long way'.[41] This sentiment would surely be shared by researchers at the Social, Technological and Environmental Pathways to Sustainability (STEPS) Centre based at Sussex University, which to my mind is one of the most groundbreaking research programmes in international development. Led by Melissa Leach and Ian Scoones, the Centre's core themes are health, agriculture, energy and climate change, and water and sanitation. Across all of this work it has found that it is precisely the dynamic nature of development contexts that results in the failure of prescriptive models. A key focus, therefore, is to really get to grips with 'the multi-scale, complex dynamic nature of change'[42] as a means of understanding how social, environmental, and political factors interact in a variety of local conditions, then using this understanding to explore different pathways to sustainable development. We can see this illustrated vividly by tracing how the STEPS team has explored the area of health and pandemics, with specific reference to avian influenza.

The researchers argue that narratives focus largely on the outbreak event rather than the reasons it happened. This then powerfully shapes the response: information systems report the outbreak; responses focus on treatment of animals, people, or areas; emergency work tries to mitigate the impacts after the fact. Standardized, universal responses act as the mainstay of work against the disease: they are 'rolled out' across the world according to plans, programmes, strategies backed up by protocols, manuals, and regulations, and overseen by a technically-equipped and well resourced, benevolent international system.

It is almost as though the underlying epidemiological dynamics of the disease are irrelevant, instead of fundamental to, the outbreak. Those dynamics that are acknowledged are generally the ones that describe how the outbreak might progress, and how the intervention might work to stop this, often based on 'heroic assumptions'—for example the idea that the disease will spread in concentric circles, that all people are equally vulnerable, and so on. This is not just a technical and intellectual issue: it is intimately bound up with the politics of health and disease response and the variety of individual, professional, and institutional interests involved in defining and resolving the problem.[43]

As one expert told the team, 'I keep looking for that pump handle solution.'[44] This is a reference to the work of pioneering nineteenth-century British epidemiologist John Snow, who identified that the source of a cholera outbreak in London was not in fact 'bad air', as was widely believed at the time.[45] Snow instead traced it to the water supply, and in particular a public pump on Broad Street, Soho. After hearing his argument, the local council removed the handle on the pump, preventing any further use of contaminated water. This has become widely known as the founding event of modern epidemiology, with a commemorative pump installed near the original in Soho. There is even an annual Pumphandle Lecture given in memory of John Snow, where participants remove and replace a pump handle as a symbol of the continuing struggles of public health.

The reality, however, as Snow himself argued, was that the removal of the pump handle was not the principal or even the most important reason for diminished cholera mortality, but rather 'the flight of the population, which commenced soon after the outbreak ... the attacks had so far diminished before the use of the water was stopped, that it is impossible to decide whether the well still contained the cholera poison in an active state, or whether, from some cause, the water had become free from it'.[46] In other words, even in this classic work, the dynamics of human–disease interactions were more important than the widely celebrated 'simple fix'. Readers will note that this resonates strongly with the health case studies already looked at in this part of the book, including the smallpox eradication effort and the malaria examples.

One respondent to the STEPS research made the following insightful point:[47]

> With avian influenza there is slow realisation that it is no longer an emergency. It is a deep-rooted issue underlying the disease. But this is very slow and is resisted. It is more attractive to be doing something in emergency mode rather than investing in strategic thinking... Avian influenza to my mind is more a symptom of... massive increases in poultry and duck production. An avian influenza was bound to arise. The question is how to improve the management of these sectors. Not just about the disease. Overall, we should be aiming for a framework for other viruses... But we are not there yet. Far from it.

In a formative study, the STEPS health team, led by Gerry Bloom, set out alternatives to this prevailing approach, which emphasize the importance of a dynamic understanding of the interactions between humans, disease, and ecology. Quite simply, this means acknowledging the capacity for rapid, non-linear evolution among disease pathogens: 'The evolutionary "trial and error" approach of pathogens will typically defeat the most carefully thought out human defence strategies.'[48] The most important implication of this is that there is scope for non-linear dynamics of disease spread within human populations as a result of economic, social, and ecological change. As the authors of the STEPS flu study argue,

> Complex disease dynamics mean that we don't know what is going to happen when, and when outbreaks do occur, their pattern and impact is highly context specific. Such complexity is not amenable to simple outbreak models, and requires a deeper understanding of changing ecologies, demographies and socio-economic contexts – and, in particular, their interactions and dynamics in particular places. This field level understanding of dynamic contexts is startlingly absent in much of the work on avian influenza.[49]

This field-level understanding of dynamics is exactly what shaped the collaboration between MSF and the Niger government around the measles outbreaks in Niamey. At a more global level, this kind of thinking is evident in a major review that attempted to trace the global migration dynamics that underpin the evolution and transmission of human influenza.[50] In this context, eradication and control may be wishful thinking: there will always be scope for old diseases to re-emerge and new ones to arise. There needs therefore to be a joint effort, on the one hand to further a scientific understanding of what is happening, and on the other to develop a pragmatic and adaptive response. The challenge of applying such principles in the emergent monster that is climate change is what I want to move on to look at next.

The Science of Surprise...

Lake Dal in Kashmir is regularly described as one of the wonders of India. It was the summer resort for the Mughals through to the British several centuries later. Home to floating gardens, lotuses, and many hundreds of species of birds and fish, surrounded by architectural magnificence from the Mughal period, it is little wonder it is seen as the jewel in the Indian tourism crown.

Sadly, it is in grave danger. Every day 1.5 tonnes of waste is trawled from its waters. Levels of nitrogen and phosphorus have rocketed in the past 50 years. This has led to explosive growth in algae and weeds, with their removal underpinning a thriving industry employing a thousand workers and two large mechanical barges. Alarmingly, the lake's surface area has diminished by almost 20 per cent. Thankfully, the Indian government has invested several hundred million dollars in dealing with the issue, although some of its actions—like forcible eviction of local populations—have been criticized.

One of the problems with managing pollution in lakes like Dal—and many others—is that the assumptions being made about what constitute acceptable levels of pollution are often based on flawed models. Agro-ecological research on levels of pollution in lakes using both linear and non-linear models suggests linear models allow for a higher threshold of contamination than is in fact allowable, because of the non-linear interactions that play out once polluting agents—like phosphorus from fertilizers—are introduced.[51] Ecologists have found this to be a general problem in pollution management, at both the local and the global level—so much so that the lake has become a classic example of a non-linear system.

Precisely the same issue has been identified in what is perhaps the single biggest pollution issue for the modern era: greenhouse emissions and their link to climate change. In a 2003 study for the Organisation for Economic Co-operation and Development Working Party on Global and Structural Policies,[52] Stephen Schneider, a towering figure in climate science and lead author of several of the Intergovernmental Panel on Climate Change (IPCC) quadrennial reports, focused on surprises and shocks in climate change and the implications for policymakers. The IPCC had by 1996 developed a scientific definition of surprises as 'rapid, non-linear responses of the climatic system to anthropogenic forcing'[53]—that is, to greenhouse gas increases. Indeed, climatic records suggest change is characterized by non-linear dynamics: oscillations, regime shifts, and abrupt, widespread transformations.[54]

Schneider made direct reference to the ideas of complex systems (specifically those explored in Chapters 8, 10, and 11) to substantiate his points. The climate, like other global systems, has multiple interacting parts, and this 'real-world coupling' leads to all kinds of unpredictable emergent behaviours. By way of example, Schneider discussed the potential non-linear impact of temperature rises on thermohaline circulation—the process of global ocean circulation that is often described as the global conveyor belt and seen as one of the most important features of our current climate regime. He also illustrated the potential impact of different levels of carbon taxation on the collapse, or otherwise, of the system.

Schneider noted that, despite the growing scientific awareness of the potential and importance of such non-linear aspects of climate change, most assessments rarely considered the low-probability high-consequence events, instead containing scenarios that 'bracket the uncertainty' rather than taking account of unlikely events at the 'tails of the distribution'.[55] The implication for decision makers was that much of the literature on climate change failed to take account of the full range of possible outcomes of change—which then had implications for the repertoire of policy responses.

The same general point applies to the multitude of interlinked systems on which climate change has an impact. A synthesis of ten case studies of non-linear impacts of climate change across the Americas concluded that non-linear relationships are more often the rule than the exception, and that more work was urgently needed to move an understanding of such relationships into empirical realms.[56] Climate change has been shown to have an impact on a whole host of ecosystems already, through a variety of mechanisms. For example, it can diminish the coupling between a species and its food source—as with numerous birds and their insect prey; it can disrupt symbiotic relationships between species, such as between flowering plants and pollinating agents like bees; and it can affect evolved behaviours, such as migration patterns and mating seasons, and threshold levels such as species extinction boundaries. Because of the complex food webs that exist between species—of precisely the kind I showed in Chapter 11 on networks—the knock-on impacts of such changes are likely to be both cascading and unpredictable.

Among agricultural researchers, the evidence is starting to point in the same direction. Studies on US agricultural data gathered over a 55-year period show that climate-related temperature changes are likely to have substantial negative impacts on the major crops, and moreover that the relationship between temperature change and yields is 'highly non-linear'[57]—with steady decreases up to certain threshold temperatures followed by catastrophic collapses. Much of this data is reported using monthly, seasonal, or annual averages, which dilutes the understanding of the precise dynamics of change.[58]

The same finding recurs in studies of the impact of climate change in African agricultural systems. For example, a study looking at the potential effects of climate change on national productivity levels covering 10,000 farms in 11 different countries found that the potential impacts were considerable, but varied considerably by country (highest in Niger; lowest in South Africa). The overall finding across countries was that temperature and precipitation changes would have strongly non-linear impacts. These patterns were more forthcoming through the use of more precise data—in this case using seasonal rather than annual averages.[59]

It is not just ecosystems and agriculture that are vulnerable to the non-linear dynamics of climate change: the UK Stern Review concluded that, if dynamic non-linearities were taken into account, the economic cost of climate change would rise from 5 per cent of gross domestic product to 20 per cent, in perpetuity.[60] Studies of the security implications raise the potential for non-linear impacts on political systems. And the UK government's Foresight project on migration and global environmental change[61]—which employed the agent-based model of the likely impact on climate refugees cited in Chapter 15—again showed non-linear change was likely to be the norm and not the exception.[62]

However powerful and evidence based the arguments, the message is not especially popular—whether among scientists, practitioners, or policymakers. Schneider argued that scientists often attempt to model complex systems in isolation and along disciplinary lines, thus 'producing internally stable and predictable behaviour'.[63] The ecosystem impact research I described earlier found that natural resource managers planned for change by relying on linear relationships between ecological processes and outcomes. This was despite the fact that the dynamics of impact identified in the case studies were not 'additive nor proportional to the magnitude of environmental change associated with a changing climate'.[64] As we shall see shortly, agricultural and food security specialists have been found to rely on static, linear, and deterministic assessments of change. Ultimately, the assumption that the effects of change will be linear allows actors to think of changes as proportional, additive, and reducible to the sum of the parts—'The various components of natural linear systems may each be described and, in some cases, managed separately'[65]—when this patently is not the case. Faulty assumptions lead to dodgy data collection, inappropriate interpretations, misguided analysis, poor understanding of reality, delays and distortions in decision making, and massive waste in scarce resources directed towards flawed responses.

So what is to be done? The answer has at least three elements: better knowledge, better anticipation and adaptation, and better response. On the knowledge side, better understanding of non-linear dynamics is essential, but, scientifically speaking, this is easier said than done. Non-linear dynamics cannot be predicted: they can be analysed *ex post*, patterns can be discerned, and these can be simulated.[66] But our 'existing methodological toolbox is sparsely equipped to facilitate and sustain such adaptive and anticipatory learning in the face of complex risks and uncertainties'.[67]

A common argument is therefore that, in the absence of understanding of non-linearity, 'Greater emphasis should be placed upon the precautionary principle to avoid catastrophic collapses.'[68] How this principle is articulated and implemented varies considerably. Interestingly, much of the diversity hinges on the extent to which the approach in question takes account of non-linear dynamics.

Resilience Thinking

In the field of climate change adaptation, for example, much of the work is seen to focus on responding to 'predicted impacts of future climate change' rather than adaptive capacity to changes in underlying factors that determine poverty and vulnerability.[69] This leads to 'a linear, largely self-limiting trajectory that favors readily identifiable and discrete adaptation actions, both anticipatory and reactive (before and after a shock), often presented in lists or inventories'.[70] Similarly, researchers examining disaster risk reduction have found that 'present approaches to address vulnerability...fail to recognise the complexities of population vulnerability to multiple hazards. The popular assumption is that natural hazards act in a linear fashion and therefore disaster response and risk reduction strategies could be crafted or formalised based on standard assumptions.'[71]

The implications are sobering. A multi-country study led by researchers associated with the Stockholm Resilience Centre shows that that such conceptual simplifications of resilience can have considerable downsides; in the extreme, they can lead to interventions that actually diminish resilience.[72] The authors assessed a number of adaptation efforts, with particular attention to how measures taken were affecting the resilience of various social–ecological systems. They found that, of the nine approaches, two-thirds had effects that predominately reduced resilience, precisely because they were narrowly focused on simple technological fixes to problems that were more complex and dynamic. Responses designed with a focus on one single risk factor can inadvertently undermine the capacity to address other stresses and 'create bizarre distortions in public policy':[73]

> [In] situations in which system stresses were defined as narrow, technical problems with short-term horizons... governance structures were top-down, did little to link actors at different scales, masked system feedbacks, and did not provide incentive or structure to promote learning... In contrast, in the two examples where the issue was framed in a broader manner, policy implementation tended to enhance characteristics that supported the ability to manage resilience, including flexibility and learning.[74]

Neil Adger, lead author of the study and one of the leading researchers of resilience in the development sector, made the point succinctly in interview: 'It's a complex area: it isn't something [for which] there'll be a set of Newtonian laws.'[75]

The study attributes this widespread focus on single risk factors to a number of factors:

- A desire for readily observable metrics.
- Existing political structures and incentives.
- Entrenched institutional cultures.
- Long histories of dealing with social and ecological problems in narrow and limited ways.

All of these were identified in Part 1 as systemic problems in international aid agencies. Indeed, some of the most troubling manifestations of the push for simplification were found in developing country case studies. For example, fisheries management in Uganda and drought responses in Kenya both highlighted the importance of local sources of resilience-based knowledge of local ecosystems and social networks; in both cases, actors and forces working at the wider level were diminishing such sources. The study suggests we are left with a simple choice: do we want efficient and effective adaptation measures, narrowly and technologically defined? Or do we want strategies that are more open-ended and innovative and seek to build resilience by understanding and strengthening local capacities?

The answer may seem obvious, but, as global climate policy debates have repeatedly highlighted, in this realm the obvious choices are often the hardest to agree on, with politics and special interests clearly playing a major role. That said, here again there are growing numbers of applications of a more systemic and dynamic understanding of resilience and its contributing factors, which highlight the importance of adaptation that is itself dynamic in nature. I look at two short and one longer example here, from across the scientific methodological spectrum, ranging from formal and quantitative to participatory learning processes. What they all share, though, is a sense that 'The goal is not to be well adapted but to adapt well.'

Researchers working across a number of US and European universities have called for 'a multi-faceted, iterative way of analyzing and learning about changes and uncertainties to manage for resilience rather than learning by shock'.[76] Drawing on a number of examples from climate change adaptation programmes, they argue that scientists and communities need to co-create knowledge about adaptation efforts. In Ghana, for example, community-based monitoring of rain levels has enabled the identification of a range of ecosystem-based early warnings for looming rains and dry spells. The researchers suggest the capacity to cope with non-linearities depends largely on openness to learning, willingness to accept change as inevitable, and ability to engage in interventions as experiments. At the heart of the approach is participatory scenario building—which serves as both a methodological tool to explore 'interconnectedness, surprises, and uncertainties' and a learning and policymaking tool 'where multiple voices, experiences, and constraints can be heard'.[77]

Surprises and uncertainties may also include daily life and livelihood stressors and larger-level economic, environmental, and policy disturbances and risks. They are best investigated through alternative storylines and different iterations (cycles), each focusing on subsets of driving forces of change. Learning and innovative thinking are expected to occur by exploring what is not known, often through the use of management or learning probes (envisioning a disturbance that exceeds actual experiences, for instance drought and flooding back to back), deliberating scenario outcomes, anticipating consequences, and planning adaptive responses.

The approach is being rolled out across several African countries, in collaboration with Red Cross National Societies. A key lesson so far is one that all agencies seeking to do such work would do well to heed: 'Managing for resilience is hard work, not simply a twist of fate.'[78]

The same philosophy underpins an emerging approach called ecosystem-based adaptation (EBA), which seeks to bring ecological understanding more firmly into adaptation efforts. This shifts towards more of a 'beginning of the pipe' approach, by engaging with the need for more flexible, systemic, and change-responsive approaches. It is also seen as increasing the agency of adaptation efforts, making them an intelligent, anticipatory response to the stimulus of climate change. Because of their focus on ecosystem-based measures, the approaches—much like the eco-health approaches described in Chapter 14— deliver win-win-wins: for people, ecologies, and economies. They have been found to enhance natural systems and deliver improved quality of life, and are also more cost effective when assessed across a range of social, ecological, and economic criteria.[79] Echoing concerns about systems approaches, however, work by the Institute of Development Studies has warned that the EBA approach should not be treated as a silver bullet: 'EbA will at best be a workable trade-off between conservation and development objectives, not the making of a new Eden.'[80]

The EBA projects implemented to date vary considerably in scope and scale, precisely because they are all focused on climate change, which has different types, scales, and combinations of impacts in different contexts. In South Africa, a variety of actors have launched a decent-sized portfolio of local-level adaptation projects, which researchers at Durban University have reviewed. The success of these has been attributed to the willingness to experiment, reinforced by 'the wicked complexity' of the problem, which has meant actors have been unable 'to define a clear and overarching vision for the adaptation work stream ... particularly as the assumptions, conditions and expectations at the start of each adaptation intervention are unlikely to remain true for its duration or beyond'.[81]

Instead, 'Local level adaptation is proving to be an incremental, iterative and non-linear process that relies on experimentation, flexibility and innovation as the means of achieving progress. Using the lessons learned from both past failures and successes, future action is refined, planned and undertaken, and the cycle repeated as the understanding of the problems and solutions increases and deepens.'[82]

On the quantitative side, Luca Alinovi, of the Food and Agricultural Organization (FAO), led work on understanding food systems using dynamic, evolutionary methods of analysis.[83] Making extensive use of the work of mathematical ecologists like Simon Levin and Buzz Holling, Alinovi et al argued that were two broad kinds of resilience: engineering resilience, which is about returning to previous steady states and based on efficiency, predictability, and constancy after a shock or stress, and ecological resilience, which is more attuned to the non-linear dynamics of complex systems. The ecological resilience approach emphasizes capacity to respond to shocks and stresses 'constructively and creatively' over the idea of long-run equilibria.[84]

Alinovi et al argued that food security systems have multiple social and ecological elements: they are a classic example of a coupled social–ecological system. All food systems, however big or small, have these elements: the ecological resource base that ensures food supply and the socioeconomic structures that are built on this resource base. Although they are frequently analysed separately, research has shown these elements co-evolve and therefore should not be analysed in separation. This co-evolving system is described as having the following features relating to dynamics and diversity:

- *Path dependency*: History matters, and the current status of a system is determined largely by the sequence of states that the system has gone through in the past.

- *Discontinuous changes*: Observed changes tend not to be continuous or gradual, but involve more or less sudden alterations around critical threshold values.

- *Non-linearity*: System dynamics and stability tend to vary non-linearly according to the scale of the system.

- *Multiple equilibria*: The functionally different states of a system involve different equilibria, that is, systems tend to evolve by switching equilibria.[85]

The ability of food systems to retain stability in the face of these changes is ultimately shaped by their ability to maintain self-organization in the face of shocks and stresses. Alinovi et al argue that the value of resilience analysis is that it explicitly enables acknowledgement of the dynamic nature of food systems, as well as allowing for the capture of diversity in resilience approaches different groups adopt.[86]

> Analysis should focus less on the steady or near-equilibrium states and more on the conditions that ensure the maintenance of system functions in the face of stress and shock. This ultimately means moving from a static, deterministic analysis towards a dynamic, stochastic analysis. These conclusions have profound implications for the analysis of food systems and food security.[87]

Alinovi built a model that would take account of these dynamics and complexities, starting with the idea that any such tool would need to assume change is the only constant feature: '[This] lays the groundwork for policies which help socioeconomic systems cope with, adapt to and even shape change.'[88] With support from the European Union, Alinovi and his teams used the approach to examine in a more systematic way household resilience to food insecurity in the Middle East and Africa. In both settings, the overall conceptual framework was validated, and what was notable was the power of the tool to capture the diversity of resilience levels and contributing factors in different settings and among different groups. For example, in Palestine, where the tool has been tested most extensively, female-headed households were far more reliant on public services and social safety nets, because of their lack of assets and sources of income. This in turn cast shadows on the targeting approaches aid agencies took, with many groups and regions that scored poorly on resilience found not to be recipients of adequate assistance. Findings in Kenya echo those from Palestine.

By equipping communities with the ability to manage and respond to shocks in the early stages of a crisis, strategic livelihoods interventions allow for more timely and appropriate responses to disasters than is possible with typical emergency relief assistance. In addition, the early protection and promotion of people's livelihoods significantly reduces the need for massive food aid operations when malnutrition and disease reach acute levels.[89]

Alinovi's work is clear about the challenges of such analysis, especially in terms of doing it in real time in order to inform decision making. In both cases, a clear limitation was that data were not available to allow for a dynamic analysis of resilience, so a 'first approximation' was made using what was available. The authors argue, however, just like the ecological community whose work inspired the approach, that lack of knowledge and understanding about system dynamics suggests that at minimum a precautionary principle approach be adopted. This means policies

> [. . .] safeguarding the range of options open to future generations by protect-ing thresholds of resilience in desirable states of nature; [and] containing the fundamental uncertainty associated with human activities either by restricting the level of activity to preserve a degree of system predictability or by ensuring that the risks associated with innovative activities/experiments that test the resilience of the system are bounded.[90]

In a subsequent examination of the kinds of policies that assist rather than diminish resilience, the teams found that resilient-friendly policies were those that 'adaptively monitor key variables of the jointly determined system', that 'provide and sustain ecological, economic and cultural diversity', that 'provide and sustain appropriate natural and social capital', and that 'seek integrative understanding'.[91]

Of course, such work is useful only if it can be shown to have been absorbed into efforts on the ground. Alinovi's work appears to be permeating into FAO's work on resilience: in its 2012 policy position on working in protracted crises, it is easy to see the fruits of Alinovi's thinking:[92]

> Building resilience is both an outcome and a dynamic process that unfolds in response to stresses and shocks, singly or more often in combination. This implies that programmes that seek to enhance resilience will need to embrace dynamic change. Rather than prescribing activities aimed solely at the achieve-ment of specific outputs, interventions should focus on fostering the character-istics that enable resilient outcomes from household to national levels. Particular emphasis should be placed on facilitating processes that empower local actors to prepare for inevitable change and adapt to evolving risk and vulnerability contexts.[93]

Alinovi himself now holds what must be one of the most challenging jobs in the whole aid world: Chief of FAO Somalia. There too, it is possible to see these ideas coming to fruition, notably in a recent joint resilience strategy developed by FAO, the World Food Programme, and the UN Children's Fund and a major international appeal launched in 2011:

> As the Somali people themselves have learned over the millennia, flexibility and opportunism are necessary tools for survival ... as well as the sustainable utilization and maintenance of the resource base. Historically, the Somali people have developed systems that allow them to adjust to floods, drought and other disasters. The mobile nomadic livestock system, water harvesting, spate irrigation and cropping on flooded areas as the water recedes are examples of adapted coping strategies. These systems have three characteristics in common: flexibility, opportunism and knowledge handed down from generation to generation and continuously refined through daily experience. Today, the delivery of emergency and development interventions must also be adaptive and opportunistic and for this real time knowledge and information is essential.[94]

As Alinovi's earlier work concluded, the most important aspect to keep in mind is that no single mechanism can guarantee the maintenance of resilience. As he puts it: 'The adoption of resilience as a criterion for policy design shifts the focus of policies from controlling change in systems assumed to be stable, to managing the capacity of social-ecological systems to cope with, adapt to and shape change.'[95]

Alinovi's work is starting to have a broader influence on food security strategies. In 2012, the WFP published a concept paper, which sought to set out preliminary thoughts for that organization's next four-year strategy. The paper cites Alinovi's work in a section on complexity, and noted that the very idea of a 'linear development path' had been fundamentally challenged by events: 'the world has seen some countries suffer extended periods of fragility, while seemingly stable and rapidly growing economies experience dramatic reversals ...'. It argued that 'the path from relief to recovery and development is non-linear and characterized by discontinuous change' and that, as a result, there was a need to move toward more dynamic management approaches that 'view food systems as complex systems and that seek to ... build lasting resilience to shocks'.[96] Whether such an understanding informs the forthcoming WFP strategy in a substantial way remains to be seen, but the initial signals are encouraging.

While the international community is starting to acknowledge the importance of resilience through growing numbers of studies, programmes, and dedicated staff members, it seems that, all too often, the linear mentalities of traditional approaches to disaster risk reduction, climate change adaptation, food security, and social protection are still prevailing. When I spoke to Elinor Ostrom about this, she was dismissive about the contribution of aid agencies, suggesting many of them were using the language of resilience without having any idea what it actually meant. Repeated statements by managers and leaders in the aid world about 'how *we* are going to build *their* resilience' reinforce this.

Unless we can take on the findings from the work of Alinovi and others like him, it is likely that the majority of lessons arising from the development community about dynamic changes in programme contexts will remain—like those around Lake Dal—late ones from early warnings.

Performance Dynamics, Dynamic Performance

> Using measures of performance is like listening to a symphony one note at a time; any harmony or discord becomes apparent only when the notes are combined into a rhythm, a pattern of change. We are resolute in our commitment to measures of performance; we are trained in them, we feel comfortable with them, and in some cases, we are legally obligated to them. But our commitment is mostly the result of knowing no alternative. We've been studying the notes and have not yet heard a symphony.[97]

Rick Davies, whose work we looked at in the previous chapter, argues that 'There are a number of types of change processes, which can be tentatively located on a continuum...At the one end there are relatively simple linear processes, and at the other end there are complex networks.'[98] He asserts that many problems of performance and accountability frameworks derive from difficulties in representing this diversity. As he asks: 'are the ways in which aid organizations seek to represent change sophisticated enough...given the nature of the change processes they are involved in?'[99]

Olivier Serrat of the Asian Development Bank has argued that, although development is a complex, adaptive process, it has on the whole not been conducted as such. The implications of this are stark: 'If the assumptions are based on *invalid theories of change* (including cause-and-effect relationships) and on inappropriate tools, methods, and approaches derived from those, development agencies jeopardize the impacts they seek to realize'[100] (emphasis added). A new wave of approaches, some of which have been informed by a qualitative understanding of complex systems research, include participatory and adaptive learning and planning approaches such as outcome mapping, constituency feedback, most significant change, positive deviance techniques, appreciative enquiry, and many others. For example, outcome mapping, developed by the Evaluation Department of IDRC, is based on the idea that for the most part, development change is non-linear and unpredictable. Therefore, in trying to bring about change, development actors need to focus less on attribution of impacts ('we achieved this!'), but on the more modest and realistic goals of contribution to outcomes ('here is how we helped change knowledge, attitudes, relationships and behaviours'), the impacts of which are largely determined by actors and factors outside of any given agencies control.

Common to all is the idea that traditional theories of change used by development and humanitarian actors are not appropriate; these all in different ways try to 'marry methodological rigor with techniques that lend themselves to a variety of complex and non-linear contexts'.[101]

There are also various ways in which such ideas are being applied. Some thinkers are arguing for similar approaches in reforming the MDGs.[102] Dani Rodrik talks of 'one economics, many recipes'; David Booth of the move from best practice to best fit; Merilee Grindle of 'good enough governance'; Bill Easterly of moving 'from planners to searchers'; Sue Unsworth of an upside-down view of governance. Matt Andrews, Lant Pritchett, and Michael Woolcock aimed to synthesize all this into their proposal for problem-driven iterative adaptation, which I looked at in Chapter 15.[103]

While growing numbers of development thinkers have sought to address this issue, and a range of new methods and philosophies have been developed, the strong tendency towards the linear and the static, the reductionist and the simplified, prevails. As a result, what should be a measured and evidence-based discussion conducted on more scientific grounds has become a cultural war, a face-off in which the hostility and difference in attitudes and values are getting more and more pronounced. As a result, 'the landscape for accountability struggles is becoming more complex and the strategies and tactics of those seeking accountability are becoming more diverse.'[104] This is echoed by Overseas Development Institute research carried out in 2008:

> Accountability is . . . complex, dynamic and systemic. That is, given the interdependent nature of different levels and forms of accountability – for instance, public, political, parliamentary, financial, etc. – and increased non-state involvement in accountability, the functioning of any one accountability relationship, or the effectiveness of a donor intervention relating to such a relationship, is likely to be shaped by other accountability relationships.[105]

Alnoor Ebrahim is a world-leading authority on the accountability and performance of aid agencies. In 2010, he was asked to give evidence to the US Congress on the accountability or otherwise of the World Bank. His is one of the few voices in this space that calmly calls for an objective perspective on the challenges of accountability. Specifically, he suggests that what is needed is a contingency model that takes account of the nature of the change being sought and of the intervention being implemented. He builds on the work of Rick Davies and some of my own earlier efforts in putting this together, and suggests that what is most important about a given approach to results and accountability is its appropriateness to the context. At the heart of this are two deeper questions. The first concerns the *theories of change* an organization uses to understand the links between its work and the wider world (as discussed above), which range from linear (or simple) to complex. The second is about 'what an organization actually does in implementing its mission'.[106] This varies

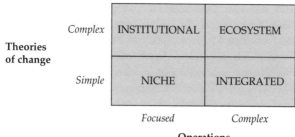

Figure 17.1 Contingency framework for different types of accountability

Source: Ebrahim A. and Kasturi Rangan V. (2010) 'The Limits of Nonprofit Impact: A Contingency Framework for Measuring Social Performance'. Working Paper 10–099 (Cambridge, MA: Harvard Business School).

from focused (on a specific task or intervention) to complex—where an organization 'expands its boundaries to absorb other key functions or niches that it deems important to achieving its mission'.[107]

> A complex theory of change refers to cause–effect relationships that are only weakly understood, and where there may be multiple causal factors at play. Many emergency and basic services operate on a linear, or focused, theory of change: get shelter, food and water to people facing a crisis in order to avert further disaster... The logistics and process of doing so can be highly complicated, but the basic intervention logic is fairly straightforward. Efforts to influence public policy, however, are typically more complex, and they are shaped by many factors which may be poorly understood and non-linear. In such contexts, it is hard to know how much of a difference a particular intervention makes [and] to attribute a policy change to the actions of any single organization.[108]

The framework in Figure 17.1 sets out the range of approaches Ebrahim has identified.

In *niche areas*—where activities are operationally focused and there are simple theories of change—efforts can be shaped by linear or well-understood causal chains implemented through very specific and well-defined interventions. In *integrated areas*—where operations may be complex but there are still simple theories of change—organizations will occupy several niches in the causal chain, and thus have more control of both outputs and outcomes. Such organizations will be able to measure their outputs and also outcomes, and, where they can isolate their interventions, they may be able to use quasi-experimental methods such as randomized control trials to test for effectiveness.

In *institutional areas of work*, organizations will have focused institutional approaches, but their theories of change are more complex. Advocacy organizations, such as Amnesty International, fall into this category. Organizations here may reasonably measure their outputs and their 'influence' on key policies, rights, and freedoms (i.e. intermediate outcomes), but not necessarily their impacts, which are arguably more likely to be achieved by networks or coalitions of actors working in concert. Approaches designed to help organizations identify and measure results in 'messy' environments may be appropriate.

Finally, in the *ecosystem* quadrant, organizations focus on problems that are not well understood (complex theory of change) while also engaging in multiple interventions and roles (complex operational strategy). They aim for results that affect entire systems, for example to contribute to overall development or address the root causes of poverty or vulnerability. Measuring the impacts of such work is likely to require long timeframes, and attributing results to any single organization is unlikely to be possible. Again, as in the institutional quadrant, impacts are more likely to be achieved through collaboration.

Another tool from complex systems research, the fitness landscape, has been used to get a deeper appreciation of the possibilities in the ecosystem quadrant. Lant Pritchett has built on his work on problem driven iterative adaptation to suggest a set of principles for engaging with results amid complexity in a systematic way. The key is to apply what Lant Pritchett calls 'structured experiential learning' which builds learning objectives into the cycle of project design, implementation, completion, and evaluation. Inspired by the work of Stuart Kauffman on fitness landscapes, Pritchett and his colleagues argue that the impact of a development project is best thought of as a fitness function much like the biological equivalent: it is an evaluative function that determines the success or otherwise of a project. For simple projects, this fitness function is relatively straightforward. However, for more complex projects, it is important to explore the fitness space: 'learning about the efficacy of development projects is an attempt to empirically characterize fitness functions'. Implementers first need to establish the overall space of possibilities for a given project, programme, or policy and then 'dynamically crawl the design space by simultaneously trying out design alternatives and then adapting the project sequentially based on the results'.[109] The transformation needed is: to move from 'experiments' as a tool to 'experimentation' as a mindset. As Pritchett puts it:

> The reality is that with complex endeavors – projects in high dimensional design spaces over rugged and contextual fitness functions – no one can know what will work in advance. Development project managers do not know if the inputs will lead to useful outputs (internal area within their control) or if the outputs created will in turn lead to outcomes and impacts (not within their control)...Development projects are not like chemistry – where we can predict exactly how interactions will work under specified conditions because we have empirically validated invariance laws that cover all the relevant contingencies...Some projects have to be authorized as a structured crawl over the promising parts of the design space...

Contingency frameworks are powerful precisely because they anticipate and help navigate the challenges faced by established development tools like the logical framework. They highlight the areas in which aid agencies have been experimenting, through tools like outcome mapping, and also point to future possibilities, such as those suggested by Lant Pritchett and his colleagues. And they do so by using an approach that allows us to hold the whole portfolio of approaches—from simple to complex—in mind simultaneously.

As Ebrahim warns, however, such frameworks should not be used as a 'be-all-and-end-all framework', but rather should be seen as a powerful aid in working out when certain approaches are more or less likely to be appropriate. As he concludes,

> Our normative argument is that it is not feasible, or even desirable, for all organizations to develop metrics at all levels on the logic chain. The more important challenge is one of alignment: building systems and structures for measurement that support the achievement of organizational mission, especially the goals that an organization can reasonably control or influence. We contend that organizational efforts extending beyond this scope are a misallocation of scarce resources.[110]

The contingency-based approach provides a way of understanding that, in the area of accountability, there are few, if any, silver bullets that are going to be appropriate to all settings: 'There are no panaceas to results measurement in complex social contexts.'[111]

This is the point on which I want to conclude this chapter. We have seen how inhabitants of slums display unpredictable, dynamic behaviour, as do entire populations of people. We have seen that technologies work best when they tap into the existing non-linear dynamics that characterize human relationships and networks. We have seen that crises—from localized disease outbreaks to global climate change—also follow such dynamics. New breeds of social–ecological scientists have focused on how some systems have managed to build resilience through processes of internal adaptation and learning that echo the external dynamics against which they are buffeted. Conversely, they have also illuminated how such unpredictable dynamics can prove disastrous for fragile systems.

We have seen that a focus on narrow, time-limited, linear interventions in complex settings have not helped deal with such problems: they have simply proved ineffectual, or have even served to make things worse. Worryingly, we have also seen that many existing approaches to performance measurement reinforce such narrow, linear approaches. By focusing on what can be directly measured and managed, the performance agenda often leaves or discards those things that are most important for effecting change.

However, by taking a more scientific approach to the problems faced, by following in the footsteps of Warren Weaver and asking if a particular conceptual approach is relevant to the problem being faced, and adapting ideas and actions accordingly, some dramatic successes have been achieved.

Reflect back on the cases in this chapter: emergent, networked learning among illiterate children, to M-PESA's meteoric rise, to the resilience of communities, to combating disease outbreaks. These remarkable successes all came about because of how the protagonists involved opened themselves up to the possibilities—and risks—of dynamic, non-linear change.

CHAPTER 18

Part 3 Epilogue—Beyond Panaceas

In the 1960s and 1970s, there was a rise in studies that linked social science issues with broader environmental dynamics. Although there are a number of contenders, perhaps the most important of these for the way that people thought about foreign aid was the handful of studies that focused on the inevitable but largely unconsidered feedback between the way human beings were increasingly living and the world around us. Over a five-year period, Garret Hardin published 'Tragedy of The Commons', Paul Ehrlich *The Population Bomb*, and The Club of Rome *Limits to Growth*. Hardin's 'Tragedy of the Commons'[1] was an influential work that illustrated how, simply by thinking in a self-centred manner, the feedbacks between individual actions and the wider environment could lead to wholesale destruction of common areas. Hardin's thesis revealed a truth that resonated with many: that humanity was trapped in a vicious feedback loop, spiralling downwards towards our inevitable destruction. It had a profound influence on a whole generation of social planners and scholars.

However, his argument has been largely superseded by the work of Elinor Ostrom on what some have called the 'strategy of the commons'. Her work, which won her a Nobel Prize in Economics in 2009, was rich and has many facets that are of relevance for this book. She argued that understanding a complex whole meant not shying away from understanding the different elements of a given system. The key—as we have heard throughout this book—was not to try and eliminate complexity, but rather to analyse and harness it.

A driving motivation for Ostrom was what she saw as the plague of panaceas. Simplistic analyses of complex systems led researchers, practitioners, and policymakers to lose sight of what was actually happening. Simplistic analysis often justifies the adoption of standardized blueprints, and this is often to the advantage of certain groups, and to the detriment of overall outcomes. When the blueprints fail—as they often do—this leads to scepticism as to whether *any* solution is in fact possible; as she put it: 'The advantaged then vigorously organize to resist efforts to learn from past mistakes and to adopt new rules.'[2]

Readers will already be seeing the resonance of these ideas with the examples I have drawn on throughout this book about how aid agencies think, learn, and act. Ostrom also points to the alternatives that might be embraced if we are willing to give up our familiar, comfortable, known failures.

One set of panaceas Ostrom deconstructed over the course of her career entailed the host of approaches developed by Hardin's followers. In the face of the inability of communities to self-govern common pool resources, the key guiding principle was for government to take action and impose rules to prevent the inevitable destruction of such spaces, or else the shift towards private ownership needed to happen.

Ostrom argued that, instead of being an inevitable consequence of commonly held goods, the tragedy narrative played out only in certain situations. In Hardin's pasture, there was no system of governing use of the common resource; there was no investment to improve the common resource; the animals using the common resource were privately owned; there was a relatively large number of users; and there was no local leadership, shared norms, or even communication between users. Empirical and experimental research has shown that, more generally, situations where these assumptions hold true do indeed conform to the tragedy narrative. At the heart of this result is the classic prisoners' dilemma model from game theory.

However, this is only one set of circumstances for the commons. Using a variety of real world settings from fisheries to irrigation, Ostrom showed that Hardin had indeed dramatically oversimplified the situation. Ostrom showed experimentally that, if just one factor was tweaked, the tragedy did not result. If resource users were allowed to have direct interactions between decisions, subsequent decisions changed to become more socially optimal. Norms emerged, and given the opportunity, so too did sanctions for inappropriate behaviours and rules for resource management. Allowing interactions leads to the emergence of institutions for self-governance that would achieve efficient and sustainable use of the resource. Negative feedback loops were only one of the possible outcomes: actors could under certain situations, given certain incentives, self-organize, creating virtuous beneficial feedback loops. In light of Ostrom's work, Garrett Hardin conceded that he should have called his paper 'The Tragedy of the Unmanaged Commons'.[3]

Ostrom argued that 'The answers are not simple because we have just begun to develop the concepts, technology and methods that can address the generic nature of the problems.'[4] But the reality is that the answers may remain complex. The key is the power of emergent behaviour—as she once said, 'Little by little, bit by bit...so much good can be done on so many levels.'[5] Ostrom published an article on the day she passed away, in which she argued again for putting aside the fixation on panaceas, and for a more evolutionary approach to policymaking. She wrote:

> We have never had to deal with problems of the scale facing today's globally interconnected society. No one knows for sure what will work, so it is important to build a system that can evolve and adapt rapidly...Such an evolutionary approach to policy provides essential safety nets should one or more policies fail. The good news is that evolutionary policymaking is already happening organically.[6]

It is clear that Ostrom's decades of rich and insightful work carry a range of specific insights for aid agencies and the way they go about their work. But her work also carries broader messages that go beyond aid, but are of tremendous relevance.

Ostrom's work tells us something about the nature of collective action, about shared spirit, about altruism. It says something about the nature of aid as an institution in its own right.

As she said to me in conversation, just because we have a certain emphasis in our institutions, it doesn't mean we are stuck with it.

This message is perhaps the common strand that runs through all of the examples of complex systems thinking applied to foreign aid that I have covered in Part 3. Even if a narrow, simplistic, mechanistic, reductionist form of global altruism is our legacy, it needn't be our fate.[7]

CHAPTER 19

Aid on the Edge of Chaos

'The dogmas of the quiet past are inadequate to the stormy present. The occasion is piled high with difficulty, and we must rise – with the occasion. As our case is new, so we must think anew, and act anew. We must disenthrall ourselves.'

Abraham Lincoln.[1]

As I noted at the start of this book, foreign aid is at a crossroads. Different paths forward have been suggested by numerous parties—which might be simplified as: expansion, reduction, or transformation. While these are not mutually exclusive, the arguments in this book have been firmly in the third of these areas.

The argument for transformation is based partly on internal issues—a growing understanding of the frequent mismatch between aid and the problems it seeks to address; and of the second-best, limited, and uncertain nature of the impact of aid. There are also external imperatives: an awareness of the fundamental importance of domestic institutions and political economy in developing countries, the fact that development comes about because of political transformations which are always 'opened and closed through historic, dynamic and iterative processes',[2] and the accelerating changes happening in the world around us.

As a much respected former colleague, Andrew Rogerson, has argued, 'Development processes are led by complex, uncertain, context-specific social and political dynamics and responses to national challenges ... Aid is marginal to these dynamics in most country contexts unless, by fortunate positioning or even accident as much as good design, it happens to align with them.'[3]

How might aid become better aligned with these dynamics? My argument in this book points to changes in the fundamental assumptions, ideas, and actions of aid. Conventional aid conceives of systems and problems, behaviours, relationships and organizations, and dynamics of change in highly abstract, idealized, and simplified ways. These are, as I argued in Part 1, poorly matched to the reality of the world.

But this mismatch doesn't need to persist. There are many ideas and insights emerging from the work of complex systems researchers that provide sound scientific alternatives to these assumptions, as I argued in Part 2. The legacy of Warren Weaver is alive and thriving: his Third Great Advance is very much in progress.

And there are numerous examples of foreign aid that have taken on board these ideas in a deliberate fashion. These have started to demonstrate the potential value of a more systemic, adaptive, networked, dynamic approach, as I showed in Part 3. Taken together these examples point towards what I see as a fundamental shift in the mental models, strategic approaches, organizational philosophies, and performance approaches of foreign aid.

Complexity thinking implies that the role of 'aid' in development and humanitarian assistance would shift from 'external push'—filling gaps in a predictable and linear fashion—to 'internal catalyst'.[4] Catalytic aid would not create development, but it would identify, expand, and sustain the space for change. Such aid can challenge the existing *status quo*, and release new energies into unconsidered and unforeseen directions. Every aid initiative, from this perspective, is a new opportunity—to experiment, prototype, get a foothold in the new reality. Such aid would not seek simply to expand on the current model with minor adjustments and yet more technical silver bullets. It would encourage us to anticipate, adapt, learn, and transform our thinking and our actions in light of the complex realities we face.

But the ideas of complexity should not themselves be seen as some kind of all-purpose fix to aid problems. To argue that they are would be counter to the overall narrative in this book, and the lesson that comes through in so many ways: that the desire for panaceas, and their unthinking application, is a large part of the problems faced in development and humanitarian efforts.

Stuart Kauffman has described complex systems research as helping reconnect us to the immense and unknowable cosmos of which we are a part. Because of the ubiquity of the patterns revealed in complexity research—from our own backyard to the formation of galaxies—he says that understanding these patterns can make us feel more 'at home in the universe'.[5] On a somewhat smaller scale, I think these ideas can help make sense of our existing realities, enable more open conversations about the challenges we face, and generate new ways of thinking about problems. Complex interconnections, behaviours, relationships, and dynamics are everywhere around us, if we are willing to change *how* we see the world: to not just discover new landscapes but to also see through new eyes. To my mind, this transformation can contribute to a form of familiarity just as important as Kauffman's grander vision. Acknowledging rather than denying complexity can make us feel more at home in our *own* world.

It can help us understand the world better than we do, in some key areas where our understanding, ways of thinking, and ways of acting are lacking.

It can help us ask the right kinds of questions, it can serve as an engine for intuition, and it can help us critically engage with the answers. It can point to possibilities we might not have otherwise considered, ideas we may have discarded, approaches that could be more relevant and appropriate. However, complexity research, like all scientific endeavours, may be limited in what it can tell us about *what* to do about the implications it generates.

The physicist Richard Feynman once made a similar point, after observing the water systems working in the adjacent rich and poor neighbourhoods on a mountainside in Rio de Janeiro, and discussing the implications with American colleagues working on Truman's Point 4 programme. He alluded to the fact that science can tell us how water runs through a tributary, about the effects of gravity and hill-slope contours, about how to build the network of pipes up a hill. It can tell us about the potential for contamination and the impact of growing and changing population. It can tell us what a fair distribution of water would be. But it can't make the decision for us. It cannot ensure that water—or any resource—is accessed equitably, fairly, humanely. Only our shared values can do that.

As the Bali *subak* story with which I opened this book shows, complexity research can tell us how a fair social system might work, and why it is important. It can show why a balanced system might be the most resilient and sustainable outcome for people and for the environment. It can make the case for why altruism is vital, and why institutions matter.

Complexity thinking can help describe and explain our world, our relationship to it, and to each other far better—with far greater realism and fidelity—than the tools we have had handed down to us from nineteenth-century physics. It seems clear that complex systems research will prove of growing interest and value for those dealing with problems of the twenty-first century—in aid and further afield. Whether we collectively have the humility and the courage to face up to its implications remains to be seen.

I opened this last chapter with a well-known Abraham Lincoln quote that sums up my mood as I write it. So what might aid, disenthralled, look like? To paraphrase a famous speech by another great American leader, John F. Kennedy, I think that complexity thinking calls for a more practical, attainable development. This would be based not on a sudden revolution in human nature but on the adaptive evolution in human institutions. There is no single, simple key to this development, no grand or magic formula to be adopted. Genuine development should be the networked product of many nations, the emergent sum of many acts. It must be dynamic, not static, changing to meet the challenge of each country, and each new generation. Development should be seen as a process, a way of thinking about and navigating complex problems.[6]

Building on the arguments and examples in this book, I would suggest that there would be more space for thinkers who discover ways of working with the hidden strength and fragility of the systems we seek to change, finding new and creative ways of looking at old problems. There would be more practitioners who are finding new ways of tapping into the dynamic potential inherent within communities, of asking the right questions rather than providing the right solutions. There would be more policymakers who are willing to acknowledge that the world we live and work in requires a different kind of leadership, one which calls for strength, not power. There would be more innovative organizations trialling new approaches, putting out probes in complex settings, and learning tirelessly—fearlessly, even—from the outcomes. More hard-headed, hard-nosed idealists who can look into the worst and best of humanity; who can work together with others to create cooperative strategies for success. Who are able to move beyond ideas of assistance to embrace mutual adaptation; who think not about delivering to others but co-evolving and learning with them.

As Elinor Ostrom told me, the ideal aid system of the future would 'reward people for developing imaginative ideas that draw on the complexity of the real world, that leave people in developing countries more autonomous, less dependent, and more capable of crafting their own future'.[7] More people in more countries—be they in government or civil society, tiny villages or sprawling slums, female or male, young or old—would be supported by aid, to innovate, to explore, to discover what *they* might do best to further their own development.

Aid in the future would not be an export industry, sclerotic and rigid, shaped by politics of supply and the mental models of early Fordism. Aid would resemble the world of which it is a part: fluid, dynamic, emergent. It would be as open to change on the inside as it was hungry for change outside. It would be an open innovation network, catalysing and leveraging change in countries around the world. Aid would exist on the border between order and chaos: a product of human innovation, of scientific realism, and of our shared values.

A system to change the system? Let's hope.

ENDNOTES

Preface

1. Adams, D. and Carwardine, M. (1991), *Last Chance to See* (New York: Harmony), p. 99
2. Pratchett, T. (1986), *Mort* (London: Victor Gollancz), p. 11
3. King, M.L. (1963), *Letter from a Birmingham Jail* (Philadelphia, PA: African Studies Center, University of Pennsylvania), http://www.africa.upenn.edu/Articles_Gen/ Letter_Birmingham.html (accessed October 2012)
4. Beinhocker, E.D. (2006), *Origin of Wealth: Evolution, Complexity, and the Radical Remaking of Economics* (Cambridge, MA: Harvard Business School)
5. Rodrik, D. (2011), 'New Rules for the Global Economy'. Project Syndicate Commentary, 10 January, http://www.project-syndicate.org/commentary/new-rules-for-the-global-economy (accessed October 2012)
6. Personal communication (2012)
7. See Ghosh, P. (2011), 'Nature's Lessons for Bank Crises', BBC Science and Environment News, 19 January, http://www.bbc.co.uk/news/science-environment-12228065 (accessed October 2012)
8. Stiglitz, J. (2011), 'Gambling with the Planet'. Project Syndicate Commentary, 6 April, http://www.project-syndicate.org/commentary/gambling-with-the-planet (accessed October 2012)
9. Crutchfield, J.P. (2009), 'The Hidden Fragility of Complex Systems—Consequences of Change, Changing Consequences', in Ascione, G., Massip, C., and Perello, J. (eds) *Cultures of Change: Social Atoms and Electronic Lives* (Barcelona: ACTAR D Publishers, Barcelona), pp. 98–111
10. Rifkin, J. (2010), *The Empathic Civilization: The Race to Global Consciousness in a World in Crisis* (Cambridge: Polity)
11. BPS (2003), Harvested Area, Yield Rate and Production of Paddy by Province, 2001, Statistics Indonesia
12. Arthawiguna, W., Lorenzen, R. and Lorenzen, S. (2005), 'Past, Present and Future: Perspectives of Balinese Rice Farming'. International Rice Conference, New Delhi, 12–14 September 2005
13. Atwood, J.B. (1998), 'The Future of United States Foreign Assistance', in Grant, R. and Nijman, J. (eds) *The Global Crisis in Foreign Aid* (Syracuse, NY: Syracuse University Press, pp. 145–51), p. 149
14. Ginzburg, O. (2005), *There You Go* (London: Hungry Man Books)
15. Personal communication (2010)

Chapter 1

1. Smith, A. (1759), *The Theory of Moral Sentiments* (London: A. Millar), <http://www.econlib.org/library/Smith/smMS1.html> (accessed October 2012)
2. UNDP (2011), 'Ethiopia HDI Values and Rank Changes in the 2011 Human Development Report'. Explanatory Note on 2011 HDR Composite Indices (New York: UNDP)
3. Barder, O. (2010), 'Aid Effectiveness: Where is it Going, and What Could You Do?' 19 May 2010, <http://www.owen.org/wp-content/uploads/100519-DAG-Ethiopia.pdf> (accessed October 2012)
4. Schumacher, E.F. (1973), *Small Is Beautiful: Economics as if People Mattered* (New York: Harper & Row)
5. OECD (2009), *Reaching Our Development Goals: Why Does Aid Effectiveness Matter?* (Paris: OECD)
6. *The Economist* (2008), 'A Scramble in Africa', 4 September <http://www.economist.com/node/12060397> (accessed October 2012)
7. Deutscher, E. and Fyson, S. (2008), 'Improving the Effectiveness of Aid'. *Finance and Development* 14(3), <http://www.imf.org/external/pubs/ft/fandd/2008/09/deutscher.htm> (accessed October 2012)
8. Djankov, S., Montalvo, J.G., and Reynal-Querol, M. (2009), 'Aid with Multiple Personalities'. *Journal of Comparative Economics* 37(2): 217–29, p. 217
9. Ralston, N. (2011), 'States Send in Their Rescue Teams', *The Age*, 14 January, <http://www.theage.com.au/environment/states-send-in-their-rescue-teams-20110113-19pub.html> (accessed October 2012)
10. OECD (2012), 'Development: Aid to Developing Countries Falls Because of Global Recession', 4 April, <http://www.oecd.org/newsroom/developmentaidtodeveloping-countriesfallsbecauseofglobalrecession.htm> (accessed October 2012)
11. Lancaster, C. (2006), *Foreign Aid: Diplomacy, Development, Domestic Politics* (Chicago: University of Chicago Press)
12. Lancaster, C. (2006), *Foreign Aid: Diplomacy, Development, Domestic Politics* (Chicago: University of Chicago Press)
13. Reisen, H. (2009), 'The Multilateral Donor Non-System: Towards Accountability and Efficient Role Assignment'. Discussion Paper (Paris: OECD)
14. Personal communication (2012)
15. Taylor, G., Stoddard, A., Harmer, A., et al (2012), *The State of the Humanitarian System* (London: ALNAP, ODI)
16. Riddell, R. (2008), *Does Foreign Aid Really Work?* (Oxford: OUP)
17. Personal communication (2012)
18. Ellerman, D. (2002), 'Should Development Agencies Have Official Views?' *Development in Practice* 12(3&4): 285–97
19. Calderisi, R. (2012), 'Turning on the Lights: A Short History of Foreign Aid in Africa' (Montreal: Montreal Institute for Genocide and Human Rights Studies), p. 2
20. Barnard, G. (2003), 'Knowledge Sharing in Development Agencies: Knowledge Fortress or Knowledge Pool?' *Information Development* 19(4): 280–8

21. Smillie, I. (2000), *Mastering the Machine Revisited: Poverty, Aid and Technology* (London: ITDG)

22. Porter, D., Allen, B., and Thompson, G. (1991), *Development in Practice: Paved with Good Intentions* (London: Routledge), p. 213

23. Riddell, R. (2008), *Does Foreign Aid Really Work?* (Oxford: OUP)

24. Morgenthau, H. (1962), 'A Political Theory of Foreign Aid'. *American Political Science Review* 56(2): 301–309, p. 301

25. World Bank (2011), *Global Monitoring Report 2011: Improving the Odds of Achieving the MDGs: Heterogeneity, Gaps, and Challenges* (Washington, DC: IBRD and World Bank)

26. UNESCO (2006), *Education for All, Global Monitoring Report: Literacy for Life* (Paris: UNESCO)

27. Social Watch (2006), *When Will Dignity for All Be Achieved?* <http://www.social-watch.org/sites/default/files/statistics06/en/whatbeyond2015/downloads/when_will_dignity_for_all_be_achieved.pdf> (accessed October 2012)

28. Rogerson, A., with Hewitt, A. and Waldenberg, D. (2004), *The International Aid System 2005–2010: Forces For and Against Change* (London: ODI)

29. Hulme, D. (2007), 'The Making of the Millennium Development Goals: Human Development Meets Results-Based Management in an Imperfect World'. Working Paper 16 (Manchester: BWPI), p. ii

30. UNDESA (2006), *Social Justice in an Open World: The Role of the United Nations* (New York: UNDESA), p. 10

31. Annan, K. (2006), 'Farewell Address to the UN General Assembly', 19 September, <http://www.un.org/News/Press/docs/2006/sgsm10643.doc.htm> (accessed October 2012)

32. Sen, A. (2006), 'The Man Without a Plan'. *Foreign Affairs*, March/April

33. Manning, R. (2012), Aid as a Second-Best Solution UNU-WIDER Working Paper No. 2012/24, p. 2

34. Manning, R. (2012), Aid as a Second-Best Solution UNU-WIDER Working Paper No. 2012/24, p. 3

35. Eyben, R. (2008), 'Power, Mutual Accountability and Responsibility in the Practice of International Aid: A Relational Approach'. Working Paper 305 (Brighton: IDS), p. 7

36. Cosgrave, J. (2007), 'Expanded Summary: Joint Evaluation of the International Response to the Indian Ocean Tsunami'. Tsunami Evaluation Coalition Synthesis Report

37. OECD (2011), 'Evaluation of the Paris Declaration—Phase II' (Paris: OECD)

38. Riddell, R. (2008), *Does Foreign Aid Really Work?* (Oxford: OUP)

39. Ackoff, R. (1999), 'A Lifetime of Systems Thinking', *Leverage Points* 115, <http://www.pegasuscom.com/levpoints/ackoff_a-lifetime-of-systems-thinking.html> (accessed October 2012)

Chapter 2

1. Truman, H.S. (1949), 'Inaugural Address', 20 January, <http://www.let.rug.nl/usa/presidents/harry-s-truman/inaugural-address-1949.php> (accessed October 2012)

2. Rostow, W.W. (1960), *The Stages of Economic Growth: A Non-Communist Manifesto* (Cambridge: CUP)

3. *The Economist* (2007), 'Flood, Famine and Mobile Phones: Technology Is Transforming Humanitarian Relief and Shifting the Balance of Power between Donors and Recipients', 26 July, 2007, <http://www.economist.com/node/9546242?story_id=9546242> (accessed October 2012)

4. Coyle, D. and Meier, P. (2009), 'New Technologies in Emergencies and Conflicts: The Role of Information and Social Networks'. Discussion Paper/White Paper (New York: UN Foundation/Vodafone Foundation)

5. Gratton, L. (2007), *Hot Spots: Why Some Teams, Workplaces, and Organizations Buzz with Energy—and Others Don't* (London: FT Prentice Hall)

6. Tsoukas, H. (2005), *Complex Knowledge: Studies in Organizational Epistemology* (New York: OUP)

7. Kemmis, S. and McTaggart, R. (eds) (1988), *The Action Research Planner* (Victoria: Deakin University)

8. OECD (2001), 'STI Scoreboard', <http://www.oecd.org/science/scienceandtechnologypolicy/1900544.pdf> (accessed October 2012)

9. Bacon, F. (1597), 'Religious Meditations, Of Heresies', in (1985) *The Essays* (Harmondsworth: Penguin)

10. Eliot, T.S. (1934), *The Rock*, <http://www.wisdomportal.com/Technology/TSEliot-TheRock.html> (accessed October 2012)

11. Argyris, C. and Schön, D. (1978), *Organizational Learning: A Theory of Action Perspective* (London: McGraw-Hill)

12. WanderLust (2010), 'Embracing the Chaotic',<http://morealtitude.wordpress.com/2010/07/08/embracing-the-chaotic-cynefin-and-humanitarian-response/> (accessed October 2012)

13. Senge, P. (1992), *Systems Thinking: A Language for Learning and Acting* (Farmington, MA: Innovation Associates), p. 63

14. Jantzi, T. and Ressler, E. (2012), 'Four Strategic Evaluations on the Transition from Food Aid to Food Assistance: A Synthesis', Report OE/2012/S002 Commissioned by the Office of Evaluation (Rome: WFP)

15. WFP (2006), 'An SOS Phone Text from a Disaster Zone'. Press Release, <http://www.wfp.org/stories/sos-phone-text-disaster-zone> (accessed October 2012)

16. Currion, P. (2007), 'Flood, Famine and Mobile Phones in the Economist', humanitarian.info, 28 July, <http://www.humanitarian.info/2007/07/28/flood-famine-and-mobile-phones-in-the-economist/> (accessed October 2012)

17. Egren, G. (2000), 'Donorship, Ownership and Partnership: Issues Arising from Four Sida Studies of Donor-Recipient Relations'. Studies in Evaluation 03/03 (Stockholm: Sida)

18. Ellerman, D. (2002), 'Should Development Agencies have Official Views?' *Development in Practice* 12(3&4): 285–97, p. 286

19. Scoones, I. and Wolmer, W. (2004), 'Workshop Report'. Policy Processes for Veterinary Services in Africa, Mombasa, 20–2 September, p. 9

20. Sutton, R. (1999), 'The Policy Process: An Overview'. Working Paper 118 (London: ODI), p. 29

21. Roe, E. (1991), 'Development Narratives, Or Making the Best of Blueprint Development'. *World Development* 19(4): 287–300

22. Eade, D., personal communication (2012)

23. Hancock, D. and Holt, R. (2003), *Tame, Messy and Wicked Risk Leadership* (Farnham: Ashgate), p. 50

24. Sutton, R. (1999), 'The Policy Process: An Overview'. Working Paper 118 (London: ODI), p. 11

25. Sutton, R. (1999), 'The Policy Process: An Overview'. Working Paper 118 (London: ODI), p. 11

26. Ellerman, D. (2002), 'Should Development Agencies Have Official Views?'

27. Mosse, D. (2004), 'Is Good Policy Unimplementable? Reflections on the Ethnography of Aid Policy and Practice', *Development and Change* 35(4): 639–71, p. 640

28. Leach, M. and Mearns, R. (1996), 'Environmental Change and Policy', in Leach, M. and Mearns, R. (eds) *The Lie of the Land: Challenging Received Wisdom on the African Environment* (Oxford: James Currey), pp. 1–33

29. Baker, J.L. (2008), 'Urban Poverty: A Global View'. Urban Paper 5 (Washington, DC: World Bank)

30. Sanderson, D. (2002), 'The Urbanisation of Poverty'. Working Paper (London: CARE), p. 2

31. IRIN (2007), 'In-depth: Tomorrow's Crises Today: The Humanitarian Impact of Urbanisation', 1 October, <http://www.irinnews.org/IndepthMain.aspx?InDepth-ID=63&ReportID=74568> (accessed October 2012)

32. Ramalingam, B., Scriven, K., and Foley, C. (2009), *Innovations in Humanitarian Action* (London: ODI)

33. Kahneman, D. (2011), *Thinking, Fast and Slow* (New York: Farrar, Straus and Giroux), p. 62

34. Douglas, M. (1986), *How Institutions Think* (Syracuse, NY: Syracuse University Press)

35. Autesserre, S. (2012), 'Dangerous Tales: Dominant Narratives on the Congo and Their Unintended Consequences', *African Affairs* 111(443), <http://afraf.oxfordjournals.org/content/early/2012/02/09/afraf.adr080.abstract> (accessed October 2012)

36. Stiglitz, J. (2002), *Globalization and Its Discontents* (New York: W.W. Norton), pp. xiii–iv

37. Ramalingam, B., Scriven, K., and Foley, C. (2009), *Innovations in Humanitarian Action* (London: ODI)

38. Schabbel, C. (2007), *The Value Chain of Foreign Aid: Development, Poverty Reduction, and Regional Contributions* (New York: Physica), p. 7

39. Powell, M. (2006), 'Which Knowledge? Whose Reality?' *Development in Practice* 16(6): 518–32

40. World Bank (1999), *World Development Report 1998/99: Knowledge for Development* (Washington, DC: World Bank), p. ix

41. Birchard, B. (n.d.), 'Knowledge Review', <http://xenia.media.mit.edu/~brooks/storybiz/storytelling-in-business.pdf, p.2> (accessed October 2012)

42. Easterly, W. (2006), *The White Man's Burden: Why the West's Efforts to Aid the Rest Have Done So Much Ill and So Little Good* (Oxford: OUP)

43. Gwin, C. (2003), 'Sharing Knowledge Innovations and Remaining Challenges'. OED Evaluation (Washington, DC: World Bank)

44. Parcell, C. and Collison, G. (2001), *Learning to Fly: Practical Knowledge Management from Leading and Learning Organizations* (Oxford: Capstone), p. 6

45. Riddell, R. (2008), *Does Foreign Aid Really Work?* (Oxford: OUP), p. xvii

46. Personal communication (2011)

47. Court, J., Hovland, I., and Young, J. (eds) (2005), *Bridging Research and Policy in Development: Evidence and the Change Process* (Rugby: ITDG)

48. Carlsson, J. and Wohlgemuth, L. (2000), *Learning in Development Co-operation* (Stockholm: Almqvist & Wiksell International)

49. Chambers, R. (1997), *Whose Reality Counts: Putting the First Last* (London: Intermediate Technology Publications)

50. Trench, P., Rowley, J., Diarra, M., Sano, F., and Keita, B. (2007), 'Beyond Any Drought: Root Causes of Chronic Vulnerability in the Sahel'. The Sahel Working Group (London: IIED)

51. Senge, P.M. (2008), *The Necessary Revolution: How Individuals and Organizations Are Working Together to Create a Sustainable World* (New York: Doubleday)

52. Easterby-Smith, M. and Lyles, M.A. (2003), *The Blackwell Handbook of Organizational Learning and Knowledge Management* (New York: Wiley)

53. Slim, H. (2006), 'Global Welfare: A Realistic Expectation for the International Humanitarian System?' in ALNAP, *ALNAP Review of Humanitarian Action: Evaluation Utilisation* (London: ODI)

54. This sub-section draws on and rewrites material originally published on <http://aidontheedge.info/2011/01/27/how-do-you-solve-a-problem-like-malaria/>

55. WHO (2010), *World Malaria Report 2010* (Geneva: WHO)

56. Pogue, J. (2011), 'General Anopheles', *Guernica*, 15 January, <http://www.guernicamag.com/features/pogue_1_15_11/> (accessed October 2012)

57. Attaran, A. (2000), 'Promises Once, Promises Twice: A View on the Abuja Declaration and a New Opportunity for African Malaria Control'. Issues Framework for the Roll Back Malaria for African Prosperity Meeting, Cambridge, MA, 29–30 June, p. 3

58. Pearson Commission (1969), *Partners in Development* (New York, Washington DC, and London: Pearson Commission)

59. Bynum, B. (2008), 'The Making of a Tropical Disease: A Short History of Malaria', Book Review, *The Lancet* 371(9622): 1407–8, p. 1408

60. Carter, R. and Mendis, K.N. (2002), 'Evolutionary and Historical Aspects of the Burden of Malaria'. *Clin. Microbiol. Rev.* 15(4): 564–94

61. Read, A.F., Lynch, P.A., and Thomas, M.B. (2009), 'How to Make Evolution-Proof Insecticides for Malaria Control'. *PLoS Biology* 7(4), <http://www.plosbiology.org/article/info:doi/10.1371/journal.pbio.1000058> (accessed October 2012)

62. Imperial College London (2010), 'Malarial Mosquitoes Are Evolving into New Species, Say Imperial Researchers'. News Release, 22 October, <http://www3.imperial.ac.uk/newsandeventspggrp/imperialcollege/newssummary/news_22-10-2010-10-27-22> (accessed October 2012)

63. WHO (2010), *World Malaria Report 2010* (Geneva: WHO)

64. Janssen, M.A. and Martens, W.J.M. (1997), 'Modeling Malaria as a Complex Adaptive System'. *Artificial Life* 3: 213–36, p. 220

65. UNDP (2011), *Human Development Report 2011* (New York: UNDP)

66. <http://cpi.transparency.org/cpi2011/>

67. <http://en.wikipedia.org/wiki/Transport_in_the_Democratic_Republic_of_the_Congo#Highways>

68. <http://www.nationmaster.com/country/be-belgium/tra-transportation>

69. <http://www.un.org/en/peacekeeping/missions/monusco/facts.shtml>

70. Autesserre, S. (2012), 'Dangerous Tales: Dominant Narratives on the Congo and Their Unintended Consequences'. *African Affairs* 111(443), <http://afraf.oxfordjournals.org/content/early/2012/02/09/afraf.adr080.abstract> (accessed October 2012)

71. Autesserre, S. (2012), 'Dangerous Tales: Dominant Narratives on the Congo and Their Unintended Consequences'. *African Affairs* 111(443), <http://afraf.oxfordjournals.org/content/early/2012/02/09/afraf.adr080.abstract> (accessed October 2012)

72. Autesserre, S. (2012), 'Dangerous Tales: Dominant Narratives on the Congo and Their Unintended Consequences', *African Affairs* 111(443): 10, <http://afraf.oxfordjournals.org/content/early/2012/02/09/afraf.adr080.abstract> (accessed October 2012)

73. Autesserre, S. (2012), 'Dangerous Tales: Dominant Narratives on the Congo and Their Unintended Consequences', *African Affairs* 111(443): 10, <http://afraf.oxfordjournals.org/content/early/2012/02/09/afraf.adr080.abstract> (accessed October 2012)

74. Autesserre, S. (2012), 'Dangerous Tales: Dominant Narratives on the Congo and Their Unintended Consequences', *African Affairs* 111(443): 10, <http://afraf.oxfordjournals.org/content/early/2012/02/09/afraf.adr080.abstract> (accessed October 2012)

75. Autesserre, S. (2012), 'Dangerous Tales: Dominant Narratives on the Congo and Their Unintended Consequences', *African Affairs* 111(443): 8, <http://afraf.oxfordjournals.org/content/early/2012/02/09/afraf.adr080.abstract> (accessed October 2012)

76. Autesserre, S. (2012), 'Dangerous Tales: Dominant Narratives on the Congo and Their Unintended Consequences', *African Affairs* 111(443): 8, <http://afraf.oxfordjournals.org/content/early/2012/02/09/afraf.adr080.abstract> (accessed October 2012)

77. Autesserre, S. (2012), 'Dangerous Tales: Dominant Narratives on the Congo and Their Unintended Consequences', *African Affairs* 111(443): 6

78. Autesserre, S. (2012), 'Dangerous Tales: Dominant Narratives on the Congo and Their Unintended Consequences', *African Affairs* 111(443): 7

79. Autesserre, S. (2012), 'Dangerous Tales: Dominant Narratives on the Congo and Their Unintended Consequences', *African Affairs* 111(443): 6

80. Autesserre, S. (2012), 'Dangerous Tales: Dominant Narratives on the Congo and Their Unintended Consequences', *African Affairs* 111(443): 6

81. Autesserre, S. (2012), 'Dangerous Tales: Dominant Narratives on the Congo and Their Unintended Consequences', *African Affairs* 111(443): 6

82. Autesserre, S. (2012), 'Dangerous Tales: Dominant Narratives on the Congo and Their Unintended Consequences', *African Affairs* 111(443): 7

83. Autesserre, S. (2012), 'Dangerous Tales: Dominant Narratives on the Congo and Their Unintended Consequences', *African Affairs* 111(443): 7

84. Grice, A.C. and Hodgkinson, K.C. (eds) (2002), *Global Rangelands: Progress and Prospects* (Oxford: CABI Publishing)

85. Niamir-Fuller, M. (2000), *Managing Mobility in African Rangelands* (Rugby: Practical Action)

86. Niamir-Fuller, M. (2000), *Managing Mobility in African Rangelands* (Rugby: Practical Action)

87. Scoones, I. (2007), 'Dynamic Systems and Development Challenges'. Briefing 1 (Brighton: STEPS Centre), p. 3

88. Perrier, G.K. (1990), 'The Contextual Nature of Range Management'. Paper 30C (London: ODI)

89. Perrier, G.K. (1990), 'The Contextual Nature of Range Management'. Paper 30C (London: ODI), p. 3

90. Perrier, G.K. (1990), 'The Contextual Nature of Range Management'. Paper 30C (London: ODI), p. 6

91. Perrier, G.K. (1990), 'The Contextual Nature of Range Management'. Paper 30C (London: ODI), p. 3

92. Bateson, G. (1972), *Steps to an Ecology of Mind* (Chicago: University of Chicago Press)

93. Scoones, I. (2007), 'Dynamic Systems and Development Challenges'. Briefing 1 (Brighton: STEPS Centre)

94. Scoones, I., Leach, M., Smith, A., Stagl, S., Stirling, A., and Thompson, J. (2007), 'Dynamic Systems and the Challenge of Sustainability'. Working Paper 1 (Brighton: STEPS Centre), p. 6

95. Morgan, G. (2006), *Images of Organization: The Executive Edition* (Thousand Oaks, CA: Sage), p. 90

96. Mosse, D. (2007), 'Notes on the Ethnography of Expertise and Professionals in International Development'. Paper for Ethnografeast III: Ethnography and the Public Sphere. Lisbon, 20–3 June, p. 4

97. Riddell (2008), *Does Foreign Aid Really Work?* (Oxford: OUP), p. xvi

98. Kahneman, D. (2011), *Thinking, Fast and Slow* (New York: Farrar, Straus and Giroux)

99. Powell, M. (2006), 'Which Knowledge? Whose Reality?' *Development in Practice* 16 (6): 518–32

100. Carlsson, J. and Wohlegemuth, L. (2000), *Learning in Development Co-operation* (Stockholm: Almqvist & Wiksell International), p. 9

101. <http://www.wfp.org/aid-professionals/blog/three-waves-innovation-food-assistance> (accessed March 2013)

102. <http://www.ifad.org/events/gc/31/speech/wfp.htm> (accessed March 2013)

103. Parsons, W. (2002) 'From Muddling Through to Muddling Up: Evidence Based Policy-Making and the Modernisation of British Government'. *Public Policy and Administration* 17(3): 43–60

Chapter 3

1. PIU (2005), 'Strengthening Leadership in the Public Sector'. Research Study (London: PIU)

2. Paarlberg, L. and Bielefeld, W. (2009), 'Complexity Science—An Alternative Framework for Understanding Strategic Management in Public Serving Organizations'. *International Public Management Journal* 12: 2236–60

3. Easterly, W. (2006), *The White Man's Burden: Why the West's Efforts to Aid the Rest Have Done So Much Ill and So Little Good* (Oxford: OUP)

4. Hopkins, J.W. (1989), *The Eradication of Smallpox: Organizational Learning and Innovation in International Health* (Boulder, CO: Westview Press)

5. Mintzberg, H., Ahlstrand, B., and Lampel, J. (2002), *Strategy Safari: A Guided Tour through the Wilds of Strategic Management* (London: Prentice Hall)

6. Mintzberg, H., Ahlstrand, B., and Lampel, J. (2002), *Strategy Safari: A Guided Tour through the Wilds of Strategic Management* (London: Prentice Hall), p. 57

7. Mintzberg, H., Ahlstrand, B., and Lampel, J. (2002), *Strategy Safari: A Guided Tour through the Wilds of Strategic Management* (London: Prentice Hall), p. 49

8. *The Economist* (2009), 'Robert McNamara, Systems Analyst and Defence Secretary, Died on July 6th, Aged 93', 9 July, <http://www.economist.com/node/13983224> (accessed October 2012)

9. Smalter, D.J. and Ruggles, R.L. (1966), 'Six Business Lessons from the Pentagon'. *Harvard Business Review* 44(2): 70–4

10. Natsios, A, (2010), 'The Clash of the Counter-bureaucracy and Development'. Essay (Washington, DC: CGD), p. 15

11. Powell, C., with Persico, J. (1996), *My American Journey* (New York: Ballantine Books), p. 103

12. Powell, C., with Persico, J. (1996), *My American Journey* (New York: Ballantine Books), p. 103

13. Amadae, S.M. (2003), *Rationalizing Capitalist Democracy: The Cold War Origins of Rational Choice Liberalism* (Chicago: University of Chicago Press), p. 75

14. *The Economist* (2009), 'Robert McNamara'

15. *The Economist* (2009), 'Robert McNamara'

16. *Financial Times* (2006), 'The Leadership Debate with Henry Mintzberg: Community-ship is the Answer', 23 October, <http://www.ft.com/intl/cms/s/2/c917c904-6041-11db-a716-0000779e2340.html#axzz28nGfz6mg> (accessed October 2012)

17. Kenny, C. (2011), *Getting Better: Why Global Development Is Succeeding—And How We Can Improve the World Even More* (New York, Basic Books)

18. Pritchett, L., Samji, S., and Hammer, J. (2012) It's All About MeE: Using Structured Experiential Learning ('e') to Crawl the Design Space, UNU-WIDERWorking Paper No. 2012/104 <http://www.wider.unu.edu/publications/workingpapers/2012/en_GB/wp2012-104/> p. 19

19. Foster, R. and Kaplan, S. (2001), *Creative Destruction: Why Companies That Are Built to Last Under Perform the Market, and How to Successfully Transform Them* (New York: Doubleday), p. 212

20. Kaiser, E., Godschalk, D., and Chapin, S.F. (1995), *Urban Land Use Planning* (Chicago: University of Chicago Press), p. 40

21. Micklethwait, J. and Wooldridge, A. (1996), *The Witch Doctors: Making Sense of the Management Gurus* (New York: Times), p. 343

22. Powell, C., with Persico, J. (1996), *My American Journey* (New York: Ballantine Books)

23. <http://choo.fis.utoronto.ca/fis/courses/lis2102/k0.who.case.html> (accessed October 2012)

24. Bhattacharya, S. (2008), 'The World Health Organization and Global Smallpox Eradication'. *Journal of Epidemiology and Community Health* 62(10): 909–12, p. 909

25. Bhattacharya, S. (2008), 'The World Health Organization and Global Smallpox Eradication'. *Journal of Epidemiology and Community Health* 62(10): 909–12, p. 909

26. Kenny, C. (2011), *Getting Better: Why Global Development Is Succeeding—And How We Can Improve the World Even More* (New York, Basic Books)

27. Lindblom, C. (1968), *The Policy Making Process*, (London: Prentice-Hall), p. 38

28. Lindblom, C. (1959), 'The Science of "Muddling Through"'. *Public Administration Review* 19(2): 79–88, p. 80

29. Mintzberg, H., Ahlstrand, B., and Lampel, J. (2002), *Strategy Safari* (London: Prentice-Hall), p. 177

30. Lindblom, C. (1958), 'Policy Analysis'. *American Economic Review* 48: 298–312, p. 307

31. Woodhouse, E.J. and Collingridge, D. (1993), 'Incrementalism, Intelligent Trial-and-error, and the Future of Political Decision Theory', in Redner, H. (ed.), *An Heretical Heir of the Enlightenment: Politics, Policy and Science in the Work of Charles E. Lindblom* (Boulder, CO: Westview Press)

32. Arrow, K.J. (1964), 'Review of a Strategy of Decision by Braybrooke and Lindblom'. *Political Science Quarterly* 79: 584–88, p. 588

33. Dror, Y. (1964), 'Muddling Through—Science or Inertia?' *Public Administration Review* 24(3): 153–57, p. 155

34. Forester, J. (1984), 'Bounded Rationality and the Politics of Muddling Through'. *Public Administration Review* 44(1): 23–30, p. 23

35. <http://choo.fis.utoronto.ca/fis/courses/lis2102/ko.who.case.html> (accessed March 2013)

36. <http://www2.cdc.gov/nip/isd/spoxclincian/contents/video10_transcript.htm> (accessed October 2012)

37. <http://www2.cdc.gov/nip/isd/spoxclincian/contents/printable_version.htm> (accessed October 2012)

38. Henderson, D. (1999), 'Eradication: Lessons from the Past'. *MMWR Supplements* 48 (SU01), <http://www.cdc.gov/mmwr/preview/mmwrhtml/su48a6.htm> (accessed October 2012)

39. Bhattacharya, S. (2008), 'The World Health Organization and Global Smallpox Eradication'. *Journal of Epidemiology and Community Health* 62(10): 909–12, p. 909

40. Harford, T. (2011), *Adapt: Why Success Always Starts with Failure* (London: Little, Brown)

41. Kilcullen, D. (2006), 'Counterinsurgency Redux', <http://smallwarsjournal.com/documents/kilcullen1.pdf> (accessed October 2012)

42. Harford, T. (2011), 'Lessons from War's Factory Floor'. *Financial Times*, 23 May

43. Allison, G. (1969), 'Conceptual Models and the Cuban Missile Crisis'. *American Political Science Review* 63(3): 689–718, p. 689

44. Hurst, D. (2012), *The New Ecology of Leadership: Business Mastery in a Chaotic World* (New York: Columbia University Press)

45. Brilliant, L.B. (1985), *The Management of Smallpox Eradication in India* (Ann Arbor, MI: University of Michigan Press)

46. Hopkins, J.W. (1989), *The Eradication of Smallpox: Organizational Learning & Innovation in International Health* (Boulder, CO: Westview Press), p. 74

47. Office of the UN Commissioner for Human Rights (2000), 'United Nations Millennium Declaration'. General Assembly Resolution 55/2, 8 September, <http://www2.ohchr.org/english/law/millennium.htm> (accessed October 2012)

48. Hulme, D. (2007), 'The Making of the Millennium Development Goals: Human Development Meets Results-based Management in an Imperfect World'. Working Paper 16 (Manchester: BWPI), p. 2

49. Kanbur, R. (2010), 'Some Notes on the Conceptual Foundations of the MDG Process Paper'. Paper for the CPRC Panel on the MDGs, Manchester, 8 September, p. 1

50. Poston, M., Conway, T., and Christiansen, K. (2004), *The Millennium Development Goals and the IDC: Driving and Framing the Committee's Work* (London: ODI)

51. Manning, R. (2009), 'Using Indicators to Encourage Development: Lessons from the MDGs'. Report 2009:01 (Copenhagen: DIIS), p. 15

52. Manning, R. (2009), 'Using Indicators to Encourage Development', p. 16

53. Saith, A. (2006), 'From Universal Values to Millennium Development Goals: Lost in Translation'. *Development and Change* 37(6): 1167–99, p. 1188

54. <http://www.publications.parliament.uk/pa/cm201213/cmselect/cmintdev/writev/post2015/m14.htm> (accessed February 2103)

55. <http://www.odi.org.uk/events/3103-jeffrey-sachs-post-2015-development-framework-reflections-challenges> (accessed February 2013)

56. <http://www.guardian.co.uk/global-development/2012/nov/16/mark-malloch-brown-mdgs-nuclear> (accessed February 2013)

57. <http://www.publications.parliament.uk/pa/cm201213/cmselect/cmintdev/writev/post2015/m14.htm> (accessed February 2013)

58. Manning, R. (2010), 'The Impact and Design of the MDGs: Some Reflections'. *IDS Bulletin* 41(1): 7–14

59. <http://www.publications.parliament.uk/pa/cm201213/cmselect/cmintdev/writev/post2015/m14.htm> (accessed February 2013)

60. Bourguignon, R., Bénassy-Quéré, A., Dercon, S., Estache, A., Gunning, J.W., Kanbur, R., Klasen, S., Maxwell, S., Platteau, J.P., and Spadaro, A. (2008), 'Millennium Development Goals at Midpoint: Where Do We Stand and Where Do We Need to Go?' Background Paper for the ERD, p. 31

61. Hulme (2007), 'The Making of the Millennium Development Goals' Brooks World Poverty Institute Working Paper No. 16. Available at SSRN: <http://ssrn.com/abstract=1246696> or <http://dx.doi.org/10.2139/ssrn.1246696> (accessed February 2013)

62. Manning, R. (2009), 'Using Indicators to Encourage Development: Lessons from the Millenium Development Goals' (Copenhagen: Danish Institute for International Studies), p. 7

63. Minority Rights Group International (2005), 'The Millennium Development Goals: Helping or Harming Minorities?' Presentation to UN Commission on Human Rights Sub-Commission on Promotion and Protection of Human Rights, Working Group on Minorities, New York, 30 May, p. 8

64. Pritchett, L., Woolcock, M., and Andrews, M. (2010) 'Capability Traps? The Mechanisms of Persistent Implementation Failure'. Working Paper 234 (Washington, DC: CGD)

65. Nielson, H.D. (2006), From Schooling Access to Learning Outcomes: An Unfinished Agenda An Evaluation of World Bank Support to Primary Education (Washington,

DC: Independent Evaluation Group, World Bank), <http://lnweb90.worldbank.org/oed/oeddoclib.nsf/DocUNIDViewForJavaSearch/DB332E8D5FF2968E852571-A800797D10/$file/primary_education_evaluation.pdf>, p. 6 (accessed February 2013)

66. Nielson, H.D. (2006), From Schooling Access to Learning Outcomes: An Unfinished Agenda An Evaluation of World Bank Support to Primary Education (Washington, DC: Independent Evaluation Group, World Bank), <http://lnweb90.worldbank.org/oed/oeddoclib.nsf/DocUNIDViewForJavaSearch/DB332E8D5FF2968E852571-A800797D10/$file/primary_education_evaluation.pdf>, p. x (accessed February 2013)

67. Freeman, T. and Faure, S. (2003), 'Local Solutions to Global Challenges: Towards Effective Partnership in Basic Education'. Joint Evaluation of External Support to Basic Education in Developing Countries (The Hague: Netherlands Ministry of Foreign Affairs), p. 15

68. <http://www.oecd.org/countries/burkinafaso/35148468.pdf> (accessed February 2013)

69. <http://www.oecd.org/countries/burkinafaso/35148468.pdf> (accessed February 2013)

70. UN-HABITAT, UNDP, and UCLG (n.d.), 'Urban Millennium Partnership: Localizing MDGs Meeting the challenge of MDGs in Cities', p. 2

71. Government Office for Science (2011), 'DFID Science and Engineering Assurance Review: Annex D—DFID Headquarter Interview Findings', <http://www.bis.gov.uk/assets/goscience/docs/science-review-dfid/11-1260d-dfid-science-engineering-review-headquarter-interview> (accessed October 2012)

72. Nielson, H.D. (2006), From Schooling Access to Learning Outcomes: An Unfinished Agenda An Evaluation of World Bank Support to Primary Education (Washington, DC: Independent Evaluation Group, World Bank), <http://lnweb90.worldbank.org/oed/oeddoclib.nsf/DocUNIDViewForJavaSearch/DB332E8D5FF2968E852571-A800797D10/$file/primary_education_evaluation.pdf>, p. 50 (accessed February 2103)

73. Haddad, W.D., with Demsky, T. (1995), 'Education Policy-planning Process: An Applied Framework'. Fundamentals of Educational Planning 51 (Paris: International Institute for Educational Planning, UNESCO), p. 88

74. Stone, D. (2008), 'Global Public Policy, Transnational Policy Communities, and Their Networks'. *Policy Studies Journal* 36(1): 19–38, p. 21

75. Hulme, D. (2009), 'The Millennium Development Goals (MDGs): A Short History of the World's Biggest Promise'. Working Paper 100 (Manchester: BWPI), p. 6

76. Maxwell, S. (2003), 'Heaven or Hubris: Reflections on the New "New Poverty Agenda"'. *Development Policy Review* 21(1): 5–25

77. World Bank (2004), 'The Poverty Reduction Strategy Initiative: An Independent Evaluation of the World Bank's Support through 2003' (Washington, DC: World Bank), p. viii

78. Marshall, R. and Walters, B. (2011), 'Evaluating Ten Years of "Strategizing" for Poverty Reduction: A Cross-Sectional Appraisal of the Poverty Reduction Strategy Paper (PRSP) Initiative'. Working Paper 143 (Manchester: BWPI), p. 4

79. World Bank (2004), 'The Poverty Reduction Strategy Initiative: An Independent Evaluation of the World Bank's Support through 2003' (Washington, DC: World Bank), p. vii

80. Personal communication (2011)

81. Focus on the Global South (2003) *Anti Poverty or Anti Poor? The Millennium Development Goals and the Eradication of Extreme Poverty and Hunger* (Bangkok: Focus on the Global South), p. 18

82. World Bank (2005), 'The Poverty Reduction Strategy Initiative: Findings from 10 Country Case Studies of World Bank and IMF Support' (Washington DC: World Bank), p. 5

83. World Bank (2005), 'The Poverty Reduction Strategy Initiative: Findings from 10 Country Case Studies of World Bank and IMF Support' (Washington DC: World Bank)

84. World Bank (2005), 'The Poverty Reduction Strategy Initiative: Findings from 10 Country Case Studies of World Bank and IMF Support' (Washington DC: World Bank), p. 5

85. World Bank (2005), 'The Poverty Reduction Strategy Initiative: Findings from 10 Country Case Studies of World Bank and IMF Support' (Washington DC: World Bank), p. 5

86. Booth, D. (2005), 'Missing Links in the Politics of Development: Learning from the PRSP Experiment'. Working Paper 256 (London: ODI)

87. World Bank (2004), 'The Poverty Reduction Strategy Initiative: An Independent Evaluation of the World Bank's Support through 2003' (Washington, DC: World Bank), p. 45

88. Marshall, R. and Walters, B. (2011), 'Evaluating Ten Years of "Years of Strategizing" for Poverty Reduction: A Cross-Sectional Appraisal of the Poverty Reduction Strategy Paper (PRSP) Initiative'. Working Paper 143 (Manchester: BWPI)

89. Cunningham, G. (1974), *The Management of Aid Agencies: Donor Structures and Procedures for the Administration of Aid to Developing Countries* (London: Croom Helm), p. 18

90. Barr, J. and Barnett, C. (2006), 'Synthesis of 2005/2006 Evaluations'. DFID Country Programme Evaluations (London: DFID), p. 13

91. Batkin, A., Chapman, N., Toonen, J., Sultan, M., and Visser, M. (2006), 'Country Study: Bangladesh 2000–2005'. Evaluation of DFID Country Programmes (London: DFID), p. xi

92. Barr, J. and Barnett, C. (2006), 'Synthesis of 2005/2006 Evaluations'. DFID Country Programme Evaluations (London: DFID), p. 12

93. Barr, J. and Barnett, C. (2006), 'Synthesis of 2005/2006 Evaluations'. DFID Country Programme Evaluations (London: DFID), p. 12

94. Barr, J. and Barnett, C. (2006), 'Synthesis of 2005/2006 Evaluations'. DFID Country Programme Evaluations (London: DFID), p. 13

95. Barr, J. and Barnett, C. (2006), 'Synthesis of 2005/2006 Evaluations'. DFID Country Programme Evaluations (London: DFID), p. 13

96. OECD (2006), 'United Kingdom'. Development Assistance Committee Peer Review (Paris: OECD), p. 17

97. Barr, J. and Barnett, C. (2006), 'Synthesis of 2005/2006 Evaluations', p. 15

98. Wuyts, M., Dolyny, H., and O'Laughlin, B. (2007), 'Assumptions and Partnerships in the Making of a Country Strategy: An Evaluation of the Swedish-Mozambican Experience Institute of Social Studies'. Sida Evaluation Report 01/07 (Stockholm: Sida), p. 18

99. Wuyts, M., Dolyny, H., and O'Laughlin, B. (2007), 'Assumptions and Partnerships in the Making of a Country Strategy: An Evaluation of the Swedish-Mozambican Experience Institute of Social Studies'. Sida Evaluation Report 01/07 (Stockholm: Sida), p. 18

100. Wuyts, M., Dolyny, H., and O'Laughlin, B. (2007), 'Assumptions and Partnerships in the Making of a Country Strategy: An Evaluation of the Swedish-Mozambican Experience Institute of Social Studies'. Sida Evaluation Report 01/07 (Stockholm: Sida), p. 21

101. Wuyts, M., Dolyny, H., and O'Laughlin, B. (2007), 'Assumptions and Partnerships in the Making of a Country Strategy: An Evaluation of the Swedish-Mozambican Experience Institute of Social Studies'. Sida Evaluation Report 01/07 (Stockholm: Sida), p. 21

102. Wuyts, M., Dolyny, H., and O'Laughlin, B. (2007), 'Assumptions and Partnerships in the Making of a Country Strategy: An Evaluation of the Swedish-Mozambican Experience Institute of Social Studies'. Sida Evaluation Report 01/07 (Stockholm: Sida), p. 45

103. Wuyts, M., Dolyny, H., and O'Laughlin, B. (2007), 'Assumptions and Partnerships in the Making of a Country Strategy: An Evaluation of the Swedish-Mozambican Experience Institute of Social Studies'. Sida Evaluation Report 01/07 (Stockholm: Sida), p. 45

104. Wuyts, M., Dolyny, H., and O'Laughlin, B. (2007), 'Assumptions and Partnerships in the Making of a Country Strategy: An Evaluation of the Swedish-Mozambican Experience Institute of Social Studies'. Sida Evaluation Report 01/07 (Stockholm: Sida), p. 45

105. Wuyts, M., Dolyny, H., and O'Laughlin, B. (2007), 'Assumptions and Partnerships in the Making of a Country Strategy: An Evaluation of the Swedish-Mozambican Experience Institute of Social Studies'. Sida Evaluation Report 01/07 (Stockholm: Sida), p. 45

106. Wuyts, M., Dolyny, H., and O'Laughlin, B. (2007), 'Assumptions and Partnerships in the Making of a Country Strategy: An Evaluation of the Swedish-Mozambican Experience Institute of Social Studies'. Sida Evaluation Report 01/07 (Stockholm: Sida), p. 62

107. Egerö, S., Schill, G., and Vadnjal, D. (2002), 'Country Plans: The Missing Middle of Sida's Country Strategy Process'. Sida Evaluation 02/37 (Stockholm: Sida), p. 1

108. IADB (2009), 'Evaluation Findings Regarding IDB-8 Guidance and Implications for Future Capital Increase Agreements' (Washington, DC: Office of Evaluation and Oversight, Inter-American Development Bank), p. 15

109. IADB (2003), 'Overview of OVE's Work on Strategy Evaluation' (Washington, DC: Office of Evaluation and Oversight, Inter-American Development Bank)

110. IADB (2003), 'Overview of OVE's Work on Strategy Evaluation' (Washington, DC: Office of Evaluation and Oversight, Inter-American Development Bank)

111. Olin, A., Florin, L., and Bengtsson, B. (2008), 'Study of the International Organization for Migration and its Humanitarian Assistance'. Sida Evaluation 2008:40 (Stockholm: Sida), p. 57

112. IADB (2009), 'Evaluation Findings Regarding IDB-8' (Washington, DC: IADB), various pages

113. Olin, A., Florin, L., and Bengtsson, B. (2008), 'Study of the International Organization for Migration and its Humanitarian Assistance'. Sida Evaluation 2008:40 (Stockholm: Sida), p. 17

114. Olin, A., Florin, L., and Bengtsson, B. (2008), 'Study of the International Organization for Migration and its Humanitarian Assistance'. Sida Evaluation 2008:40 (Stockholm: Sida), p. 57

115. Olin, A., Florin, L., and Bengtsson, B. (2008), 'Study of the International Organization for Migration and its Humanitarian Assistance'. Sida Evaluation 2008:40 (Stockholm: Sida), p. 17

116. GFATM (2009), 'The Five-year Evaluation of the Global Fund to Fight AIDS, Tuberculosis, and Malaria'. Synthesis of Study Areas 1, 2 and 3 (Geneva: GFATM), p. 54

117. GFATM (2009), 'The Five-year Evaluation of the Global Fund to Fight AIDS, Tuberculosis, and Malaria'. Synthesis of Study Areas 1, 2 and 3 (Geneva: GFATM), p. 54

118. GFATM (2009), 'The Five-year Evaluation of the Global Fund to Fight AIDS, Tuberculosis, and Malaria'. Synthesis of Study Areas 1, 2 and 3 (Geneva: GFATM), p. 55

119. GFATM (2009), 'The Five-year Evaluation of the Global Fund to Fight AIDS, Tuberculosis, and Malaria'. Synthesis of Study Areas 1, 2 and 3 (Geneva: GFATM), p. 54

120. SDC (2009), 'Evaluation of SDC's Performance in Mainstreaming Gender Equality'. Evaluation 2009/1 (Bern: SDC), p. 32

121. SDC (2004), 'SDC'S Human Rights and Rule of Law Guidance Documents: Influence, Effectiveness and Relevance within SDC'. Evaluation 2004/1 (Bern: SDC), p. 4

122. UNDP (2006), 'Evaluation of UNDP's Role and Contributions in the HIV/AIDS Response in Southern Africa and Ethiopia' (New York: Evaluation Office, UNDP), p. 14

123. UNDP (2006), 'Evaluation of UNDP's Role and Contributions in the HIV/AIDS Response in Southern Africa and Ethiopia' (New York: Evaluation Office, UNDP), p. 14

124. UNDP (2006), 'Evaluation of UNDP's Role and Contributions in the HIV/AIDS Response in Southern Africa and Ethiopia' (New York: Evaluation Office, UNDP), p. 39

125. UNDP (2006), 'Evaluation of UNDP's Role and Contributions in the HIV/AIDS Response in Southern Africa and Ethiopia' (New York: Evaluation Office, UNDP), p. 47

126. Sanchez de Ocaña, M. (2011), 'A Review of Oxfam Joint Country Analysis and Strategy Documents'. *JCAS Review*, 22 December, p. 3

127. Narayan, D., Pritchett, L., and Kapoor, S. (2009), *Moving Out of Poverty: Success from the Bottom-Up* (Washington, DC: Palgrave Macmillan and World Bank)

128. Sen, A. (2006), 'The Man Without a Plan'. *Foreign Affairs*, March/April, <http://www.foreignaffairs.com/articles/61525/amartya-sen/the-man-without-a-plan> (accessed October 2012)

Chapter 4

1. Ohno, I. and Niiya, Y. (2004), 'Good Donorship and the Choice of Aid Modalities—Matching Aid with Country Needs and Ownership'. Tokyo, December, p. 3
2. Mamman, M. and Rees, C.J. (2007), Towards the Understanding of Development Policy Failures through the Eyes of Management and Organisational Theories'. Working Paper 18 (Manchester: IDPM), p. 13
3. Mamman, M. and Rees, C.J. (2007), 'Towards the Understanding of Development Policy Failures through the Eyes of Management and Organisational Theories'. Working Paper 18 (Manchester: IDPM), p. 5
4. Eyben, R. (2010), 'Hiding Relations: The Irony of "Effective Aid"'. *European Journal of Development Research* 22(3): 382–97, p. 3
5. Gow, D. (1991), 'Collaboration in Development Consulting: Stooges, Hired Guns or Musketeers?' *Human Organisation* 50(1): 1–15, p. 1
6. Maxwell, S. (2001), 'Organisational Issues in Food Security Planning', in Maxwell, S. and Devereux, S. (eds) *Food Security in Sub-Saharan Africa* (London: ITDG Publishing)
7. Doyle, A.C. (1892), 'Silver Blaze', in *The Memoirs of Sherlock Holmes* (London: George Newnes Ltd)
8. Mamman, M. and Rees, C.J. (2007), 'Towards the Understanding of Development Policy Failures through the Eyes of Management and Organisational Theories'. Working Paper 18 (Manchester: IDPM)
9. Personal communication (2009)
10. Gow, D. (1991), 'Collaboration in Development Consulting: Stooges, Hired Guns or Musketeers?' *Human Organisation* 50(1): 1–15, p. 1
11. Mamman, M. and Rees, C.J. (2007), 'Towards the Understanding of Development Policy Failures through the Eyes of Management and Organisational Theories'. Working Paper 18 (Manchester: IDPM), p. 12
12. Burnes (2009), *Managing Change*, (London: Prentice Hall), p. 11
13. King, K. and McGrath, S. (2004), *Knowledge For Development? Comparing British, Japanese, Swedish and World Bank Aid* (London and New York: Zed Books; Cape Town: HSRC Press)
14. Vernon, P. (2009), 'Overseas Development Aid: Is It Working?', 9 November, <http://www.opendemocracy.net/phil-vernon/overseas-development-aid-is-it-working> (accessed October 2012)
15. Hammersley, M. (2009), personal communication
16. In Koch, P. and Hauknes, J. (2005), 'Innovation in the Public Sector'. Public Report D20 (Oslo: NIFU STEP), p. 30
17. Clarke, P. and Ramalingam, B. (2008), 'Organisational Change in the Humanitarian Sector', in *ALNAP Review of Humanitarian Action* (London: ALNAP), p. 33
18. Clarke, P. and Ramalingam, B. (2008), 'Organisational Change in the Humanitarian Sector', in *ALNAP Review of Humanitarian Action* (London: ALNAP), p. 33
19. Burns, T. and Stalker, G.M. (1961), *The Management of Innovation* (London: Tavistock)

20. Boisot, M. and Cohen, J. (2000), 'Shall I Compare Thee to an Organization?' *Emergence* 2(4): 113–35, p. 116

21. Morgan, G. (1986), *Images of Organization* (Thousand Oaks, CA: SAGE), p. 31

22. Morgan, G. (1986), *Images of Organization* (Thousand Oaks, CA: SAGE)

23. Morgan, G. (1986), *Images of Organization* (Thousand Oaks, CA: SAGE)

24. Begun, J., Zimmerman, B., and Dooley, K. (2003), 'Health Care Organizations as Complex Adaptive Systems', in Mick, S.S. and Wyttenbach, M.E. (eds), *Advances in Health Care Organization Theory* (San Francisco, CA: Jossey-Bass), p. 253

25. Mosse, D. (2003), 'The Making and Marketing of Participatory Development', in Quarles van Uffard, P. and Giri, A. (eds), *A Moral Critique of Development: In Search of Global Responsibilities* (London and New York: Routledge), pp. 43–75

26. Dichter, T.W. (2003), *Despite Good Intentions: Why Development Assistance to the Third World Has Failed* (Boston: University of Massachusetts Press), p. 6

27. Mosse, D. (2004), 'Is Good Policy Unimplementable? Reflections on the Ethnography of Aid Policy and Practice'. *Development and Change* 35(4): 639–71, p. 671

28. de Renzio (2005), 'Incentives for Harmonisation', ODI Working paper 248 (London: ODI), p. 7

29. Morgan, G. (1986), *Images of Organization* (Thousand Oaks, CA: Sage)

30. Mosse, D. (2004), 'Is Good Policy Unimplementable? Reflections on the Ethnography of Aid Policy and Practice'. *Development and Change* 35(4): 639–71, p. 5

31. Ford, H. and Crowther, S. (1922), *My Life and Work* (New York: Garden City Publishing Company), p. 52

32. Ellerman, D. (2002), 'Should Development Agencies Have Official Views?' *Development in Practice* 12(3&4): 285–97, p. 286

33. Chambers, R. (1997), *Whose Reality Counts? Putting the Last First* (London: Intermediate Technology Publications), p. 67

34. Watts, D.J. (2003), *Six Degrees: The Science of a Connected Age* (New York: Norton)

35. Pascale, R.T., Millemann, M., and Gioja, L. (2000), *Surfing the Edge of Chaos: The Laws of Nature and the New Laws of Business* (New York: Three Rivers), p. 13

36. UNDP (2006), 'Evaluation of UNDP's Role and Contributions in the HIV/AIDS Response in Southern Africa and Ethiopia' (New York: Evaluation Office, UNDP), p. 51

37. Buchanan-Smith, M. with Scriven, K. (2011), 'Leadership in Action: Leading Effectively in Humanitarian Operations' (London: ALNAP, ODI)

38. In Riddell, R. (2008), *Does Foreign Aid Really Work?* (Oxford: OUP), p. 209

39. Ternstrom, B., Yamato, M., Myint, S., and Khin Maung Lwin, U. (2008) 'Evaluation of CARE Myanmar's Cyclone Nargis Response' (Stockholm: Ternstrom Consulting AB), p. 31

40. Ternstrom, B., Yamato, M., Myint, S., and Khin Maung Lwin, U. (2008) 'Evaluation of CARE Myanmar's Cyclone Nargis Response' (Stockholm: Ternstrom Consulting AB), p. 23

41. Ternstrom, B., Yamato, M., Myint, S., and Khin Maung Lwin, U. (2008) 'Evaluation of CARE Myanmar's Cyclone Nargis Response' (Stockholm: Ternstrom Consulting AB), p. 32

42. Ternstrom, B., Yamato, M., Myint, S., and Khin Maung Lwin, U. (2008) 'Evaluation of CARE Myanmar's Cyclone Nargis Response' (Stockholm: Ternstrom Consulting AB), p. 32

43. Buchanan-Smith, M. (2011), 'Leadership in action. Where next for effective leadership in humanitarian operations?' (London: ALNAP)

44. Eyben (2010), 'Hiding Relations: The Irony of 'Effective Aid'' *European Journal of Development Research* 22, 382–97

45. Serrat (2009), 'Overcoming Roadblocks to Learning'. International Publication 4-1-2009 (Cornell, NY: ILR School, Cornell University), p. 7

46. ICVA (2009) 'Changing the Humanitarian Community', Conference Background Paper, <http://www.icva.ch/doc00003353.doc> (accessed October 2012)

47. Ramalingam, B. and Barnett, M. (2010), 'The Humanitarian's Dilemma: Collective Action or Inaction in International Relief?' Background Note (London: ODI), p. 4

48. Binder, A. and Witte, J.M. (2007), 'Business Engagement in Humanitarian Relief'. HPG Background Paper (London: ODI)

49. Dowden, R. (2009), *Africa: Altered States, Ordinary Miracles* (New York: Public Affairs)

50. Personal communication (2011)

51. World Bank (2005), 'World Bank Support for Capacity Building in Africa' (Washington, DC: World Bank), p. 7

52. <http://www.odi.org.uk/sites/odi.org.uk/files/odi-assets/publications-opinion-files/5840.pdf> (accessed February 2013)

53. Mansuri, G. and Rao, V. (2011), 'Localizing Development: Does Participation Work?' Policy Research Report (Washington, DC: World Bank), p. 256

54. Cornwall, A. (2009), 'Changing Ideals in a Donor Organisation: "Participation" in Sida'. Working Paper 317 (Brighton: IDS), p. 28

55. Cavalcanti, J.G. (2007), 'Development versus Enjoyment of Life: A Post-Development Critique of the Developmentalist Worldview'. *Development in Practice* 17(1): 85–92

56. Cavalcanti (2007), 'Development versus Enjoyment of Life: A Post-Development Critique of the Developmentalist Worldview'. *Development in Practice* 17(1): 85–92, p. 85

57. Cavalcanti (2007), 'Development versus Enjoyment of Life: A Post-Development Critique of the Developmentalist Worldview'. *Development in Practice* 17(1): 85–92, p. 92

58. Mansuri and Rao (2011), 'Localizing Development: Does Participation Work?' Policy Research Report (Washington, DC: World Bank), p. 284

59. Kenny, C. (2012), 'Why Don't They Want What We Know They Need?' CGD Blog, 16 May, <http://blogs.cgdev.org/globaldevelopment/2012/05/why-dont-they-want-what-we-know-they-need.php> (accessed October 2012)

60. Pascale, R.T., Millemann, M., and Gioja, L. (2000), *Surfing The Edge of Chaos: The Laws of Nature and the New Laws of Business* (New York: Three Rivers), p. 13

61. Gibson, C.C., Anderson, K., Ostrom, E., and Shivakumar, S. (2005), *The Samaritan's Dilemma: The Political Economy of Development Aid* (Oxford: OUP), p. 73

62. Desai, M. (2003), 'Speech in the House of Lords'. House of Lords Hansard Column 459, 12 June

63. Desai, M. (2003) speaking at the Overseas Development Institute, London, 18 June, <http://www.odi.org.uk/RAPID/Meetings/Presentation_17/_Desai.html> (accessed October 2012)

64. Acemoglu, D. and Robinson, J. (2012), *Why Nations Fail: The Origins of Power, Prosperity, and Poverty* (New York: Crown Business), pp. 451–52

65. Haines, G. (2007), 'Matrix Structures that Work!', <http://www.bpisurveys.com.au/Articles/Article%2040/Article%2040%20-%20matrix%20structures%20that%20work.pdf> (accessed October 2012)

66. de Renzio, P., with Booth, A., Rogerson, A., and Curran, Z. (2005), 'Incentives for Harmonisation and Alignment in Aid Agencies'. Working Paper 248 (London: ODI)

67. de Renzio, P., with Booth, A., Rogerson, A., and Curran, Z. (2005), 'Incentives for Harmonisation and Alignment in Aid Agencies'. Working Paper 248 (London: ODI)

68. Clarke, P. and Ramalingam, B. (2008), 'Organisational Change in the Humanitarian Sector', in *ALNAP Review of Humanitarian Action* (London: ALNAP)

69. de Renzio, P., with Booth, A., Rogerson, A., and Curran, Z. (2005), 'Incentives for Harmonisation and Alignment in Aid Agencies'. Working Paper 248 (London: ODI)

70. OECD DAC (2009), 'Managing Aid—Taking a Look at Donor Practices'. Seminar Report (Paris: OECD DAC), p. 2

71. Keidanren Nippon (2007), 'Recommendations on Japan's International Cooperation Policy and Expectations on the new JICA', Japan Business Federation, 15 May, <http://www.keidanren.or.jp/english/policy/2007/040.html> (accessed October 2012)

72. Riddell, R. (2008), *Does Foreign Aid Really Work?* (Oxford: OUP), p.xvi

73. Dawson, R. (2009), 'An Argument for Heterarchy: Creating More Effective Organizational Structures'. *People and Strategy* 32(1): 4–13, p. 9

74. Judge, A. (1977) 'International Organization Networks: A Complementary Perspective', in Groom, A. and Taylor, P. (eds), *International Organizations: A Conceptual Approach* (London: Frances Pinter), pp. 381–413, p. 404

75. Corkingdale, G. (2008), 'Lost in Matrix Management', Harvard Business Review Blog Network, 4 June, <http://blogs.hbr.org/corkindale/2008/06/lost_in_matrix_management.html> (accessed October 2012)

76. Corkingdale, G. (2008), 'Lost in Matrix Management', Harvard Business Review Blog Network, 4 June, <http://blogs.hbr.org/corkindale/2008/06/lost_in_matrix_management.html> (accessed October 2012)

77. Christoplos, I., Mitchell J., and Liljelund, A. (2001), 'Re-framing Risk: The Changing Context of Disaster Mitigation and Preparedness'. *Disasters* 25(3): 185–98, p. 185

78. Cape, G. (2002) 'Growth, Change and Organizational Structure: The Evolving Relationship between Form and Function', <http://www.pdfio.com/k-1038009.html#> (accessed October 2012)

79. Serrat, O. (2009), 'Overcoming Roadblocks to Learning'. International Publication 4-1-2009 (Cornell, NY: ILR School, Cornell University)

80. Personal communication (2010)

81. Woods, N. (2001), 'Who Should Govern the World Economy: The Challenges of Globalization and Governance'. *Renewal* 9(2/3): 73–82, p. 77

82. Veillette, C. (2007), 'Foreign Aid Reform: Issues for Congress and Policy Options'. CRS Report for Congress, 7 November

83. <https://www.devex.com/en/news/29184/print> (accessed March 2013)

84. Haines (2007), 'Matrix Structures that Work!', <http://www.bpisurveys.com.au/Articles/Article%2040/Article%2040%20-%20matrix%20structures%20that%20work.pdf> (accessed October 2012)
85. Gerstner, L. (2003), *Who Says Elephants Can't Dance? How I Turned Around IBM* (London: Harper Collins), p. 249
86. Douglas, M. (1986), *How Institutions Think* (Syracuse, NY: Syracuse University Press)
87. <http://www.youtube.com/watch?v=zDZFcDGpL4U> (viewed October 2012)
88. Slim, H. (2007), 'Global Welfare: A Realistic Expectation for the International Humanitarian System?', in ALNAP *Review of Humanitarian Action* (London: ALNAP, ODI)
89. Vernon (2009), 'Overseas Development Aid: Is It Working?', 9 November, <http://www.opendemocracy.net/phil-vernon/overseas-development-aid-is-it-working> (accessed October 2012)

Chapter 5

1. Hosking, G. (2008), 'The "Credit Crunch" and the Importance of Trust', October, <http://www.historyandpolicy.org/papers/policy-paper-77.html> (accessed October 2012)
2. Giddens, A. (1990), *The Consequences of Modernity* (Stanford, CA: Stanford University Press)
3. Calnan, M. and Rowe, R. (2008), *Trust Matters in Health Care* (Buckingham: Open University Press)
4. Calnan, M. and Rowe, R. (2008), *Trust Matters in Health Care* (Buckingham: Open University Press) p. 158
5. Chen, S. and Ravallion, M. (2012), 'An Update to the World Bank's Estimates of Consumption Poverty in the Developing World'. Briefing Paper (Washington, DC: Development Research Group, World Bank)
6. UNICEF and WHO (2012), 'Millennium Development Goal Drinking Water Target Met; Sanitation Target Still Lagging Far Behind'. News Release, 6 March
7. Burke, S. (2003), 'Stats on Poverty? Or the Poverty of Stats?', <http://www.gloves-off.org/ringside_reports/poverty_040603.html> (accessed October 2012)
8. Rodrik, D. (2012), 'After the Millennium Development Goals'. Project Syndicate blog, 10 September, <http://www.project-syndicate.org/commentary/after-the-millennium-development-goals-by-dani-rodrik> (accessed October 2012)
9. Reddy, S.J. and Minoiu, C. (2007), 'Has World Poverty *Really* Fallen?' *Review of Income and Wealth* 53(3), 484–502
10. UNICEF and WHO (2012), 'Millennium Development Goal Drinking Water Target Met; Sanitation Target Still Lagging Far Behind'. News Release, 6 March
11. UNICEF and WHO (2012), 'Progress on Drinking Water and Sanitation, 2012 Update' (New York and Geneva: UNICEF and WHO)

12. Skinner, J. (2012), 'Clean Drinking Water Is about People, Not Pipes'. *The Guardian* blog, 15 March, <http://www.guardian.co.uk/global-development/poverty-matters/2012/mar/15/clean-drinking-water-people-pipes> (accessed October 2012)

13. <http://www.huffingtonpost.com/ned-breslin/clean-water-millennium-development-goal_b_1343292.html?ref=tw> (accessed February 2013)

14. UNICEF and WHO (2012), 'Millennium Development Goal Drinking Water Target Met; Sanitation Target Still Lagging Far Behind'. News Release, 6 March

15. UNICEF and WHO (2012), 'Millennium Development Goal Drinking Water Target Met; Sanitation Target Still Lagging Far Behind'. News Release, 6 March

16. Mayne, J. (1999), 'Addressing Attribution Through Contribution Analysis: Using Performance Measures Sensibly'. Discussion Paper (Ottawa: Office of the Auditor General of Canada)

17. Luhmann, N. (1979), *Trust and Power* (Chichester: Wiley), p. 4

18. O'Neill, O. (2002), 'Spreading Suspicion: We May Have Our Doubts on Many Fronts, but We Cannot Get by Without Trust'. *The Focus* XII/I: 35–40, p. 1

19. O'Neill (2002), 'Spreading Suspicion: We May Have Our Doubts on Many Fronts, but We Cannot Get by Without Trust'. *The Focus* XII/I: 35–40, p. 1

20. O'Neill (2002), 'Spreading Suspicion: We May Have Our Doubts on Many Fronts, but We Cannot Get by Without Trust'. *The Focus* XII/I: 35–40, p. 1

21. O'Neil, T., Foresti, M., and Hudson, A. (2007), 'Evaluation of Citizens' Voice and Accountability: Review of the Literature and Donor Approaches' (London: DFID), p. 5

22. Dixon, J., Kouzmin, A., and Korac-Kakabadse, N. (1998), 'Managerialism—Something Old, Something Borrowed, Little New'. *International Journal of Public Sector Management* 11(2/3): 164–87, p. 169

23. Lloyd, R. (2005), *The Role of NGO Self-Regulation in Increasing Stakeholder Accountability* (London: One World Trust)

24. Radin, B. (2006), *Challenging the Performance Movement: Accountability, Complexity, and Democratic Values* (Washington, DC: Georgetown University Press)

25. Zadek, S. (2005), 'Reinventing Accountability for the 21st Century', openDemocracy blog, 12 September, <http://www.opendemocracy.net/globalization-accountability/peer_to_peer_2823.jsp> (accessed October 2012)

26. Hilhorst, D. (2002), 'Being Good at Doing Good? Quality and Accountability of Humanitarian NGOs'. *Disasters* 26(3): 193–214, p. 194

27. Riddell, R. (2008), *Does Foreign Aid Really Work?* (Oxford: OUP)

28. Evans, A. (2010), 'The Humanitarian Innovation Fund: Catalysing Improvements in Disaster Response', ODI Article, 1 December, <http://www.odi.org.uk/news/details.asp?id=389&title=humanitarian-innovation-fund> (accessed October 2012)

29. Mitchell, J. (2003), 'Accountability: The Three-lane Highway'. *Humanitarian Exchange Magazine* 24, <http://www.odihpn.org/humanitarian-exchange-magazine/issue-24/accountability-the-three-lane-highway> (accessed October 2012)

30. Ebrahim, A. and Kasturi Rangan, V. (2010), 'The Limits of Nonprofit Impact: A Contingency Framework for Measuring Social Performance'. Working Paper 10-099 (Cambridge, MA: Social Enterprise Initiative, Harvard Business School)

31. Eyben, R. (2008), 'Power, Mutual Accountability and Responsibility in the Practice of International Aid: A Relational Approach'. Working Paper 305 (Brighton: IDS), p. 37

32. Simon, R. (1994), *Levers of Control: How Managers Use Innovative Control Systems to Drive Strategic Renewal* (Boston, MA: Harvard Business School Press), p. 5

33. Cosgrave, J. (2007), 'Synthesis Report: Expanded Summary. Joint Evaluation of the International Response to the Indian Ocean Tsunami' (London: TEC), p. 29

34. Easterly, W. (2006), *The White Man's Burden: Why the West's Efforts to Aid the Rest Have Done So Much Ill and So Little Good* (Oxford: OUP), pp. 150–51

35. Ebrahim, A. (2003), 'Accountability in Practice: Mechanisms for NGOs'. *World Development* 31(5): 813–29, p. 814

36. Bourguignon, F. and Sundberg, M. (2007), 'Aid Effectiveness—Opening the Black Box'. *American Economic Review* 97(2): 316–21

37. Bourguignon, F. and Sundberg, M. (2007), 'Aid Effectiveness—Opening the Black Box'. *American Economic Review* 97(2): 316

38. Bourguignon, F. and Sundberg, M. (2007), 'Aid Effectiveness—Opening the Black Box'. *American Economic Review* 97(2): 316

39. OECD DAC (2000), 'Sweden's Development Cooperation Programme in Tanzania'. Note by the Secretariat DCD/DAC/AR(2000)2/18/ADD3, 14 September (Paris: OECD DAC), p. 11

40. Carlssen, J., Eriksson-Baaz, M., Fallenius, A.M., and Lövgren, E. (1999), 'Are Evaluations Useful? Cases from Swedish Development Co-operation'. Studies in Evaluation 99/1 (Stockholm: Department for Evaluation and Internal Audit, Sida)

41. The Listening Project (2008), 'Why Being Here Matters'. Issue Paper (Cambridge, MA: CDA Collaborative Learning Projects), p. 4

42. Jacobs, A. (2006), 'Helping People Is Difficult: Growth and Performance in Social Enterprises Working for International Relief and Development', in Nicholls, A. (ed.), *Social Entrepreneurship: New Models of Sustainable Social Change* (Oxford: OUP), pp. 247–69, p. 250

43. Bakewell, A. and Garbutt, O. (2005), *The Use and Abuse of the Logical Framework Approach* (Stockholm: Sida), p. 12

44. Ebrahim, A. (2003), *NGOs and Organizational Change: Discourse, Reporting and Learning* (Cambridge: CUP), p. 90

45. Personal communication (2011)

46. Reeler, D. (2007), 'A Three-fold Theory of Social Change and Implications for Practice, Planning, Monitoring and Evaluation' (Cape Town: CDRA), p. 5

47. ALNAP (2003), *Annual Review 2003. Humanitarian Action: Improving Monitoring To Enhance Accountability and Learning* (London: ODI), p. 107

48. O'Neil, T., Foresti, M., and Hudson, A. (2007), 'Evaluation of Citizens' Voice and Accountability: Review of the Literature and Donor Approaches' (London: DFID), p. 44

49. Flint, M., Cameron, C., Henderson, S., Jones, S., and Ticehurst, D. (2003), 'How Effective is DFID? An Independent Review of DFID's Organisational and Development Effectiveness'. EVSUM EV640 (London: DFID), pp. 2–3

50. Flint, M., Cameron, C., Henderson, S., Jones, S., and Ticehurst, D. (2003), 'How Effective is DFID? An Independent Review of DFID's Organisational and Development Effectiveness'. EVSUM EV640 (London: DFID), p. 45

51. Faust, J. (2010), 'Reliable Evidence of Impact'. *D+C Focus* (2009/01): 14–17, p. 16, <http://www.dandc.eu/en/article/development-agencies-need-more-solid-knowledge-effect-their-work> (accessed February 2013)

52. Faust, J. (2010), 'Reliable Evidence of Impact', *D+C Focus* (2009/01): 14–17, p. 16, <http://www.dandc.eu/en/article/development-agencies-need-more-solid-knowledge-effect-their-work> (accessed February 2013)

53. Carden, F. (2010), personal communication

54. Easterly, W. (2009), 'Development Experiments: Ethical? Feasible? Useful?' Aid Watchers, 16 July, <http://aidwatchers.com/2009/07/development-experiments-ethical-feasible-useful/> (accessed October 2012)

55. Toyama, K. (2012), 'Can Better Data End Global Poverty?' *The Atlantic*, 28 March, <http://www.theatlantic.com/business/archive/2012/03/can-better-data-end-global-poverty/255143/> (accessed October 2012)

56. OECD and World Bank (2006), *Emerging Good Practice In Managing For Development Results* (Paris and Washington, DC: OECD and World Bank), p. 6

57. Meier, W. (2003), 'Results-based Management, Towards a Common Understanding among Development Cooperation Agencies'. Discussion Paper for CIDA

58. Wood, B., Kabell, D., Muwanga, N, and Sagasti, F. (2008), 'Evaluation of the Implementation of the Paris Declaration, Phase 1 Synthesis Report' (Copenhagen: Kabell Konsulting ApS)

59. Scott, A. (2005), 'DFID's Assessment of Multilateral Organisational Effectiveness: An Overview of Results' (London: DFID), p. 5

60. Scott, A. (2005), 'DFID's Assessment of Multilateral Organisational Effectiveness: An Overview of Results' (London: DFID), p. 5

61. Scott, A. (2005), 'DFID's Assessment of Multilateral Organisational Effectiveness: An Overview of Results' (London: DFID), p. 14

62. Scott, A. (2005), 'DFID's Assessment of Multilateral Organisational Effectiveness: An Overview of Results' (London: DFID)

63. Hulme, D. (2007), 'The Making of the Millennium Development Goals: Human Development Meets Results-based Management in an Imperfect World'. Working Paper 16 (Manchester: BWPI)

64. Hulme, D. (2007), 'The Making of the Millennium Development Goals: Human Development Meets Results-based Management in an Imperfect World'. Working Paper 16 (Manchester: BWPI), p. 20

65. Hulme, D. (2007), 'The Making of the Millennium Development Goals: Human Development Meets Results-based Management in an Imperfect World'. Working Paper 16 (Manchester: BWPI), p. 20

66. Carlssen, J., Eriksson-Baaz, M., Fallenius, A.M., and Lövgren, E. (1999), 'Are Evaluations Useful? Cases from Swedish Development Co-operation'. Studies in Evaluation 99/1 (Stockholm: Department for Evaluation and Internal Audit, Sida), p. 41

67. Saith, S. (2006), 'From Universal Values to Millennium Development Goals: Lost in Translation'. *Development and Change* 37(6): 1167–99

68. Saith, S. (2006), 'From Universal Values to Millennium Development Goals: Lost in Translation'. *Development and Change* 37(6): 1167–99, p. 1188

69. Maxwell, S. (n.d.), 'International Targets for Poverty Reduction and Food Security', FAO Corporate Document Repository, <http://www.fao.org/docrep/004/X6728E/x6728e08.htm> (accessed October 2012)

70. Vaes, R. (2008), 'Workshop on Results-based Country Portfolio Management and Review' (Manila: Results Management Unit, Strategy and Policy Department, ADB), p. 5

71. Natsios, A. (2010), 'The Clash of the Counter-Bureaucracy and Development'. Essay (Washington, DC: CGD), p. 9

72. Hilhorst, H. (2005), 'Dead Letter or Living Document? Ten Years of the Code of Conduct for Disaster Relief'. *Disasters* 29(4): 351–69, p. 364

73. Ebrahim, A. (2003), 'Accountability in Practice: Mechanisms for NGOs'. *World Development* 31(5): 813–29

74. OECD DAC (2005), *Paris Declaration on Aid Effectiveness* (Paris: OECD), p. 1

75. OECD DAC (2012), 'Workshop on Lessons Learned from International Joint Evaluations, Paris, 6–7 February 2012' (Paris: OECD DAC)

76. Wood, B., Betts, J., Etta, F., Gayfer, J., Kabell, D., Ngwira, N., Sagasti, F., and Samaranayake, M. (2011), 'The Evaluation of the Paris Declaration Final Report' (Copenhagen: DIIS), p. xiv

77. Cosgrave, J. (2007), 'Synthesis Report: Expanded Summary. Joint Evaluation of the International Response to the Indian Ocean Tsunami' (London: TEC), p. 29

78. Edwards, M. and Hulme, D. (1995), *NGOs—Performance and Accountability: Beyond the Magic Bullet* (London: Earthscan), p. 197

79. Personal communication (2009)

80. Smillie, I. and Helmich, H. (eds) (1996), *Non-governmental Organisations and Governments: Stakeholders for Development* (Paris: OECD Development Centre), p. 19

81. Keystone and AccountAbility (2006), 'A BOND Approach to Quality in Non-Governmental Organisations: Putting Beneficiaries First', August (London: Bond), p. 8

82. Townsend, S. (2009), 'Survey Finds Weaknesses in Transparency and Accountability', Third Sector, 3 February, <http://www.thirdsector.co.uk/news/Article/877897/survey-finds-weaknesses-transparency-accountability/> (accessed October 2012)

83. Reeler, D. (2007), 'A Three-fold Theory of Social Change and Implications for Practice, Planning, Monitoring and Evaluation' (Cape Town: CDRA), p. 4

84. Crawford, S. (2007), 'The Impact of Rights-based Approaches to Development Evaluation/Learning Process Bangladesh, Malawi and Peru'. UK Interagency Group on Human Rights-based Development

85. Ritchie, B. and Haggith, M. (2004), 'The Push-Me-Pull-You of Forest Devolution in Scotland'. Workshop on Decentralization, Federal Systems in Forestry and National Forest Programs, Interlaken, 27–30 April

86. Finger, M. and Ruchat, B. (2003), 'The Transformation of International Public Organizations', in Beigbeder, Y. and Dijkzeul, D. (eds) *Rethinking International Organizations: Pathology and Promise* (New York and Oxford: Berghahn Books), p. 154

87. Eade, D. (1993), 'Editorial'. *Development in Practice* 3(3): 161–62

88. Zadek, S. (2005), 'Reinventing Accountability for the 21st Century'. OpenDemocracy, 15 September, <http://www.opendemocracy.net/node/2823/pdf> (accessed October 2012)

89. O'Neil, T., Foresti, M., and Hudson, A. (2007), 'Evaluation of Citizens' Voice and Accountability: Review of the Literature and Donor Approaches' (London: DFID), p. 2

90. O'Neil, T., Foresti, M., and Hudson, A. (2007), 'Evaluation of Citizens' Voice and Accountability: Review of the Literature and Donor Approaches' (London: DFID), p. 2

91. Ramalingam, B. (2011), 'Why the Results Agenda Doesn't Need Results, and What to Do About It', 31 January, <http://aidontheedge.info/2011/01/31/why-the-results-agenda-doesnt-need-results-and-what-to-do-about-it/> (accessed October 2012)

92. Priesmeyer, H.R. (1992), *Organizations and Chaos: Defining the Methods of Nonlinear Management* (Westport, CT: Quorum), p. 3

Chapter 6

1. <http://www.thehenryford.org/research/rubberPlantations.aspx> (accessed October 2012)

2. Bellows, A. (2006), 'The Ruins of Fordlandia'. Article 238, 3 August, <http://www.damninteresting.com/the-ruins-of-fordlandia/> (accessed October 2012)

3. Natsios, A. (2010), 'The Clash of the Counter-Bureaucracy and Development'. Essay (Washington, DC: CGD)

4. Natsios, A. (2010), 'The Clash of the Counter-Bureaucracy and Development'. Essay (Washington, DC: CGD), p. 28

5. Dichter, T. (2003), *Despite Good Intentions: Why Development Assistance to the Third World has Failed* (Amherst and Boston, MA: University of Massachusetts Press), p. 7

6. Hjertholm, P. and White, H. (2000), 'Foreign Aid in Historical Perspective: Background and Trends', in Tarp, F. (ed.) *Foreign Aid and Development: Lessons Learned and Directions for the Future* (New York: Routledge), p. 80

7. Mahoney, J. and Thelen, K. (2009), 'A Theory of Gradual Institutional Change', in Mahoney, J. and Thelen, K. (eds) *Explaining Institutional Change: Ambiguity, Agency, and Power* (Cambridge: CUP), pp. 1–10

8. Malloch-Brown, M. (2011), *The Unfinished Global Revolution: The Pursuit of a New International Politics* (New York: Penguin), p. 189

9. Hancock, D. and Holt, R. (2003), *Tame, Messy and Wicked Risk Leadership* (Farnham: Ashgate), p. 34

10. Ormerod, P. (2012), *Positive Linking: How Networks Can Revolutionise the World* (London: Faber and Faber), p. 265

11. Lo, A.W. and Mueller, M.T. (2010), 'WARNING: Physics Envy May Be Hazardous to Your Wealth!', <http://arxiv.org/pdf/1003.2688.pdf> (accessed October 2012), pp. 6–7

12. Lo, A.W. and Mueller, M.T. (2010), 'WARNING: Physics Envy May Be Hazardous to Your Wealth!', <http://arxiv.org/pdf/1003.2688.pdf> (accessed October 2012), pp. 6–7

13. Easterly, W. (2010), 'Physics Envy in Development (Even Worse than in Finance!)', 28 October, <http://aidwatchers.com/2010/10/physics-envy-in-development-even-worse-than-in-finance/> (accessed October 2012)

14. Reinert, E.S. (2007), *How Rich Countries Got Rich—and Why Poor Countries Stay Poor* (New York: Carroll & Graf), p. 35

15. Reinert, E.S. (2007), *How Rich Countries Got Rich—and Why Poor Countries Stay Poor* (New York: Carroll & Graf), p. 35

16. The STEPS Centre (n.d.), 'Dynamic Systems and Development Challenges'. STEPS Briefing 1 (Brighton: IDS), p. 1

17. Christiansen, K. (2009), 'Building Shared Understanding of Wicked Problems: Interview with Jeff Conklin'. *Rotman Magazine*, Winter, <http://www.cognexus.org/Rotman-interview_SharedUnderstanding.pdf> (accessed October 2012)

18. Crutchfield, J.P. (2009), 'The Hidden Fragility of Complex Systems—Consequences of Change, Changing Consequences' (Santa Fe, NM: SFI)

19. Eyben, R. (2010), 'The Big Push Back [and Push Forward!]', 27 September, <http://www.aidontheedge.files.wordpress.com/2010/09/meeting_report.pdf> (accessed October 2012)

20. Reinert, E.S. (2007), *How Rich Countries Got Rich—and Why Poor Countries Stay Poor* (New York: Carroll & Graf), p. 204

21. Natsios, A. (2010), 'The Clash of the Counter-Bureaucracy and Development'. Essay (Washington, DC: CGD), p. 68

22. Personal communication (2011)

23. Evans, P. (2004), 'Development as Institutional Change: The Pitfalls of Monocropping and the Potentials of Deliberation'. *Studies in Comparative International Development* 38(4): 30–52

24. Pritchett, L. and Woolcock, M. (2002), 'Solutions when the Solution is the Problem: Arraying the Disarray in Development'. Working Paper 10 (Washington, DC: CGD), p. 5

25. Pritchett, L. and Woolcock, M. (2002), 'Solutions when the Solution is the Problem: Arraying the Disarray in Development'. Working Paper 10 (Washington, DC: CGD), p. 17

26. Mosse, D. (2007), 'Ethnography and the Public Sphere'. Ethnografeast III, Lisbon, 20–3 June, p. 4

27. Frej, B. and Ramalingam, B. (2011) Foreign Policy and Complex Adaptive Systems, Santa Fe Institute Working Paper. This paragraph and argument that follows draws heavily from this paper.

28. Set up by the Smithsonian Institution, Futures Group International, and the UN University

29. <http://www.millennium-project.org/millennium/challeng.html> (accessed October 2012). The Millennium Project has also developed the largest ever collection of techniques for thinking about futures issues—some 1,300 pages of material. Warren Weaver would likely have approved, as the methods are categorized with reference to the different kinds of complexity of the problem being addressed

30. <http://www.millennium-project.org/millennium/Global_Challenges/chall-09.html> (accessed October 2012)

Chapter 7

1. Weaver, W. (1948), 'Science and Complexity'. *Scientific American* 36: 536–44

2. Johnson, S. (2001), *Emergence: The Connected Lives of Ants, Brains, Cities, and Software* (New York: Scribner), p. 46

3. O'Connor, J.J. and Robertson, E.F. (2005), 'Warren Weaver', <http://www-history. mcs.st-andrews.ac.uk/Biographies/Weaver.html> (accessed October 2012)

4. Weaver, W. (1948), 'Science and Complexity'. *Scientific American* 36: 536–44, p. 536

5. Weaver, W. (1948), 'Science and Complexity'. *Scientific American* 36: 536–44, p. 536

6. Weaver, W. (1948), 'Science and Complexity'. *Scientific American* 36: 536–44, p. 541

7. Weaver, W. (1948), 'Science and Complexity'. *Scientific American* 36: 536–44, p. 537

8. Weaver, W. (1948), 'Science and Complexity'. *Scientific American* 36: 536–44, p. 540

9. Hayek, F. (1974) 'Nobel Acceptance Speech', <http://www.nobelprize.org/nobel_ prizes/economics/laureates/1974/hayek-lecture.html> (accessed October 2012)

10. Simon, H. (1962), 'The Architecture of Complexity'. *Proceedings of the American Philosophical Society* 106(6): 46–82

11. Mirowski, P. (2002), *Machine Dreams: Economics Becomes a Cyborg Science* (Cambridge: CUP), p. 455

12. Jacobs, J. (1961), *Death and Life of Great American Cities* (Visalia, CA: Vintage), p. 50

13. Wirth, R. (2004), 'Classical Papers—Science and Complexity'. *E:CO* 6(3): 65–74

14. Crutchfield, J. and Wiesner, K. (2010), 'Simplicity and Complexity'. *Physics World*, February, p. 36

15. Gell-Mann, M. (2011), personal communication

16. Khun, T. (1959), 'The Essential Tension: Tradition and Innovation in Scientific Research'. Third University of Utah Research Conference on the Identification of Scientific Talent, Alta, 11–14 June, p. 234

17. Dorit, R.L. (2011), 'The Humpty-Dumpty Problem: Even When We Understand Their Parts, Living Things Are Hard to Put Back Together'. *American Scientist* 99(4): 293

18. Johnson, N. (2007), *Two's Company, Three Is Complexity* One World Publications

19. Dorit, R.L. (2011), 'The Humpty-Dumpty Problem: Even When We Understand Their Parts, Living Things Are Hard to Put Back Together'. *American Scientist* 99(4): 293

20. Dorit, R.L. (2011), 'The Humpty-Dumpty Problem: Even When We Understand Their Parts, Living Things Are Hard to Put Back Together'. *American Scientist* 99(4): 293

21. Homer-Dixon, T. (2011), 'Complexity Science'. *Oxford Leadership Journal* 2(1), <http://www.oxfordleadership.com/journal/vol2_issue1/homerdixon.pdf> (accessed October 2012)

22. Ramalingam, B. and Jones, H., with Reba, T. and Young, J. (2008), 'Exploring the Science of Complexity: Ideas and Implications for Development and Humanitarian Efforts'. Working Paper 285 (London: ODI), p. 11

23. Kok, K. and Easterling, W.E. (2002), 'Emergent Properties of Scale in Global Environmental Modeling—Are There Any?' *Integrated Assessment* 3(2–3): 233–46

24. Weaver, W. (1948), 'Science and Complexity'. *Scientific American* 36: 536–44, p. 540

25. Wilson, A. (2010), 'Knowledge Power: Ambition and Reach in a Reinvented University', in Munck, R. and Mohrman, K. (eds) *Reinventing the University* (Dublin: Glasnevin)

26. Wilson, A. (2011), personal communication

27. Bourgon, J. (2010), personal communication

28. Prirogine, I. (1997), 'The End of Certainty', translated on <http://www.connected. org/is/prigogine.html> (accessed October 2012)

29. Kohler, T. (2011), 'Complex Systems and Archaeology'. CCSS Working Paper 09-005 2009 (Santa Fe, NM: SFI), p. 1

30. Mitchell, M. (2006), 'Complex Systems: Network Thinking' (Santa Fe, NM: SFI), p. 1

31. IIASA (1992), *Science and Sustainability: Selected papers on IIASA's 20th Anniversary* (Laxenburg: IIASA), p. ii

32. Tomlinson, R. and Kiss, I. eds (1984), *Rethinking the Process of Operational Research and Systems Analysis: Frontiers of Operational Research and Applied Systems Analysis Volume 2* (Oxford: Pergamon Press), p. 46

33. Sornette, D. (2009), 'Dragon-Kings, Black Swans and the Prediction of Crises', *International Journal of Terraspace Science and Engineering* 2(1): 1–18, p. 1

34. Gell-Mann, M. and Lloyd, S. (2003), 'Effective Complexity' (Santa Fe, NM: SFI)

35. <http://en.wikipedia.org/wiki/Complex_adaptive_system> (accessed October 2012)

36. Newman, M.E.J. (2011), 'Complex Systems: A Survey' (Ann Arbor, ML: Department of Physics and Center for the Study of Complex Systems, University of Michigan)

37. Beinhocker, E. (2012), 'New Economics, Policy and Politics', in Dolphin, T. and Nash, D. (eds), *Complex New World: Translating New Economic Thinking into Public Policy* (London: IPPR), p. 136

38. Sornette, D. (2009), 'Dragon-Kings, Black Swans and the Prediction of Crises', *International Journal of Terraspace Science and Engineering* 2(1): 1–18, p. 1

39. Simon, H.A. (1978), 'Rational Decision-Making in Business Organizations'. Nobel Memorial Lecture, Pittsburg, PA, 8 December, <http://www.nobelprize.org/nobel_prizes/economics/laureates/1978/simon-lecture.pdf> (accessed October 2012)

40. Beinhocker, E.D. (2006), *Origin of Wealth: Evolution, Complexity, and the Radical Remaking of Economics* (Cambridge, MA: Harvard Business School), p. xii

41. Personal communication, 2012

42. Wilson, A. (2011), personal communication

43. Beinhocker, E.D. (2006), *Origin of Wealth: Evolution, Complexity, and the Radical Remaking of Economics* (Cambridge, MA: Harvard Business School), p. xii

44. Mitchell, M. (2006), 'Complex Systems: Network Thinking'. *Artificial Intelligence* 170(18): 1194–212, p. 1194

45. Ball, P. (2012), '2011 and All That: The Case for Treating Society as a Complex System'. Public Evening Talk, London, 28 May

Chapter 8

1. Simon, H.A. (1962), 'The Architecture of Complexity'. *Proceedings of the American Philosophical Society* 106(6): 467–82, p. 468

2. Crutchfield, J.P. and Machta, J. (2011), 'Introduction to Focus Issue on "Randomness, Structure, and Causality: Measures of Complexity from Theory to Applications"'. *Chaos* 21(3): 308–12

3. Teare, P. (2012), personal communication

4. Miller, J.H. and Page, S.E. (2007), *Complex Adaptive Systems* (Princeton, NJ: Princeton University Press), p. 50

5. Miller, J.H. and Page, S.E. (2007), *Complex Adaptive Systems* (Princeton, NJ: Princeton University Press), p. 50

6. Reynolds, C.W. (1987), 'Flocks, Herds, and Schools: A Distributed Behavioral Model'. *Computer Graphics* 21(4): 25–34

7. Kauffmann, S. (1995), *At Home in the Universe: The Search for the Laws of Self-Organization and Complexity* (Oxford: OUP), p. 15

8. Langton, C.G. (1990), 'Computation at the Edge of Chaos'. *Physica D* 42: 12–37

9. Kauffmann, S. (1995), *At Home in the Universe: The Search for the Laws of Self-Organization and Complexity* (Oxford: OUP), p. 15

10. Personal communication (2012)

11. Bonabeau, E. (2002), 'Predicting the Unpredictable'. *Harvard Business Review*, March, <http://www.hbr.org/2002/03/predicting-the-unpredictable/ar/4> (accessed October 2012)

12. Bonabeau, E. (2002), 'Predicting the Unpredictable'. *Harvard Business Review*, March, <http://www.hbr.org/2002/03/predicting-the-unpredictable/ar/4> (accessed October 2012)

13. Bonabeau, E. (2002), 'Predicting the Unpredictable'. *Harvard Business Review*, March, <http://www.hbr.org/2002/03/predicting-the-unpredictable/ar/4> (accessed October 2012)

14. Martinez, J. (2005), 'Spatial Dynamics of Human Populations: Some Basic Models' (San Bernadino, CA: California State University)

15. In Ramalingam, B. (2009), 'Aid on the Edge of Chaos: Exploring Complexity & Evolutionary Sciences in Foreign aid', 4 December, <http://www.aidontheedge.info/2009/12/04/lessons-in-distributed-leadership-from-the-obama-campaign/> (accessed October 2012)

16. In Ramalingam, B. (2009), 'Aid on the Edge of Chaos: Exploring Complexity & Evolutionary Sciences in Foreign aid', 4 December, <http://www.aidontheedge.info/2009/12/04/lessons-in-distributed-leadership-from-the-obama-campaign/> (accessed October 2012)

17. In Ramalingam, B. (2009), 'Aid on the Edge of Chaos: Exploring Complexity & Evolutionary Sciences in Foreign aid', 4 December, <http://www.aidontheedge.info/2009/12/04/lessons-in-distributed-leadership-from-the-obama-campaign/> (accessed October 2012)

18. Bonabeau, E. (2002), 'Predicting the Unpredictable'. *Harvard Business Review*, March, <http://www.hbr.org/2002/03/predicting-the-unpredictable/ar/4> (accessed October 2012)

19. Bonabeau, E. (2002), 'Predicting the Unpredictable'. *Harvard Business Review*, March, <http://www.hbr.org/2002/03/predicting-the-unpredictable/ar/4> (accessed October 2012)

20. Jacobs, J. (1961), *Death and Life of Great American Cities* (Visalia, CA: Vintage), p. 433

21. *The Economist* (1997), 'Planned Cities: Capital Punishments', 18 December, <http://www.economist.com/node/455959> (accessed October 2012)

22. Holland, J. (1995), *Hidden Order: How Adaptation Builds Complexity* (New York: Helix Books), p. 1

23. Batty, M. (2003), 'The Emergence of Cities: Complexity and Urban Dynamics'. Working Paper 64 (London: Centre for Advanced Spatial Analysis), p. 2

24. Batty, M. (2008), 'The Size, Scale, and Shape of Cities'. *Science* 319(769): 769–71

25. Batty, M. (2005), *Cities and Complexity: Understanding Cities with Cellular Automata, Agent-Based Models, and Fractals* (Cambridge, MA: MIT), p. 66

26. Batty, M. (2005), *Cities and Complexity: Understanding Cities with Cellular Automata, Agent-Based Models, and Fractals* (Cambridge, MA: MIT), p. 478

27. Helbing, D. and Mukerji, P. (2012), 'Crowd Disasters as Systemic Failures: Analysis of the Love Parade Disaster'. *EPJ Data Science* 1(7), <http://www.arxiv.org/abs/1206.5856> (accessed October 2012)

28. Helbing, D. and Mukerji, P. (2012), 'Crowd Disasters as Systemic Failures: Analysis of the Love Parade Disaster'. *EPJ Data Science* 1(7), <http://www.arxiv.org/abs/1206.5856> (accessed October 2012)

29. Ball, P. (2004), *Critical Mass: How One Thing Leads to Another* (New York: Farrar, Straus and Giroux), p, 182

30. Ball, P. (2004), *Critical Mass: How One Thing Leads to Another* (New York: Farrar, Straus and Giroux), p, 182

31. Liu, J., Dietz, T., Carpenter, S.R., et al (2005), 'Complexity of Coupled Human and Natural Systems'. *Science* 317: 1513–16, p. 1513

32. Ehrlich, P. (1968), *The Population Bomb* (New York: Ballantine Books)

33. Liu, J., Daily, G.C., Ehrlich, P.R., and Luck, G.W. (2003), 'Effects of Household Dynamics on Resource Consumption and Biodiversity'. *Nature* 421(30): 530–3

34. Steffen, W. (2006), 'The Arctic in an Earth System Context: From Brake to Accelerator of Change'. *Ambio* 35(4): 153–9, p. 156

35. <http://chans-net.org/> (accessed March 2013)

36. Byrne, M. (2011), 'Sustainability Scholar Jack Liu on Globalization and "Telecoupling"'. Motherboard, 3 March, <http://motherboard.vice.com/2011/3/3/sustainability-scholar-jack-liu-on-globalization-and-telecoupling> (accessed October 2012)

37. Liu, J., Dietz, T., Carpenter, S., Alberti, M., et al (2007), 'Complexity of Coupled Human and Natural Systems'. *Science* 317(5844): 1513–16

38. Liu, J., Dietz, T., Carpenter, S., Alberti, M., et al (2007), 'Complexity of Coupled Human and Natural Systems'. *Science* 317(5844): 1513–16, p. 1514

39. Liu, J., Dietz, T., Carpenter, S.R., et al (2007), 'Complexity of Coupled Human and Natural Systems'. *Science* 317: 1513–16, p. 1513

40. Liu, J., Dietz, T., Carpenter, S., Alberti, M., et al (2007), 'Complexity of Coupled Human and Natural Systems'. *Science* 317(5844): 1513–16, p. 1514

41. CSIS (2011), ' "Telecoupling" Explains Why It's a Small (and Fast) World, After All'. 18 February, <http://csis.msu.edu/news/telecoupling%E2%80%9D-explains-why-it%E2%80%99s-small-and-fast-world-after-all> (accessed October 2012)

42. CSIS (2011), ' "Telecoupling" Explains Why It's a Small (and Fast) World, After All'. 18 February, <http://csis.msu.edu/news/telecoupling%E2%80%9D-explains-why-it%E2%80%99s-small-and-fast-world-after-all> (accessed October 2012)

43. Walsh, B. (2011), 'The New Science of Telecoupling Shows Just How Connected the World Is—For Better and For Worse', 23 February, <http://science.time.com/2011/02/23/the-new-science-of-telecoupling-shows-just-how-connected-the-world-is%E2%80%94for-better-and-for-worse/> (accessed October 2012)

44. Reenberg, A. and Fenger, N.A. (2011), 'Globalizing Land Use Transitions: The Soybean Acceleration'. *Danish Journal of Geography* 111(1): 85–92, p. 85

45. Walsh, B. (2011), 'The New Science of Telecoupling Shows Just How Connected the World Is—For Better and For Worse', 23 February, <http://science.time.com/2011/02/23/the-new-science-of-telecoupling-shows-just-how-connected-the-world-is%E2%80%94for-better-and-for-worse/> (accessed October 2012)

46. Arctic Council (2004), *Arctic Climate Impact Assessment*. Fourth Arctic Council Ministerial Meeting, Reykjavik, 24 November, p. 83

47. Arctic Council (2004), *Arctic Climate Impact Assessment*. Fourth Arctic Council Ministerial Meeting, Reykjavik, 24 November, p. 83

48. Dyer, G. (2010), *Climate Wars: The Fight for Survival as the World Overheats* (Oxford: Oneworld)

49. Harrison, S. (2007), 'Predicting Future Climate Change: Lessons from Palaeoclimatology' (London: Environmental Research Group, Kings College), p. 4

50. Majda, A. and Gershgorin, B. (2010), 'Quantifying Uncertainty in Climate Change Science through Empirical Information Theory'. *PNAS* 107(34): 14958

51. Johnson, N. (2009), *Simply Complexity: A Clear Guide to Complexity Theory* (Oxford: Oneworld)

52. Fuerth, L., in Dyer, G. (2010), *Climate Wars: The Fight for Survival as the World Overheats* (Oxford: Oneworld), pp. 21–2

53. Fuerth, L., in Dyer, G. (2010), *Climate Wars: The Fight for Survival as the World Overheats* (Oxford: Oneworld), pp. 21–2

54. Jervis, R. (1997), 'System Effects: Complexity in Political and Social Life' (Princeton, NJ: Princeton University Press), p. 125

55. IPCC (2012), 'Glossary of Terms', in Field, C.B., Barros, V., Stocker, T.F., Qin, D., et al (eds), *Managing the Risks of Extreme Events and Disasters to Advance Climate Change Adaptation*. Special Report of Working Groups I and II of the IPCC (Cambridge and New York: CUP), pp. 555–64, p. 557

56. Corell, R.W., Hassol, S.J., and Melillio, J. (2011), 'Emerging Challenges: Methane from the Arctic, Global Warming Wildcard', in UNEP (ed.), *UNEP Year Book 2008* (Geneva: UNEP)

57. Parry, M.L., Canziani, O.F., Palutikof, J.P., et al (eds), *IPCC Fourth Assessment Report: Climate Change 2007*. Working Group II: Impacts, Adaptation and Vulnerability. Contribution to the Fourth Assessment Report of the IPCC, <http://www.ipcc.ch/publications_and_data/ar4/wg2/en/ch151-2-1-2.html> (accessed October 2012)

58. Hansen, J., Sato, M., Kharechal, P., et al (2008), 'Target Atmospheric CO_2: Where Should Humanity Aim?' *The Open Atmospheric Science Journal* 2: 217–31

59. Campbell, K.M., Gulledge, J., McNeill, J.R., et al (2007), *The Age of Consequences: The Foreign Policy and National Security Implications of Global Climate Change* (Washington, DC: CSIS), p. 39

60. Rial, J.A., Pielke, R., Beniston, M., et al (2004), 'Nonlinearities, Feedbacks and Critical Thresholds within the Earth's Climate System'. *Climatic Change* 65: 11–38, p. 12

61. OECD DAC (2009), *Future Global Shocks: Improving Risk Governance* (Paris: OECD). This whole box is extracted, with some small edits, from the OECD report.

62. OECD DAC (2009), *Future Global Shocks: Improving Risk Governance* (Paris: OECD), p. 56

63. <http://www.amap.no/acia/> (accessed March 2013)

64. <http://www.amap.no/> (accessed March 2013)

65. Griffiths, P. (2009), 'Arctic to Be Ice-free in Summer in 20 Years: Scientist'. Reuters, 15 October, <http://www.reuters.com/article/GCA-GreenBusiness/idUSTRE59E18-W20091015> (accessed October 2012)

66. Hansen, J., Sato, M., Kharechal, P., et al (2008), 'Target Atmospheric CO2: Where Should Humanity Aim?' *The Open Atmospheric Science Journal* 2: 217–31

67. Price, M.V. and Waser, N.M. (1998), 'Effects of Experimental Warming on Plant Reproductive Phenology in a Subalpine Meadow'. *Ecology* 79: 1261–71

68. Yarris, L. (2006), 'Feedback Loops in Global Climate Change Point to a Very Hot 21st Century'. Berkeley Lab Research News, 22 May, <http://www.lbl.gov/Science-Articles/Archive/ESD-feedback-loops.html> (accessed October 2012)

69. Dyer, G. (2010), *Climate Wars: The Fight for Survival as the World Overheats* (Oxford: Oneworld), p. 92

70. Rial, J.A., Pielke, R., Beniston, M., et al (2004), 'Nonlinearities, Feedbacks and Critical Thresholds within the Earth's Climate System'. *Climatic Change* 65: 11–38, p. 15

71. Quiggin, J. (2007), 'Complexity, Climate Change and the Precautionary Principle'. Working Paper C07-3 (Brisbane: Risk & Sustainable Management Group, Schools of Economics and Political Science, University of Queensland)

72. Bretherton, F. et al (1988), *Earth System Science: A Closer View* (Washington, DC: NASA)

73. Beringer, J. (2010), 'Earth Systems Science'. PowerPoint presentation (Melbourne: Monash University)

74. Jones, R. (2000), 'Analysing the Risk of Climate Change Using an Irrigation Demand Model'. *Climate Research* 14: 89–100

75. Jervis, R. (1997), 'System Effects: Complexity in Political and Social Life' (Princeton, NJ: Princeton University Press), p. 125

76. Rial, J.A., Pielke, R., Beniston, M., et al (2004), 'Nonlinearities, Feedbacks and Critical Thresholds within the Earth's Climate System'. *Climatic Change* 65: 11–38, p. 15

77. Jenkins, J., Nordhaus, T., and Shellenberger, M. (2011), 'Energy Emergence: Rebound and Backfire as Emergent Phenomena. A Review of the Literature' (Oakland, CA: Breakthrough Institute), p. 25

78. Kupers, R. and Mangalagiu, D. (2010), 'Positive or Negative Economic Impact? Why?' Working Paper 1 (Brussels: ECF)

79. Cox, P.M. and Nakicenovic, N. (2004), 'Assessing and Simulating the Altered Functioning of the Earth System in the Anthropocene', in Schellnhuber, H.J., Crutzen, P.J., Clark, W.C., and Claussen, M. (eds) *Earth System Analysis for Sustainability* (Cambridge, MA: MIT Press)

80. Whittle, D. (2011), 'Ben Ramalingam on Aid and Complexity'. TheHuffingtonPost.com, Inc., 7 January, <http://www.huffingtonpost.com/dennis-whittle/ben-ramalingam-on-aid-and_b_805838.html> (accessed October 2012)

81. Dyer, G. (2010), *Climate Wars: The Fight for Survival as the World Overheats* (Oxford: Oneworld), pp. 21–2

82. García Márquez, G. (1988), *Love in the Time of Cholera* (New York: Alfred A. Knopf)

Chapter 9

1. Spence, J. (1820), *Observations, Anecdotes and Characters of Books and Men* (London: J. Murray), p. 368

2. Kornbluh, P. (1998), 'The Cuban Missile Crisis', in Chang, L. and Kornbluh, P. (eds), *A National Security Archive Documents Reader* (New York: The New Press), <http://www.gwu.edu/~nsarchiv/nsa/cuba_mis_cri/declass.htm> (accessed October 2012)

3. Chang, L. and Kornbluh, P. (eds) (1998), *The Cuban Missile Crisis 1962* (New York: The New Press)

4. <http://www.nationalcoldwarexhibition.org/explore/biography.cfm?name=LeMay,%20Curtis> (accessed October 2012)

5. <http://www.errolmorris.com/film/fow_transcript.html> (accessed October 2012)

6. <http://www.errolmorris.com/film/fow_transcript.html> (accessed October 2012)

7. <http://www.presidency.ucsb.edu/ws/?pid=9421> (accessed October 2012)

8. Allison, G. (1971), *The Essence of Decision: Explaining the Cuban Missile Crisis* (Boston: Little, Brown)

9. Rabin, M.A. (2002), 'Perspective on Psychology and Economics'. Working Paper E02–313 (Berkeley, CA: Department of Economics, University of California, Berkeley)

10. Beinhocker, E.D. (2006), *Origin of Wealth: Evolution, Complexity, and the Radical Remaking of Economics* (Cambridge, MA: Harvard Business School)

11. Weick, K. (2001), *Making Sense of the Organization* (Oxford: Blackwell), pp. 344–5

12. Friedman, M. (1953), 'The Methodology of Positive Economics' (Chicago: University of Chicago Press), p. 12

13. Simon, H.A. (1978), 'Rational Decision-Making in Business Organizations'. Nobel Memorial Lecture, Pittsburgh, PA, 8 December, p. 367

14. Simon, H.A. (1978), 'Rational Decision-Making in Business Organizations'. Nobel Memorial Lecture, Pittsburgh, PA, 8 December, p. 367

15. Allison, G. (1971), *The Essence of Decision: Explaining the Cuban Missile Crisis* (Boston: Little, Brown), p. 35

16. <http://www.errolmorris.com/film/fow_transcript.html> (accessed October 2012)

17. Cramer, C. (2002), '*Homo Economicus* Goes to War: Methodological Individualism, Rational Choice and the Political Economy of War'. *World Development* 30(11): 845–64

18. Cramer, C. (2002), '*Homo Economicus* Goes to War: Methodological Individualism, Rational Choice and the Political Economy of War'. *World Development* 30(11): 845–64, p. 857

19. Arrow, K.J. (1986), 'Rationality of Self and Others in an Economic System'. *The Journal of Business* 59(4): S385–99

20. Sen, A. (1990), 'Rational Behavior', in Eatwell, J., Milgate, M., and Newman, P. (eds) *Utility and Probability* (New York: W.W. Norton & Company), pp. 1998–2216

21. Beunza, D. and Stark, D. (2003), 'Heterarchical Search in a Wall Street Trading Room'. Economics Working Paper 735 (Barcelona: Department of Economics and Business, Universitat Pompeu Fabra)

22. Beunza, D. and Stark, D. (2003), 'Heterarchical Search in a Wall Street Trading Room'. Economics Working Paper 735 (Barcelona: Department of Economics and Business, Universitat Pompeu Fabra), p. 19

23. Lo, A. (2011), 'Presentation at IIASA Meeting on FemtoRisks', June 2012

24. Mills, M. (2010), 'Complexity Science: An Introduction (and Invitation for Actuaries)', 1 June, <http://www.scribd.com/doc/64162240/Research-Complexity-Report-v1a> (accessed October 2012)

25. Harford, T. (2012), 'Believe the Hype in Hyperinflation', 20 October, <http://timharford.com/2005/12/lunch-with-the-ft-thomas-schelling-and-the-game-of-life/> (accessed October 2012)

26. Carvalho, J. (2000), 'Using Agent Sheets to Teach Simulation to Undergraduate Students'. *J. Artificial Societies Social Simulation*, Vol. 3, <http://jasss.soc.surrey.ac.uk/3/3/forum/2.html> (accessed March 2013)

27. Schelling, T. (2006), *Micromotives and Macrobehaviour: With a New Preface and the Nobel Lecture* (New York: W.W. Norton)

28. Gilbert, N. (2002), 'Varieties of Emergence'. Ecology, Exchange, and Evolution Conference, 11–12 October

29. Brookings Institution (2008), 'Q&A with Joshua Epstein on Computational Modeling', 19 March, <http://www.brookings.edu/interviews/2008/0319_csed_epstein.aspx> (accessed October 2012)

30. Epstein, J.M. and Axtell, R. (1996), *Growing Artificial Societies: Social Science from the Bottom up* (Washington, DC: Brookings Institution)

31. Bigbee, A., Cioffi-Revilla, C., and Luke, S. (2007), 'Replication of Sugarscape Using MASON'. *Springer Series on Agent Based Social Systems* 3: 183–90

32. ISCID (2005), 'Encyclopedia of Science and Philosophy', <http://www.iscid.org/about.php> (accessed October 2012)

33. This list is drawn from Macy, M.W. and Willer, R. (2002), 'From Factors to Actors: Computational Sociology and Agent-based Modeling'. *Annual Review of Sociology* 28: 143–66 and Gell-Mann, M. (1994), *The Quark and the Jaguar: Adventures in the Simple and the Complex* (London: St Martin's Griffin)

34. Simon, H.A. (1956), 'Rational Choice and the Structure of the Environment'. *Psychological Review* 63(2): 129–38

35. Klein, G.A. (1998), *Sources of Power: How People Make Decisions* (Cambridge, MA: MIT), p. 114

36. National Institute of General Medical Sciences (2011), 'Modeling Infectious Diseases Fact Sheet: Using Computers to Prepare for Disease Outbreaks', <http://www.nigms.nih.gov/Research/FeaturedPrograms/MIDAS/Background/Factsheet.htm> (accessed October 2012)

37. *The Economist* (2010), 'Economics Focus: Agents of Change', 22 July, <http://www.economist.com/node/16636121> (accessed October 2012)

38. *The Economist* (2010), 'Economics Focus: Agents of Change', 22 July, <http://www.economist.com/node/16636121> (accessed October 2012)

39. Brown, M. and Darley, V. (1995), 'The Future of Trading: Biology-Based Market Modeling at Nasdaq' (Santa Fe: SFI), p. 7

40. Brown, M. and Darley, V. (1995), 'The Future of Trading: Biology-Based Market Modeling at Nasdaq' (Santa Fe: SFI), p. 7

41. In Darley, V., and Outkin, A.V. (2007), *A NASDAQ Market Simulation: Insights on a Major Market from the Science of Complex Adaptive Systems* (Hackensack, NJ: World Scientific)

42. Bonabeau, E. (2002), 'Predicting the Unpredictable'. *Harvard Business Review*, March, <http://hbr.org/2002/03/predicting-the-unpredictable/ar/4> (accessed October 2012)

43. Simon, H.A. (1956), 'Rational Choice and the Structure of the Environment'. *Psychological Review* 63: 129–38

44. Wright, S. (1932), 'The Roles of Mutation, Inbreeding, Crossbreeding, and Selection in Evolution'. *Proceedings of the Sixth International Congress on Genetics*: 355–66

45. Mills, M. (2010), 'Complexity Science: An Introduction (and Invitation for Actuaries)', 1 June, <http://www.scribd.com/doc/64162240/Research-Complexity-Report-v1a> (accessed October 2012)

46. Harford, T. (2011), *Adapt: Why Success Always Starts with Failure* (London: Little, Brown)

47. Ostrom, E. (2007), 'Sustainable Social-ecological Systems: An Impossibility?' Annual Meeting of the American Association for the Advancement of Science, 'Science and Technology for Sustainable Well-Being', San Francisco, CA: 15–19 February

48. Kauffman, S. (1995), *At Home in the Universe: The Search for Laws of Self-Organization and Complexity* (Oxford: OUP), p. 208

49. Dawkins, R. (1996), *Climbing Mount Improbable* (New York: W. W. Norton)

50. Gould, S.J. (1989), *Wonderful Life: The Burgess Shale and the Nature of History* (New York: W. W. Norton Company)

51. Kauffman, S. (1995), *At Home in the Universe: The Search for Laws of Self-Organization and Complexity* (Oxford: OUP), p. 26

52. Kauffman, S. (1995), *At Home in the Universe: The Search for Laws of Self-Organization and Complexity* (Oxford: OUP), p. 247

53. Jervis, R. (1997), *System Effects: Complexity in Political and Social Life* (Princeton, NJ: Princeton University Press)

54. Wadhawan, V. (2009), 'Complexity Explained: Evolution of Chemical Complexity', 29 October, <http://nirmukta.com/2009/10/29/complexity-explained-8-evolution-of-chemical-complexity/> (accessed October 2012)

55. <http://boinc.bakerlab.org/rah_about.php> (accessed October 2012)

56. Yong, E. (2011), 'Computer Gamers Solve Problem in AIDS Research that Puzzled Scientists for Years', 18 September, <http://blogs.discovermagazine.com/notrocketscience/2011/09/18/computer-gamers-solve-problem-in-aids-research-that-puzzled-scientists-for-years/> (accessed October 2012)

57. Khatib, F., Cooper, S., Tyka, M.D., et al (2011), 'Algorithm Discovery by Protein Folding Game Players'. *PNAS* 22(108): 18949–53

58. <http://boinc.bakerlab.org/rah_about.php> (accessed October 2012)

59. Nelson, R.R. and Winter, S.G. (1982), *An Evolutionary Theory of Economic Change* (Cambridge, MA: Belknap of Harvard University Press)

60. Lewin Arie, Y., Long, C.P., and Carroll, T.N. (1999), 'The Coevolution of New Organizational Forms'. *Organization Science* 10(5): 535–50

61. Laver, E. and Sergenti, E. (2011), *Party Competition: An Agent-Based Model* (Princeton, NJ: Princeton University Press)

62. Kollman, K., Miller, J.H., and Page, S.E. (1998), 'Political Parties and Electoral Landscapes'. *British Journal of Political Science* 28(1): 139–58

63. Laver, E. and Sergenti, E. (2011), *Party Competition: An Agent-Based Model* (Princeton, NJ: Princeton University Press)

64. Kollman, K., Miller, J.H., and Page, S.E. (1998), 'Political Parties and Electoral Landscapes'. *British Journal of Political Science* 28(1): 139–58

65. Coleman, P.T. (2011), *The Five Percent: Finding Solutions to Seemingly Impossible Conflicts* (New York: Public Affairs)

66. Kauffman, S. (1995), *At Home in the Universe: The Search for Laws of Self-Organization and Complexity* (Oxford: OUP), p. 27

67. Kauffman, S. (1995), *At Home in the Universe: The Search for Laws of Self-Organization and Complexity* (Oxford: OUP), p. 27

68. Marion, R. (1999), *The Edge of Organization: Chaos and Complexity Theories of Formal Social Systems* (Thousand Oaks, CA: Sage Publications)

69. Miller, J.H. and Page, S.E. (2007), *Complex Adaptive Systems: An Introduction to Computational Models of Social Life* (Princeton, NJ: Princeton University Press), p. 140

70. Ostrom, E. (2007), 'Sustainable Social-ecological Systems: An Impossibility?' Annual Meeting of the American Association for the Advancement of Science, 'Science and Technology for Sustainable Well-Being', San Francisco, CA: 15–19 February, p. 4

71. Axelrod, R. (1984), *The Evolution of Cooperation* (New York: Basic Books)

72. Axelrod, R. (1984), *The Evolution of Cooperation* (New York: Basic Books), p. 87

73. Prigogine, I., in Ramalingam, B. and Jones, H., with Toussaint, R. and Young, J. (eds) (2008), 'Exploring the Science of Complexity: Ideas and Implications for Development'. Working Paper 285 (London: ODI)

74. Ostrom, E. (2007), 'Biography of Robert Axelrod'. *Political Science and Politics* 40(1): 171–4

75. Krugman, P.R. (1996), *The Self-Organizing Economy* (Cambridge, MA: Blackwell)

76. Bhavnani, R. (2006), 'Agent-based Models in the Study of Ethnic Norms and Violence', in Harrison, N.E. and Rosenau, J.N. (eds), *Complexity in World Politics: Concepts and Methods of a New Paradigm* (New York: SUNY Press)

77. Kahneman, D. and Renson, J. (2006), 'Why Hawks Win'. *Foreign Policy*, 27 December, <http://www.foreignpolicy.com/articles/2006/12/27/why_hawks_win> (accessed October 2012)

78. Barrett, F.J. (1998), 'Coda—Creativity and Improvisation in Jazz and Organizations: Implications for Organizational Learning'. *Organization Science* 9(5): 605–22

79. Kiefer, C. (2012), 'Multiparametric Interfaces for Fine-Grained Control of Digital Music'. DPhil Dissertation, University of Sussex

80. Johnson, N. (2007), 'Two's Company, Three's Complexity' (London: Oneworld), p. 63

81. Clinton, W.J. (2011), Speech given at 3rd Nobel Laureate Symposium on Global Sustainability, Stockholm, 16–19 May 2011

Chapter 10

1. Gribbins, J. (2004), *Deep Simplicity: Bringing Order to Chaos and Complexity* (London: Random House), p. 163

2. Haldane, A.G. (2009), 'Rethinking the Financial Network'. Speech delivered at the Financial Student Association, Amsterdam

3. May, R., Levin, S., and Sugihara, G. (2008), 'Complex Systems: Ecology for Bankers'. *Nature* 451(21): 893–95

4. Ghosh, P. (2011), 'Nature's Lessons for Bank Crises', BBC Science and Environment News, 19 January, <http://www.bbc.co.uk/news/science-environment-12228065> (accessed October 2012)

5. Yodzis, P. (2001), 'Must Top Predators Be Culled for the Sake of Fisheries?' *Trends in Ecology and Evolution* 16(2): 76–83

6. Darwin, C. (1859), *On the Origin of Species* (London: J. Murray), p. 490

7. May, R., Levin, S., and Sugihara, G. (2008), 'Complex Systems: Ecology for Bankers'. *Nature* 451(21): 893–95, p. 895

8. Kambhu, J., Weidman, S., and Krishnan, N. (2007), 'New Directions for Understanding Systemic Risk'. *Economic Policy Review* 13(2): 1–83, p. 3

9. Greenspan, A. (2008), 'Testimony to the House Committee of Government Oversight and Reform', 23 October, <http://clipsandcomment.com/wp-content/uploads/2008/10/greenspan-testimony-20081023.pdf> (accessed October 2012)

10. Klein, E. (2011), 'What "Inside Job" Got Wrong'. *The Washington Post*, 22 June, <http://www.washingtonpost.com/blogs/ezra-klein/post/what-inside-job-got-wrong/2011/05/19/AGgGoJgH_blog.html> (accessed October 2012)

11. Klein, E. (2011), 'What "Inside Job" Got Wrong'. *The Washington Post*, 22 June, <http://www.washingtonpost.com/blogs/ezra-klein/post/what-inside-job-got-wrong/2011/05/19/AGgGoJgH_blog.html> (accessed October 2012)

12. Ghosh, P. (2011), 'Nature's Lessons for Bank Crises', BBC Science and Environment News, 19 January, <http://www.bbc.co.uk/news/science-environment-12228065> (accessed October 2012)

13. Ghosh, P. (2011), 'Nature's Lessons for Bank Crises', BBC Science and Environment News, 19 January, <http://www.bbc.co.uk/news/science-environment-12228065> (accessed October 2012)

14. Ghosh, P. (2011), 'Nature's Lessons for Bank Crises', BBC Science and Environment News, 19 January, <http://www.bbc.co.uk/news/science-environment-12228065> (accessed October 2012)

15. Haldane, A.G. and May, R.M. (2011), 'Systemic Risk in Banking Ecosystems'. *Nature* 469: 351–55

16. Miller, J.H. and Page, S.E. (2007), *Complex Adaptive Systems: An Introduction to Computational Models of Social Life* (Princeton, NJ: Princeton University Press), p. 15

17. Haldane, A.G. and May, R.M. (2011), 'Systemic Risk in Banking Ecosystems'. *Nature* 469: 351–55, p. 355

18. Haldane, A. (2012), 'The Dog and the Frisbee'. Speech given at the Federal Reserve Bank of Kansas City's 36th Economic Policy Symposium, 'The Changing Policy Landscape', Jackson Hole, WY, 31 August, p. 24

19. Lo, A. (2011), Presentation at IIASA, June 2011

20. Borgatti, S.P., Mehra, A., Brass, D.J., and Labianca, G. (2009), 'Network Analysis in the Social Sciences'. *Science* 323(5916): 892–95

21. <http://en.wikipedia.org/wiki/Jacob_L._Moreno> (accessed October 2012)

22. Simon, H.A. (1962), 'The Architecture of Complexity'. *Proceedings of the American Philosophical Society* 106(6): 467–82, p. 469

23. Stewart, I. (2004), 'Networking Opportunity'. *Nature* 427(6975): 601–4

24. Stewart, I. (2004), 'Networking Opportunity'. *Nature* 427(6975): 601–4, p. 601

25. Newman, M. (2010), *Networks: An Introduction* (New York: OUP)

26. Mitchell, M. (2006), 'Complex Systems: Network Thinking'. *Artificial Intelligence*, 170(18): 1194–212

27. Mitchell, M. (2006), 'Complex Systems: Network Thinking'. *Artificial Intelligence*, 170(18): 1194–212, p. 4

28. Hidalgo, C.A. (2010), 'The Value in the Links: Networks and the Evolution of Organizations', in Allen, P., Maguire, S., and McKelvey, B. (eds) (2011) *Sage Handbook on Management and Complexity* (Thousand Oaks, CA: Sage Publications)

29. Buchanan, M. (2002), *Nexus: Small Worlds and the Science of Networks* (New York: Norton), p. 55

30. Watts, D.J. (2003), *Six Degrees: The Science of a Connected Age* (New York: W.W. Norton); Watts, D.J. and Strogatz, S.H. (1998), 'Collective Dynamics of "Small-world" Networks'. *Nature* 393: 440–42

31. Barabási, A.-L. and Albert, R. (1999), 'Emergence of Scaling in Random Networks'. *Science* 286: 509–12, p. 512

32. Barabási, A.-L. and Albert, R. (1999), 'Emergence of Scaling in Random Networks'. *Science* 286: 509–12, p. 512

33. Easley, D. and Kleinberg, J. (2012), *Networks, Crowds, and Markets: Reasoning About a Highly Connected World* (Cambridge: CUP)

34. Simon, H.A. (1955), 'On a Class of Skew Distribution Functions'. *Biometrika* 42(3–4): 425–40

35. Solé, R.V., Fernández, P., and Kauffman, S.A. (2003), 'Adaptive Walks in a Gene Network Model of Morphogenesis: Insights into the Cambrian Explosion'. *Int. J. Dev. Biol.* 47: 685–93

36. Watts, D.J. (2003), *Six Degrees: The Science of a Connected Age* (New York: W.W. Norton), p. 109

37. Haldane, A.G. (2009), 'Rethinking the Financial Network'. Speech delivered at the Financial Student Association, Amsterdam, pp. 12–13

38. Kauffman, S.A. (1995), *At Home in the Universe: The Search for Laws of Self-organization and Complexity* (New York: OUP)

39. McKelvey, B. (1999), 'Avoiding Complexity Catastrophe in Coevolutionary Pockets: Strategies for Rugged Landscapes'. *Organization Science* 10(3): 294–321

40. Kauffman, S.A. (1993), *The Origins of Order: Self-Organization and Selection in Evolution* (New York: OUP)

41. Much of this draws on Ramalingam, B. (2010), 'Slime Mould, Simple Rules and the Politics of Self-organisation', 15 February, <http://aidontheedge.info/2010/02/15/slime-mould-simple-rules-and-the-politics-of-self-organisation/> (accessed October 2012)

42. Yong, E. (2010), 'Slime Mould ~~Attacks~~ Simulates Tokyo Rail Network', 21 January, <http://scienceblogs.com/notrocketscience/2010/01/21/slime-mould-attacks-simulates-tokyo-rail-network/> (accessed October 2012)

43. *The Economist* (2010), 'A Life of Slime: Network-Engineering Problems Can Be Solved by Surprisingly Simple Creatures', 21 January, <http://www.economist.com/node/15328524> (accessed October 2012)

44. Crabtree, J. (2010), 'Let's All Be Friends', *Prospect Magazine*, 24 February, <http://www.prospectmagazine.co.uk/magazine/let's-all-be-friends/> (accessed October 2012)

45. Hidalgo, C.A. (2010), 'The Value in the Links: Networks and the Evolution of Organizations', in Allen, P., Maguire, S., and McKelvey, B. (eds) (2011) *Sage Handbook on Management and Complexity* (Thousand Oaks, CA: Sage Publications)

46. Hidalgo, C.A. (2010), 'The Value in the Links: Networks and the Evolution of Organizations', in Allen, P., Maguire, S., and McKelvey, B. (eds) (2011) *Sage Handbook on Management and Complexity* (Thousand Oaks, CA: Sage Publications)

47. Hidalgo, C.A. (2010), 'The Value in the Links: Networks and the Evolution of Organizations', in Allen, P., Maguire, S., and McKelvey, B. (eds) (2011) *Sage Handbook on Management and Complexity* (Thousand Oaks, CA: Sage Publications)

48. <http://www.orgnet.com/slumlords.html> (accessed October 2012)

49. <http://drpop.org/2010/04/how-to-research-a-slumlord/> (accessed October 2012)

50. Hidalgo, C.A. (2010), 'The Value in the Links: Networks and the Evolution of Organizations', in Allen, P., Maguire, S., and McKelvey, B. (eds) (2011) *Sage Handbook on Management and Complexity* (Thousand Oaks, CA: Sage Publications)

Chapter 11

1. Priesmeyer, R.H. (1992), *Organisations and Chaos* (Westport, CT: Quorum Books), p. 3

2. US Department of Agriculture (2001), 'U.S. Forest Facts and Historical Trends' (Washington, DC: Forest Service, US Department of Agriculture)

3. Moritz, M.A., Morais, M.E., Summerell, et al (2005), 'Wildfires, Complexity, and Highly Optimized Tolerance'. *PNAS* 102(50): 17912–17

4. Gunderson, L.H. and Holling, C.S. (2002), *Panarchy* (Washington, DC: Island)

5. Stephens, S.L. and Ruth, L.W. (2005), 'Federal Forest-Fire Policy in the United States'. *Ecological Applications* 15(2): 532–42, p. 533

6. Pyne, S.J. (1982), *Fire in America: A Cultural History of Wildland and Rural Fire* (Seattle, WA: Washington University Press)

7. Berry, A. (2010), 'Forest Policy Up in Smoke: Fire Suppression in the United States' (Bozeman, MT: Property and Environment Research Center); Franklin, F. J. and Agee, J.K. (2003), 'Forging a Science-based National Forest Fire Policy'. *Issues in Science and Technology Online* 20(1): 59–66

8. Marsh Wolfe, L.M. (ed.) (1938), *John of the Mountains: Unpublished Journals of John Muir* (Boston: Houghton Mifflin), p. 433

9. Berry, A. (2010), 'Forest Policy Up in Smoke: Fire Suppression in the United States' (Bozeman, MT: Property and Environment Research Center)

10. Berry, A. (2010), 'Forest Policy Up in Smoke: Fire Suppression in the United States' (Bozeman, MT: Property and Environment Research Center), pp. 10–11

11. Berry, A. (2010), 'Forest Policy Up in Smoke: Fire Suppression in the United States' (Bozeman, MT: Property and Environment Research Center), p. 11

12. Muir, J. (1913), *The Story of My Boyhood and Youth* (Whitefish, MT: Kessinger), p. 186

13. Simon, H.A. (1962), 'The Architecture of Complexity'. *Proceedings of the American Philosophical Society* 106(6): 467–82

14. Weick, K. (1976), 'Educational Organizations as Loosely Coupled Systems'. *Administrative Science Quarterly* 21: 1–19

15. Casti J.L. (1998), 'Developing and Applying Complex Adaptive Models'. Strategy and Complexity Seminar, London, 15 May

16. Simon, H.A. (1962), 'The Architecture of Complexity'. *Proceedings of the American Philosophical Society* 106(6): 467–82

17. <http://www.resalliance.org/> (accessed October 2012)

18. Silva, J., Moench, M., Tyler, S., and Kernaghan, S. (2010) 'Urban Resilience Framework'. Arup/ISET Working Document for ACCCRN Program

19. Dorit, R.L. (2011), 'The Humpty-Dumpty Problem: Even When We Understand Their Parts, Living Things Are Hard to Put Back Together'. *American Scientist* 99 (4), <http://www.americanscientist.org/issues/pub/the-humpty-dumpty-problem/1> (accessed October 2012)

20. Dorit, R.L. (2011), 'The Humpty-Dumpty Problem: Even When We Understand Their Parts, Living Things Are Hard to Put Back Together'. *American Scientist* 99(4), <http://www.americanscientist.org/issues/pub/the-humpty-dumpty-problem/1> (accessed October 2012)

21. Bak, P., Tang, C., and Weisenfeld, K. (1988), 'Self-Organized Criticality'. *Physical Review* A38: p. 364

22. Paczuski, M., and Bak, P. (1999), 'Self-Organization of Complex Systems'. Proceedings of the 12th Chris Engelbrecht Summer School, <http://msdl.cs.mcgill.ca/people/indrani/socpapers/paczuski_bak.pdf> (accessed October 2012)

23. Paczuski, M., and Bak, P. (1999), 'Self-Organization of Complex Systems'. Proceedings of the 12th Chris Engelbrecht Summer School, <http://msdl.cs.mcgill.ca/people/indrani/socpapers/paczuski_bak.pdf> (accessed October 2012), p. 1

24. Paczuski, M., and Bak, P. (1999), 'Self-Organization of Complex Systems'. Proceedings of the 12th Chris Engelbrecht Summer School, <http://msdl.cs.mcgill.ca/people/indrani/socpapers/paczuski_bak.pdf> (accessed October 2012)

25. Ramalingam, B. and Jones, H., with Reba, T. and Young, J. (2008), 'Exploring the Science of Complexity: Ideas and Implications for Development and Humanitarian Efforts'. Working Paper 285 (London: ODI), p. 9

26. Perrow, C. (1984), *Normal Accidents: Living with High-risk Technologies* (New York: Basic)

27. Tainter, J.A. (1988), *The Collapse of Complex Societies* (Cambridge: CUP)

28. Bertrand, K.Z. and Bar-Yam, Y. (2011), 'Contagion and Cascades through the Middle East: Tunisia, Egypt, Jordan, Syria . . .', NECSI Technical Report 2011-2-01, <http://www.necsi.edu/research/social/middleeastcontagion.html> (accessed October 2012)

29. Porterie, B., Zekri, N., Clerc, J.P., and Loraud, J.C. (2007), 'Modeling Forest Fire Spread and Spotting Process with Small World Networks'. *Combustion and Flame* 149(1–2): 63–78

30. Lo, A. (2011), Presentation at IIASA, June

31. Groszmann, M. (2012), personal communication

32. Bertrand, K.Z. and Bar-Yam, Y. (2011), 'Contagion and Cascades through the Middle East: Tunisia, Egypt, Jordan, Syria . . .', NECSI Technical Report 2011-2-01, <http://www.necsi.edu/research/social/middleeastcontagion.html> (accessed October 2012)

33. <http://en.wikipedia.org/wiki/Vilfredo_Pareto> (accessed October 2012)

34. Buchanan, M. (2007), 'Power Laws and the New Science of Complexity Management', <http://www.optimalenterprise.com/docs/Power%20Laws%20-%20Complexity%20Mgmt%20sb34_04107.pdf> (accessed October 2012)

35. Schumpeter, J. (1949), 'Vilfredo Pareto (1848–1923)'. *Quarterly Journal of Economics* 63: 147–72, p. 155

36. Zipf, G.K. (1949), *Human Behavior and the Principle of Least Effort* (Cambridge, MA: Addison-Wesley)

37. Richardson, L.F. (1960), *Statistics of Deadly Quarrels* (Pittsburgh, PA: Boxwood Press)

38. Gutenberg, B. and Richter, C.F. (1954), *Seismicity of the Earth and Associated Phenomena* (Princeton, NJ: Princeton University Press)

39. Simon, H.A. (1955), 'On a Class of Skew Distribution Functions'. *Biometrika* 42(3/4): 425–40

40. Beinhocker, E. (2011), personal communication

41. Sornette, D. (2005), 'Dragon-Kings, Black Swans and Prediction of Crises'. Working Paper CCSS-09-005 (Zurich: ETH)

42. Buchanan, M. (2007), 'Power Laws and the New Science of Complexity Management', <http://www.optimalenterprise.com/docs/Power%20Laws%20-%20Complexity%20Mgmt%20sb34_04107.pdf> (accessed October 2012)

43. Andriani, P. and McKelvey, B. (2009) 'Beyond Gaussian Averages: Redirecting Organization Science Toward Extreme Events and Power Laws'. *Organization Science* 20(6): 1053–71

44. Buchanan, M. (2007), 'Power Laws and the New Science of Complexity Management', <http://www.optimalenterprise.com/docs/Power%20Laws%20-%20Complexity%20Mgmt%20sb34_04107.pdf> (accessed October 2012)

45. Obrist, H.U. (2010), 'The Father of Long Tails: Interview with Benoît Mandelbrot', *The Edge*, <http://www.edge.org/3rd_culture/obrist10/obrist10_index.html> (accessed October 2012)

46. Taleb, N.N. (2007), *The Black Swan: The Impact of the Highly Improbable* (New York: Random House)

47. Ball, J. (2011), 'September 11's Indirect Toll: Road Deaths Linked to Fearful Flyers'. *The Guardian*, 5 September, <http://www.guardian.co.uk/world/2011/sep/05/september-11-road-deaths> (accessed October 2012)

48. Clauset, A., Shalizi, C.R., and Newman, M.E.J. (2009), 'Power-Law Distributions in Empirical Data'. *SIAM Review* 51(4): 661–703
49. Buchanan, M. (2007), 'Power Laws and the New Science of Complexity Management', <http://www.optimalenterprise.com/docs/Power%20Laws%20-%20Complexity%20Mgmt%20sb34_04107.pdf> (accessed October 2012)
50. Sornette, D. (2005), 'Dragon-Kings, Black Swans and Prediction of Crises'. Working Paper CCSS-09-005 (Zurich: ETH)
51. Allen, C.R. and Holling, C.S. (2008), *Discontinuities in Ecosystems and Other Complex Systems* (New York: Columbia University Press)
52. Awati, K. (2010), 'Power Laws', *Eight to Late.* 28 July, <http://eight2late.wordpress.com/category/power-laws/> (accessed October 2012)
53. Anderson, P.W. (1997), 'Some Thoughts about Distribution in Economics', in Arthur, W.B., Durlaf, S.N., and Lane, S.A. (eds) *The Economy as an Evolving Complex System II* (Reading, MA: Addison-Wesley), p. 566
54. Eldridge, N. and Gould, S.J. (1972), 'Punctuated Equilibria: An Alternative to Phyletic Gradualism', in Schopf, T.J.M. (ed.) *Models in Paleobiology* (San Francisco, CA: Freeman Cooper), pp. 82–115
55. Holling, C.S. (1973), 'Resilience and Stability of Ecological Systems'. *Annual Review of Ecology and Systematics* 4: 1–23
56. Raup, D. (1994), 'The Role of Extinction in Evolution'. *PNAS* 91: 6758–73
57. Bak, P. and Sneppen, K. (1993), 'Punctuated Equilibrium and Criticality in a Simple Model of Evolution'. *Physical Review Letters* 71(24): 4083–6, p. 4085
58. Prigogine, I. and Nicolis, G. (1977), *Self-Organization in Non-Equilibrium Systems* (New York: Wiley)
59. Gould, S.J. (1989), *Wonderful Life. The Burgess Shale and the Nature of History* (New York: W. W. Norton), p. 383
60. Fontana, W. and Schuster, P. (1998), 'Continuity in Evolution: On the Nature of Transitions'. *Science* 280: 1451–5
61. Gladwell, M. (2002), *The Tipping Point: How Little Things Can Make a Big Difference* (Boston, MA: Back Bay Books)
62. Kauffman, S. (1995), *At Home in the Universe: The Search for Laws of Complexity* (New York: OUP), p. 28
63. Lamberson, P.J. and Page, S.E. (2012), 'Tipping Points: Essay'. *Quarterly Journal of Political Science* 7: 175–208
64. Lamberson, P.J. and Page, S.E. (2012), 'Tipping Points: Essay'. *Quarterly Journal of Political Science* 7: 175–208, p. 200
65. Lamberson, P.J. and Page, S.E. (2012), 'Tipping Points: Essay'. *Quarterly Journal of Political Science* 7: 175–208
66. Gould, S.J. (1989), *Wonderful Life: The Burgess Shale and the Nature of History* (New York: W. W. Norton), p. 289
67. David, P.A. (2000), 'Path Dependence, Its Critics and the Quest for "Historical Economics"'. Working Paper (Oxford: All Souls College)
68. Jervis, R. (1997), *System Effects: Complexity in Political and Social Life* (Princeton, NJ: Princeton University Press), p. 156
69. Homer-Dixon, T. (2011), 'Complexity Science'. *Oxford Leadership Journal* 2(1): 1–15, p. 7

70. Ouellette, J. (2011), 'Teetering on the Edge of Chaos'. *Scientific American*, 2 August, <http://blogs.scientificamerican.com/cocktail-party-physics/2011/08/02/teetering-on-the-edge-of-chaos/> (accessed October 2012)

71. Crutchfield, J.P. (2003), 'What Lies between Order and Chaos', in Casti, J. and Karlqvist, K. (eds), *Art and Complexity* (Amsterdam: Elsevier), pp. 31–45, p. 39

72. Crutchfield, J.P. (2003), 'What Lies between Order and Chaos', in Casti, J. and Karlqvist, K. (eds), *Art and Complexity* (Amsterdam: Elsevier), pp. 31–45, p. 41

73. Crutchfield, J.P. (2003), 'What Lies between Order and Chaos', in Casti, J. and Karlqvist, K. (eds), *Art and Complexity* (Amsterdam: Elsevier), pp. 31–45, p. 42

74. Prigogine, I. and Stengers, I. (1979), 'The New Alliance Gallimard', translated at <http://www.connected.org/is/prigogine.html> (accessed October 2012)

75. Homer-Dixon, T. (1996), 'Strategies for Studying Causation in Complex Ecological-Political Systems'. *Journal of Environment and Development* 5(2): 132–48

76. Bass, T.A. (1999), *The Predictors* (New York: H. Holt and Co.), p. 65

77. Strogatz, S. (2003), *Sync: The Emerging Science of Spontaneous Order* (New York: Hyperion)

78. Bass, T.A. (1999), *The Predictors* (New York: H. Holt and Co.), p. 66

79. Paczuski, M., and Bak, P. (1999), 'Self-Organization of Complex Systems'. Proceedings of the 12th Chris Engelbrecht Summer School, <http://msdl.cs.mcgill.ca/people/indrani/socpapers/paczuski_bak.pdf> (accessed October 2012)

80. Bass, T.A. (1999), *The Predictors* (New York: H. Holt and Co.), pp. 65–66

81. Campbell, K.M. (2008), *Climatic Cataclysm: The Foreign Policy and National Security Implications of Climate Change* (Washington DC: Brookings Institution Press), p. 170

82. Jervis, R. (1997), *System Effects: Complexity in Political and Social Life* (Princeton, NJ: Princeton University Press), p. 52

83. Jervis, R. (1997), *System Effects: Complexity in Political and Social Life* (Princeton, NJ: Princeton University Press), p. 52

84. Khandani, A., Lo, A., and Merton, R. (2010), 'Systemic Risk and the Refinancing Ratchet Effect'. Working Paper (Cambridge, MA: Harvard Business School)

85. Lo, A. (2011) Presentation at IIASA

86. Milikan, R.A. and Maxwell, R. (1990), 'Visions of a Sustainable World'. Introductory Talk at Meeting on Sustainable World Project, Santa Fe, NM, May, p. 6

87. Milikan, R.A. and Maxwell, R. (1990), 'Visions of a Sustainable World'. Introductory Talk at Meeting on Sustainable World Project, Santa Fe, NM, May, p. 6

88. Strogatz, S. (2003), *Sync: The Emerging Science of Spontaneous Order* (New York: Hyperion)

89. Sabloff, J. (2012), 'Speech'. SFI Public Lecture, August

90. Campbell, K.M. (2008), *Climatic Cataclysm: The Foreign Policy and National Security Implications of Climate Change* (Washington DC: Brookings Institution Press), p. 72

91. HM Treasury (2006), *Stern Review of Climate Change* (London: HM Treasury)

92. Note that the previously cited increase from 5 per cent to 14.4 per cent owed to natural, known feedbacks and does not include non-linear feedbacks.

93. Jenkins, J., Nordhaus, T., and Shellenberger, M. (2011), 'Energy Emergence: Rebound and Backfire as Emergent Phenomena' (Oakland, CA: The Breakthrough Institute), p. 4

94. Jenkins, J., Nordhaus, T., and Shellenberger, M. (2011), 'Energy Emergence: Rebound and Backfire as Emergent Phenomena' (Oakland, CA: The Breakthrough Institute), p. 7

95. Jenkins, J., Nordhaus, T., and Shellenberger, M. (2011), 'Energy Emergence: Rebound and Backfire as Emergent Phenomena' (Oakland, CA: The Breakthrough Institute), p. 12

96. Jenkins, J., Nordhaus, T., and Shellenberger, M. (2011), 'Energy Emergence: Rebound and Backfire as Emergent Phenomena' (Oakland, CA: The Breakthrough Institute), p. 7

97. Jenkins, J., Nordhaus, T., and Shellenberger, M. (2011), 'Energy Emergence: Rebound and Backfire as Emergent Phenomena' (Oakland, CA: The Breakthrough Institute), p. 10

98. Strogatz, S. (2003), *Sync: The Emerging Science of Spontaneous Order* (New York: Hyperion), p. 182

99. Cordis Europa (2012), 'Designing Together to Unshock the New'. Workshop on Future Technology and Society, Brussels, 19 November, p. 14

Chapter 12

1. Ramo, J. (2009), *The Age of the Unthinkable: Why the New World Disorder Constantly Surprises Us And What We Can Do About It* (New York: Little, Brown)

2. Mr Y (2011), 'A National Strategic Narrative' (Washington, DC: Woodrow Wilson International Center for Scholars), p. 3. Mr Y is a pseudonym for US Navy Captain Wayne Porter and US Marine Corps Colonel Mark Mykleby, who both worked for the Chairman of the Joint Chiefs of Staff in the Pentagon

3. La Force, T. (2009), 'Farewell, Dr Kissinger'. *The New Yorker*, 7 May, <http://www.newyorker.com/online/blogs/books/2009/05/last-night-at-the-river.html#ixzz29-PKcj4yZ> (accessed October 2012)

4. Homer-Dixon, T. (2011), 'Complexity Science'. *Oxford Leadership Journal* 2(1): 1–15, p. 12

5. Homer-Dixon, T. (2011), 'Complexity Science'. *Oxford Leadership Journal* 2(1): 1–15, p. 12

6. Mitchell, M. (2006), 'Complex Systems: Network Thinking'. *Artificial Intelligence* 170(18): 1194–212, p. 1194

7. Personal communication (2012)

8. Peake, S. (2010), 'Policymaking as Design in Complex Systems—the International Climate Change Regime'. *Emergence: Complexity and Organization* 12(2), pp. 15–22, p. 19

9. Boisot, M. (2003), in Mitleton-Kelly, E. (ed.), *Complex Systems and Evolutionary Perspectives on Organisations: The Application of Complexity Theory to Organisations* (Oxford: Pergamon), p. 200

10. The Health Foundation (2010), *Evidence Scan: Complex Adaptive Systems* (London: The Health Foundation), p. 24

11. Gould, S.J. (2007), *Punctuated Equilibrium* (Cambridge, MA: Belknap of Harvard University Press), p. 234

12. Gell-Mann, M. (2011), personal communication

13. Boyd, E. (2008), 'Weathering the Drought: Strategies for Adaptation under Extreme Risk and Uncertainty'. PowerPoint presentation, 2 October

14. Crutchfield, J.P. (2003), 'What Lies between Order and Chaos', in Casti, J. and Karlqvist, K. (eds), *Art and Complexity* (Amsterdam: Elsevier), pp. 31–45, p. 43

15. Crutchfield, J.P. (2003), 'What Lies between Order and Chaos', in Casti, J. and Karlqvist, K. (eds), *Art and Complexity* (Amsterdam: Elsevier), pp. 31–45, p. 43

16. Crutchfield, J.P. (2003), 'What Lies between Order and Chaos', in Casti, J. and Karlqvist, K. (eds), *Art and Complexity* (Amsterdam: Elsevier), pp. 31–45, p. 43

17. Ramo, J. (2009), *The Age of the Unthinkable: Why the New World Disorder Constantly Surprises Us And What We Can Do About It* (New York: Little, Brown), pp. 39–40

Chapter 13

1. ADB (1990), 'Bali Irrigation Sector Project'. Project Completion Report, June (Manila: ADB), p. 17

2. Smillie, I. (2000), *Mastering the Machine* (Rugby: ITDG), p. 45

3. Lansing, S. (2006), *Perfect Order: Recognizing Complexity in Bali* (Princeton, NJ: Princeton University Press)

4. Lansing, S. (2006), *Perfect Order: Recognizing Complexity in Bali* (Princeton, NJ: Princeton University Press), p. 11

5. Lansing, S. (1991), *Priests and Programmers: Technologies of Power in the Engineered Landscape of Bali* (Princeton, NJ: Princeton University Press), p. 120

6. Lansing, S. and Kremer, J.N. (1993), 'Emergent Properties of Balinese Water Temple Networks: Coadaptation on a Rugged Fitness Landscape'. *American Anthropologist, New Series* 95(1): 97–114

7. Lansing, S. and Miller, J.H. (2003), 'Cooperation in Balinese Rice Farming'. Working Paper (Sante Fe, NM: SFI)

8. Lansing, S. (2006), *Perfect Order: Recognizing Complexity in Bali* (Princeton, NJ: Princeton University Press), p. 84

9. Lansing, S. (2006), *Perfect Order: Recognizing Complexity in Bali* (Princeton, NJ: Princeton University Press), p. 86

10. Cheong, F. and Corbittt, B.J. (2010), 'From Childhood Poverty to Catfish: A Conceptual Participatory Modelling Framework for Strategic Decision Making'. *International Journal of Strategic Decision Sciences* 1(3): 14–32

11. ADB (1990), 'Bali Irrigation Sector Project'. Project Performance Audit Report, June (Manila: ADB); ADB (1992), 'Bali Irrigation Sector Project'. Project Performance Audit Report, June (Manila: ADB)

12. ADB (1990), 'Bali Irrigation Sector Project'. Project Performance Audit Report, June (Manila: ADB)

13. ADB (1992), 'Bali Irrigation Sector Project'. Project Performance Audit Report, June (Manila: ADB), p. 8

14. ADB (1990), 'Bali Irrigation Sector Project'. Project Performance Audit Report, June (Manila: ADB), p. 10

Chapter 14

1. Shah, R. (2012), 'Remarks at the Aspen Institute', 1 August, <http://www.usaid.gov/news-information/speeches/remarks-usaid-administrator-dr-rajiv-shah-aspen-institute> (accessed October 2012)
2. A lot of this section draws on ideas originally posted on Ramalingam, B. (2010), 'Land Is Not Linear: Towards the Brown Revolution', 22 October, <http://aidontheedge.info/2010/10/22/land-is-not-linear-towards-the-brown-revolution/> (accessed October 2012) and on Thackara, J. (2010), 'Greener Pastures'. *Seed Magazine*, 3 June
3. Thackara, J. (2010), 'Greener Pastures'. *Seed Magazine*, 3 June
4. UN (1994), 'UN Convention to Combat Desertification', <http://www.unccd.int/main.php> (accessed October 2012)
5. Reynolds, J.F., Stafford Smith, M., and Lambin, E. (2003), 'Do Humans Cause Deserts? An Old Problem through the Lens of a New Framework: The Dahlem Desertification Paradigm'. Proceedings of the VIIth International Rangelands Congress, Durban, 26 July–1 August
6. Stafford Smith, D.M. and Reynolds, J.F. (2002), 'Desertification: A New Paradigm for an Old Problem', in Reynolds, J.F. and Stafford Smith, D.M. (eds), *Global Desertification: Do Humans Cause Deserts?* (Berlin: Dahlem University Press)
7. Stafford Smith, D.M. and Reynolds, J.F. (2002), 'Desertification: A New Paradigm for an Old Problem', in Reynolds, J.F. and Stafford Smith, D.M. (eds), *Global Desertification: Do Humans Cause Deserts?* (Berlin: Dahlem University Press), pp. 406–7
8. Neely, C.L. and Butterfield, J. (2004), 'Holistic Management of African Rangelands'. *Leisa Magazine*, December
9. Savory, A. (2012), personal communication
10. Savory, A. (2012), personal communication
11. Savory, A. (2012), personal communication
12. Adapted from Thackara, J. (2010), 'Greener Pastures'. *Seed Magazine*, 3 June
13. Thackara, J. (2010), 'Greener Pastures'. *Seed Magazine*, 3 June
14. Thackara, J. (2010), 'Greener Pastures'. *Seed Magazine*, 3 June
15. Thackara, J. (2010), 'Greener Pastures'. *Seed Magazine*, 3 June
16. Bingham, S. (2004), 'A Short History of the West African Pilot Pastoral Program 1993–2002', <http://managingwholes.com/bingham-wappp.htm> (accessed October 2012)
17. Thackara, J. (2010), 'Greener Pastures'. *Seed Magazine*, 3 June
18. UNCDD Secretariat (2012), 'Zero Net Land Degradation: A Sustainable Development Goal for Rio + 20'. Policy Brief, May, p.19
19. Ramalingam, B. (2010), 'Land Is Not Linear: Towards the Brown Revolution', 22 October, <http://aidontheedge.info/2010/10/22/land-is-not-linear-towards-the-brown-revolution/> (accessed October 2012)
20. <http://globalhealth.kff.org/Daily-Reports/2010/October/14/GH-101410-World-Food-Prize.aspx?p=1> (accessed October 2012)
21. Altieri, M.A. (1987), *Agroecology* (Boulder, CO: Westview), p. 5

22. Altieri, M.A. (1987), *Agroecology* (Boulder, CO: Westview), p. 5
23. Benyus, J. M. (1997), *Biomimicry: Innovation Inspired By Nature* (New York: William Morrow)
24. De Schutter, O. (2010), 'Report Submitted by the Special Rapporteur on the Right to Food'. 16th Session of the HRC, New York, 20 December
25. Australian Government (n.d.), 'Tackling Wicked Problems: A Public Policy Perspective' (Canberra: Australian Public Service Commission), p. 3
26. Concha-Eastman, A. (2008), 'Comprehensive Health Strategies', in Hauswedell, C. and Kurtenbach, S. (eds), *In War as in Peace: Youth Violence—A Challenge for International Cooperation* (Berlin: Loccummer Protokol), p. 233
27. Concha-Eastman, A. (2005), 'Ten Years of a Successful Violence Reduction Programme in Bogota, Columbia'. Speech at Preventing Violence: From Global Perspectives to National Action, 10–11 March
28. Kilcullen, D. (2010), *Counterinsurgency* (Oxford: OUP), p. 196
29. Ricigliano, R. (2011), 'A Systems Approach to Peacebuilding', <http://www.c-r.org/sites/c-r.org/files/Accord%2022_5A%20systems%20approach%20to%20peacebuilding_2011_ENG.pdf> (accessed October 2012), p. 17
30. Ricigliano, R. (2011), 'A Systems Approach to Peacebuilding', <http://www.c-r.org/sites/c-r.org/files/Accord%2022_5A%20systems%20approach%20to%20peacebuilding_2011_ENG.pdf> (accessed October 2012), p. 19
31. Ricigliano, R. (2011), 'A Systems Approach to Peacebuilding', <http://www.c-r.org/sites/c-r.org/files/Accord%2022_5A%20systems%20approach%20to%20peacebuilding_2011_ENG.pdf> (accessed October 2012), p. 19
32. Gell-Mann, M. (1994), *The Quark and the Jaguar: Adventures in the Simple and the Complex* (New York: W.H. Freeman)
33. Track 1 is official, involving politicians and military, focusing on ceasefires, treaties, and peace talks; Track 2 is unofficial dialogue and problem solving aimed at building relationships and typically involves civil society, academics, religious groups, and so on; and Track 1.5 denotes informal dialogue and problem solving between high-ranking officials and decision makers
34. Ricigliano, R. (2012), personal communication
35. Ricigliano, R. (2012), personal communication
36. Brand-Jacobsen, K. (n.d.), 'Palestine and Israel: Improving Civil Society Peacebuilding Strategies, Design and Impact', <http://www.novatrainings.org/userfiles/files/Peacebuilding_ANG.pdf> (accessed October 2012), p. 10
37. Ricigliano, R. (2011), 'A Systems Approach to Peacebuilding', <http://www.c-r.org/sites/c-r.org/files/Accord%2022_5A%20systems%20approach%20to%20peacebuilding_2011_ENG.pdf> (accessed October 2012), p. 18
38. Haushofer, J., Biletzki, A., and Kanwisher, N. (2010), 'Both Sides Retaliate in the Israeli–Palestinian Conflict'. *PNAS* 107(42): 17927–32
39. Haushofer, J., Biletzki, A., and Kanwisher, N. (2010), 'Both Sides Retaliate in the Israeli–Palestinian Conflict'. *PNAS* 107(42): 17927–32, p. 17927
40. Brand-Jacobsen, K. (n.d.), 'Palestine and Israel: Improving Civil Society Peacebuilding Strategies, Design and Impact', <http://www.novatrainings.org/userfiles/files/Peacebuilding_ANG.pdf> (accessed October 2012)

41. Coleman, P.T., Vallacher, R., Nowak, A., and Bui-Wrzosinska, L. (2007), 'Intractable Conflict as an Attractor: Presenting a Dynamical Model of Conflict, Escalation, and Intractability'. *American Behavioral Scientist* 50(11): 1454–75, p. 1455

42. Coleman, P.T., Vallacher, R., Nowak, A., and Bui-Wrzosinska, L. (2007), 'Intractable Conflict as an Attractor: Presenting a Dynamical Model of Conflict, Escalation, and Intractability'. *American Behavioral Scientist* 50(11): 1454–75, p. 1455

43. Coleman, P.T., Vallacher, R., Nowak, A., and Bui-Wrzosinska, L. (2007), 'Intractable Conflict as an Attractor: Presenting a Dynamical Model of Conflict, Escalation, and Intractability'. *American Behavioral Scientist* 50(11): 1454–75, p. 1456

44. Brand-Jacobsen, K.F. (2009), 'Palestine and Israel: Improving Civil Society Peacebuilding Strategies, Design and Impact' (Madrid: AECID)

45. Ricigliano, R. (2011), 'A Systems Approach to Peacebuilding', <http://www.c-r.org/sites/c-r.org/files/Accord%2022_5A%20systems%20approach%20to%20peacebuilding_2011_ENG.pdf> (accessed October 2012), p. 17

46. *The Economist* (2012), 'Pray for the Doves', 28 July, <http://www.economist.com/node/21559616> (accessed October 2012)

47. Conciliation Resources (2008), 'Delivering Peace in Aceh: An Interview with President Martti Ahtisaari', <http://www.c-r.org/accord-article/delivering-peace-aceh-interview-president-martti-ahtisaari> (accessed October 2012)

48. Conciliation Resources (2008), 'Delivering Peace in Aceh: An Interview with President Martti Ahtisaari', <http://www.c-r.org/accord-article/delivering-peace-aceh-interview-president-martti-ahtisaari> (accessed October 2012)

49. Conciliation Resources (2008), 'Delivering Peace in Aceh: An Interview with President Martti Ahtisaari', <http://www.c-r.org/accord-article/delivering-peace-aceh-interview-president-martti-ahtisaari> (accessed October 2012)

50. Ricigliano, R. (2012), *Making Peace Last* (Boulder, CO: Paradigm Publications), p. 62

51. Charron, D.J. (2011), *Ecohealth Research in Practice: Innovative Applications of an Ecosystem Approach to Health* (New York: Springer), p. 10

52. Robbins, J. (2012), 'The Ecology of Disease'. *The New York Times Sunday Review*, 14 July

53. Lebell, J. (2003), 'Health: An Ecosystem Approach' (Ottawa: IRDC)

54. Waltner-Toews, D. (2001), 'An Ecosystem Approach to Health and its Applications to Tropical and Emerging Diseases'. *Cad. Saúde Pública, Rio de Janeiro* 17 (Suplemento): 7–36

55. Bradley, D. (2007), 'Malaria in Africa: Ecohealth Projects'. IDRC Evaluation (Ottawa: IDRC)

56. Pepall, J. (2003), 'Malaria and Agriculture in Kenya: A New Perspective on the Links between Health and Ecosystems' (Ottawa: IRDC)

57. Lebell, J. (2003), 'Health: An Ecosystem Approach' (Ottawa: IRDC), p. 43

58. Okech, B.A., Mwobobia, I.K., Kamau, A., et al (2008), 'Use of Integrated Malaria Management Reduces Malaria in Kenya'. *PLoS ONE* 3(12), <http://www.plosone.org/article/info%3Adoi%2F10.1371%2Fjournal.pone.0004050> (accessed October 2012)

59. Bradley, D. (2007), 'Malaria in Africa: Ecohealth Projects'. IDRC Evaluation (Ottawa: IDRC)

60. Pepall, J. (2003), 'Fighting Malaria without DDT: Better Management of the Environment a Key to Disease Control'. Health: An Ecosystem Approach Case Study (Ottawa: IDRC)

61. Ferguson, H.M., Dornhaus, A., Beeche, A., et al (2010), 'Ecology: A Prerequisite for Malaria Elimination and Eradication'. *PLoS Med* 7(8), <http://www.plosmedicine.org/article/info%3Adoi%2F10.1371%2Fjournal.pmed.1000303> (accessed October 2012)

62. Alliance for Health Policy and Systems Research (2009), *Systems Thinking for Health Systems Strengthening* (Geneva: WHO)

63. Pruyt, E. (2010), 'Using Small Models for Big Issues: Exploratory System Dynamics Modelling and Analysis for Insightful Crisis Management' in Moon, T.-H. (2010), *Proceedings of the 18th International Conference of the System Dynamics Society, Seoul, 25–9 July* (Seoul: The System Dynamics Society)

64. McMichael, A.J. (1998), 'Prisoners of the Proximate: Loosening the Constraints on Epidemiology in an Age of Change'. *Am. J. Epidemiol* 149(10): 887–97

65. <http://www.undp-aap.org/sites/undp-aap.org/files/Kenya%20Threshold%2021%20Climate%20Change%20Impact%20Sectoral%20Briefs_0.pdf> (accessed October 2012)

66. Ostrom, E. (2007), 'A Diagnostic Approach for Going beyond Panaceas'. *PNAS* 104 (39): 15181–7, p. 15187

67. Holling et al (1998), in Ostrom, E. (2007), 'A Diagnostic Approach for Going Beyond Panaceas'. *PNAS* 104(39): 15181–7

68. Ostrom, E. (2007), 'A Diagnostic Approach for Going beyond Panaceas'. *PNAS* 104 (39): 15181–7, p. 15187

69. Personal communication (2010)

70. Capra, F. (2002), *The Hidden Connections: Integrating the Hidden Connections among the Biological, Cognitive, and Social Dimensions of Life* (New York: Doubleday), p. 201

71. Personal communication (2012)

72. Mittleton-Kelly, E. (2003), *Complex Systems and Evolutionary Perspectives on Organisations: The Application of Complexity Theory to Organisations* (London: Pergamon)

73. Hulme, M. (2009), *Why We Disagree about Climate Change* (Cambridge: CUP), p. 334

74. Nepal Climate Vulnerability Study Team (2009), *Vulnerability through the Eyes of the Vulnerable* (Kathmandu: Institute for Social and Environmental Transition), p. 91

75. Hulme, M. (2009), *Why We Disagree about Climate Change* (Cambridge: CUP), p. 363

76. Rittel, H.W.J. and Webber, M.M. (1973), 'Dilemmas in a General Theory of Planning'. *Policy Sciences* 4(1973): 155–69

77. Batty, M. (2007), 'Complexity in City Systems: Understanding, Evolution, and Design'. Working Paper 117-07 (London: UCL), pp. 25–6

78. Australian Government (n.d.), 'Tackling Wicked Problems: A Public Policy Perspective' (Canberra: Australian Public Service Commission), p. 3

79. Rittel, H.W.J. and Webber, M.M. (1973), 'Dilemmas in a General Theory of Planning'. *Policy Sciences* 4(1973): 155–69, p. 155

80. Howes, S. and Wyrwoll, P. (2012), 'Asia's Wicked Environmental Problems'. Working Paper 348 (Manila: ADBI)

81. Ellerman, D. (2002), 'Should Development Agencies have Official Views?' *Development in Practice* 12(3&4): 285–97, p. 286
82. Task Force on Impact Assessment and Evaluation (2007), 'Impact Assessment and Evaluation in Agricultural Research for Development' (Brussels: EIARD), p. 5
83. Task Force on Impact Assessment and Evaluation (2007), 'Impact Assessment and Evaluation in Agricultural Research for Development' (Brussels: EIARD)
84. Howes, S. and Wyrwoll, P. (2012), 'Asia's Wicked Environmental Problems'. Working Paper 348 (Manila: ADBI)
85. Easton, N. (2011), 'Raj Shah: The Young Gun Fixing USAID'. *Fortune Magazine*, 21 September, <http://money.cnn.com/2011/09/20/news/economy/raj_shah_usaid.fortune/index.htm> (accessed October 2012)
86. <http://aidontheedge.files.wordpress.com/2010/09/meeting_report.pdf, p.2> (accessed October 2012)
87. Gates, W.H. (2007), 'To Turn Caring into Action'. *Harvard Magazine*, 7 June <http://harvardmagazine.com/2007/06/bill-gates-harvard-commencement-address> (accessed October 2012)
88. Lester, R.K. and Piore, M.J. (2004), *Innovation, the Missing Dimension* (Cambridge, MA: Harvard University Press), p. 42
89. Rittel, H.W.J. and Webber, M.M. (1973), 'Dilemmas in a General Theory of Planning'. *Policy Sciences* 4(1973): 155–69, p. 161
90. Walker, B., Barrett, S., Polasky, S., et al (2009), 'Looming Global-scale Failures and Missing Institutions'. *Science* 325(5946): 1345
91. Lester, R.K. and Piore, M.J. (2004), *Innovation, the Missing Dimension* (Cambridge, MA: Harvard University Press), p. 49
92. Howes, S. and Wyrwoll, P. (2012), 'Asia's Wicked Environmental Problems'. Working Paper 348 (Manila: ADBI), p. 36
93. Howes, S. and Wyrwoll, P. (2012), 'Asia's Wicked Environmental Problems'. Working Paper 348 (Manila: ADBI), p. 37
94. Howes, S. and Wyrwoll, P. (2012), 'Asia's Wicked Environmental Problems'. Working Paper 348 (Manila: ADBI), p. 35
95. Andrews, M., Pritchett, L., and Woolcock, M. (2012), 'Escaping Capability Traps through Problem-driven Iterative Adaptation'. Working Paper 299 (Washington, DC: CGD), p. 19
96. Peter, L.J. (1982), *Peter's Almanac* (New York: Morrow)
97. Riddell, R. (2008), *Does Foreign Aid Really Work?* (Oxford: OUP), p. k

Chapter 15

1. UN Multimedia (2012), 'United Nations Needs to Adapt to 21st Century: Ban Ki-moon', 10 September, <http://www.unmultimedia.org/radio/english/2012/01/united-nations-needs-to-adapt-to-21st-century-ban-ki-moon-2/> (accessed October 2012)
2. Positive Deviance Initiative (n.d.), 'The Viet Nam Story: Narrated by Jerry Sternin', <http://www.positivedeviance.org/about_pd/Monique%20VIET%20NAM%20CHAPTER%20Oct%2017.pdf> (accessed October 2012), p.1

3. Zeitlin, M., Ghassemi, and Mansour, M. (1990), *Positive Deviance in Child Nutrition—With Emphasis on Psychosocial and Behavioural Aspects and Implications for Development* (Helsinki: UNU), <http://archive.unu.edu/unupress/unupbooks/80697e/80697E01.htm#Executive%20summary> (accessed October 2012)

4. Zeitlin, M., Ghassemi, H., and Mansour, M. (1990), 'The Literature and its Policy and Programme Implications',<http://archive.unu.edu/unupress/unupbooks/80697e/80697E02.htm> (accessed October 2012)

5. Zeitlin, M., Ghassemi, H., and Mansour, M. (1990), 'The Literature and its Policy and Programme Implications', <http://archive.unu.edu/unupress/unupbooks/80697e/80697E02.htm> (accessed October 2012)

6. Zeitlin, M., Ghassemi, H., and Mansour, M. (1990), 'The Literature and its Policy and Programme Implications', <http://archive.unu.edu/unupress/unupbooks/80697e/80697E02.htm> (accessed October 2012)

7. Sternin, M. (2012), personal communication

8. Sternin, M. (2012), personal communication

9. Sternin, M. (2012), personal communication

10. Positive Deviance Initiative (n.d.), 'The Viet Nam Story: Narrated by Jerry Sternin', <http://www.positivedeviance.org/about_pd/Monique%20VIET%20NAM%20CHAPTER%20Oct%2017.pdf> (accessed October 2012), p. 5

11. Positive Deviance Initiative (n.d.), 'The Viet Nam Story: Narrated by Jerry Sternin', <http://www.positivedeviance.org/about_pd/Monique%20VIET%20NAM%20CHAPTER%20Oct%2017.pdf> (accessed October 2012), p. 5

12. Positive Deviance Initiative (n.d.), 'The Viet Nam Story: Narrated by Jerry Sternin', <http://www.positivedeviance.org/about_pd/Monique%20VIET%20NAM%20CHAPTER%20Oct%2017.pdf> (accessed October 2012), p. 5

13. Sternin, M. (2012), personal communication

14. Pascale, R., Sternin J. and Sternin, M. (2010), *The Power of Positive Deviance: How Unlikely Innovators Solve the World's Toughest Problems* (Cambridge: MA: Harvard Business Press), p. 38

15. Positive Deviance Initiative (n.d.), 'The Viet Nam Story: Narrated by Jerry Sternin', <http://www.positivedeviance.org/about_pd/Monique%20VIET%20NAM%20CHAPTER%20Oct%2017.pdf> (accessed October 2012), p. 8

16. Pascale, R., Sternin J. and Sternin, M. (2010), *The Power of Positive Deviance: How Unlikely Innovators Solve the World's Toughest Problems* (Cambridge: MA: Harvard Business Press), pp. 8–9

17. Sternin, J. (2007), 'The Positive Deviance Initiative Story', 5 January, <http://www.policyinnovations.org/ideas/innovations/data/PositiveDeviance> (accessed October 2012)

18. Sternin, J. (2007), 'The Positive Deviance Initiative Story', 5 January, <http://www.policyinnovations.org/ideas/innovations/data/PositiveDeviance> (accessed October 2012)

19. Sternin, J. (2007), 'The Positive Deviance Initiative Story', 5 January, <http://www.policyinnovations.org/ideas/innovations/data/PositiveDeviance> (accessed October 2012)

20. Pascale, R., Sternin J. and Sternin, M. (2010), *The Power of Positive Deviance: How Unlikely Innovators Solve the World's Toughest Problems* (Cambridge: MA: Harvard Business Press), p. 13

21. Pascale, R., Sternin J. and Sternin, M. (2010), *The Power of Positive Deviance: How Unlikely Innovators Solve the World's Toughest Problems* (Cambridge: MA: Harvard Business Press), p. 13

22. Sternin, M. (2012), personal communication

23. Sternin, M. (2012), personal communication

24. Buchanan, M. (2007), 'Power Laws and the New Science of Complexity Management', <http://www.optimalenterprise.com/docs/Power%20Laws%20-%20Complexity%20Mgmt%20sb34_04107.pdf> (accessed October 2012)

25. Sternin, J. (2007), 'The Positive Deviance Initiative Story', 5 January, <http://www.policyinnovations.org/ideas/innovations/data/PositiveDeviance> (accessed October 2012)

26. Herschbach, D. and Baird, F.B. (2007), 'Understanding the Outstanding: Zipf's Law and Positive Deviants', in Lewis, J. (ed.) *Academic Excellence: The SourceBook*, (Tuscon, AZ: Research Corporation), pp. 70–4

27. Herschbach, D. (2010), personal communication

28. Easterly, W. and Reshef, A. (2010), 'African Export Successes: Surprises, Stylized Facts, and Explanations'. Working Paper 16597 (Cambridge, MA: NBER), p. 50

29. Easterly, W. and Reshef, A. (2010), 'African Export Successes: Surprises, Stylized Facts, and Explanations'. Working Paper 16597 (Cambridge, MA: NBER), p. 50

30. Sternin, J. (2007), 'The Positive Deviance Initiative Story', 5 January, <http://www.policyinnovations.org/ideas/innovations/data/PositiveDeviance> (accessed October 2012)

31. Personal communication (2012)

32. Andrews, M., Pritchett, L., and Woolcock, M. (2012), 'Escaping Capability Traps through Problem-driven Iterative Adaptation'. Working Paper 299 (Washington, DC: CGD), p. 2

33. Andrews, M., Pritchett, L., and Woolcock, M. (2012), 'Escaping Capability Traps through Problem-driven Iterative Adaptation'. Working Paper 299 (Washington, DC: CGD), p. 2

34. Hopkins, J.W. (1989), *The Eradication of Smallpox: Organizational Learning and Innovation in International Health* (Boulder, CO: Westview Press)

35. Brilliant, L.B. (1985), *The Management of Smallpox Eradication in India* (Ann Arbor, MI: University of Michigan Press)

36. This draws on my own blog post on the topic: Ramalingam, B. (2011), 'How Do you Solve a Problem Like Malaria?', 27 January, <http://aidontheedge.info/2011/01/27/how-do-you-solve-a-problem-like-malaria/> (accessed October 2012)

37. Trape, J.-F., Tall, A., Diagne, N., et al (2011), 'Malaria Morbidity and Pyrethroid Resistance after the Introduction of Insecticide-treated Bednets and Artemisinin-based Combination Therapies: A Longitudinal Study'. *The Lancet Infectious Diseases* 11(12): 925–32

38. Newton, G. (2002), 'The Evolution of Malaria Parasites', 1 October, <http://malaria.wellcome.ac.uk/doc_WTD023858.html> (accessed October 2012)

39. Janssen, M.A. and Martens, W.J.M. (1997), 'Modelling Malaria as a Complex Adaptive System'. *Artificial Life* 3(3): 213–36

40. Gu, W. and Novak, R.J. (2009), 'Predicting the Impact of Insecticide-Treated Bed Nets on Malaria Transmission: The Devil is in the Detail'. *Malaria Journal* 8(1): 256

41. Rogerson, A. and Maxwell, S. (2004), 'Aid: What's Next?' Opinion 27 (London: ODI), p. 2

42. Drawn from Nunberg, B., and Abdollahian, M. (2005), 'Operationalizing Political Analysis for Development: An Agent Based Stakeholder Model for Governance Reform'. International Studies Association Annual Meeting, Honolulu, 2–6 March; Nunberg, B., Barma, N., Abdollahian, M., Green, A., and Perlman, D. (2010), 'At the Frontier of Practical Political Economy: Operationalizing an Agent-based Stakeholder Model in the World Bank's East Asia and Pacific Region'. Policy Research Working Paper 5176 (Washington, DC: World Bank)

43. Nunberg, B., and Abdollahian, M. (2005), 'Operationalizing Political Analysis for Development: An Agent Based Stakeholder Model for Governance Reform'. International Studies Association Annual Meeting, Honolulu, 2–6 March, p. 4

44. Nunberg, B., and Abdollahian, M. (2005), 'Operationalizing Political Analysis for Development: An Agent Based Stakeholder Model for Governance Reform'. International Studies Association Annual Meeting, Honolulu, 2–6 March

45. Nunberg, B., Barma, N., Abdollahian, M., Green, A., and Perlman, D. (2010), 'At the Frontier of Practical Political Economy: Operationalizing an Agent-based Stakeholder Model in the World Bank's East Asia and Pacific Region'. Policy Research Working Paper 5176 (Washington, DC: World Bank)

46. Nunberg, B., Barma, N., Abdollahian, M., Green, A., and Perlman, D. (2010), 'At the Frontier of Practical Political Economy: Operationalizing an Agent-based Stakeholder Model in the World Bank's East Asia and Pacific Region'. Policy Research Working Paper 5176 (Washington, DC: World Bank), p. 4

47. Nunberg, B., and Abdollahian, M. (2005), 'Operationalizing Political Analysis for Development: An Agent Based Stakeholder Model for Governance Reform'. International Studies Association Annual Meeting, Honolulu, 2–6 March

48. Nunberg, B., Barma, N., Abdollahian, M., Green, A., and Perlman, D. (2010), 'At the Frontier of Practical Political Economy: Operationalizing an Agent-based Stakeholder Model in the World Bank's East Asia and Pacific Region'. Policy Research Working Paper 5176 (Washington, DC: World Bank), p. 7

49. Nunberg, B., Barma, N., Abdollahian, M., Green, A., and Perlman, D. (2010), 'At the Frontier of Practical Political Economy: Operationalizing an Agent-based Stakeholder Model in the World Bank's East Asia and Pacific Region'. Policy Research Working Paper 5176 (Washington, DC: World Bank), p. 4

50. Nunberg, B., Barma, N., Abdollahian, M., Green, A., and Perlman, D. (2010), 'At the Frontier of Practical Political Economy: Operationalizing an Agent-based Stakeholder Model in the World Bank's East Asia and Pacific Region'. Policy Research Working Paper 5176 (Washington, DC: World Bank), p. 6

51. Nunberg, B., Barma, N., Abdollahian, M., Green, A., and Perlman, D. (2010), 'At the Frontier of Practical Political Economy: Operationalizing an Agent-based Stakeholder Model in the World Bank's East Asia and Pacific Region'. Policy Research Working Paper 5176 (Washington, DC: World Bank), p. 2

52. Nunberg, B., Barma, N., Abdollahian, M., Green, A., and Perlman, D. (2010), 'At the Frontier of Practical Political Economy: Operationalizing an Agent-based Stakeholder Model in the World Bank's East Asia and Pacific Region'. Policy Research Working Paper 5176 (Washington, DC: World Bank) p. 19

53. Nunberg, B., Barma, N., Abdollahian, M., Green, A., and Perlman, D. (2010), 'At the Frontier of Practical Political Economy: Operationalizing an Agent-based

Stakeholder Model in the World Bank's East Asia and Pacific Region'. Policy Research Working Paper 5176 (Washington, DC: World Bank), p. 2

54. Nunberg, B., Barma, N., Abdollahian, M., Green, A., and Perlman, D. (2010), 'At the Frontier of Practical Political Economy: Operationalizing an Agent-based Stakeholder Model in the World Bank's East Asia and Pacific Region'. Policy Research Working Paper 5176 (Washington, DC: World Bank), p. 27

55. Nunberg, B. (2012), personal communication

56. Nunberg, B. (2012), personal communication

57. Arrow, K. (2012), personal communication

58. Arrow, K. (2012), personal communication

59. Arrow, K. (2012), personal communication

60. Gonçalves, P. (2008), 'System Dynamics Modeling of Humanitarian Relief Operations'. Working Paper 4704-08 (Cambridge, MA: MIT Sloan School), <http://www.worldresourcesreport.org/responses/putting-vulnerable-people-center-communication-adaptation-case-knowledge-sharing-through-p> (accessed October 2012)

61. Bousquet, F., Barnaud, C., Barreteau, O., et al (2006), 'Companion Modeling for Resilient Water Management: Stakeholders' Perceptions of Water Dynamics and Collective Learning at the Catchment Scale', in Rocchi, D. (ed.) *France and the CGIAR: Delivering Scientific Results for Agriculture Development* (Montpellier: CGIAR), pp. 98–101

62. Bousquet, F., Barnaud, C., Barreteau, O., et al (2006), 'Companion Modeling for Resilient Water Management: Stakeholders' Perceptions of Water Dynamics and Collective Learning at the Catchment Scale', in Rocchi, D. (ed.) *France and the CGIAR: Delivering Scientific Results for Agriculture Development* (Montpellier: CGIAR), pp. 98–101, p. 98

63. Gurung, T.R., Bousquet, R., and Trébuil, G. (2006), 'Companion Modeling, Conflict Resolution, and Institution Building: Sharing Irrigation Water in the Lingmuteychu Watershed, Bhutan'. *Ecology and Society* 11(2): 36

64. Bousquet, F., Trébuil, G., and Hardy, B. (2005), *Companion Modeling and Multi-Agent Systems for Integrated Natural Resource Management in Asia* (Los Baños: IRRI), p. 171

65. Bousquet, F. (2012), personal communication

66. Hoanh, C.T., Le Page, C., Barreteau, O., Trébuil, G., Bousquet, F., Cernesson, F., Barnaud, C., Gurung, T.R., Promburom, P., Naivinit, W., Dung, D.C., Dumrongrojwatthana, P., and Thongnoi, M., (n.d.) 'Agent-based Modeling to Facilitate Resilient Water Management in Southeast and South Asia'. Findings from the CGIAR/EU PN25 Coastal Companion Modelling and Water Dynamics Project, p. 1

67. Gurung, T.R., Bousquet, R., and Trébuil, G. (2006), 'Companion Modeling, Conflict Resolution, and Institution Building: Sharing Irrigation Water in the Lingmuteychu Watershed, Bhutan'. *Ecology and Society* 11(2): 36, p. 8

68. Gurung, T.R., Bousquet, R., and Trébuil, G. (2006), 'Companion Modeling, Conflict Resolution, and Institution Building: Sharing Irrigation Water in the Lingmuteychu Watershed, Bhutan'. *Ecology and Society* 11(2): 36

69. Gurung, T.R., Bousquet, R., and Trébuil, G. (2006), 'Companion Modeling, Conflict Resolution, and Institution Building: Sharing Irrigation Water in the Lingmuteychu Watershed, Bhutan'. *Ecology and Society* 11(2): 36, p. 8

70. Gurung, T.R., Bousquet, R., and Trébuil, G. (2006), 'Companion Modeling, Conflict Resolution, and Institution Building: Sharing Irrigation Water in the Lingmuteychu Watershed, Bhutan'. *Ecology and Society* 11(2): 36, p. 15

71. Kopainsky, B., Pedercini, M., Davidsen, P.I., and Alessi, S.M. (2010), 'A Blend of Planning and Learning: Simplifying a Simulation Model of National Development'. *Simulation and Gaming* 41(5): 641–62

72. Kniveton, D., Smith, C., and Wood, S. (2011), 'Agent-based Model Simulations of Future Changes in Migration Flows for Burkina Faso'. *Global Environmental Change* 21(24): 6498–6520

73. Kniveton, D., Schmidt-Verkerk, K., Smith, C., and Black, R. (2008), 'Climate Change and Migration: Improving Methodologies to Estimate Flows'. Migration Research Series 33 (Geneva: IOM), p. 53

74. Nunberg, B. (2012), personal communication

75. Cummings, S. and Wilson, D.C. (2003) *Images of Strategy* (New York: John Wiley)

76. Faulkner, D. and Campbell, A. (2003), *The Oxford Handbook of Strategy* (Oxford: OUP), p. 48

77. Mintzberg, H., Ahlstrand, B. and Lampel, J. (2002), *Strategy Safari: A Guided Tour through the Wilds of Strategic Management* (London: Prentice Hall) p. 11

78. Ostrom, E. (2007), 'A Diagnostic Approach for Going beyond Panaceas'. *Proceedings of the National Academy of Science* 104(39): 15181

79. Faulkner, D. and Campbell, A. (2003), *The Oxford Handbook of Strategy* (Oxford: OUP), p. 50

80. Hopkins, J.W. (1989), *The Eradication of Smallpox: Organizational Learning and Innovation in International Health* (Boulder, CO: Westview Press)

Chapter 16

1. Zoellick, R. (2010), 'End of the Third World? Modernizing Multilateralism for a Multipolar World' (Washington, DC: Woodrow Wilson Center for International Scholars), 14 April, <http://go.worldbank.org/MI7PLIP8U0> (accessed October 2012)

2. Schiffer, E. and Waale, D. (2008), 'Tracing Power and Influence in Networks: Net-Map as a Tool for Research and Strategic Network Planning'. Discussion Paper 00772 (Washington, DC: IFPRI), p. vi

3. Coffman, J. (2012), 'Eva Schiffer and Net-Map'. Center for Evaluation Innovation Interview, <http://www.evaluationinnovation.org/publications/newsletter/issue-archive/2010/aug/advocacy-evaluation-update-issue-9/eva-schiffer-and-n> (accessed October 2012)

4. Schiffer, E. and Waale, D. (2008), 'Tracing Power and Influence in Networks: Net-Map as a Tool for Research and Strategic Network Planning'. Discussion Paper 00772 (Washington, DC: IFPRI)

5. von Braun, J., in CGIAR (2008), 'Top Innovations and Achievements in Global Agricultural Research Honored'. CGIAR 2008 AGM, p. 3

6. Foley, C. (2007), 'Mozambique: A Case Study in the Role of the Affected State in Humanitarian Action'. HPG Working Paper (London: ODI), p. 5

7. OECD (1999), *Guidance for Evaluating Humanitarian Assistance in Complex Emergencies: OECD Handbook* (Paris: OECD), p. 33

8. Moore, S., Eng, E., and Daniel, M. (2003), 'International NGOs and the Role of Network Centrality in Humanitarian Aid Operations: A Case Study of Coordination during the 2000 Mozambique Floods'. *Disasters* 27(4): 305–18

9. Ramalingam, B. and Barnett, M. (2010), 'The Humanitarian's Dilemma: Collective Action or Inaction in International Relief?' Background Note (London: ODI)

10. Christie, F. and Hanlon, J. (2001), *Mozambique & the Great Flood of 2000* (International African Institute in association with Oxford: James Currey; Bloomington, IN: Indiana University Press), p. 137

11. Reindorp, N. and Wiles, P. (2001), 'Humanitarian Coordination: Lessons from Recent Field Experience'. Report for OCHA (London: ODI), p. xi

12. Moore, S., Eng, E., and Daniel, M. (2003), 'International NGOs and the Role of Network Centrality in Humanitarian Aid Operations: A Case Study of Coordination during the 2000 Mozambique Floods'. *Disasters* 27(4): 305–18

13. Tataryn, M. and Blanchet, K. (2010), 'Giving with One Hand . . . Evaluation of Post-earthquake Physical Rehabilitation Response in Haiti, 2010—a Systems Analysis' (London: International Centre for Evidence in Disability and London School of Hygiene and Tropical Medicine), p. 13

14. Valid International and Ansa (2001), 'Independent Evaluation of Expenditure of DEC Mozambique Floods Appeal Funds March to December 2000 Expanded Executive Summary' (London: DEC), p. 4

15. Hilhorst, D. (2003), 'Responding to Disasters: Diversity of Bureaucrats, Technocrats and Local People'. *International Journal of Mass Emergencies and Disasters* 21(1): 37–55

16. Zhao, Y. (2010), 'Social Networks and Reduction of Risk in Disasters: An Example of Wenchuan Earthquake'. *International Conference on Economic Stress, Human Capital, and Families in Asia*: 3–4

17. Dale, P. (2011), 'Ties that Bind: Studying Social Networks in Timor-Leste'. People, Spaces, Deliberation blogs.worldbank.org, 28 June, <http://blogs.worldbank.org/publicsphere/node/5763> (accessed October 2012)

18. Caeyers, B. and Dercon, S. (2011), 'Political Connections and Social Networks in Targeted Transfer Programmes: Evidence from Rural Ethiopia'. Working Paper WPS/2008 33 (Oxford: CSAE)

19. Magsino, S.L. (2009), 'Applications of Social Network Analysis for Building Community Disaster Resilience: Workshop Summary', <http://www.nap.edu/catalog.php?record_id=12706> (accessed October 2012)

20. Blanchet, K. (2012), 'The Role of Social Networks in the Governance of Health Systems: The Case of Eye Care Systems in Ghana'. *Health Policy Plan* (Epub ahead of printing), <http://www.ncbi.nlm.nih.gov/pubmed/22411882> (accessed October 2012)

21. Blanchet, K. (2012), 'The Role of Social Networks in the Governance of Health Systems: The Case of Eye Care Systems in Ghana'. *Health Policy Plan* (Epub ahead of printing), <http://www.ncbi.nlm.nih.gov/pubmed/22411882> (accessed October 2012)

22. Blanchet, K. (2012), 'The Role of Social Networks in the Governance of Health Systems: The Case of Eye Care Systems in Ghana'. *Health Policy Plan* (Epub ahead of printing), <http://www.ncbi.nlm.nih.gov/pubmed/22411882> (accessed October 2012)

23. Blanchet, K. (2012), 'The Role of Social Networks in the Governance of Health Systems: The Case of Eye Care Systems in Ghana'. *Health Policy Plan* (Epub ahead of printing), <http://www.ncbi.nlm.nih.gov/pubmed/22411882> (accessed October 2012)

24. Chemonics International Inc. (2008), 'Moving from Subsistence to Commercial Farming in Uganda'. Agricultural Productivity Enhancement Program Final Report (Washington, DC: USAID), p. 24

25. Bender-deMoll, S. (2008), 'Potential Human Rights Uses of Network Analysis and Mapping'. Report to the Science and Human Rights Program of the American Association for the Advancement of Science, 28 April

26. Bloom, E., Reeves, M., Sunseri, A., and Nyhan-Jones, V. (2008), 'Strengthening Networks: Using Organizational Network Analysis to Promote Network Effectiveness, Scale, and Accountability'. Capacity Development Brief 28 (Washington, DC: World Bank Institute), p. 5

27. Krebs, V. and Holley, J. (2006), 'Building Smart Communities through Network Weaving', <http://www.orgnet.com/BuildingNetworks.pdf> (accessed October 2012)

28. Riddell, R. (2008), *Does Foreign Aid Really Work?* (Oxford: OUP)

29. IMF (2010), 'Understanding Financial Interconnectedness' (Washington, DC: Strategy, Policy, and Review Department and Monetary and Capital Markets Department, IMF)

30. IMF (2010), 'Understanding Financial Interconnectedness' (Washington, DC: Strategy, Policy, and Review Department and Monetary and Capital Markets Department, IMF), p. 5

31. IMF (2011), 'Mapping Cross-border Financial Linkages: A Supporting Case for Global Financial Safety Nets' (Washington, DC: Strategy, Policy, and Review Department, IMF)

32. Haldane. A. and May, R. (2011), 'Systemic Risk in Banking Ecosystems'. *Nature* 469 (7330): 351–5

33. IMF (2011), 'Mapping Cross-Border Financial Linkages: A Supporting Case for Global Financial Safety Nets' (Washington, DC: Strategy, Policy, and Review Department, IMF), p. 4

34. IMF (2010), 'Understanding Financial Interconnectedness' (Washington, DC: Strategy, Policy, and Review Department and Monetary and Capital Markets Department, IMF), p. 37

35. Minoiu, C. and Reyes, J.A. (2010), 'A Network Analysis of Global Banking: 1978–2009'. Working Paper 11/74 (Washington, DC: IMF); and Minoiu, C. (2012), 'Caught in the Web'. *Finance and Development* 49(3), <http://www.imf.org/external/pubs/ft/fandd/2012/09/minoiu.htm> (accessed October 2012)

36. Minoiu, C. (2012), 'Caught in the Web'. *Finance and Development* 49(3), <http://www.imf.org/external/pubs/ft/fandd/2012/09/minoiu.htm> (accessed October 2012)

37. Minoiu, C. (2012), 'Caught in the Web'. *Finance and Development* 49(3), <http://www.imf.org/external/pubs/ft/fandd/2012/09/minoiu.htm> (accessed October 2012)

38. Minoiu, C. (2012), 'Caught in the Web'. *Finance and Development* 49(3), <http://www.imf.org/external/pubs/ft/fandd/2012/09/minoiu.htm> (accessed October 2012)

39. Fold, N. and Whitfield, L. (2012), 'Developing a Palm Oil Sector: The Experiences of Malaysia and Ghana Compared'. Working Paper 2012/08 (Copenhagen: DIIS)

40. Hidalgo, C., Klinger, B., Barabási, A.-L., and Hausmann, R. (2005), 'The Product Space Conditions the Development of Nations'. *Science* 317: 482–7, p. 482

41. Hidalgo, C., Klinger, B., Barabási, A.-L., and Hausmann, R. (2005), 'The Product Space Conditions the Development of Nations'. *Science* 317: 482–7, p. 482

42. Hidalgo, C. (2011), personal communication

43. Hidalgo, C., Klinger, B., Barabási, A.-L., and Hausmann, R. (2005), 'The Product Space Conditions the Development of Nations'. *Science* 317: 482–7, p. 484

44. *The Economist* (2011), 'The Building Blocks of Economic Growth: Complexity Matters', 27 October, <http://www.economist.com/blogs/freeexchange/2011/10/building-blocks-economic-growth> (accessed October 2012)

45. Hausmann, R., Hidalgo, C.A., Bustos, S., et al (2011), *The Atlas of Economic Complexity: Mapping Paths to Prosperity* (Boston, MA: Center for Institutional Development, Harvard University, MIT Media Lab)

46. *The Economist* (2011), 'The Building Blocks of Economic Growth: Complexity Matters', 27 October, <http://www.economist.com/blogs/freeexchange/2011/10/building-blocks-economic-growth> (accessed October 2012)

47. Visualign Consulting (2012), 'The Atlas of Economic Complexity', 10 November <http://visualign.wordpress.com/2011/11/10/the-atlas-of-economic-complexity/> (accessed October 2012)

48. Yusof, Z.A. (2010), 'Economic Growth in Malaysia—Some Possible Lessons for Ghana'. Discussion Paper 10/0827 (London and Oxford: ICG)

49. Yusof, Z.A. (2010), 'Economic Growth in Malaysia—Some Possible Lessons for Ghana'. Discussion Paper 10/0827 (London and Oxford: ICG)

50. WEF (2012), *The Future of Manufacturing: Opportunities to Drive Economic Growth* (Geneva: WEF)

51. Kali, R., McGee, J., Reyes, J., and Shirrell, S. (2009), 'Networks in Growth: Product Space, Small World Networks, and Growth Acceleration'. Discussion Paper (Little Rock, AK: University of Arkansas)

52. Giuliani, E. and Pietrobelli, C. (2011), *Social Network Analysis Methodologies for the Evaluation of Cluster Development Programs* (Washington, DC: IADB)

53. Buys, P., Deichmann, D., and Wheeler, D. (2006), 'Road Network Upgrading and Overland Trade Expansion in Sub-Saharan Africa'. Policy Research Working Paper 4097 (Washington, DC: World Bank)

54. *The Economist* (2011), 'The Building Blocks of Economic Growth: Complexity Matters', 27 October, <http://www.economist.com/blogs/freeexchange/2011/10/building-blocks-economic-growth> (accessed October 2012)

55. Hidalgo, C. (2011), personal communication

56. Hausmann, R., Hidalgo, C.A., Bustos, S., et al (2011), *The Atlas of Economic Complexity: Mapping Paths to Prosperity* (Boston, MA: Center for Institutional Development, Harvard University, MIT Media Lab), preface

57. Hausmann, R., Hidalgo, C.A., Bustos, S., et al (2011), *The Atlas of Economic Complexity: Mapping Paths to Prosperity* (Boston, MA: Center for Institutional Development, Harvard University, MIT Media Lab), p. 18

58. Cross, R. and Parker, A. (2004), *The Hidden Power of Social Networks: Understanding How Work Really Gets Done in Organizations* (Cambridge, MA: Harvard Business School)

59. Clarke, P. and Ramalingam, B. (2008), 'Organisational Change in the Humanitarian Sector', in ALNAP (ed.) *Seventh Review of Humanitarian Action* (London: ALNAP, ODI)

60. Cross, R. and Parker, A. (2004), *The Hidden Power of Social Networks: Understanding How Work Really Gets Done in Organizations* (Cambridge, MA: Harvard Business School)

61. Cross, R. and Zenner, D. (2008), 'Applying Network Analysis for Insights into the Decentralization Strategy at the International Finance Corporation'. PowerPoint presentation

62. Quaggiotto, G., in Cross, R. and Zenner, D. (2008), 'Applying Network Analysis for Insights into the Decentralization Strategy at the International Finance Corporation'. PowerPoint presentation

63. Personal communication (2012)

64. Bloom, E., Reeves, M., Sunseri, A., and Nyhan-Jones, V. (2008), 'Strengthening Networks: Using Organizational Network Analysis to Promote Network Effectiveness, Scale, and Accountability'. Capacity Development Brief 28 (Washington, DC: World Bank Institute), p. 6

65. Levinger, B. and Bloom, E. (2011), 'Fulfilling the Promise: How National Societies Achieve Sustainable Organizational Development. A Multi-Country Study.' American Red Cross, IFRC, and Root Change

66. Levinger, B. and Bloom, E. (2011), 'Fulfilling the Promise: How National Societies Achieve Sustainable Organizational Development. A Multi-Country Study.' American Red Cross, IFRC, and Root Change, p. 24

67. <http://iipdigital.usembassy.gov/st/english/publication/2009/03/20090304102443-ebyessedoo.6759455.html#axzz2MsP2MKEM> (accessed March 2013)

68. Davies, R. (2003), 'Network Perspectives in the Evaluation of Development Interventions: More than a Metaphor'. EDAIS Conference on New Directions in Impact Assessment for Development: Methods and Practice, 24–5 November

Chapter 17

1. Mitra, S. (2010), 'The Hole in the Wall: Self-Organising Systems in Education'. Keynote Speech, Conference on Into Something Rich and Strange: Making Sense of the Sea-change, Nottingham, 8 September, p. 10

2. Mitra, S., Dangwal, R., Chatterjee, S., Jha, S., Bisht, R.S., and Kapur, P. (2005), 'Acquisition of Computing Literacy on Shared Public Computers: Children and the "Hole in the Wall"'. *Australasian Journal of Educational Technology* 21(3): 407–26, p. 408

3. Mitra, S., Dangwal, R., Chatterjee, S., Jha, S., Bisht, R.S., and Kapur, P. (2005), 'Acquisition of Computing Literacy on Shared Public Computers: Children and the "Hole in the Wall"'. *Australasian Journal of Educational Technology* 21(3): 407–26, p. 408

4. Mitra, S. (2012), personal communication

5. Mitra, S., Dangwal, R., Chatterjee, S., Jha, S., Bisht, R.S., and Kapur, P. (2005), 'Acquisition of Computing Literacy on Shared Public Computers: Children and the "Hole in the Wall"'. *Australasian Journal of Educational Technology* 21(3): 407–26

6. Judge, P. (2000), 'Interview with Sugata Mitra'. Businessweek Online Daily Briefing, <http://www.greenstar.org/butterflies/Hole-in-the-Wall.htm> (accessed October 2012)

7. Mitra, S., Dangwal, R., Chatterjee, S., Jha, S., Bisht, R.S., and Kapur, P. (2005), 'Acquisition of Computing Literacy on Shared Public Computers: Children and the "Hole in the Wall"'. *Australasian Journal of Educational Technology* 21(3): 407–26

8. Chambers, R. (1997), *Whose Reality Counts* (London: ITDG Publishing), p. 61

9. Filmer, D., Hasan, A., and Pritchett, L. (2006), 'A Millennium Learning Goal: Measuring Real Progress in Education'. Working Paper 97 (Washington, DC: CGD)

10. *The Hindu* (2009), 'Hole in Wall project inspiration of Slumdog Millionaire: Vikas', 18 January, <http://www.hindu.com/thehindu/holnus/009200901181121.htm> (accessed October 2012)

11. Mitra, S., Dangwal, R., Chatterjee, S., Jha, S., Bisht, R.S., and Kapur, P. (2005), 'Acquisition of Computing Literacy on Shared Public Computers: Children and the "Hole in the Wall"'. *Australasian Journal of Educational Technology* 21(3): 407–26, p. 424

12. Personal communication (2012)

13. Eagle, N. (2009), 'Txteagle: Mobile Crowdsourcing', <http://reality.media.mit.edu/pdfs/hcii_txteagle.pdf> (accessed October 2012)

14. *The Economist* (2010), 'Mobile Work: A Way to Earn Money by Texting', 28 October, <http://www.economist.com/node/17366137> (accessed October 2012)

15. Berman, M.S. (2011), 'The Development, Use and Cultural Context of MPESA in Costal Kenya'. Independent Study Project, SIT Graduate Institute

16. Eagle, N. (2009), 'Txteagle: Mobile Crowdsourcing', <http://reality.media.mit.edu/pdfs/hcii_txteagle.pdf> (accessed October 2012)

17. Kokolis, K. (2012), 'Media (R)evolutions: Mobile Money in Africa'. People, Spaces, Deliberation blogs.worldbank.org, 22 August, <http://blogs.worldbank.org/public-sphere/media-revolutions-mobile-money-africa> (accessed October 2012)

18. Berman, M.S. (2011), 'The Development, Use and Cultural Context of MPESA in Costal Kenya'. Independent Study Project, SIT Graduate Institute, p. 6

19. Berman, M.S. (2011), 'The Development, Use and Cultural Context of MPESA in Costal Kenya'. Independent Study Project, SIT Graduate Institute; see also *The Economist* (2010), 'Out of Thin Air: The Behind-the-scenes Logistics of Kenya's Mobile-money Miracle', 10 June, <http://www.economist.com/node/16319635> (accessed October 2012)

20. Johnson, S., with Brown, G.K. and Fouillet, C. (2012), 'The Search for Inclusion in Kenya's Financial Landscape: The Rift Revealed' (Bath: CSD), p. vi

21. Omwamsa, T. (2009), 'M-PESA: Progress and Prospects'. Innovations Case Discussion, Mobile World Congress 2009, Barcelona, 16–19 February

22. Stuart, G. and Cohen, M. (2011), 'Cash In, Cash Out Kenya: The Role of MPESA in the Lives of Low Income People'. Financial Services Assessment, September

23. On the origins of M-PESA, see Hughes, N. and Lonie, S. (2007), 'M-PESA: Mobile Money for the "Unbanked" Turning Cellphones into 24-Hour Tellers in Kenya'. *Innovations* Winter/Spring

24. Shah, R. (2012), 'Remarks at the Aspen Institute', 1 August, <http://www.usaid. gov/news-information/speeches/remarks-usaid-administrator-dr-rajiv-shah-aspen-institute> (accessed October 2012)

25. Wesolowski, A.P. and Eagle, N. (2010), 'Parameterizing the Dynamics of Slums'. AAAI Spring Symposium on Artificial Intelligence, Stanford, CA, 23–5 March

26. Wesolowski, A.P. and Eagle, N. (2010), 'Parameterizing the Dynamics of Slums'. AAAI Spring Symposium on Artificial Intelligence, Stanford, CA, 23–5 March, p. 5

27. UN-HABITAT and UNEP (2010), *State of African Cities Report: Governance, Inequality and Urban Land Markets* (Nairobi: UN-HABITAT)

28. Bengtsson, L., Lu, S., Thorson, A., et al (2011), 'Improved Response to Disasters and Outbreaks by Tracking Population Movements with Mobile Phone Network Data: A Post-Earthquake Geospatial Study in Haiti', *PLoS Med* 8(8), <http://www.mobileac-tive.org/files/file_uploads/journal.pmed_.1001083.pdf> (accessed October 2012), p. 7

29. Dougherty, E. (2012), 'Mobilizing a Revolution: How Cellphones Are Transforming Public Health'. *Harvard Public Health Review* Winter: 14–21, p. 15

30. Dougherty, E. (2012), 'Mobilizing a Revolution: How Cellphones Are Transforming Public Health'. *Harvard Public Health Review* Winter: 14–21, p. 17

31. Palmer, J. (2009), 'Aid Agencies "Must Use New Tools"', 11 December, <http://news.bbc.co.uk/1/hi/technology/8406509.stm> (accessed October 2012)

32. Ferrari, M.J., Grais, R.F., Bharti, N., et al (2008), 'The Dynamics of Measles in Sub-Saharan Africa'. *Nature* 451: 679–84

33. In Penn State Live (2008), 'Dry Season Brings on Measles in Sub-Saharan Africa', 6 February, <http://live.psu.edu/story/28633> (accessed October 2012)

34. In Penn State Live (2008), 'Dry Season Brings on Measles in Sub-Saharan Africa', 6 February, <http://live.psu.edu/story/28633> (accessed October 2012)

35. In Penn State Live (2008), 'Dry Season Brings on Measles in Sub-Saharan Africa' 6 February, <http://live.psu.edu/story/28633> (accessed October 2012)

36. In Penn State Live (2008), 'Dry Season Brings on Measles in Sub-Saharan Africa', 6 February, <http://live.psu.edu/story/28633> (accessed October 2012)

37. Bharti, N., Bjørnstad, O., Grenfell, B., et al (n.d.), 'Spatial Patterns on the Edge of Stability: Measles in the Sahel'. PowerPoint Presentation

38. Ferrari, M. (2012), personal communication

39. Ferrari, M. (2012), personal communication

40. Ferrari, M. (2012), personal communication

41. Personal communication (2012)

42. Scoones, I., Leach, M., Smith, A., et al (2007), 'Dynamic Systems and the Challenge of Sustainability'. STEPS Working Paper 1 (Brighton: STEPS Centre), p. 2

43. Scoones, I. and Forster, P. (2008), 'The International Response to Highly Pathogenic Avian Influenza: Science, Policy and Politics'. STEPS Working Paper 10 (Brighton: STEPS Centre)

44. Scoones, I. and Forster, P. (2008), 'The International Response to Highly Pathogenic Avian Influenza: Science, Policy and Politics'. STEPS Working Paper 10 (Brighton: STEPS Centre), p. 39

45. Frerichs, R.R. (n.d.), 'John Snow', <http://www.ph.ucla.edu/epi/snow.html> (accessed October 2012)

46. Snow, J. (1885), *On the Mode of Communication of Cholera* (London: John Churchill), p. 55

47. Scoones, I. and Forster, P. (2008), 'The International Response to Highly Pathogenic Avian Influenza: Science, Policy and Politics'. STEPS Working Paper 10 (Brighton: STEPS Centre), p. 40

48. Bloom, G., Edström, J., Leach, M., et al (2007), 'Health in a Dynamic World'. STEPS Working Paper 5 (Brighton: STEPS Centre), p. 10

49. Scoones, I. and Forster, P. (2008), 'The International Response to Highly Pathogenic Avian Influenza: Science, Policy and Politics'. STEPS Working Paper 10 (Brighton: STEPS Centre), p. 39

50. Bedford, T., Cobey, S., Beerli, P., and Pascual, M. (2010), 'Global Migration Dynamics Underlie Evolution and Persistence of Human Influenza A (H3N2)'. *PLoS Pathog* 6(5), <http://www.plospathogens.org/article/info%3Adoi%2F10.1371%2Fjournal.ppat.1000918> (accessed October 2012)

51. Burkett, V.R., Wilcox, D.A., Stottlemyer, R., et al (2005), 'Nonlinear Dynamics in Ecosystem Response to Climatic Change: Case Studies and Policy Implications'. *Ecological Complexity* 2: 357–94

52. Schneider, S.H. (2004), 'Abrupt Non-Linear Climate Change, Irreversibility and Surprise'. *Global Environmental Change* 14: 245–58

53. Working Group II: Impacts, Adaptation and Vulnerability (2007), 'Developing and Applying Scenarios', (Geneva: IPCC), <http://www.ipcc.ch/ipccreports/tar/wg2/index.php?idp=146> (accessed October 2012)

54. Burkett, V.R., Wilcox, D.A., Stottlemyer, R., et al (2005), 'Nonlinear Dynamics in Ecosystem Response to Climatic Change: Case Studies and Policy Implications'. *Ecological Complexity* 2: 357–94

55. Schneider, S.H. (2004), 'Abrupt Non-Linear Climate Change, Irreversibility and Surprise'. *Global Environmental Change* 14: 245–58, p. 250

56. Burkett, V.R., Wilcox, D.A., Stottlemyer, R., et al (2005), 'Nonlinear Dynamics in Ecosystem Response to Climatic Change: Case Studies and Policy Implications'. *Ecological Complexity* 2: 357–94

57. Bedford, T., Cobey, S., Beerli, P., and Pascual, M. (2010), 'Global Migration Dynamics Underlie Evolution and Persistence of Human Influenza A (H3N2)'. *PLoS Pathog* 6(5), <http://www.plospathogens.org/article/info%3Adoi%2F10.1371%2Fjournal.ppat.1000918> (accessed October 2012)

58. Schlenkera, W. and Roberts, M.J. (2009), 'Nonlinear Temperature Effects Indicate Severe Damages to U.S. Crop Yields under Climate Change'. *PNAS* 106(37): 15594–8

59. Maddison, D., Manley, M., and Kurukulasuriya, P. (2006), 'The Impact of Climate Change on African Agriculture'. Discussion Paper 15 (Cape Town: CEEPA)

60. HM Treasury (2006), *Stern Review of Climate Change* (London: HM Treasury)

61. http://www.bis.gov.uk/foresight/our-work/projects/published-projects/global-migration (accessed October 2012)

62. Kniveton, D., Smith, C., and Wood, S. (2011), 'Agent-Based Model Simulations of Future Changes in Migration Flows for Burkina Faso'. *Global Environmental Change* 21(24): 6498–520.

63. Schneider, S.H. (2004), 'Abrupt Non-Linear Climate Change, Irreversibility and Surprise'. *Global Environmental Change* 14: 245–58, p. 5

64. Burkett, V.R., Wilcox, D.A., Stottlemyer, R., et al (2005), 'Nonlinear Dynamics in Ecosystem Response to Climatic Change: Case Studies and Policy Implications'. *Ecological Complexity* 2: 357–94, p. 385

65. Burkett, V.R., Wilcox, D.A., Stottlemyer, R., et al (2005), 'Nonlinear Dynamics in Ecosystem Response to Climatic Change: Case Studies and Policy Implications'. *Ecological Complexity* 2: 357–94, p. 385

66. Burkett, V.R., Wilcox, D.A., Stottlemyer, R., et al (2005), 'Nonlinear Dynamics in Ecosystem Response to Climatic Change: Case Studies and Policy Implications'. *Ecological Complexity* 2: 357–94

67. Tschakert, P. and Dietrich, K.A. (2010), 'Anticipatory Learning for Climate Change Adaptation and Resilience'. *Ecology and Society* 15(2), <http://www.ecologyandsociety.org/vol15/iss2/art11/> (accessed October 2012)

68. Burkett, V.R., Wilcox, D.A., Stottlemyer, R., et al (2005), 'Nonlinear Dynamics in Ecosystem Response to Climatic Change: Case Studies and Policy Implications'. *Ecological Complexity* 2: 357–94, p. 361

69. Tschakert, P. and Dietrich, K.A. (2010), 'Anticipatory Learning for Climate Change Adaptation and Resilience'. *Ecology and Society* 15(2), <http://www.ecologyandsociety.org/vol15/iss2/art11/> (accessed October 2012)

70. Tschakert, P. and Dietrich, K.A. (2010), 'Anticipatory Learning for Climate Change Adaptation and Resilience'. *Ecology and Society* 15(2), <http://www.ecologyandsociety.org/vol15/iss2/art11/> (accessed October 2012)

71. Santha, S. and Sreedharan, R. (2010), 'Population Vulnerability and Disaster Risk Reduction: A Situation Analysis among the Landslide Affected Communities in Kerala, India'. *Journal of Disaster Risk Studies* 3(1): 367–80, p. 377

72. This account draws heavily on the following blog post: Ramalingam, B. (2011), 'Climate Change Adaptation, Resilience and Complexity', 1 December, <http://aidontheedge.info/2011/12/01/climate-change-adaptation-efforts-must-embrace-complexity-to-build-long-term-resilience/> (accessed October 2012) and the paper on which it is based: Adger, W.N., Brown, K., Nelson, D.R., et al (2011), 'Resilience Implications of Policy Responses to Climate Change'. *WIREs Clim Change* 2: 757–66

73. Adger, W.N., Brown, K., Nelson, D.R., et al (2011), 'Resilience Implications of Policy Responses to Climate Change'. *WIREs Clim Change* 2: 757–66, p. 758

74. Adger, W.N., Brown, K., Nelson, D.R., et al (2011), 'Resilience Implications of Policy Responses to Climate Change'. *WIREs Clim Change* 2: 757–66, p. 765

75. Hopkins, R. (2010), 'An Interview with Neil Adger: Resilience, Adaptability, Localisation and Transition', 26 March, <http://transitionculture.org/2010/03/26/an-interview-with-neil-adger-resilience-adaptability-localisation-and-transition/> (accessed October 2012)

76. Tschakert, P. and Dietrich, K.A. (2010), 'Anticipatory Learning for Climate Change Adaptation and Resilience'. *Ecology and Society* 15(2), <http://www.ecologyandsociety.org/vol15/iss2/art11/> (accessed October 2012)

77. Tschakert, P. and Dietrich, K.A. (2010), 'Anticipatory Learning for Climate Change Adaptation and Resilience'. *Ecology and Society* 15(2), <http://www.ecologyandsociety.org/vol15/iss2/art11/> (accessed October 2012)

78. Tschakert, P. and Dietrich, K.A. (2010), 'Anticipatory Learning for Climate Change Adaptation and Resilience'. *Ecology and Society* 15(2), <http://www.ecologyandsociety.org/vol15/iss2/art11/> (accessed October 2012)

79. Devisscher, T. (2010), 'Ecosystem-based Adaptation in Africa: Rationale, Pathways, and Cost Estimates'. Sectoral Report for the AdaptCost Study (Stockholm: SEI)

80. Newsham, A. (2012), 'Ecosystems-Based Adaptation: Have We Been Here Before?' (Brighton: IDS), <http://www.ids.ac.uk/news/ecosystems-based-adaptation-have-we-been-here-before> (accessed October 2012)

81. Roberts, D., Boon, R., Diederichs, N., et al (2012), 'Exploring Ecosystem-based Adaptation in Durban, South Africa: "Learning-by-doing" at the Local Government Coal Face'. *Environment and Urbanization* 24(1): 167–95

82. Devisscher, T. (2010), 'Ecosystem-Based Adaptation in Africa: Rationale, Pathways, and Cost Estimates'. Sectoral Report for the AdaptCost Study (Stockholm: SEI)

83. Alinovi, L., Mane, E., and Romano, D. (2009), 'Measuring Household Resilience to Food Insecurity: Application to Palestinian Households'. EC-FAO Food Security Programme (Rome: FAO)

84. Alinovi, L., Mane, E., and Romano, D. (2009), 'Measuring Household Resilience to Food Insecurity: Application to Palestinian Households'. EC-FAO Food Security Programme (Rome: FAO), p. 9

85. Alinovi, L., Mane, E., and Romano, D. (2009), 'Measuring Household Resilience to Food Insecurity: Application to Palestinian Households'. EC-FAO Food Security Programme (Rome: FAO), p. 9

86. Alinovi, L., D'Errico, M., Mane, E., and Romano, D. (2010), 'Livelihoods Strategies and Household Resilience to Food Insecurity: An Empirical Analysis to Kenya'. Conference on Promoting Resilience through Social Protection in Sub-Saharan Africa, Dakar, 28–30 June

87. Alinovi, L., Mane, E., and Romano, D. (2009), 'Measuring Household Resilience to Food Insecurity: Application to Palestinian Households'. EC-FAO Food Security Programme (Rome: FAO), p. 4

88. FAO (2008), 'Measuring Resilience: A Concept Note on the Resilience Tool' (Rome: FAO), p. 3

89. Alinovi, L., D'Errico, M., Mane, E., and Romano, D. (2010), 'Livelihoods Strategies and Household Resilience to Food Insecurity: An Empirical Analysis to Kenya'. Conference on Promoting Resilience through Social Protection in Sub-Saharan Africa, Dakar, 28–30 June, p. 34

90. Alinovi, L., Mane, E., and Romano, D. (2009), 'Measuring Household Resilience to Food Insecurity: Application to Palestinian Households'. EC-FAO Food Security Programme (Rome: FAO), p. 28

91. Alinovi, L., Mane, E., and Romano, D. (2009), 'Measuring Household Resilience to Food Insecurity: Application to Palestinian Households'. EC-FAO Food Security Programme (Rome: FAO), p. 29

92. FAO (2010), 'Resilience of Individuals, Households, Communities and Institutions in Protracted Crises', in *The State of Food Insecurity in the World 2010: Addressing Food Insecurity in Protracted Crises* (Rome: FAO and WFP)

93. FAO (2012), 'Resilience of Individuals, Households, Communities and Institutions in Protracted Crises'. Food Security in Protracted Crises High-level Expert Forum, Rome, 13–14 September, p. 3

94. FAO Somalia (2011), 'FAO Strategy and Plan of Action, 2011–2015' (Mogadishu: FAO Somalia), p. 57

95. Alinovi, L., Mane, E., and Romano, D. (2009), 'Measuring Household Resilience to Food Insecurity: Application to Palestinian Households'. EC-FAO Food Security Programme (Rome: FAO), p. 29

96. <http://documents.wfp.org/stellent/groups/public/documents/resources/wfp252679.pdf> (accessed March 2013)

97. Priesmeyer, H. (1992), *Organizations and Chaos: Defining the Methods of Nonlinear Management* (Westport, CT: Quorum Books), p. 3

98. Davies, R. (2002), 'Improved Representations of Change Processes: Improved Theories of Change'. 5th Biennial Conference of the European Evaluation Society. Three Movements in Contemporary Evaluation: Learning, Theory and Evidence, Seville, p. 3

99. Biennial Conference of the European Evaluation Society. Three Movements in Contemporary Evaluation: Learning, Theory and Evidence, Seville, p. 2

100. Serrat, O. (2009), 'Understanding Complexity'. *Knowledge Solutions* 66: 1–9, p. 5

101. Ebrahim, A. and Kasturi Rangan, V. (2010), 'The Limits of Nonprofit Impact: A Contingency Framework for Measuring Social Performance'. Working Paper 10-099 (Cambridge, MA: Harvard Business School), p. 15

102. Manning, R. (2009), 'Using Indicators to Encourage Development Lessons from the Millennium Development Goals'. DIIS Report 2009:01 (Copenhagen: DIIS); Hulme, D. and Wilkinson, R. (2012), 'Brave New World: Global Development Goals after 2015'. Working Paper 168 (Manchester: BWPI)

103. Barder, O. (2012), 'Complexity, Adaptation, and Results'. Global Development: Views from the Center, <http://blogs.cgdev.org/globaldevelopment/2012/09/complexity-and-results.php> (accessed October 2012)

104. O'Neil, T., Foresti, M., and Hudson, A. (2007), 'Evaluation of Citizens' Voice & Accountability: Review of the Literature & Donor Approaches Report' (London: DFID), p .6

105. O'Neil, T., Foresti, M., and Hudson, A. (2007), 'Evaluation of Citizens' Voice & Accountability: Review of the Literature & Donor Approaches Report' (London: DFID), p. 6

106. Ebrahim, A. and Kasturi Rangan, V. (2010), 'The Limits of Nonprofit Impact: A Contingency Framework for Measuring Social Performance'. Working Paper 10-099 (Cambridge, MA: Harvard Business School), p. 23

107. Ebrahim, A. and Kasturi Rangan, V. (2010), 'The Limits of Nonprofit Impact: A Contingency Framework for Measuring Social Performance'. Working Paper 10-099 (Cambridge, MA: Harvard Business School), p. 23

108. Ebrahim, A. and Kasturi Rangan, V. (2010), 'The Limits of Nonprofit Impact: A Contingency Framework for Measuring Social Performance'. Working Paper 10-099 (Cambridge, MA: Harvard Business School), p. 23

109. Pritchett, L., Samji, S., and Hammer, J. (2012) It's All About MeE: Using Structured Experiential Learning ('e') to Crawl the Design Space UNU-WIDER Working Paper No. 2012/104 <http://www.wider.unu.edu/publications/working-papers/2012/en_GB/wp2012-104/> (accessed March 2013)

110. Ebrahim, A. and Kasturi Rangan, V. (2010), 'The Limits of Nonprofit Impact: A Contingency Framework for Measuring Social Performance'. Working Paper 10–099 (Cambridge, MA: Harvard Business School), p. 4

111. Ebrahim, A. and Kasturi Rangan, V. (2010), 'The Limits of Nonprofit Impact: A Contingency Framework for Measuring Social Performance'. Working Paper 10–099 (Cambridge, MA: Harvard Business School), p. 30

Chapter 18

1. Hardin, G. (1968), 'The Tragedy of the Commons'. *Science* 162: 1243–8
2. Ostrom, E. (2007), 'Sustainable Social-Ecological Systems: An Impossibility?' Annual Meeting of the American Association for the Advancement of Science, San Francisco, CA, 15–19 February
3. Hardin, G. (1994), 'The Tragedy of the Unmanaged Commons'. *Trends in Ecology & Evolution* 9(5): 199
4. Ostrom, E (2007), 'A Diagnostic Approach for Going beyond Panaceas'. *PNAS* 4(39): 15181–7
5. Associated Press (2012), 'Elinor Ostrom, First Woman to Receive Nobel Prize in Economics, Dies', 14 June, <http://www.northjersey.com/obituaries/Elinor_Ostrom_first_woman_to_receive_nobel_prize_in_economics_dies.html?c=y&page=3> (accessed October 2012)
6. Ostrom, E. (2012), 'Green from the Grassroots'. Project Syndicate, 12 June, <http://www.project-syndicate.org/commentary/green-from-the-grassroots> (accessed October 2012)
7. Bowles, S. (2009), 'The Coevolution of Institutions and Preferences: History and Theory' (Santa Fe, NM: SFI)

Chapter 19

1. Lincoln, A. (1862), 'Second Annual Message', 1 December, <http://www.presidency.ucsb.edu/ws/index.php?pid=29503> (accessed October 2012)
2. Gaventa, J. and McGee, R. (2010), 'Introduction: Making Change Happen—Citizen Action and National Policy Reform', <http://www.drc-citizenship.org/system/assets/1052734655/original/1052734655-gaventa_etal.2010-making.pdf, p.15> (accessed October 2012)
3. Rogerson, A. (2011), 'What if Development Aid Were Truly "Catalytic"?' Background Note (London: ODI), p. 1
4. Sumner, A. and Mallett, R. (2012), 'Aid: A Survey in Light of Changes in the Distribution of Global Poverty' (Brighton: IDS)
5. Kauffman, S. (1995), *At Home in the Universe: The Search for Laws of Self-Organization and Complexity* (New York: OUP)
6. Adapted from Kennedy, J.F. (1963), 'Towards a Strategy of Peace'. Address at The American University, Washington, DC, 10 June
7. Personal communication (2010)

INDEX